CW01558662

THE POWER OF INCLUSIVE EXCLUSION

ANATA, EAST JERUSALEM, 2007 [ACTIVESTILLS.ORG/KEREN MANOR]

THE POWER OF INCLUSIVE EXCLUSION

Anatomy of Israeli Rule in the Occupied Palestinian Territories

edited by

Adi Ophir, Michal Givoni, and Sari Hanafi

ZONE BOOKS · NEW YORK

2009

The editors would like to thank the Van Leer Jerusalem Institute
for their support of the research for this book.

The revised and updated chapter "The Illegality of the Occupation
Regime: The Fabric of Law in the Occupied Palestinian Territory"
included by permission of the Regents of the University of
California © 2005.

Printed in the United States of America.

Distributed by The MIT Press,
Cambridge, Massachusetts, and London, England

Library of Congress Cataloging-in-Publication Data

The power of inclusive exclusion : anatomy of Israeli rule
in the occupied Palestinian territories / edited by Adi Ophir,
Michal Givoni, and Sari Hanafi.
     p. cm.
  Includes bibliographical references (p.).
  ISBN 978-1-890951-92-4 (alk. paper)
     1. Arab-Israeli conflict, 1993—Occupied territories.
2. Gaza Strip—Politics and government. 3. West Bank—Politics
and government. 4. Israel—Politics and government—1993–
I. Ophir, Adi. II. Givoni, Michal. III. Hanafi, Sari.

    DS119.76.P69 2009
    956.95'3044—dc22

                 2009010813

Contents

Acknowledgments

Work on this volume was made possible thanks to the generous support of the Van Leer Jerusalem Institute, which hosted the research group *Israel-Palestine, a Catastrophe in the Making* and funded its activities, and of its succeeding directors, Shimshon Zelniker and Gabriel Motzkin. We wish to thank the scholars, practitioners, and activists who took part in the activities of the research group over the years—Caroline Abu-Sada, Sheerin Al-Araj, Merav Amir, Tal Arbel, Danna Bader, Yael Berda, Gail Boling, David Enoch, Corinna Gayer, Hunaida Ghanim, Ruthie Ginsburg, Neve Gordon, Connie Hackbarth, Ariel Handel, Shir Hever, Ruchama Marton, Nicolas Pelham, Galia Plotkin-Amrami, Maya Rosenfeld, and Judith Soussan—for their contribution to a stimulating body of scholarship and to a vibrant discussion that helped us consolidate the ideas behind this book. Danna Bader and Judith Soussan were charged with the often unrewarding task of tracking the occupation's paper trail, and we are grateful for their determination and creativity in conducting this documentary research. We also wish to thank Itamar Mann and Liron Mor for their help with additional research. Galit Eilat, Eyal Danon, and Ariella Azoulay provided us with creative advice that helped us conceptualize the project of the occupation's paper trail in its various stages. Finally, we are indebted to the members of the research group, as well as to the following individuals and organizations for providing us with documents from their archives or with helpful leads: Attorney Dana Alexander and Attorney Limor Yehuda from the Association for Civil Rights in Israel, Yehezkel Lein and Ofir Feuerstein from B'tselem, Meir Margalit from the Israeli Committee against House Demolitions, Salwa Alenat from Kav La'oved, Sylvia Piterman from MachsomWatch, David Shearer and Yehudith Harel from the United Nations Office for the Coordination of Humanitarian Affairs (OCHA) in the Occupied

Palestinian Territory, Dror Etkes and Hagit Ofran from the Peace Now Settlement Watch Program, Hadas Ziv from Physicians for Human Rights-Israel, Akiva Eldar, M.P. Dov Khenin, Amira Hass, Attorney Tamar Peleg-Shrik, Einat Podgorny, Attorney Michael Sfard, the Alternative Information Center, and HaMoked— Center for the Defence of the Individual.

Introduction

Adi Ophir, Michal Givoni, and Sari Hanafi

The nature of the Jewish national movement since the end of the nineteenth century and of the Palestinian struggle to counter Jewish immigration to Palestine and later to put an end to Israeli domination in Palestine have been hotly debated among scholars, ideologues, politicians, and the public at large. Strong, conflicting ideological and religious commitments seem to determine one's perspective and basic presuppositions on the matter and burden any theoretical point of entry into its study. Some think about these issues in terms of a binational conflict, others in terms of a forced Western colonization of Arab land, and yet others in terms of a slow, miraculous process of Jewish redemption in which the Palestinians are a stumbling block. Within these theoretical or ideological frameworks, some describe Israel's ongoing occupation of the Palestinian territories as a tragedy in which the most moral, most justified "solution" to "the Jewish problem" has taken a perverted, accidental turn; for others, it is an inevitable continuation and culmination of a long process of conquest and destruction of Palestinian society and the creation of a Jewish state on its ruins; yet others conceive the occupation as a certain moment in the story of the Jewish return into history—an inevitable problem that will not be resolved without dividing the land of Israel-Palestine between the two peoples; for others, it is but a phase in the history of Western colonization and hegemony in the Middle East that will come to an end with the rise of an Arab or Islamic nation.

This book does not attempt to adjudicate between these conflicting positions and does not offer a new perspective on the history of "the conflict" or on the debate itself. Its focus is not on the origins or the historical significance of the occupation, but on its nature as a sui generis regime or political system, a cluster of state and nonstate apparatuses, a frame of mind, and a series of political technologies that should be studied in their own right. The aim of the book is to turn attention from the past (the history of the conflict, of colonization, or of Jewish renewal and Palestinian struggles and disasters) and from the future (possible solutions to the conflict, directions for a peace process, the goal of the national struggle) to the present. If history enters the analytic frame that this book offers, it does so only by way of the genealogies of the technologies of power studied in it. If the future is projected here, it is projected only through the foreseeable effects of these technologies.

A basic presupposition of this book is that the debates about the history of Zionism and of the Palestinian national movement, and even more so about possible solutions to the conflict, suffer from a similar blindness to the current state of affairs. Moreover, it is presupposed here that this blindness is an effective element in the occupation machinery itself. People who tend to ignore the present often talk about the past as if it has never culminated in the current state of affairs, or they project into an indeterminate future what appears to be a devastating situation—a humanitarian crisis, an apartheid state, Islamization, or the fragmentation of Palestinian society—that is actually taking place already. In the same vein, they read a speculative future (especially the "two-states solution," the establishment of a Palestinian state in the West Bank and Gaza alongside Israel) into the present, as if it has already happened or at least has been agreed upon and hence has become a historical necessity, something that will happen inevitably.

Most Israelis, many Palestinians, and many friends and critics of Israel or of the Palestinians are trapped in conceptual frameworks offered by nationalized histories or by a pragmatic problem-solving set of mind oriented toward the future without taking proper account of the present. "Occupation" itself has become a shorthand way of speaking about the Israeli domination over the Palestinian non-citizens without ever bothering to consider exactly what kind of political power is involved in and manufactured as part of this domination and without questioning two key implications of this term: It happens elsewhere, and it is temporary.

The series of studies gathered in this book are wary of considering the occupation as a political and legal fetish and as a self-explanatory category that makes Israel's policies, past and present, transparent. Even if they do not address the nature of the Israeli political system directly, they are careful not to presuppose the externality of the occupation in relation to it or its temporariness vis-à-vis other, seemingly fixed and solid characteristics of this system. They are also careful not to frame the occupation as a particular form of something known already, for example, colonialism, apartheid, ethnic war, or national liberation, without, however, adhering to the myth that portrays it as a unique and incomparable phenomenon. Various aspects of the Israeli rule in the Occupied Territories may be the result of a long colonizing process or of a process of national liberation that has gone astray, but the conceptual framework offered by such conflicting narratives fails to explain or even to describe its specificities, let alone to analyze its logic of operation and the mechanisms of its reproduction. If historical analogies are invoked in this book, they are not used to condemn the occupation as an instantiation of notorious political forms, but rather are employed as a heuristic device that helps explicate the modus operandi of both regimes that are thus juxtaposed.

The occupation is understood here as an unstable set of technologies of power that open and limit a space of action and reaction for their subjects.[1] The essays collected in this volume explore ways in which such technologies of power exert constraints on those who think they are in command of that power, but who all too often are its products, and the ways in which these technologies yield unintended consequences that tend to thwart seemingly rational decision making and to jeopardize political plans of all sorts. While describing and questioning different aspects of the military-judicial-civil apparatuses that have maintained Israeli domination in the Occupied Territories for more than four decades, the studies gathered in this book focus for the most part on the most recent transformation that the Israeli system of rule has undergone following the eruption of the second Palestinian intifada in October 2000. At stake in this volume are the current modalities of Israeli control of the West Bank and Gaza Strip that were amply documented in the media and in reports by human rights organizations in recent years, such as the regimentation of movement, the fragmentation of space, the checkpoint system, creeping colonization, and extrajudicial assassinations. While this book does not pretend to bring to light unknown facts on the occupation or to unravel issues that were not hitherto discussed by activists, human rights practitioners, and engaged journalists, its mission consists of trying to fill the gaps between disparate accounts that foreground particular aspects of the occupation, but that rarely strive to probe the type and nature of the regime in which they coalesce. The attempt made here to examine the occupation as a unique political configuration derives from a belief that such an inquiry is essential for forming effective resistance to the occupation and for coming to terms with the real prospects of bringing it to an end.

The analysis ventured in this book is predicated on the observation that sheer, brutal military violence may be one operational conduit of the occupation regime, but does not represent the sophistication of means and diversification of ends involved in its control of the population as a whole and of each individual within it. In addition, our analytical framework leans toward the view that the more or less abrupt moments in which military might is unleashed and in which the occupation's use of power becomes excessive and the regime seems to lose control, foregoing any attempt at regulating its effects, are actually symptomatic of a skewed relation between the regime and its subjects. This relation can also be found at the basis of the occupation's more mundane modes of operation, and it is only accentuated and becomes more visible during military attacks.

Although they are subjects of the occupation regime, the Palestinians are actually cast as noncitizens of the Israeli state. They have been ruled for more than four decades by a power that denies their political rights and that too often violates their basic human rights under the pretext of an indefinite state of exception justified by Israel's "belligerent occupation" that has become part of the framing and justification of the annual renewal of a formal state of emergency. The essays collected here look into the relation of the exception that constitutes Palestinians as bare life and exposes them to the whims of a sovereign power whose agents may violate Palestinian integrity and dignity of body and mind with impunity.[2] They discuss extensively the radicalization of the sovereign exception in Israel/Palestine today, the shifting balance between military violence and other forms of control of everyday life, and the changing forms of the legal and ethical regulation of military violence. At the same time, the essays collected in this volume leave unheeded the possibility that the occupation might be transformed, if it has not been transformed already, into a pure and simple war machine that is indistinguishably directed against civilians and noncivilians alike.

Rather than studying Israeli warfare in the Occupied Territories per se, this book concentrates for the most part on the deployment of the occupying forces and on the strategies that they promote before, after, and beyond the moment of warfare. By so doing, it provides maps that make it possible to trace the routes that lead to outbursts of extreme political violence, whose fiercest manifestation to date has been Israel's assault on the Gaza strip in December 2008–January 2009, in which more than thirteen hundred Palestinians have been killed, more than half of them civilians.

Many in the West have considered Israel's assault on Gaza to be justified in its aims, even though not necessarily in its means. Under a critical gaze of the kind we offer here, it is necessary to ask first what it is exactly that one justifies. Justifications, like intentions, are bracketed here more or less systematically to make room for descriptions. When the occupation is viewed as a rationalized system that encompasses diverse and sometimes conflicting techniques of domination and control, the seasonal outbursts of military violence that have recurred periodically since 2002 can no longer be considered in isolation from one another and from the occupation regime as a whole. From this viewpoint, the latest assault on Gaza appears to be embedded in a calculated process of "catastrophization" that Israel has wreaked on the Gaza Strip. This process started with Israel's imposition of a general closure during the Gulf War in 1991, a closure that was relaxed somewhat during the Oslo years, tightened forcefully with the second intifada, and then, after the disengagement in August 2005, turned into a full-fledged military siege. Without employing much power, simply by closing the Gaza Strip, preventing the movement of people and commodities, restricting the flow of gas and electricity, letting the already failing sewer system collapse completely, Israel has turned the strip into a zone of emergency.

Without denying the possibility that the assault on Gaza may be a sign of another transformation of the occupation regime, this volume sets out to elucidate the logics of power and rule from which such deadly attacks have emanated and that stand a high chance of being reinstated after the fog of war will have faded away. It is the task of this book to offer a point of view that enables one to understand how extreme violence and much less brutal techniques of governmentality are woven together to produce the occasional eruptions of "wars" and the ongoing course of submission, resistance, and "peace talks" that characterize not only the recent phase of the conflict, but the occupation as a special type of regime. It is worth remembering, for example, that the assault on Gaza has been conducted on the basis of extremely close surveillance of the territory and its population and of detailed knowledge of streets, people, and social groups that has been gathered during forty-one years of Israel's domination (the digital database that Israel constructed during the last two decades was never given to the Palestinian Authority when it took limited control over the Gaza Strip following the Oslo Accords). The relation between the mundane forms of the occupation power described in this book and its delicate balance of the administration of life and death, on the one hand, and the military operations it wages against the Palestinians, where lethal force becomes the rule, on the other, parallels Carl Schmitt's depiction of the relation between enmity and war. "War," claims Schmitt, "has its own grammar…but politics remain its brain. It does not have its own logic."[3] The more "civilized" regime of occupation, with its ongoing modes of domination and control, is the brain behind the periodical outbursts of violence, even when they radically depart from the arsenal of the everyday means of coercion. For this reason, as much as the analysis advanced here is surpassed by the pace of events in Israel/Palestine, its historical and structural account of the occupation acquires an even more critical relevance vis-à-vis the recent military operation in Gaza at the beginning of 2009.

This book has been conceived in an atmosphere that is generally hostile to the kind of political questions and theoretical perspectives it strives to open. In Israel and among many foreign observers, the occupation, which has been conceived as both temporary and external, is generally understood as an inevitable project of the Israeli state, and not as a political system in its own right that to a large extent determines the nature of this state. Military violence is usually dissociated from the ongoing operation of the apparatus of domination and discussed in terms of the "security needs" of a peaceful society facing terrorist attacks or examined in terms of the legal dictates of human rights and proportionality in the use of force. Clichés taken from ideological narratives about the history of the Jewish people, the Zionist movement, the Holocaust, and the Israeli-Arab conflict are too often mobilized to close questions that call for theory-guided analysis and hinder the consideration of the occupation as a system of power with its own history, structure, and logic.

As a system of power, the occupation became an object of study for a variety of academic disciplines only in the late 1980s. The forerunners who initiated this line of inquiry were the Palestinian National Lawyers Guild and later El Haq and the Palestinian Association for Human Rights, which already in the late 1970s and early 1980s issued reports not only on human rights violations, but also on various techniques of the occupying power.[4] In the early 1980s, Meron Benvenisti, an Israeli geographer and for a short while deputy mayor of Jerusalem, started collecting data on the colonial projects of the occupying power and its governmental practices and regulations. His detailed reports issued until the end of that decade were the first in-depth studies of the occupation.[5] The Israeli-Palestinian joint project of the Alternative Information Centre contributed to these early efforts of a radical leftist perspective through which daily Palestinian life was analyzed alongside major political events within a coherent theoretical context.

The academic research that followed these early attempts at documenting and understanding the occupation has always been much indebted to the corpus of documentation produced by human rights groups and political activists, both local, Palestinian and Israeli, and international. This corpus started to grow rapidly with the first intifada and the mushrooming of nongovernmental organizations working in the Occupied Territories. However, the theoretical framework used for the collection of data and its analysis was often too narrow, formally legalistic, or solely concerned with the moves and statements of major political players. Very little attention was given to the fast consolidation of a new regime that incorporates and constrains the production of knowledge about its various aspects. A towering exception was the work of Meron Benvenisti, who has been assiduously examining the structural components of this regime and who offered new models for analyzing it. In the late 1980s, in a groundbreaking work, the late Israeli sociologist Baruch Kimmerling joined Benvenisti and insisted on the need to analyze the occupation not as a temporary project external to the Israeli state, but as an essential part of its "system of control."[6]

The work done in the Israeli academy by sociologists, political scientists, geographers, and jurists did not follow this direction and usually failed to address the occupation as a system of power, let alone as an essential part of Israeli state apparatuses. Outside Israel, there have been several attempts to cope with Israel's ongoing rule in the Occupied Territories, but most of these were usually framed within a politico-theoretical perspective—either nationalist or anticolonialist—that determined the answers before opening the questions. Some exceptions nevertheless can be mentioned that have done a refined analysis on the relationship between power structures and social classes inside the Occupied Palestinian Territories and on the Israeli control and surveillance regime, notably the work of Salim Tamari and Jamil Hilal.[7] Only in the mid-1990s did works start to appear in which scholars were seriously looking for new approaches for gathering information and new theoretical models to analyze and explain it. Ian Lustick developed a comparative model for analyzing colonial conflicts over land that colonizers consider part of their homeland;[8] Sara Roy studied the economic "de-development" of Gaza;[9] Juval Portugali used a geographical model of "inclusive relations" to analyze the social and geographical implications of Palestinian labor in the Israeli economy.[10]

More new, important studies appeared in the last decade. David Kretzmer analyzed the deep implication of Israel's Supreme Court in ruling the territories,[11] and James Ron suggested a comparative model for understanding different types of violence used by Israel to rule the Palestinians within the Occupied Territories and to fight them outside the Israeli system of control, mainly in Lebanon.[12] After the failure of the Oslo Accords and the eruption of the second intifada, a new wave of studies has appeared with a wide range of interests, disciplinary orientations, and theoretical perspectives. Palestinian scholars have mainly followed two directions of research. The first has been to analyze the small dramas of the daily life of the Palestinians, taking into account the political reality of the occupation as a basic backdrop. This approach has yielded multiauthor volumes on the first and second intifada,[13] the work of Salim Tamari on the emerging new Palestinian elite,[14] and the work of Rema Hammami on the emerging economy in the checkpoint areas.[15] The second trend of research has invested in the production of a new form of knowledge very dear to the donor community and to the many international organizations active in the territories since the late 1980s. This genre of research has relied quite heavily on surveys and opinion polls that have yielded rather descriptive accounts of the living conditions, attitudes, and expectations of Palestinians under the occupation, accounts that have often been devoid of critical interpretation.[16] During the same period, there has appeared in-depth research by Israeli, Palestinian, and international scholars on the military court system,[17] on the interpretation of international law by the Israeli legal system,[18] on the presence of nongovernmental organizations in the territories,[19] on the economy under the occupation,[20] and on the geography of colonization and separation.[21] The works collected in this book owe a particular debt to this recent wave of studies, in which they, too, take part.[22]

The various essays in the book represent a concerted effort to extricate from the empirical reality of the occupation several basic principles that may account for the regularities in its modus operandi. It is those principles that inform the comparison with other historical regimes, as well as the genealogical analysis of the occupation with which some of the essays engage. The essays gathered here diverge with regard to the prevailing modalities of the occupation regime in various periods and their order of significance. They examine shifts in and of these modalities and highlight their different conditions or ramifications. The principles that emerge from the studies do not convey a uniform and coherent portrait of the occupation. Instead, they highlight disparate rationalities and mechanisms of power whose heterogeneity reinforces the overall effectiveness and perseverance of this regime.

According to the analyses advanced here, the salient features of the occupation can be briefly summarized as submission without rights, separation, colonization, normalization of the state of exception, and humanitarian concern. Submission without rights emerges as the underlying rationality of the occupation regime and the regular outcome produced by its other operational principles, whatever their more immediate aims. If the intentionality of the occupying power is bracketed, neither separation nor colonization can be considered as its telos and should instead be perceived as modalities through which submission is articulated, on which it relies, and what it reciprocally enables and reinforces. Several essays in this volume dissect the subjugation of the Palestinian noncitizens by the Israeli ruling apparatus as an interminable process that relies not only on the tight, bureaucratized control of movement but also on other means of coercion that pursue a more ambitious reframing of bodies and minds. They show that in the current phase of the occupation, submission is mainly generated by a unique logic of withheld or suspended violence, in which the means of violence are on display rather than in actual use, and by the systematic production of uncertainty that strips the subject of rational mastery of her future and destiny.[23]

When viewed as the regular and calculated outcome of the occupation regime, submission without rights sheds critical light on the Israeli project of separation and on its professed agenda of severing the links between the Israeli polity inside the Green Line and the mass of Palestinian noncitizens in the Occupied Territories.

The analyses ventured here show that rather than to a clear-cut division between territories and between populations, separation points to a series of inclusive exclusions that expand the links of the disenfranchised Palestinian population to the Israeli ruling apparatus while cutting this population off from its territory. Separation sets in motion an unending project that combines the meticulous administration of Palestinian movement and the colonial fragmentation of Palestinian space.[24] While the material outcome of separation and its twin pillars of paper persecution and enclave geography is an inflation of domestic borders and muddled spatialities, as a mental condition, separation translates into endemic disorientation for occupier and occupied alike.[25] In both respects, separation is an irreversible political process that preceded the occupation of the West Bank and Gaza Strip, and whose consequences are bound to outlive the occupation regime.

Intimately interwoven with the separation principle, the colonization principle entails the promotion of economic dependence, systematic dispossession, and "de-development" that severely undermine the Palestinian social fabric. Several essays in this volume probe the rationalization of the colonizing power under the aegis of the Oslo "peace process" that paradoxically served to institutionalize entrenched asymmetries between Israelis and Palestinians.[26] In addition to these socioeconomic analyses, other studies highlight two basic conditions for operation of the colonizing power that are often overlooked: its dependency on the instrumentalization of economic deprivation and social misery within Israeli society,[27] and its inscription in a skewed bureaucratic apparatus that operates not through rationalized rules, but rather through miraculous interventions, and whose unpredictability is the key to its effectiveness.[28]

Indeed, colonization and separation both presuppose the exclusion of the Occupied Palestinian Territories and their inhabitants from the pale of law and the normalization of a state of exception in which the Palestinian population as a whole and individuals within it are exposed to arbitrary violence and coercive regulation of daily life. The most vivid expression perhaps of this protracted state of exception is the Palestinian refugee camp that currently functions as an experimental laboratory for control and surveillance exercised by Israeli authorities and international agencies alike.[29] Pace Giorgio Agamben, the thick description of the occupation regime in this volume shows that the suspension of law and the forsaking of life do not completely overlap. The denial of Palestinian citizenship and the replacement of the rule of law by a tapestry of regulations, procedures, and decrees characterized the occupation regime from its inception and set the stage for its more active and violent abandonment of Palestinian life in recent years.[30] At the same time, as several essays here demonstrate, the normalization of the state of exception is a facilitating framework that is moderated, legitimized, and reproduced by the logic of humanitarian concern that is driven by an inverse moral aspiration and yet assumes an analogous structure of exception. Rather than studying humanitarianism as an autonomous, external force that strives to alleviate emergency conditions in the Occupied Territories without affecting relations of power, studies in this book attest to the significant role humanitarian considerations have come to play as an integral part of the machinery of the occupying power itself.[31] A residue of Israel's abandonment of its legal duty toward the welfare of the occupied Palestinians, humanitarian concern is designed to attenuate the repercussions of military violence, creeping colonization, the restrictions on movement, and the fragmentation of space, while giving them a moral and legal seal of approval.

In addition to the scholarly articles, the book contains three projects that experiment with less conventional modes of documentation and analysis while directly confronting the orders of representation and memory that underpin the occupation regime. The three projects are "Chronology of the Occupation Regime, 1967–2007," researched and composed by Ariel Handel; "The Occupation's Paper Trail," a selection of documents put together by Michal Givoni; and "The (In)Human Spatial Condition," a visual essay in five chapters with photographs selected and annotated by Ariella Azoulay.

The chronology of the first forty years of the occupation is designed to provide a background for the analyses put forward in the essays, but it can also be used as an independent reference tool. It tracks the emergence, the evolutions, the disappearance, and the transformation of modalities, techniques, and devices of power implemented in the West Bank and Gaza Strip since June 1967. The chronology departs from traditional histories of the Israeli-Palestinian conflict that are usually framed by overarching narratives of war and peace, punctuated by dramatic moments of military operations and diplomatic negotiations, and that consider the courage or shortsightedness of statesmen as decisive factors. Rather, this chronological account attempts to uncover and to group together the traces of political practices that framed the everyday existence of Palestinians under the occupation, practices that correspond to and are sometimes influenced by attempts at reconciliation or by violent escalations and that yet follow independent courses of evolution. Those practices may be cruel or banal, successful or failed, designed to repress certain behaviors or to encourage others. The items that relate to them are collated in a deliberately crude and laconic manner that reflects the piecemeal and tentative operation of the occupation regime, the interplay of domination and resistance that shapes its changing strategies, and the interaction of seemingly incongruous apparatuses—military, administrative, legal, and humanitarian— in the production and reproduction of its commanding power. Wide coverage of the occupation in the press and in human rights reports since the first Palestinian uprising has made the documentation of its last two decades thicker than the reconstruction of its early history, regarding which much has still to be recovered from closed archives.

The annotated collection of documents entitled "The Occupation's Paper Trail" represents a similar effort to put together an anatomy of the current power structures of the occupation. This mode of representation privileges crude documentations over argumentative theses and construes the banality of the occupation as the primary source of its horror. While not pretending to be innocent of political bias, this selection of letters, forms, orders, procedures, and other original documents presents an attempt to imagine the future archive of the occupation and to assemble and preserve its exhibits as of now. It involves an exercise in projecting from the future into the present the figure of the moral spectator who stands astonished in front of showcases in museums dedicated to the commemoration of historical catastrophes. This archival project reclaims the logic of evidence that informs human rights discourse and that is invariably employed by political authorities as a means to silence their victims. It reinscribes this logic in a political stance that disentangles factuality and detachment. Here again, the fact that the paper trails that we could follow were incredibly short, that many regular policies did not seem to leave textual traces behind, and that only a tiny segment of the gray materials that the occupation regime produces on a daily basis could be accessed is itself indicative of the type of political power in question. The difficulties of documenting the occupation can be read as signs of the increasing arbitrariness of the regime, as well as of the calculated obfuscation of the transparency that characterized the Civil Administration in earlier periods in favor of an unaccountable and at times denialist approach.

In Ariella Azoulay's photographic essay, "The In(Human) Spatial Condition," photographs are not used as illustrations attached to things already said elsewhere, but as a sui generis field of observation that forces new questions upon the observer and opens new points of view. In the five chapters of her essay, Azoulay presents visual claims that address two modes of intervention in space operated by the occupying power: destruction and the administration of movement. Using a handful of photographs selected out of an immense and growing corpus of visual evidence, Azoulay seeks to construct a typology of the modes and techniques of the ruling power. The seeming aestheticization of brutal acts of control and events of destruction denaturalizes categories such as "illegal construction," "operational needs," and "house demolition" used to describe and justify various acts of the Israeli state. The display of the photographs and their analytic interpretation helps even the more learned student of the occupation, who is usually keen on reading and deconstructing official documents, to observe certain regularities in the operation of power that often go unnoticed.

Work on this volume started in the framework of a research project on the humanitarian aspects of the Israeli occupation that was inaugurated in 2003 under the auspices of the Van Leer Jerusalem Institute. The idea behind the project was to bring together Israeli, Palestinian, and international scholars and activists to reflect on the most recent phase of the occupation, which corresponded more or less—and this time frame was to be put to question as part of the broader interrogation—to the period of the second intifada. The initial observation that guided the group's activities was that the occupation was in the process of morphing into a low-intensity humanitarian crisis in which social suffering was both produced at unprecedented levels and used and abused as a primary strategic consideration by the occupation regime while gradually taking over other frames of reference of international response. The growing numbers of civilian causalities, the soaring rates of impoverishment, poverty, and unemployment, and the increasing level of dependence upon humanitarian assistance in the West Bank and Gaza Strip indicated that Israel had openly adopted a policy of active carelessness toward the lives and safety of the Palestinians. At the same time, the violent and destructive measures that Israel was implementing were intermeshed with institutionalized forms of humanitarian sensibility that were more ubiquitous than ever before and that had infiltrated the very logic of the occupation regime. Humanitarian agencies, human rights organizations, and even solidarity movements, all of whose operations in the region had increased dramatically since the outbreak of the second intifada, seemed to be interlocked into Israel's underlying project of undermining the Palestinian social fabric while preventing a full-fledged humanitarian disaster. The catastrophe was to remain an ever-present possibility, a constant threat for occupier and occupied alike, and both governmental and nongovernmental agencies, Israeli and international, were to join forces in holding it in check.

The group was initially preoccupied with the unwitting collaboration of humanitarian agencies in the politics of the occupation and with the cooptation of the discourse and practice of humanitarianism into the logic of "catastrophe in the making" that became the occupation's new face. Gradually, research was drawn into a broader interrogation of the rationalities, tools, and mechanisms that inform Israel's rule in and of the Palestinian territories, of which humanitarian practices and sensibilities came to be seen as but one aspect. The group focused on the modes of Israeli domination and for the most part did not venture to look into the consequences of these modes of domination from the perspective of Palestinian society and Palestinian daily life. This shift in orientation from the politics of humanitarianism to a broader and more ambitious analysis of the occupation regime was a response to the absence of a systematic and comprehensive account of the occupation regime and the tendency to regard it as a set of repressive measures and policies or as a prolonged series of humanitarian problems.

But the decision to privilege a structural analysis of the occupation regime, rather than a more traditional ethnographic or sociological study of its experienced reality, also came as a response to the composition of the research group. Our efforts to create a joint multinational team in which Israeli and Palestinian scholars would be equally represented were soon thwarted by the mundane reality of the occupation. As a result of Israel's restrictions on movement, access to Jerusalem has been extremely difficult for Palestinian scholars, who were forced to go through the hardship and humiliation involved in applying for a movement permit and in passing through the various checkpoints that separate Jerusalem from the West Bank. While some Palestinian scholars have not considered their participation in the joint Israeli-Palestinian research group to undermine their call for boycotting Israeli academic institutions (because the boycott campaign has explicitly encouraged cooperation and meeting with Israelis who oppose the occupation), others have considered the group as a legitimate target of the boycott and refused to cooperate with it. The partial and inevitably biased portrait of the occupation regime traced in this volume is therefore a reflection of the conditions of separation that it attempts to analyze and to challenge. A group of scholars composed exclusively of Palestinians or a team in which Israeli and Palestinians hold equal shares would have probably produced a quite different analysis of the occupation and might have prioritized other fault lines altogether in the history of the Israeli-Palestinian conflict. While the political obstructions designed to tear Israelis and Palestinians apart determine the setting in which each and every encounter takes place, this book is a living proof that their control of social relations is never complete.

NOTES

1   This technological analysis of the occupation regime is inspired by the works of Michel Foucault. For Foucault's own analyses of political technologies see mainly Michel Foucault, *Discipline and Punish: The Birth of the Prison,* trans. Alan Sheridan (New York: Vintage, 1979); *Security, Territory, Population: Lectures at the Collège de France, 1977–78,* ed. Michel Senellart, trans. Graham Burchell (New York: Palgrave Macmillan, 2007).

2   On the relation of the exception, see Giorgio Agamben, *Homo Sacer: Sovereign Power and Bare Life,* trans. Daniel Heller-Roazen (Stanford, CA: Stanford University Press, 1998).

3   Carl Schmitt, *The Concept of the Political,* trans. George Schwab (Chicago: University of Chicago Press, 1996), p. 34.

4   National Lawyers Guild, *Treatment of Palestinians in Israeli-occupied West Bank and Gaza: Report of the New York National Lawyers Guild,* Middle East delegation, 1977; National Lawyers Guild, *Treatment of Palestinians in Israeli-occupied West Bank and Gaza: Report of the New York National Lawyers Guild,* Middle East delegation, 1978.

5   Meron Benvenisti, The West Bank Data Project: A Survey of Israel's Policies, West Bank Data Base Project Report (Washington, D.C.: American Enterprise Institute for Public Policy Research, 1984); *Demographic, Economic, Legal, Social, and Political Developments in the West Bank,* West Bank Data Base Project Report (Jerusalem: Jerusalem Post, 1986); *Demographic, Economic, Legal, Social and Political Developments in the West Bank,* West Bank Data Base Project Report (Jerusalem: Jerusalem Post, 1987).

6   Baruch Kimmerling, "Boundaries and Frontiers of the Israeli Control System," in Baruch Kimmerling (ed.), *The Israeli State and Society: Boundaries and Frontiers* (Albany: State University of New York Press, 1989), pp. 265–84.

7   See Salim Tamari, "Israel's Search for A Native Pillar: The Village Leagues," in Nasser Aruri (ed.), *Occupation: Israel over Palestine* (Belmont, MA: Association of Arab American University Graduates, 1989); Jamil Hilal, *West Bank: Economic and Social Structure 1948–1974* (Beirut: Research Center, 1975) (in Arabic).

8   Ian S. Lustick, *Unsettled States, Disputed Land: Britain and Ireland, France and Algeria, Israel and the West Bank–Gaza* (Ithaca, NY: Cornell University Press, 1993).

9   Sara Roy, *The Gaza Strip: The Political Economy of De-Development* (Washington, D.C.: Institute of Palestinian Studies, 1995).

10 Juval Portugali, *Implicate Relations: Society and Space in the Israeli-Palestinian Conflict* (Dordrecht: Kluwer Academic Publishers, 1993).

11 David Kretzmer, *The Occupation of Justice: The Supreme Court of Israel and the Occupied Territories* (Albany: State University of New York Press, 2002).

12 James Ron, *Frontiers and Ghettos: State Violence in Serbia and Israel* (Berkeley: University of California Press, 2003).

13 See, for example, Jamal R. Nasser and Roger Heacock (eds.), *Intifada: Palestine at the Crossroads* (New York: Praeger, 2007) and Lisa Tarak (ed.), *Living Palestine: Family Survival, Resistance, and Mobility under Occupation* (Syracuse, NY: Syracuse University Press, 2007).

14 For example, Salim Tamari, "Authority and Society in the Interim Phase," in Ibrahim Abu-Lughod et al. (eds.), *The Palestinian-Israeli Declaration of Principles* (Birzeit: Birzeit University Publications, 1995), pp. 62–66.

15 Rema Hammami, "On the Importance of Thugs: The Moral Economy of a Checkpoint," *Middle East Report,* no. 231 (Summer 2004).

16 See, for example, Marianne Heiberg and Geir Øvensen, *Palestinian Society in Gaza, West Bank and Arab Jerusalem: A Survey of Living Conditions,* Fafo Report 151 (1993); R. Bocco, M. Brunner, L. De Martino, J. al-Husseini and F. Lapeyre, "Mesurer la fièvre palestinienne: Notes sur une expérience de monitoring des conditions de vie de la population civile palestinienne pendant la deuxième Intifada, 2000–2006," in *Annuaire Suisse des Politiques de Développement* 25, no. 2 (October 2006): pp. 79–94, as well as reports by the Palestinian Academic Society for the Study of International Affairs (PASIA) and the Birzeit University Community Health Unit.

17 Lisa Hajjar, *Courting Conflict: The Israeli Military Court System in the West Bank and Gaza* (Berkeley: University of California Press, 2005).

18 Aeyal M. Gross, "The Construction of a Wall between The Hague and Jerusalem: The Enforcement and Limits of Humanitarian Law and the Structure of Occupation," *Leiden Journal of International Law* 19, no. 2 (2006): pp. 393–440; "Human Proportions: Are Human Rights the Emperor's New Clothes of the International Law of Occupation?" *The European Journal of International Law* 18, no. 1 (2007): pp. 1–35; Orna Ben-Naftali and Keren R. Michaeli, "'We Must Not Make a Scarecrow of the Law': A Legal Analysis of the Israeli Policy of Targeted Killings," *Cornell International Law Journal* 36 (2003): pp. 233–92.

19 Sari Hanafi and Linda Tabar, *The Emergence of a Globalized Palestinian Elite: Donors, International Organizations and Local NGOs* (Jerusalem: Institute of Jerusalem Studies and Muwatin, 2005).

20 Arie Arnon, Sara Roy, and Leila Farsakh, *Palestinian Labour Migration to Israel: Labour, Land and Occupation* (London: Routledge, 2005); Arie Arnon, Israel Luski, Avia Spivak, and Jimmy Weinblatt, *The Palestinian Economy: Between Imposed Integration and Voluntary Separation* (Leiden: Brill, 1997).

21 Elisha Efrat, *The West Bank and Gaza Strip: A Geography of Occupation and Disengagement* (London: Routledge, 2006); Eyal Weizman, *Hollow Land: Israel's Architecture of Occupation* (London: Verso, 2007); Stephen Graham, "Constructing Urbicide by Bulldozer in the Occupied Territories," in Stephen Graham (ed.), *Cities, War, and Terrorism: Towards an Urban Geopolitics* (Oxford: Blackwell, 2004).

22 Two comprehensive studies of the occupation were written and published by three of this volume's contributors during the time in which the book was in the making. Neve Gordon's *Israel's Occupation* (Berkeley: University of California Press, 2008) is a thorough historical and analytical account of the major technologies of power developed by and incorporated into the occupation regime and the dialectics of their transformation. Ariella Azoulay and Adi Ophir's *This Regime Which is Not One: Occupation and Democracy between the Sea and the River* (Tel Aviv: Resling, 2008) (in Hebrew) surveys the history of the occupation, analyzes the modus operandi of the Israeli apparatuses of power since the second intifada, and seeks to explain the relatively peaceful and often disavowed coexistence of a semiliberal "ethnic democracy" and oppressive separatist regime within the framework of the Israeli political system.

23 See, respectively, Ariella Azoulay and Adi Ophir, "The Order of Violence," and Neve Gordon and Dani Filc, "The Destruction of the Risk Society and the Ascendancy of Hamas," in this volume.

24 See Hilla Dayan, "Regimes of Separation: Israel/Palestine and the Shadow of Apartheid," and Ariel Handel, "Where, Where to, and When in the Occupied Territories: An Introduction to Geography of Disaster," in this volume.

25 See Ronen Shamir, "Occupation as Disorientation: The Impossibility of Borders," in this volume.

26 See Leila Farsakh, "From Domination to Destruction: The Palestinian Economy under the Israeli Occupation," and Caroline Abu-Sada, "Cultivating Dependence: Palestinian Agriculture under the Israeli Occupation," in this volume.

27 See Gadi Algazi, "Matrix in Bil'in: Colonial Capitalism in the Occupied Territories," in this volume.

28 See Yehouda Shenhav and Yael Berda, "The Colonial Foundations of the State of Exception: Juxtaposing the Israeli Occupation of the Palestinian Territories with Colonial Bureaucratic History," in this volume.

29 See Sari Hanafi, "Palestinian Refugee Camps in the Palestinian Territory: Territory of Exception and Locus of Resistance," in this volume.

30 On the fabric of law in the Occupied Territories see Orna Ben-Naftali, Aeyal M. Gross, and Keren Michaeli, "The Illegality of the Occupation Regime: The Fabric of Law in the Occupied Palestinian Territory," in this volume. On the violent escalation of the occupation regime in recent years see Neve Gordon, "From Colonization to Separation: Exploring the Structure of Israel's Occupation," in this volume.

31 See for example Eyal Weizman, "Thanato-tactics," in this volume.

The Illegality of the Occupation Regime:
The Fabric of Law in the Occupied Palestinian Territory

Orna Ben-Naftali, Aeyal M. Gross, and Keren Michaeli

And what will be the case if examination of the alternative route leads to the conclusion that the only route that provides the minimum required security is the existing route? Without it, there is no security for the Israelis. With it, there is a severe injury to the *fabric of life* of the [Palestinian] residents of the villages. What will the case be in such a situation? That is the most difficult of the questions...it seems to us that the time has not yet come to confront this difficulty, and the time may never come.
—The Israeli High Court of Justice

The fabric of life under an occupation is tailor-made by law to fit the design of any particular occupation regime. That design varies, but the legal imagination has stopped short of conceiving of an occupation regime—as distinct from specific actions undertaken to sustain it—as illegal.[1] In this essay, we advance three interrelated propositions: a general proposition that an occupation regime may be illegal, regardless of whether it was occasioned by a lawful use of force in self-defense or by aggression; a specific proposition that the continued Israeli control over the occupied Palestinian territory conquered in 1967 is an illegal occupation,[2] even if the Israeli narrative of a war in self-defense is accepted universally; and a derivative proposition according to which the defining feature of this illegal regime is its indeterminacy, an indeterminacy that functions to legitimize what would otherwise be clearly illegal: obfuscating the boundaries between occupation and nonoccupation, between annexation and nonannexation, between the temporary and the indefinite and, indeed, between the rule and the exception. This regime sustains an indefinite occupation that amounts to de facto annexation. In this manner, the international regime of occupation, a regime designed to ensure that the fabric of life in an occupied territory remains as intact as possible, premised on as quick as possible a return to the normal order of the international society (built normatively around sovereign states each exercising effective control over the people within its territory) has been manipulated in a manner that legitimizes the tearing apart of the fabric of Palestinian life while advancing the political agenda of Israeli expansionism.

BASIC DEFINITIONS

The above propositions refer to two terms that need to be defined: "occupation" and "occupied Palestinian territory."

The phenomenon of occupation is currently defined as "the effective control of a power (be it one or more states or an international organization, such as the United Nations) over a territory to which that power has no sovereign title, without the volition of the sovereign of that territory."[3]

There are two notable features to this widely accepted definition: First, it is expansive in a manner designed to cover varied types of occupation. The rationale behind this expansiveness is clear: The moment an occupation exists, the normative regime of occupation applies. This regime comprises a host of humanitarian rules, incorporated into the 1907 Fourth Hague Convention and annexed regulations, the 1949 Fourth Geneva Convention, and the 1977 First Additional Protocol of the Geneva Conventions.[4] Bearing in mind that occupying powers are notoriously reluctant to abide by these rules, their first line of defense being the denial that the specific situation qualifies as an occupation,[5] the broad definition is designed to curb any such defiance. Israel's rejection of the applicability of the Fourth Geneva Convention to the situation underscores the point.[6]

The second notable feature of the definition is that it incorporates the principle of the inalienability of sovereignty. This principle is the fundamental tenet of the law of occupation in three senses: First, it indicates that occupation does not confer title.[7] Second, it recognizes that the situation of occupation is exceptional, because it deviates from the normal order of sovereign states insofar as it reflects the suspension of the link between sovereignty and effective control. It is this exceptionality, in turn, that defines both the substantive and the temporal nature of the relationship between the occupying power and the sovereign.[8] Taken together, these principles demarcate the boundaries of the phenomenon in relation to the normal order of the international state system.

It should finally be noted that the proviso to the definition "without the volition of the sovereign of that territory" presents a legal presumption that underscores the distinction between "effective control" and "sovereignty": It is presumed that the severance of the link between sovereignty and effective control is always without the volition of the sovereign, but this presumption may be refuted at any particular point in time. Thus, for instance, the initial presence of foreign troops in a certain territory may have the blessing of the local population, but over time, it is presumed that the latter would prefer to effect their legal sovereignty through the effective exercise of self-government.

The "occupied Palestinian territory" refers to the areas conquered by Israel in 1967 and over which Israel exercises effective control. The territory conquered by Israel in 1967 is composed of the West Bank, the Gaza Strip, and East Jerusalem. Since 1999, the United Nations has gradually substituted the term "occupied Palestinian territory" for the terms the West Bank, the Gaza Strip, and East Jerusalem and "the Palestinian occupied territories" to connote the contiguous nature of the area where the Palestinians are entitled to exercise their right of self-determination.[9]

The 2005 unilateral disengagement from the Gaza Strip gave rise to the Israeli contention that that area is no longer under occupation.[10] This contention is designed to relieve Israel of its legal obligations as an occupying power. In this and in other instances that may arise in the future, the legal question is what constitutes "effective control."

Current international law seems to be polarized between two approaches to this question: One maintains that "effective control" is closely associated with the *presence of troops* on the ground; the other holds that the decisive criterion is the *potential power* to exercise exclusive governmental authority over individuals, a potential which depends inter alia on the inability of the lawful sovereign to exercise such power. The International Court of Justice (ICJ) has recently taken the approach that occupation requires establishing and exercising authority. While this approach is about establishing authority, rather than about the presence of troops on the ground, it can still be contrasted with the approach focusing on the potential to exercise authority, which was actually the approach taken by the Israeli High Court of Justice already in the early 1980s.[11]

It seems to us that a flexible approach, less concerned with status and more concerned with the scope of obligations that a governmental authority should shoulder vis-à-vis people who are affected by its actions, is both reasonable and supported by the relevant jurisprudence.[12] The parameters for determining, in each particular case, the scope of said obligations include the de-facto relations of power (its nature, intensity, and effect) between the authority and individuals subject to its power; the context of the specific power relations (historical, geographic, economic, cultural, and political factors relative to its duration, consequential relations of dependence, and so on); and the need to avoid a vacuum in humanitarian protection offered to individuals. The application of these criteria to the Gaza Strip suggests that as of the autumn of 2007, Israel's effective control over the Gaza Strip, entailed broad humanitarian obligations and indeed amounts to an occupation.[13]

The proposition that an occupation regime in general—and that the Israeli occupation in particular—could be illegal may appear self-evident to nonlawyers who are critical of the occupation. Not so to international lawyers, even if they are critical of the occupation. Indeed, while there is a wealth of legal writings on various aspects of this occupation, primarily concerned with the manner with which specific Israeli actions comply—or fail to comply—with Israel's obligations as an occupying power under the law of occupation, virtually no attention has been paid to the question of the legality of the occupation itself.[14]

Thus, when the secretary-general of the United Nations, in a statement made to the Security Council on March 12, 2002, called on Israel to "end the illegal occupation,"[15] this reference was immediately characterized as a "redefinition of the Middle East conflict.... A new and provocative label of 'illegality' is now out of the chute and running loose."[16] This presumed genie, however, was soon put back in the bottle when the spokesman for the secretary-general clarified that the word "illegal" referred to Israel's refusal to accept the legal obligation that the status of an occupying power entails and to its actions that run contrary to those obligations, actions that have been declared illegal by the Security Council and the General Assembly.[17] As a result, the discourse resumed its habitual focus on specific actions undertaken within the normative regime of the occupation, as distinct from the nature of the occupation itself. Even the advisory opinion rendered by the International Court of Justice in *Construction of a Wall*,[18] while critical of both this construction and of the related settlement enterprise, and while decreeing their illegality, still focused on these specific actions and did not question the legality of the occupation regime as such.

The virtual immunity from critical discussion conferred on the regime of this occupation cannot be explained away on political grounds. Indeed, the Israeli occupation has been subject to a widespread political as well as moral critique, both internationally and domestically. The reason lies in the occupation being perceived as a phenomenon that is defined in factual, rather than in normative, terms. Thus posited, the fact of occupation generates normative results—the application of the international laws of occupation—but in itself does not seem to rank within that or any other normative order.

One might understand this practically axiomatic perception in three ways. The first would be to conceive of the phenomenon of occupation as a mere fact of power, a kind of *Grundnorm*, as formulated by Hans Kelsen in *General Theory of Law and State,* which itself is grounded in an extralegal domain.[19] The second alternative is to situate the phenomenon within the sphere of law as a negative arrangement: Since there is no norm that prohibits occupation, the phenomenon is legally permissible.[20] The third option is to identify a norm that governs the phenomenon, differentiating between a legal and an illegal occupation. This identification involves a legal construction relating to both the normative order that is generated by an occupation and to the normative order that generates the legal regime of the occupation.

Clearly, the first two alternatives exclude the propositions this article wishes to advance. Both, however, are problematic: The barren beauty of the Kelsian formalism underlying the first option offers a vision of law far too narrow to account for the substantive interaction of form with function, structure with substance, fact with norm, and power with law.[21] The splendid "majesty of law"[22] implicit in the second option is equally deceptive in purporting to subject power to law in a manner that may well disregard the many other ways and means of their interaction.[23] Both thus generate the same troubling result, that is, the rendering of international law as an apology for power,[24] and the consequential exclusion of the very phenomenon of occupation from a critical legal review. Such exclusion is an invitation for excessive power.

This essay posits the third approach. This approach locates the occupation within a normative framework that differentiates between legality and illegality. It thus redefines the contours of the legal discourse on occupation. That discourse is in dire need of development.

CURRENT DISCOURSE ON THE LEGALITY OF OCCUPATION REGIMES

Post–World War legal history records only one instance in which a particular occupation was construed as illegal, that is, as a phenomenon subject to a legal standard that determines its legality or lack thereof. That instance was the advisory opinion rendered by the International Court of Justice on the continued presence of South Africa in Namibia following the revocation of the mandate by the General Assembly.[25] The court's starting point was the historical fact of South Africa's presence in South West Africa / Namibia, and it proceeded to deduce its illegality from various pertinent components that had characterized this fact. Our inquiry proposes to complement this historical approach with an analytical perspective that focuses on the legal and political structure of the phenomenon of occupation in the hope of thereby contributing not merely to the legal qualification of the Israeli occupation of the territory, but also to the international legal discourse on occupation in the political space we all inhabit.

Current "interventions"—the euphemistic term used for "occupation"—require the development of this discourse. The occupation of Iraq indicates that the phenomenon of occupation, far from becoming obsolete, is being revived and claims legitimacy on the basis of purposes otherwise foreign to belligerent occupations, that is, as the liberation of a people from an abusive regime. Since the occupation is perceived as a fact, rather than as a norm, the discourse surrounding the invasion and occupation of Iraq focused primarily on the legality and legitimacy of the use of force by the United States and not on that of the occupation. Underlying these arguments, however, is the implicit presumption that the legitimacy accorded to the U.S. action extends to the occupation itself.[26] At the same time, the little discussion that the issue has generated thus far seems to be both polarized and lacking specificity. Thus, the inherent tension between the right to self-determination and the legality of the occupation has led Antonio Cassese to conclude that "self-determination is violated whenever there is a military invasion or belligerent occupation of a foreign country, except where the occupation—although unlawful—is of a minimal duration or is solely intended as a measure of repelling, under Article 1 of the UN Charter, an armed attack initiated by the vanquished Power and consequently is not protracted."[27] This view, then, regards all occupations as inherently unlawful, but admits that the legitimacy of an occupation's initial act—that is, the use of force in self-defense—may provide a justification for its existence, subject to a strict temporal limitation.[28]

Eyal Benvenisti advances a different position, positing that the notion of "illegal occupation" could amount to "major qualifications if not a revolution in the law of occupation."[29] This notion, observes Benvenisti, has its roots in various international documents, wherein an occupation was grouped together with unlawful modalities of governance such as colonialism and apartheid.[30] The latter, however, should not be read as advocating the outlawing of the modality of occupation in its entirety. Rather, only an occupier who uses this modality as an indefinite grant of power and refuses to negotiate its withdrawal "abuses its power and might taint its continuing presence in the occupied territory with illegality."[31] An occupation that has not been thus abused retains its legal validity. Support for this limited notion of illegality, says Benvenisti, is found in Security Council Resolution 1483 of May 22, 2003, which recognized the authorities, responsibilities, and obligations under applicable international law of the "occupying powers" in Iraq and called upon all concerned to comply fully "with their obligations under international law including in particular the Geneva Conventions of 1949 and the Hague Regulations of 1907,"[32] thereby reviving the neutral connotation of the doctrine of belligerent occupation and relieving it of its derogatory undertone.[33]

Practice has echoed, to a large extent, this scholarly debate. Thus, the inherent tension between the full enjoyment of human rights and the situation of occupation has led the special rapporteur of the United Nations Commission of Human Rights, John Dugard, to conclude in one of his reports on "the violation of human rights in the occupied Arab territories," that "violations of human rights are a necessary consequence of military occupation."[34] Israel understood this conclusion to imply that "while military occupation may not itself be inherently illegal, it necessarily leads to violations of human rights and so presumably must be illegal, if not directly then, at least, indirectly," and proceeded to assert that this is "an attempt to rewrite international law" and to characterize it as "a remarkable legal thesis [that] contravenes the entire body of humanitarian law dealing with belligerent occupation."[35]

The above polarized positions underscore the need to clarify and develop the legal discourse on the matter and to refine the criteria by which the legality of an occupation may be measured. Torn between the position that all occupations are inherently illegal and the position that an occupation is a neutral fact that defies any such characterization, the criteria that have been advanced in this context seem to focus on either the legitimacy of the initial act of occupation or on the legality of specific actions undertaken during the course of an occupation. This essay proposes to advance the discussion by positing that an occupation, while neither initially nor inherently illegal, is not neutral. Occasioned by and extending the use of force, regardless of its initial justification and notwithstanding the prohibition on this use,[36] it is to be viewed and monitored critically, lest the very necessary law of occupation becomes a shield for the violation of its own extrinsic purpose and intrinsic principles. The specification of these principles and purpose provide adequate criteria for determining the legality or illegality of any specific occupation. Lack of such criteria may well generate a legitimizing effect, allowing this precarious, albeit not necessarily illegal situation to become illegal.

THE CRITERIA FOR THE DETERMINATION OF THE LEGALITY
OF AN OCCUPATION REGIME

The underlying principle of the international legal order rests on a presumption of sovereign equality between states.[37] Under current international law, that sovereignty is understood as vested in the people, giving expression to the right to self-determination.[38] Analytically, the phenomenon of occupation presents this order with the challenge of the extraordinary. The severance of the link between sovereignty and effective control entailed in an occupation suspends this order as it relates to the occupied territory.[39] This exceptional situation cannot thus be defined as either a fact or a norm, because it exists only by virtue of the suspension of the norm.[40] It partakes of both. The international law of occupation enters the picture signifying both the need to distinguish between order and chaos and the need to distinguish between orders: between the rule and the exception. In distinguishing between order and chaos, its function is to manage the situation, to eliminate chaos through control of the exceptional situation. In distinguishing between orders, its function is to create an orderly space that is defined by its exceptionality, by its suspension of the rule.

It is our position that the legal validity of the phenomenon of occupation as it relates to the function of managing the situation is to be measured in relation to three interrelated fundamental legal principles.

First, sovereignty and title in an occupied territory are not vested in the occupying power. The roots of this principle emanate from the principle of the inalienability of sovereignty through actual or threatened use of force. Under contemporary international law and in view of the principle of self-determination, sovereignty is vested in the population under occupation.[41]

Second, the occupying power is entrusted with the management of public order and civil life in the territory under control. In view of the principle of self-determination, the people under occupation are the beneficiaries of this trust. The dispossession and subjugation of these people is thus a violation of this trust.[42]

Third, the occupation is temporary.[43] It may be neither permanent nor indefinite.

The violation of each of these principles, as distinct from the violation of a specific norm that reflects an aspect of these principles, renders an occupation illegal. Further, these principles interrelate: the substantive constraints on the managerial discretion of the occupier elucidated in the first and second principles, respectively, generate the conclusion that it must necessarily be temporary, and the violation of the temporal constraints expressed in third principle cannot but violate the first two, thereby corrupting the normative regime of occupation. This occupation is illegal. This is the nature of the Israeli occupation. The discussion below under "The Intrinsic Dimensions of the Israeli Occupation of the Occupied Palestinian Territory" substantiates this argument.

We further submit that the legal validity of the phenomenon of occupation in its functioning to create an orderly space that is nevertheless distinct from the normal political order of sovereign equality between states is to be measured by its exceptionality. Once the boundaries between the exception and the rule are blurred, the occupation becomes illegal. The nexus between the two functions is clear: An occupation that is illegal from the perspective of managing an otherwise chaotic situation is also illegal in that it obfuscates the distinction between the rule and its exception. Yet the distinction between the two forms of illegality is important. The former is grounded in the intrinsic principles of the law of occupation, while the latter is extrinsic to this law and delineates its limits. The Israeli occupation is illegal both intrinsically and extrinsically. The discussion below under "The Extrinsic Dimensions of the Israeli Occupation of the Occupied Palestinian Territory" substantiates this argument.

Finally, the concluding discussion in "The Matrix of Illegal Occupation" below focuses on the third proposition—the indeterminacies of this occupation as reflecting both its essential feature and its legitimizing mechanism—and proceeds to relate them to the political aspirations of the Israeli occupation and to consider the normative consequences of an illegal occupation.

THE INTRINSIC DIMENSIONS OF THE ISRAELI OCCUPATION OF THE OCCUPIED PALESTINIAN TERRITORY: THE NORMS OF OCCUPATION

The Israeli occupation violates the three basic tenets of the normative regime of occupation and is therefore intrinsically illegal. This section discusses the basic principles informing the normative regime and then applies them to the Israeli occupation. Each of its three subsections focuses on one of the three basic tenets of the normative regime of occupation. In each subsection, the normative conclusions generated by the discussion are then applied to the Israeli occupation.

THE SUSPENSION OF SOVEREIGNTY: OCCUPATION DOES NOT CONFER TITLE

"The foundation upon which the entire law of occupation is based," writes Benvenisti, "is the principle of inalienability of sovereignty through the actual or threatened use of force. Effective control by foreign military force can never bring about by itself a valid transfer of sovereignty."[44] The rule of nonrecognition, forbidding states to recognize title thus acquired, is the normative consequence of this principle.[45]

This basic tenet of the law of occupation rests on and reflects the well-established general international legal principle that the acquisition of territory by force does not confer a valid title to the territory. This principle holds, even if force is used legally (i.e., in self-defense) and even if the status of the territory under consideration is disputed.[46]

This principle is articulated in all relevant documents: Article 43 of the Fourth Hague Convention limits the occupier's authority to maintaining public order and civil life while "respecting, unless absolutely prevented, the laws in force in the country." This proviso precludes the annexation of the territory by the occupier.[47] This preclusion was further made clear in Article 47 of the Fourth Geneva Convention, which emphasizes that annexation of an occupied territory during wartime, before any peace treaty had been concluded, does not deprive the protected persons of the rights guaranteed by the convention, that is, annexation does not alter the status of the territory or its population.[48] The latest affirmation of the principle can be found in Article 4 of the Protocol I, restating that neither occupation of a territory nor the application of the protocol's provisions shall affect the legal status of the territory under dispute.[49]

As stated above, even if the occupation has been occasioned by a legal use of force, it cannot confer legal title. Thus, the UN Declaration on Principles of International Law concerning Friendly Relations and Cooperation among States does not distinguish between legal and illegal use of force when it states that "no territorial acquisition resulting from the threat or use of force shall be recognized as legal."[50] Despite Israel's adamant claim that the 1967 War was pursued in self-defense, the same rationale underlies the UN Security Council's Middle East Resolution 242, which reiterated the inadmissibility of the acquisition of territory by war.

One conclusion to be drawn from the above is that the legality of an occupation—or lack thereof—cannot be grounded in a determination that an occupation has been occasioned as a result of a war of self-defense. Thus, the debate about the legality of Israel's original action in occupying the occupied Palestinian territory during the 1967 War—a debate reflected in the different narratives that shape the conflict—is irrelevant to the question with which we are concerned here.[51] Indeed, even if the Israeli narrative of a war fought in self-defense was accepted as the shared assumption of the conflict, it is irrelevant to both the determination of the legality of the continued occupation and the principle of the inalienability of sovereignty.

Another conclusion to be drawn from the above is that the Israeli annexation of East Jerusalem—expanding gradually its boundaries from 6.5 to 71 square kilometers—is illegal.[52] This illegality was affirmed by both the Security Council and the General Assembly, with the consequence that under international law, the area is still considered occupied.[53] The International Court of Justice's *Construction of the Wall* advisory opinion confirms this conclusion.[54]

Complementing the principle that use of force of any kind cannot confer legal title to territory is the principle of self-determination, which informs not only the United Nations decisions regarding Israel's annexation of occupied East Jerusalem and its settlements in the occupied Palestinian territory,[55] but also the Security Council's vision of "a region where two states, Israel and Palestine, live side by side within secure and recognized borders."[56] The rationale underlying this determination is that if peoples, according to Common Article 1 (1) of the International Covenants on Human Rights, have the right to "freely determine their political status,"[57] then sovereignty belongs to the people, and no valid title can be transferred in disregard of the will of the population of the territory.[58] This point was wholeheartedly approved by the *Construction of a Wall* advisory opinion with respect to the de facto annexation of vast Palestinian territories entailed by the establishment of the settlements and the construction of the Wall by Israel.[59]

An occupation thus suspends sovereignty insofar as it severs its ordinary link with effective control, but it does not—indeed, cannot—alter sovereignty.

Effective control must be exercised in a manner that accords with the obligations of the occupying power as a trustee. The meaning of this form of trust is detailed in the following subsection.

TRUST MATTERS: AN OCCUPATION IS ESSENTIALLY A FORM OF TRUST

The notion of trusteeship is implicit in the principle that occupation does not confer title and that the occupier is vested with the authority, in the words of Article 43 of the 1907 Fourth Hague Convention, "to take all the measures in his power to restore, and ensure, as far as possible, public order and safety/civil life, while respecting, unless absolutely prevented, the laws in force in the country."[60] Occupied territories thus "constitute...a sacred trust, which must be administered as a whole in the interests both of the inhabitants and the legitimate sovereign or the duly constituted successor in title."[61] This trust, however, is of a particular nature.

The framework of the trust consists of two features: the security needs of the occupying power, on the one hand, and the maintenance of civil life, on the other. It thus carries with it a potential conflict of interests between those of the population and those of the occupier. In the nineteenth-century context, when governmental involvement in the life of the population was minimal, this framework produced two primary rules: The occupier mainly was tasked with the negative duty of refraining from infringing on the basic rights of the inhabitants, while the latter were tasked with a duty of obedience to the occupier, a duty that can be derived from three possible sources: municipal law (that is, the population was to follow the laws of the land because they were the laws of the legitimate sovereign), international law (meaning that the duties incumbent upon the sovereign gave rise to corollary rights), and the physical ability of the occupier to enforce such obedience.[62]

With the continued evolution of the law of occupation, the scale began to tip to the side of the inhabitants. The Fourth Geneva Convention seems to reject the idea that the population of an occupied territory is under any international legal obligation to obey the occupier.[63] In parallel, the convention considerably expands the protection due to the inhabitants, establishing obligations to respect their persons, honor, family life, religious convictions, and customs, and requiring their humane treatment at all times. Women should be especially protected, and discrimination is prohibited.[64] The convention also prohibits the infliction of physical suffering, corporal punishment, medical experiments, collective punishment, pillage, reprisals, the taking of hostages, deportations, and retroactive criminal legislation and punishment. The right of the occupier to compel the inhabitants to work is restricted. The convention further imposes positive duties on the occupier with regard to the protection of children, ensuring food and medical supplies,[65] maintaining hospitals, and providing for certain due-process rights and the rights of imprisoned persons.[66] The convention also restricts the right of the occupier to detain protected persons and stipulates substantial protection for detainees.[67]

This expanded protection of the inhabitants culminates in the currently prevailing view that international human rights law applies concurrently with international humanitarian law to occupied territories: The latter is the *lex specialis,* but the former is resorted to either in cases of lacunae or for interpenetrative purposes.[68] Indeed, the longer the occupation, the heavier is the weight to be accorded to the human rights of the population of an occupied territory.[69] The inseparability of human rights guarantees from the concept of trust rests at the heart of the International Court of Justice advisory opinion titled *Legal Consequences for States of the Continued Presence of South Africa in Namibia (South-West Africa) Notwithstanding Security Council Resolution 276 (1970).* The court construed the relationship between South Africa and Namibia as a "sacred trust" and found South Africa's continued infringement of the rights and well-being of the inhabitants of Namibia to destroy "the very object and purpose of that relationship."[70] Therefore, the court held that the termination of the mandate by the UN General Assembly to be valid and the continuing presence of South Africa in Namibia—a presence that thereafter was a foreign occupation—to be illegal.[71]

It is interesting to note in this context that the court reiterated this position in its recent *Construction of a Wall* advisory opinion. In the part of the opinion dealing with the status of the occupied Palestinian territory, the court narrates the history of the conflict, the roots of which are described as follows: "Palestine was part of the Ottoman Empire. At the end of the First World War, a class 'A' Mandate for Palestine was entrusted to Great Britain by the League of Nations."[72] The court recalled that in its 1950 opinion, *The International Status of South West Africa,*[73] it held that "two principles were considered to be of paramount importance" with respect to territories that were placed under the mandate system, "the principle of non-annexation and the principle that the well-being and development of... peoples [not yet able to govern themselves] form 'a sacred trust of civilization.'"[74]

The court returned to this point in a later part of the opinion concerned with determining the relevant international legal rules applicable to the issue at hand. Recalling its 1971 opinion *Legal Consequences for States of the Continued Presence of South Africa in Namibia (South-West Africa) Notwithstanding Security Council Resolution 276 (1970),* the court stated that "current developments in 'international law in regard to non-self governing territories'...made the principle of self-determination applicable to all [such territories]" and "these developments leave little doubt that the ultimate objective of the sacred trust...was the self-determination of the people concerned."[75] What the court seems to be doing, then, is to construct the concept of "a sacred trust," the origins of which are rooted in the mandate system, as the common denominator of all situations where people are not self-governing, occupations included. That construction is facilitated by the historical fact that Palestine was a mandate territory and that the roots of the Israeli-Palestinian conflict rest in the dissolution of the mandate. This construction enables the court to emphasize not only the principle of self-determination, but also the related notion of a "sacred trust" as applicable to the occupied Palestinian territory.[76]

It is nevertheless clear that the notion of an occupation as a trust, especially as a trust emanating from a belligerent type of occupation, rather than from a mandate, does not abrogate the security interests of the occupying power.[77] The convention explicitly subjects some of the guarantees afforded to the population to military necessity and conditions.[78] Furthermore, the occupier is allowed to take measures against protected persons in the form of promulgating penal laws and assigning residence and internment.[79] That being said, such authority seems to have fallen out of favor in recent years in light of pronouncements by the international community endorsing the right of the population of an occupied territory to rise against the occupier in its pursuit of self-determination. Security measures are thus subject to strict scrutiny.

The balance between humanitarian and human rights concerns—pouring content into the notion of trust, on the one hand, and by military necessity delimiting, but never substituting anything for this trust, on the other—is thus a hallmark of the current law of occupation. The working assumption behind this arrangement is that an occupation is of a relatively short duration.[80] The restriction on the occupier's authority to amend the laws of the country so as to make necessary reforms, which might be called for throughout the years, underscores this point. In long-term occupations, the result may well be the stagnation of all aspects of life: economic, political, cultural, and social existence, with harsh consequences for the population. It is, in fact, hard to reconcile such an outcome with the occupier's general duty to ensure civil life in the occupied territory.[81] Furthermore, the longer the occupation lasts, the higher the likelihood of an uprising by the population, acting in pursuit of its right to self-determination. This, in turn, is likely to generate stricter security measures by the occupier to the detriment of the population. The net result would thus be less, rather than more weight given to the humanitarian and human rights concerns of the population, and unless the uprising is successful, a further frustration of the right to self determination, that is, a sacrifice of the trust at the altar of security. Such indeed is the sorry story of the Israeli occupation of the occupied Palestinian territory.[82]

That story had been framed by law even before it became a fact of power. Much like a would-be parent carefully furnishing a nursery long before a child is conceived, already in the early 1960s, the then military advocate-general—and eventually chief justice of the Israeli Supreme Court—Meir Shamgar, had designed the legal framework within which the Israeli Defense Forces (IDF) were to exercise their power as an occupier. By June 1967, there was a cadre of trained military lawyers accompanying the forces and ready to put the normative regime of occupation into effect.[83] The objective, said Shamgar, was to guarantee respect for the legal rights of the population in the occupied territory.[84] The means were innovative: to subject the actions of the IDF to judicial review by allowing the occupied people to appeal to the highest judicial authority in Israel, the High Court of Justice. The effect was, alas, the judicial blurring of boundaries between the occupied and the occupying territories and the legalization and legitimization of the dispossession of the Palestinians. The fact that over 99 percent of the Palestinian petitions to the court have been rejected, the fact that the initial military directive applying the Fourth Geneva Convention was soon cancelled and replaced by a thesis that the convention does not apply (a thesis never refuted by the Supreme Court, which ever since has applied the conventions humanitarian provisions on the basis of the willingness of the state—rather than its legal obligation—to abide by these provisions),[85] and the fact that already in 1967, the territory was being considered as "administered," rather than as "occupied" (with references to "Judea and Samaria" substituting for references to "the West Bank") all underscore the point. The story of the occupation, then, is inseparable from the story of law. It is also inseparable from the settlement enterprise.

The settlements, we submit, generate both dispossession of and discrimination against the Palestinians, thereby signifying Israel's breach of the trust entailed in the normative regime of occupation. In order to substantiate this argument, it is necessary to discuss the genesis of the settlements and the debate concerning their legality and to analyze the various aspects that their construction and maintenance entail—ranging from the confiscation of land to the existence of two separate legal systems in the area, operating along ethnic lines—as well as their effect on some select aspects of the daily life of the population of the occupied Palestinian territory. While God—or the Devil—may well be in the details, for the purposes of this discussion, we are less concerned with specific violations of the law of occupation occasioned by any particular action, violations that have indeed attracted attention elsewhere in the relevant literature, but rather with identifying the basic structure and nature of this occupation regime.

Immediately following the 1967 War, the Labor government then in power initiated the settlement project, based ostensibly on security considerations.[86] When the Likud Party, headed by Menachem Begin, formed a government in 1977, the security motive gave way to an ideological claim to the entire occupied Palestinian territory based on historical and religious grounds. The settlement enterprise thus became a "holy work," which Prime Minister Shamir, who took office after Begin in 1983, vowed to pursue.[87] That year, the Ministry of Agriculture and the World Zionist Organization, a quasi-governmental organization entrusted with furthering the political objectives of Zionism, jointly prepared a master plan for the development of the settlements designed "to achieve the incorporation [of the West Bank] into the [Israeli] national system."[88] A comparison between its details and current on-the-ground realities indicates a high degree of geographical, if not demographical realization of this plan.[89] This has been achieved by the expropriation of land from the Palestinians, coupled with economic incentives to the settlers.[90] As a result of this policy, there are at present some 120 settlements in the West Bank with over 230,000 settlers. The much ado that occurred about the "disengagement" from the Gaza Strip involved the dismantling of a mere 16 settlements and the evacuation of fewer than 10,000 settlers. About 180,000 settlers live in the neighborhoods of the expanded area of East Jerusalem. The population growth in the settlements is three times that of Israel.[91]

The land upon which the settlements are built in the West Bank, in addition to adjacent confiscated land, settlement bypass roads and other land controlled by the military, amounts to 59 percent of the West Bank. The settlements and the bypass roads connecting them to each other as well as to Israel have divided the West Bank into some sixty discontinuous zones and Gaza (before the disengagement) into four parts. East Jerusalem has been severed from the rest of the West Bank.[92]

The legal debate concerning the Israeli settlements has focused primarily on Article 49, paragraph 6 of the Fourth Geneva Convention, which prohibits the occupier from transferring parts of its own civilian population into the territory it occupies.[93] The Israeli government has always maintained that the prohibition does not include voluntary transfer by citizens to occupied territory because the prohibition was informed by and should be interpreted in light of the policies practiced by Germany during World War II, to which the Israeli policy cannot be compared.[94] This position is not entirely consistent with the International Committee of the Red Cross commentary on the Fourth Convention, according to which the intent of the drafters was to maintain a general demographic status quo in occupied territory.[95] Further pronouncement by the parties to the convention rejected the Israeli interpretation by declaring the settlements to be illegal.[96] This is the context for understanding the different version of this prohibition adopted in Article 8 (2) (b) (viii) of the Rome Statute, which criminalizes such transfers whether they are undertaken directly or *indirectly*. This provision might well identify Israel's incentive policy as an "indirect transfer" and largely explains Israel's decision not to ratify the statute.[97] However, given the fact that the Israeli government built the settlements, and given further the financial incentives provided to settlers, the settlement project is a "direct transfer" and thus falls within the scope of the original prohibition of article 49 (6).[98] The International Court of Justice had an opportunity to opine on this matter in its advisory opinion *Construction of a Wall*, because the "wall's sinuous route has been traced in such a way as to include within that area the great majority of the Israeli settlements in the occupied Palestinian Territory (including East Jerusalem)."[99] Noting that "since 1977, Israel has conducted a policy and developed practices involving the establishment of settlements in the Occupied Palestinian Territory, contrary to the terms of Article 49 paragraph 6," it concluded that "the Israeli settlements in the Occupied Palestinian Territory (including east Jerusalem) have been established in breach of international law."[100]

Israel's extensive confiscation of Palestinian land, carried out to satisfy the needs of the continuing expansion of the settlements,[101] might also amount to a grave breach under Article 147. Article 147 prohibits "extensive appropriation of property, not justified by military necessity and carried out unlawfully and wantonly."[102] Such action is criminalized by Article 8 (2) (a) (iv) of the Rome Statute.

The method and effect of this expropriation merit attention. Following a determination by the High Court of Justice that private land could not be confiscated for the establishment of civilian settlements,[103] the Israeli government moved quickly to define ever greater portions of the occupied territory as "state land." Such a definition was facilitated by the lack of a comprehensive land ownership registration in the occupied Palestinian territory, which made it quite difficult for individuals to prove their land ownership, as well as by a governmental decision to designate all uncultivated rural land as "state land."[104] The effect of these practices has been twofold: first, the de facto dispossession of individual Palestinians, and second, the dispossession of the Palestinian population of land reserves that should have primarily served its interests. Instead, these lands are administered by the Israel Land Administration, a body set up under Israeli law to administer state land in Israel proper and now being used for settlements.[105]

Israel has also used control over planning to restrict the growth of Palestinian towns and villages while expanding the settlements.[106] This control has been exercised by omission, that is, by refraining from "preparing updated regional outline plans for the West Bank. As a result, until the transfer of authority to the Palestinian Authority (and, to this day, in Area C), two regional plans prepared in the 1940s by the British Mandate continue to apply."[107] Subsequent "special partial outline plans" for some four hundred villages, far from alleviating the problem of inadequate planning schemes, underscored its rationale, because they constituted demarcation plans that prohibited construction outside existing lines. This administrative and legal structure has then been used both to justify the rejection of Palestinians' applications for building permits on private land, and to issue demolition orders for houses that were constructed without a permit.[108] Thus, the law that vested the occupier with the power to ensure the welfare of the population of the occupied Palestinian territory has been used by the former to advance its own interests to the detriment of the latter.

Indeed, while different phenomena are associated with the settlements, such as inequality in the allocation of water resources, coupled with acute water shortages in the Palestinian villages,[109] or acts of violence committed by settlers against the Palestinian population that receive no proper response from the Israeli security forces,[110] it is the legal terrain wrought by the occupation that is of special relevance to our analysis. There are separate legal systems operating concurrently in the West Bank, effectively dividing the population along ethnic lines: Jewish settlers are extraterritorially subject to Israeli civilian law, whereas the Palestinians are subject to Israeli military law and to local law.[111] Two methods are used to generate this situation. First, the application of Israeli law *in personam* to Israeli citizens and Jews in the occupied Palestinian territory, and second, the partial application of Israeli law, on a supposedly territorial basis, to the Jewish settlements in the occupied Palestinian territory. Each of these arrangements merits our brief attention.

The personal application of Israeli law works in myriad ways. For example, emergency regulations issued by the Israeli government and renewed regularly through legislation determine that Israeli courts will have jurisdiction over criminal offences committed by Israeli citizens (and in general by people who are present in Israel) in the occupied Palestinian territory, even if the offence took part in areas under the control of the Palestinian Authority.[112] Further, the law extending the emergency regulations determines that for certain statutes, people who live in the occupied Palestinian territory will be considered residents of Israel if they are Israeli citizens *or* are "entitled to immigrate to Israel under the Law of Return" (i.e. Jews and family members of Jews).[113] These statutes, seventeen in total, include the Income Tax Ordinance, the Social Security Law of 1968, and the National Health Care Law of 1994.[114] The net result is that there is a different set of rights and duties applying to different groups in the occupied Palestinian territory divided along ethnic lines. Finally, in this context, we should note the extension, on a personal basis, of Israel's Election Law, which determines that Israelis who reside in territory held by the IDF will be able to vote in their places of residence.[115] This provision is significant, especially when considered against the lack of an absentee ballot in Israel.[116] Its effect is to allow Israeli settlers in the occupied Palestinian territory to take part in choosing the government that rules this territory as an occupying power, whereas the Palestinian residents of the same territory, who are also subject to the actions of this very same government, do not take part in choosing it.[117]

Whereas the personal application of Israeli law to Israelis—and in some cases, to non-Israeli Jews—in the occupied Palestinian territory is effected through emergency regulations issued by the Israeli government and extended by the Israeli legislature, territorial application occurs through orders issued by the Israeli military commander in the territory.[118] These orders give special status to Jewish settlements in the occupied Palestinian territory by applying to those territorial units certain aspects of Israeli law in various spheres, such as education, giving them the privileges enjoyed by localities within Israel. The same mechanism further prohibits Palestinians from entry into the settlements unless they possess a special permit. Israelis are exempt from the need for a special permit to enter the settlements. Israelis are defined for this purpose as residents of Israel, residents of the territory who are Israeli citizens or who are allowed to immigrate to Israel under the Law of Return, and people who are not residents of the territory, but who have a valid visa to enter Israel. This definition extends the privilege of entering the settlements beyond Israeli citizens and Jews to tourists who are neither Israelis nor Jewish.[119] Given this last qualification, the supposedly territorial application of these laws may also be seen as personal. The net result is the creation of two separate legal regimes based on a combination of personal and territorial factors.

It should finally be noted that in a decision concerning the rights of Israeli settlers evacuated from the Gaza Strip, the High Court of Justice decided that the Israeli Basic Laws (which make up the nascent Constitution of Israel), including the Basic Law: Human Liberty and Dignity, apply *in personam* to Israelis in the occupied Palestinian territory, leaving open the question of the application of these laws to the Palestinian residents of the same territory.[120]

As the leading Israeli constitutional law scholar Amnon Rubinstein already had observed in 1988, this partial application of Israeli law to the occupied Palestinian territory blurred the boundaries between Israel and the territory and drastically changed the status of the territory from an "escrow" to a "legal mongrel." Once perceived as an "escrow" under the rules of international law—that is, as a trust—the occupied Palestinian territory gradually had "incorporated in practice into the realm of Israel's rule."[121] The substitution of the status of "legal mongrel" for that of an "escrow" clearly signifies the breach of trust by the occupier and the veiled annexation of the territory. Given that the violation of trust and the veiled annexation violate the two basic tenets of the normative regime of occupation, it would be more appropriate to conclude that the transition effected was from an "escrow" to an "illegal mongrel." Indeed, a "legal mongrel," at least in this context, seems to be an oxymoron. The "mongrel" is illegal.

Furthermore, closer scrutiny reveals that, from a legal perspective, the Israeli government's actions actually constitute a greater violation of international law than what would have been created by a straightforward annexation, because they confer the benefits of annexation to the occupier without requiring it to incorporate the people under occupation to its polity and thus without according them the rights and privileges that would follow. When combined with the different treatment and rights accorded to settlers,[122] often at the expense of the Palestinians, the occupation appears to resemble a form of colonial regime, the hallmark of which is the exploitation of the resources of the territory for the benefits of the home country and its citizens, rather than a belligerent occupation.[123] Indeed, it may well amount to prohibited discrimination as defined by Article 1 of the Convention on the Elimination of All Forms of Racial Discrimination (CERD) and of the International Convention on the Suppression and Punishment of the Crime of Apartheid.[124] In its extreme form, that is, if practiced as a widespread or systematic policy, apartheid is criminalized in Article 7 (1) (j) of the Rome Statute as a crime against humanity.[125]

It is interesting to mention in this context that in the *Construction of a Wall* advisory opinion, the court noted that the construction of the Wall had been accompanied by the creation of a new administrative regime and that under this regime, part of the West Bank lying between the Green Line and the Wall had been designated as a "Closed Area": "Residents of this area may no longer remain in it, nor may nonresidents enter it, unless holding a permit or identity card issued by the Israeli authorities.... Israeli citizens, Israeli permanent residents and those eligible to immigrate to Israel in accordance with the Law of Return may remain in, or move freely to, from and within the Closed Area without a permit."[126] These references to a regime that operates on the basis of ethnic distinctions seem to suggest the prima facie relevance of the CERD.[127]

While there are many differences between the former regime of apartheid in South Africa and the occupation regime of the occupied Palestinian territory, it is interesting to note here that a prevailing discourse regarding the Israeli-Palestinian peace process in Israel is one of "separation." The question arises whether this "separation" may not resemble the separation entailed in the regime of apartheid. This discussion brings up complex questions about the possible solutions to the Palestinian-Israeli conflict and the viability of the "separation" thesis that does not amount to apartheid. The problem of resemblance to apartheid did not go away, but to some extent was extenuated during the years of the Oslo process.[128] In this sense, it is interesting to compare the peace processes in Israel/Palestine and in South Africa. Both processes probably continued traditional approaches to the solution of these conflicts: incorporation in South Africa and partition in the Israeli-Palestinian context. The question for the Israeli-Palestinian situation is how to create partition that does not entail apartheid.[129]

For the purposes of the argument advanced in this section, however, it is not necessary to determine whether or not the occupation of the occupied Palestinian territory has become a form of colonialism or resembles an apartheid regime. Rather, it is sufficient to conclude that inasmuch as the legal structure of the occupation regime is *designed* to and in fact *does* serve the interests of the settlers more than it does the interests of the population of the occupied Palestinian territory, and, indeed, at the latter's expense, it breaches the obligations of the occupier under Article 43 of the 1907 Fourth Hague Convention, thus violating the basic tenet of trust inherent in the law of occupation.[130] Inasmuch as the justness of an occupation is determined by its political direction and the distribution of benefits it provides, as Michael Walzer recently has suggested in the context of the American occupation of Iraq,[131] the occupation of the occupied Palestinian territory appears to be neither legal nor just.

DISRUPTING THE FABRIC OF LIFE OF THE POPULATION OF THE OCCUPIED PALESTINIAN TERRITORY

The injustice of the political geography created by the complex legal system of the occupation is most poignant in its effect on the daily life of the population of the occupied territory, particularly because it severely restricts Palestinian freedom of movement. An intricate network of some three hundred checkpoints and roadblocks divides the occupied Palestinian territory internally into a patchwork of cantons. Permits are required to travel from one to the other. Gaza is completely isolated from the rest of the Palestinian territory. These divisions constitute an enormous constraint on the ability of Palestinians to get to work, schools, hospitals, friends, and family. Assessing this situation, the special rapporteur of the Human Rights Commission concluded:

> Settlements are linked to each other by a vast system of bypass roads that have a 50-to-70 meter buffer zone on each side in which no building is permitted. These settlements and roads, which separate Palestinian communities and deprive Palestinians of agricultural land, have fragmented both land and the people. In effect, they foreclose the possibility of a Palestinian State as they destroy the territorial integrity of the Palestinian Territory.[132]

Further measures thus affecting movement and, indeed, any resemblance of a normal life are closures that prohibit Palestinian movement without special permits and curfews that compel inhabitants to stay in their homes.[133] Curfews and closures constitute the primary cause for Palestinian economic loses.[134] The cumulative effect of checkpoints and curfews is a sharp decline in access to health care and in health standards due to shortages of food, clean water, and access to hospitals, as well as rising rates of unemployment and poverty.[135]

It is clear that these and other measures not only violate fundamental norms of both humanitarian and human rights law, but also render the very conduct of civil life in the occupied Palestinian territory practically impossible.[136] It is, indeed, "a human tragedy that is unfolding in Palestine."[137] The construction of the Wall signifies the culmination of these policies, their devastating effect on life in the territory, and the violation of the notion of trust that underlies the occupying power's responsibilities vis-à-vis the population of the territory.[138] The International Court of Justice's reading of this situation is quite pertinent:

> the route chosen for the wall gives expression *in loco* to the illegal measures taken by Israel with regard to Jerusalem and the settlements, as deplored by the Security Council.... There is also a risk of further alterations to the demographic composition of the Occupied Palestinian Territory...inasmuch as it is contributing to the departure of Palestinian population from certain areas.... That construction, along with the measures taken previously, thus severely impedes the exercise by the Palestinian people of its right to self-determination.[139]

The destruction of the fabric of life of the Palestinian residents of the occupied Palestinian territory is evident. It is equally clear, however, that an occupying power, while required to maintain civil life in the territory under its effective control, is not required to forsake its own security interests. Indeed, Israel contends that the Palestinians, having responded to Israel's offer to end the conflict with the al-Aqsa intifada's indiscriminate terrorist attacks against Israeli citizens, attacks constituting crimes against humanity,[140] are to be held responsible for their situation.[141] Israel argues further that "many of the Palestinian terrorist groups perpetrate their atrocities not to put an end to Israel's presence, but rather to frustrate any political progress that may do just that."[142]

Israel's thesis thus rests on an attempt to sever the nexus between the occupation and the intifada and, indeed, between its obligations as an occupying power and its right and duty to protect its own citizens and security. In doing so, it challenges, inter alia, the observation of the special rapporteur of the United Nations Commission of Human Rights that "violations of human rights are a necessary consequence of military occupation."[143] As was noted above, Israel regards this observation as "an attempt to rewrite international law" and as a "remarkable legal thesis" that "contravenes the entire body of humanitarian law dealing with belligerent occupation, which establishes standards to be maintained by States that find themselves in a situation of occupying territory."[144]

Israel is right in maintaining that the international law of occupation establishes such standards and that therefore an occupation does not, ipso facto, entail the violation of either human rights or its own governing regime, because such a construction would have rendered the normative regime that governs the situation not only redundant, but illegal *ab initio*. It does not follow, however, that the violations of human rights and of humanitarian law in the occupied Palestinian territory are not a necessary consequence of this specific occupation, that is, that they are generated by Israel's breach of the basic tenets of the law of occupation, rather than by the mere fact of occupation.

IT'S ABOUT TIME: AN OCCUPATION IS TEMPORARY

In order to assess this issue and to evaluate the respective positions articulated above, it is necessary to inquire into the last tenet of the normative regime — its temporal dimension. The two basic principles discussed above — that is, the inalienability of sovereignty vested in the people and its management as a form of trust — generate the third principle of occupation: its temporality. Indeed, the very essence of occupation decrees so. Thus, writes Doris A. Graber:

> The modern law of belligerent occupation is anchored in the concept that occupation differs in its nature and legal consequences from conquest. It is therefore not surprising that the early definitions of the modern concept of occupation are chiefly concerned with the main aspects of this difference, namely the temporary nature of belligerent occupation as contrasted with the permanency of conquest, and the limited, rather than the full powers which belligerent occupation entails for the occupant.[145]

It is in this light that one should understand the various provisions in the documents detailing the law of occupation that have, *ab initio,* imposed constraints on the managerial powers of the occupier, evidencing the temporary nature of its control. Indeed, the Lieber Code, commissioned by President Abraham Lincoln for training Union forces during the U.S. Civil War and considered the first milestone in the genesis of the law of belligerent occupation, already provided that martial law imposed by the occupier only *suspends* criminal and civil law, as well as domestic administration and government during the period of occupation.[146]

Article 43 of the 1899 and 1907 Hague Conventions imposed a duty on the occupier to respect, unless "absolutely prevented," the laws in force in the country.

Although not expressly defining the authority of the former sovereign as "suspended," the Hague Convention altered neither the concept of an occupation as temporary nor its underlying rationale, that the occupier does not acquire sovereignty, but exercises a temporary right of administration until the status of the territory is finally determined.[147] This understanding of the provisional, nonsovereign status of the occupier is reaffirmed by Article 55 of the 1907 Fourth Hague Convention, which states that the occupier is merely to administer and safeguard public buildings, real estate, and the agriculture estates belonging to the state.[148]

The idea of occupation as a temporary form of control underlies the provisions of the Fourth Geneva Convention. Due, however, to the shift in emphasis of the convention from the rights of the ousted sovereign to the welfare of the population of the occupied territory, the temporal restrictions on the occupying authority are more implicit than explicit when compared with earlier codes. Thus, for instance, the nonrecognition of annexation stipulated in Article 47 of the Fourth Convention is informed by, but does not explicitly state the temporary nature of an occupation.[149] This may also be said with regard to paragraph 6 of Article 49, which prohibits the settlement of the occupier's nationals in the occupied territory: In addition to the World War II experience with the mass transportation of populations, which informed the article, the provision was also designed to ensure that the sociological and demographic structure of the territory will be left unchanged.[150]

Further indication of the temporary nature of the occupation and its limitation to the preservation of the status quo is found in Article 54 of the convention, which stipulates that the status of judges and public officials in the territory shall not be altered. This proscription reaffirms the maintenance of the country's judicial and administrative structure, which is expected to go on functioning without hindrance,[151] and enhances the conclusion that the occupier's authority is temporary and nonsovereign. Article 64 contains a similar provision with respect to the laws in place and, as suggested by the convention's commentary, "expresses, in a more precise and detailed form, the terms of Article 43 of the Hague regulations, which lays down that the Occupying Power is to respect the laws in force in the country 'unless absolutely prevented.'"[152]

However, it is Article 6 of the Fourth Geneva Convention that relates most directly to the temporal limits of occupation, and thus it merits special attention. It provides in paragraph 3:

In the case of occupied territory, the application of the present Convention shall cease one year after the general close of military operations; however, the Occupying Power shall be bound, for the duration of the occupation, to the extent that such

Power exercises the functions of government in such territory, by the provisions of the following Articles 1 to 12, 27, 29 to 34, 47, 49, 51, 52, 53, 59, 61 to 77, 143.

The International Court of Justice considered this provision in the *Construction of a Wall* advisory opinion. The court opined that:

> A distinction is also made in the Fourth Geneva Convention between provisions applying during military operations leading to the occupation and those that remain applicable throughout the entire period of occupation.... Since the military operations leading to the occupation of the West Bank in 1967 ended a long time ago, only those Articles of the Fourth Geneva Convention referred to in Article 6, paragraph 3, remain applicable in that occupied territory.[153]

> We submit that this textual interpretation, leading to the conclusion that long-term occupations reduce the responsibilities of Occupying Powers *vis-à-vis* the occupied civilian population, is an absurd conclusion: it is unwarranted by the text and is further incongruent with the purpose and legal practice of the normative regime of occupation, confusing a problem with a solution.[154]

> Textually, Article 6 refers to a "general close of military operations." It does not refer to military operations "leading to the occupation."[155] The latter is a judicial insertion. The realities of the occupation in general, and in particular the circumstances surrounding the construction of the wall (itself a military operation), attest to the fact of on-going military operations. Thus, even a literal reading of the text of Article 6 should have revealed its inapplicability on its own terms. Indeed, Article 6 lends itself to an entirely different reading.

According to the language of Article 6, in an occupation that lasts longer than one year after the close of military operations, only twenty-three of the thirty-two articles comprising Section III of the convention that deal with occupied territories would continue to apply.[156] The nine articles that would cease to apply include, for instance, the obligation incumbent on the occupying power to "facilitate the proper working of all institutions devoted to the care and education of children" and "the duty of ensuring the food and medical supplies of the population."[157] It is unreasonable to assume that the drafters of the convention intended for children to be deprived of proper schooling or for the population to be deprived of medical supplies and food in long-term occupations, because such an intention would defy the convention's main objective. The only reasonable conclusion, therefore, is that the working assumption behind Article 6 was that the situation of an occupation is bound to be relatively short and that responsibilities of this kind would be transferred to local authorities in a process leading to the end of the exceptional situation of occupation. The *travaux préparatoires* and the commentary confirm this assumption.[158] Once reality defies the assumption, however, the rationale informing Article 6 disappears, and, insofar as law is to make sense, it should no longer apply.

Subsequent developments in both law and legal practice lend support to our proposed reading of the provision. Once it became clear that the drafters' assumption regarding the short duration of occupations was not supported by reality and that this provision may be construed by occupying powers as limiting their responsibilities under the convention precisely in situations where the latter should be expanded, the provision was abrogated: Article 3 (b) of Additional Protocol I provides for the application of the protocol's provisions until the termination of the occupation.[159]

The argument that Article 6 of the Fourth Geneva Convention limits the convention's scope of applicability was never raised before Israeli courts, and indeed the Israeli High Court of Justice had applied provisions that would have otherwise become inapplicable in light of the language of Article 6.[160] This practice characterizes other prolonged occupations,[161] thereby lending support to the proposition that Article 3 (b) of Protocol I enjoys customary status.

Further, the court's determination regarding the limited scope of applicability of the Fourth Geneva Convention is incongruent with—and defies the rationale behind—its determination regarding the applicability of various human rights instruments, together with humanitarian law in occupied territories. This coapplication is designed to offer greater protection to the civilian population. It is this incongruence that explains the odd conclusion of the court that Israel had violated some of its human rights obligations, but not the very same obligations—only far clearer and specifically designed for the situation of an occupation—as they appear in the Fourth Geneva Convention.[162] The implication is that human rights law came into play to fill a lacuna in the Geneva Convention, whereas in fact, the latter contains relevant provisions. The lacuna, therefore, is constructed, only to be filled by another and less suitable normative source. This does not make much sense.

It follows from the above that a proper reading of Article 6 should have generated the conclusion that this provision, as Adam Roberts has suggested, has "correctly identified a problem," the problem of prolonged occupation, but not a proper solution.[163] It is regrettable that the court confused the solution with the problem. Had it engaged in a discussion of the temporal assumption informing the Fourth Geneva Convention, it not only could have produced a better reading of Article 6, but could have further shed light on the temporal limitations of an occupation. The remaining part of this section offers such a discussion.

As was discussed above, there is overwhelming evidence for the proposition that the normative regime of occupation requires that it be temporary.[164] The absence of exact time limits set on the duration of occupation has been explained—indeed, explained away—by Justice Meir Shamgar, the legal architect of the occupation,[165] as being reflective of "a factual situation," generating the conclusion that "pending an alternative political or military solution this system of government could, from a legal point of view, continue indefinitely."[166]

A legal point of view is not merely reflective of a factual situation, nor does it sanction the substitution of "indefinite" for "temporary." A temporary situation definitely has an end. An indefinite situation may or may not have an end. The two situations are very different. In order to appreciate the point, it is useful to reflect momentarily on the human condition: It is largely controlled by our awareness that our existence is temporary. Had we conceived of our existence as indefinite, it is quite likely that the human condition would have altered significantly. "Under heaven," we may hopefully presume, there is "a time for every purpose," but on Earth, we humbly acknowledge, time is a limited resource.[167] Time thus affects us individually and socially, and it is our awareness of the temporary nature of human existence that shapes, inter alia, our social institutions, including our law.

Far from reflecting time as naturally indefinite, law allocates, distributes, and mediates time as a "commodity, the supply of which is not inexhaustible."[168] Law shapes our perceptions of the realities of time as a historical, social, cultural, and political construct.[169] Law thus defines not only the supposedly natural time of birth and of death, of childhood and of adulthood, but also incorporates certain assumptions about individual and collective time to delineate rights and duties.[170] Indeed, the very principle of legality, as well as foundational legal presumptions, signify embedded conceptions of demarcated time without which they, and law itself, would be meaningless.[171]

Law, then, is preoccupied with time. Given that the distribution of limited resources is a major legal function, the construction of time as a limited resource implies that law is interested in the distribution of time. Time, however, unlike other natural commodities, is *construed* as limited. As such, it cannot be distributed *in abstracto,* but only in relation to a concrete action. Indeed, it is the very conception of time as a limited resource that endows the concrete action with meaning and requires time allocation relative to competing interests.

An example may illustrate this point. Administrative detention is a concrete action that involves two competing interests: the public safety, on the one hand, and the human right to liberty, on the other. Because time is understood as a limited resource, the individual cannot be detained indefinitely, and it is for this reason that a reasonable time limit is set on the action. Clearly, if temporality were not of the essence of administrative detention, the competing interests would be meaningless. In this sense, it is time that delineates liberty and renders it meaningful. If administrative detention were permitted indefinitely, liberty would have lost its meaning.

It is equally unreasonable to place the concrete situation of occupation within an indefinite time frame. If occupation "could, from a legal point of view, continue indefinitely," the interests it is designed to protect—the interest of the occupied people in reaching the point in time where they regain control over their life and exercise their right to self determination and the interest of the international system in resuming its normal order of sovereign equality between states—would be rendered meaningless. This, indeed, is the rationale behind the temporary—as distinct from the indefinite—nature of an occupation.[172]

The notion of "reasonable time" thus underlies any concrete limits set by law on the duration of an action. The very same rationale holds for setting limits on the duration of actions that are not defined in concrete temporal terms. The conclusion that actions not defined in concrete temporal terms somehow transform the temporary into the indefinite is unreasonable. Indeed, in such situations, the concrete time limit is determined by the legal construct of "reasonable time," which derives from the legal principle of "reasonableness."[173] What is a reasonable time for an action depends on the nature, purpose, and circumstances of the action.[174]

Given the preceding discussion regarding the inalienability of sovereignty, the nature of the relationship between the population of the occupied territory and the occupying power as a form of trust, and the related rationale for the temporary nature of an occupation, it is clear that the purpose of the regime of occupation is to manage the situation in a manner designed to bring about political change and to generate a resumption of the normal order of international society. Relevant international norms further decree that this change should come about by peaceful means and realize the principle of self-determination.[175] The standing taken by the International Court of Justice, the General Assembly, and the Security Council with respect to the illegality of South Africa's postmandate presence in Namibia all serve to underscore the point.

The purpose of occupation would therefore be frustrated if its normative regime would be construed as indefinite in duration, because that construction may well generate political stagnation, rather than the desired change. Such an interpretation, then, is unreasonable, and the observation that the law of occupation, essentially designed for a relatively brief period, arguably lends itself to it should not obscure its unreasonableness relative to the purpose of that law. Israel's indefinite occupation frustrates the purpose of this regime.

It is not only the purpose of the regime of occupation, but also its essential nature that may well be defied if it is allowed to continue indefinitely. The population of an occupied territory does not enjoy the full range of human rights, in the very least insofar as it is deprived of citizenship and the rights attached to that status. The prolongation of such a situation may well be in the interests of an occupying power who may rely on the provisions of the law relative to the maintenance of the status quo, as well as to its security concerns, to the detriment of the population. Given that the occupier is likely to treat its own citizens in a manner vastly different from the manner with which it treats the population of an occupied territory, the result may well be the the de facto institutionalization of an apartheid of some sort.[176] Such a scenario, while ostensibly legal in terms of a "rule-book" conception of the rule of law, is manifestly illegal in terms of a "right" conception of the rule of law.[177] Indeed, in making the very rule of law a casualty of an indefinite occupation, it corrupts the law.[178]

Finally, we come to the circumstances of the occupation. The achievement of the purpose of a peaceful political change leading to a new sovereign state is a major policy issue. Matters of policy necessitate planning designed to achieve the desired result. Such planning, especially in respect to complicated and bitterly contested political issues that are not within the absolute control of one party, as is the case in the Israeli-Palestinian conflict, is neither a trivial nor an immediate matter. It is a long-term process. It may be incremental. It may, indeed, fail. It is possible, however, to evaluate whether such a policy was in the making *ex-ante*. This evaluation requires the examination of the circumstances of the specific occupation.

The most relevant circumstances to be examined in this respect are whether the occupying power has annexed the occupied territory or has otherwise indicated an intention to retain its presence there indefinitely. The examination of Israel's annexation of East Jerusalem, the expropriation of vast portions of Palestinian land to establish settlements in the occupied Palestinian territory, to construct the bypass roads, and, most recently, to erect the Wall, all suggest such an intention. The Wall, especially, merits our brief attention. As previously noted, its route does not follow the 1967 border. While its final path is yet unclear and, indeed, changes regularly in response to internal and external pressures, it is clearly designed to incorporate major settlements and many settlers into the Israeli side of it.[179] In some areas, it creates a barrier that encircles Palestinian villages. In others, it isolates them from the rest of the West Bank. The special rapporteur of the UN Commission on Human Rights concluded that "the construction of the Barrier within the West Bank, and the continued expansion of settlements, which, on the face of it have more to do with territorial expansion, de facto annexation or conquest, raise serious doubts about the good faith of Israel's justifications in the name of security."[180] The International Court of Justice's conclusion on this issue is quite pertinent:

> Whilst the Court notes the assurance given by Israel that the construction of the wall does not amount to annexation and that the wall is of a temporary nature...it

nevertheless cannot remain indifferent to certain fears expressed to it that the route of the wall will prejudge the future frontier between Israel and Palestine, and the fear that Israel may integrate the settlements and their means of access. The Court considers that the construction of the wall and its associated regime create a "fait accompli" on the ground that could well become permanent, in which case, and notwithstanding the formal characterization of the wall by Israel, it would be tantamount to *de facto* annexation.[181]

Had the International Court of Justice entertained the notion that the space between the "temporary" and the "permanent" is inhabited by the "indefinite," its conclusion would have been that such a construction is indicative less of a de facto annexation that may happen in the (permanent) future and more of an annexation that has been effected in the (indefinite) present.

When the above-described actions are coupled with the huge investments entailed therein,[182] as well as with the expansionist ideas that they realize within Israel, the only reasonable conclusion is that Israel, far from treating the occupied Palestinian territory as a negotiation card to be returned in exchange for peace, has intended to—and de facto did—annex a substantial part thereof. Unlike the de jure annexation of East Jerusalem, the actions described in the court's text lack the official act of annexation, but nevertheless amount to a de facto annexation, effected without giving the Palestinians the rights of citizenship and made visibly and materially clear by the planned path of the Wall. As noted by the special rapporteur of the UN Commission on Human Rights, John Dugard, "Language is a powerful instrument. This explains why words that accurately describe a particular situation are often avoided." Focusing merely on the barrier, the special rapporteur observed:

> the Barrier that Israel is presently constructing within the territory of the West Bank...goes by the name of "Seam Zone"; "Security Fence" or "Wall." The word "annexation" is avoided as it is too accurate a description and too concerned about the need to obfuscate the truth...the fact must be faced that what we are presently witnessing in the West Bank is a visible and clear act of territorial annexation under the guise of security.... Annexation of this kind goes by another name in international law: conquest.[183]

The resulting political geography of the occupied Palestinian territory, having been thus divided into a multitude of noncontiguous cantons, would not allow the Palestinians to exercise their right to self-determination in a viable sovereign state,[184] frustrating the desired political change clearly articulated by the Security Council.[185] The question remains whether Israel's security concerns justify the settlements and the chain of actions generated by their establishment. As we have noted, Israel claims that its actions are justified by legitimate security concerns, especially in the light of suicide bombing, and that they are simply temporary measures evidencing no intention to alter political boundaries.[186] This argument, however, is untenable on the basis of both substantive law and evidence.

As a matter of substantive law, while it is clear that the law of occupation recognizes the legitimate security concerns of the occupying power, such recognition does not extend to all means and methods arguably used to further this security. Indeed, it does not extend to settlements. Paragraph 6 of Article 49 of the Fourth Geneva Convention contains no exception to its prohibition of settlements on the grounds of such security considerations, and the latter, therefore, do not render the settlements a valid security measure.[187]

Even if, for the sake of argument, one dissociates the construction of the Wall from the settlements and examines the legality of this one measure in isolation, it would be hard to sustain the security claim legally in view of two factors. First, the principle of proportionality: The harm its construction entails for the Palestinian population is disproportionate relative to the security Israel may thereby achieve. This point is strengthened when the second factor is added: The Wall does not actually separate Palestinians from Israelis. Rather, it separates them from other Palestinians. Given that the Wall, much like the bypass roads and, indeed, the settlements themselves, are as inseparable in reality as they are in applicable law, the legal grounds for the Israeli position are tenuous at best.

Clearly, the concept of military necessity is not without its limits. One of those notable limitations is the customary principle of proportionality, the meaning of which is that the loss of life and damage to property not be out of proportion to the expected military advantage.[188] It thus imposes the obligation to balance between the desired aim and the damage inflicted, thereby subjecting the means and methods used to the standard of reasonableness. In his 2003 report, the special rapporteur to the UN Secretary General states unequivocally that such a balance was lacking in the way Israel exercised military power in the occupied territory:

> The Special Rapporteur finds it difficult to accept that the excessive use of force that disregards the distinction between civilians and combatants, the creation of a humanitarian crisis by restrictions on the mobility of goods and people, the killing and inhuman treatment of children, the widespread destruction of property and, now, territorial expansion can be justified as a proportionate response to the violence and threats of violence to which Israel is subjected.[189]

Further, the credibility of the "temporary" label that Israel attaches to these allegedly security measures is seriously questionable, given the relevant legal history. It is through allegedly temporary "requisition for military needs" orders that Palestinian lands were seized. These lands were never returned.[190] It is quite instructive, in this context, to ponder the state attorney's response to the Israeli High Court of Justice in the context of an appeal against the construction of the Wall: "The State is not prevented from seizing land by means of temporary seizure orders even for the purpose of erecting structures that are not necessarily temporary in nature. By way of illustration: in Judea and Samaria, temporary seizure orders have been used to erect permanent structures of many kinds, such as bypass roads and Israeli communities."[191]

This language game between the "temporary" act ("seizure") and its "permanent" effects ("structures") functions to legitimize actions that would have been otherwise prohibited and is, in fact, made possible once an occupation has ceased to be and to be conceived as temporary. Such an occupation, as the discussion pertaining to its purpose, nature, and circumstances demonstrates, has exceeded its reasonable duration. Such an occupation, in substituting an indefinite for a temporary control, violates the basic principle of temporariness underlying the normative regime of occupation.

The above does not suggest that the occupation is permanent. The "disengagement" from the Gaza Strip shows that a political decision can effect the dismantling of settlements and, perhaps, lead to the end of an occupation. The discussion does suggest, however, that in substituting the "indefinite" for a "temporary" occupation, Israel has violated the normative regime of occupation. It is instructive to note in this context that following the political decision to withdraw military forces from and dismantle the settlements in the Gaza Strip, the High Court of Justice emphasized the temporary—as distinct from the indefinite—nature of the occupation to deny the settlers' claim to remain in the settlements.[192] This decision is normatively sound. The fact that it was never made in order to question the legality of the settlements enterprise in the preceding decades demonstrates that temporary/indefinite indeterminacy is being used to legitimize power, not to contain it. The temporary nature of occupation was resurrected to replace the "indefinite" construction only when a political will to pull out was reached.

In conclusion, the very same actions that indicate that the occupation can no longer be regarded as temporary also disclose the violation of the substantive constraints imposed by the law of occupation on the managerial discretion of the occupying power. They amount to a de facto annexation of large portions of the occupied territory, entail gross violations of humanitarian and human rights norms, and defy both the principle of the inalienability of sovereignty and the principle of trust. The violation of the temporal constraints cannot but violate the two other basic tenets of the law of occupation, and the latter necessarily generate the conclusion that an occupation must be temporary. The Israeli occupation, having thus violated the three basic principles underlying the normative regime of occupation, is a conquest in disguise. It is, therefore, intrinsically illegal. The examination of its legality from an extrinsic perspective is undertaken in the section that follows.

THE EXTRINSIC DIMENSIONS OF THE ISRAELI OCCUPATION OF THE OCCUPIED PALESTINIAN TERRITORY: THE *NOMOS* OF OCCUPATION

The above discussion of the intrinsic dimensions of the Israeli occupation of the occupied Palestinian territory concentrated on the way Israel has managed the occupation in the light of the foundational normative standards set by the law of occupation. Its focus, thus, is the *substance* of the normative regime of occupation. It serves as a measuring rod for assessing various actions undertaken by the occupier. Here, the focus is different. It is on the normative and political *structure* of the occupation, a situation distinct from the regular order of the international society. We focus here on its exceptionality.[193]

Structurally, the law of occupation bears strong resemblance to an emergency regime. This regime, the roots of which date back to the Roman commissarial model, rests on three precepts: exceptionality, limited scope of powers, and temporary duration.[194] In this discourse a situation of emergency is separated and distinguished from the ordinary state of affairs because it signifies an occurrence that does not conform to the rule. The ordinary state of affairs is the general norm— this is what makes it "normal." The emergency is the exception—this is why its duration must be limited and generate no permanent effects. This is also why the norm is regarded as superior to the exception. The existing legal order defines the terms under which it is suspended, and the powers granted in such a situation are to be used for the purpose of an expeditious reestablishment of the status quo, that is, of a return to normalcy.[195]

The basic tenets of the normative regime of occupation largely conform to this constitutional model, transporting it to the international arena. The normal order of affairs is based on the principle of sovereign equality between states that are, at least to some extent, presumed to be founded on the ideas of self-government and self-determination. The severance of the link between sovereignty and effective control and life under foreign rule—both features of occupation—constitute an exceptional situation, and the law of occupation recognizes it as an exception. It is to be managed so as to ensure expeditious return to normalcy. This is why the occupier has only limited powers in terms of both scope and time and is not permitted to act in a manner designed to yield permanent results.[196]

Indeed, the conclusion of modern studies of emergency situations concerned with the derogation from human rights law thereby occasioned have concluded that "above and beyond the rules…one principle, namely, the principle of provisional status, dominates all others. The right of derogation (of human rights) can be justified solely by the concern to return to normalcy."[197] This conclusion holds true and equally applies to occupations.

A reversal of the relationship between the norm and the exception generates, of necessity, the terminus of every normative system.[198] Carl Schmitt's political theology, wherein the norm becomes subservient to the exception, is both a precedent and a warning point: "the rule", says Schmitt, "proves nothing; the exception proves everything: it confirms not only the rule but also its existence, which derives only from the exception."[199] The state of emergency, which in German is called a "state of exception" (*Ausnahmezeustand*), is one where the rule of man prevails over the rule of law and where the Leviathan reigns supreme.[200] The result is a Hobbesian state of war—indeed, the clearest case of an exception—where, bereft of any rights, the only meaningful distinction for a person to make is between the reified constructs of "friend" and "'foe."[201] This situation signifies the destruction of both the normative regime of the exception and the general rule. From a normative perspective, it is thus as meaningless as it is indefensible.

One lesson to be drawn from the above is the importance of retaining a clear distinction between fact and norm, between the rule and the exception, lest the exception becomes a new rule and generates a new conception of reality. This is important because in this new conception of reality, one's security habitually, uncritically, overrides one's enemy's human rights. Indeed, the reversal of the relationship between the rule and the exception operates as a legitimizing device. It allows for a discussion of various specific violations of human rights carried out in the name of security, as if they are the exception to the normal order of things, thereby obfuscating the fact that said violations are the rule, not the exception.

It is in order to contain the eruption of a Schmittian "friend/enemy" politics that the international rule of law recognized the situation of occupation as an exception and created a normative regime designed to ensure that the effective control of the occupying power is exercised in a manner that is temporary, respectful of the humanitarian needs and the human rights of the population of the occupied territory, and leads to an expeditious return to normalcy based on sovereign equality. An occupation that fails to do this is substantively and intrinsically illegal in terms of the law of occupation, but also, as well as structurally and extrinsically illegal in terms of the international legal order that provides the normative framework within which the law of occupation operates. The Israeli occupation of the occupied Palestinian territory has thus failed.

THE MATRIX OF AN ILLEGAL OCCUPATION AND ITS
NORMATIVE CONSEQUENCES: CONCLUDING OBSERVATIONS

In light of the above conclusion, one should revisit Israel's arguments regarding its security concerns and the measures taken to ensure that they are met. It is beyond dispute that terrorist attacks present a major challenge to the conduct of normal life. This has become painfully evident in many parts of the world following 9/11. What should be disputed, however, is the equation that Israel has drawn between the Palestinians and al-Qaeda, and indeed between the former and worldwide Islamic fanaticism. The Palestinians are engaged in a struggle for freedom by an occupied people; al-Qaeda is an amorphous and transnational group intent on destroying the Western way of life. The Israeli equation lends support to the Israeli argument, discussed above, that the Palestinian response to Israel's most generous peace offerings at Camp David is evidence of the lack of good-faith engagement in the peace process on the part of the Palestinians and exposes their true motivation: the destruction of the only democratic state in the Middle East, Israel. What is missing from the equation, however, is the occupation. The equation is thus self-serving, because it allows for the obfuscation of the cause-and-effect relations that exist between this occupation and Palestinian violence. These relations do not justify terrorist attacks against civilians — there is no justification for such attacks — but they do contextualize them and refocus the attention on the nature of the Israeli occupation of the occupied Palestinian territory.

It should be recalled in this context that the essential features of the occupation regime of the occupied Palestinian territory date back to at least 1977, thus preceding both the second and the first intifadas and making the assignment of blame for the failure of the peace process to the Palestinians, its accuracy notwithstanding, irrelevant to the present discussion. The establishment of the Palestinian Authority did not alter the fact of the occupation, not least because Israel neither ceased to exercise effective control over the territory nor ceased to allow the expansion, or "natural growth," of the settlements.[202] These facts indeed, have led some observers to compare the creation of the Palestinian Authority to the creation of Bantustans in apartheid South Africa.[203]

Furthermore, our argument regarding the illegality of the continued Israeli occupation of the occupied Palestinian territory rests on the violation by Israel of the basic tenets of the normative regime of occupation. The various arguments advanced in support of Israeli actions in the territory in the name of security thus fail to counter our argument. The question whether a particular action by the IDF undertaken to advance Israel's security has violated certain rights of the protected population should not be confused with and is indeed separate from the question of the illegality of the regime of occupation.

Focusing on the nature of this regime—as distinct from analyzing specific actions undertaken within it—reveals that obfuscation and the blurring of boundaries is the defining feature of this occupation. Its indeterminacy has operated to legitimize what otherwise would have been determined as illegal. Thus, while Israel has consistently argued that the West Bank and the Gaza Strip are not occupied territory, the state's attorneys have sought to justify Israel's actions in the territory that restrict the rights of Palestinians on the basis of the law of occupation.[204] Similarly, the High Court of Justice, while never confirming the applicability of the Fourth Geneva Convention to the territory, has nevertheless decided to apply its humanitarian provisions in a manner that has allowed the IDF to exercise the powers of a belligerent occupier, but has rejected the vast majority of Palestinian petitions. This is most significant in the context of two major issues on which the court rejected Palestinian petitions and allowed the army to act in ways that de facto negated protections that the Geneva Convention sought to give: deportations, and home demolitions.[205] In the context of both issues, the High Court of Justice interpreted the Geneva Convention in a highly controversial way that allowed the Israeli Army to use these measures, notwithstanding the specific prohibitions on them in the text of the convention.[206]

In this manner, Israel has been able to enjoy the credit for applying international humanitarian law while at the same time violating its essential tenets. This credit should be noted particularly for its rarity, insofar as it has been the practice of occupying powers to deny the very applicability of the law of occupation.[207] There is a difference, however, between admitting the relevance of and referring to international humanitarian law and applying it in a manner consistent with its purpose. While the High Court of Justice does apply this law in a manner that occasionally has favored a Palestinian petition directly and, perhaps more significantly, indirectly, by exercising its "shadow" function to encourage the state to retreat from a contested action before a decision is rendered, it has not, in the main, applied this law in a manner that advances the law's main purpose.[208]

This occupation/nonoccupation indeterminacy is complemented by its twin annexation/nonannexation indeterminacy. Israel acts in the occupied territory as a sovereign insofar as it settles its citizens there and extends to them its laws on a personal and on a mixed personal/territorial basis, yet insofar as the territory has not been formally annexed and insofar as this exercise of sovereignty falls short of giving the Palestinian residents citizenship rights, Israel is not acting as a sovereign. In this manner, Israel enjoys in the occupied Palestinian territory both the powers of an occupier and the powers of a sovereign, while the Palestinians enjoy neither the rights of an occupied people nor the rights of citizenship. This indeterminacy thus, allows Israel to avoid the wrath of the international community for having illegally annexed the territory while pursuing the policies of "greater Israel" without jeopardizing its Jewish majority.[209]

It is important to note in this context that demography plays a significant role not only in relation to the Palestinians in the occupied Palestinian territory, but also in relation to the Palestinian minority within Israel proper. The latter, while enjoying the myriad rights associated with citizenship, are nevertheless discriminated against, most notably with respect to land rights as they most directly pertain to the "Judaization" process of the land of Israel. This process has led to the characterization of the Israeli regime as an "ethnic democracy"—a concept that appears to be an oxymoron—or as an "ethnocracy." Seen in this context, the occupation regime attempts to replicate the same process by extending the ethnic regime that exists within Israel's recognized borders. The result is an Israeli state whose existence as a democracy is put in doubt.[210]

Finally, the blurring of the boundaries between the temporary and the indefinite and, indeed, between the rule and the exception, has conferred a mantle of legitimacy on this occupation and has made possible the continuous interplay of occupation/nonoccupation, annexation/nonannexation. This mantle, however, much like the emperor's new clothes, should not obfuscate our vision of the naked illegality of this regime.

"The qualification of a situation as illegal," observed the International Court of Justice, "does not itself put an end to it. It can only be the first necessary step in an endeavour to bring the illegal occupation to an end."[211] While law, in itself, is surely no substitute for statesmanship and cannot therefore "bring the illegal occupation to an end," there are normative results that do follow from illegality. A state "whose conduct constitutes an internationally wrongful act having a continuing character is under an obligation to cease that conduct, without prejudice to the responsibility it has already incurred."[212]

The advisory opinion of the International Court of Justice regarding the legal consequences emanating from the continued presence of South Africa in Namibia is quite pertinent to the case at hand: "By maintaining the present illegal situation, and occupying the territory without title," opined the court, "South Africa entails international responsibilities arising from a continuing violation of an international obligation.... Physical control of a territory, and not sovereignty or legitimacy of title, is the basis of state liability for acts affecting other States."[213] The court, having stated that there is an obligation on the members of the United Nations to bring that situation to an end,[214] proceeded to detail that obligation, indicating a range of measures designed to recognize the illegality and to put pressure on

South Africa with reference to its "occupation of Namibia."[215] The court was further mindful that such measures should not have a boomerang effect on the people of Namibia and thus concluded that "as to the general consequences resulting from the illegal presence of South Africa in Namibia, all States should bear in mind that the injured entity is a people which must look to the international community for assistance in its progress towards the goals for which the sacred trust was instituted."[216] The same normative consequences, mutatis mutandis, follow from the illegality of the Israeli occupation of the occupied Palestinian territory.

Further, the qualification of the occupation as "illegal," while it does not affect the continued application of both humanitarian and human rights law (so as to avoid a legal vacuum and to offer protection to the population of the occupied territory as long as the illegal situation persists), does affect the legality of the security measures taken in its defense—because such measures are thereby illegal themselves.[217] This consequence is relevant both to the legal assessment of various security measures undertaken by Israel, including but not limited to the Wall, and to the legal validity of the arguments raised within Israel by soldiers who refuse to partake in the defense of the occupation. Indeed, the perception of the Israeli occupation as illegal and illegitimate might well have been the main factor that informed the court's perception of the Wall in the *Construction of a Wall* advisory opinion. While refraining from commenting on the occupation regime itself, the court was well aware of the "greater whole" of which the Wall is but one aspect.[218] This might explain, for example, its offhand rejection of Israel's self-defense argument, based on Article 51 of the UN Charter, on the ground that Israel was not reacting in response to force used by another state, but rather to force emanating from within its territory in light of the control it is exercising in the occupied Palestinian territory.[219]

It may, however, be possible to construe additional normative consequences emanating from an indefinite occupation that, as discussed above, necessarily constitutes an assault on both sovereign integrity and fundamental human rights. Such an occupation defies the basic tenets of both the laws of occupation and the normal order of international society. The time has come for the international community to promulgate clear time limitations for the duration of an occupation, thereby offering a solution to the problem identified in, but not resolved by, Article 6 of the Fourth Geneva Convention. The international community may wish to entertain the thought that in cases of occupations the duration of which lasts longer than a year, and pending a comprehensive political solution, effective control over the occupied territory be transferred from the occupying power to an appropriate international authority.[220] It may further wish to consider the possibility that a refusal by an occupying power thus to transfer control be construed as a form of aggression.[221] Indeed, the rationale underlying the criminalization of aggression, that is, that it is a framework for an entire body of international crimes, as explained by the Nuremberg International Military Tribunal, seems to apply here, as well.[222] This notion is, perhaps, somewhat baffling and difficult to accept, given the nearly axiomatic conception of occupation as a fact of life.[223] But, then, was not aggression, too, before World War II, perceived as an acceptable, albeit regrettable fact of life regulated by the Covenant of the League of Nations?

Whether or not the international community, by taking any of the measures recommended above, decides to deter similar instances where the boundaries between the rule and the exception become blurred, leading to the *nomos* of occupation, remains to be seen. Such speculation is clearly outside the scope of our present concern. What we posit, however, as a matter of legal analysis, is that once the law is used in order to obfuscate the distinction between the rule and the exception, the very fabric of law is being corrupted, and the rule of law becomes subverted. It becomes a legal fabrication. The result is the (il)legal sanctioning of the destruction of "the *fabric of life* of the [Palestinian] residents" of the occupied Palestinian territory. The time has indeed come to confront this difficulty.

NOTES

This article is a revised and updated version of Orna Ben-Naftali, Aeyal M. Gross, and Keren Michaeli, *Illegal Occupation: The Framing of the Occupied Palestinian Territory* 23 (3) Berkeley J. Int'l. L. 551 (2005), which includes a more detailed discussion of some of the legal issues at stake. The epigraph is taken from HCJ 7957/04, Mara'abe v. The Prime Minister of Israel, available on-line in English at http://www.alhaq.org/pdfs/Petition%20HCJ-1960-07.pdf (last accessed February 28, 2009), para. 116 (emphasis added). The Mara'abe case concerned an appeal against the legality of a portion of the "Separation Wall," the construction project begun in 2003 by the Israeli government within the Palestinian territory occupied by its military, cutting Palestinians off from their livelihoods, schools, clinics, and social services. It was the first case to have been rendered by the Israeli High Court of Justice (HCJ) after the International Court of Justice (ICJ) had rendered its advisory opinion on the legality of the Wall. See International Court of Justice, *Legal Consequences of a Wall in the Occupied Palestinian Territory,* 2004 ICJ 131 (July 9) (hereafter, *Construction of a Wall*). There are various terms used to describe this construction, for example, "wall," "fence," and "separation barrier." The term "wall" will be used in this paper in accordance with the language of the advisory opinion of the International Court of Justice.

1   Adam Roberts, *What is a Military Occupation?* 55 Brit. Y.B. Int'l. L. 249 (1984). Roberts lists seventeen types of occupations and includes "illegal occupation" as a category, but puts this term in quotation marks and raises a doubt about its validity: the term is used to refer to

an occupation that is perceived as being the outcome of aggression, but this position is not tenable, given that the law of war, including the law of occupation, equally applies to all states, whether aggressors or victims of aggression. *Id.,* at 293–94.

2   The term "occupied Palestinian territory," in the singular, is what is employed by the United Nations to denote the territorial contiguity of the would-be Palestinian polity and will be employed throughout the present essay.

3   Eyal Benvenisti, *The International Law of Occupation* 4 (1992). For a discussion of the evolutionary development of the law of occupation, see Ben-Naftali, Gross, and Michaeli, *Illegal Occupation.*

4   Convention (IV) respecting the Laws and Customs of War on Land and its annex: Regulations Concerning the Laws and Customs of War on Land, Oct. 18, 1907, Reg. 42, 36 Stat. 2277, 1 Bevans 631; Geneva Convention Relative to the Protection of Civilian Persons in Time of War, Aug. 12, 1949, 75 UNTS 287 (hereafter, Fourth Geneva Convention); Protocol Additional to the Geneva Conventions of 12 August 1949, and relating to the Protection of Victims of International Armed Conflicts (Protocol I), 8 June 1977, Article 1 (4), 1125 UNTS 3 (hereafter, Protocol I).

5   Richard R. Baxter, *Some Existing Problems of Humanitarian Law,* 14 Revue de Droit Penal Militaire et de Droit de la Guerre 297, 288 (1975).

6   The Israeli position has been widely rejected, most recently by the International Court of Justice in *Construction of a Wall,* at para. 101. It should be noted that Israel had declared early on that it would apply the humanitarian provisions of the Geneva Convention, a declaration relied on by the High Court of Justice in petitions pertaining to various measures undertaken in the occupied Palestinian territory. For a comprehensive discussion of both the Israeli position and its rejection, see Ben-Naftali, Gross, and Michaeli, *Illegal Occupation,* pp. 567–70.

7   This principle is discussed in "The Intrinsic Dimensions of the Israeli Occupation of the Occupied Palestinian Territory" below.

8   Likewise discussed in "The Intrinsic Dimensions of the Israeli Occupation of the Occupied Palestinian Territory."

9   See, for example, GA Res. ES-10/6, UN GAOR, 54th Sess., Supp. No. 49, UN Doc. A/ES-10/6 (1999).

10   The question of the continuation of the occupation in the face of changes in control was also raised in relation to the territory over which Israel transferred administrative powers to the Palestinian Authority under the Oslo Accords. With the demise of the Oslo agreement after 2000, the point became moot.

11   See *Case Concerning Armed Activities on the Territory of the Congo (Democratic Republic of the Congo v Uganda)* (19 Dec. 2005) para. 167–180; HCJ 102/82 Tsemel v. Minister of Defense, 37 (1) P.D. 365.

12   For an analytical review of relevant jurisprudence, see Orna Ben-Naftali and Yuval Shany, *Living in Denial: the Application of Human Rights in the Occupied Territories,* 37 Isr. L. Rev. 17, 70–87; 96–100.

13   See Sari Bashi and Kenneth Mann, *Disengaged Occupiers: The Legal Status of Gaza,* GISHA: Center for the Legal Protection of Freedom of Movement (January 2007). The report points to the facts of the control Israel exercises over Gaza's air, water, and land borders, the transfer of goods and people, Gaza's residents' registry, customs and thereby the ability of public institutions to receive foreign donations and salaries of civil servants through taxation as all indicating its continuing control of Gaza. However, in January 2008, the Israeli Supreme

Court held that Israel no longer has effective control over what takes place within Gaza, given that its soldiers are no longer present there on an ongoing basis and that the Israeli military government that existed there was abolished. Thus, the court held that Israel no longer bears a general obligation to concern itself with the welfare of Gaza's residents and that the duties prescribed in the law of occupation no longer applied to it. The primary obligations of Israel regarding Gaza, the court held, derive from the state of armed conflict that exists between Israel and Hamas, from the degree of control Israel has over the border crossing between it and Gaza, to and from the situation that was created between Israel and Gaza due to the years of Israeli military control of the area. See HC 9132/07 Jaber al-Basyuni Ahmed et al. v. The Prime Minister et al. (not yet published).

14   A search in Lexis-Nexis on the topic of the Israeli occupation of the Palestinian territory generated over 100 entries concerned with various Israeli actions and positions as an occupying power and no entry relative to the legality of the occupation itself. Similar results were obtained from West Law.

15   The Secretary-General Statement to the Security Council on the Middle East, New York, March 12, 2002.

16   George Fletcher, "Annan's Careless Language," *New York Times,* March 21, 2002, at A37.

17   Frederic Eckhard, "A Delicate Word in the Mideast," letter to the editor, *New York Times,* March 23, 2002, at A16.

18   *Construction of a Wall.*

19   Hans Kelsen, *General Theory of Law and State* 116 (1945). This text does not suggest that Kelsen would have regarded occupation as a basic norm, which is therefore not subject to the test of validity. On the contrary, under Kelsen's theory, the occupation would be considered a legal norm within a normative system, the basic norm of which authorizes the creation by states of customary and conventional international laws.

20   *The Case of the S.S. Lotus* (Fr. v. Turk.), 1927 P.C.I.J. (Ser. A) No. 9, at 18 (Sep. 7).

21   For a critique of Kelsen's pure theory of law, see Ronald M. Dworkin, *Comments on the Unity of Law Doctrine (a Response),* in *Ethics and Social Justice* 200 (Howard E. Kiefer and Milton K. Munitz eds., 1970); Joseph Raz, *The Concept of a Legal System* 93–120 (1970).

22   To borrow the famous term coined by Justice Oliver Wendell Holmes, *The Path of the Law,* 10 Harv. L. Rev. 457 (1897). The conception of law implied in this alternative is majestic, or reflective of imperialistic positivism, inasmuch as it conceives of the law as governing all human actions, either forbidding or authorizing each and every action, thereby rejecting the theoretical possibility of legal lacunae.

23   Such interaction is one of the major elements in the Critical Legal Studies (CLS) critique of legal liberalism. See Duncan Kennedy, *A Critique of Adjudication: Fin De Siècle* (1997). In the context of international law, see Martti Koskenniemi, *From Apology to Utopia: The Structure of International Legal Argument* (1989, 2006).

24   In reference to Koskenniemi's terms, *id.* See also, Martti Koskenniemi, *The Politics of International Law,* 1 Eur. J. Int'l. L. 4 (1990).

25   *Legal Consequences for States of the Continued Presence of South Africa in Namibia (South-West Africa) Notwithstanding Security Council Resolution 276* (1970), 1971 ICJ 16 (June 21), This was followed by a decision of the Security Council which declared the continued presence of South Africa in Namibia to be illegal. See SC Res. 276, UN SCOR, 25th Sess., Res. & Dec., at 1, 2, UN Doc. s/INF/25 (1970).

26 Thus, writes Anne-Marie Slaughter, "the United States and its allies can justify their intervention if the Iraqi people welcome their coming and if they turn immediately back to the United Nations to help rebuild the country." Anne-Marie Slaughter, "Good Reasons for Going around the UN," *New York Times,* March 13, 2003, at A33. For criticism, see Richard A. Falk, *Future Implication of the Iraq Conflict: What Future for the UN Charter System of War Prevention?* 97 Am. J. Int'l. L. 590, 596–97 (2003). Falk criticizes claims that a regime change constitutes a legal basis for humanitarian intervention. See also David J. Scheffer, *Future Implication of the Iraq Conflict: Beyond Occupation Law,* 97 Am. J. Int'l. L. 842, 851 (2003). Scheffer indicates that since the law of occupation is ill suited for the purposes of changing a regime or rebuilding a country, a nation-building policy by the UN is called for, rather than an American occupation.

27 Antonio Cassese, *Self-Determination of Peoples* 238–39 (1995) 99.

28 Cf. Judge Elaraby, *Construction of a Wall,* Separate Opinion of Judge Elaraby, para. 3.1. Judge Elaraby cites with approval an article authored by Professors Richard Falk and Burns Weston that argues that occupation, as an illegal and temporary situation, is at the heart of the whole problem. Judge Elaraby does not explain why an occupation is illegal and does not make a connection between its temporary duration and illegality. His reliance on Falk and Weston suggests that the illegality stems from the original act of force that generated the occupation. See Richard A. Falk and Burns H. Weston, *The Relevance of International Law to Israeli and Palestinian Rights in the West Bank and Gaza,* in *International Law and the Administration of Occupied Territories* 125 146–47 (Emma Playfair ed., 1992).

29 See Eyal Benvenisti, *The Security Council and the Law of Occupation: Resolution 1483 on Iraq in Historical Perspective,* 1 IDF L. Rev. 19 (2003), at 33.

30 Benvenisti lists the following documents: The Charter of Economic Rights and Duties of States of December 12, 1974 (Article 16 (1) of GA Res. 3281, 29 UN GAOR, 29th Sess., Supp. No. 31, at 52, UN Doc. A/9631 (1974)); GA Res. 3171, section 2, UN GAOR, 28th Sess., Supp. No. 30, at 52, UN Doc. A/9030 (1973); Protocol I; Article 12 (12) of the 1979 International Convention Against the Taking of Hostages (UN Doc. A/C.6/34/L.23, reprinted in 18 ILM 1456 (1979). Benvenisti, *id.,* at 32–33.

31 *Id.,* at 33–34.

32 United Nations S/RES/1483 (2003), Article 5.

33 Benvenisti, *The Security Council and the Law of Occupation,* at 36–38.

34 Question of the Violations of Human Rights in the Occupied Arab Territories, Including Palestine, Report of the Special Rapporteur of the Commission of Human Rights on the Situation of Human Rights in the Palestinian Territories Occupied by Israel Since 1967 (A/57/366), August 29, 2002, para. 21, hereafter *2002 Report on the Violations of Human Rights in the Occupied Arab Territories.*

35 Question of the Violation of Human Rights in the Occupied Arab Territories, Including Palestine, Note Verbale Dated 16 December 2002 from the Permanent Representative of Israel to the United Nations Office at Geneva, Addressed to the Secretariat of the Commission of Human Rights, Commission of Human Rights, 59th Sess., E/CN.4/2003.G/21 para. 9 (December 23, 2002).

36 See in this context Adam Roberts's discussion of a possible grounding of an argument made by the Palestinians on the illegality of the Israeli occupation on the presumed fact that Israel was an aggressor in 1967. Adam Roberts, *Prolonged Military Occupation: The Israeli Occupied*

Territories Since 1967, 84 Am. J. Int'l. L. 44, 49–51 (1990).

37 Enshrined in Article 2 (1) of the Charter of the United Nations, June 26, 1945, 59 Stat. 1031, T.S. No. 993, 3 Bevans 1153.

38 Benvenisti, *The Security Council and the Law of Occupation,* at 28.

39 This notion of suspension was already recognized in the first attempt to codify the international law of occupation in the Final Protocol and Project of an International Declaration Concerning the Laws and Customs of War, August 27, 1874, reprinted in *The Laws of Armed Conflict: A Collection of Conventions, Resolutions and Other Documents* 25 (Dietrich Schindler and Jiri Toman, eds., 3rd ed. 1988).

40 The tension between the rule and the exception formed one of the basic tenets of Carl Schmitt's critique of the liberal state and, indeed, of the very rule of law. See Carl Schmitt, *Political Theology: Four Chapters on the Concept of Sovereignty* (George Schwab trans., 1988). A critical discussion of Schmitt's concept of the exception is offered in "The Extrinsic Dimensions of the Israeli Occupation of the Occupied Palestinian Territory" below.

41 Traditionally, sovereignty was attached to the state that held title to the territory prior to occupation. Currently, the focus has shifted to the rights of the population under occupation. See Eyal Benvenisti, *The Security Council and the Law of Occupation.* For a review of the recognition of the Palestinian right to self-determination, see Cassese, *Self-Determination of Peoples,* at 238–39. It is further important to note that Israel itself seems to have recognized this right, albeit implicitly, at least since the Oslo Accords of 1993, as can be inferred from both the text and the context of the Declaration of Principles signed between Israel and the PLO in 1993. See *Declaration of Principles on Interim Self-Government Arrangements,* September 13, 1993, 32 ILM 1525 (1993). In the *Construction of a Wall* advisory opinion, the Palestinian right to self-determination was explicitly recognized, the court opining that "the existence of a 'Palestinian people' is no longer an issue" and noting that Israel itself has recognized this right. *Construction of a Wall,* at para. 118. It is significant in this context to note that the court further opined that Israel has a right to exist within the Green Line. *Id.,* at para. 71; 162.

42 A discussion of the principle of trust as embedded in the normative regime of occupation is offered in "The Intrinsic Dimensions of the Israeli Occupation of the Occupied Palestinian Territory" below.

43 See *Construction of a Wall,* Separate Opinion of Judge Elaraby, para. 3.1; Separate Opinion of Judge Koroma, para. 2. A discussion of the temporal constraints of the normative regime of occupation is offered in "The Intrinsic Dimensions of the Israeli Occupation of the Occupied Palestinian Territory" below.

44 Benvenisti, *The International Law of Occupation,* at 5.

45 Surya P. Sharma, *Territorial Acquisition, Disputes and International Law* 148 (1997).

46 Partial Award, Central Front, Ethiopia's Claim 2, April 28, 2004, para. 28–29, available on-line at http://www.pca-cpa.org/upload/files/ET%20Partial%20Award(1).pdf (last accessed September 12, 2008).

47 Georg Schwarzenberger, *International Law as Applied by International Courts and Tribunals* 166–67 (3rd. ed., 1957).

48 Jean S. Pictet, *Commentary — The Geneva Convention Relative to the Protection of Civilian Persons in Time of War,* 275–76 (1958). Pictet emphasizes the fact that the reference to annexation in the article cannot be considered as implying recognition of it as a means to acquire territory and that the contrary is true.

49 *Commentary on the Additional Protocols of 8 July 1977 to the Geneva Conventions of 12 August 1949* 73–74 (Yves Sandoz et al., eds., 1987)

50 See *The Declaration on Principles of International Law concerning Friendly Relations and Co-operation among States in Accordance with the Charter of the United Nations,* GA Res. 2625, UN GAOR, 25th Sess., Supp. No. 28, at 121, UN Doc. A/8028 (1970).

51 See Fletcher, "Annan's Careless Language" and Eckhard, "A Delicate Word in the Mideast."

52 Israel extended its law to East Jerusalem on June 26, 1967. See The Law and Administration Ordinance (Amendment No. 11) Law, 21 LSI 75 (1967); The Municipalities Ordinance (Amendment No. 6) Law, 21 LSI. 75 (1967). It formally annexed that area on June 30, 1980; see The Basic Law: Jerusalem, Capital of Israel, 34 LSI 209 (1980).

53 See SC Res. 478, UN SCOR, 35th Sess., 2245th mtg. At 14, UN Doc. S/INF/36 (1980); GA Res. 35/169E, UN GAOR, 35th Sess., Supp. No. 48, at 208–9, UN Doc. A/35/48 (1981); SC Res. 673, UN SCOR, 46th Sess., 2949 mtg. at Res. & Dec. 7, UN Doc. S/INF/46 (1991). Israel based its claim to sovereignty over East Jerusalem essentially on its right to fill the sovereignty vacuum that existed since the termination of the mandate, an argument that generated a debate among Israeli international lawyers and that failed to gain the support of the international community. On the debate within Israel, see, for example, Yehudah Blum, *The Redemption of Zion in International Law,* 3 Isr. L. Rev. 279 (1968) and Yoram Dinstein, *The Future Redemption of Zion in International Law,* 27 Hapraklit 5 (1971). For a discussion on the legal status of Jerusalem, see John Quigley, *The Future of Jerusalem: A Symposium.* Sovereignty in Jerusalem, 45 Cath. U. L. Rev. 765 (1996). Similar reactions followed Israel's annexation of the Golan Heights, a Syrian territory occupied by Israel during the Six-Day War of 1967. See the Golan Heights Law, 36 LSI 7 (5742-1981/2); SC Res. 497 (1981); GA Res. 36/226A (1981); GA Res. 39/146A (1984).

54 *Construction of a Wall,* at para. 74–75, 120–22.

55 GA Res. 37/88C, UN GAOR, 37th Sess., Supp. No. 51, at 93, UN Doc. A/37/51 (1982–83); SC Res. 465, UN SCOR, 35th Sess., 2203d mtg. at 5, UN Doc. S/INF/36 (1980).

56 SC Res. 1397, UN SCOR, 4489th mtg., UN Doc. S/RES/1397 (2002).

57 See Declaration on the Granting of Independence to Colonial Countries and Peoples, GA Res. 1514, 15 UN GAOR Supp. (No. 16), at 66, UN Doc. A/4684 (1960).

58 Ardi Imseis, *On the Fourth Geneva Convention and the Occupied Palestinian Territory,* 44 Harv. Int'l. L. J. 65, 97 (2003); Benvenisti, the *International Law of Occupation,* at 183.

59 *Construction of a Wall,* at para. 118–22.

60 Roberts, *What Is a Military Occupation?* at 295.

61 *Construction of a Wall,* Separate Opinion of Judge Koroma, para. 2; Arnold Wilson, *The Laws of War in Occupied Territories* 18 Transactions Grotius Soc'y 17, 38 (1933).

62 See Richard R. Baxter, *The Duty of Obedience to the Belligerent Occupant,* 27 Brit. Y.B. Int'l L. 235 (1950).

63 For example, the terms "war rebellion" and "war treason" were not incorporated in the convention. Furthermore, while providing the occupier with the right to take measures against protected persons who carry out acts detrimental to the security of the occupier, it nevertheless preserves most of their rights under the Convention. Cf. Fourth Geneva Convention, Articles 27, 64, with Articles 5, 68. Also see Baxter, *The Duty of Obedience,* at 261, 264.

64 The Fourth Geneva Convention, Articles 27, 75.

65 *Id.,* at Articles 55, 59–62.

66 *Id.,* at Articles 32, 33, 34, 49, 65, 67, 51, 52, 50, 55, 59–62, 66, 69, 71–73, 76, 77, respectively.

67 *Id.,* Articles 79–135.

68 See *Construction of a Wall,* at para. 105–13. See also *Legality of the Threat or Use of Nuclear Weapons,* 1996 ICJ. 226, 249 (July 8). See generally, Ben-Naftali and Shany, *Living in Denial.*

69 Esther R. Cohen, *Human Rights in the Israeli-Occupied Territories 1967–1982* (1985), 29; Roberts, *Prolonged Military Occupation,* at 97.

70 Roberts, *Prolonged Military Occupation,* at 28–32; *Legal Consequences for States of the Continued Presence of South Africa in Namibia,* at 47. While the special context of the relationship between South Africa and Namibia was the mandate system established by the League of Nations, the reasoning of the court nevertheless seems to be of general applicability as emphasized by the fact that the court interpreted the traditional concept of trust found in the mandate system in light of recent legal developments, namely, the self-determination and independence of the people and basic human rights. Furthermore, the court construed South Africa's presence in Namibia following the revocation of the mandate as an occupation.

71 Roberts, *What Is a Military Occupation,* at 293–94 (referring to this specific type of occupation); *Legal Consequences for States of the Continued Presence of South Africa in Namibia,* at 54.

72 *Construction of a Wall,* at para. 70.

73 *International Status of South-West Africa,* 1950 ICJ 128 1950 (July 11).

74 *Id.,* at 131; *Construction of a Wall,* at para. 70.

75 *Legal Consequences for States of the Continued Presence of South Africa in Namibia,* para. 52–54; cited in *Construction of a Wall,* at para. 88.

76 Note that some of the judges who appended separate opinions took issue with this analogy. See *Construction of a Wall,* Separate opinion of Judge Higgins, para. 2; Separate opinion of Judge Kooijmans, para. 33.

77 It is interesting to note that Allan Gerson referred to the Israeli occupation as a "Trustee Occupation." His thesis was that this type of occupation occurs when the legal status of the territory prior to the occupation was short of full sovereignty, the occupation was not generated by a war of aggression, and the occupier was seeking to develop the area positively. In such cases, the occupier should be seen as a trustee responsible for promoting the population's right of self determination and should therefore not be constrained by the law requiring the preservation of the status quo. See Allan Gerson, *Trustee Occupant: The Legal Status of Israel's Presence in the West Bank,* 14 Harv. Int'l L. J. 1 (1973). This typology, however, is problematic from the perspective of law and fact alike. From a legal perspective, as discussed in the text above, the concept of trust underlies the law of occupation in general. From a factual perspective, it is unclear whether Israel's occupation resulted from a war of self-defense, and even if it did, it is clear that it has not assumed the role of trustee fostering the Palestinian right to self-determination, as acknowledged by Gerson himself already in 1978. See Allan Gerson, *Israel, The West Bank and International Law* 78–82 (1978).

78 Fourth Geneva Convention, Article 27, second paragraph of Article 49, 51, 53.

79 *Id.,* Articles 64, 78, 42.

80 See the discussion in "The Extrinsic Dimensions of the Israeli Occupation of the Occupied Palestinian Territory" below.

81 Benvenisti, *The International Law of Occupation,* at 147; Roberts, *Prolonged Military Occupation,* at 52.

82 As emphasized by Judge Elaraby, *Construction of a Wall,* Separate Opinion of Judge Elaraby, para. 3.1.

83 See Akiva Eldar Andidit Zertal, *Lords of the Land: The Settlers and the State of Israel 1967– 2004,* 439–53 (2005). It is notable that Israel was quite familiar with the notion of a military government, having effected it with respect to its Arab citizens between October 1948 and December 1966. *Id.,* at 449.

84 *Id.,* at 451.

85 See Meir Shamgar, *The Observance of International Law in the Administered Territories,* 1 Isr. YB of HR 262 (1972). On the debate over the de-jure applicability of the Fourth Geneva Convention to the occupied Palestinian Territory see Ben-Naftali, Gross, and Michaeli, *Illegal Occupation,* at 567–70. The thesis regarding the inapplicability of the convention was widely rejected by international lawyers both within and outside Israel, including by the International Court of Justice in *Construction of a Wall,* at para. 90–101.

86 See Meron Benvenisti, *The West Bank Data Project: A Survey of Israel's Policies* 30–36 (1984); Raja Shehadeh, *Occupier's Law: The West Bank and the Rule of Law* 15–49 (1985).

87 Cited in John Quigley, *Living in Legal Limbo,* 10 Pace Int'l. L. R. 16 (1998).

88 *Id.* Note further that the first settlement plan prepared by the World Zionist Organization stated clearly that the objective of the settlements was to make it difficult for the Palestinian population "to form a territorial continuity and political unity when it is fragmented by Jewish settlements." Cited in David Kretzmer, *The Occupation of Justice,* 76 (2002).

89 Reproduced in Benvenisti, *The West Bank Data Project,* at 19–28.

90 B'Tselem, The Israeli Information Center for Human Rights in the Occupied Territories, *Land Grab: Israel's Settlement Policy in the West Bank,* available on-line at http://www.btselem. org/Download/200205_Land_Grab_Eng.pdf (last accessed July 14, 2008), hereafter *Land Grab.* The settlers and other Israeli citizens working or investing in the settlements are entitled to significant financial benefits, such as generous loans for the purchase of apartments, part of which are converted to grants, significant price reductions in leasing land, incentives for teachers, exemption from tuition fees in kindergartens and free transportation to school, grants for investors, infrastructure for industrial zones, incentives for social workers, and reductions in income tax for individuals and companies. The Ministry of the Interior provides increased grants for the local authorities in the territory relative to those provided for communities within Israel. *Id.*

91 See Question of the Violation of Human Rights in the Occupied Arab Territories, Including Palestine, Report of the Special Rapporteur of the Commission on Human Rights, John Dugard, on the situation of human rights in the Palestinian territories occupied by Israel since 1967, submitted in accordance with Commission resolution 1993/2 A, 14, UN Doc. E/ CN.4/2004/6, Sep. 8, 2003, hereafter 2003 Report on the Situation of Human Rights in the Palestinian Territories.

92 See *Question of the Violation of Human Rights in the Occupied Arab Territories, Including Palestine,* Update to the mission report on Israel's violations of human rights in the Palestinian territories occupied since 1967, submitted by Giorgio Giacomelli, Special Rapporteur, to the Commission on Human Rights at its fifth special session, para. 26, UN Doc. E/CN.4/2001/30, March 21, 2001. For a discussion of the politics of the geography and planning of the settlements, see Rafi Segal and Eyal Weizman, *The Mountain Principle of Building in Heights,* in *A Civilian Occupation: The Politics of Israeli Agriculture* 79 (Rafi Segal and Eyal Weizman, eds., 2003).

93   Such transfer further constitutes a grave breach of Protocol I. See Article 85 (4) (a) of Protocol I. Israel is not a party to Protocol I.

94   For the Israeli position, see *Israeli Settlements and International Law,* available on-line at http://www.mfa.gov.il/mfa/go.asp?MFAH0jyz0 (last accessed September 15, 2008); Ayelet Levy, *Israel Rejects Its Own Offspring: The International Criminal Court,* 22 Loy. L.A. Int'l & Comp. L. Rev. 207, 230–31 (1999); Jean-Marie Henckaerts, *Deportation and Transfer of Civilians in Time of War,* 26 Vand. J. Transnat'l L. 469, 472 (1993).

95   Pictet, commentary, at 283.

96   See *Declaration of the Conference of the Parties to the Fourth Geneva Convention,* December 5, 2001, available on-line at http://www.globalpolicy.org/security/issues/israel-palestine/2001/1205geneva.htm (last accessed February 27, 2009); Gerhard von Glahn, *Law Among Nations: An Introduction to Public International Law* 675–76 (7th ed. 1996).

97   See the statement by Israeli Foreign Ministry legal advisor Allen Baker to that effect, January 3, 2001, available on-line at http://www.mfa.gov.il/MFA/MFAArchive/2000_2009/2001/1/International+Criminal+Court+-+Press+Briefing+by+I.htm (last accessed September 15, 2008). Israel signed the statute on December 31, 2001, attaching a declaration conveying its disappointment at what was termed by it as the "politicization" of the statute by the insertion of "formulations tailored to meet the political agenda of certain states." On August 28, 2002, Israel informed the UN secretary-general of its intention not to ratify the statute. On the status of ratifications of the Rome Statute, including declarations made by Israel, see http://www.amicc.org/icc_ratifications.html#* (last accessed February 27, 2009).

98   See Catriona Drew, *Self–Determination, Population Transfer and the Middle East Peace Accords,* in *Human Rights, Self-Determination and Political Change in the Occupied Palestinian Territories* 119, 144–46 (Stephen Bowen ed., 1997).

99   *Construction of a Wall,* at para. 119.

100   *Id.,* at para. 120. The court reached this conclusion based inter alia on UN Security Council Resolution 446 (1979).

101   Such expropriation has continued during and after the Oslo process. On the expropriation methods, see, generally, Raja Shehadeh, *From Occupation to Interim Accords: Israel and the Palestinian Territories* 3–35 (1997); Imseis, *On the Fourth Geneva Convention,* at 102.

102   Note that the *Construction of a Wall* advisory opinion does not cite Article 147 of the Fourth Geneva Convention as relevant to the case at hand. This is due to the court's interpretation of Article 6 as precluding the applicability of all but 43 of the convention's 159 articles, including Article 147. We take issue with this interpretation, as is discussed in "The Intrinsic Dimensions of the Israeli Occupation of the Occupied Palestinian Territory" below.

103   HC 390/79 Dewikat v. Government of Israel, 34 (1) P.D. 1; see Kretzmer, *The Occupation of Justice,* at 85–89.

104   For a detailed account of these practices and the complex set of legal mechanisms that enable them, see *Land Grab;* Shehadeh, *Occupier's Law,* at 22–41; and Kretzmer, *The Occupation of Justice,* at 89–94.

105   Kretzmer, *The Occupation of Justice,* at 95.

106   Israel transferred planning authority from the Jordanian Ministry of the Interior to the commander of the IDF Forces in the region. Following the Oslo Accords, Israel retained this authority over Area C, comprising some 60 percent of the territory of the West Bank and some 60,000 Palestinians. See, generally, *Land Grab.*

107 *Id.*

108 *Id.*; Amnesty International, *Demolition and Dispossession: The Destruction of Palestinian Homes,* MDE 15/059/1999 (December 1999), available on-line at http://www.amnesty.org/en/library/asset/MDE15/059/1999/en/dom-MDE150591999en.pdf (last accessed September 15, 2008).

109 The average Palestinian in the West Bank residing in communities connected to a water network consumes 60 liters of water per day. The consumption of water by people not thus connected, while unknown, is certainly lower. The average consumption per capita in Israel as well as in the settlements is almost six times higher, that is, 350 liters per day. In practical terms, this discrepancy means that the settlements enjoy an unlimited supply of running water, which allows for swimming pools and green lawns, while their neighboring Palestinians often lack drinking and bathing water. See Yehezkel Lein, *Not Even A Drop: The Water Crisis in Palestinian Villages Without a Water Network* (2001); Yehezkel Lein, *Thirsty for a Solution: The Water Crisis in the Occupied Territories and Its Resolution in the Final Status Agreement* (2002), available on-line http://www.btselem.org/Download/200007_Thirsty_for_a_Solution_Eng.doc (last accessed September 15, 2008); Yehezkel Lein, *Disputed Waters: Israel's Responsibility for the Water Shortage in the Occupied Territories* (1998) http://www.btselem.org/Download/199809_Disputed_Waters_Eng.rtf (last accessed September 15, 2008).

110 See SC Res. 471 of June 5, 1980, UN SCOR 35th Sess., 2226th mtg. UN Doc. s/RES/36 (1980); SC Res. 904 of March 18, 1994, UN SCOR 49th Sess., 3351 mtg., UN Doc. s/RES/50 (1994), calling on Israel to assume its obligation to protect the civilian population and to take measures, including the confiscation of arms, to prevent illegal acts of violence by Israeli settlers. See B'tselem, *Violence of Settlers Against Palestinians,* available on-line at http://www.btselem.org/English/Settler_Violence/ (last accessed September 15, 2008); Ron Dudai, *Free Rein: Vigilante Settlers and Israel's Non-Enforcement of the Law* (2001), available on-line at http://www.btselem.org/Download/200110_Free_Rein_Eng.doc (last accessed September 15, 2008); and Yhezkel Lein, *The Performance of Law Enforcement Authorities in Responding to Settler Attacks on Olive Harvesters,* available on-line at http://www.btselem.org/Download/200211_Olive_Harvest_Eng.doc (last accessed September 15, 2008). This violence is particularly prevalent in Hebron, a city where 180,000 Palestinians live and where a population of approximately 450 Jewish settlers is allowed to humiliate, threaten, and exercise violence against Palestinian property and people. See Shlomi Swissa, Hebron, *Area H-2: Settlements Cause Mass Departure of Palestinians,* available on-line at http://www.btselem.org/Download/200308_Hebron_Area_H2_Eng.doc (last accessed September 15, 2008).

111 Imseis, *On the Fourth Geneva Convention,* at 106.

112 Law for the Extension of Emergency Regulations (Judea, Samaria and the Gaza Strip—Judging for Offences and Legal Aid) 1971. Other regulations allow Israeli courts in civil suits to engage in matters relating to residents of the occupied Palestinian Territory. Civil Procedure Regulations (Issuing of Documents to the Occupied Territories), 1969.

113 The Law of Return of 1950 gives, in Article 1, the right to immigrate to Israel to Jews (defined in Article 4B as a person who is the offspring of a Jewish mother or who has converted to Judaism and is not a member of another religion) and also to the children, grandchildren, and spouses of Jews and to spouses of children and grandchildren of Jews, unless they were born Jews and willingly converted to another religion (Article 4A).

114 This law does not apply in areas under the control of the Palestinian Authority, a fact that has no practical effect, because Israelis and Jews do not reside in these areas.

115 Article 147 of the Election Law (Consolidated Version) of 1969.

116 Israeli law does not allow Israeli citizens, with the exception of diplomats and similar official groups of people, to vote outside the geographic boundaries of Israel. See Article 6 of the Election Law (Consolidated Version) of 1969.

117 For an analysis of the Israeli legislation applying Israeli law on a personal basis to Israelis in the territory, see Amnon Rubinstein, *The Changing Status of the "Territories" (West Bank and Gaza): From Escrow to Legal Mongrel,* 8 Tel Aviv University Studies in Law, 59, 68–72 (1988). For a discussion of the significance of the difference in suffrage, see Oren Yiftachel, *'Ethnocracy': The Politics of Judaizing Israel/Palestine,* 6 Constellations 364 (1999), at 377.

118 Order regarding Management of Regional Councils (No. 783) and Order regarding Management of Local Council (No. 892), cited in *Land Grab.*

119 Order Concerning Security Instructions (Judea and Samaria) (No. 378) 1970–Announcement on a Closed Area (Israeli settlements), cited in *Land Grab.* For a discussion of the military legislation applying Israeli law on the settlements on a territorial basis, see Rubinstein, *Changing Status of the "Territories" (West Bank and Gaza),* at 72–79.

120 HCJ 1661/05, Regional Council Gaza Beach v. The Knesset, at para. 78–80, available on-line in Hebrew at http://elyon1.court.gov.il/files/05/610/016/A20/05016610.a20.pdf (last accessed February 27, 2009). See also HCJ 3278/02, The Center for the Defense of the Individual v. Commander of the IDF in the West Bank, 57 (1) PD 385, available on-line in Hebrew at http://elyon1.court.gov.il/files/02/780/032/A06/02032780.a06.pdf (last accessed February 27, 2009).

121 Rubinstein, *The Changing Status of the "Territories" (West Bank and Gaza),* at 67.

122 The different treatment is evident in myriad situations and primarily in relation to land, water, planning, protection from violence, and the rule of law. Note that even the High Court of Justice acknowledged that "the Israeli settlements (in Judea and Samaria) received special benefits, and the State invested in their construction and expansion many resources, a treatment that was not accorded to the local population." See HCJ 548/04 Amna v. IDF Commander in Judea and Samaria (February 26, 2004), available on-line in Hebrew at http://elyon1.court.gov.il/files/04/480/005/L03/04005480.l03.pdf (last accessed February 27, 2009).

123 Kretzmer, *The Occupation of Justice,* at 75, 197. Kretzmer notes the significance in this context of Israel's invocation of the law of occupation in order to justify the limitations on the rights of the Palestinians. For a discussion of this position, see Yaffa Zilbershatz, *The Control of the IDF in the Judea, Samaria and Gaza: Belligerent Occupation or Colonial Takeover* (in Hebrew), 20 Bar-Ilan Stud. 547 (2004).

124 International Convention on the Elimination of All Forms of Racial Discrimination, *opened for signature* March 7, 1966, 660 UNTS 195; Convention on the Suppression and Punishment of the Crime of Apartheid, November 30, 1973, 1015 UNTS 243. See also Samira Shah, *On the Road to Apartheid: The Bypass Road Network in the West Bank,* 29 Colum. Hum. Rts. L. Rev. 221, 283 (1997).

125 Article 7 (2) (h) defines the crime of apartheid as "inhumane acts of a character similar to those referred to in paragraph 1, committed in the context of an institutionalized regime of systematic oppression and domination by one racial group over any other racial group or groups and committed with the intention of maintaining that regime."

126 *Construction of a Wall,* at para. 85. The court returned to this point in the application part of the opinion at para. 133.

127 It is therefore surprising that the court failed to refer to it when it enumerated the human rights treaties to which Israel is a party and that are, at least potentially, applicable to the issue at hand. See Orna Ben-Naftali, *Á la Recherche du Temps Perdu: Rethinking Article 6 of the Fourth Geneva Convention in the Light of the Legal Consequences of the Construction of a Wall in the Occupied Palestinian Territory* Advisory Opinion, 38 (1–2) Isr. L. Rev. 211 (2005).

128 For a discussion see Hilla Dayan's contribution to this volume, "Regimes of Separation: Israel/Palestine and the Shadow of Apartheid," and Aeyal M. Gross, *The Constitution, Reconciliation, and Transitional Justice: Lessons from South Africa and Israel,* 40 Stan. J. Int'l. L. 47 (2004).

129 For a perspective on why these two conflicts took such different turns, despite their similar roots, see generally Ran Greenstein, *Genealogies of Conflict: Class, Identity and State in Palestine/Israel and South Africa* (1995).

130 It is worthwhile to note here that the Israeli High Court of Justice contributed to the undermining of Article 43 when it allowed large-scale changes in local law and included the settlers as part of the local population for the purposes of Article 43. See Kretzmer, *The Occupation of Justice,* at 187.

131 See Michael Walzer, *Arguing About War,* 162–65 (2004).

132 See Question of the Violations of Human Rights in the Occupied Arab Territories, Including Palestine.

133 B'tselem, *Freedom of Movement,* available on-line at http://www.btselem.org/english/Freedom_of_Movement/index.asp (last accessed September 15, 2008); *2003 Report on the Situation of Human Rights in the Palestinian Territories,* at 9, noting the slight decrease in the number of Palestinians thus affected by curfews from approximately 520,000 in 2002 to 390,000 in 2003.

134 The World Bank, West Bank and Gaza Office, Jerusalem, *Twenty-Seven Months — Intifada, Closures, and Palestinian Economic Crisis: An Assessment,* chap. 2, para. 2.5. (May, 2003).

135 See Combined report of B'tselem and Physicians for Human Rights-Israel, *Harm to Medical Personnel* (December 2003), available on-line at http://www.phr.org.il/phr/files/articlefile_1108317917290.rtf (last accessed September 15, 2008); *2003 Report on the Situation of Human Rights in the Palestinian Territories,* at 10.

136 For example, targeted killings. See Amnesty International, *Israel and the Occupied Territories: State Assassinations and Other Unlawful Killings* 9 (2001), available on-line at http://www.unhcr.org/refworld/pdfid/3c29def40.pdf (last accessed February 27, 2009). For a legal analysis of this measure, see Orna Ben-Naftali and Keren R. Michaeli, *"We Must Not Make a Scarecrow of the Law": A Legal Analysis of the Israeli Policy of Targeted Killings,* 36 Cornell Int'l. L. J. 233, 260–61 (2003). Another measure of dubious legality is administrative detention. In the beginning of March 2003, Israel held more than one thousand Palestinians in administrative detention, that is, detention without charge or trial, authorized by administrative order, rather than by judicial decree. See B'tselem, *Administrative Detention,* available on-line at http://www.btselem.org/english/Administrative_Detention/index.asp (last accessed September 15, 2008). See also Amnesty International, *Israel and the Occupied Territories: Despair, Uncertainty and Lack of Due Process* (1997), available on-line at http://www.unhcr.org/refworld/category,COI,AMNESTY,ISR,3ae6a98e8,0.html (last accessed February 27,

2009); and B'tselem, *Administrative Detention in the Occupied Territories,* available on-line at http://www.btselem.org/english/Administrative_Detention/Occupied_Territories.asp (last accessed September 15, 2008). In addition to the above, Israel has been carrying out a policy of house demolition. Since 1987, over 1000 houses have been demolished by the IDF forces and 299 sealed. See B'tselem, *House Demolitions—Statistics,* available on-line at http://www.btselem.org/english/Punitive_Demolitions/Statistics_Since_1987.asp (last accessed February 27, 2009). This is justified by Israel as necessary to prevent the houses from becoming a haven for militants opposing the IDF and the settlements, as a punishment for those who have committed crimes against Israel, and for deterrence purposes. See *2003 Report on the Situation of Human Rights in the Palestinian Territories,* at 13–14. As far as this means is exercised for deterrence purposes and for the punishment of families of suicide bombers, it might amount to prohibited reprisals, collective punishment, and extensive property damage unwarranted by military necessity under Articles 33 and 53 of the Fourth Geneva Convention, respectively.

137 As observed by the UN secretary-general special rapporteur following a visit to the occupied Palestinian territory at the end of August 2002. See *Question of the Violations of Human Rights in the Occupied Arab Territories, Including Palestine*—Report of the Special Rapporteur of the Commission of Human Rights on the Situation of Human Rights in the Palestinian Territories Occupied By Israel Since 1967—Addendum—Note by the Secretary-General, A/57/366/Add. 1, para. 2 (September 16, 2003).

138 *Construction of a Wall,* at para. 123–37.

139 *Id.,* at para. 122.

140 See Amnesty International, *Without Distinction—Attacks on Civilians by Palestinian Armed Groups* (July 2002) available on-line via http://web.amnesty.org/library/Index/ENGMDE020032002?open&of=ENG-ISR***** (last accessed February 28, 2009).

141 See, for example, Israel's Response to the Report Submitted by the Special Rapporteur on the Right to Food, submitted to the Commission on Human Rights, 60th Sess., E/CN.4/2004/G/14, para. 5, 6 (November 26, 2003), which indicates the rapporteur's failure to take into account the Palestinians' responsibility for the encouragement of terror attacks against Israel, which forms the basis of Israel's actions taken in self-defense.

142 Question of the Violation of Human Rights in the Occupied Arab Territories, Including Palestine.

143 *2002 Report on the Violations of Human Rights in the Occupied Arab Territories,* at 4.

144 Question of the Violation of Human Rights in the Occupied Arab Territories, Including Palestine.

145 Doris A. Graber, *The Development of the Law of Belligerent Occupation 1863–1914—A Historical Survey* 37 (1949).

146 Article 3, Instructions for the Government of Armies of the United States in the Field, General Order No. 100, April 23, 1863 (Lieber Code), reprinted in *The Laws of Armed Conflict: A Collection of Conventions, Resolutions and other Documents* 3 (Dietrich Schindler and Jiri Toman eds., 3rd ed. 1988).

147 Everett P. Wheeler, *Government de facto,* 5 Am. J. Int'l. L. 66 (1911); Graber, *The Development of the Law of Belligerent Occupation,* at 68–69.

148 Hans-Peter Gasser, *Protection of the Civilian Population,* in *The Handbook of Humanitarian Law in Armed Conflict* 1, 10 (Dieter Fleck ed., 1995), at 209, 246.

149 Pictet, *Commentary,* at 274; Benvenisti, *The International Law of Occupation,* at 99.

150 Gasser, *Protection of the Civilian Population,* at 246; Pictet, *Commentary,* at 283. This prohibition could also be understood as designed to prevent a situation wherein citizens of the occupying power reside in the occupied area and are subject to a different legal regime.

151 Gasser, *Protection of the Civilian Population,* at 257.

152 Pictet, *Commentary,* at 335.

153 *Construction of a Wall,* at para. 125. In para. 126, the court proceeded to identify Articles 47, 49, 52, 53, and 59 of the Fourth Geneva Convention as relevant to the question at hand. For a similar interpretation, see Yoram Dinstein, *The International Legal Status of the West Bank and the Gaza Strip—1998,* 28 Isr. Y.B. Hum. Rts. 37, 42–44.

154 For a critical review of this aspect of the advisory opinion, see Ben-Naftali, *Á la Recherche du Temps Perdu: Rethinking Article 6 of the Fourth Geneva Convention.*

155 *Construction of a Wall,* at para. 125. Note that in para. 135, where, in the context of addressing the term "military operations" in Article 53 in order to determine the existence of military exigencies, the court said that such exigencies "may be invoked in occupied territories even after the general close of military operations that led to their occupation."

156 While 43 of the 159 articles of the convention continue to apply, the emphasis is on Articles 47 through 78, which are the relevant articles in Section III.

157 Fourth Geneva Convention, Articles 50 and 55.

158 See *2a Final Record of the Diplomatic Conference of Geneva 1949* 623–25; Pictet, *Commentary,* at 63; Roberts, *Prolonged Military Occupation,* at 56. Roberts advances four arguments for the inapplicability of Article 6.

159 Protocol I. See further, *Commentary on the Additional Protocols of 8 July 1977 to the Geneva Conventions of 12 August 1949* 73–74 (Yves Sandoz et al., eds. 1987), at 66; Roberts, *Prolonged Military Occupation,* at 56. Admittedly, the language of Article 3 (b) is unclear and could be construed as suggesting that it applies the Fourth Geneva Convention subject to its own terms. See, for this construction, *The International Legal Status of the West Bank and the Gaza Strip—1998,* 28 Isr. Y.B. Hum. Rts. 37, 43 (1998). Such reading, however, defies both the drafters' intention and the teleological test of international humanitarian law.

160 For example, Article 78 of the Fourth Geneva Convention was applied by the High Court of Justice in HCJ 7015/02 Ajury v. Commander of the IDF in the Judea and Samaria, P.D. 56 (6) 352. For reviews of this judgment, see Daphne Barak-Erez, *Assigned Residence in Israel's Administered Territories: The Judicial Review of Security Measures,* Isr. Y.B. Hum. Rts. (2003); Eyal Benvenisti, *Ajuri et al.—Israel High Court of Justice,* 3 September 2002, 9 Eur. Pub. L. 481 (2003); Orna Ben-Naftali and Keren Michaeli, *The Call of Abraham: Between Man and 'Makom': Following HCJ 7015/02 Ajuri v. IDF Commander in the West Bank,* 15 Hamishpat 56 (2003) (in Hebrew). Note that while Article 78 provides less for the obligations and more for the rights of the occupying power, endowing it with the power to subject protected persons to assigned residence and to internment, the fact remains that the court applied this provision, regardless of Article 6.

161 Roberts, *Prolonged Military Occupation,* at 55.

162 See, for example, the claim that Article 50 protecting children's right to education does not apply, but that this very same right as it appears in Article 28 of the Convention on the Rights of the Child (CRC) and Articles 10, 13, and 14 of the International Convention on Economic Social and Cultural Rights (ICESCR), does apply. Similarly, Articles 55 and 56, which stipulate the duty of the occupier to ensure the population's health through the provision of

food and medical supplies and the maintenance of medical and hospital establishments, has no applicability, while similar duties, far less specific, clear, and legally binding enshrined in Articles 11 and 12 of the ICESCR (the right to adequate standard of living and the right to health, respectively) and Articles 24 and 27 of the CRC (the rights to health and adequate standard of living and development, respectively) do apply.

163 Roberts, *Prolonged Military Occupation,* at 57.

164 See *Construction of a Wall,* Separate Opinion of Judge Elaraby, para. 3.1; Separate Opinion of Judge Koroma, para. 2.

165 See Eldar and Zertal, *Lords of the Land*; Shamgar, *The Observance of International Law in the Administered Territories*; and Ben-Naftali, Gross, and Michaeli, *Illegal Occupation: Construction of a Wall.*

166 Meir Shamgar, *Legal Concepts and Problems of the Israeli Military Government — The Initial Stage,* in *Military Government in the Territories Administrated by Israel 1967–1980* 13 (Meir Shamgar ed., 1982), at 43. Justice Shamgar began serving as a judge in the Israeli High Court of Justice in 1975 and served as its chief justice from 1983 until 1995.

167 Ecclesiastes 3:1.

168 William H. Rehnquist, *Successful Lawyers Pay the Price,* 82 A.B.A.J. 100 (1996).

169 On the ways time is conceived by law, see Carol J. Greenhouse, *Just in Time: Temporality and the Cultural Legitimation of Law,* 98 Yale L. J. 1631 (1989); David M. Engel, *Time and Community,* 21 L. & Soc'y Rev. 605 (1987); Rebecca R. French, *Time in the Law,* 72 U. Col. L. Rev. 663 (2001); Todd Rakoff, *The Law of Social Time: A Time for Every Purpose: Law and the Balance of Life* (2002); Jed Rubenfeld, *Freedom and Time: A Theory of Constitutional Self-Government* (2001).

170 Statutes of limitations, jurisdictional time limits, civil and criminal procedure laws, the laws of evidence, intellectual property protections, the rule against perpetuities, and sentencing are examples that immediately come to mind, and all embody legal assumptions about human interaction with time.

171 The principle of *nullum crimen sine lege,* that is, of nonretroactivity, is meaningful only due to the centrality of the concept of time. Similarly, any legal presumption would have been rendered meaningless were it not for the temporal dimension that allows for its refutation.

172 Applying this rationale to the analogous situation of a mandate, a situation where no time limits have been explicitly set, Judge Ammoun concluded: "Mandates must have an end or are revocable." See Separate Opinion of Vice-President Ammoun, *The Case of the S.S. Lotus* (Fr. v. Turk.), 1927 P.C.I.J. (Ser. A) No. 9, at 18 (Sep. 7), at 72–73.

173 The principle of reasonableness is a general principle of international law. Its application has generated the conclusion that a right cannot be exercised in a wholly unreasonable manner causing harm disproportionate to the right holder's interests. See Bin Cheng, *General Principles of Law: As Applied by International Courts and Tribunals* 121–23 (1987); see also WTO, *Report of the Appellate Body in United States — Standard for Reformulated and Concentrated Gasoline and Like Products of National Origin,* reprinted in 35 ILM 603, 626 (1996).

174 For example, the Uniform Negotiable Instruments Law sets standards for the measurement of "reasonable time." See Richard Speidel and Steve H. Nicks, *Negotiable Instruments and Check Collections* (The New Law) in a Nutshell 60, 61, 148, 149, 152 (4th ed. 1993). Similarly, "reasonable time" for taking an action is contemplated in the Uniform Commercial Code (Colorado) as depending "on the nature, purpose and circumstances of such action." See

http://www.law.du.edu/russell/contracts/ucc/4-1-204.htm (last accessed September 15, 2008). It is interesting to note that the Israeli Supreme Court has itself resorted to the principle of reasonable time in order to determine the time limits of a judicial institutionalization order. See CA 3854/02, Anonymous v. the District Adult Psychiatric Committee, available on-line in Hebrew at http://elyon1.court.gov.il/files/02/540/038/A05/02038540.a05.pdf (last accessed February 28, 2009). This determination relied on a similar decision by the U.S. Supreme Court, Jackson v. Indiana 406 U.S. 715, 738 (1972).

175 Article 2 (3) of the UN Charter.

176 Roberts, *Prolonged Military Occupation,* at 52.

177 To use Ronald Dworkin's reference to a formal and a substantive conception of the rule of law: The former is interested in the enforceability of law, regardless of its content, that is, in order, while the latter is interested in the substance, nature, and justification of the order, determined by the balance thereby achieved between the individual and society, between liberty and security. See Ronald Dworkin, *A Matter of Principle,* 11 (1985).

178 "The rule of law is one casualty of the conflict in the occupied Palestinian Territory, but the main casualties are the people of both Palestine and Israel." See *2002 Report on the Violations of Human Rights in the Occupied Arab Territories,* at 12.

179 Internal pressures emanate from the settlers who are represented in the government, on the one hand, and from the Israeli High Court of Justice, on the other. The court, having determined that the current route in sections of the Wall that were the subject of the appeal fails to meet the proportionality test of both international humanitarian law and Israeli administrative law, ordered the rerouting of a twenty-mile section of what is termed in Israel the "separation fence." See HC 2056/04 The Village Council of Beit Surik et al. v. the Government of Israel and the Military Commander of the West Bank, available on-line in English at http://www.alhaq.org/pdfs/HCJ%20-%20Beit%20Sourik.pdf and in Hebrew at http://elyon1.court.gov.il/files/04/560/020/A28/04020560.a28.pdf (both last accessed February 28, 2009). See also HCJ 7957/04. Many similar appeals pertaining to other segments of the wall are currently pending before the HCJ. The most notable external pressure stems from the *Construction of a Wall.* The opinion, which was rendered pursuant to a request submitted by the UN General Assembly (see GA Res. A/RES/ES-10/14, UN GAOR, 10th emer. Sess. 23rd plan. Mtg. [December 8, 2003]), held that the construction of the Wall in any part of the occupied Palestinian territory is illegal and specified the legal consequences emanating from that illegality. The opinion was adopted by the General Assembly in GA Res. A/ES-10/L.18/Rev. 1 (July 20, 2004) (150 votes in favor, 6 against, and 10 absentees).

180 See *2003 Report on the Situation of Human Rights in the Palestinian Territories,* at 7 and 15.

181 *Construction of a Wall,* at para. 121.

182 While it is virtually impossible to calculate the total investment, because it runs the whole gamut from military expenditure to monetary incentives to settlers, some figures are sufficiently telling for the present discussion. During the last decade, the Israeli government invested $2.5 billion in constructing new houses in the occupied Palestinian territory, 50 percent of which was public, compared with 25 percent public financing inside the Green Line. During the same period, the government allocated to municipalities an average of 5,428 shekels per settler a year, compared to 3,807 per citizen in Israel. See Shlomo Svirski et al., *Governmental Funding of Israeli Settlement In Judea and Samaria and the Golan Heights in the Nineties: Municipalities, Housing and Roads Construction* (January 2002) (in Hebrew), on

file with the authors. Just the cost of constructing the bypass roads in the occupied Palestinian territory since Oslo has been estimated at more than $265 million. See Ze'ev Schiff, *The March of Folly of the By-Pass Roads, Ha'aretz,* B.1, February 15, 2002. The projected cost of the wall is $1.4 billion; see *2003 Report on the Situation of Human Rights in the Palestinian Territories,* at 7–8.

183 See *2003 Report on the Situation of Human Rights in the Palestinian Territories,* at 6 and 8. Schiff, a leading commentator in *Ha'aretz* newspaper, contemplating merely the cost of the bypass roads, concluded that: "three explanations stand behind this reality. The first is that these expenditures express an intention never to give up the territory, and all the rest is an illusion. The second is that we have decided to build, step by step, the road system of the Palestinian State that will be established in the territory at the expense of the Israeli tax-payer. The third possible explanation is that the governmental systems of Israel have been dragged into this as if forced by a demon and without anyone being able to stop the parade of stupidity." Schiff, *The March of Folly of the By-Pass Roads.* Given that governments are not presumed to be possessed by demons, the obvious cynicism of the second explanation, and the broader context and raison d'être of the bypass roads, that is, the settlement enterprise, the first explanation is clearly the only reasonable conclusion.

184 See *2003 Report on the Situation of Human Rights in the Palestinian Territories,* at 14–15. The International Court of Justice reiterated this position in *Construction of a Wall,* at para. 122.

185 SC Res. 1397, envisioning "a region where two states, Israel and Palestine, live side by side within secure and recognized borders."

186 *Construction of a Wall,* at para. 116.

187 *Id.,* at para. 135.

188 See John Embry Parkerson, Jr., *United States Compliance with Humanitarian Law Respecting Civilians During Operation Just Cause,* 133 Mil. L. Rev. 31, 47 (1991).

189 *2003 Report on the Situation of Human Rights in the Palestinian Territories,* at 15. For the High Court of Justice's discussion of proportionality, see *Construction of a Wall,* at para. 135–36. Cf. HC 2056/04, especially para. 48; 82–85. Note that the High Court of Justice's discussion of the proportionality requirement is ostensibly both more analytical and more specific than that of the International Court of Justice. The High Court of Justice applies that require-ment to each and every segment of the wall that was appealed and further inquires into the existence of alternative, less harmful means through which the stated security objective may be met. Nevertheless, the High Court of Justice's application of proportionality mixes vari-ous contexts of proportionality, importing into the context of occupation a proportionality analysis that is more befitting administrative law within a representative democracy. For a discussion of this move and its effects, see Aeyal Gross, *The Construction of a Wall between Jerusalem and the Hague: The Enforcement and Limits of Humanitarian Law and the Structure of Occupation,* 19 Leiden Journal of International Law 393, 405–411, 419–423 (2006).

190 *Land Grab.*

191 Comm. App./2597, Kafr 'Aqeb Development Committee et al. v. Ministry of Defense et al., response of the state, sec. 33/c, reproduced in *Behind the Barrier, B'tselem Human Rights Violation As a Result of Israel's Wall: Position Paper* (April, 2003), available on-line at http://www.btselem.org/Download/200304_Behind_The_Barrier_Eng.rtf (last accessed September 15, 2008). Note further that the High Court of Justice itself had, in the past, accepted this logic when it contemplated and authorized the *temporary* seizure of Palestinian land for the

building of *permanent* settlements. See HC 610/78 Ayun v. Minister of Defense, 33 (2) PD 113, 131 (opinion of Judge Landau); 134 (opinion of Judge Ben-Porat).

192 HCJ 1661/05 Regional Council Gaza Beach, para. 8–9, 115, 126.

193 The use of the term *nomos* in the section's title encompasses its varied meanings for Robert Cover, for Carl Schmitt, and for Giorgio Agamben. For Cover, it indicates a normative universe, comprising both rules and the narratives that give them meaning. See Robert Cover, *Nomos and Narrative,* 97 Harv. L. Rev. 4 (1983). For Schmitt, it meant that right as original violence, as difference, rather than universalistic rationality is the foundation of law. See Carl Schmitt, *Der Nomos Der Erde* (1974), discussed in Carlo Galli, *The Critic of Liberalism: Carl Schmitt's Antiliberalism. Its Theoretical and Historical Sources and Its Philosophical and Political Meaning,* 21 Cardozo L. Rev. 1597, 1601 (2000). Giorgio Agamben's analysis brings Schmitt's theory of the exception, explicated in this section, to its logical conclusion by stating that the concentration camp—as a paradigmatic structure—has become the modern political *nomos*: the space where the exception and the rule, the fact and the norm, are indistinguishable, and law becomes meaningless. See Giorgio Agamben, *Homo Sacer: Sovereign Power and Bare Life,* 166–80 (Daniel Heller-Roazen trans., 1988).

194 See Theodor E. Mommsen, *The History of Rome,* 325–26 (1908) (1864). For later references to this classical model, see, for example, Nicolo Machiavelli, *The Discourses* 194–98 (Bernard Crick ed., Leslie Walker trans., 1970) (1513–17); Jean Jacques Rousseau, *The Social Contract and Discourses,* 293–96 (G. D. H. Cole trans., Alfred A. Knopf 1993) (1762).

195 For the essential features of the traditional model of emergency powers, Oren Gross, *Exception and Emergency Powers: The Normless and Exceptionless Exception. Carl Schmitt's Theory of Emergency Powers and the "Norm-Exception" Dichotomy,* 21 Cardozo L. Rev. 1825, 1836–39 (2000).

196 As discussed in "The Intrinsic Dimensions of the Israeli Occupation of the Occupied Palestinian Territory: The Norms of Occupation" above.

197 *Study of the Implications for Human Rights of Recent Development Concerning Situations Known as State of Siege or Emergency,* UN ESCOR, 35th Sess., Agenda Item 10, 69 UN Doc. E/CN.4/Sub.2/1982/15 (1982) (N. Questiaux). See also Oren Gross and Fionnuala Ni Aolain, *To Know Where We Are We Need To Know Where We Are: Revisiting States of Emergency,* in *Human Rights: An Agenda for the 21st Century* 79 (Angela Hegarty and Siobhan Leonard eds., 1999).

198 Giacomo Marramo, *Schmitt and the Categories of the Political: The Exile of the Nomos. For a Critical Profile of Carl Schmitt,* 27 Cardozo L. Rev. 1567 (2000).

199 Schmitt, *Political Theology.*

200 Heiner Bielefeld, *Carl Schmitt's Critique of Liberalism: Systemic Reconstruction and Countercriticism,* 10 Can. J. L. & Juris. 65, 68 (1997). Schmitt was fascinated with Hobbes and regarded himself as his heir, ending his commentary on Hobbes's *Leviathan* with the words: "You shall no longer teach in vain, Thomas Hobbes." See Carl Schmitt, *The Leviathan in the State Theory of Thomas Hobbs: Meaning and Failure of a Political Symbol* (George Schwab and Erna Hilfstein, trans., 1996). On the affinity between Schmitt and Hobbes, see David Dyzenhous, *Now the Machine Runs Itself: Carl Schmitt on Hobbes and Kelsen,* 16 Cardozo L. Rev. 1 (1994); John P. McCormick, *Fear, Technology and the State: Carl Schmitt, Leo Strauss and the Revival of Hobbes in Weimar and National Socialist Germany,* 22 Pol. Theory 619 (1994).

201 For Schmitt's "friend"/"enemy" distinction, see Carl Schmitt, *The Concept of the Political,*

25–37 (J. Harvey Lomax trans., 3rd ed. 1996) (1932). For an analysis, see Andrew Norris, *Carl Schmitt on Friends, Enemies and the Political,* Telos, 68 (Summer 1998). On the odd history of Schmitt's reception in the Anglo-American academy, see Emanuel Richter, *The Critic of Liberalism: Carl Schmitt. The Defective Guidance for the Critique of Political Liberalism,* 21 Cardozo L. Rev. 1619 (2000).

202 See *Construction of a Wall,* at para. 78.

203 See, for example., Christine Bell, *Peace Agreements and Human Rights* 189–90 (2000).

204 On the state's resort to the Geneva Conventions as a basis for exercising its powers, see the arguments advanced by Kretzmer, *The Occupation of Justice,* at 197.

205 *Id.*, at 49–52, 165–86 and 145–63.

206 On the jurisprudence of the High Court of Justice, see Kretzmer, *The Occupation of Justice,* at 38. On deportations, see *id.*, at 49–52 and 165–86. On home demolitions, see *id.*, at 145–63. On the legitimizing function of the High Court of Justice in rejecting over 99 percent of Palestinian petitions, but accepting some that thereby become symbolic "landmark cases" that legitimize the authority of the High Court of Justice without significantly affecting the rights of the Palestinians, see Ronen Shamir, *Landmark Cases and the Reproduction of Legitimacy: the Case of Israel's High Court of Justice,* 24 L. & Soc'y Rev. 781 (1990). A recent change in the direction of this jurisprudence should, however, be noted, because it may well indicate a trend toward greater recognition of the humanitarian and human rights plight of the Palestinians, as is evidenced in the High Court of Justice's analysis of the proportionality requirement in connection with the construction of the wall (see HC 2056/04 and HC 7957/04), as well as in its application of human rights instruments to the occupied territory (see HC 3239/02 Mar'ab. v. The IDF Commander in Judea and Samaria, available on-line in Hebrew at http://elyon1.court.gov.il/files/02/390/032/A04/02032390.a04.pdf (last accessed February 28, 2009). For a detailed discussion of the High Court of Justice's wall cases see Gross, *The Construction of a Wall between Jerusalem and the Hague.*

207 See Baxter, *Some Existing Problems,* at 288; Roberts, *Prolonged Military Occupation,* at 46.

208 For an analysis of the "shadow function" of the court in this context, see Yoav Dotan, *Judicial Rhetoric, Government Lawyers and Human Rights: the Case of the Israeli High Court of Justice during the Intifada,* 33 L. & Soc'y Rev. 319 (1999); Kretzmer, *The Occupation of Justice,* at 189–91.

209 On "Greater Israel" (*Eretz Isreal,* Land of Israel) ideology and its implications, see Baruch Kimmerling, *Between the Primordial and the Civil Definitions of the Collective Identity: Eretz Israel or the State of Israel?* in *Comparative Social Dynamics: Essays in Honor of S. N. Eisenstadt,* 262–83 (Eric Cohen et al. eds., 1985); and Baruch Kimmerling, *Boundaries and Frontiers of the Israeli Control System: Analytical Conclusions,* in *The Israeli State and Society: Boundaries and Frontiers* 265, 277 (Baruch Kimmrling ed., 1989).

210 On discrimination against Palestinian citizens of Israel with respect to land rights, see Alexander Kedar, *The Legal Transformation of Ethnic Geography: Israeli Law and the Palestinian Landholder 1948–1967,* 33 N.Y.U. J. Int'l. L. & Pol. 923 (2001); Aeyal Gross, *The Dilemma of Constitutional Property Rights in Ethnic Land Regimes: Israel and South Africa Compared,* 121 S. African L. J. 448 (2004). On the concept of an "ethnic democracy," see Sammy Smooha, *Minority Status in an Ethnic Democracy: The Status of the Arab Minority in Israel,* 13 Ethnic & Racial Stud. 389–413 (1990). On the critique of this concept, see As'ad Ghanem et al., *Questioning "Ethnic Democracy": A Response to Sammy Smooha,* 3 Isr. Stud. 253 (1998). On the alternative concept of "Ethnocracy," see Oren Yiftachel, *'Ethnocracy': The Politics of Judaizing*

Israel/Palestine, 6 Constellations 364 (1999). For a detailed discussion of this debate, see Aeyal Gross, *Democracy, Ethnicism and Constitutionalism in Israel: Between the "Jewish State" and the "Democratic State,"* 2 Sotsyologia Israelit 647 (2000) (in Hebrew).

211 *Legal Consequences for States of the Continued Presence of South Africa in Namibia,* at 52.

212 *Draft Articles on State Responsibility,* Article 43, Report of the ILC on the Work of its 48th session, UN GAOR, 51st Sess., Supp. No. 10, at 142, UN Doc. A/51/10 (1996).

213 *Legal Consequences for States of the Continued Presence of South Africa in Namibia,* at 54.

214 *Id.* See also *Construction of a Wall,* at para. 159–60.

215 For example, to abstain from treaty relations with South Africa when it purports to act on behalf of Namibia, to abstain from sending diplomatic or special missions to South Africa, and to abstain from economic dealings with South Africa on behalf of Namibia. *Legal Consequences for States of the Continued Presence of South Africa in Namibia,* at 54–56.

216 *Id.,* at 56. "Bearing in mind that the non-recognition of South Africa's administration of the territory 'should not result in depriving the people of Namibia of any advantages derived from international co-operation.'" *Id.* A similar concern was voiced by the special rapporteur of the Human Rights Commission with respect to the Israeli Occupation of the occupied Palestinian territory. See Report of the Special Rapporteur of the Commission of Human Rights on the Situation of Human Rights in the Palestinian Territories Occupied By Israel Since 1967—Addendum—Note by the Secretary-General, A/57/366/Add.1, at para. 12–13. Discussing "the paradox of humanitarian assistance," the special rapporteur calls for international humanitarian assistance to the Palestinian people, noting, however, "at the same time, it must be made clear that, by providing aid of this kind, the international donor community relieves Israel of the burden of providing such assistance itself and in this way might be seen to be contributing to the funding of the occupation."

217 The argument does not propose that actions taken in an armed conflict are to be measured in relation to the question of whether the original use of force was legal or not. Indeed, such an argument would have blurred the important distinction between *jus ad bellum* and *jus in bello.* It merely argues that actions undertaken in defense of an illegal occupation are illegal themselves.

218 *Construction of a Wall,* at para. 54.

219 *Id.,* at para. 139. It is this assumption that raised the objection of several judges who felt the court did not take fair notice of the illegal acts performed by the Palestinians and thus disregarded the context of the question at hand. See *id.,* Separate Opinion of Judge Higgins, para. 15–18; Declaration of Judge Burgenthal, para. 3–6; Separate Opinion of Judge Owada, para. 26–29, 31. For a critique of the International Court of Justice's position on the question of self-defense, see Gross, *The Construction of a Wall between Jerusalem and the Hague,* at 400–402.

220 See Ben-Naftali, *Á la Recherche du Temps Perdu: Rethinking Article 6 of the Fourth Geneva Convention.*

221 The international law definition of aggression is yet to be decided. While criminalized in Article X of the Nuremberg Charter as a "crime against peace" (see Charter of the International Military Tribunal and Protocol of 6 October 1945, August 8, 1945, 59 Stat. 1544, 82 UNTS 279), it was not properly defined therein. Since then, the international community has struggled to define the phenomenon. See GA Res. 3314, UNGAOR, 29th Sess., Definition of Aggression, Annex, Definition of Aggression, UN Doc. A/Res./3314 (XXIX) (1974). Under

Resolution 3314, "aggression is the use of armed force by a State against the sovereignty, territorial integrity or political independence of another State, or in any other manner inconsistent with the Charter of the United Nations." This definition, however, applies only as far as state responsibility goes. No consensus exists as to the definition of aggression as a crime. For this reason, while enumerated as one of the crimes under the jurisdiction of the International Criminal Court, as stipulated in Article 5 (1) (d) of the Rome Statute, Article 5 (2) provides for the suspension of such jurisdiction until a definition is agreed upon by state parties. See Grant M. Dawson, *Defining Substantive Crimes within the Subject Matter Jurisdiction of the International Criminal Court: What Is the Crime of Aggression?* 19 N.Y.L. Sch. J. Int'l & Comp. L. 413 (2000).

222 As stated by the Nuremberg International Military Tribunal, an aggressive war is "essentially an evil thing.... To initiate a war of aggression...is not only an international crime; it is the supreme international crime differing only from other war crimes in that it contains within itself the accumulated evil of the whole. See Office of the United States Chief of Council For Prosecutions of Axis Criminality, 1 Nazi Conspiracy and Aggression 16 (1946).

223 Support for this position may be found in Separate Opinion of Vice-President Ammoun, *The Case of the S.S. Lotus* (Fr. v. Turk.), 1927 P.C.I.J. (Ser. A) No. 9, at 18 (Sep. 7), at 89–92.

Michal Givoni

SEAM ZONE REGULATIONS (EXCERPTS) The Separation Wall encompasses a complex legal and administrative regime that applies to Palestinians only. This regime regulates entry and stay in the "Seam Zone"—the area enclosed between the Separation Wall and the Green Line—which will supposedly contain, once the Wall is built, 10 percent of the West Bank. A number of military orders that were published in October 2003 declared the Seam Zone an area closed to Palestinians and stated that Palestinians who live, work, or visit there must obtain a special entry permit. The orders distinguish between several population groups: those permitted to stay in the area as a rule (Israelis and persons coming within the provisions of the Law of Return); "categories of persons" given a general permit to stay in the zone (Palestinians having a permit to enter Israel or to work in the settlements); and various categories of Palestinians who are required to obtain personal entry permits (persons living in the Seam Zone, along with workers, students, farmers, and visitors wanting to enter it—classified into twelve different categories).

Research for "The Occupation's Paper Trail"
conducted by Danna Bader and Judith Soussan
Translation by Harold Jacobson

צבא הגנה לישראל

צו בדבר הוראות ביטחון (יהודה והשומרון) (מס' 378), התש"ל - 1970
הכרזה בדבר סגירת שטח מס' 2/03/סי (מרחב התפר)

בתוקף סמכותי כמפקד כוחות צה"ל באזור יהודה והשומרון ובהתאם לסעיפים 88 ו- 90 לצו בדבר הוראות ביטחון (יהודה והשומרון) (מס' 378), התש"ל - 1970 (להלן – "הצו") ויתר סמכויותיי על פי כל דין ותחיקת ביטחון, ולנוכח הנסיבות הביטחוניות המיוחדות השוררות באזור והצורך לנקוט בצעדים הכרחיים למניעת פיגועי טרור ומניעת יציאתם של מפגעים משטחי אזור יהודה והשומרון למדינת ישראל, הנני מכריז בזאת לאמור:

הגדרות   1.   בהכרזה זו:

"המפה" – מפה בקנה מידה 150,000:1, הנושאת את השם "הכרזה בדבר סגירת שטח מס' 2/03/סי (מרחב התפר)", החתומה על ידי והמהווה חלק בלתי נפרד מהכרזה זו.

"ישראלי" – כל אחד מאלה:

א. אזרח מדינת ישראל.

ב. תושב מדינת ישראל, הרשום במרשם האוכלוסין בישראל לפי מרשם האוכלוסין, התשכ"ה – 1965, כפי תוקפו בישראל, מעת לעת.

ג. מי שזכאי לעלות לישראל לפי חוק השבות, תשי"י – 1950, כפי תוקפו בישראל מעת לעת.

"המכשול" - גדרות, חומות ודרכי פטרול, אשר נועדו למניעת פיגועי טרור ולמניעת יציאתם של מפגעים משטחי אזור יהודה והשומרון למדינת ישראל, שהוקמו מכח צווי התפיסה המפורטים בחלק אי לתוספת להכרזה זו, כפי תוקפם מעת לעת.

"מרחב התפר" – כל שטח הנתחם על-ידי המכשול, המסומן במפה בקן בצבע אדום, לכיוון מדינת ישראל.

סגירת שטח   2.   הנני מכריז כי מרחב התפר הוא שטח סגור כמשמעותו בצו.

איסור כניסה   3.   א. לא ייכנס אדם למרחב התפר ולא ישהה בו.
ושהייה
ב. אדם הנמצא במרחב התפר יהיה חייב לצאת ממנו לאלתר.

**Order Concerning Security Directives (Judea and Samaria) (No. 378), 5730—1970
Declaration Concerning the Closure of Area Number S/2/03 (Seam Zone)**

Pursuant to my authority as commander of the IDF forces in the Judea and Samaria region and in accordance with articles 88 and 90 of the Order Concerning Security Directives (Judea and Samaria) (No. 378), 5730—1970 (hereinafter "the Order"), and my other powers under any law and defense legislation, and in light of the special security situation in the region and the need to take the measures necessary to prevent terrorist attacks and the exit of terrorists from the area of Judea and Samaria into the State of Israel, I hereby declare as follows:

Definitions 1. In this order:

"**the map**"—the map with the scale of 1:150,000, bearing the name "Declaration Regarding Closing of Area No. S/2/03 (Seam Zone)," signed by me and constituting an integral part of this declaration.

"**Israeli**"—each of the following:
A. a citizen of the State of Israel.
B. a resident of the State of Israel registered in the Population Registry in Israel pursuant to the Population Registry Law, 5725—1965, as it shall be in force in Israel from time to time.
C. a person entitled to immigrate to Israel under the Law of Return, 5710—1950, as it shall be in force from time to time.

"**the barrier**"—fences, walls, and patrol roads that are intended to prevent terrorist attacks and prevent the entry of terrorists from the territory of Judea and Samaria into the State of Israel that were built pursuant to the seizure orders specified in Part 1 of the annex to this declaration, as they shall be in force from time to time.

"**the Seam Zone**"—every area demarcated by the barrier, which is marked on the map with a red line, in the direction of the State of Israel.

Closing of area 2. I hereby declare that the Seam Zone is a closed area within its meaning in the order.

Prohibition on 3. A. No person shall enter the Seam Zone or stay in it.
entry and staying B. A person staying in the Seam Zone must leave it immediately.

4. **א.** סעיף 3 לחכרזה זו לא יחול על: | **סייג לתחולה**

1. ישראלי.

2. מי שניתן לו היתר על ידי או על-ידי מי מטעמי להיכנס למרחב התפר ולשהות בו, והכל על-פי התנאים שנקבעו בהיתר. היתר לפי פיסקה זו יכול שיהיה כללי, לסוגים, אישי או מיוחד.

ב. על אף האמור בסעיף-קטן (א), מפקד צבאי ראשי לקבוע כי חורואת סעיף 3 לחכרזה זו תחול על אדם או על כל סוג בני-אדם הנכנסים למרחב התפר או השוהים בו.

5. **א.** אדם, שמלאו לו 16 שנים, שמקום מגוריו הקבוע, ביום תחילת תוקפה של הכרזה זו, | **תושבים קבועים** הוא במרחב התפר, יהיה רשאי להיכנס למרחב התפר ולשהות בו, ובלבד שבידו היתר בכתב, שניתן לו על ידי או על-ידי מי מטעמי, המעיד על כך שמקום מגוריו הקבוע הוא במרחב התפר, והכל על-פי התנאים שנקבעו בהיתר.

1. אדם, שלא מלאו לו 16 שנים, שמקום מגוריו הקבוע הוא במרחב התפר, יהיה רשאי לשהות במרחב התפר, ללא חיתר בכתב כאמור בסעיף-קטן (א).

2. אדם, שלא מלאו לו 16 שנים, שמקום מגוריו הקבוע הוא במרחב התפר, יהיה רשאי להיכנס למרחב התפר באחת הדרכים תבאות:

   א. אם בידו היתר בכתב, כאמור בסעיף-קטן (א), ובלבד שמלאו לו 12 שנים;

   ב. בלוויית אדם שכניסתו הותרה לפי סעיף-קטן (א);

   ג. בכל דרך אחרת שתיקבע על ידי או על-ידי מי מטעמי.

6. **א.** כניסה למרחב התפר ויציאה ממנו יהיו דרך המעברים המפורטים בחלק ב' לתוספת | **מעברים** לחכרזה זו, והמסומנים בצבע כחול במפה, והכל בהתאם לתאים שייקבעו על ידי או על-ידי מי מטעמי.

ב. לעניין סעיף זה:

"**כניסה למרחב התפר**" - כניסה למרחב התפר מכיוון שטחי האזור שאינם במרחב התפר.

"**יציאה ממרחב התפר**" - יציאה ממרחב התפר לכיוון שטחי האזור שאינם במרחב התפר.

7. רא:ש המנהל האזרחי מוסמך לקבוע חורואת והסדרים בכל הקשור לחכרזה זו. | **הסמכה**

8. **א.** העתקים מהכרזה זו ומהמפה המצורפת אליה יופקדו לעיונו של כל אדם בשעות | **פרסום** העבודה הרגילות של המשרדים הבאים:

1. משרדי מנהלות התיאום והקישור חגזרתיות.

2. תחנות המשטרה באזור יהודה והשומרון.

3. לשכת היועץ המשפטי לאזור יהודה והשומרון.

Exception to applicability	**4.**	A.	Section 3 of this declaration shall not apply to:

Exception to applicability   **4.**   A.   Section 3 of this declaration shall not apply to:

           1.   an Israeli.

           2.   a person given a permit by me or by a person on my behalf to enter the Seam Zone and stay in it, in accordance with the conditions specified in the permit. A permit under this paragraph may be general, for certain categories, personal, or special.

        B.   Notwithstanding the provisions of subsection (A), a military commander may specify that the provision of Section 3 of this declaration applies to a person or to any category of persons entering the seam zone or staying in it.

Permanent residents   **5.**   A.   A person who has attained the age of 16 years, whose permanent place of residence on the day this declaration enters into force is the Seam Zone, may enter the Seam Zone and stay in it, provided that he has a permit in writing, given to him by me or by a person on my behalf, testifying that his permanent place of residence is in the Seam Zone, all according to the conditions specified in the permit.

        B.   1.   A person who has not attained the age of 16 years, whose permanent place of residence is the Seam Zone, may stay in the Seam Zone without a permit in writing as stated in subsection (A).

           2.   A person who has not attained the age of 16 years and whose permanent place of residence is the Seam Zone may enter the Seam Zone in one of the following ways:

               a.   if he has a written permit, as stated in subsection (A), provided that he has attained 12 years of age;

               b.   is accompanied by person whose entry is permitted under subsection (A);

               c.   in any other manner that I, or a person on my behalf, shall specify.

Crossings   **6.**   A.   Entering the Seam Zone and exiting it shall be via the crossings specified in Part 2 of the annex to this declaration, which are marked in blue on the map, all in accordance with the conditions set by me or a person on my behalf.

        B.   For the purposes of this section:

        "entering the Seam Zone" — entry to the Seam Zone from the direction of the territory of the region that is not in the Seam Zone.

        "exiting the Seam Zone" — exiting the Seam Zone in the direction of territory of the region that is not in the Seam Zone.

Authorization   **7.**   The head of the Civil Administration is authorized to issue directives and regulations in matters pertaining to this declaration.

       [. . .]

צו בדבר הוראות ביטחון (יהודה והשומרון) (מס' 378), התש"ל - 1970

היתר כללי לכניסה למרחב התפר ולשהייה בו

בתוקף סמכותי כמפקד כוחות צה"ל באזור יהודה והשומרון ובהתאם לסעיף 4(א)(2) להכרזה בדבר סגירת שטח
מס' ס/2/03 (מרחב תפר) (יהודה והשומרון), התשס"ד - 2003 (להלן – "ההכרזה"), הנני מורה בזאת לאמור :

היתר כללי לכניסה למרחב התפר ולשהייה בו	**1**	ניתן בזה היתר כניסה למרחב התפר, כהגדרתו בהכרזה, ושהייה בו, לכל אדם הנמנה על סוגי בני אדם המפורטים בתוספת להיתר זה, בהתאם לתנאים המצויינים בתוספת.
תנאים	**2**	א. אדם הנכנס למרחב התפר והשוהה בו, מכוחו של היתר זה, ישא עימו מסמך המעיד על היותו שייך לאחד מסוגי בני האדם המפורטים בתוספת; וכן תעודה לזיהויו. ב. ראש המנהל האזרחי רשאי לשנות או להוסיף על התנאים האמורים בסעיף-קטן (א) ביחס לאדם מסוים או לסוג של בני אדם.
סייג לתחולה	**3**	על אף האמור בסעיף 1, מפקד צבאי רשאי לקבוע כי היתר זה לא יחול על אדם או סוג בני אדם הנכנסים למרחב התפר.
פרסום	**4**	א. העתקים מהיתר זה ויופקדו לעיונו של כל אדם בשעות העבודה הרגילות של המשרדים הבאים : 1. משרדי מנהלות התיאום והקישור הגזרתיות. 2. תחנות המשטרה באזור יהודה והשומרון. 3. לשכת היועץ המשפטי לאזור יהודה והשומרון. 4. משרדי ראש תחום תשתיות במנהל האזרחי לאזור יהודה והשומרון. ב. העתקים מהחיתר יוצגו על גבי לוח המודעות במשרדי מנהלות התיאום והקישור הגזרתיות, כאמור בסעיף קטן (א)(1), לתקופה של שלושה חודשים מיום תחילת תוקפו של החיתר. ג. ראש המנהל האזרחי רשאי לקבוע דרכי פרסום נוספות, מעבר למפורט בסעיפים קטנים (א) ו-(ב).
תחילת ותוקף	**5**	תחילת תוקפו של היתר זה חינה ביום חתימתו.

Order Concerning Security Directives (Judea and Samaria) (No. 378), 5730—1970
General Permit to Enter and Stay in the Seam Zone

Pursuant to my authority as commander of IDF forces in the Judea and Samaria region, and in accordance with section 4(A)(2) of the Proclamation Regarding Closing of Area No. S/2/03 (Seam Zone) (Judea and Samaria), 5764—2003 (hereinafter "the declaration"), I hereby order as follows:

General Permit to enter and stay in the Seam Zone	1.	Permit is hereby granted to enter the Seam Zone, as defined in the declaration and to stay in it, to every person in the categories set forth in the annex to this permit, in accordance with the conditions specified in the annex.
Conditions	2.	A. A person who, pursuant to such permit, enters the Seam Zone and stays in it shall carry with him, in addition to his identity card, a document indicating that he belongs to one of the categories of persons set forth in the annex.
		B. The head of the Civil Administration may alter or add to the conditions set forth in subsection (A) as regards a specific person or category of persons.
Exception to applicability	3.	Notwithstanding the provisions of Section 1, a military commander may order that this permit does not apply to a person or to a category of persons who enter the Seam Zone.
Publication	4.	A. Copies of this permit shall be deposited for public review during normal working hours of the following offices:
		1. The sector Coordination and Liaison Offices.
		2. Police stations in Judea and Samaria.
		3. The office of the legal advisor for Judea and Samaria.
		4. Offices of the head of infrastructure in the Civil Administration for Judea and Samaria.
		B. Copies of the permit shall be posted on the bulletin board in the sector Coordination and Liaison Offices, as stated in subsection (A)(1), for a period of three months from the day that this permit enters into force.
		C. The head of the Civil Administration may establish other ways to publish this permit, in addition to those set forth in subsections (A) and (B).
Commencement of validity	5.	This permit shall take effect on the day it is signed.

6. היתר זה ייקרא: "היתר כללי לכניסה למרחב התפר ולשהייה בו (יהודה והשומרון), התשס"ד - 2003".

תוספת

תנאים	סוג בני אדם
כניסה למרחב התפר ושהייה בו לכל צורך	מי שאינו תושב האזור, ושבידיו דרכון זר בתוקף ואשרת שהייה תקפה בישראל
כניסה למרחב התפר ושהייה בו לצורך תעסוקה בישוב הנקוב בהיתר התעסוקה, ובתנאים הקבועים בהיתר התעסוקה	מי שבידיו היתר תעסוקה בתוקף, בישוב ישראלי הנמצא במרחב התפר, מכוח הצו בדבר העסקת עובדים במקומות מסוימים (יהודה והשומרון) (מס' 967) התשמ"ב - 1982
מעבר במרחב התפר לצורך יציאה מהאזור לישראל	מי שבידיו היתר יציאה בתוקף מתאזור לישראל

תאריך: ___ התשס"ד
___ 2003

משה קפלינסקי, אלוף
מפקד כוחות צה"ל
באזור יהודה והשומרון

Name   6.   This permit will be called: "General Permit to Enter and Stay in the Seam Zone (Judea and Samaria), 5764—2003."

ANNEX

CATEGORY OF PERSONS	CONDITIONS
Nonresident of the region who holds a valid foreign passport and valid visa to stay in Israel.	Entry and stay in the Seam Zone allowed for every purpose.
Holder of valid permit to work in an Israeli community located in the Seam Zone, pursuant to the Order Regarding Employment of Workers in Certain Places (Judea and Samaria) (No. 967), 5742—1982.	Entry and stay in the Seam Zone for the purpose of working in the community mentioned in the employment permit and according to the conditions set forth in the employment permit.
Holder of valid permit to exit the region for Israel.	Crossing the Seam Zone for the purpose of leaving the region to enter Israel.

Date: 6 Tishrei 5764
     2 October 2003

Moshe Kaplinsky, Major General
Commander of IDF Forces in Judea and Samaria

The Order of Violence

Ariella Azoulay and Adi Ophir

The main part of this text aims to describe and to analyze the new formations of violence employed by Israeli forces in the Occupied Territories since the outbreak of the al-Aqsa intifada in October 2000 (also called the second intifada) and to examine their significance as a constructing element of the occupation regime. In order to do this, we—very briefly—present the two general formations of power relations between Israelis and Palestinians that have evolved since the onset of the occupation in 1967 and review their specific characteristics formed since the Oslo Accords.

TWO FORMATIONS OF POWER RELATIONS

Two formations of power relations have been inscribed in the Occupied Territories and have clear spatial expressions. The first, in which submission of the population of the Occupied Territories to the occupier is enacted and displayed, is distinguished by the proliferation and decentralization of contact points between Israelis and Palestinians, mostly inside the Occupied Territories, vaguely demarcated and open to the occupier's free movement. The second formation is characterized by efforts to minimize and concentrate any contact between the two sides along clearly delineated lines of separation.[1]

The outstanding characteristics of each formation have changed over time, but the formations themselves have not ceased to coexist. Their changing relations will serve as our key to describe various phases of the occupation regime. The differences in power relations between Israelis and Palestinians are manifest in the possibilities, means, and manners available to one of the two parties to act upon and within these formations in order to defeat the other or to gain advantage over it. Important milestones in the history of the occupation are an outcome of the (ever partial and temporary) success of one of the sides in changing these formations and their interrelations, making one of them more dominant than the other.

Under the Oslo Accords, separation, the second formation, appeared for the first time as a reciprocal relation between two supposedly equal parties that resolve their conflicts essentially through negotiation and agreement.[2] However, this symmetry and reciprocity did not apply to the first formation, that of submission. In fact, Israel persisted in increasing the number of contact points at which Palestinians encountered Israelis as occupiers who ruled them with no regard for coordination or agreement while minimizing the Palestinians' capacity to cross the lines of separation, both within the Occupied Territories and into Israel across the Green Line. With the division of Palestinian territory into Areas A, B, and C (and the later division of the Hebron area into Areas H-1 and H-2) as devised in the accords, a new matrix of control had taken effect: "dissection" or fragmentation.[3] Palestinian territory was literally carved up, making the area itself far more penetrable while curbing Palestinian movement within it even more extensively. As early as the spring of 1994, with implementation of the accords still in its first phase, it was already evident that while pretending to separate the two sides, Israel continued to control the Palestinian population and administer its life. As the al-Aqsa intifada broke out in the fall of 2000, the separation formation, which had previously been subject to political negotiations "toward peace" between two sides, was transformed into open warfare wherein all lines of separation become subject to a "security-first" military rationale. In 1968, Israel had defined the Occupied Territories as hostile territory, but in 2000, they became a war zone from which anyone uninvolved in the fighting was to be kept out and where anyone defined as the "enemy" was to be systematically annihilated. Martial thought pervaded all aspects of life. All Palestinian territories immediately became a kind of war-room map and thoroughly accessible to the Israeli Army, which in turn could make instant contact with the local population. Such contact aimed to destroy whoever was defined as the enemy and to impose a new formation of occupier-occupied relations along the new lines of separation formed within the deconstructed Palestinian space described above.

The military term for this form of domination on the ground is "regulation of the combat zone."[4] With such "regulation," the Israeli ruling apparatus functions in various ways to crush the Palestinian side, albeit short of its total destruction. Dissecting space and restricting movement within it have become the main means of control and domination of life in the Occupied Territories. New conditions have thus been generated for exerting violence, and this new order of violence, in turn, has necessitated a reorganization of space and new restrictions on movement. This dialectical process has been ongoing at least since the Oslo Accords and reached its epitome in Israel's disengagement from the Gaza Strip and the army's new form of power wielding there. We cannot present this process in its entirety here. We will only analyze the changes in the order of violence in view of the changes in regimentation of movement. Nor can we discuss the phase of disengagement, but rather propose a theoretical framework for such a discussion. Our interest will be mainly limited to the Israeli apparatus. We will not analyze the rationality of Palestinian violence and its various agents, from local armed groups to the Palestinian national authority. Clearly, a comprehensive analysis of the history of the conflict necessitates the inclusion of what we relegate here to the margin of our frame. However, we study the Israeli apparatuses of violence as part of our attempt to understand the occupation regime as a sui generis form of power,[5] and in this context, we believe, this framing is permissible. For brevity's sake, we will also skip here the systematic examination of separation and submission as spatial techniques and the organization of space they have dictated.

TWO KINDS OF VIOLENCE

Violence is a kind of power, and as Michel Foucault defined it, a mode of "acting upon the action of others." Foucault stressed that such action does not necessarily mean the use of physical force, but clearly, physical force is also a way to act upon the action of others.[6] Violence is physical force that acts upon the actions of people because it inflicts or threatens to inflict harm on their own persons and possessions or on those of their dear ones.

Other kinds of power, such as purchasing power or the power exercised by a ruling authority, can act without harming anyone or anything. They can move persons or things elsewhere or effect exchanges. Not so violence. Violence is the exertion of physical force to injure its object. Violence is invasive, disruptive, painful, or erosive. Disruption, penetration, erosion, and the like are forms of destruction: After the injury, the injured has difficulty existing in the state that preceded the injury. Regard for the law, central to a critical discussion of violence,[7] will always be secondary to the power of destruction. Violence destroys; law might allow or prohibit destruction, limit or ignore it, enable, restrict, or reject claims to reparation, however destruction does not result from the law or its regard, but from the actual or potential contact between the active force and its object: a body or property.

Acts of violence such as invasion, penetration, or demolition have a visible aspect par excellence—even in the absence of eye witnesses, such as instances of violent robbery in a dark alley or a massacre in a god-forsaken forest—because they are always visible events, at least in the eyes of the victim. But an act is also violent when the force is not eruptive and violence is *withheld*. Withheld violence is the presence of a violent force whose outbreak is imminent, but is not manifest. It differs from violence insinuated by words, a flag, or other symbols in the immediacy of its potential manifestation and the rapidly diminishing interval in space and time between the presence of such force and its actual outburst. In withheld violence, threatening and deterring gestures replace direct contact with the exposed body, but these are gestures of overt presence on the part of the threatening force. The difference between withheld violence and insinuated violence is a matter of degree and continuity. At times, insinuations of violence act as threats, and their deterrent effect is no less powerful, even greater than its overt presence. But in an ongoing conflict, insinuated threats tend to lose their effectiveness, and the ruling power needs to intensify the threats by means of displaying withheld violence. In any case, violence—either insinuated or withheld—is effective even when there is no outburst of physical force. Without such an outbreak, when no blow is given, there is no visible bodily contact, and yet the traces of destruction are clear.

In this respect, insinuated or withheld violence does not differ from economic power, purchasing power, the rhetorical power of persuasion, and other such acts and representations in which people "act upon the actions of others" without exerting physical force. When people act upon the actions of others, they maintain power relations. Such relations must not be described in binary terms, both because in every binary relation there is always a third—distanced—party (and such distancing is an exertion of power) and because the polarization of power relations requires the regular, ongoing exertion of force, amassing the majority of people and consolidating their interrelations around two extremities. Potential power—money and possessions, political authority, physical fitness, courage, or an arsenal of arms—has meaning as an "action upon actions" or upon the behavior of others only if something indicates it or signifies it—only if it shows its presence. Potential force acts through the discourse that represents it and through the imagination that simulates its action without necessarily being linked to the actual designated force. Potential force, like any "thing in itself," is applied merely through the mediation of whatever represents it, acting according to the effectiveness of such a representation: how it is designated, leaves traces, is expressed and symbolized, imagined, metaphorically molded, counted, and quantified. Purchasing power that has not been consummated, but is represented; knowledge that has not been demonstrated, but is signified; political authority that has not been exercised, but is declared; violence that has not been actually exerted here, but elsewhere—are all significant in defining the possible field of action of power, its range of influence. Every such form of presence of potential power partakes of the actual productive game of power.

These distinctions are true of all sources of power—physical, economic, political-governmental, or cognitive-cultural.[8] In the present context, however, attempting to understand Israel's control mechanism in the Occupied Territories, as in other contexts where violence is practiced widely and systematically alongside other control mechanisms, it would not suffice to place violence alongside other sources of power, as their equivalent. Violence in the Occupied Territories, as in many "emergency zones" throughout the world, is a comprehensive form of regulating and administering life, activity, movement, and human interrelations, and we should better understand its machinations as a ruling system in its own right, apart from other power sources and ruling systems, in order to comprehend fully the way in which it is incorporated in them.

One obvious difference between violence and other sources of power in modern society is the special weight intrinsic to the relation between the potential force and its manifest state. This difference is expressed in two aspects of the transition from potential to manifestation: the regulation of this transition and its frequency. The transition from political authority to political resolution, from purchasing power to actual purchase, from covert to overt information, is fluent, frequent, very partially regulated, determined mainly or even exclusively by the judgment of the enforcing party, restrained only within the limits of a specific activity (certain things may not be purchased, certain people are prohibited from purchasing certain things, certain things must not be known or revealed, and the like). The nature of the transition from insinuated violence, to withheld violence, to the eruption of violence is at the heart of state rule and at the base of social order, and this nature varies from regime to regime.

The prevalence of such a transition is a function of the ruling power's legitimacy in the eyes of its subjects and of the political order's stability. A stable, legitimate ruling power is one in which such transitions are rare and are regulated by law, restricted in space and time, and generally accepted by the governed. The effectiveness of violence in a political system is affected by the gap that lies between withholding force and its exertion, on the one hand, and the continuum between potential violence and its manifestation, on the other. "Proper" rule—especially political, but also the kind of rule maintained in other violence-needy contexts, such as educational facilities, industry, or the military—works mainly by means of insinuated threats of violence and not through actually applying violent force. When it is challenged, it usually chooses to deter and defeat its opponents through the display of withheld violence and would hesitate before instructing its armed forces to open fire. But the essential meaning of an insinuated threat is that it might be carried out at any moment—all the more so when withheld violence is overtly present.

When a ruling power loses its legitimacy and stability, it tends to display withheld violence on a wide scale and exert overt violence on an irregular and ad hoc basis. In actual fact, these differences are blurred, of course, but on this continuum, we find it important to maintain three distinct ideal types: proper rule under which withheld violence is an exception to the rule and its eruption a rare event; proper rule under which, in certain distinct areas, withheld violence is the rule; and unstable, illegitimate rule whose jurisdiction is typified by the daily occurrence of both forms of violence, withheld and eruptive. In spite of the differences between these three types of rule, as long as the ruling power is concerned about its legitimacy both internally and externally, it recognizes that its best interests lie in maintaining a guise of continuity and ordered transition between the two forms of violence and further in presenting its violence as a legal response to severe legal transgressions and eruptions of violence on the part of the governed. Violence thus appears before both as part of the legal order and as a condition for its existence.

Obviously, the occupation regime is not considered legitimate by the Palestinians in the Occupied Territories, but for the occupation regime, the question of legitimacy never concerns the Palestinian population, only Israelis and part of the world public. Euphemistic language that describes enlightened checkpoints, targeted eliminations and smart bombs, and the legal safety net given to all of these actions clearly express the effort made by the control apparatus there to display its restraint. It wishes to create the impression that wherever possible, its forces are concentrated only to deter, and it seeks to diminish the extent of direct violence that is exerted. Its ostensible interest in legitimizing its overt violence has characterized occupation rule since its inception. However, since the disengagement from Gaza in August 2005, a decisive change has taken place, because two entirely different arenas have been formed for the exertion of force: the Gaza Strip and the West Bank. In each, each type of violence—withheld and eruptive—has a different status. It is, as we noted, a process that began with the Oslo Accords and that was exacerbated by the "disengagement." It casts doubt on the nature of the gap and continuity of the two types of violence that the ruling power wishes to present and requires us to reexamine the relations between them in every arena where they are practiced.

Furthermore, under a regime that has no legitimacy in the eyes of the governed—certainly the case of occupation rule in the Occupied Territories—violence confuses the relation between suspending force and its eruption, and its effectiveness as a ruling apparatus does not depend on keeping them apart and continuous. Therefore, discussion of violence practiced in the Occupied Territories cannot begin by seeing violence as a potential realized by the ruling power according to law or convention. Instead, one should examine the actual forms of eruptive violence, on the one hand, and the deployment patterns of withheld violence, on the other, and discern the nature of harm inflicted by each of these two types of violence. To persist in the discussion of violence as the relations between a potential and its realization means accepting the conceptual point of view of power. Our justification for shifting the main discussion of violence from the accepted patterns for realizing withheld violence over to the victims of violence stems from our insistence on distancing ourselves from power's perspective and turning it into a part of the issue at hand.

Under Israeli occupation of the territories, these two forms of violence—withheld and eruptive—belong to two distinct spheres of action and may take place simultaneously without being related to each other. Their simultaneous exercise happened for the first time in an organized fashion toward the end of the first intifada, in the late 1980s, when special undercover army units (the Mista'arvim), acting covertly and extrajudicially to injure resistance leaders and activists, became a routine part of the ruling apparatus. It happened again, much more extensively, with the outbreak of the al-Aqsa intifada. The issue is not temporal and ontological continuity between potential and eruptive violence or between acts of flagrant violence and its retraction and freezing into structures of unexecuted threat. The issue is the simultaneous presence of violence that has not yet been exerted and eruptive violence whose menacing presence has not been felt previously. Under the control apparatus maintained in the Occupied Territories, the entire space has become penetrable to both types, whereas the relation between withheld and eruptive violence is no longer that of potential and fulfillment: The apparatus of withheld violence is constantly active and does not remain a mere potential threat, while potentially eruptive violence hovers separately and independently. The force wielded by the occupation might materialize anywhere, like a deus ex machina, and its emergence does not necessarily express the realization of potential force that the regime marks and presents in conventional codes. By the same token, the presence of withheld, contained, suspended force turns out to be the continuous infliction of violence upon objects—body and mind—that refutes the assumption that the link between suspended and flagrant force is the link between potential and activated force.

If one assumes that the two forms of violence create a continuum, then apparently the further away one moves from suspended violence, its presence is made all the more tangible. The threat that it emanates increases, and the time needed to carry out that threat is reduced. This is, of course, an assumed continuum. In actual fact, observing Israeli violence in action in the Occupied Territories, it becomes evident that on the one hand, the violent outburst, the *passage à l'acte*, does not always originate in potential violence. On the other hand, countless foci of potential violence are visible throughout the dominated space, and the mere presence of potential violence suffices to prohibit, direct, and administer life, inflict bodily injury, and crush the life texture of an entire population. Our main distinction, therefore, will be between withheld violence and eruptive violence.

There are indeed places in the Occupied Territories and situations in which continuity is evident between the two poles of violence, linked by potential-manifest relations. But we argue that such a continuity has now become the exception to the rule. The regulation of continuity between withheld violence (potential) and eruptive violence (actualization) assumes conventions known to the ruling power and its subjects—temporary or permanent zoning throughout this space of private and public, accessible and inaccessible areas, both penetrable and impenetrable to the infliction of sanctioned violence—and the grounds on which the two sides partake in preserving these conventions and their recovery, if breached. Such conventions and demarcations are no longer valid in the Occupied Territories since the outbreak of the second intifada. The ruling apparatus can breach accepted rules at any moment and penetrate defined areas (private homes and public places, the ministries of the Palestinian Authority, public institutions such as mosques, schools, hospitals, and cemeteries), and it may do so with a violence that leaves its victims helpless, unable to demand that the regime suspend this eruptive violence along accepted rules. When violence is suspended, the subject might sometimes assume or guess how close the violent force was to erupting and what could delay or escalate transition from threat to deed, but he or she knows that the attempt to decipher the order of violence is usually just so much guesswork, and in any case, the subject remains trapped in its ongoing impact.

Withheld violence is suspended violence whose potential dimension—usually invisible—is made visible and displayed conspicuously. Violent force acts by flaunting its potential. Here it is not merely a declared or referred authority, the publishing of fiscal balances, or the waving of titles and uniforms. It is the display of the "thing in itself." It is not "the thing in itself," of course (the shot or blast), only its display, but the display is real (an actual weapon-carrying body, or at times, just the weapon itself). It is not a symbolic presentation—the power is present, not just represented. It acts through its actual presence. In a gang fight or a tribal feud, dispersing demonstrators or strikers, preparing for war, or even in war itself, the display of violence plays a central role. When the display of violence is regulated through cultural and legal codes that are considered legitimate, it might be a part of the strategy of struggle between the parties to the power relations, a strategy employed without having actually to exert violence. Such a display might use decoys or simulation, of course. One can try to scare through exaggeration or belittling in order to mislead, but these possibilities stem from the role that is already assigned to the visibility of the violent force. However, lacking cultural and legal codes agreed upon by the parties, the display of violence always constitutes the exertion of violence.

The description of withheld violence as a separate kind of violence should not be understood as disconnecting the display of violent force from actual manifested violence. On the contrary, suspension means that the eruption of violence is but one possible form of withheld violence that may not necessarily be fulfilled. Suspended violence, either insinuated or withheld, is an active force;[9] as expected the outburst works because it deters, while when suspended the outburst works because it enables a space of negotiation, or retreat, or escape, or counterthreat. Unrealized potential works not only because it might be fulfilled, but also because it might not. The presence of power in withheld violence should be conceived here not as a necessary phase on the way to actually erupting, as though that were an objective that would eventually be achieved, but as a presencing of the potential either to erupt or not to erupt, to be or not to be an eruption of violence.[10] The more intense such presencing of power is, and the more effectively it is deployed in space and time, the greater the chances for potential to act as potential, to realize its power through unfulfillment: to injure, direct, and administer, urge and block, diminish and expand, abandon and grab, redivide, lay down borders and breach them—all by force of its presence as destructive potential. One should add that as soon as withheld violence replaces the insinuated violence of the "proper" regime as a major tool of domination, insinuated violence, too, becomes afflicted, is less insinuated, and functions as a display (or presencing) and not merely a representation of the potential to erupt or not to erupt.

Withheld violence tends to be contagious. During political crises such as states of emergency, wars, or occupations, when the law is suspended or imposed, and subjects persist in their resistance, there are no permanent arrangements for the presence of withheld violence, and the rules for realizing its potential are drawn up ad hoc, changing according to the "situation on the ground." In such situations, when the suspending effect of withheld violence intensifies, there is an intrinsic tendency to blur differences between this kind of violence and eruptive violence, and the governed are trapped in a state of constant threat to their well-being, their lives, and their possessions.

MAPPING THE VIOLENCE IN THE OCCUPIED TERRITORIES

Until the outbreak of the first intifada, Israel ruled the Occupied Territories with a semblance of order. The presence of withheld violence was usually sufficient to destroy political space, although violence erupted from time to time in response to attempts at political organization or acts of overt resistance, both civil and armed. In the first twenty years of the occupation, about 650 Palestinians were killed in clashes with the Israeli security forces and colonists. During the first intifada, a substantial rise was felt in the level of violence, and during the five years of uprising, over 1,400 Palestinians were killed and more than 10,000 were wounded. Even when it responded to terrorist activity that resumed following the Hebron (Cave of the Patriarchs) massacre of March 1994, Israel did not escalate its eruptive violence in the territories, where, as a rule, until the late 1990s, it had remained relatively limited. In spite of the growing number of casualties, it was still low compared with that of the years of the second intifada—more than 660 Palestinians dead and more than 4,300 wounded each year. But even this number is still a low rate compared with the number of victims in ethnic conflicts elsewhere.[11] Before the second intifada, eruptive violence was exerted in more or less distinct incidents: clashes with armed resistance fighters, dispersing demonstrators, torture, home demolitions, arresting suspects. The main change felt after the Oslo Accords was the deployment in space of withheld violence, as described above.

With the onset of the second intifada and the entrance of massive military forces into the West Bank and Gaza Strip, the ruling apparatus ceased to function as an administration of civilian life that maintains a semblance of distinction between the two types of violence and that displays potential violence or exerts eruptive violence according to fixed, known, and authorized codes. The map of violence became characterized by a wide and contiguous deployment of forces that enabled the tangible, powerful presence of withheld violence and that intensified uncertainty as to how this violence was deployed and how its subjects were expected to submit to it. The span of time needed to exert violence and the frequently changing instructions for opening fire made it difficult for Palestinians to anticipate eruptions of violence. Israeli military forces were now deployed throughout the area almost as in a state of war, but there was no war. War itself was suspended. There were "only" army operations, violent arrests, occasional incursions into residential neighborhoods, and targeted killings, with their "collateral damage" and the destruction of infrastructure and dwellings, whether as punitive measures or as a form of attack.

Following the diminishing frequency of suicide bombings and the change in the political situation as the disengagement plan was about to be implemented in summer 2005,[12] a certain reduction was felt in the force and frequency of such army activity, but it never stopped altogether and was renewed shortly after the Israeli Army left the Gaza Strip.[13] Still, in spite of the obvious number of violent clashes in general, and particularly those initiated by Israel (which has had its share of accumulating death and destruction), and in spite of the tremendous increase of the direct use of violent measures in the Gaza Strip after disengagement was completed, most of the soldiers in the Occupied Territories do not occupy anything. In spite of the growing presence of their weapons, these usually stay locked. Eruptive violence remains suspended, withheld in the club, the rifle, the armored vehicle, but also in the voice announcing a curfew, in the computer issuing the magnetic cards that serve as permits of passage, in the metal arm of the roadblock and the concrete structure that serves as an ID inspection booth—and this is precisely how this violence is exerted. It imposes its constraints upon the movement of the subjects of the Occupied Territories and upon their conduct wherever it is present and wherever it might show up. And it might show up—as we well know—anytime, anywhere.

One of the main effects of withheld violence in the Occupied Territories is suspension. It delays or prevents movement, creates waiting lines, postpones daily activities, stretches out waiting time for whatever has to be waited for, and forces people to loiter in the wrong place at the wrong time. In this manner, withheld violence encumbers, complicates, disrupts preferences, undermines plans, maddens, wounds, infests, generates disease, and kills. This is the tangible, immediate effect of the withheld presence of force. Withheld violence prevents individuals— at whom it is directed—from doing whatever is needed to avoid its harm, which is very hard to ascribe to a specific cause. Detaining women in labor at the checkpoints or refusing to grant passage to ailing patients are extreme instances that speak for themselves. But people in good health and in no need of special medical care are harmed no less than the sick and the weak. When withheld violence suspends life itself, it takes its toll without erupting and with no direct regard for the obedience of its subjects. Its outcome might prove no less disastrous— perhaps even more so—than that of exerting eruptive violence. Actually, in areas and periods when violence suspends its victims all the more forcefully, such as in the crammed pens at checkpoints—full to bursting—where the crowd inches its way to the checking posts after days of closure, in waiting lines for food after a prolonged curfew, in areas deprived of water where delays in traffic hold back water-tanker trucks and disrupt the distribution of rationed water, or in areas where the electrical power supply has been cut off for days and basic services are unattainable, the formal difference between eruption and threat is entirely erased, and the body is incessantly vulnerable to all types of harm.[14]

The Occupied Palestinian Territories have become a "zone of indistinction" between the two types of violence, which, under stable sovereign rule, are otherwise distinct. Against this background, one might understand the occasionally recurring phenomenon of "moral stock taking" by the Israeli public about the morality of exerting force in the territories. The seasonal spells of "righteous indignation" that public figures and journalists undergo in view of showcase violence exerted by the ruling apparatus aim, apparently, to rehabilitate the deteriorating distinction between the two kinds of violence. At the same time, withheld violence and a considerable part of its suspending effects are not reported. They are normalized, detached from their causes, and their visible results are publicized only in periodic reports produced by nongovernmental organizations that hardly find their way into the Israeli public sphere. While focusing on the violation of rights, it is difficult to measure the daily damage inflicted on routine life, the ability to maintain a family life, a regular social life, or to assess worsening work conditions. Reports of the deterioration of the standard of living do not reflect all the dimensions of impoverishment in Palestinian society and the havoc wrought on infrastructure of all kinds. Damage to health and education services is measured especially by their accessibility, denied through the regimentation of movement in the Occupied Territories. There is, however, no clear appraisal of the accumulating damages to health and education. Nor are there reports of the frequent arrests of many Palestinians who do not end up in jail, but are disposed of, left for hours waiting at the roadside, blindfolded, their hands cuffed in tight plastic strips—only to be released later, just as they had been picked up, without any explanation.

Erupting violence, on the other hand, emerges as an accessible topic of discourse, quantified through the tally of victims, assessed by its proportionality, examined in light of the Israeli Army's official "code of ethics," and is forever justified in the name of security. When the press occasionally bothers to deal with "immoral behavior" by Israeli soldiers in the Occupied Territories, it tends to repeat the descriptions of military operations there in light of accepted moral rules that are supposed to regulate violence, sanction some of it as a necessary evil, and condemn whatever exceeds this. Every now and then, stories are told of lethal, destructive showcase violence, erupting regardless of the accepted code. Condemnations then resound from the left, sometimes even from the right, and the issue suddenly involves military men, as well. The violent events are presented as both shocking and exceptional. Commonplace discussions in the media and politics disconnect showcase violence from its place in the economy of violence, tend to ignore withheld violence, and do not concern themselves with the destruction it inflicts upon Palestinian society.

The moral sensitivity shown by opponents of the occupation may be heightened by such instances of eruptive violence, more so, perhaps, than by others. Withheld violence, however, still tends to slip by them with relative ease, although withheld violence is not only very evasive, but also extremely widespread. Even at the height of the al-Aqsa intifada in the spring of 2002, during the Israeli operation named Defense Shield, when the Israeli Army "reconquered" most of the West Bank, once more making the local population feel its powerful presence, and changed the nature of its control in the Gaza Strip—even then, the power active in the Occupied Territories was more withheld and checked than eruptive. Even then, withheld violence had greater impact upon the lives of Palestinians than eruptive violence. After all, withheld violence is the kind that controls everyday life. Eruptive violence is short-lived. Whether as an unexpected reaction or as a premeditated operation, the eruption of force is meant to end by reaffirming the presence of withheld violence, which at times—though not necessarily—happens through a new deployment of forces and a reorganization of the space, time, and living arrangements of the dominated. Usually, the subject chooses to obey, retreat, pass or refrain from passage, go out of his or her way, work or refrain from working, strip, stand in front of the camera, wait in line, clam up, become resigned to the verdict (without trial), keep quiet, maintaining order, polite speech, or silence.

For those who operate the ruling apparatus, this preference on the part of the subjects proves the success of the apparatus's functioning principle, for resistance is checked without any eruption of violence. But such proof has only temporary validity and must be produced again and again. This requires both the reintroduction of withheld violence and direct action through eruptive violence. Sporadic bursts of violence, random in space and time, bear witness to the continuous existence of the withheld presence, to its homogeneity in space and time. These eruptions must take place more and more frequently as the threat contained in suspended force gradually erodes. The threat is eroded not necessarily because the threatening force has weakened or retreated, for the threat is not only a result of the introduction of armed forces, but also of the way in which their withheld violence is perceived by the threatened party. The more violence is exerted against it, the less the threatened side has anything left to lose. The less it has left to lose, the greater the threat against it must become in order to achieve the same result: destroying the threatened's power and will to resist. In 1971, the army razed dozens of homes in refugee camps in Gaza in order to "air the camps out" and prevent the sheltering of armed people while inflicting relatively small damage on their residents and without any signs of resistance; 2002 saw the army in Operation Defense Shield raze 140 homes at the Jenin refugee camp alone during its fierce battles against Palestinian fighters who showed great determination and caused the army numerous casualties.

RULING APPARATUSES

Violence, in both its forms, is the main ruling apparatus active in the Occupied Territories. But in order to comprehend how violence functions, we must step back and place it in the context of other ruling apparatuses. Following Foucault's work in the 1970s, one may distinguish three ruling apparatuses involved on a daily basis in the rule of a modern state: the judicial-sovereign apparatus that establishes general law, interprets it, and enforces it in particular cases; the disciplinary apparatus that forms individuals into subjects and citizens; and the governmental apparatus that focuses on administering territories and populations, assuring the well-being and security of society at large.[15] Despite Foucault, it seems to us correct to locate in each of these three apparatuses an ideological component, as Althusser defined the term: practices meant to shape the individual as a subject of power. The subject of power, having internalized power relations, sees himself or herself as a recipient of power's instructions, however much he or she opposes it, and experiences the world as mediated by conceptual categories, metaphors, and images shared with others taking part in the same web of power relations.[16]

Retreat to violence may take place in all three apparatuses, in their more or less ideological components, but only the judicial-sovereign apparatus functions by regularly combining violence and the law, because some of its organs sanction the violence exercised by the others. Within this framework, violence usually appears in some relation to law, as a war that aims to destroy existing law and instate new law or as policing to preserve the existing law. The law, in its turn, might legitimize war or preparations for it, the various forms of police violence, as well as its own retreat and abandonment of land and population in states of emergency.

The flagrant presence of withheld violence in the Occupied Territories is explained by the fact that Israel acts there without the ability to make significant use of ideology, law, or disciplinary mechanisms that reduce its need for violence. In the late 1980s, the Palestinian uprising already diminished this ability to a great extent. In spite of the fact that the occupying power, of its own accord, rescinded laws as its modus operandi, it has been operating in the territories (and since August 2005, only in the West Bank) a quasi-sovereign apparatus that attempts to create a semblance of law and order. Despite the fact that the occupying power has rescinded—either on its own initiative or unwillingly—disciplinary venues destined to shape the disciplined Palestinian subject, it has not ceased trying to operate the disciplinary apparatus, particularly and individually wherever the security forces encounter Palestinians in their activity at the checkpoints, in the offices handling applications for permits, in patrols, and during arrests. Both judicial and disciplinary practices act as mere simulations of similar apparatuses of regulated sovereign rule. Of the three apparatuses mentioned above, the only one functioning properly in the Occupied Territories is the governmental apparatus. But because of the transfer of responsibilities to the Palestinian Authority that followed the Oslo Accords and because of the population's sweeping resistance, this apparatus has been completely reduced to its functions of counting and classification at the service of "security," entirely giving up its caring functions (for example, the provision of health, education, infrastructure, and so on).[17] For the same reason—the resistance of the governed—this apparatus can be maintained only through violent enforcement. Since, with the exception of apparatuses of violence, the reduced governmental apparatus is the only one still functioning, and since its function is absolutely conditioned by its possible violent enforcement, relying on the governmental apparatus only enhances the need for violence, for neither the judicial nor the disciplinary mechanisms can be of any help.

THE JUDICIAL APPARATUS The overwhelming majority of actions by the ruling apparatus in the Occupied Territories is still performed with ruling authorization that is subject to the law and withstands judicial scrutiny. Commanders and officials usually act according to authority that has been vested in them by law. But legal authorization is more or less the only remaining vestige of law in the ruling apparatus of the territories, and it, too, has been breached lately, because the army avoids obeying explicit orders of the High Court of Justice in the rare cases where rulings have favored the Palestinians.[18]

Israeli law in the Occupied Territories is suspended both due to the state of occupation and military rule declared there in June 1967 and due to the suspension of military rule by emergency regulations and ad hoc regulations that are changed sporadically by announcements of military commanders on the ground.[19] Recently, the law has also been suspended due to the simple fact that the army has been knowingly and intentionally acting contrary to court rulings, especially on different occasions in the Hebron area. Still, the law in the Occupied Territories proliferates incessantly by force of edicts and regulations that are produced now and then, as well as by force of the occasional review of various policies and particular actions by the Supreme Court. This judicial criticism questions the lawfulness, reasonableness, or "proportionality" of actions undertaken with the authorization to exert violence, to destroy and confiscate property, and to arrest, detain, grant permits, and deny them. Such criticism is always heard in retrospect and has mainly one effect: giving the occupation regime a semblance of lawfulness and thus enabling the continuity of the two ruling apparatuses without revoking the difference between them. Usually, when judicial criticism delivers constraints upon the security forces, the latter ignore them or find ways to avoid them. When, however, judicial criticism refers to damages on the Palestinian side, this almost always results in legally justifying damage already done. Still, there are rare cases in which the court has ruled in the Palestinians' favor, and these are precisely the cases that uphold the semblance of the lawfulness and sovereignty of the judicial system, as well as the legitimacy of the entire occupation regime—in the eyes of the occupiers, of course.[20]

De facto rulings take place through an elaborate system of "ruling by decrees" that has characterized colonial regimes since the late nineteenth century.[21] A similar format of control was maintained in the Gaza Strip until the disengagement. Since the outbreak of the second intifada, most orders deal with the movement of Palestinians in a Palestinian space that has become a cluster of distinct land cells. Thus, these orders actually belong to the governmental apparatus of control (see above). The law in the Occupied Territories is not an effective device of control not only because the Palestinians do not recognize its legitimacy, but because the Israeli regime changes it incessantly by suspending laws and annulling them. The military command inundates the area under its control and its subjects with orders and regulations that keep changing and often does not follow its own regulations.[22]

The Occupied Territories are not a legal vacuum. The abuse of life at the hands of the ruling power is not due to some withdrawal of the law, but occurs thanks to a savage proliferation of legalities and illegalities and the creation of an extensive judicial patchwork that has no lawfulness of its own and that keeps changing the law itself, the regime's authorities and immunity, and the subject's own status before the law.[23] Under such conditions, subjects cannot—and are not supposed to—internalize the law. Under such conditions, the difference between law and decree, decree and order, and between order and the presence of the uniformed person who administers it greatly diminishes and at times disappears altogether. Even under less duress, ruling by decree is chronically and outstandingly unstable, and in the Occupied Territories, this instability has been on the increase since the first intifada. Because the rules that the subjects are supposed to follow change rapidly, it is impossible to rely on the validity of anything that is not accompanied by withheld violence. No order is worth the paper it is written on without the actual presence of the force that can implement it. The regime needs the massive presence of withheld violence in order to announce the rules and with them direct and dictate the behavior of its subjects. But the subjects, too, need this presence in order to be informed of the rules and to know how to calculate their everyday moves. In order to know which route to take to work, one must know where the checkpoint is placed; in order to decide whether even to bother going to work, one must know whether or not a curfew has been imposed during the night—and thus on and on, with every activity in every aspect of life.

DISCIPLINARY SITES AND PRACTICES Ever since the Oslo Accords, the Israeli regime no longer maintains disciplinary sites in the Occupied Territories. Prisons and detention centers are meant mainly to isolate the inmates, rather than to shape them as disciplined subjects.[24] In their capacity as disciplining sites, prisons have paradoxically served the Palestinian rebels, and not the Israeli ruling power. Incarcerated Palestinian prisoners have used these closed disciplining sites to shape the disciplined subject of the Palestinian uprising. The disciplinary apparatuses functioning within Palestinian society are not subject to Israeli rule. As in an inverted mirror image of the way in which such apparatuses in Israel train and recruit their "subjects" for the struggle against Palestinians, the Palestinian apparatuses recruit their own "subjects" into the struggle against Israel (and since the Hamas takeover in the Gaza Strip, against Fatah or Hamas, respectively). They shape nearly every boy and girl, man and woman in whose lives they are involved into subjects who see this struggle as inevitable, as an arena of excellence, and as a vital dimension of any public activity.

Disciplinary practices are still maintained in nearly any encounter between Palestinians and the forces that exert withheld violence, and especially at the institutionalized points of friction: the checkpoints, questioning rooms, and whatever is left of the Civil Administration. But this disciplining—which takes place under absolutely illegitimate conditions set by the disciplining power—fulfills a local, ad hoc role. The Palestinians are taught how to behave when crossing a checkpoint, how to address an official in the district coordination office, how to gain benefits in detention cells. What the Palestinian learns in an encounter with the regime in one venue, however, does not teach him or her what to expect in other encounters in other venues. Moreover, he or she ought to learn precisely this: that it is pointless to internalize rules of conduct, for these constantly change and must be forever deciphered anew in every encounter with the regime. Only two things will be repeated in nearly every encounter: the absolute submission of the Palestinian to the agents of the Israeli ruling power and the need to relearn again and again what is expected in order to either please or avoid them. The sporadic disciplinary practices that do occur do not serve to teach the subject how to internalize the regime's perspective and embody it in his or her relations with others when not under surveillance. More importantly, they do not construct a reliable subject. Quite the contrary, perhaps: The almost unlimited authority that security forces have to change the rules is a way to produce a subject that is inherently unreliable. Therefore, any unaccounted-for Palestinian is suspect and must be supervised. The rules of discipline, like the law, need the immediate presence of withheld violence. The judicial apparatus, as well as the disciplinary practices, cannot produce the "remote-control" effect that typifies disciplinary apparatuses in a modern state. Therefore, paradoxically, instead of reducing violence (at least withheld violence) by means of nonviolent governing apparatuses, any appeal to the letter of the law and to disciplinary norms in the Occupied Territories requires the intensification of with-held violence, without which the law and disciplinary norms would be ineffective.

Under conditions of political stability, the main contributions of disciplinary apparatuses and ideological representation are to cause subjects to internalize the power relations and accept their position and status within such relations and to shape every individual as a subject of the ruling power. Without the rule of law, when power does not maintain effective disciplining sites or ideological mecha-nisms, the Palestinians in the Occupied Territories cannot be made subjects of the Israeli regime—blatantly unlike Palestinian citizens of Israel. The Palestinian is neither citizen of the regime nor submitted to it as *subjectus*,[25] and when he or she obeys, he or she does so only out of fear, neither willingly nor due to faith or conviction. He or she bows to a ruling power that, as far as the Palestinian is con-cerned, is the embodiment of arbitrariness. For the Palestinian, Israeli rule does not cease also to be an imaginary other who institutes the law. But as already stated, this is law that is impossible to internalize without the violent presence of the rul-ing power and impossible to formulate as an inner edict, even if one is willing to accept the absolute submission it involves, because it is impossible to formulate as a rule what appears ad hoc, sporadically, except the rule of hopeless arbitrariness itself, of violence that might emerge at any moment, anywhere. The subjects in spite of themselves, the noncitizens, who are ruled by means of violent force that suspends the law and that acts in ways that are unmediated do not internalize a thing. As far as they are concerned, power must always be overt, be just what it is on the surface of the area in its grip, in the endless game between the intensifying presence of withheld violence and the showcase instances of eruptive violence.

Without disciplining and ideological mediation, without legitimacy, when law is perceived as an arbitrary force that does not regulate violence, but that rather sanctions it, the ruling apparatus is called upon to empower the presence of with-held violence, to accompany it with eruptive violence (which, in addition to its specific purpose, is always intended to remind the subject what he or she might expect when "overstepping" and exactly what his or her place is in the relations of domination) and shorten the time needed to exert it. Instead of disciplining subjects or educating them, the ruling apparatus injures their bodies and posses-sions. Instead of punishing them in corrective frameworks when they resist (or are perceived by it as resisters, or as intending to resist), the ruling apparatus kills, bombs, and demolishes. The need for rapidity is expressed in a denser deploy-ment of violence in the Occupied Territories and the absolute penetrability of the whole area to Israeli forces, regardless of the geographical or urban route of move-ment. This need has led to the development of new techniques of warfare in built-up areas, including razing and "swarming": The troops avoid moving in familiar routes—familiar, also, to the Palestinians who might ambush them there—and proceed in as straight lines as possible, literally through house walls, equipped with gear and professionals whose purpose is to remove any obstacle in their way to their target. Anyone they encounter on the way—standing in or crossing the straight line that connects them to their target—risks being directly hit, risks his or her life. He or she will be injured for having been in the wrong place at the wrong time.

Still, mention should be made of the fact that most cases of destruction in the Occupied Territories—the razing and blasting of buildings, the digging of trenches, the laying of obstacles, the sealing of wells, everything that Amira Hass has called "weapons of light construction," which have totally changed the Palestinian habitat—all of them are not a result of an uncontrolled eruption of direct violence in response to resistance, but rather an outcome of the calculated use of tools meant to damage buildings, objects, and space without directly affecting humans.[26] The harm to humans is a byproduct of using these tools, but usually not its direct purpose. The rationale behind such harm is demographic: separating, assembling, and compressing populations, which at times includes transferring individuals or relatively small groups in what human rights groups have called "quiet transfer." Such acts are carried out by changing the law and using loopholes in it to make a population lose its residency rights,[27] or through the widespread destruction accompanying warfare and the creation of "buffer zones" close to fences in the Gaza Strip, or through space-shaping "civilian" enterprises such as the construction of the Separation Wall and the paving of bypass roads in the West Bank. The most expansive destruction so far was carried out next to the border at Rafah, where 116 houses were demolished during Operation Rainbow and 1,160 people had to evacuate the area. During this activity, 55 Palestinians were killed. This ratio—55 dead versus 1,160 people who were made refugees and forced to relocate—clearly expresses the relation between the means, violence, and the end, evacuating territory and transferring population.

The Israeli regime acts in the Occupied Territories first and foremost as a demographic ruling apparatus through the systematic separation of Jewish citizens (colonists, soldiers, and visitors from Israel) from Palestinian subjects, through the territorial separation of Jews and Palestinians, and through the separation of the various habitats of the Palestinians, a separation that has been progressively enhanced since the 1990s. Until the outbreak of the first intifada, this apparatus— first presided over by military governors and military administration and later by the misnamed Civil Administration and submitted to army commanders in the territories—consisted of various ruling apparatuses that were in charge of different aspects of the life of the dominated population: the economy and trade, agriculture, health, infrastructures, education, traffic, communications, even welfare. Most government ministries were represented in these apparatuses. Budgets were allocated to deal with the Palestinian population, and various negotiation channels were maintained between residents and their local leadership and functionaries of the ruling apparatus. Care for the Palestinian population was limited, of course. Hardly any steps were taken to develop the Occupied Territories or Palestinian society in any realm, and measures were taken to curb their development in many realms. However, the occupation regime still bore minimal responsibility to administer a normal everyday life and to address particular problems that arose from time to time.

Since the first intifada, this apparatus has been retracted and has gradually deteriorated. The Oslo Accords gave responsibility for the governing systems in Areas A and B to the Palestinian Authority, while the services provided by the occupation regime to residents of Area C were further reduced. As the al-Aqsa intifada broke out, Israel nearly ceased any governing activity whatsoever that meant providing care for the subjugated Palestinian population. Since April 2002, Israel has been systematically destroying Palestinian administrative apparatuses. But the demographic apparatus has not been removed. It has only changed its purpose. It now works to hone and perfect the separation mechanisms and regime of movement that was implemented in the Occupied Territories sporadically since the First Gulf War, at times following the suicide bombings of the 1990s and systematically and continuously since the outbreak of the second intifada, in order to achieve as full as possible control and surveillance over the entire volume of movement of all Palestinians in the Occupied Territories. The regime of movement needs the classification, tracking, counting, and locating supplied by the demographic apparatus, and this demand creates an incessant supply of more and more "demographic" distinctions, some made on the basis of space (geographical location), others on biology (gender, age, state of health), employment, and "security" —a separate category that might, at any given moment, include any one of the other categories or all of them at once.

This is a highly perfected system that combines detailed spatial knowledge and detailed demographic knowledge, movement procedures and practices of classification, arrest, detention, and surveillance, investigation, reconnaissance, informing, incrimination, and more. Nothing in this system can exist without withheld violence, while eruptive violence tends to be used with caution and only up to a limit. Violence, when it erupts, disrupts movement arrangements, makes information gathering cumbersome, mixes up what has been sorted out and sorts out what should be mixed, makes it necessary to count again, to locate, classify, and reclassify. People disappear, while others appear unexpectedly, and at times, the system even causes Jews to mingle with Arabs. In short, from the demographic apparatus's point of view, eruptive violence has a dimension of lost control. All the more important, then, is withheld violence. This measured, precise presence of the security forces—along traffic routes, at checkpoints, in flash patrols, at the entrances of homes, the planned and meticulous combination of computerized soldiers and armed soldiers, of the magnetic card and the rifle, of passage permits and checkpoints that deny movement, of the sweeping blockage of movement throughout an entire region and the filtering of traffic by personal supervision of each and every individual passenger—promises maximal control by applying withheld violence at the lowest price. This is the price measured both in financial terms and (as we will explain) in human lives, both Jewish and Arab. There is an enormous price paid for Israel's primary, ruling resolution to separate citizens and subjects and to maintain in the Occupied Territories a ruling apparatus whereby relations between the two kinds of violence are neither regulated nor foreseen. But under the conditions created by this resolution, the apparatus of withheld violence is meant to maintain Israeli rule at the lowest possible direct price. This primary resolution is not self-evident. It constitutes the rejection of two other possibilities that always loom on the horizon: to withdraw from the territories occupied in 1967 and thus give up control of the local population or to annex the territories and naturalize its Palestinian residents.

VIOLENCE-PREVENTING VIOLENCE

The daily price that withheld violence demands of the Palestinians is exorbitant. As noncitizens, the Palestinians lack the legal shield that enables citizens to negotiate legally and politically the means by which they are ruled. Their access to the Israeli legal system is curbed, and the help it can provide them is negligible. Nor does the Palestinian—as a nonsubject—see himself or herself as a part of some social whole that the ruling power is supposed to represent. The Palestinian is a subject who only may submit or resist and force the ruling apparatus to intensify the presence of withheld violence or respond directly in violent eruptions. The persistence of Palestinian resistance shows an unusual degree of resilience in the face of such violence, which forces the apparatus to deploy its withheld violence ever more broadly and to instigate more frequent eruptions of direct violence. The Palestinians in the West Bank—and until the disengagement, in the Gaza Strip as well—cannot publicly display withheld violence for fear of its means being destroyed by Israel. The violence they direct toward Israelis is nearly always eruptive, for withheld violence has an overt, ongoing presence that is markedly lacking in the violence of the terrorist or guerilla warrior. The terrorist's violence is not associated with withheld violence, except as ever-present in the imagination of Israelis, which turns any Palestinian into a potential terrorist. In circumstances of absolute inferiority, both guerilla actions and terrorism reflect the acknowledgement of weakness and an understanding that other channels of resistance (political, legal, or civil) cannot bring about any change in power relations. Under such circumstances, these two forms of resistance, especially suicide terrorism, provide the ruling apparatus with its principal excuse to intensify its use of violence, both withheld and eruptive.

The truth, however, is that most of the time, the majority of Palestinians are afraid to resist by resorting to withheld violence of their own. Since they also cannot totally give in to the dictates of the ruling apparatus, they try to survive through improvisation and manipulation, looking for ways out, smuggling, calculating the costs of daily activity, deciding every morning anew which path to take, how to dress for the inspection at the checkpoint, which permits to bring along, how to avoid encounters with the forces on the ground and how to address the soldiers. They must not be perceived as threatening, yet they cannot afford to remain without resources for coping with the situation. But this is precisely what happens to them all the time. They are forever suspect, at least as long as they retain their ability to speak back to the ruling power in its own tongue—force—and at times only for taking the liberty of a leveled gaze, and at any moment they might remain empty-handed. For the ruling apparatus, their resistance is not just their actions, but their mere presence, their insistence on staying.

According to the official Israeli conception, all Israeli mechanisms of violence active in the Occupied Territories are meant to fulfill "security needs," namely, preventing direct Palestinian violence against Israeli citizens. Observation of many of the situations in which the two kinds of violence are exerted shows that they were intended to prevent direct or indirect Palestinian violence against the ruling apparatus. Despite the fact that this is not a sovereign regime, and despite the fact that this regime does not operate disciplining venues, the ruling apparatus in the Occupied Territories maintains permanent, ongoing mechanisms of self-preservation, finalizing the form of power relations in the minds of the subjects. [See, for example, the leaflet on page 121.] Official Israeli spokespersons tend to ignore the possibility that the continuous massive exertion of violence, both withheld and eruptive, boosts violent resistance on the other side and that under the existing conditions of rule and in the absence of a tradition of civil disobedience, violent resistance tends to erupt time and again and is no less and sometimes more destructive than what the ruling apparatus successfully prevents. With every terrorist attack, official spokespersons hurry to announce that deterrence is never total, and as such, Israel has no choice but to persist in trying to prevent violent

A **LEAFLET** distributed in the Gaza Strip by the IDF following the abduction of the soldier Gilad Schalit, summer 2006.

إلى سكان قطاع غزة

في الأيام الأخيرة قام جيش الدفاع الإسرائيلي بعمليات ضد منفذي الأعمال الإرهابية ومن ساعدهم في إطلاق الصواريخ وتخزين الذخيرة والعتاد العسكري .

ستستمر هذه العمليات ما دام الجندي جلعاد شليط مخطوفاً وعمليات إطلاق الصواريخ مستمرة باتجاه أراضي دولة إسرائيل.

جيش الدفاع الإسرائيلي لديه أنواع مختلفة من الوسائل القتالية التي لم يستخدمها بعد. لكن في حال استمرار الأعمال الإرهابية سيبحث في استخدام الملائم منها .

تذكروا ان الهدوء يجلب الهدوء وهكذا يمكنكم العيش بحياة كريمة آمنة انتم وعائلاتكم

قيادة جيش الدفاع الإسرائيلي

To Residents of the Gaza Strip

In recent days, Israeli security forces took action against persons who engaged in terrorism and persons who aided them in firing missiles and in storing ammunition and weapons.

This activity will continue so long as Gilad Schalit remains abducted and missile fire at Israel persists.

Israeli security forces have a variety of combat means that have not yet been used. In the event that the acts of terrorism continue, use of the appropriate means will be considered.

Remember that quiet will bring quiet, enabling both you and your family to live your lives in dignity and security.

resistance, and journalists and politicians echo them repeatedly. Violence thus is presented as violence-preventing violence, as violence exerted in order to enable the apparatus to be the last one to exert violence and vice versa. But the latest violent eruption is always the last of an infinite series—another will follow shortly, a new "last one."

The lull between one outburst and another has grown longer since 2005. Most Palestinian violence today is practiced by the relatively small Islamic Jihad organization and by Hamas, and it focuses on Israeli towns and villages near the Gaza Strip. But the dynamic has remained the same. Nearly every eruption of Palestinian violence provokes an outburst of Israeli violence and vice versa. The latest outburst usually creates the conditions for the next eruption, and thus again and again, ad infinitum. Victory will follow the latest blow, but the latest blow contains defeat (it, too, only temporary, of course), which will follow the next eruption of the other side. The real difference, at least as regards violence, is not between victory and defeat, but rather between more and less lethal and destructive showcase violence. By this token, the Palestinians are losing, naturally: 4,274 dead and over 30,000 wounded since the beginning of the intifada and until August 2007, as opposed to 1,024 Israeli dead and about 6,000 wounded.[28]

Is there at least a connection between cause and effect, the means and the end? "Cause" should be understood here as motive: the motive to choose violence as a means. In both cases, the explicit motive explains only a small part of the outcome, and the effect is much greater than the end. In both cases, the decision to continue resorting to violence is not influenced by the extent to which violent means succeed in achieving the ends to which they were used to begin with (destroying terrorist infrastructure; destroying the Zionist entity, or at least scaring the Israelis into leaving the Occupied Territories). In both cases, the choice of violent means seems more affected by the place that the economy of violence takes in the political order of each of the sides and in its political imagination. On the Palestinian side, the issue is the struggle between Fatah, Hamas, and Islamic Jihad, on the one hand (the political order), and the role of violence in the reconstruction of the Palestinian as a subject of sovereign rule resisting the Israeli regime, on the other (the political imagination). On the Israeli side, the issue is choosing to administer the Occupied Territories by means of violence, rather than by other state mechanisms (the political order) and the separation of the territories from "Israel proper" as a form of containing the territories within the Israeli regime (the political imagination). The Palestinians resort to violence because they do not feel they have other effective means of removing the occupier, and their acts of resistance or terrorism express a refusal to make a distinction between the occupier as military force or as a civil force. Most Israeli soldiers and policemen (but not necessarily most colonists) exert violence according to orders given by their commanders and those who authorize them. The instructions change constantly, however, leaving vast room for the judgment of officers and soldiers, who in time have become nearly immune to legal charges, even in cases of deviation from explicit instructions.[29] Violence is always justified by the need to preserve security, but "security" has become a general, abstract term that hides the fact that the ruling apparatus in the Occupied Territories exerts violence because the primary ruling resolution does not leave it any other means of controlling the Palestinian population there. Most of the Israeli public and its political leadership are willing—in the name of security—to accept the reduction of relations with Palestinians to various forms of violence and to live with the vast injuries inflicted upon Palestinian subjects, but also on Israeli citizens—a direct result of this reduction. They accept risking Israeli soldiers as self-evident and prefer to ignore the mental and moral damages that follow military service in the Occupied Territories.

Both parties in this struggle are in each other's grip, conditioning each other, and the reacting force adopts the reasoning of the acting force, even as it attempts to free itself of the deadlock. But the relations between Israeli violence and Palestinian violence are not symmetrical, and not only because of the relations of submission and the obvious difference in armed might. In most cases, the Palestinians have neither the ability nor the means to respond violently to the violence exerted against them, and the violence that they do resort to erupts in places where they recognize openings in the web of withheld violence in which they are caught. This use of violence against Israelis is not the regime they wish to establish or the power by which they wish to be ruled. It is not meant to preserve an existing regime, but rather to free them of its hold. Therefore, it does not necessarily express recognition of the authority of central Palestinian ruling institutions or the authority of any regime whatsoever. On the other hand, when Israeli security forces apply violence, withheld or eruptive, they act on behalf of the state and as a part of it, authorized by it in the name of the law and for the preservation of law and order. In their actions, they assert themselves as subjects of this regime and endow both recognition and legitimacy both to the regime and to its ruling apparatus, to forms of exerting violence as well as to the models of justification that accompany it and the recruitment mechanisms that enable it.

Not all Palestinians resort to violence. The majority still try to act in a civil mode. A few of them still—or again—try to affect Israeli public discourse. Others pursue a legal struggle, and since petitions have been heard regarding the Separation Wall, they have known a few successes—whose significance is limited because the legal procedure takes years, and in the meantime, the ruling apparatus is free to act, and no one reimburses the victims for the damages inflicted upon them all that time. Moreover, many verdicts are not implemented at all, and the cases in which the state is obliged to change "facts established on the ground" are few and far between. They are the exception to the rule that reaffirms the rule and that actually enables it, since in every case where the local action of the ruling apparatus is condemned, the rest of the "facts on the ground" established and sheltered through withheld violence are condoned retroactively by the judiciary.[30] At the same time, as though not to leave any doubt about the futility of civil struggle, the army exerts unprecedented violence—both withheld and eruptive, spectacular—to disperse or altogether to prevent nonviolent demonstrations protesting the construction of the Wall, which have recently become very frequent. The Palestinians who take part in them alongside Israelis and international volunteers insist on developing modes of unarmed civil struggle, but the ruling apparatus seems to insist on preventing this, and every week it displays its force in new ways, using new tools to throw the civilizing arena back into the heart of the economy of violence.

What has happened since February 2005 near the village of Bil'in, where weekly nonviolent protests have been taking place, proves that the economy of violence, feeding on the terrorist attacks and expanding because of them, is similarly maintained without them.[31] To this, one should add the many cases of random shooting at suspects, which has killed about 180 Palestinians—only 97 of them armed—in the time span between the Palestinian declaration of cease-fire and the disengagement from Gaza. The tag "armed" has long become a license to kill—meaning that at the slightest insinuation of possible Palestinian violence, violence-preventing violence is called for. Whether it will indeed emerge and in what form is subject to military considerations. Political considerations, on the rare occasions in which they are taken into account, might delay an eruption of violence or hurry it along, but in any case, they come only after the military need for action has been established. Legal considerations, if they enter into the picture at all, appear mainly in retrospect, when an action needs to be justified that inflicted greater "collateral damage" than expected.

Contrary to the popular opinion that "the merry-go-round of violence" is a direct result of terrorist attacks, Israelis do not resort to violence because they are subject to terrorism, but rather because using violence is a fundamental part of their ruling apparatus in the Occupied Territories, all the more so when they define the area as a war zone. Terrorist attacks and Qassam rockets change the intensity of reprisal, not its basic format: an endless game of withheld and eruptive, spectacular violence that depend on each other and feed off each other and that together compensate for the lack of other functioning ruling apparatuses. The division of labor between the two kinds of violence has no expression in the language of the ruling power, which tends to present its withheld violence as the opposite of eruptive violence, a part of the natural order of things and a tool of domination that is used legitimately in order to supervise and regulate the subjects' lives. The ruling power will always describe its eruptive violence as an unavoidable response to Palestinian violence, whereas its withheld violence will be presented as an unavoidable substitute for "law and order" and as a preventive and defensive measure against the outburst of Palestinian violence.

In fact, the issue at hand is an apparatus of withheld violence and a parallel active apparatus of eruptive violence. Eruptive violence is often exerted independently of the visible forces that display their presence and yet withhold their violence. It emerges out of the blue and vanishes just as arbitrarily. It tends to appear and disappear without any evident rationale. Withheld violence is present, changes its deployment, or becomes invisible according to an explicit rationale that changes incessantly. Some of the rules of this violence may be learned and become familiar in time, while others must always be guessed anew. Civil struggle against withheld violence takes a clear toll: It cannot appeal against the illegality of the ruling apparatus. However, because of the semblance of legality that is still assumed in acts such as land dispossession or road blockage, it is still possible (in principle) to reduce withheld violence by judicial and political means. Eruptive violence, however, has no obvious link to withheld violence and if there are rules that guide it, they remain clandestine, and eruptive violence is thus all the harder to rein in, control, or resist in legal ways.

This economy of violence offers the dominated population countless opportunities to touch upon the threshold of eruptive violence. Thus it realizes the assumption on the basis of which the ruling apparatus functions: Every Palestinian is a possible source of eruptive and unbridled violence (terrorism)—if not right now, then yesterday or tomorrow. If not he himself or herself, then his or her neighbors and relatives. In the perspective of the occupation regime, the Palestinian by his or her mere presence is both an object of violence and an accumulation of withheld violence that is just waiting for the right moment to erupt. But unlike the flagrant presence of withheld violence that the Israeli regime exercises under a lawful façade, withheld violence on the part of the Palestinian is both forbidden and a challenge to such lawfulness and is thus necessarily concealed and requires efforts to be exposed. One needs to threaten, constrict, restrict movement and monitor it, penetrate in order to carry out surveillance, carry out surveillance in order to penetrate, make arrests in order to investigate and investigate in order to make arrests, ruin cultivated farmland (razing for the sake of exposing), impose closures and curfews. Violence-preventing violence produces violence just as much as it reduces violence. It constantly inflicts injuries on bodies, alive and inert, and destroys their common spaces. But it shapes new spaces and establishes new structures. It invents mechanisms and methods, sows anxieties and fears, beliefs and opinions, agents and dangers galore. This violence has a totalizing nature—without it, so we are told, everyone would be vulnerable. For its sake, everyone can be made vulnerable. It does not cease to act. It can hardly stop or accept agreements that declare a ceasefire. A pause in this cycle of violence always means just a longer stay at the pole of withheld violence—no attempt is made to stop the pendulum swinging between the two poles, hiding their simultaneous existence and thwarting every effort to construct alternative ruling apparatuses that should enable the sublimation of violence. In this economy of violence, violence is withheld without going through sublimation and erupts without any relief. The borders of this economy are temporary and fluid. Fencing is its permanent practice,[32] but wherever necessary, it breaks walls and fences. No border is immune to it, and in fact, the entire dominated territory is subjected to its reasoning.

THE SUBSTITUTE

The distinction we have proposed here between eruptive and withheld violence echoes an important distinction formulated (and deconstructed) by Walter Benjamin when he differentiated "lawmaking" violence (through a revolution or coup, for example) and "law-preserving" violence (through police and military forces acting on behalf of the law).[33] However, ours is not congruent with his distinction, but rather crosses it via the concepts of eruptive, suspended, and withheld violence. One might thus say that our formulation is already contained in Benjamin's: Lawmaking violence is always joined by vast eruptions of force acting directly upon bodies, whereas in law-preserving violence, force is both suspended and present in the form of the policeman or soldier, the billy club or the rifle, and such suspended presence is a necessary condition for the enforcement of law and the maintenance of "the rule of law" in all senses of this phrase. This is all true, but not sufficient. At any moment, violence constructing law anew must *also* be preserved as *withheld* violence, lest it dissipate before establishing the new political order. Law-preserving violence, on the other hand, always contains traces of eruptive violence, too, as Benjamin himself pointed out when discussing the police.[34]

The duality inherent in both eruptive and suspended violence is displayed in the acts of the police that invariably both declare the law and participate in its reconstruction through the acts intended to preserve it, also preserving the law through the acts intended to construct it. However, this duality is precisely what cannot be attributed to withheld violence in the Occupied Territories. While the army or police violence to which Benjamin refers both constructs the law and preserves it, withheld violence, which we locate in the ruling apparatus, does not construct the law, nor does it preserve it. It is not a tool of the law at all. On the contrary, the law is a tool in the hands of withheld violence. It uses the law to give legal guise—either in advance or in retrospect—to orders and edicts that give it shelter and sanction and that legitimize it in cases where legality is questionable. The situations in which we observe withheld violence are those in which the law is recruited to sanction an area not originally under its jurisdiction, where orders and edicts of one of the military authorities replace the law. Force is exerted under the authority vested in the military commander, and his actions are—in principle— under legal scrutiny, but that is precisely all that is left of legality. The authority vested in the ruling power to damage, destroy, and kill is vast, and its victims have almost no way of knowing the rules guiding the actions that harms them or how possibly to defend themselves against it. The law—as a differentiated sphere of texts and practices, the rules of which can be known a priori and whose players all enjoy essentially equal access to its resources and negotiating positions within it— this law is no longer applicable. It is suspended without any proper warning (therefore, one cannot speak of the violence involved as law-preserving), and no other law is constructed (therefore one cannot speak of it as law-instating violence), except for the ad hoc orders that contain the entire judicial and enforcement systems *in potentiam,* from the authority to arrest all the way through the authority to execute, barring any actual juridical procedure itself.

The violent struggle under such conditions is not for instating alternative laws or preserving an existing legal system, but rather *to preserve the suspension* of the realm of right as described here and the conditions under which such a suspension will persist within the law itself. The meaning of "suspending" the realm of right here is twofold—the preservation of territory from which the law has been withdrawn, and the preservation of the territory's link with the law, its definition as a territory where the law has not yet been altogether retracted and where it exists through suspension. We are referring to the preservation of occupied territory as an emergency zone, an area that has been made exceptional and abandoned, but is constantly referred to by law as what has been taken out of the reach of the law: an abandoned no-man's land.

We distinguish here between deferment (*hashhaya* in Hebrew) and suspension (*hash'aya*). Deferment indicates a temporary absence of what may or might appear, or be realized, or vanish at any moment. In the meantime, its appearance or disappearance is deferred. Suspension indicates the declaration by a ruling or bureaucratic authority of the temporary inapplicability or in validity of a rule or a law, which themselves are not altogether canceled. Under "normal" conditions of rule by a lawful regime, when the need arises to exercise violence in order to preserve both the regime and the law, what is suspended, but not deferred, is "law itself" (or the legislator's intention, or the constitution). Under normal conditions, every juridical clarification is based on the deferred display of "law itself," whose validity in a certain singular case is yet to be clarified. Any juridical ruling is a temporary apparition of the law, embodied in the ruled case, but this embodiment is temporary until the next court ruling, until the next controversy or the next case that will demand that the ruling be delayed and that the interpretation that had previously appeared clear and final be suspended. The deferred law and suspended interpretation are part and parcel of a properly functioning judicial system. They hover above bustling legal-interpretative activity like a seductive ghost, an unfixed signified over whose representation numerous signifiers are busy competing. Law-preserving violence—both withheld and eruptive—has to keep this signified hovering in order to maintain an open space for discussing the question "What does the law say?" But when civil law is suspended in favor of an elaborate system of decrees, procedures and ad hoc orders, the deferment of eruptive violence is a substitute for the role played by deferring the presence of the law itself in a proper ruling and judicial system.

Israeli law has crept into the Occupied Palestinian Territories through several channels: enforcement of Israeli law in the areas annexed to Jerusalem, but in a way that left the Palestinian residents of Jerusalem with the status of "permanent residents,"[35] a hybrid status between that of subjects and citizens; a gradual—by now almost full—application of the law to all Jewish colonies in the territories;[36] the authorization of the military commander in the territories (and some of his subordinates), by force of emergency regulations, to issue regulations and edicts that regulate the everyday lives of Palestinians there;[37] subjecting such authority to the juridical criticism of the High Court of Justice;[38] and finally, disarming such criticism by a long series of rulings in which the court avoids interfering in the state's considerations (such as on the issue of targeted killings) or sanctions them retroactively (such as the ruling to construct the Separation Wall beyond the Green Line). It would seem that the fact that the Knesset itself had applied the emergency regulations to the territories and is renewing their application every year, as well as the fact that the military commander's decisions are subject to criticism of the High Court of Justice, leave the Occupied Territories and their inhabitants within the jurisdiction of Israeli law. But in fact, this was also the way both to leave the Palestinians within the confines of the Israeli judicial system while ignoring their protection by international law and to keep them outside that jurisdiction, ignoring Israel's responsibilities as the actual sovereign in the Occupied Territories.[39]

Both establishing rules and suspending them are validated by the emergency regulations that are supposed to regulate an exceptional situation, but have long since become a permanent tool of control in a *permanent* state of emergency. In fact there is no permanent distinction between the rule and the exception to the rule, for the rule that applies to Palestinians in a certain matter at a certain place is itself the exception to the rule that applies to Israeli citizens in the Occupied Territories or to Palestinian residents in other matters in other places. Furthermore, the higher the level of violence—systematically, since the outbreak of the second intifada—the more decentralized is the authority to establish rules and suspend them, to make exceptions to the rule, or to act regardless of any rules under rapidly changing circumstances. Not just at any checkpoint, and not even in any encounter between the security forces and Palestinian subjects, but wherever such encounters are to be anticipated—namely, at any point where the security forces are or will be active—the local military commander and any of his subordinates have the authority to exercise their own judgment and break previous rules—under the circumstances.

With such conditions, when civil law is suspended and the subjects are defined as noncitizens, the escalation of withheld violence does not preserve the law, but rather replaces it. More precisely, withheld violence enables the system of rules and regulations, exceptions and ad hoc rulings, to replace the suspended judicial system while sporting a semblance of legality as well as while gaining sanction from time to time on behalf of the very same judicial system that has been suspended. Within that system, the differences between a regulation and a momentarily issued order and between the latter and an order on the ground have been almost completely erased. Eventually, the presence of withheld violence—the soldier at the checkpoint, the policeman at the inspection post, the troops securing the bulldozer—establishes the rule: where traffic stops, who is permitted to proceed, what is to be demolished. This rule has already been disconnected from the judicial system and lacks any legal rationale. It is indeed dependent on some haphazard accumulation of authorizations, partially known edicts, and regulations that are revised time and again "to suit operational circumstances."

Essentially, withheld violence can turn into an eruption of violence directed at bodies at any moment, but must not be considered in terms of unfulfilled potential. The potential of withheld violence is fulfilled in its noneruption at least as much as in its eruption, and in fact, the institutionalization of such violence marks a systematic separation of suspension and eruption. Usually, the people whose presence embodies withheld violence are not particularly adept at using the weapons they wield, and they make fairly rare use of them. One must not confuse the mentality and practices of the checkpoint with those of killing. If something goes wrong, they will summon others more skilled than themselves. Naturally, there are exceptions; soldiers at a checkpoint, like policemen on patrol, do occasionally exercise direct force unprovoked. But such exceptions, however frequent,[40] are usually the result of overexertion in a lawless zone and of regarding lives as already abandoned. They have no systemic rationale and are sometimes simply perceived as a sign of a failure of the control system, indication that the apparatus is overburdened.

Essentially, withheld violence can be rationalized to a certain extent and might become the object of civil negotiation over "humanitarianizing" the regime of movement by placing officers in charge of humanitarian matters and introducing humanitarian training for checkpoint operators.[41] One might always try to teach the armed forces to speak politely, respect others, take the trouble not to violate rights unnecessarily, avoid superfluous humiliation, and follow instructions as long as they are in force. The ruling power even expects the subjects to appreciate the protection they receive from these armed troops, for everyone knows that with their conduct—be it more or less rational, more or less polite—they are a buffer between the bare bodies of the subjects and the thing itself.

THE PERMANENT SOLUTIONS

The thing itself, whose nonpresence must be enabled and ensured—and if that is impossible, then its appearance should be mellowed or diluted—the thing itself is not the law, but an emergence of a different order. Violence in the Occupied Territories does not uphold the law, nor does it enable its nonpresence. Violence— both withheld and eruptive, in their unique interplay, with their typical division of labor—does not relate to the (suspended) law. The thing itself that violence both defers and suspends, this different order, may consist of an emergence of total lawlessness, of sweeping violence that threatens to destroy everything, or alternately, in the return of an entirely different law, the law that abolishes the state of occupation and makes the state of emergency obsolete. We would like to name this other thing "the permanent solution." The permanent solution is what continues to hover, ghostlike, over the entire economy of violence, just as law itself hovers over withheld violence in a normal civil regime. What is suspended is not only the realm of right, but also the declaration of total war—or, alternately, the total abolition of the occupation. Every local act of withheld violence, every act of control by means of suspension, draws its power from the ongoing suspension of the permanent solution. The permanent solution is a singular point that is composed of two opposite virtual states that might essentially develop equally in each of these opposite directions, and it is equally wary of both: annexation, naturalization of the Palestinian residents, and full implementation of the rule of law, on the one hand, and total war, on the other. These are two potential "final" states of the ruling apparatus that constructs ruling relations and interferes with them by suspending/deferring their presence and "presencing" their suspension/deferment.

The occupation, essentially a provisionary state, has become a permanent ruling structure, an entire system of power and a regime that already has its own self-preserving principle, the urge to remain just what it is: an Israeli occupation regime in the Palestinian Territories. So-called "temporariness" lends this structure its legitimacy, at least in the eyes of most Israelis, as well as those of most Americans, because it is utterly impossible to reach agreement—neither Israeli nor, of course, Palestinian or international—about either one of the two contradictory states that might replace it. The occupation protects the Israelis—but also the Palestinians—from something worse: a final regulation through war that would include Nakba-like ethnic cleansing and a final termination of the Palestinian national struggle or a final settlement through Israel's annexation of land and making the Palestinians its citizens.

The sophisticated use of withheld violence does have a restraining effect, but this restraint must be understood here in two opposing senses: as the restraining not just of Palestinian terrorism, but also of the Israeli power of destruction, not just as replacing the law, but also as preserving a "lawful" situation. The massive presence of withheld violence everywhere allows the suspension of an outburst of much more widespread military violence and the suspension of declared, total war. It enables the ruling apparatus to function lawlessly, without any judicial form, with no education or disciplining, but also *without war*. Such a war, were it to break out under the present circumstances, with the Palestinians lacking any kind of military force, would mean either their expulsion or their annihilation. It would lead to one or another form of "permanent solution" of the conflict, for the territories are already occupied, and there is no enemy regime to be defeated. But the Palestinians are not being annihilated, just as they are not being assimilated. They are neither eradicated nor made citizens. The deferment of full-fledged annexation is the flip side of suspension. Annexation would formally change the Israeli regime and by turning 3.5 million non-Jewish subjects into citizens, would force this regime to give up its proclaimed "Jewish" identity and perhaps recover its proclaimed "democratic" identity. Withheld violence replaces the law, but also maintains the constitutional framework that enables withdrawal of the law. And who provides for the Palestinians? They remain temporary humans who are a part of the state of Israel as its noncitizens, submitted to its military authority, nonsubjects on the threshold of both law and catastrophe, subjects and patients of a ruling apparatus, abandoned with neither care nor supervision.

The occupation was a result of a brief war between states, but the Golan was annexed and cleansed of its Syrian residents, and Israel withdrew from the Sinai Peninsula after the peace agreement with Egypt. Hence, the term "occupation" has applied only to the West Bank and the Gaza Strip. The all-out struggle against their Palestinian residents was consolidated into a total military campaign only after the Camp David peace talks of the summer of 2000 failed and the second intifada broke out, and even then, it was not war. Until the 1982 War in Lebanon, Israel managed to neutralize any political organizing and uprising in the Occupied Territories, as well as the influence of Palestinian national organizing outside the territories upon life within them. In 1982, however, on Lebanese ground, Israel fought a total war against the Palestinian national movement, explicitly intending to annihilate it.[42] This war included a massive ground invasion, bombing heavily populated areas with aircraft and artillery, and a lengthy siege of Beirut, capital of a sovereign state. In this war, thousands of Palestinians and Lebanese citizens were killed, the civil and economic fabric of life in southern Lebanon was seriously damaged, and leaders of the Palestinian national movement and its official bodies were forced to leave Lebanon and settle for exile in Tunisia. James Ron distinguishes between administering a population of noncitizens in a "ghetto" and reckless war against a "frontier" population, and he identifies the Lebanese arena as Israel's frontier since the 1980s. But Ron does not stress the main issue in the context of the occupation: the 1982 War in Lebanon was meant to enable Israel to continue administering what he calls a Palestinian ghetto in the Occupied Territories. The war against Palestinians in Lebanon was meant—precisely like withheld violence in the territories—to replace war in the territories and to enable further control of the Palestinians there without naturalizing them, neither expelling nor annihilating them.

In the Occupied Territories, warfare has remained tentative. For many years now, the Israeli struggle against Palestinians living in the territories has been an all-out struggle—not just the takeover of a regime or land, annexation or dispossession, but a total change in the overall fabric of life of the Palestinians. This struggle has caused a transformation in Palestinian space and a drastic narrowing of Palestinians' freedom of movement within it by turning Palestinian territory into a mosaic of enclaves and compressing the population inside them. It has taken over the means of production and has interfered with the relations of production while denying access to various resources, systematically dismantling social institutions, and eroding the authority of others. But all-out struggle is not total war, in spite of the wide use of armed forces and various means of warfare and in spite of the various "operations" and, from time to time, the massive mobilization of troops. This struggle has never been conducted as a real war between two armies or an army and a fighting population. At least not in the Occupied Territories.

Such an all-out struggle against an indigenous population is a familiar characteristic of colonization processes in different parts of the world, no less than the pendulum of relations between withheld and eruptive violence in which this struggle takes place. Under typical colonial European modes of control from the sixteenth until the late nineteenth centuries, all-out struggle did occasionally turn into total war: across North America and Australia, in South Africa, and throughout the Soviet Empire, entire regions were cleansed of their indigenous populations. "Natives" were crowded into reservations, their social frameworks shattered, their social strata collapsed, their family dynasties terminated, their cultures turned into laboratories for anthropologists and into a collection of folklore objects for tradesmen and tourists. The geopolitical conditions under which Israeli rule has been maintained in the Occupied Palestinian Territories since the late twentieth century, as well as the nature of Jewish Israeli society's recruitment into its colonization project (a recruitment often tormented, self-righteous, and full of contradictions), place enormous obstacles against any attempt to conduct the all-out struggle against the Palestinians in the Territories as a total war. In 1982, the first war in Lebanon could—just barely—be presented as a survival struggle in a way that never really gained widespread public legitimacy, because the PLO was presented as a hostile army posing a threat to the actual existence of the state, and a distinction was made (verbally, not necessarily on the battlefield) between the Palestinian national movement and the Palestinian population. In the Occupied Territories, such separation is impossible, or has been at least since the first intifada. Therefore, the struggle has to be an all-out one, but cannot—for the time being—be conducted as a war.

But this is not sufficient to remove the total war option completely. Total war hovers as a permanent option over any local confrontation and has turned into a routine issue in the discourse over necessary responses to Palestinian aggression in the Gaza Strip. Since preparations began for the "disengagement," Israel's spokespeople have never ceased their threats of total war if the Qassam rocket launchings resume or intensify.[43] These indeed have resumed and intensified, and have been followed by Israeli operations to eliminate Palestinian resistance. The threat of total war hovers anew over every such operation ("reoccupation" of the Gaza Strip in order to "drain the swamp," or "purge the area of terrorist nests"). There are plenty of examples. The military operations are often perceived and presented as preparatory actions for far more sweeping campaigns, still held back as contingency plans. An operation lasting several hours might eventually go on for weeks or months. At any moment, the number of detainees, the expelled, or the dead might double or triple. Instead of demolishing a row of houses in the heart of a city, the whole city could be ruined. Instead of hundreds of dunams of farm land, thousands could be razed. But in the meantime, there are always political, moral, even military reasons for the decision not to extend the operation, in spite of the temptation to do so, reasons to postpone its second or third phase for the time being, to withdraw before the announced date and still assure us that "all our objectives were achieved." Total war and the utter disaster it would wreak are always kept as a distant threat, whereas the line between the reckless phantasm of violence and restrained violence actually exerted is drawn more flexibly than ever. The threshold of violence that the Israeli public conceives of as unbearable and unjustifiable is modified again and again according to operational circumstances, circumstances in which Palestinian terrorism plays an important role, but not a decisive one. As a result, more people are willing to comply and live with deeds that were previously regarded "inconceivable."

POSTPONING ANNEXATION

In order to understand this point, we should reiterate the regime's primary decision. In every modern state, this is a dual decision, both sovereign-juridical and demographic, that combines the legal status of various population groups and the regime's treatment of the lives of its subjects, respectively. The primary decision is the separation of citizen and noncitizen subject. The second decision is the choice between care for life and abandonment of life. Every such decision splits into further decisions between groups of citizens who are more or less defective in their citizenship and various types of care for life and abandonment of life.[44] The citizen is a participant in the political system. He or she has access to power and to the arenas where the struggle of seizing and shaping it takes place. He or she has "elbow room" for negotiating with the ruling power. The control that this power has over the citizen is mediated and limited by the law. Noncitizen subjects do not take part in the ruling power. They cannot legitimately struggle to seize it, have almost no access to it, their freedom to negotiate with the regime is most limited, and they are directly exposed to the control of armed forces, military and otherwise, that is exercised every so often when the law is suspended or entirely removed. Usually they are denied all possibility of organizing in alternative political modes for participation in the centralist game of the ruling power. Naturally, not all subjects are equally dispossessed and distanced from the ruling power (just as not all citizens have equal access to it), but even those who are totally dispossessed are still persons to whom the state apparatuses are not indifferent, working to control and administer their lives. The decision to abandon life and retract modes of life care that characterize the modern state might be directed toward (defective) citizens just as much as toward noncitizen subjects.

The Israeli reaction to the al-Aqsa intifada was the exacerbation of a process that had already begun during the period of the Oslo Accords: turning the state of emergency into a permanent condition, reducing the number of ruling apparatuses in charge of the lives of its subjects and (as a matter of security) diminishing their existence to the mere potential for terrorist activity that they embody, on the one hand, and to their mere survival (a matter of humanitarian concern), on the other. Until the outbreak of the second intifada, the Palestinian's political existence, as perceived by the ruling apparatus, was reduced to his or her status as a subject in the literal meaning of the term: he or she who is subjected or should be subjected to the ruling power. This reduction process has been ongoing and has intensified since the beginning of the second intifada, and it peaked during the "disengagement" from the Gaza Strip. The Palestinian ceased to be he or she who is subjected to power. His or her existence was reduced to that of a moving body that interests the ruling power in two ways only: as a humanitarian case, because of anxiety over the possible consequences (in Israel and abroad) of their (massive) death in a "humanitarian crisis," which forces the ruling power to let others—nongovernmental and international organizations—provide the minimum conditions to keep the Palestinian alive, and as a suspect, a nuisance, a disturbance, or threat, someone who is placed as the recipient of withheld or eruptive violence. In any other sense, in the eyes of the ruling power, the Palestinian's life world has turned into a no-man's land. The Palestinian is not a subject, but rather an abandoned individual. The ruling apparatus treats the Palestinian with double irresponsibility. It abandons the Palestinian and shirks its responsibility for his or her condition, and it also treats the Palestinian irresponsibly when it shows interest in him or her as a suspect or even just as someone seen around suspects. This lack of responsibility, this act of abandonment, stems not from neglect, negligence, or failure. It is inherent, systematic irresponsibility that brings to perfection the separation between citizens and noncitizens, and between noncitizens ruled as subjects and those ruled precisely by being abandoned, ruled according to the ways and means of their abandonment.

The abandoning of Palestinians takes place between two death threats—the individual death of the suicide bomber and mass death resulting from a humanitarian disaster. The former threat is a pretext for containing the abandoned Palestinians within a ruling and surveillance apparatus more rigorous than ever before, while the latter threat is an excuse for making the area in which the abandoned Palestinians are enclosed accessible to welfare organizations the world over for active participation in the globalization of the conflict in general and for administering Palestinian life in particular. Although the Oslo Accords passed part of the responsibility for the administering of Palestinian life over to the Palestinian

Authority, Israeli reaction to the al-Aqsa intifada shattered the ability to function of that administration and placed the main responsibility for running Palestinian life on welfare bodies, nongovernmental organizations, UN agencies, and local charities, both civil-secular and religious. The ruling apparatus takes the liberty to deter and even sabotage the activity of these groups whenever it spots a threat to security, familiarly a sweeping consideration, while explicitly encouraging their activity whenever it fears an approaching humanitarian crisis. The Palestinians, especially those living in the Gaza Strip, constantly remain "on the verge of a humanitarian catastrophe."[45]

The catastrophe is avoided for the same reasons that war is deferred, perhaps, but why are the Palestinians allowed to remain on the verge of catastrophe? Surely not for the same reasons that they are made to remain noncitizens. Denial of citizenship does not necessitate abandonment to disaster conditions, and as we have seen, for a long time, the occupation regime did treat Palestinians as subjects whose existence must be facilitated no less than their lives administered.[46] The first intifada, no less than a popular Palestinian uprising against the occupation, marked the emergence of a political space whose existence Israel had not previously allowed. In the Oslo Accords, Israel recognized this space and enabled its institutionalization. Thus it destroyed, in fact, though not officially, the option that had been left open in the first twenty years of the occupation: to naturalize the Palestinians and assimilate them into Israel's political sphere. Abandoning the Palestinians to disaster conditions, especially in the Gaza Strip, is a consequence not of the decision to deny them citizenship, but of the decision not to wage total war against them. Since the outbreak of the al-Aqsa intifada, creating disaster conditions has become a form of struggle with and control of the Palestinian population.

NOTES

This chapter is an excerpt from the third part of *This Regime Which Is Not One: Occupation and Democracy between the Sea and the River* (Tel Aviv, Resling 2008) (in Hebrew). Translation by Tal Haran. We would like to thank Michal Givoni, Miki Kratsman, Neve Gordon, Sari Hanafi, Ariel Handel, Udi Edelman, and Liron Mor for helpful comments and information.

1   Until the outbreak of the first intifada, Israel allowed Palestinian workers entry into "Israel proper," but after working hours, it drew the lines of separation shut again, with very few exceptions.

2   See Azmi Bishara, "On the Intifada, Sharon's Aims, 48 Palestinians and NDA/Tajamu' Strategy," *Between the Lines* 3, nos. 23–24 (2003): pp. 3–16.

3   Jeff Halper, "Matrix of Control," *Middle East Report* 216 (Fall 2000).

4   Haggai Golan and Shaul Sahy (eds.), *Low-Intensity Conflict* (Tel Aviv: Maaracot—Ministry of Defense, Israel, 2004) (in Hebrew).

5   This regime is part of the Israeli regime, which also includes a more or less democratic system of government in "Israel proper," albeit a distorted one, hampered by the structural separation of and discrimination against Palestinians and other non-Jewish citizens. The present chapter is part of a larger argument about the nature of the Israeli regime, a regime that contains both democracy and occupation, and precisely for this reason "is not one." Ariella Azoulay and Adi Ophir, *This Regime Which Is Not One*.

6   Michel Foucault, "The Subject and Power," in *Power: The Essential Works of Foucault, 1954–1984*, vol. 3, ed. James D. Faubion, trans. Robert Hurley (New York: The New Press, 2000), 340. Vis-à-vis a long tradition of political thought, Foucault wishes to emphasize nonviolent means of control and administration and thus change the understanding of ruling power itself. The concealment of violence, justified in the historical and theoretical context of Foucault's writing, is unjustified in the present context.

7   Walter Benjamin, "Critique of Violence," trans. Edmund Jephcott, in *Selected Writings, Volume 1, 1913–1926*, ed. Marcus Bullock and Michael W. Jennings (Cambridge, MA: Harvard University Press, 1996), p. 236.

8   See also Michael Mann's classification of four sources of social power: ideological, economic, political, and military. Michael Mann, *The Sources of Social Power, Vol. 1: A History of Power from the Beginning to A.D. 1760* (Cambridge: Cambridge University Press, 1986), pp. 22–28.

9   On the dialectic between potential force and its eruption, see the classic discussion in Louis Marin, *The Portrait of the King*, trans. Martha M. Houle (Minneapolis: University of Minnesota Press, 1987).

10   We assume here Agamben's analysis of "potentiality." See, for example, Giorgio Agamben, *Homo Sacer: Sovereign Power and Bare Life*, trans. Daniel Heller-Roazen (Stanford, CA: Stanford University Press, 1998), part 1, chap. 3, and *Potentialities: Collected Essays in Philosophy*, ed. and trans. Daniel Heller-Roazen (Stanford, CA: Stanford University Press, 1999), chap. 11.

11   See Neve Gordon, "From Colonization to Separation: Exploring the Structure of Israel's Occupation," in this volume. For data provided by B'Tselem on the first intifada, see http://www.btselem.org/english/Statistics/First_Intifada_Tables.asp (last accessed September 16, 2008). For data on the second intifada, see http://www.btselem.org/english/statistics/casualties.asp (last accessed September 16, 2008). For an army-related source, see http://www.terrorism-info.org.il/site/home/default.asp (last accessed September 16, 2008).

12   According to statistics provided by several Israeli and international organizations, Israeli deaths from suicide attacks have steadily decreased: from 230 in 2002 to 139 in 2003, 29 in 2005, 15 in 2006, and 3 in 2007.

13   See the archive of B'Tselem's reports on the Gaza Strip beginning in August 2005 at http://www.btselem.org/english/ota/index.asp?WebbTopicNumber=30&image.x=44&image.y=14 (last accessed October 24 2008).

14   See, for example, Gideon Levi, *The Twilight Zone: Life and Death under Israeli Occupation* (Tel Aviv: Babel, 2004) (in Hebrew); Rema Hammami, "On the Importance of Thugs: The Moral Economy of a Checkpoint," *Middle East Report* 231 (Summer 2004). On water shortages, see Yehezke Lein, "Disputed Waters: Israel's Responsibility for the Water Shortage in the Occupied Territories," B'Tselem report, 1998, available on-line at http://www.btselem.org/english/Publications/Summaries/199809_Disputed_Waters.asp (last accessed September 16,

2008). On conditions at the checkpoint, see the nine-minute film *Qalandiya Report* by Tamar Goldschmidt, available on-line at http://www.mahsanmilim.com/qalandiyareportHE.htm (last accessed September 16, 2008).

15   Michel Foucault, *Society Must Be Defended: Lectures at the Collège de France, 1975–76,* ed. Mauro Bertani, Alessandro Fontana, and François Ewald, trans. David Macey (New York: Picador, 2003), and *Security, Territory, Population: Lectures at the Collège de France, 1977–78,* ed. Michel Senellart, trans. Graham Burchell (New York: Palgrave Macmillan, 2007).

16   Louis Althusser, *Lenin and Philosophy and Other Essays,* trans. Ben Brewster (London: New Left Review, 1971). We question the position of Foucault, who rejected Althusser's concept of ideology, and propose to present Foucault's concept of *assujetissement*—shaping the individual as subject—as a critical interpretation and refinement of Althusser's concept of ideology.

17   In every respect connected with the responsibility for administering the life of Palestinians, Israel acts as though the Palestinian Authority were a foreign sovereign government. But whenever Palestinian governance matters touch upon Israeli presence in the Occupied Territories outside of Area A or upon any other issue defined as an Israeli interest, the control apparatus persists in its conduct as a sovereign. For its part, the Palestinian Authority, since the Oslo Accords, has established ruling institutions and supposedly maintains three functioning ones (a legislature, a judiciary, and an executive) under sovereign rule. However, in countless matters of legislation and government, customs, import and export, infrastructure, construction, industrialization, and, of course, enforcement mechanisms, its hands are tied. Amal Jamal, *The Palestinian National Movement: Politics of Contention, 1967–2005* (Bloomington: Indiana University Press, 2005). Since the outbreak of the al-Aqsa intifada, most of these matters are not addressed when the Palestinian Authority and Israeli rule come in contact. Encounters are mostly devoted to "security issues," with Israel repeatedly demanding of the Palestinian Authority to play the role designated it by the Oslo Accords: to provide security services. Neve Gordon, *Israel's Occupation—Sovereignty, Discipline, and Control* (Berkeley: University of California Press, 2008). In any case, whether or not the Palestinian Authority has any role mediating between the control apparatus and the Palestinian subjects, this control is not implemented through legislation or law enforcement.

18   A case in point is the army's not opening Shuhada Street in Hebron in spite of an explicit court order to do so. See a joint report by B'Tselem and the Association for Civil Rights in Israel, May 2007, at http://www.btselem.org/english/Publications/Summaries/200705_Hebron.asp (last accessed October 24, 2008). Another is the army's shirking its instruction to dismantle a 41-kilometer-long low concrete wall built along a main road in the South Hebron hills. Amos Harel, *Ha'aretz,* July 24, 2007.

19   See Orna Ben-Naftali, Aeyal M. Gross, and Keren Michaeli, "The Illegality of the Occupation Regime: The Fabric of Law in the Occupied Palestinian Territory," in this volume.

20   David Kretzmer, *The Occupation of Justice: The Supreme Court of Israel and the Occupied Territories* (Albany: State University of New York Press, 2002); Aeyal M. Gross, "The Construction of a Wall between The Hague and Jerusalem: The Enforcement and Limits of Humanitarian Law and the Structure of Occupation," *Leiden Journal of International Law* 19, no. 2 (2006): pp. 393–440, and "Human Proportions: Are Human Rights the Emperor's New Clothes of the International Law of Occupation?" *The European Journal of International Law* 18 no. 1 (2007): pp. 1–35.

21   Hannah Arendt, *The Origins of Totalitarianism* (New York: Harcourt Brace & Company 1979), part 2, pp. 243–50.

22 For example, the army regulations regarding the opening times of the farming gates in the Separation Wall are breached on a regular basis. B'Tselem report "Not All It Seems: Preventing Palestinians Access to Their Lands West of the Separation Barrier in the Tulkarm-Qalqiliya Area," available on-line at http://www.btselem.org/Download/2004_Qalqiliya_Tulkarm_Barrier_Eng.pdf (last accessed September 16, 2008).

23 We do not subscribe to Agamben's position in *Homo Sacer* on suspension of the law and abandonment of life per se, but suggest a more reserved formulation. See Agamben, *Homo Sacer*, pp. 83–85.

24 On prisons as the hothouse of the Palestinian uprising, see Lisa Hajaar, *Courting Conflict: The Israeli Military Court System in the West Bank and Gaza* (Berkeley: University of California Press, 2005), pp. 207–10.

25 See Étienne Balibar, "Citizen Subject," in *Who Comes after the Subject,* ed. Eduardo Cadava, Peter Connor, and Jean-Luc Nancy (New York: Routeldge, 1991), pp. 33–57, esp. 40–44.

26 Amira Hass, personal conversation, Van Leer Jerusalem Institute, April 2004.

27 Eyal Weizman, *Hollow Land: Israel's Architecture of Occupation* (London: Verson, 2007), chap. 7.

28 See B'Tselem's data on-line at http://www.btselem.org/english/statistics/casualties.asp (last accessed September 16, 2008). Since the ratio of the two populations is about 1:2, the real ratio of fatalities is not 4:1 but rather 8:1. This is an average ratio for the seven years from 2000 to 2007. In the last three years the ratio of death has changed quite significantly and is now about 10:1 (or 20:1 in relative terms).

29 This majority does not include small groups of colonists who violently assault Palestinians living and working next to their colonies. They regularly refute the Israeli ruling power's assumed monopoly on violence in the Occupied Territories. This phenomenon is so widespread that one cannot clearly tell whether it stems from helplessness on the part of law-enforcement authorities or from an institutionalized division of labor among the security forces and colonists' would-be militias. James Ron wrote of such division of labor in *Frontiers and Ghettos: State Violence in Serbia and Israel* (Berkeley: University of California Press, 2003), chap. 8.

30 Talia Sasson has elaborated on this in her report to Israel's Prime Minister Ariel Sharon on March 8, 2005. For the full report in Hebrew, see http://www.pmo.gov.il/NR/rdonlyres/0A0FBE3C-C741-46A6-8CB5-F6CDC042465D/0/sason2.pdf (last accessed October 2008). For an English summary see Talia Sasson, *Summary of the Opinion concerning Unauthorized Outposts* (March 2005), available on-line at http://www.mfa.gov.il/MFA/Government/Law/Legal+Issues+and+Rulings/Summary+of+Opinion+Concerning+Unauthorized+Outposts+-+Talya+Sason+Adv.htm (last accessed July 17, 2008).

31 For more on Bil'in, see Gadi Algazi, "Matrix in Bil'in: Colonial Capitalism in the Occupied Territories," in this volume.

32 Ronen Shamir, "Without Borders? Notes on Globalization as a Mobility Regime," *Sociological Theory* 23, no. 2 (2005): pp. 197–217; Yael Padan and Shuli Hartman, *Fences, Walls, and Environmental Justice* (Bimkom — Planners for Planning Rights, 2006) (in Hebrew), available on-line at http://www.bimkom.org/dynContent/articles/walls,%20fences,%20justice.pdf (last accessed September 17, 2008).

33 Benjamin, "Critique of Violence," p. 243.

34 The power of the police "is formless, like its nowhere-tangible, all-pervasive, ghostly presence in the life of civilized states." *Ibid.*

35 As soon as these permanent residents leave Jerusalem, this permanence becomes temporary. Stein, *The Quiet Deportation.*

36 Amnon Rubinstein, "The Changing Status of the "Territories" (West Bank and Gaza): From Escrow to Legal Mongrel," Tel Aviv University Studies in Law 8 (1988), pp. 68–67; Menachem Hofnung, Democracy, Law, and National Security in Israel (Aldershot, UK: Dartmouth, 1996), pp. 229–37.

37 Shlomo Gazit, *Trapped Fools: Thirty Years of Israeli Policy in the Territories* (London: F. Cass, 2003); Hajaar, *Courting Conflict,* p. 253.

38 The decision to grant residents of the Occupied Territories the right to petition the High Court of Justice was made shortly after their occupation. Kretzmer, *The Occupation of Justice,* p. 20.

39 Meron Benvenisti, *The Sling and the Club* (Jerusalem: Keter, 1988) (in Hebrew), p. 77.

40 Yael Stein, "Standard Routine: Beatings and Abuse of Palestinians by Israeli Security Forces during The al-Aqsa *Intifada,*" B'Tselem Report, May 2001, available on-line at http://www.btselem.org/Download/200105_Standard_Routine_Eng.doc (last accessed October 2008).

41 Hagar Kotef and Merav Amir, "(En)Gendering Checkpoints: Checkpoint Watch and the Repercussions of Intervention," *Signs: Journal of Women in Culture and Society* 32, no. 4 (2007): pp. 973–96; Daniella Mansbach, "Protest on the Border: The Power of Duality in the Protest Practices of Machsom Watch," *Theoria ve-Bikoret* 31 (2008) (in Hebrew).

42 Baruch Kimmerling, *Politicide: Ariel Sharon's War against the Palestinians* (London: Verso, 2003), chap. 10.

43 See, for example, Amos Harel, "Preparations for the Third Round Have Begun," *Ha'aretz,* April 29, 2005; Ari Shavit, "Ya'alon: After the Disengagement, a Second War of Terror Is To Be Expected, with Bombings and Qassam Launchings against the Center of the Country," *Ha'aretz,* January 6, 2005; Aluf Ben, "The Second Qassam Test," *Ha'aretz,* September 9, 2005.

44 For the notion of "defective" or "impaired" citizenship see Ariella Azoulay, *The Civil Contract of Photography* (New York: Zone Books, 2008), chap. 1. For a thorough analysis of the system of differential citizenship in Israel, Yoav Peled and Gershon Shaffir, *Being Israeli: The Dynamics of Multiple Citizenship* (Cambridge: Cambridge University Press, 2002).

45 The difference between the West Bank and the Gaza Strip, which has always existed, was exacerbated by the disengagement. The phrase "on the verge of a humanitarian disaster" was coined by Jean Ziegler, special envoy of the United Nations, whose report *The Right to Food* was presented to the UN General Secretary in September 2003. Under Israeli-American pressure, its original version was kept from the public, and it was publicized only in 2004 after certain sections were kept out. Similar data and expressions documenting a humanitarian disaster in the Occupied Territories have appeared in many reports made by various international organizations, as well as by foreign governments and parliaments. The proliferation of such reports is notable. The Occupied Palestinian Territories are probably one of the world's most widely documented disaster areas. See Jean Ziegler, *The Right to Food: Report by the Special Rapporteur, Jean Ziegler. Addendum: Mission to the Occupied Palestinian Territories* (2003), available on-line http://www.unhchr.ch/pdf/chr60/10add2AV.pdf (last accessed September 17, 2008).

46 The reports of the military government and the Civil Administration from the 1970s and 1980s take much pride in their achievements in developing health, agriculture, public hygiene, employment, and more. See also Neve Gordon, *Israel's Occupation* and his "From Colonization to Separation: Exploring the Structure of Israel's Occupation," in this volume.

WITHHELD AND ERUPTIVE VIOLENCE Since the outbreak of the al-Aqsa intifada and after the situation in the Occupied Territories was classified an "armed conflict," the IDF ceased distributing the *Soldier's Pocket Booklet,* which specifies the open-fire regulations, to soldiers serving in the Occupied Territories. Although in the past, the IDF did not enforce the law on soldiers who injured or killed Palestinians in violation of the regulations, in recent years, an even more lenient attitude has been officially encouraged, with the rules for opening fire changing in place and time without obeying any written, clear, and binding regulations. The flexibility of the open-fire rules epitomizes a logic of military violence whose exercise is both systematic and calculated (from the point of view of the occupiers) and opaque, capricious and unpredictable (from the point of view of the occupied).

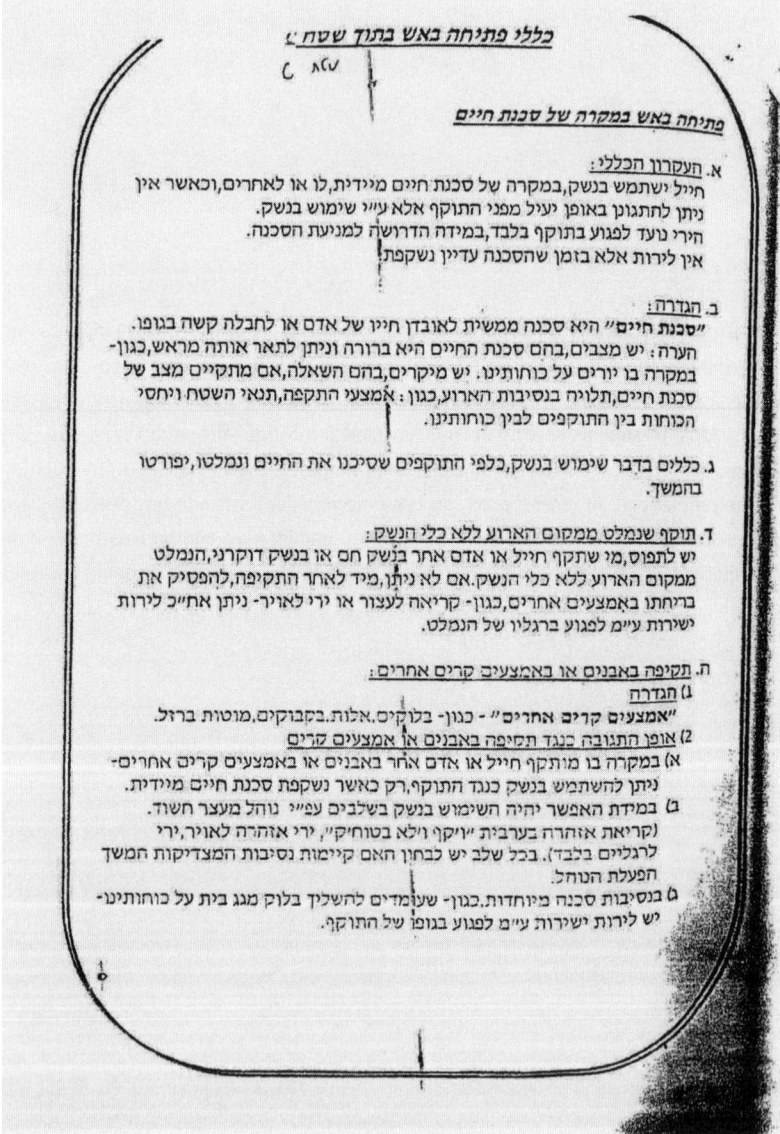

כללי פתיחה באש בתוך שטח ע
C אלו

פתיחה באש במקרה של סכנת חיים

א. העקרון הכללי:
חייל ישתמש בנשק,במקרה של סכנת חיים מיידית,לו או לאחרים,וכאשר אין
ניתן להתגונן באופן יעיל מפני התוקף אלא ע"י שימוש בנשק.
הירי נועד לפגוע בתוקף בלבד,במידה הדרושה למניעת הסכנה.
אין לירות אלא בזמן שהסכנה עדיין נשקפת.

ב. הגדרה:
"סכנת חיים" היא סכנה ממשית לאובדן חייו של אדם או לחבלה קשה בגופו.
הערה: יש מצבים,בהם סכנת חיים היא ברורה וניתן לתאר אותה מראש,כגון-
במקרה בו יורים על כוחותינו. יש מיקרים,בהם השאלה,אם מתקיים מצב של
סכנת חיים,תלויה בנסיבות הארוע,כגון: אמצעי התקפה,תנאי השטח ויחסי
הכוחות בין התוקפים לבין כוחותינו.

ג. כללים בדבר שימוש בנשק,כלפי התוקפים שסיכנו את החיים ונמלטו,יפורטו
בהמשך.

ד. תוקף שנמלט ממקום הארוע ללא כלי הנשק:
יש לתפוס,מי שתקף חייל או אדם אחר בנשק חם או בנשק דוקרני,הנמלט
ממקום הארוע ללא כלי הנשק.אם לא ניתן,מיד לאחר התקיפה,להפסיק את
בריחתו באמצעים אחרים,כגון: קריאה לעצור או ירי לאויר- ניתן אח"כ לירות
ישירות ע"מ לפגוע ברגליו של הנמלט.

ה. תקיפה באבנים או באמצעים קרים אחרים:
1) הגדרה
"אמצעים קרים אחרים" - כגון- בלוקים.אלות.בקבוקים.מוטות ברזל.
2) אופן התגובה כנגד תקיפה באבנים או אמצעים קרים
א) במקרה בו מותקף חייל או אדם אחר באבנים או באמצעים קרים אחרים-
ניתן להשתמש בנשק כנגד התוקף,רק כאשר נשקפת סכנת חיים מיידית.
ב) במידת האפשר יהיה השימוש בנשק בשלבים עפ"י נוהל מעצר חשוד.
(קריאת אזהרה בערבית "ויקף" ולא בטוחיקי, ירי אזהרה לאויר,ירי
לרגליים בלבד). בכל שלב יש לבחון האם קיימות נסיבות המצדיקות המשך
הפעלת הנוהל.
3) בנסיבות סכנה מיוחדות.כגון- שעומדים להשליך בלוק מגג בית על כוחותינו-
יש לירות ישירות ע"מ לפגוע בגופו של התוקף.

<h1 style="text-align:center">Open-Fire Regulations in Area C</h1>

Opening fire in the case of danger to life

A. The general principle

A soldier will use a weapon in the event of immediate danger to his life or that of another person when it is impossible to defend himself effectively from the assailant other than by the use of a weapon. The firing is intended to hit the assailant only, to the extent necessary to prevent the danger.

Shooting is permitted only while the danger continues to exist.

B. Definition

"**Danger to life**" means a real danger of death or serious bodily injury of a person.
Note: There are situations in which the danger to life is clear and can be specified in advance, such as firing at our forces. There are cases in which the question of whether danger to life exists depends on the circumstances—for example, the means of the attack, the conditions on the ground, and the balance of forces between the assailants and our forces.

C. Rules relating to the use of weapons against assailants who endangered life and escaped are specified below.

D. Assailant who escapes from the scene of the event without the weapon

Anyone who attacked a soldier or person with a firearm or a sharp weapon and flees the scene without the weapon must be captured. If it is impossible immediately after the attack to prevent his escape by other means, such as a call to stop or firing in the air, it is then permitted to fire directly at the legs of the fleeing assailant.

E. Attack with stones or other cold implements

1) Definition

"**Other cold implements**" means, for example, blocks, clubs, bottles, steel rods.

2) Manner of response against an attack with stones or other cold implements

a) In the event that a soldier or another person is attacked with stones or other cold implements, it is permitted to use a weapon against the assailant only when there is an immediate danger to life.

b) To the extent possible, the use of weapons shall be executed gradually, in accordance with the Procedure for Arresting a Suspect (warning call in Arabic: "Waqef wala bit-wakhek," a warning shot in the air, firing at the legs only). At each stage, it is necessary to determine whether circumstances exist justifying the continued use of the procedure.

c) In circumstances of special danger, such as when a block is about to be thrown from a rooftop onto our forces, soldiers shall fire directly to hit the body of the assailant.

תנאים ודגשים לשימוש בנשק:

1) אסור לפתוח באש,לעבר מי שחשוד בעבירה פלילית "רגילה",כגון- סירוב להזדהות,גניבה,הברחה.

2) אסור לפתוח באש,לעבר אדם המסרב לדרישה לעצור ונמלט,אלא אם כן הוא "חשוד בביצוע פשע מסוכן",עצם הבריחה כשלעצמה אינה הופכת את הבורח לחשוד בפשע מסוכן.

3) אסור לפתוח באש לעבר נשים וילדים (במקרה של ירי לעבר רכב,אין לירות לעבר רכב שנראים בו נשים וילדים).

4) אסור לפתוח באש לעבר חשוד,כאשר קיימת סכנה ממשית,כי אנשים אחרים עלולים להפגע.

5) אסור לפתוח באש כאשר התנאים במקום אינם מאפשרים לזהות בוודאות את החשוד ואת נקודת המכוון (רגלי החשוד או גלגלי רכב).

6) אין לבצע ירי לעבר אדם ממצב נסיעה אלא ממצב נייח בלבד.

7) הפתיחה באש תבוצע במידת האפשר ע"י מפקד בשטח,או לפי הוראתו. הפתיחה באש תהיה,במידת האפשר,ע"י יורה אחד בלבד.

8) הפתיחה באש תבוצע, רק כאשר עפ"י הערכת היורה יש לו סיכוי ממשי לפגוע ברגלי החשוד.
   במסדר יציאה למשימה יתדרכו מפקדי הכוחות את חייליהם בדבר מגבלות הטווחים עפ"י סוגי הנשק כמפורט בדף תדריך לשימוש בנשק בנוהל מעצר חשוד (של א/מ ענף סנים ואבטחה: מב-2- כ- 5273 מיום 1 אפריל 93').

9) נתפס החשוד- יעצר,ותיפתח נגדו חקירה פלילית.

Conditions and emphases for the use of weapons

1) It is prohibited to open fire at a person suspected of having committed a "regular" criminal offense, such as refusal to identify oneself, theft, smuggling.

2) It is prohibited to open fire at a person who resists an order to stop and flees, unless the person is "suspected of having committed a dangerous crime." The act of fleeing per se does not turn the escapee into a person suspected of a dangerous crime.

3) It is prohibited to open fire at women and children (when shooting at a vehicle, it is prohibited to shoot at a vehicle in which women and children are seen).

4) It is prohibited to open fire at a suspect when a real danger exists that other people might be hurt.

5) It is prohibited to open fire when the conditions at the scene do not permit the certain identification of the suspect and the point at which the firing is to be aimed (the legs of the suspect or the wheels of the vehicle).

6) It is forbidden to shoot at a person when driving, and the shooting is to be done only from a stationary position.

7) Opening fire will be done, to the extent possible, by the commander in the field, or on his order. Opening fire will be done, to the extent possible, by one shooter only.

8) Opening fire will be done only when, according to the shooter's assessment, he has a real chance to hit the legs of the suspect. At the assembly before setting out on the mission, the commanders of the forces will brief the soldiers on the limitations of ranges according to types of weapons as specified in the guidelines for the use of weapons in the Procedure for Arresting a Suspect.

9) When a suspect is captured, he is to be arrested and a criminal investigation against him will be opened.

אמצעים לפיזור התפרעויות

א. העיקרון הכללי:

ההתפרעויות האלימות ביהודה ושומרון מעלות את הצורך לתת בידי החיילים אמצעים שונים,שיאפשרו להם לחתמודד‎ במול ההתפרעות האלימה,גם במצבים בהם אין נשקפת סכנת חיים מיידית.השימוש באמצעים אלה יהיה באופן מדורג,כאשר המטרה היא לפזר את ההתפרעות האלימה מבלי לגרום לאובדן חיים ולפגיעות קשות בגוף.

ב. תגדרה:

"התפרעות אלימה"

1) התקהלות אלימה של אנשים, המלווה בידוי אבנים,או אמצעים קרים אחרים לרבות הנחת מחסומים והבערת צמיגים בנתיבי תחבורה.
2) זריקת אבנים או אמצעים קרים אחרים, ע"י יחיד או רבים,בכוונה לפגוע באדם,ברכב נוסע,או ברכוש.

ג. נוהל פיזור התפרעות - הכלל

לפיזור התפרעות אלימה יש לקרוא.תחילה למתפרעים להתפזר. לא פסקה ההתפרעות האלימה תוך זמן סביר,ניתן להפעיל אמצעים לפיזור הפגנות לפי הדרוג הבא :

1) אמצעים כגון : גז מדמיע,סילוני מים,חזיזים,רימוני הלם.
2) ירי אזהרה לאויר.

3) ירי תחמושת גומי (רדרני"מ ורומה ג"ג).

המעבר משלב לשלב יבוצע,רק אם חשלב הקודם לא הביא להפסקת ההתפרעות האלימה. ניתן לדלג על שלב,אם אמצעים מסוויימים אינם עומדים לרשות הכח, או שאין הם ישימים בנסיבות הארוע.

ד. השימוש באמצעים לפיזור ההתפרעות,והמעבר משלב לשלב,יחין בהתאם להוראות המפקד.

ה. דגשים:

1) יש בכוחם של האמצעים לפיזור ההתפרעות כדי לגרום לפגיעה בגופו של אדם ואף לגרום בנסיבות מסוויימות לתוצאה קטלנית. לפיכך חלה חובה להשתמש באמצעים אלה בזהירות רבה ובהתאם לכל התנאים והמגבלות שיפורטו בסעיף זה.
2) בכל מיקרה ישקול המפקד היטב,אם ראגי לעשות שימוש באמצעים לפיזור הפגנת,בהתחשב בתומרת ההתפרעות האלימה ובנסיבות הארוע.

Methods for dispersing riots

A. The general principle

The violent riots in Judea and Samaria raise the need to provide the soldiers with various means that will enable them to deal with the violent riot, also in situations in which no immediate danger to life is foreseen. These means shall be used in a gradual manner, the objective being to disperse the violent riot without causing the loss of life and serious bodily harm.

B. Definition

"Violent riot" means—

1) a violent gathering of people, accompanied by stone throwing or other cold means, including erecting barricades and burning tires on traffic arteries.
2) throwing stones or other cold means, by an individual or a group, with the intent of harming a person, a moving vehicle, or property.

C. Procedure for dispersing a riot—the rule

In dispersing a violent riot, a call to the rioters to disperse shall be made first. If the riot does not cease within a reasonable period of time, it is permitted to use means to disperse demonstrations according to the following stages:

1) means such as tear gas, water jets, blasting caps, stun grenades.
2) warning shots in the air.
3) firing of rubber ammunition.

Passage from one stage to the next is allowed only if the previous stage did not result in cessation of the violent riot. A stage may be skipped if certain means are not at the disposal of the force or if they are not applicable in the circumstances of the event.

D. The use of means for dispersing the riot and the passage from one stage to the next shall be carried out according to the orders of the commander.

[...]

OPEN-FIRE NORMS AS RECONSTRUCTED IN SOLDIERS' TESTIMONIES Excerpt from a report by Breaking the Silence, an Israeli organization of veteran soldiers, which uses a style similar to the *Soldier's Pocket Booklet.* [Document source: "Combatants' Testimonies on the Open-Fire Regulations in Judea and Samaria and in the Gaza Strip," April 2005]

Testimonies presented in this pocket booklet indicate that over the past four years of IDF activity in the Occupied Territories, commanders have given verbal orders that, had they been made in writing, would state as follows:

1. **Shoot to kill anyone who is found outside his house/on the street between 1:00 A.M. and 4:00 P.M.** (See Testimony No. 1.)

2. **Shoot to kill anyone whom the commander of the force in the field classifies a "lookout," i.e., a person positioned on the roof of his house, on the balcony, or at the window of the house, with or without a means for making observations.** (See Testimony No. 2.)

3. **Shoot to kill anyone who is dragging bodies or is approaching bodies.** (See Testimony No. 3.)

4. **Shoot to kill anyone who raises a rock in both hands to throw it—adult or child.** (See Testimony No. 4.)

5. **Shoot to kill anyone who enters an area classified as "extermination areas" of the military post.** (See Testimony No. 5.)

6. **Where an armored troop vehicle is placed in a populated area as a lure—shoot to kill anyone trying to get into it.** (See Testimony No. 6.)

7. **Shoot to kill anyone seen carrying a gas balloon in the street.** (See Testimony No. 7.)

8. **For deterrence, shoot live ammunition randomly at populated Palestinian neighborhoods.** (See Testimony No. 8.)

9. **Arrest will start with the massive machinegun/missile fire at walls, the objective being to display presence in the area.** (See Testimony No. 9.)

PRESSURE COOKER PROCEDURE The following document is copied from the Hebrew edition of Wikipedia. The entry in the virtual encyclopedia, which was possibly written by soldiers engaged in arrest operations in the Occupied Territories, states that the IDF increased use of the procedure after the High Court of Justice forbade the use of Palestinians as "human shields" in carrying out such operations.

The Pressure Cooker Procedure is a multistage technique for capturing a wanted person barricaded in a house, each stage being of increased intensity and used if the preceding stage is ineffective, i.e., the wanted person refuses to surrender. The stages are as follows:

1. IDF forces surround the house and ensure innocent persons are not inside.

2. A call is given to the wanted person to come out. Sometimes, a relative of the person is used to get him to surrender (see the Neighbor Procedure). This stage is vital, particularly from the legal point of view, and is intended to give the terrorist an opportunity to surrender voluntarily, before force is used.

3. The forces fire a number of antitank rockets (such as Lau and Shipon rockets) at the house and sometimes use grenades and light gunfire. This stage is intended to cause the terrorist to come out, either out of psychological fear or in an attempt to flee the gunfire.

4. The forces shell the house with tank gunfire (when a tank is available). The immense noise and the shaking of the house resulting from the tank fire are intended to frighten the wanted person and make him give up.

5. An engineering mechanical device (D-9 bulldozer, wheeled shovel, protected excavator) is driven toward the house, threatening to demolish it if the terrorist doesn't come out. Sometimes, the psychological effect of this measure is sufficient to get the wanted person to surrender.

6. The forces cause the house to shake by knocking down a part. They simply take a bulldozer and stick the "knife" (nickname for the shovel) into one of the walls of the house. With an earth-mover, they begin to scrape the walls of the floor on which the terrorist is located.

7. The forces demolish the house. If the terrorist has not yet surrendered, he might be buried under the ruins of the house in which he barricaded himself.

PROCEDURE FOR DETAINING PALESTINIANS AT PERMANENT CHECKPOINTS Although
its immediate objective is to prevent the misuse of power, the following document
exposes a small bit of the arbitrary transition between various levels of withheld violence at checkpoints, and of its fuzzy official sanction. According to a letter sent

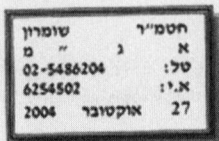

חטמ"ר שומרון מח"ט, ק.אג"מ, ק.חמ"ל
גדוד שב"ש- מג"ד, קמב"ץ
גדוד חורון- מג"ד,קמב"ץ
גוש 101- מג"ד קמב"ץ
איו"ש 877 ק. אג"מ, קמב"ץ

הנחיית מח"ט- נוהל עיכוב פלס' במחסומי הקבע
(עדכון מס' 2)

1. הנחייה זו יוצאת כתבהרה להנחיית המח"ט בדבר עיכוב פלס' במחסומים, וזאת בעקבות עיכובים ממושכים החורגים מהמותר שאירע בתקופה האחרונה.

2. במחסומי הכתר, למעט המחסומים הקבועים, ניתן לעכב פלס' למשך של עד 4 שעות, כשבתומן יש לשחרר את הפלס' במידה ואינו דורש מעצר.

3. מפירי כתר יעוכבו למשך של עד **שעתיים** באישור מג"ד, ועיכוב למשך **ארבע שעות** יהיה באישור חטיבה.

4. הארכת משך זמן העיכוב מעבר לשעתיים תהיה באישור **מח"ט בלבד.**

5. פלסטינאים "יתקינים", העוברים מחסומי הקבע ע"פ חוק- ניתן לעכבם למשך של **עד שעה לבדיקת ת.ז.**

6. הנחייה זו תקפה ומחודדת מרגע הפצתה.

7. לידיעתכם, טיפולכם,

סיון ניזלס, סגן
קמב"ץ שומרון

from the Office of the Judge Advocate for Judea and Samaria to MachsomWatch in February 2005, the wording of the directive had changed, "and it clarifies, explicitly and unequivocally, that it is absolutely forbidden to detain persons as punishment."

[Document source: MachsomWatch]

Shomron Regional Brigade
Operations Branch
Tel: 02-5486204
Army Tel: 6254502
27 October 2004

Shomron Regional Brigade—Brigade Commander, Operations Branch officer, War Room officer
SVS Battalion—Battalion Commander, Operations Officer
Horon Battalion—Battalion Commander, Operations Officer
Battalion 101 – Battalion Commander, Operations Officer
Judea and Samaria 877 K Operations Branch, Operations Officer

Battalion Commander's Directive—
Procedure for Detaining Pales' [Palestinians] at Permanent Checkpoints
(Revision No. 2)

1. This directive is issued to clarify the battalion commander's directive on detaining Pales' at checkpoints and follows recent cases of detention longer than the time permitted.

2. At the encirclement checkpoints, except for the permanent checkpoints, a Pales' may be detained for up to 4 hours, during which time the Pales' is to be released if his arrest is not required.

3. Violators of the encirclement will be detained for up to **two** hours with the approval of the battalion commander and detention of **four hours** with brigade approval.

4. Detention for a period exceeding two hours requires the approval of the **brigade commander alone**.

5. "Proper" Pales', who cross the permanent checkpoints lawfully—may be detained for **up to one hour for I.D. inspection**.

6. This directive takes force and is clarified from the moment it is circulated.

7. For your information, for your handling.

Sivan Gizels, Lieutenant
Operations Officer Shomron

The (In)Human Spatial Condition: A Visual Essay

Ariella Azoulay

The image of the sovereign as a founder of cities who imports architects and engineers from far and wide to help him leave his own stamp in space is familiar to us from ancient history. Something of this dimension of ruling power is perpetuated in our times by the sovereign's right to initiate and build monuments that transform urban space and to do it without any competition, contract, or civil consent.

Such an architectural privilege, in modern France, for example, belongs to the president of the republic and has an explicit monarchic connotation: *fait du prince*. In a democratic state, the sovereign may enjoy this privilege only as long as he makes measured and careful use of it. In such states, the monument glorifies the president through the pleasure and benefit he extends to the general citizenry.

In the forty years of its rule, the occupation regime has made extensive use of this privilege reserved for the sovereign, massively disrupting Palestinian space through three forms of intervention: construction, the administration of movement, and destruction. The fact that Israeli occupation rule is not recognized as sovereign and its subjects do not recognize its authority has not kept it from expecting absolute and sweeping application of this privilege while depriving the subjects of any status that would allow them to negotiate over the changes in their habitat. In each of these three forms, the occupation regime has conducted itself as foreign rule whose sole purpose is to establish its control and possession of space, rather than to develop that space to improve the living conditions of the local population. The three forms of intervention have deepened and reflected the polarized, conflictual power relations between the occupiers and the population of noncitizens living in the Occupied Territories. Land use, movement restriction, development, and the use of resources were all subjugated to these polarized relations from the very beginning in a gradual and escalating process and have turned the Palestinians into provisional residents of a space whose shape and transformation are forever subject to the whims of the regime and its Israeli citizens. Almost nothing in Palestinian space has remained constant, and many of its inhabitants live displaced in their homes, a new type of internal exile in their homeland. Where once orchards and orange groves grew, roads are now paved. Houses previously Palestinian have been confiscated and used to build colonies or army bases. Familiar thoroughfares have been blocked. Use of new ones has not been allowed, public space has become out of bounds for civilian use, movement is subject to constant surveillance, and even house walls have not protected their dwellers from various types of invasion and penetration of their living spaces. The enforcement of power relations between the occupiers and the population of the Occupied Territories has meant not only the Palestinians' dispossession. It has also meant taking over strategic sites throughout the space and spreading forces over points numerous enough to control and perpetuate these polarized relations in space.[1]

Since the first intifada, much information has been collected by various bodies and organizations about these three forms of spatial intervention by the sovereign. Much has been written about construction, which has changed the appearance of space under occupation—construction in the colonies and the checkpoint system, in particular. However, the major part of the occupation regime's activity in space since the second intifada, activity that has received relatively little attention in its implications on Palestinian habitat, is expressed in the way the sovereign has reversed its prerogatives over the power of construction. Instead of promoting construction in the Occupied Territories, the occupation regime has utterly changed space through destruction—not whimsical, ad hoc random destruction, but rather methodical, controlled, and administered destruction, present everywhere. Both construction (by Jews and for Jews), and destruction (for Palestinians) inflict permanent damage on the local population, interfere with its ability to travel to work, school, and medical clinics, and provoke its resistance.[2] To neutralize such resistance or to reduce it, the ruling power must exercise extensive military might, and in order to shape space, it needs soldiers more than it needs architects, engineers, and builders.

The Oslo Accords divided the Occupied Territories into distinct areas of Israeli and Palestinian control. But even after the accords, the occupation regime did not cease to apply massive military force as the final authority regarding the administration and organization of space in the Palestinian Authority's domain, as well. Apparently the regime needs to prove publicly and unequivocally that no walls can stand in its way and that it has no respect for the privacy of dwellings. The homes of those it suspects of resisting the occupation are the preferred venue for its show of force: "Let them learn their lesson." Often, the residents of these demolished homes are not the suspects themselves, but members of their families. However, resistance to the occupation's might is not its only pretext for demolishing houses. Thousands of houses, gardens, orchards, and groves are destroyed merely because their location disrupts the occupation's operations or prevents some colony or other from developing and expanding. In areas that have remained under its full control, the occupation regime applies legal and civil tools to demolish the homes of thousands of Palestinians whose petitions for building permits it has persistently rejected, dooming their dwellings to the status of illegal constructions.

From 1967 to the present, the Israeli Defense Forces have demolished about eighteen thousand houses in the West Bank and the Gaza Strip.[3] This number does not include houses damaged by gunfire or stray shells and not intentionally demolished. Beyond devastating the foundations of public space and its relations with the private sphere, the occupation regime has developed its own unique spatial language of blockage, separation, and subjugation, preventing its subjects from maintaining a public space in which speech, gaze, and action are supposed to take place as free, spontaneous, and unpredictable play.

Such disruptions of spatial order afflict what Hannah Arendt has described as "the human condition" and generate an inhuman spatial condition. The Palestinians are deprived of the free use of space in all three forms of their *vita activa*: They are not free to move about spontaneously and find their way into and out of places; they are not free to use space in their work, commerce, and other forms of economic and professional activities; and they are not free to create open spaces for public gatherings, free speech, and free association without being limited, controlled, and monitored by the occupying authorities. This severe and ongoing disruption of social space produces a unique situation: The main options for public gatherings and the relatively free use of space are the various sites of destruction, right after the dramatic event of destruction wrought by the occupying power, which transforms the damages into spatial scars.

During the actual demolition, Palestinians are ordered away from the site and allowed back only after the irreversible has become fact—the three-dimensional house has turned into a mere two-dimensional texture, the street has become unusable as a street, and a kind of new square has been opened in its midst. The ruling power justifies the disasters it wreaks and shirks its responsibility for the victims who have become dispossessed and displaced. The void left behind by the sovereign power is partially filled by the Palestinian Authority, by the residents themselves under the harsh restrictions that the army imposes upon their freedom of movement and action, and by the various aid organizations such as the United Nations Relief and Works Agency, UNRWA, the agency that cares for refugees of the past as well as for new types of refugees that Israel produces in the present, or the Red Cross.

The disaster taking place in public space takes two forms: the spectacle at its moment of occurrence and its ongoing results, which most of the time the subjects cannot reverse on their own. These two appearances help perpetuate the power relations between the occupier and the population of the Occupied Territories and the subjugation they constitute and reduce the possibilities Palestinians have for conducting the various forms of their praxis in their common space. The sovereign pulling the strings that produce the disaster is both present and absent from the scene. He acts as one who relies on the disaster and the emergencies that it produces to magnetize the subjects in his absence, to administer and supervise their movement, to rivet them to their basic needs, and to paralyze their ability to act. Thus, the gathering around a site of disaster inflicted by the occupier has become the permissible and most common type of public gathering in the Occupied Territories—a gathering around an "image" or "spectacle." The products of destruction scattered everywhere thus function like public squares. The occupier, as inherently stupid as occupiers are, assumes he can determine how the spectators in the public square will gaze at the horror show he has generated and what moral and lesson will be drawn from it. He assumes that he can "etch their consciousness" with the following conclusion: "We have delivered an unequivocal message to the population—any person involved in terrorism, as well as their next of kin, will pay a steep price for it."

Destruction requires immediate care and ways and means to provide for the urgent basic needs of the victims. But the flagrant ongoing presence of the results of destruction in their space, at times not removed for months or even years, creates a "world" in the sense that Arendt has lent this term. Its forms are the stable, permanent environment that the inhabitants know and in the textures of which they dwell. The disaster scene, from which the sovereign has withdrawn and which he abandoned, is the only environment where he hardly ever forbids their public gathering: the site transforms into a political space where the three domains of the vita activa, otherwise partially forbidden, take place.[4] In the photographs distributed throughout this volume, one might see that the gathering of Palestinians around the site of destruction is not harnessed only for the urgent needs of survival: They are rescuing victims and providing urgently needed care, but also professionally administrating their affairs and restoring their public space as a space of freedom.

In this public square, where Palestinians convene around a common object of their gaze and whose limits they establish during their encounter, they create a bond between the disaster site and the rest of the city. Thus, for example, for those standing at the rim of the huge pit opened under Sami al-Shaer's home, there is more than a gaze of wonder at the extent of its destruction. Their faces are sealed and distant. At times, they show contempt toward those who forced them to act within a public space whose basic form is disaster. With the unfathomable patience of those who recognize the limits of the occupier's intervention and who know he will never be able to destroy their public space completely and deny them their basic political right to assemble in it, they scrutinize disaster and deny its perpetrators' pretension of thus delivering an unequivocal message. They face the power of human destructiveness with awe. But they also confront the stupidity of the occupiers, who invest such enormous efforts and means in practices of blockage and separation that mean, among other things, limiting disaster to one side of the space so that the occupiers could imagine themselves as outside the space of disaster, separate from it, safe and immune.

The Palestinians' observation of the feats of destruction transcends the urgency that disaster produces, opening a wider perspective. Through it, disaster may be seen not only as a particular event at a given point in time, but as a form of continuous control. The more the occupier devastates space and tears it asunder with events that bring disaster, blockages, and separation, its grip deepens, becoming more and more impossible to unravel. The population of the Occupied Territories, doomed to observe their own disaster, look through it at the occupiers who observe disaster from afar and deny their own active part in generating it. In disaster itself, they refute the occupiers' pretension to control the limits of disaster and to deny the way in which it touches them, too, gripping them in spite of all their efforts to detach themselves from it.

The five series of photographs presented here, interspersed throughout—five visual claims, as it were—address the destruction of the built environment in Palestinian space and the administration of movement as related policies. The first and the last series—"The Architecture of Destruction" and "Textures of Destruction"—attempt to characterize destruction without assuming or accepting the categories offered by the ruling power. The ruling power's military and legal language distinguishes between various cases of destruction according to the many justifications that the army provides for the havoc it wreaks: "illegal construction," "dwellings harboring individuals suspected of terrorism," or even its own "operational needs." Presenting side by side a photograph of a concrete ruin and an architectural scheme that illustrates the type of ruin at hand is part of the effort to deconstruct the category that has become too general and abstract—"house demolition"—and in its stead propose a primary typology of the sovereign's actions in the Occupied Territories. The categories offered here instead are based on distinctions in various types of destruction resulting from the techniques applied and the different textural types of the "architectural" stamp that destruction leaves upon Palestinian space. This initial sorting enables one to shift one's gaze from the population of the Occupied Territories as the reason for or justification of destruction to the language of the occupier who has turned destruction into a sophisticated and available toolbox. This sorting enables one to see how different forms of destruction that were applied at specific points and that may have been perceived at a given point in time as unbearable eventually became an obvious tool to be honed and used by trained soldiers.

The second and the third series "Types of Blockage" and "The Architecture of Separation"—focus on procedures by which the occupation regime actually produces a disorientation of space in which legibility and coherence have been totally disrupted. Most of these procedures, if not all of them, slow down Palestinians' movement in space nearly to a halt. They also show how these procedures allow Palestinians only measured movement amid "architectural" components such as slabs of concrete, parts of walls, barbed-wire fences, plastic barriers, and other elements that generate an entirely new cartography.

"Types of Blockage" shows how what is near at hand, always within seeing distance, and accessible in remembered past becomes inaccessible to Palestinians. The architectural syntax of different types of blockage points reflects this effect par excellence, but is also apparent wherever Palestinians find themselves at the threshold of their own homes, but prevented from entering, whether because the homes have been physically blocked or have been turned into army outposts.

"The Architecture of Separation" emphasizes the spatial delineation of separation between Jews and Palestinians. In addition to the discriminatory partition that grants Israelis relative freedom of movement and leaves Palestinians with space that is fragmented and blocked, this partition reorganizes the field of vision, a field no longer to be shared. In this split field of vision, Israelis' and Palestinians' gazes are no longer supposed to meet.

The fourth series, "The Architecture of Fear/The Language of Subjugation," focuses on various blocking points and presents the spatial and design language used by the occupation regime to administer the movement of Palestinians in space. It shows how the occupation regime ensures that crowds will not be allowed to form, but rather must continue to move or stand in single file. As they drag themselves along, one by one, their movement is controlled and supervised individually. The photographs provide extensive information related to time and space, technology and movement, demography and administration, topography and control.

Like the keys of a map, icons of the temporary components of the architecture, spread throughout space, accompany this series and the series showing the architecture of blockage. The icons present the gamut of temporary, mobile components used by the sovereign's minor-ranking authority bearers. These components now constitute a "kit" that can be rapidly deployed at any point in space to change, limit, or block the movement of people, wares, and vehicles. These components have become totally familiar, incorporated in Jewish Israelis' bodies as protective devices while embodying subjugation in the Palestinians themselves.

These series of photographs attempt to illuminate the dual injury inflicted by the occupation regime upon Palestinian space, both public and private. Public space is administered and controlled by the explicit military presence of the ruling power, and the inhabitants' potential civil actions within it are totally reduced. The private sphere is penetrable, vulnerable, and perforated, and its inhabitants are liable at any time to become homeless and unable to dream of more than filling their basic existential needs. The sovereign demonstrates his power and might by publicly demolishing the limits of the Palestinian home, crushing its intimacy. What was just now indoors—where only relatives and family members were welcome—is suddenly bared amid the ruins: ceilings collapsed, belongings crushed and torn and scattered about. The private indoors is projected onto the public outdoors, and public space is administered centrally as though possessed by the ruling power, emptying it of its political nature.

With these series of photographs, I mean to characterize the inner grammar of the faits du prince responsible for the inhuman spatial conditions in the Occupied Territories. The photographs insist that Israeli Jews observe Palestinian space together with the Palestinians in the way this fragmented and blocked space is imposed on them, unraveling the illusion of total separation that is the occupier's basic principle.

It is this illusion alone that enables the infliction upon Palestinians of injustices that Israeli citizens would never tolerate were they ever to be inflicted upon them. The separation is actually between what is bearable and even justifiable (that is, in the eyes of the Israelis and inflicted upon the Palestinians) and the unbearable and unjustifiable (that is, what should not be inflicted upon the Israelis). Behind the illusion of physical separation, the occupation regime keeps raising the threshold of the unbearable, along with the Separation Wall between the two regimes. The occupation regime exercises enormous power in checking and limiting the extent of destruction to the one side, and indeed, the landscape shown here remains mostly that of the Occupied Territories. But the ruling power is required to apply force not only upon the populations of the territories, but upon its own citizens as well, in order to make destruction's unbearable sights seem bearable by token of their remaining limited to the one side. At the same time, actual participation in this destruction, presumably a heinous crime were it perpetrated on the other side, is regarded as an honorable duty. But here the occupation regime's inherent weakness, its blind spot, is exposed. The effort it invests in destroying Palestinian space and the Palestinians' public space are viral, as it were. The public sphere flawed by the ongoing disaster inflicted by the occupation regime upon its Palestinian noncitizens seeps into the Israeli side: the mobilization of Israeli citizens to take part in the production of the disaster and its justification, as well as its erasure and denial. On the Palestinian side, directly affected by disaster, the public sphere is flawed by the way in which it is controlled and by its constant state of emergency.

NOTES

English translation by Tal Haran. Special thanks to Liron Mor, Itamar Mann, Daniel Mann, and Mikhael Mankin for their research assistance

1   Jeff Halper, head of the Israeli Committee Against House Demolitions, compares the Israeli takeover of Palestinian space to the game of Go, in which the goal is not defeating one's opponent, but rather to block his ability to move. Jeff Halper, "Matrix of Control," *Middle East Report* 216 (Fall 2000).

2   I have pointed out various practices of spatial resistance in the exhibition *Act of State: 1967– 2007* at the Minshar Gallery, Tel Aviv, Spring 2007.

3   See the Web site of the Israeli Committee Against House Demolitions on the history of house demolitions at http://www.icahd.org/eng/projects.asp (last accessed September 8, 2008). The committee, together with Palestinians and international volunteers, rebuilds some of the demolished houses; BADIL Resource Center for Palestinian Residency an Refugee Rights, "A History of Destruction," (May 18, 2004), available on-line at http://electronicintifada.net/ v2/article2700.shtml (last accessed September 8, 2008).

4   Instead of identifying the political only with freedom and with the third domain of action, as does Arendt, I rely here on my discussion of the political as taking place in all three domains: Ariella Azoulay, *The Civil Condition* (Tel Aviv: Resling, forthcoming) (in Hebrew). Paper presented at the Second Workshop for Visual Studies, Bar-Ilan University, May 2008.

Ariella Azoulay

MIKI KRATSMAN

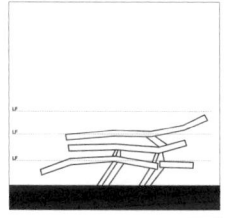

1.1 RAFAH, 2005 Most of the apartments in this building had been deserted sometime before it was demolished.
Its location not far from the Qatif colony block made it an
easy target for shooting and shelling, and life in it became
unbearable. According to the army, Palestinian fighters
used its deserted apartments for hiding, and that sufficed
to doom it to destruction. During the al-Aqsa intifada,
home demolition practices were enhanced into a sort of assembly-line procedure in
an accelerated process of operational effectiveness by which thousands of buildings
are demolished in the Occupied Territories every year. A principal condition for this

Architectonic schemes by Meira Kowalsky

161

operational efficiency is to detach the process from nonoperational considerations that might delay and encumber it. Such detachment enables the regional commander to decree demolition without waiting for the confirmation of his superiors and even to skip the early warning phase that allows the owners to appeal to the courts for an injunction or interim order. No one asks why that particular house is being blasted or why houses are being blasted at all. The building is selected by the General Security Service (GSS). The soldiers accept the mission unquestioningly and the necessity of blasting a residential building as a matter of course.

The extensive technological and operational know-how that the defense forces have accumulated as a result of the frequent observation of house demolitions in real time has enabled them to simplify the process of destruction and to break it up into regular phases, so that just a handful of soldiers is able to carry it out in a mere quarter of an hour. They can do this without depending on an engineer or the crack-unit members who have been especially trained for such missions. The procedure is clear and explicit, and the operation of the equipment is known to all combat soldiers. The destruction workers arrive in several armored personnel carriers that move into civilian space, approach the building destined for demolition, and surround it. After breaking in the door, the first group of soldiers enters and begins by identifying the beams and foundations. With a nail gun, one of the soldiers "hammers" size 10 nails into the center of each of the beams and supporting columns. A second group of soldiers carries explosive charges into the building (each containing about 10 kilograms of advanced-type explosives) and hangs them on the nails, while other soldiers chain the explosives to each other with a detonator connected to a wireless operation system. The soldiers retreat a few hundred meters away and count down until the blast is heard. It lasts several seconds and shakes the entire area. Hanging the explosives on beams and support walls makes ceilings collapse, and the entire building implodes as if made of some flexible material. In some cases, the army sends in bulldozers the next day to finish up the job, grinding the building to dust. In others, it leaves the destruction incomplete, indifferent to the fact that the half-hanging structure constitutes a safety hazard.

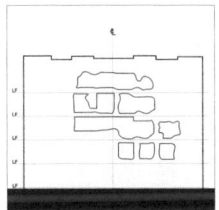

1.2 RAFAH, 2005 At the center of the photograph, a five-story apartment building. Two of the stories have been totally ruined, and another two have been partially damaged. The "targeted" blast spared the first story. It is perforated from ongoing exchanges of fire in the area, which have not been considered assaults or included in the statistics of home demolitions. Advanced technologies of targeted destruction enable the army to carry out "controlled demolition," which ruins "only" the apartments of those it suspects of terrorism. The fact that the rest of the building's residents are forced to live in a ruined, mangled building is irrelevant to military logic. The army continues to provide ready-made pretexts for its actions and boasts of maximal precision and gradually minimized damage to innocents. This operational discourse remains coherent because the security forces have the exclusive authority to determine who are guilty and who are innocent. The security forces announce their possession of evidence that remains largely confidential, and they are the ones to carry out the sentence under military considerations, leaving no room for appeal. (When appeal was possible, it would nearly always be rejected.) An Amnesty International 2004 report investigated and doubted the army's claims that Palestinians used the houses it demolished for shooting or assaults or were partly "deserted," "empty," or "uninhabited."

Outer walls made of bare, unplastered cement in the Occupied Territories cannot attest to a building's being uninhabited, as is plainly visible, for example, in the two bare buildings seen behind the building in the foreground of the photograph. The constant threat that looms over Palestinian construction and the ongoing economic depression are some of the reasons why Palestinians commonly dwell in buildings bare of outer plaster layers, from whose roofs iron rods still protrude so that construction work might be resumed as soon as resources are available again. The specter of future destruction haunts them constantly, scarring the present and shaping norms of spatial organization, dwelling, and movement in both private and public space. The holes blasted in these classical dwelling "boxes" are a constant, present reminder of the likelihood that any Palestinian, regardless of his or her activity, might be instantly thrown out of his or her dwelling and witness its demolition.

NIR KAFRI

1.3 TUL KAREM REFUGEE CAMP, 2002 In their pioneering days of "Wall and Watchtower," Jewish settlers new to Palestine would erect an entire environment within a few hours, between midnight and dawn, unilaterally creating facts on the ground in the face of the British Mandate and the local Palestinian population. The demolition of homes of suspected terrorists now takes place like some inverted projection of this "Wall and Watchtower" operation. The soldiers surprise the residents when they appear at night at the house destined for demolition. They have about six hours, until sunrise, to make the building uninhabitable and then get back to their base. They leave behind dispossessed families whose belongings usually are also turned to dust. The demolition is not an arbitrary act, but a result of a complex preparation that involves planning, tools, means, edicts, justifications, and precautionary measures. The army arrived at midnight at the home of Sirhan Sirhan, a Palestinian suspected of murdering five Israelis at Kibbutz Metzer. They concealed dynamite "fingers" in the house's inner walls without damaging its beams and foundations. The action lasted ten minutes. This, too, was the time allotted the residents to salvage some of their belongings. Precise engineering planning and the calculated use of explosives enabled the army to focus the demolition on one specific apartment in an apartment building, sparing neighbors: "So far, we did not touch Sirhan's place, because it is on the third floor, and we were concerned about the floors underneath and adjacent buildings. We chose a controlled, microscopic blast that would make the ceiling of a certain floor implode." The concern for "focus" of which the commander of this demolition boasted resembles the army's focus on targeted assassinations. Such concern attracts most of the attention to targeting the demolition itself and on ways to obtain higher precision, oblivious to the fact that the target for such a focus is determined by a "field jury" that unilaterally passes sentence and determines the limits of this focus. Thus, for example, after the army "surgically" targeted and assassinated Sirhan Sirhan himself, it proceeded to demolish his parents' house "precisely," without damaging neighboring houses. After evacuating the family and finishing their preparations, including a thorough videotaping of the home and of the father who confirmed that this was indeed the home of Sirhan Sirhan, the soldiers vacated the house and waited for the blast. The blast took place as planned, and the damage was done "only" to the family dwelling. The commander of the action confirmed by radio that "the relevant floor is no longer usable, while the rest of the building is intact," and the destruction forces withdrew. *photograph on the opposite page*

ACTIVESTILLS.ORG/KEREN MANOR

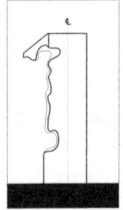

1.4 THE BULLDOZER, SUR BAHR, 2007 Use of bulldozers is usually reserved for the demolition of illegal construction. The building is crumbled slowly and methodically. Destruction begins at the building's right angles and outer walls. Once the outer shell is removed and the volume of the separate apartments is reduced to the various strata of floors and ceilings, the bulldozers pursue their gnawing like children savoring each layer of a chocolate-coated wafer. The duration of the work varies according to the height of the building and the number of rooms on each floor. Normally, no more than a day is required to turn the building into a texture of stone rubble and another few hours to complete pulverization and removal.

1.5 THE PILE, WADI QADDUM, EAST JERUSALEM, MARCH 2007 The bulldozers usually commence their work only after the residents and their belongings have been removed from the building. Since the demolition order applies only to the building, execution includes evacuation, as well. The inhabitants usually evacuate themselves, and the security forces make sure they are kept away while army employees identifiable on the spot in their orange-colored vests are busy removing belongings. These are packed by alien—sometimes very crude—hands: mattresses, beds, chairs, refrigerator, a baking oven, a wash basin, cushions, a table, and games are all heaped next to the building soon to be demolished, absorbing layers of dust that will be etched into them for an eternity of shame, a reminder of having been salvaged courtesy of the occupier kindly sparing the owners' unnecessary suffering.

1.6 THE SPECTATORS, SUR BAHR, EAST JERUSALEM, 2007 The residents who have evacuated themselves for fear of the law's long arm are distanced from the site. Usually, they find an opening through which they peek at the destruction of their home to the unfinished symphony of bulldozers. A group of neighbors share their witnessing, perhaps practicing for their own near future. Some of them might be standing there throughout the hours of demolition, while others emerge every time the house changes its material state. Seemingly at this last stage, when the rubble has been nearly flattened and evenly covers the ground, they assemble for a last farewell.

1.7 SURROUNDING THE BUILDING, A-TUR, EAST JERUSALEM, 2007 To protect the act from possible resistance expected from the evacuees, a huge crowd of policemen and soldiers is posted at several foci around a building destined for demolition.

1.8 THE TENT, A-TUR, EAST JERUSALEM, JANUARY 2007 The location of the Red Cross–supplied tent marks the outer circumference of the rubble. The tent is too small to contain belongings, so these are all piled up in front of it, objects accumulated over the years. In the small yard created in front of the tent sit the evacuees, bracing themselves for the coming hours.

MIKI KRATSMAN

1.9 BRAZIL CAMP, GAZA STRIP, 2007 Late at night, several days before they were photographed standing on the rim of the crater, at the sound of the familiarly chilling roar of a fighter plane, many of them opened their windows in order to minimize the damage from the blast that would soon rock their dwellings. They know the outcome of F-16s penetrating the camp's sky, their bodies and possessions having refuted time and again the Israeli Army's pretensions at sophistication and precision. With their utterly meager means, they try to protect themselves from the horror and to minimize as much as possible the span of injuries. Daem al-Az Hamad, a fourteen-year-old girl living about three hundred meters from the spot where the bomb fell, turning the house into a crater, was killed by a house beam flying toward her parents' home. The army insists that it is not responsible for her fate, claiming that destruction was precise, wrought "only" on Sami al-Shaer's house. This house was targeted because the army thought its yard contained a tunnel for smuggling arms. The spectators (over twenty people) standing at the rim of the enormous crater (about thirty meters in diameter, seven meters in depth) gaze at various focal points of destruction (most of the house walls along the Philadelphie Road adjacent to the camp are perforated sieves by now), embodying the gap between the laundered, semilegal language the army uses to justify its actions and the appearance of this space in which destruction looks anything but focused. The pure human violence exercised here, swallowing the house and leaving hardly a trace, interests this audience, in its amazement not letting it vanish, but holding onto it, a wake of memory: No spectator is safe from it, and it might reappear and surprise them at any time.

Spectators standing together around the crater is one of the few forms of public gathering in a public space that the occupation regime not merely tolerates, but even initiates and supplies with ample spectacle.

MIKI KRATSMAN

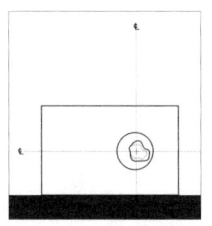

1.10 EIN BEIT ILAMA REFUGEE CAMP, NABLUS, 2007 The hole frames Mrs. Rajab, who is moving in her home across the wall. Today she passes the hole by as if she is already accustomed to its presence and accepts it. This hole was broken violently one night last September, taking her whole family by surprise. Immediately after the hammering and slight blast, they heard dogs barking and strangers moving around—Hebrew-speaking Israeli soldiers. The soldiers use dogs to move ahead and be the first to take gunfire and blows expected on their movement through the "tunnel" they produce inside the houses. This hole in her home, throwing her together with her next-door neighbors in unfamiliar ways, is one of a series of several dozen holes broken by Israeli combatants during nights of searching for a suicide bomber. The holes in the walls at the homes of the Rajab, Namruti, Taha, and other families enable the soldiers to proceed unseen inside the crowded camp in a relatively straight line. The walls do not constitute an obstacle, nor does the privacy of families living inside the houses that they devastate on their mission merit any respect. Moving through walls is part of the novel warfare developed by the Israeli Army during the second intifada. In a sense, this warfare is the inverse of the methods developed by the army in the early 1970s to crush resistance among refugee-camp dwellers. This inversion of space relations between open and closed, solid and air, mobile and static seems to resonate with various postmodern theories. In fact, this type of warfare, like the theories that inspired it, is produced by circumstances of a postmodern situation that sometimes threatens to obliterate the distance between the practices of power and the theories that address it. In the early 1970s, the army looked for ways to clear swathes inside the dense texture of the camp, through which it would move undisturbed, visible to all, obtaining deterrence and control of the space, razing whole building blocks in the process. Now the army seeks rapid contact with individuals targeted amid the civilian population and minimal friction while present in Palestinian territory. The two kinds of warfare differ greatly, but they share a significant common denominator—the Palestinian home is no obstacle to the army's movement. *photograph on the opposite page*

1.11 RAFAH, 2004 The D9 bulldozer moves forward, devastating anything in its way. It acts relatively quickly to "clear the area" of anything the army has designated as a target. It does so with a cast-steel blade installed in front, pushing anything in its way, piling up soil and stone, uprooting obstacles, while a ripper in its rear cracks open hard objects and material. Side blades resembling sharp fingernails installed on some bulldozers enable them to apply concentrated force on small objects. The bulldozer is very powerful, and its upgraded protective armor turns it into a terrifying tool capable of enormous damage and injury without its operator even sensing its extent. In the twelve days in May 2004 of Operation Rainbow, army D9 bulldozers demolished 183 houses in Rafah, partially damaging dozens of other buildings, razed miles of paved road, and devastated electricity, water, and sanitation infrastructures. Cameras installed in the bulldozers' front parts recorded the destruction.

Were the army to hand over to the public even a single one of these photographs taken by those cameras installed in the bulldozer's front, we could know something about what the army sees and the kinds of visual material it wishes to scrutinize. Perhaps we could also have in full action the photographer who took the photograph we are viewing now. But this photography is courtesy of the army, which released it for publication through a Wikipedia site, the Hebrew version of the free encyclopedia, to which the army apparently must be generously contributing. Here, then, is a photograph that the army wants us to view and to use without even needing its approval or copyright.

What is it about this photograph that the army chose to publicize? What exactly is the link between the act of photography that produced it and the action it describes—home demolition? The most obvious answer lies on the performance level: through the photograph, the army states that home demolition is not a contemptible act, but rather a justified action taking place in broad daylight, in view of the camera. But that is not all. The photograph, like the act of destruction, is meant not only for the eyes of the community in whose ears justifications are recited and waiting for approval. It is also destined for the eyes of the community being deterred and horrified. Home demolition, in the words of the deputy to the state attorney, advocate Shai Nitzan, is a way of "aiming, among other things, to deter potential terrorists, after having clearly learned that family is a central motive for them." The photograph, especially chosen by the army, with a Palestinian boy at its center—he, too, being a "potential terrorist," according to the self-same operational logic, like any other Palestinian boy—is supposed to serve as a deterrent for people whose family is important to them. The boy looking at the might of the Israeli Army is supposed to internalize the military logic that chooses targets of destruction and to acknowledge its justifications. If he does internalize this, the army implies, he will give up his resistance to the occupation and his struggle for his civil aspirations (being governed like others) and his nationalist hopes (enjoying self-determination or at least participation in the regime to which he is subject). But the army cannot control the way in which a young boy, forced to escape the jaws of this terrifying tool that wreaks destruction everywhere, will appear to the viewers. The boy is familiar with these scenes of devastation—he has probably seen too many already and still does not seem willing to accept them or to recognize their movement as the embodiment of justice. While his body is terrified of the powerful D9 and runs forward, he cannot tear his gaze away from the colorful shreds of houses mangled in the dirt.

1.12 AL-MUQATA'A, JENIN, 2001 The contingency plan to demolish the government building in Jenin was prepared long before the order was issued. Many contingency plans to demolish public buildings or other "strategic" structures in Palestine exist and have been waiting for the right moment to execute them, already having been practiced by soldiers. Those soldiers supposed to carry out this demolition in Jenin waited a few days at the "assembly area" as long as it remained unclear whether the plan would be carried out. Then the Twin Towers came down. The army recognized a window of opportunity while the attention of the world was riveted on the Manhattan horror scene. This is how one of the men of the Engineering Corps among the building's destroyers described it: "As soon as the second plane hit the second tower, we got the okay to go ahead. The army always does this when there is something special on the world scene. Say, for example, when Princess Diana was killed and world attention suddenly went elsewhere, they [the army] give us the 'Go ahead.' There are a thousand and one contingency plans that would eventually make a lot of noise, and this way no one even hears about it."

Indeed, destruction of the al-Muqata'a compound, built of three wings, as well as the inner yard where its residents used to grow vegetables for their consumption and the neighboring mosque (and the killing of nineteen Palestinians by bombing from the air) raised not a murmur in the local and international media. This photograph was taken accidentally by a journalist who happened to come to Jenin about a month later. He first heard of the destruction from Palestinians: "Here at this place there was a garden and decorative fish pond. For years, we received Israeli officers here royally [under the coordination arrangements between Israeli and Palestinian security forces in the days of the Oslo Accords]. This is how they reciprocated." The demolition of al-Muqata'a was a combination of bombing from the air and a ground operation by the Engineering Corps. Inside the building handed over to the Palestinians when the Israelis withdrew from the city under the Oslo Accords, an electronic surveillance device was concealed, and only an Engineering Corps crew could see to its destruction, so that it would not be suddenly revealed in the rubble. The various wings of the building became unusable, but the fact that their destruction was not completed turned it into a safety hazard and an additional monument of devastation.

Where, Where to, and When in the Occupied Territories: An Introduction to Geography of Disaster

Ariel Handel

Over the past nineteen months since the Intifada began my space has been constantly narrowing. First it became too dangerous to go for walks in the hills around Ramallah, then I stopped being able to drive to Israel, then driving between the Palestinian towns and villages was prohibited. Now I cannot even step outside the door of my house. The perimeters of my house are all that is left for me of Palestine that I can call my own, and even this is not secure.

— Raja Shehadeh, *When the Bulbul Stopped Singing: A Diary of Ramallah under Siege*

Therefore, the people planning weddings in this country—may their numbers increase—designed invitations that included all the information about their beloved daughter or son...the announcement of the wedding and its location, everything except the details of when the joyous event would take place—the day of the week, the date, and the hour. All these were to be added by hand, in keeping with the circumstances.... Only when the curfew was lifted would they fill in the missing details on the invitation and send it as quickly as possible to the invitees.... This new custom includes writing three or four dates, and the invitee knows that should a curfew be called on the first date...then the event will take place on the next date, and so on.

—Azmi Bishara, *Yearning in the Land of Checkpoints*

Space has been at the core of the Palestinian-Israeli conflict since the beginning of Zionism. That is why maps and tables of land area are often used to describe the conflict. From the United Nations partition map, through that of the 1948 state of Israel, up to the sophisticated maps presenting the depth of Israel's control of the Occupied Palestinian Territories (OPT), one can see the Palestinian space shrinking as the Israeli space keeps growing. According to these cartographic depictions, the

OPT makes up about 22 percent of Mandatory Palestine, the territory of the former League of Nations British Mandate of Palestine, and large parts of it are taken up by settlements, roads, military zones, and nature reserves. Of the West Bank's land, 41.9 percent is under direct control of the settlements; Area C, in which full military and civilian Israeli control still prevails, forms an additional 18.1 percent of the overall land space of the Occupied Territories.

These maps present concretely Israel's expansion at the expense of the Palestinians, and their importance is clear. Nevertheless, this manner of mapping has a few weaknesses and is even more remarkable in light of the state of affairs in the OPT today. First, these maps assume that both sides—Palestinian and Israeli—share the same space. This is a problematic assumption, which will be discussed below. Second, underlying the maps is the assumption that the conflict is a zero-sum game in which every piece of land taken from one side is added to the balance of the other. That assumption—which makes it possible to portray areas in the map as "Israeli" or "Palestinian" and to mark clear boundaries distinguishing one from another—causes confusion by creating an imaginary symmetry between the two sides. The significance for Palestinians of a defined Palestinian area is not the same as the significance for the Israelis of a defined Israeli area. These weaknesses derive from the fact that the maps present the *absolute value* of the space instead of its *use value*.

The absolute value of space is what can be measured by uniform distance units, for example, the aerial distance between two points, which is basically indifferent to occurrences in the measured space. The use value, however, refers to the actual possibilities for using a given space. If an impassable wall stands between points A and B, no matter what the absolute distance is between them, the actual distance taking into account the use value would be infinite.

Although one may consider as well the *economic* use value of a space (for example, whether it contains minerals or is located in an attractive real-estate zone), the *political* use value of a public space, and so on, I wish to deal with the basic use of space: how one can move in it. All other use values presuppose that primary value and are conditioned by it. Accessibility and centrality produce political and economic value; transportation expenses over space are embodied in the price of goods and are dependent upon movement possibilities in the space. Since my main concern is movement—specifically, human movement in space—it is clear that the spatial use value always embodies *time*. Road paving between two points doesn't change the distance in kilometers, but shortens significantly the actual time it takes to travel between them. In the same manner, a blockage on the road lengthens that time, since the blockage contains an inherent postponement. The mode of movement, therefore, greatly influences the use value. Flying in a jet plane bears no similarity to walking or riding a horse on the ground, either in terms of the speed of movement or in terms of the route. Another important primary assumption is that human time is always a scarce resource. In the twenty-four hours of a day, one must sleep, eat, work, and so on. From the basic fact that each movement in space is also a movement in time, it follows that scarcity of time disables space, as well. That is, there is a limit to the possible distance between one's home and work, since one must move between them and allow sufficient time in each for sleep and work.[1]

Mapping use values is much more complicated than mapping absolute values, but people do it regularly. Every departure of a person from their house assumes a more or less clear idea of the place, direction, and estimated time to the destination. People moving in space use cognitive (imaginary) maps that reflect their acquaintance with an area, that is, a sense of orientation, knowledge of different locations, routes, and bypasses, and tacit assumptions about different use values of distinct spatial units within that area. Having such a map in mind, they may gauge their movement according to its mode and speed, the destination's location, the time of departure, and so on.[2] That map's stability—the routinization of daily activity in space and time—is the very basis of what Anthony Giddens calls "ontological security." Repetitiveness connects the individual and the outside world and gives the former the faith in the continuity and stability of the latter. It is critical for the individual's sense of security and stability, as well as for the building and preservation of *long durée* social institutions.[3]

Two main limitations dictate modes of spatial use: the organization of physical space and the regulations that govern its use. The organization of physical space includes possible movement routes (entrances, streets, highways, railways, and so on) and the limits imposed on them (doors, barriers, traffic lights, and so on). The regulations that limit the use of space are those defining movement options and restrictions within the given physical possibilities (cars are not allowed on sidewalks, train travel requires a valid ticket, driving is on the right side of the road, and so on). A knowledge of both the physical organization and the rules governing use is a necessary condition for the creation of a cognitive map of a person's =environment.

In the OPT, as I will argue, due to constant changes in both the physical space and the regulations governing its use, the stability of the space dissipates, and it is nearly impossible to create a map of use values. Therefore I will describe the spatial conflict in Israel/Palestine in a different way: as a dispute not over land units, but over the very possibility of *using* the space. From the fact that the built area of the settlements is 1.7 percent of the West Bank's land, that the "settlements' boundaries" are 6.8 percent of the land, and that the sum of Israel's direct holdings in the West Bank is 42 percent,[4] it is impossible to understand how life and movement are distorted in *the rest* of the area. What follows will show how the Israeli side, with its combined military and civilian occupation, strengthens its own spatial stability at the expense of that of the Palestinians. While Israeli use values in the OPT, with the fenced settlements and the wide, fast, and blockage-free roads that they enjoy there, are more stable than ever, the effective Palestinian space disintegrates and dissipates.

This leads to an inversion of the usual arguments concerning space and society. Public space is usually treated as structured, planned, supervised, and controlled (or at least, such are the pretensions of the ruling power), while human movement is treated as something that resists structured, planned, rational control. Michel de Certeau, for example, describes the way pedestrians use unplanned shortcuts or avoid moving in places where they should be moving according to rational plans.[5] Plans can never predict all movement possibilities, and down-up deviations occur even in the most planned space. In the OPT, in contrast, the ruling power itself produces rhizomatic, changing, and fluid space, while the users are the ones who struggle to reintroduce predictable features into their living space.

The first part of what follows will try to demonstrate the current spatial state of affairs in the OPT, and, paradoxically, will try to draw a map of the unmappable and present averages of the unaveragable. All the maps to be shown will be contingent and temporary and represent only the principle of temporariness and contingency. These are maps that, in principle, are not up to date even on the day of publication and that actually were not accurate at any time.

The second part will suggest a historical reading of the Israeli domination of Palestinian spatial use values from the occupation of the Palestinian territories in June 1967 until the situation developed that is described in the first part. This second part will shed light on the process of producing physical space that is gradually charged with usage regulations. Those involved in the production of Israeli space, I will argue, understood the importance of the *point* and the *line* when loaded with both active and passive spatial control and management practices. The deployment of settlements, outposts, and of roads, coupled with differential rules governing the use of space, enabled control technologies to develop in the OPT.

THE SPATIAL STATE OF AFFAIRS

Various kinds of movement restrictions have been imposed in the OPT over the years. Most of them were personal (that is, prohibiting specific people from moving in certain parts of the OPT or from entering Israel) or limited in time (a curfew on a specific village or a limited blockade for the duration of a specific military operation). Generally speaking, beginning in 1972, when the "general exit permit" was granted, Palestinian movement was not limited within or outside the OPT. The situation changed in the First Gulf War, when a total closure of the OPT was imposed for forty-one days. During the 1990s, closure became institutionalized as the rule, with the exit permit as the exception. At the same time, restrictions were imposed on passage between the Gaza Strip and the West Bank.

During the middle of the 1990s, Israel began imposing internal closures (*keter*) on various parts of the OPT. These closures were neither permanent nor stable, but the very idea of the division of the land and the institutionalization of checkpoints became permanent features. The division of the territory required movement-control technologies, which became refined with the passage of time. They included many kinds of barriers (manned checkpoints and physical obstacles, such as earth mounds, concrete cubes, empty or sewage-filled trenches, iron gates, fences, and walls), as well as various, frequently changing passage regulations (some of them official and requiring numerous permits, others imposed ad hoc, without being published or institutionalized in any form).

Following the outbreak of the second intifada in September 2000, movement restrictions increased drastically, and the OPT was dissected into many dozens of frequently changing "land cells." As of January 2006, in the West Bank, there were fifty-eight manned checkpoints and 471 unmanned blocks.[6] "Surprise checkpoints," consisting of a jeep or armored vehicle and a small number of soldiers, are not included in these numbers, though their disruption of life is even greater than that of the permanent roadblocks, for which it is possible to prepare and to estimate the time needed to get through them. According to a report of the United Nations Office for the Coordination of Humanitarian Affairs (OCHA), at the beginning of 2006, there were, on average, 100 surprise checkpoints per week. In addition to all the aforementioned barriers are dozens of kilometers of fences alongside roads on which Palestinian movement is prohibited and, of course, the Separation Wall.

The checkpoints map, printed by OCHA every two to three months, is not only out of date by the time it is published, but cannot be up to date at any given moment. Since data collection takes time, and the array of barriers changes so quickly, by the time the Nablus segment of the map is being prepared, the data collected in the Hebron region are no longer accurate. According to the organization, ninety-five physical barriers were added between November 2005 and January 2006. As stated above, however, there is no way of knowing when these were added or what the real data were at the time of printing. Local newspapers and radio broadcasts report the daily barrier situation along with the weather forecast in order to give the closest possible approximation of the movement options for the day.

The outcome of the barriers is that the space becomes divided into small cells, and passage between them is nearly impossible. In the West Bank, there are some areas to which entry is nearly impossible: East Jerusalem, the Jordan Valley, the "Seam Zone" (the area trapped between the Wall and the Green Line). In the northern part of the West Bank (especially from Nablus to the north), entry is permitted only to inhabitants of the area. At night, the IDF raids East Jerusalem neighborhoods as well as villages in the Jordan Valley and in the Seam Zone, expelling to the other side of the checkpoint Palestinians who cannot produce an ID card bearing the same address as the location where they are found.

The rest of the West Bank is divided into dozens of cells, and movement between cells, as will be discussed below, is difficult, slow, and unpredictable. As a result, Palestinians decrease their affinities to "distant" areas (usually no more than a few kilometers away). People choose work and attend schools in accordance with the location of checkpoints. Housing prices "before the checkpoint" rise drastically in comparison to those "beyond the checkpoint."[7] In Hebron, a few weeks before their due date, pregnant women move from the Israeli-controlled part (H-2) to the Palestinian side (H-1) so as to be able to reach the hospital in time and avoid giving birth at one of the checkpoints.[8]

For a realistic view of the division of space, on the closures map, we can draw the cells whose inhabitants must get through certain checkpoints (Map 1). Since each checkpoint is located on a specific crossroad through which the population of the cell must pass, the picture that emerges is reminiscent of a stream-drainage basin. As of January 2006, there were 101 cells. Since this map represents the movement of vehicles, it shows all unmanned barriers (such as gates, trenches, mounds of earth) as impassable.

Map 2 presents the possible movement routes between the cells. Points signify land cells. Lines signify possible passage routes—for example, if the two cells are separated by a manned checkpoint allowing vehicles to pass. Where the road leading out of a cell is blocked by a physical barrier, the cell is marked as being closed. We must, however, qualify this map. First, it is reasonable to assume that there are roads that bypass these blocks. Not every dirt road is marked on the maps, and it is impossible to indicate all possibilities of movement. But the bypass roads are far from being a solution to the problem. There are few of them, they are difficult to traverse, and the IDF is constantly on the lookout for them so as to block them, as well. The second qualification is that in a few places, there are underpasses below the Israelis-only road, which allow the movement of cars between cells by avoiding the barriers at road level.[9] But this qualification has its own qualification and has to be limited, as well. Each of these underpasses has a built-in-advance iron gate, which means that passage through them is always conditioned. The third

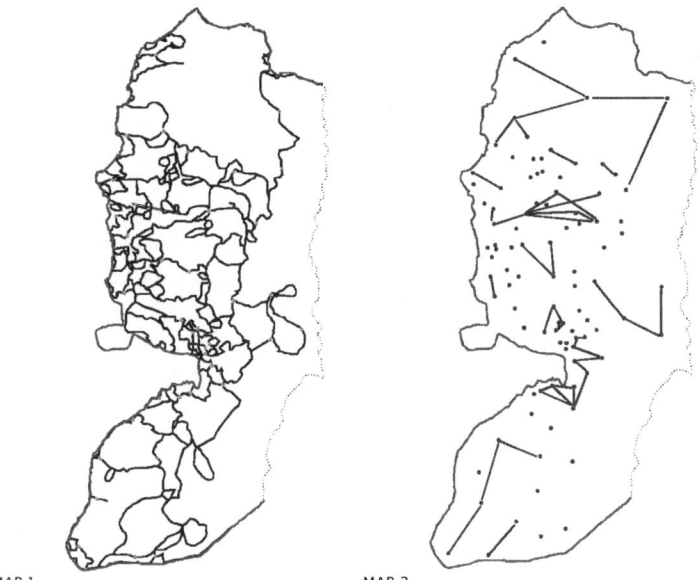

MAP 1   MAP 2

qualification is that movement between cells is not always strictly impossible, but it is discontinuous. That is, at many of the barriers there are "back-to-back" taxis; passengers get out of one taxi, cross the barrier on foot, and get into another taxi. Clearly, however, this mode of travel lengthens the travel time and increases its cost significantly.

Some important things can be learned from Map 2. The most obvious of these is the number of cells that are completely cut off from neighboring cells. Most West Bank inhabitants cannot drive their own cars or travel continuously beyond their immediate surroundings. Moreover, the cells that are connected to others are arranged like a train, so that one cell is connected to the second, which is connected to the third, and so on. Hardly any land cell is connected to more than one other cell. The significance of this fact for the Palestinian wishing to pass through several land cells is that the possibility of movement through each cell is essentially "contained" in the preceding cell. Thus, a blockage in one cell will prevent movement overall. It should be noted that in at least some of the places in which it seems that there is free passage (such as the Jordan Valley, East Jerusalem, the Seam Zone, and the northern West Bank), this freedom applies only to inhabitants of the area. Thus, the power of the surprise checkpoints becomes clearer, because they can further reduce the connection between different areas and divide each land cell into many subcells.

Let us now take a small segment of the map (Map 3) and test its spatial use values for a Palestinian and for a settler traveling on similar routes between adjacent points (Beit Furik to Salfit for the Palestinian; Itamar to Ariel for the settler).

As can be seen quite easily, the Palestinian has much less space per time unit. And since time, as we have pointed out, is a limited resource (there is a fixed number of hours available for work, study, family, sleep, and so on), the Palestinian has absolutely less space than his neighbor the settler. The situation only worsens under a curfew or tight internal closures. In addition, passing through checkpoints with a private vehicle requires a permit that is available only to a few. Only 3,412 Palestinians (of 2.3 million West Bank inhabitants) hold a valid permit for passing with their vehicles through internal West Bank checkpoints.[10] Thus, taxis have become the major enablers of movement, especially between cells. Since in many

Road prohibited
for Palestinians

MAP 3 Comparison of distance and travel time for a settler traveling from Itamar to Ariel and a Palestinian traveling from Beit Furik to Salfit. [Background map: United Nations Office for the Coordination of Humanitarian Affairs.]

	ITAMAR–ARIEL	BEIT FURIK–SALFIT	CHANGE PERCENTAGE
Aerial distance	~ 14 km	~ 17 km	21%
Road distance	~ 17 km	~ 24 km	41%
Travel time	~ 11 minutes (at an estimated speed of 90 km/h on a fast road)	~ 3 hours, 24 minutes (at an estimated speed of 60 km/h on an old, narrow road and factoring in three checkpoints involving delays of about one hour each)	1854%

places taxis work in "back-to-back" mode, requiring passengers to change taxis at each checkpoint, the time for pedestrian passage and taxi exchange must be added to the total travel time.

An even bigger problem than the long travel time for the 24-kilometer journey is the inability to predict the probable length of that time. I have calculated the passage time through each of the checkpoints as one hour, but this number has no significance. In many reports concerning the movement regime in the OPT one can find a statement of the kind "the journey that once took fifteen minutes now takes more than two hours." From the point of view of a Palestinian passenger, these averages, too, are essentially meaningless. When travel from point A to point B can take between one hour and two days, there is no practical purpose in calculating averages. In a few areas, movement has been institutionalized in a way that creates a reasonable standard deviation for travel time. But for a person needing to pass through several checkpoints, uncertainty is multiplied by the number of checkpoints, thus making planning a day nearly impossible.

Map 4 shows the journey of Litfiyeh Jaludi, a woman with kidney problems, from the village of Faqqu'a, near Jenin, to Altuni Hospital in Nablus, on June 7, 2001.[11]

What is the distance between Faqqu'a and Nablus? The aerial distance is about 35 kilometers, but as we have already seen, aerial distances are not useful

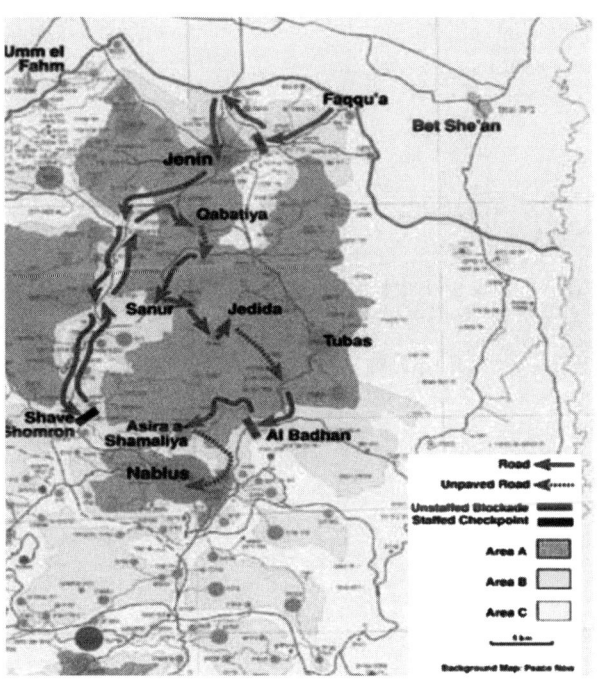

MAP 4 Journey of Litfiyeh Jaludi from Faqqu'a to Nablus. [Source: B'Tselem]

to the average person. Let us look, then, at the distance by paved road. It is about 10 kilometers longer. On June 7, 2001, however, the real distance for Jaludi was 125 kilometers!

It is reasonable to assume that Jaludi, a sick woman who needs dialysis three times a week, knows the shortest and most efficient way to get to the hospital. Let us follow her route on that day. Jaludi and B'Tselem investigators left Faqqu'a and headed south. Near the Shavei Shomron settlement, they encountered a manned checkpoint where the IDF soldiers refused to allow them to pass. Although Jaludi and the investigators made clear that she is sick, the soldiers steadfastly refused her passage. Jaludi and the investigators had to drive back and try to find an alternate route to the hospital. Only after encountering two unmanned barriers, which lengthened their journey significantly, and driving over rough dirt bypass roads, did they manage to reach the hospital.

It is clear that on any given day—when temporary or permanent checkpoints are removed or added, when other soldiers man the checkpoint, when the level of alert is different, when the checkpoint bypass road is open or blocked, and so on—the distance will vary greatly. The distance can vary from forty-five kilometers to infinity, which occurs when the road is blocked, and reaching Nablus from Faqqu'a is impossible. The time is even more variable than the distance, since the waiting time at any of the checkpoints can range from minutes to weeks,[12] and there is no way of estimating it in advance.

Torsten Hägerstrand, a Swedish geographer, developed a graphic method for describing human movement in space and time.[13] A schematic graph of this kind looks like this:

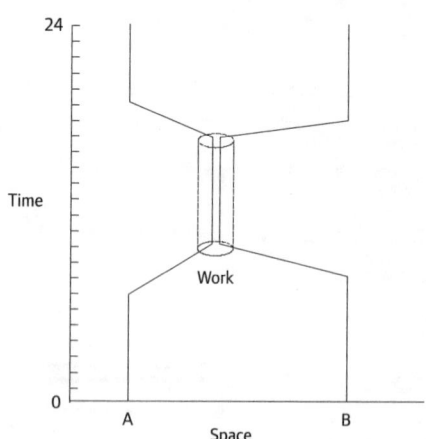

ILLUSTRATION 1

The horizontal axis indicates space and the vertical axis indicates time in twenty-four hourly units. Person A sleeps at his home until 7:00, then drives to work (moving in both space and time), stays there until 16:00 and then drives back home. As can be seen, the traffic load is greater in the morning, so the travel time is longer, and the graph's gradient is steeper. Person B, who works with person A, lives farther away from the workplace, but since he owns a fast motorcycle, he can leave his home at a later hour and still reach work on time, and his movement gradient will be more moderate. These graphs can be drawn at different resolutions for both time and space. Graphs can be sketched in units of seconds and meters or, as done by Hägerstrand himself, in "life routes" of people, from birth to death, where the space resolution is on the level of migration between cities and countries. Illustration 2 is a schematic representation of the spatial movement of a settler and a Palestinian.

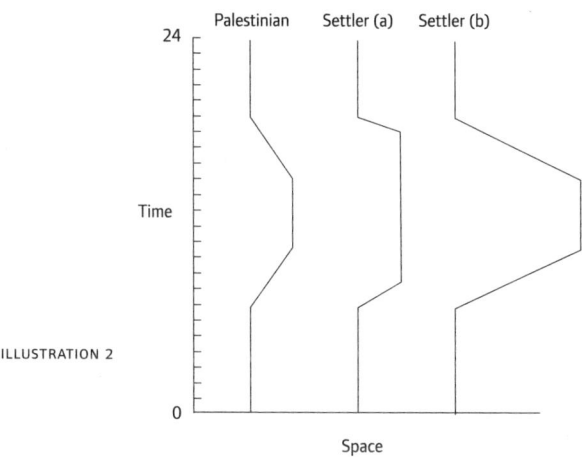

ILLUSTRATION 2

The settler in option (a) drives the same *distance* to work as the Palestinian, but can work more hours. In option (b), the settler devotes the same amount of *time to travel* as the Palestinian, but can work farther away (that is, this settler has more options regarding the place of work).

But this graph, again, is misleading. The fact that *on average* it takes more time for a Palestinian to traverse the same distance as the settler does not describe the real situation. Let us have a look at a higher-resolution graph, describing several possible situations of at a checkpoint.

Illustration 3A shows slow, but steady movement; 3B shows a one-hour delay of nonmovement and then quick release of the jam; 3C shows an encounter with a

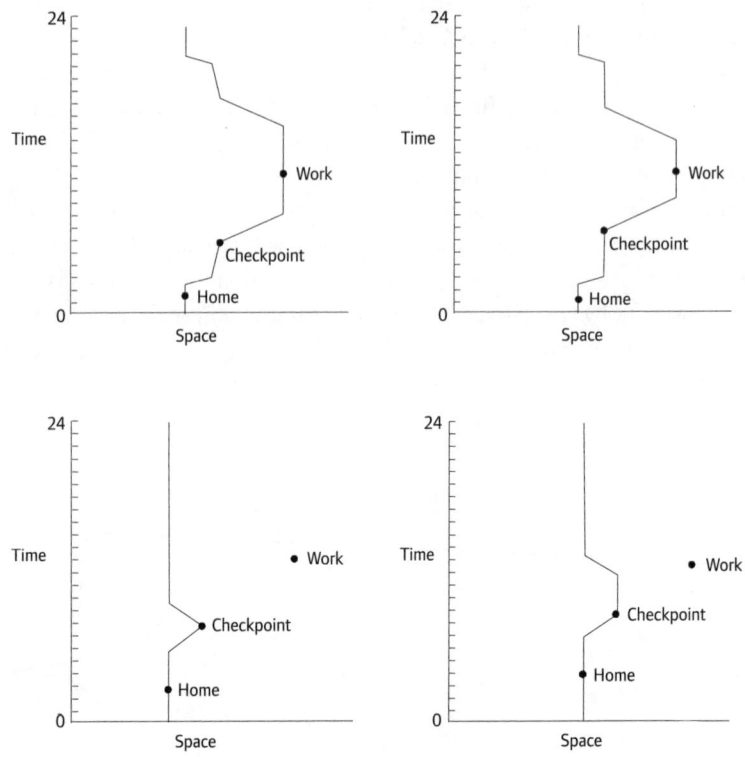

ILLUSTRATION 3 (A top left; B top right; C bottom left; D bottom right)

closed checkpoint; 3D shows an encounter with an open checkpoint, but just as the person reaches it, after an hour's delay, he finds that he is not allowed to pass. In both of the last cases, the workplace remains beyond the person's reach.

These four situations, of course, do not cover all possible options, and many variations could be made in each of them. Illustration 4 will show one possible variation of a man moving through four different checkpoints from his home to work, the university, or the hospital.

Illustration 5 shows what happened at the a-Tufah checkpoint when many inhabitants of the al-Mawasi area of the Gaza Strip were unable to return home while the checkpoint was closed for fifty consecutive days. These people, nevertheless, came every day, from morning to evening, to see whether the checkpoint had opened.[14]

The cumulative implication of the facts reviewed above is that Palestinians spend most of their time in movement (standing in line, in that model, is movement at zero speed). A Palestinian must wake up earlier and returns home later in order to work fewer hours. The Palestinian wastes his day in moving for the sake of waiting and in waiting for the sake of moving, without knowing whether he will even manage to arrive and if so, when. The ordinary person, or for that matter the settler, leaves one place,[15] such as home, on the way to another place in pursuit of work, family, entertainment, or study. For the settler, the way itself, short or long, is only a road, a *placeless place* connecting different places. This contrasts with the Palestinian, who leaves home very early and wastes most of the day in placeless places, lacking in interest or in significance as reference points. As Azmi Bishara puts it in *Yearning in the Land of Checkpoints,* "The question 'Where are you?'" loses its meaning, "because life in the shadow of the checkpoints [has] turned it into a foolish, at times even taunting question. For where else could one be under such circumstances? If a curfew was imposed, people would be at home, and if there was no curfew, there was the choice of their immediate surroundings or the checkpoint, since moving from city to city had become nearly impossible."[16] The question "Where are you?" becomes foolish simply because the Palestinian is actually always in a *nonplace*. Absurdly, the checkpoint itself, the ultimate placeless place, becomes the main reference point. Everything, both space and time, is measured in terms of before and after the checkpoint, and there are no assurances that another checkpoint will not pop up around the bend. This situation makes attempts at movement nearly absurd. In despair, Palestinians reduce movement to the necessary minimum. Many Palestinians have not been beyond their village entrance for years. Illustration 6 shows the remaining space left for an ordinary Palestinian with respect to various closure situations. The settler is used as a "control group" in order to show the potential of spatial movement without forced closures.

The question "Where?" is not the only one to lose its meaning. The question "Where to?" becomes obsolete, as well, in a place where one does not know whether to head east or north to reach a destination in the south (see Litfiyeh Jaludi's route on Map 4). Given that the roads that actually connect points change frequently and that planning the day ahead is nearly impossible, it is hard to ask "Where to?" Regarding the question "When?" there is no need for further discussion. Palestinians cannot say when they will reach work or come back home from it. The standard deviation around the average is so high that the answer will be almost meaningless.

Every human activity takes place in time and space, and the questions "Where?" "Where to?" and "When?" are both the trivial and the necessary conditions

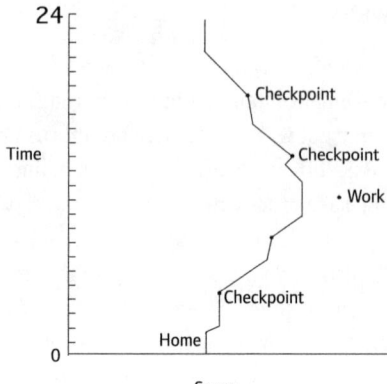

ILLUSTRATION 4

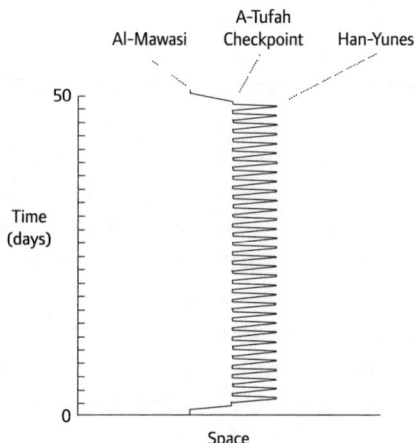

ILLUSTRATION 5

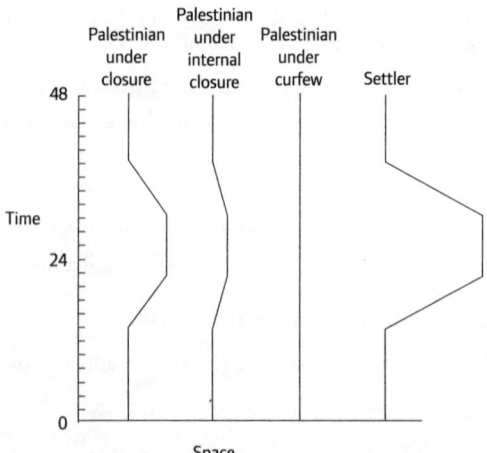

ILLUSTRATION 6

for any individual or social activity and social coordination. Changes in time and space, therefore, affect the human activities occurring in them. According to Anthony Giddens, routine in space and time is a basic element of daily social activity.[17] Routinization is crucial for creating ontological security, which is established and preserved by these daily activities. Repetitiveness connects a person with the outside world by making the former believe in the continuity and stability of the latter. Routinization is crucial, then, for both the individual and for *long durée* social institutions; its absence is harmful to both the individual and society. When there is no routine, one's faith in one's own stability and in the existence of one's inner core seems to dissipate. The same happens in relation to society. Giddens analyzes situations in Nazi concentration camps in order to show the extent to which the breach of routine produces radical ontological insecurity. He cites Bruno Bettelheim: "It was…the inability to plan ahead because of the sudden changes in camp policies that was so deeply destructive."[18]

Hägerstrand talks about another kind of limitation on human movement above the purely physiological—the need for sleep or for food at regular intervals, and so on—which he calls "coupling constraints." These refer to activities undertaken jointly with other people. Physiological constraints are thus further limited by the need to coordinate activities with other individuals in order to achieve a goal that can be done only in a group. Therefore, to the hardships of the uncertainty and unplanability of time, one must add the impossibility of coordinating a joint activity, let it be work, school, research, or a purely social meeting.

The decomposition of space by Israeli policies in the OPT undermines the ability of Palestinians there to work, to produce, to sell, to buy, to study, to heal, to know someone, to keep in touch, to organize, to coordinate, to resist, and to fight. The limits on movement imposed by both physiological and coupling constraints in the OPT have produced what must be called a "geography of disaster." A disaster in this sense is defined as a large-scale event in which suffering and loss occur together with partial or total collapse of the systems of space and time.[19] In periods of disaster, regular patterns and rules are suspended, but not canceled or permanently changed, since the disaster is, by definition, limited in time (and space). During that time, however, it is hard, if not impossible, to discuss patterns or rules, to coordinate, and to synchronize expectations. A government in a disaster zone is expected to restore routine and order and is judged, among other things, by the amount of time it takes to achieve this. The situation in the OPT can be defined as a "continuous disaster," since, as noted above, uncertainty has become the only true certainty, and its end is nowhere in sight.

The geography of disaster, in our case, is not the description of the spatial characteristics of a disaster area, but rather the main source of the disaster. Exerting control *by means of* space aims mainly at preventing organization, coordination, resistance, and fighting, but it necessarily also prevents people from working, producing, selling, buying, studying, healing and being healed, socializing, being intimate, and being friendly. The authorities, in this case, are not trying to restore order, but are acting instead as the main producers of chaos. In other words, Israeli order is preserved by the systematic destruction of Palestinian order.

I began by drawing a distinction between the absolute value of space as measured in square kilometers and the use value of that space. As we now can see, Israel controls the OPT by means of a systematic suspension of Palestinian spatial use values in that space. From this spatial analysis, it becomes clear that the Palestinians and the Israelis do not share the *same* space. Israeli use values in the OPT are completely different from Palestinian ones, and actually, as will be shown in the next section, the former were created purposely in order to reduce the latter. The two spaces, Israeli and Palestinian, overlap, both being limited in absolute terms by the same reference points, yet the difference in use values nullifies the argument that these are actually parts of the same space.

The tight control of the Palestinians attained through the systematic destruction of the continuity of space and time would be hard to achieve otherwise. Relatively speaking, Israel does not invest a lot of money in direct military occupation. The control technology is simple and nearly primitive, consisting of mounds of earth, trenches, and a few jeeps.[20] In relative terms, not much violence is invested in the economy of domination.[21] The number of Palestinian fatalities, when seen in light of the duration of the conflict, is not high in comparison with the numbers in other armed conflicts.[22] The generation of uncertainty has been found to be a simple, cheap, and effective technology. It is simpler and cheaper to impose arbitrary and highly fluid movement prohibitions while intentionally avoiding signposting, documentation, or notification to the controlled population about the prohibitions, than to build walls and fences. When a Palestinian does not have a clue as to which zones are open for passage and what the open-fire orders are regarding someone passing through a prohibited zone,[23] it is reasonable to assume that this Palestinian will avoid movement altogether. Next, I will address how control has been refined to the point of maintaining this situation of continuous disaster.

A BRIEF HISTORY OF THE DOMINATION OF PALESTINIAN SPACE

As we saw above, use values for a space are determined by two main factors: the physical organization of the space and the rules governing its use. Both are determined, with varying levels of success, by the power that controls public space. In other words, the possession of space and the right to formulate the rules for its use give the authorities the power to determine the spatial use values. Thus, an efficient ruling power can overcome numerical and territorial inferiority. In the OPT, space has been organized and rules have been fixed in a way that enables Israel to dominate effectively a territory in which it seems to be inferior. The settlers make up less than one-tenth of the West Bank's population, and the built area of the settlements are less than 2 percent of its land, and yet Israel rules with the penetration and intensity that we have discussed above.

The purpose of this historical overview is not to examine former modes of control and space management or even to provide a chronological description of the limitations on Palestinian movement, including what existed prior to the current situation. The goal here is to show how the spatial array of the OPT (as determined by the IDF, the settlements, and legislation) made possible the current use of movement-disruption technology.

The description, therefore, should not begin with al-Nakba, the "disaster," as the Palestinians call the events that led to the creation of the state of Israel in 1948, or with the military administration of the Palestinian citizens of Israel (1948–66). All these fall under the classic category of the struggle over territory and tell us little about the current situation of numerous cells, barriers, and borderlines. The history presented here is important for understanding how one jeep can close an entire land cell and how a tiny outpost can exert influence over a large space. In other words, what follows aims to show the power of the clever use of dots and lines.

To explain better how a space can be dominated by clever deployment and use practices, I will begin with a historical example. In his book about the history of barbed wire, Reviel Netz describes how it was used to take control of space.[24] When the barbed-wire fence was first invented during the 1870s, it was designed for containing herds of cattle and delimiting their grazing. The first time it was used explicitly to control people and to win a war over space was during the Boer War (1899–1902).[25] In that war, Britain fought to protect its interests in South Africa, particularly the newly discovered gold mines. The first battles against the Dutch settlers were quickly settled in favor of Britain. Then, however, the Boers started to organize in small "commando" units of horseback-mounted riflemen who attacked the British forces and bombed the railways, the major means of conveying goods and military forces at the time.

To protect the railways, the British used barbed wire, which at the time was used to keep trains from crashing into animals. Thick barbed-wire fences were stretched along the rails, which, as in every other British-dominated area, crisscrossed the territory. Small guard posts, about one kilometer apart, dotted the wire fences. The method succeeded beyond all expectations. The new technology had created spatial enclaves, allowing domination over a large territory with relatively few troops. A few soldiers could now successfully delay and even fend off a quite large commando unit.

Netz discusses the manner in which the railway network was converted into a tool of spatial control by means of lines (railways) that connected dots (train stations). Once the linear network was surrounded by barbed wire, a "topological inversion" occurred, so that the lines *connecting* the stations became lines *separating* one area from another. The South African savanna was divided into relatively small land cells, enclosed on all sides by barbed wire. The network of fenced railways was later used as the passive base from which British military forces were deployed for "sweeping activities" in which they "cleared" the villages out of the separate land cells. The inhabitants were moved to "concentration camps," which also were surrounded by barbed wire. The space was divided and cleared, the inhabitants were restricted to specific areas where they could live, and thus the entire land became British.

This historical example resonates strongly with how Israel exerted control over the OPT. In the OPT, this process began with a freezing of spatial organization and a limiting of legitimate Palestinian space solely to the built areas. After these Palestinian "islands" were delineated, major portions of the remaining land were declared to be Israeli by defining them as "state lands," "fire zones," or "nature reserves." This gave Israel a hold that was sufficient for organizing the continuous space in which the Palestinian villages were scattered.

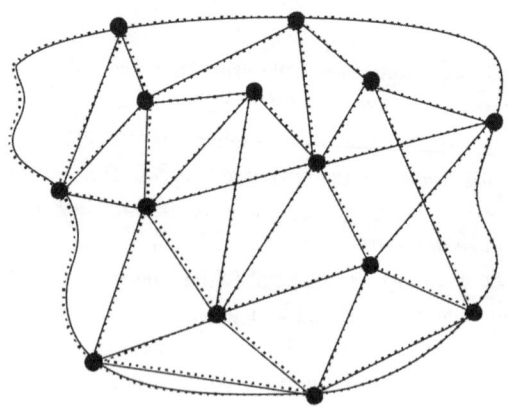

ILLUSTRATION 7 Once the railways are fenced they become separation lines, dividing the savanna into relatively small cells.

The isolated settlement points, sowed by Israel over the years, grew in a strange manner, with an emphasis on maximal linear spread, so as to divide the Palestinian areas. Connecting those dots by lines—wide paved roads—completed the topological inversion to create isolated land cells, with movement between them controlled, if not prohibited. Starting from the relatively passive formation of lines and dots, the IDF developed an offensive approach to defense. Eventually, this led to the IDF's pulling the small amount of land still left to the Palestinians out from under their feet by declaring some of them illegal residents in their own homes.[26]

The Israeli takeover must be understood as a *combined* military and civilian occupation; neither a military nor a civilian occupation alone could explain the extreme situation that characterizes the control of Palestinian space. The situation arose from the ongoing process of acquiring land in order to build a settlement, then acquiring more land in order to protect it. The newly acquired "defense area" is quickly settled by civilians, prompting the army to acquire more land in order to protect the civilians, and so on. The combined civilian-military process of achieving domination over the territories thus involved possessing a growing amount of land, coupled with changing the manner of possession from de jure to de facto, and taking advantage of the possession of the land to impose spatial-use regulations that make possible additional spatial takeovers. All this results in a reduction of Palestinian use values: from building restrictions, to movement restrictions, and finally to residency restrictions.

LIMITING THE PALESTINIAN "ISLANDS"

Two legislative orders from the early years of the occupation begin the takeover story. The first, in 1968, froze registration of land titles by West Bank inhabitants.[27] Israel justified this move by citing the need to avoid harming the rights of Palestinians who had left the West Bank during the 1967 War and who therefore would not be able to prevent the title from being registered in someone else's name.[28] For various historical reasons involving, among other things, the wish to avoid tax payments and the existence of traditional communal agricultural practices, more than 70 percent of West Bank lands were not registered in any way before the order was given.

The second order, in 1971, changed the 1966 Jordanian planning law known as City, Village, and Building Planning Law, No. 79.[29] This change in the planning legislation had a great impact on spatial growth in the West Bank, because it redefined permitted locations for building and development. Actually, this was not a matter of replanning, but rather of adopting unplanning as a policy. The Supreme Planning Council became a unit of the Civil Administration once all authority for planning was handed over to the IDF area commander and all the Jordanian and

Palestinian officials on the council were replaced by Israelis, most of whom were either military officers or representatives of the settlers.[30]

The council received exclusive and complete authority over outline plans, detailed plans, building permits, setting the boundaries for villages and cities, and so on. The regional and rural planning committees were disbanded, leaving all authority in the hands of the Supreme Planning Council, whose decisions could no longer be appealed.

Thus, Palestinian planning and development were frozen. Since the Israeli occupation, not a single outline plan has been made, and the only valid regional outline plans are those for the regions of Jerusalem and Nablus dating from 1942. Though needs and the social and economic realities have changed drastically since 1942, these outline plans still form the guidelines for permit approvals. Of 424 villages in the West Bank, only one, Taibeh, has an approved outline plan. Most of the cities that are run by municipalities have valid outline plans, but these date back to the British Mandate before the creation of the state of Israel and are long outdated. Because so much time has elapsed since the plans were drawn up, and because a great part of the West Bank was defined by the British as an "agricultural area" or "nature reserve," the land allocated for building has long since been exhausted. In addition, the plans declare 1000 square meters as the basic, indivisible unit for a house, thereby preventing division of the land into smaller portions and severely limiting even the options for in-fill construction and development.[31]

Fixing the spatial configuration as that of the late 1960s and early 1970s limited Palestinian living space to extant places, essentially prohibiting additional development. This was accomplished by denying building permits, thereby laying a legal foundation for destruction and for the arbitrary use of force. This limiting, both in theory and in practice, divided the Palestinian space, that is, the built areas, from the space of potential Israeli development—that is, all the rest.

Palestinian expansion was limited also by reserving widespread areas for military purposes, enacting aberrant building restrictions near main roads, and prohibiting the construction of residential buildings near settlements and military bases. In addition, many areas were declared nature reserves in which construction and agricultural activities were prohibited.[32] Thus, Israel succeeded in prohibiting building in nearly 70 percent of the West Bank.[33]

In the early 1990s, the Central Planning Bureau of the Civil Administration prepared Special Partial Outline Plans for some four hundred villages in the West Bank.[34] These plans were meant to replace the detailed plans required by Jordanian law. Instead of being a means of development, however, these new plans were actually limitation plans, formed as they were by taking aerial photographs of each village, drawing a line around the built areas, and prohibiting construction beyond that line. According to these plans, construction in the villages was to be in-fill, that is, vertical construction in available areas within the line and a gradual increase of population density.

Using outline plans as a means of limiting Palestinian construction and as a tool for increasing construction in the settlements was very common in East Jerusalem, too, despite institutional and legal differences between this area and the rest of the West Bank. Upon the annexation of East Jerusalem in 1967, and contrary to what happened in the rest of the West Bank, all the Jordanian outline plans were canceled, creating a planning vacuum that was filled gradually only in later years. During the first ten years of Israeli annexation, only ad hoc building permits were given, and these only in extremely limited areas of the town.

At the beginning of the 1980s, the Jerusalem municipality decided to prepare outline plans for all the Palestinian neighborhoods in East Jerusalem, most of which were completed, and some of which are still in the process of preparation and approval. The most significant characteristic of these plans is the huge amount of land, roughly 40 percent, labeled as "open landscape," upon which construction is prohibited. According to the plans approved by the end of 1999, only 11 percent of East Jerusalem land, *excluding* the expropriated land, was available for Palestinian construction. In keeping with the other demarcation plans of the West Bank, construction is allowed mainly in the existing built areas.[35]

Today, authority for planning and building in Area C, about 60 percent of the West Bank, is exclusively in Israeli hands. Palestinian applications to the Civil Administration for building permits on their own private lands that fall outside the demarcation boundaries have been rejected in most cases. The arguments for the rejection are based upon the demarcation plans (in which the land is beyond the plans' boundaries), as well as upon the British Mandate's outline plans (in which the land is defined as an agricultural area or as a nature reserve). The legal counselor of the Civil Administration, Colonel Shlomo Politis, has admitted that "in practice…there are no building permits for Palestinians."[36]

In some parts of the West Bank, especially in the western hills, the boundaries of Areas A and B overlap almost completely with the boundaries of the built Palestinian areas, which serve as the boundaries of the demarcation plans. Most of the available land is therefore in Area C, where the planning authorities are Israeli. As this illustrates, transferring to the Palestinian Authority the mandate for planning and building in Areas A and B is meaningless in many cases.[37]

The planning vacuum was filled by Israel. Planning policy for the West Bank is guided by two main bodies that coordinate their efforts. The first is the government, acting through various ministries, and the second is the Jewish Agency, acting through the Settlement Department of the Zionist Organization. The 1980

Drobless Plan, the master plan of the Jewish Agency for settlement in the OPT, defined its goals as "reducing the spread of uncontrolled Arab settlement." This is an application to planning of the view that Palestinian space must be restricted to existing homes and villages and that all growth is an uncontrolled invasion into Jewish space.[38] Thus, the demarcation of Palestinian space and the creation of the tools that made possible Israeli domination of the remainder of the space have resulted in a topological inversion. The Palestinian villages were no longer part of the continuous space of the West Bank, but rather became isolated islands in an open frontier reserved exclusively for Israelis.

The main tool Israel used to acquire Palestinian land was declaring it "state land."[39] This method is based on the Ottoman Land Law of 1858. According to this law, the sovereign can seize ownerless land, defined as land that is not private property, that has been cultivated for less than ten successive years, that has not been cultivated for at least three years, or that is rocky land so far away that "the loudest voice made by a man in the nearest settled area would not be heard there." As noted above, the registration procedures for more than 70 percent of the West Bank's land had not been completed by the time of the order that froze registration, making this land easy prey. It must be noted that Israel had significantly increased the burden of proof concerning land cultivation. In addition, the actual marking of the land on maps was very inaccurate. The primary marking was made on aerial photographs, which have a distortion effect that increases as one moves from the center of the photograph to the perimeter. Apparently, more than 30 percent of the lands declared as state land should not have been so declared, even according to the strict criteria set by Israel.[40]

Here we must emphasize the inversion of the burden of proof. A Palestinian wishing to appeal against his land's seizure must pass through the Appeals Committee. The main principle according to which the committee works is that the burden of proof lies on the person claiming that the land *is not* state land. According to the Order Regarding Government Property (Judea and Samaria) of 1967, "If the Custodian has confirmed, in a written declaration bearing his signature, that a given property is government property, that property shall be considered government property for so long as the contrary has not been proven."[41] The first obstacle facing Palestinians wishing to object to such labeling of their lands was that, in many cases, they did not even know about the procedure. Many Palestinian landowners discovered that their lands had been declared as state land only when construction of a settlement began.[42] In most cases, the actual building started months and sometimes years after the declaration, and therefore they could not appeal to the committee, since appeals are accepted only within forty-five days of the declaration. In addition, an appeal is costly, because the appellant must pay an appeals fee, a certified surveyor for a precise mapping of the land, and a lawyer to draw up the affidavit and present the case to the Appeals Committee.

Even if the appellant manages to fulfill all requirements and to convince committee members of his ownership of the land in question, there are still cases in which the committee will reject the appeal. This is because sometimes the deliberations take place after the custodian has already signed an authorization for one of the bodies engaged in settlement and after preparatory work for a settlement has already begun. To prevent the reversal of such a situation, section 5 of Order No. 59 Regarding Government Property includes the following provision: "No transaction undertaken in good faith by the Custodian and another person regarding any property that the Custodian believed, at the time of the transaction, to be government property shall be nullified, and it shall continue to be valid even if it is proven that the property was not at that time government property."[43]

TAKING CONTROL OF THE CONTINUOUS SPACE

Geographer Elisha Efrat argues that the settlements did not create a critical demographic mass, and that their geographic dispersal made them weak and vulnerable. "It is hard to say that after a few decades of creeping civil occupation, there is now Jewish domination of the territories,"[44] he claims. Efrat's attitude, derived from the classic geographic view, misses the complexity of the spatial expansion process described here. True, the number of settlers at mid-2007 was 267,500,[45] or around 10 percent of the West Bank's population, and the constructed areas of settlement were only 1.7 percent of the West Bank's land. Indeed, by these measures, the settlers are clearly inferior numerically. But these measures ignore highly important factors of space arrangement and usage regulations: the location of the settlements, their municipal area, their shape and form of development, the roads connecting them, and the military defense practices in the settlements and on the roads. These are the factors that describe the real scale of Israeli domination of the OPT.

THE LOCATION OF THE SETTLEMENTS The spread of the settlements was very calculated. The settlers of Gush Emunim, the flagship movement of religious-ideological settlement in the Occupied Territories, understood well that their "control of a region is a function not only of the size of the population residing there, but also of the size of the area in which this population exercises its impression and influence."[46] The map of the settlements shows how they spread throughout the land, often intentionally in the heart of Arab population centers. Many of the settlements were built very close to Palestinian settlements, blocking further Palestinian urban development. In some cases, the settlement was purposely built in a location that, due to topographic circumstances, would be the natural direction for expansion of the Palestinian settlement.[47]

The proximity of the settlements to main roads was of major importance. Road 60 is the main north-south artery in the West Bank, connecting the six main Palestinian cities. Spreading the settlements along this axis was meant to enable Israeli control over the main road while blocking possible Palestinian construction that would have linked Palestinian settlements on both sides of the road. As the master settlement plan for Judea and Samaria states, "Jewish settlement along this road will create a mental barrier with regard to the mountain ridge and may also limit the uncontrolled expansion of Arab settlement."[48] In most cases, the settlements are isolated and control relatively short segments of the road. In a few cases, however, Israel created a block of settlements that dominate a significant area of Road 60. One example is the settlement block of Shilo, Eli, and Ma'ale Levona, whose municipal boundaries cover some 1,925 acres around the road.

The settlement of Ma'ale Adumim exemplifies the importance of settlements' location. Its municipal area is only 0.8 percent of the total land of the West Bank, but its location near the west-east road from Jerusalem to Jericho cuts the West Bank horizontally into two parts that are almost totally separated.

THE MUNICIPAL AREA With regard to Jewish settlements, the manner of demarcation is the inverse of that applied to Palestinian settlements. Whereas for Palestinian settlements the municipal area is de facto never more than the built area, the municipal boundaries for Jewish settlements can be dozens of times the size of the built area.[49] The inversion is most salient in the Arvot Hayarden Regional Council (along the Jordan valley), where the municipal boundaries were defined as "all the Jordan Valley excluding the Palestinian settlements." Here the entire continuous space has become Israeli, excluding only the already built Palestinian areas, thereby preventing any future Palestinian development.

Two important concepts are the "area of the community," that is, the municipal boundaries of a specific settlement, and the "municipal area," which is the area under the jurisdiction of a regional council that oversees several settlements. The areas within the municipal area's boundaries include all the lands that Israel has laid claim to over the years. Therefore, the boundaries of most of the Jewish local authorities in the West Bank are curved and include noncontinuous patches of land. The municipal areas of the regional councils contain huge tracts of empty space that are not part of the "area of community" of a specific settlement. The built Jewish area in the West Bank is 1.7 percent of the total land, while the community areas are four times that size. An *additional* 35.1 percent (nearly 500,000 acres) has been put under the jurisdiction of the regional councils. Thus, the settlements directly control 41.9 percent of the West Bank.[50] The municipal areas were significantly increased in the mid-1990s, the period of the Oslo Accords, and as stated by an official report, "the municipal boundaries were broadened without any connection to the urban needs of the existing settlements."[51]

THE SHAPE AND FORM OF DEVELOPMENT As stated above, the municipal boundaries of most of the regional councils in the OPT are winding and, at times, include noncontiguous tracts of land. At first glance, these boundaries seem totally unreasonable and indeed, they do not meet any standard of classic geography-based planning. Let us take Itamar as an example. This settlement, inhabited by 540 people, has an area of the community of more than 1,750 acres, or fourteen times the built area, of hilly, winding, narrow, and long tracts of land, surrounding "islands" that are not part of its municipal area.

It is even harder to comprehend the form of construction within that area. Instead of erecting new buildings adjacent to the existing built area, more and more outposts have been built (six so far) at the edges of the settlement boundaries. Although the last "official" settlement, Modi'in Illit, was established according to an Israeli governmental decision in 1996, since the mid-1990s, more than one hundred illegal outposts have been erected all around the West Bank and in Gaza Strip before the evacuation. Although these outposts are indeed considered

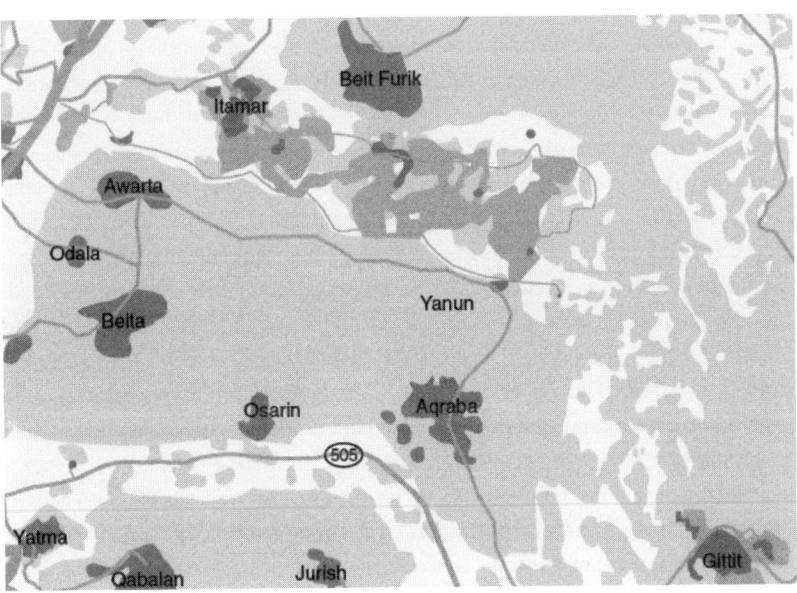

MAP 5 The settlement of Itamar, its outposts (dark dots) and roads, and the Palestinian surroundings.
[Source: B'Tselem]

"illegal," most of them receive a full service from the Israeli authorities: defense by means of soldiers, weapons and fences; electricity and telephones; paved roads; budgets for education and religious services, and more. Building outposts thus necessitates paving more roads through difficult terrain, additional security, and so on. Broadening one's view from the settlement itself to its Palestinian surroundings makes clear the reason for such an odd form of expansion. Itamar directly blocks the growth of three Palestinian villages: Beit Furik, Awarta, and Yanun. Preventing Palestinian contiguity is the only reason for such a development.

Another example can be seen in the city of Ariel. Its municipal boundaries stretch 11 kilometers from east to west, and its maximum breadth is 2.5 kilometers. Here, again, we can see an intentional blocking of Palestinian continuity, because the settlement was stretched out as long as possible by means of building from the outside in, that is, starting at the edges and only then building the central area. The length of Ariel's built area is 5 kilometers, but its width is only 700 meters. From a planning perspective, this is an unreasonable spread.

The unreasonableness is even more glaring in light of the fact that adjacent to where the first of the houses were built, especially to the south, there are extensive available lands that could have served to widen the settlement. Construction in outlying areas indicates that the Israeli planning authorities were not concerned with urban planning, but rather acted to create a buffer, as long as possible, separating the Palestinian villages on both sides of the Cross-Samaria Road and disrupting their territorial continuity.

ROADS "The roads in Judea and Samaria have always been notable for their close connection to the topography, the conditions of the agricultural land, and the distribution of rural and urban Arab areas."[52] The settlement roads totally differed from this pattern from their inception. Every settlement built in the OPT entailed construction of a road leading to it, even when this involved breaking through difficult, rocky terrain or dealing with steep slopes. Ten kilometers of road were needed to connect the settlements of Kadim and Ganim to the Jenin bypass road, fourteen kilometers were paved for 300 people living in Shim'a, and more than thirty kilometers of road were paved between Teko'a and the Dead Sea in order to connect to 550 settlers in Ma'ale Amos and Mitzpe Shalem.[53] These roads required land that was obtained through widespread confiscation of Palestinian lands.

In addition, the roads adhered to the logic of erecting barriers in the heart of Palestinian population centers. Contrary to the common purpose of roads—connecting people in different locations—the Israeli roads in the West Bank were meant to do the exact opposite to the Palestinians. Some of these roads were planned as physical boundaries limiting the urban development of Palestinian settlements. These roads prevent the natural coalescence of Palestinian settlements in

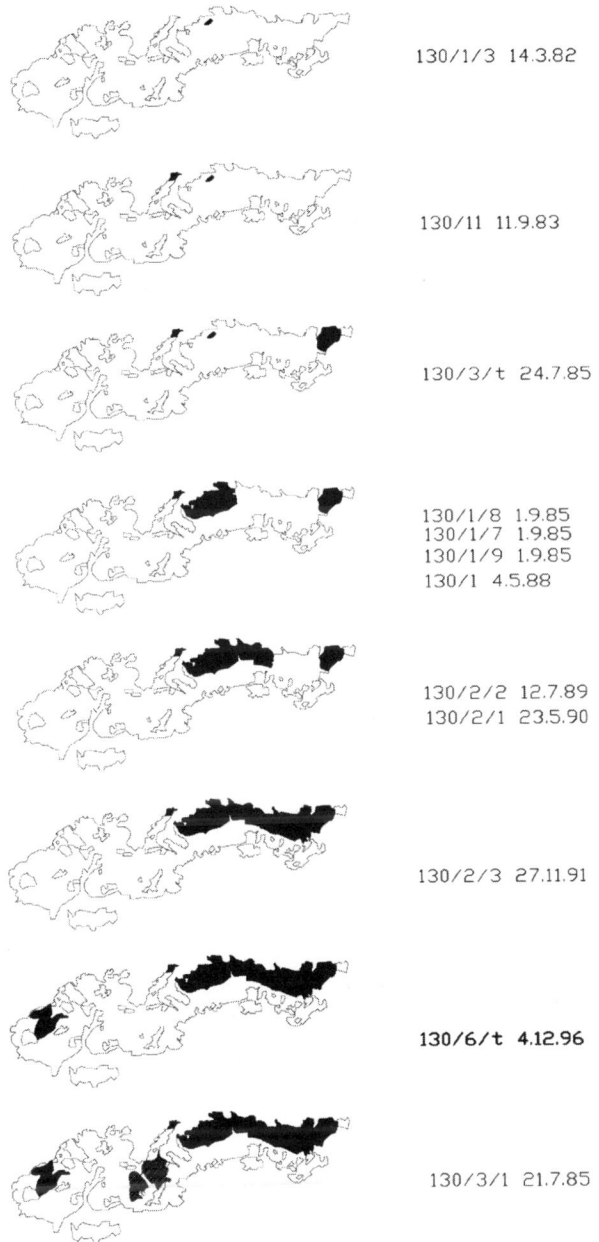

130/1/3 14.3.82

130/11 11.9.83

130/3/t 24.7.85

130/1/8 1.9.85
130/1/7 1.9.85
130/1/9 1.9.85
130/1 4.5.88

130/2/2 12.7.89
130/2/1 23.5.90

130/2/3 27.11.91

130/6/t 4.12.96

130/3/1 21.7.85

MAP 6 Growth of the built area in Ariel. The last illustration is based on a plan from 1985, which so far has not materialized. [Source: B'Tselem, "Land Grab" (see note 4)]

areas over which Israel wants to maintain its control for military or civil purposes. Amira Hass wrote in January 2003:

> A person can drive all over the West Bank without knowing not only the names of the villages and the towns whose lands were taken for the building of Jewish settlements and neighborhoods, but also the very fact of their existence. The names of most of them do not appear on the road signs.... A Jew driving on the little-traveled roads of the West Bank might think that there are no more Arabs; they do not drive on the wide roads he uses....
>
> Whoever planned the settlements, both big and small, 20 years ago knew that it was imperative to prevent any attacks on them and their inhabitants by the "natives," primarily achieved through building roads that would isolate every Palestinian village and town, distancing them from one another and from the main roads. This was done to such an extent that a mound of earth became sufficient for blocking access from the village to the road.... Israeli decision makers...knew how to plan a dividing web of roads that would become the main weapon against the Palestinians.[54]

Citing security as an excuse, since the outbreak of the second intifada, Israel has prevented the Palestinians from using a major part of West Bank roads. A B'Tselem report divided the restricted roads into three types: those on which travel by Palestinians is completely prohibited, partially prohibited, or restricted.[55] The completely prohibited roads are further divided into roads with a military manned checkpoint that allows Jews to pass, but prohibits Palestinian passage (defined as a "sterile road") and roads that are blocked with physical barriers preventing access. In some cases, even crossing the road by car is prohibited. Consequently, Palestinians are limited in their ability to use even nonprohibited roads. In such cases, a Palestinian traveling on a permitted road who reaches an intersection with a prohibited road must exit the vehicle, cross the prohibited road on foot, and take another vehicle for the rest of the journey. A B'Tselem survey shows seventeen roads and road segments in the West Bank that are completely prohibited to Palestinian vehicular movement. Their total length is 120 kilometers.

The partially prohibited roads include those on which only Palestinians holding a "Special Movement Permit for Internal Checkpoints in Judea and Samaria"[56] may drive. This category also includes roads on which driving is permitted only for Palestinians with the special permit or who live (as their ID cards testify) in villages or towns that are otherwise inaccessible. There are ten roads or segments in this category with a total length exceeding 245 kilometers.

The restricted-use category includes roads that are accessible only through a manned checkpoint because all other access roads have been blocked by physical barriers. Generally speaking, Palestinians do not have to show a movement permit in order to pass through these checkpoints. Nevertheless, Palestinians must undergo certain inspections. At some of these checkpoints, the small number of soldiers relative to the amount of traffic results in long waits. As a result, many drivers avoid using these roads. In addition, police enforce traffic laws rigorously in Palestinian areas and impose many fines. From time to time, the IDF imposes additional restrictions, such as allowing only public-transportation or commercial vehicles access to the road. Fourteen roads and road segments in the West Bank fall into this category. Their total length is 365 kilometers. Map 7 shows how these prohibited and restricted-use roads are distributed over the West Bank.

DEFENSE PRACTICES "Our basic assumption always is that wherever Jews are, the army must ensure their well-being," declared Ron Schechner, assistant to the defense minister.[57] Since there are Jews everywhere in the OPT—in the settlements, at outposts and on the roads—the army must employ defensive practices at any point where Jews live or pass.

MAP 7 Israeli-controlled roads in the West Bank. [Source: Applied Research Institute, Jerusalem]

Initially, Palestinians were restricted from entering the settlements themselves. This restriction was not published as an official order, but it was clear that a Palestinian had no business within a settlement, with the exception of Palestinian laborers employed in construction, cleaning, and so on. In 1996, the entire municipal area of the settlements was declared a closed military zone.[58] The order states, naturally, that "the declaration's orders do not apply to Israelis." In a later phase, the military declared sterile "special security zones" around the settlements and around the outposts, as well. The special security zone includes a paved "security road" and a barbed-wire fence encompassing the settlement at a distance of 400 meters from the perimeter of the built area. In many places, however, the fences were put up farther than 400 meters from the perimeter.[59] The spatial defense framework was upgraded again in January 2003, when the Central Command brigadier general ordered that "the boundaries of any settlement's security envelope extend to the most outlying houses of the neighboring Arab villags."[60]

The term "defense" is misleading. The IDF's conception of defense has always been active and offensive. "Going outside the fence" was the basic practice for defending a fence from the time of the pre-IDF organizations of the 1930s. The real meaning of the term "security zone" is a sterile, Palestinian-free zone. In many of these places, this translates into a shoot-to-kill policy against anyone who enters. It is important to note that these areas are not declared, signposted, or marked in any way, on a map or on the ground. No wonder, then, that Palestinians prefer to stay far from whatever might be a "security zone." When that zone extends to the houses of the neighboring Palestinian village, the only safe space for inhabitants lies within the village boundaries themselves.[61] Since these offensive-defense practices are also imposed on roads used by Jews, Palestinians avoid approaching the roads, even on foot, as much as possible.[62]

To the "defensive practices" we must add actions of the settlers. These, in keeping with the military rationale, but in a less restrained manner, move "defense" outside settlements and roads and into the shrinking Palestinian space. Thus, a complementary mechanism is created: "security measures" declared by the army are used by the settlers to enlarge the area they control; this, in turn, begets an enlarging of the area affected by security measures, and so forth. According to one of the settlers, "There are officers who expect us, as they even told us themselves, to enter nearby villages and go wild. I can understand them; it is hard for them to act with their arms and legs tied, and in many cases the politicians indeed fetter them."[63]

In many parts of the West Bank, settlers sow terror and fear in their surroundings, thus preventing Palestinians from approaching their own lands, roads, and olive groves. Many Palestinians are afraid of getting near areas where they may encounter settlers. In some areas, mainly around Nablus, in southern Mount

Hebron, and in the city of Hebron, such violent behavior by the settlers has become routine, and many Palestinians are abandoning their lands and limiting or changing their daily routes.[64]

The topological inversion is thus complete. The lines that connect the dots have become too dangerous to cross, either on foot or by car, and thus are delineated as isolated islands.[65] This situation has been perpetuated, both politically and graphically, by dividing the West Bank into Areas A, B, and C. Area C, which is under full Israeli control, constitutes a continuous 60 percent of the West Bank's territory. Within it are no fewer than 190 islands of Areas A and B.[66] The roads and settled Jewish points determined this map on the clear assumption that "whatever is not Palestinian will now be Israeli." In many cases, the boundaries of areas under Palestinian rule are congruent with the built areas and always are at a great distance (the "defense area") from Jewish settlements and roads.

The settlements were not built with the intention of reducing Palestinian *movement*, but rather to limit the expansion of built areas and to prevent the establishment of an independent Palestinian entity, just as the railroad lines were not laid in South Africa in order to divide the space and to play a role in the Boer War. But in both cases, the original intent is irrelevant. From the moment a division of the space was needed, the settlements and the roads formed an excellent basis for barriers and separations. The fences and the checkpoints, which are relatively new, are the embodiment of the potential for closure and limitation that existed in the organization of space from the beginning. All that was needed was a redefinition of movement regulations, coupled with enforcement by means of trenches and mounds of earth. According to Olivier Razac, "The perfection of a tool of power is not measured so much by its technical refinement as by its economic adaptation. The instruments which serve authority best are those which expend the smallest amount of energy possible to produce the effects of control or domination."[67]

THE REGULATION OF SPACE

As we have just seen, spatial analysis is a powerful tool for examining the development, application, and consequences of movement-disruption technology proceeded in the OPT. It can illuminate a number of other topics related to the use of that technology in the regulation of space there, topics whose importance usually has been reduced or ignored in other modes of analysis and that merit deeper critical scrutiny. These topics are the outposts, the "Seam Zone," the various disengagement plans, and the separation of Palestinian movement from Israeli movement.[68]

In early 2008 there were 122 "official" settlements in the OPT, inhabited, as of mid-2007, by 267,500 settlers. The last settlement built with permission of the government, Modi'in Illit, established in 1996, is the second-most populated city in the West Bank. As of 2004, its population was 27,300. In addition to "official" settlements, more than 100 outposts have been established in the OPT since the 1990s. Their total population is no more than several thousand.[69] Comparing the city of Modi'in Illit to the outposts emphasizes the difference between considering the size of a population and considering its location and distribution.[70]

While the population of Modi'in Illit is five to six times that of all the outposts combined, a map shows the essential difference in their spatial claims. Modi'in Illit, located close to the Green Line, has a sufficiently large mass of inhabitants to bring about a change in the route of the Separation Wall so as to include the settlement on the Israeli side, swallowing up large parts of the land of the Palestinian village of Bil'in.[71] Without disregarding the harm caused to Bil'in, we can say that this harm is mainly local and that its effect is more similar to that depicted by the conservative spatial description of the conflict. That is, it does not prevent the existence of Palestinian space, but rather limits and reduces it. The outposts, on the other hand, in spite of their tiny size, at times even unmanned, fulfill their objective of taking over the space. Just as the train stations, despite their being no more than uninhabited passage points between places, played a significant role in the British domination of South Africa, so the main importance of the outposts lies in the lines stretched to them and in the defense practices with regard to the points and lines.[72]

The settlement Itamar again provides an excellent example (see Map 5). The winding, space-blocking municipal area of the settlement was not enough. Six tiny outposts were spread out on a line eight kilometers long.[73] A road was paved and security was established between the points,[74] defining the abstract municipal areas de facto. Sometimes these additions even provide an excuse for enlarging the municipal areas, as in the case of the municipal area of the settlement Shim'a, which was enlarged in 2005 so as to include the Sansana outpost located more than an aerial distance of five kilometers away.

THE "SEAM ZONE"

The "Seam Zone" is the Israeli-named region between the Separation Wall and the Green Line, in which Israeli domination and Palestinian exclusion reach their maximal point. The first article in the order creating the Seam Zone states that "no one may enter the Seam Zone or stay in it" and that "anyone in the Seam Zone must leave it immediately."[75] The next article allows all other "kinds of people" into the zone, with the exception of its Palestinian inhabitants.

In keeping with this draconian regulation of space, every stay in it requires a permit. The trapped villagers must have a "permanent resident permit," which must be renewed every three months, in order to continue living in their own houses. Noninhabitants wishing to enter the Seam Zone must request a special permit from the District Coordination Office (DCO). There are a dozen categories of people who may request a permit: agricultural workers, teachers, irrigation technicians, and others. In general, the permit gives its holder the right to stay within the closed zone only during the day; sleeping in the zone requires separate approval, marked on the back of the permit. Also, the permit is valid only at the specific entrance gate named on it.

A "spatial table" is thus constituted in the Seam Zone. Instead of arranging information, data, and people's files in columns and rows on a piece of paper or in office drawers, the table here is created on the ground. Each item is put in its specific place according to the rational justification of the narrow categories set by Israel. Movement, allowed only at one named gate and only during its specific hours of operation, is also bound to specified patterns. The other aspect of the table is its ability to exclude and eliminate. The moment an item fails to fit into its prescribed location, it is considered dispensable and is discarded.

Unique to the Seam Zone is the physico-geographical existence of this table. The imposition of bureaucratic documents onto a concrete territory makes the classification much more violent than it is ordinarily. It is a sophisticated method that prepares the ground (or at least produces the potential) for a gradual "bureaucratic combing action" by means of which the land will be emptied of its inhabitants by a reduction of the number of permits and the eligibility for them. The spatial imposition of the table allows not only the removal of a person's papers from a drawer, but also the removal of the individual from the land.[76] A situation will be created that is similar to that of the concentration camps of the Boer War. The remaining inhabitants will stay in villages that are actually isolated pens, encircled by barbed wire or walls, cut off from their lands and from any possible space for expansion.

"DISENGAGEMENTS"

The ground withdrawal from the Gaza Strip and the dismantling of the settlements there, known as "the disengagement plan," was marketed to the Israelis, as well as to the world, as the first step toward the end of the occupation. In fact, all that happened was a change in the mode of control. True, at this moment, Israel is no longer settled in the Gaza Strip, but it still controls it effectively. First, the passages between the Gaza Strip and Israel are working on a very irregular basis,[77] a situation that creates an acute scarcity of basic goods, such as flour, sugar, and construction materials. At the same time, the export of goods and the entry of workers to Israel are prohibited. As of December 2005, 65 percent of the Gaza Strip's inhabitants earned less than $2.10 per day.[78] According to OCHA's data, Gaza is on the verge of a humanitarian catastrophe.[79]

The aerial and marine spaces of the Gaza Strip are exclusively controlled by Israel. Small unmanned aircraft patrol the skies constantly, relaying data and targets for liquidation. IDF combat planes assassinate "wanted" men and produce sonic booms in the middle of the night to frighten the populace. Artillery units shell the periphery of the cities and systematically destroy the infrastructure of the roads in the northern Gaza Strip, to the extent of severing the town of Beit Hanoun from the rest of the strip. There are even threats of bombing inhabited neighborhoods (after warning residents that to avoid harm they are advised to leave), in response to Qassam rockets fired at Israel.[80] In April 2006, the IDF reduced the "safety range" for artillery bombing from 300 meters to 100 meters from built areas. One hundred meters is the known error for an artillery shell of the kind used in Gaza. In other words, the IDF is shelling with clear knowledge that civilians will be hit. The destruction in northern Gaza Strip neighborhoods is great, and several civilians have already been killed in their homes.[81]

All future disengagement plans for the West Bank mention continuing all military activities, liquidations, and raids "if necessary." In fact, "disengagement" gives Israel an opportunity to increase the severity of military practices used against Palestinian inhabitants. James Ron distinguishes between two spatial patterns: the "frontier," defined as a peripheral region unincorporated into a powerful state's legal zone of influence and, as such, more prone to acts of lawless nationalist violence, and the "ghetto," defined as a repository of unwanted and marginalized populations but that is nonetheless included within the dominant state's legal sphere of influence, with inhabitants classified as quasi-members of the polity.[82] Ghetto populations are more likely to be policed than forcefully deported.[83] The space of the OPT is gradually being transformed from a ghetto into a frontier. This is the true meaning of the "Lebanonization" that security authorities talk about in Israel. This is the shift of the status of the Occupied Territories from a space policed and governed rigidly to a space of warlike methods in which almost everything is allowed in order to allow the ruling power to "restore order." The Gaza Strip has passed into the last phase before becoming a total frontier, according to Ron. This stage is marked by effective control coupled with a renunciation of responsibility, alienation, and elimination. This is the apparent path in store for areas from which Israel will disengage in the future, especially, it appears, the most populated areas of the West Bank, located between the Separation Wall and the Jordan Valley.

Concurrent with increasingly limited possibilities of movement in the heart of the West Bank, other, seemingly opposite processes are taking place in the periphery. Here I refer mainly to the "passages" in the Separation Wall and the plans for segregated roads for Jews and Palestinians in the West Bank.[84] The passages, according to spokespeople of the control array, exhibit a conspicuous change in the army's attitude toward checkpoints. The change is manifested first of all in their names. These sites are designated as passages, and not as barriers to prohibit passage.[85] The defense minister's adviser on matters of the Palestinian "fabric of life," Baruch Spiegel, claimed that this change would be expressed in the fact that the passages would operate on a principle of being "usually open," as opposed to checkpoints, which operate on the basic assumption of being "usually closed." Also, these passages would have fixed passage regulations, "something which has never existed."[86] The passages are even defined as a humanitarian issue, receiving $50 million of American financing as "aid for humanitarian needs."[87]

The passages, in keeping with this approach, have been privatized and are operated by private security companies on the assumption that these can ensure better "customer service" to the Palestinians and that competition between the companies will bring about an "improvement in service." The aim of privatization is to "change the management culture of the checkpoints."[88] The company indeed emphasized service and even set maximal time spans for the passage of Palestinians in the various categories.[89] Passage will be by means of a biometric "smart card," available for purchase at the passage itself (and valid for one to three months). A Palestinian would not see a soldier or other official until the final phase, when the photograph on the card is compared with the individual who presents it.

Segregating the road system is also presented as a humanitarian solution to the harsh situation of the Palestinians. According to the plan, code named by the military Everything Flows, a continuous Palestinian space *parallel* to that of the Israelis will be made possible by means of interchanges, bridges, and underpasses. As of January 2006, twenty-seven underpasses and overpasses had been built along the Jewish-only main roads. An additional nineteen are being planned or under construction. In addition, two new Palestinian road systems are planned.[90] The first road, called "East Villages Road," will allow Palestinian movement from Hebron to Bethlehem east of Gush Etzion, continuing to Ramallah through an underpass below the Jericho-Jerusalem main road. From Ramallah to the northern cities, mainly Tulkarem, the connection will be the "Western Villages Road," passing west of the Beit-El–Tapuah main road.[91] The total length of the new roadways is planned to be 140 kilometers (out of 2,000 kilometers of roads in the West Bank), spread over thirty-four roads.

But all of these nice words conceal a very different reality and are no more than euphemisms. The day after the inauguration of the Qalandia checkpoint as a "border passage," *Ha'aretz* declared: "The significance of opening this passage is mainly to tighten checks on Palestinians and to conform to the policy that these passages signify the future border between Israel and the territories."[92] Daniela Mansbach shows how the privatization of the passages worsened their "service" to the Palestinians. One of the important issues is the prohibition on Machsom-Watch and other humanitarian organizations members from entering the passage. The architecture of the passage allows the Palestinians to be checked one by one, in a "sterile" zone, thus avoiding the critical gaze of the activists, leaving the arbitrary behavior of the soldiers unchecked.[93]

The same is true for the Heraclitian Everything Flows plan. Just as the spatial uncertainty described above does not signify freedom, but rather a technology of control, Everything Flows means channeling the flow in a way that makes supervision and control easier. Palestinian movement is channeled into alternative side roads on which a barrier can be opened or closed for regulation. Iron gates are installed at the entrance to most of the underpasses and overpasses, a permanent reminder of the potential for closure.

In reality, the more that movement is organized, the easier it is to disrupt it. As Gilles Deleuze once noted, "Guattari has imagined a city where one would be able to leave one's apartment, one's street, one's neighborhood, thanks to one's electronic card that raises a given barrier; but the card could just as easily be rejected on a given day or between certain hours; what counts is not the barrier but the computer that tracks each person's position—licit or illicit—and effects a universal modulation."[94] Pedestrian space is harder to regulate than that of highways and railroads. When movement is prohibited on all roads, bypass routes spring up, making movement less predictable for the ruler. Diverting the flow onto roads declared to be "usually open" will help prevent the formation of bypasses, will avoid rhizomization, and will ultimately increase control. Like the city under the surveillance of Guattari's computer, the planned space in the OPT will allow relatively unhindered Palestinian movement. The point, however, is that with the same ease as in Guattari's example, the biometric card can be rejected or the tunnel can be locked without explanation and without any option of argument or appeal. Arbitrariness will not be reduced, but rather will be refined, in that there will be no need for mechanisms of justification and no room left for bypass options.

CONCLUSION: EVERYDAY RESISTANCE

Resistance is inherent in movement. As Michel de Certeau noted, "the crossing, drifting away, or improvisation of walking privilege, transform or abandon spatial elements" because "the walker transforms each spatial signifier into something else." Thus, "on the one hand he actualizes only a few of the possibilities fixed by the constructed order (he goes only here and not there)," while "on the other he increases the number of possibilities (for example, by creating shortcuts and detours) and prohibitions (for example, he forbids himself to take paths generally considered accessible or even obligatory)."[95] The resistance to the spatial state of affairs that allows continuity of life in the OPT is of two types: physical and communicative. Creating new bypasses is an example of physical resistance. Actually, since most Palestinian-restricted roads originated as bypass roads (that is, allowing settlers to bypass Arab population centers), the new roads are bypass roads bypassing bypass roads. Every checkpoint and every prohibited road generates new bypasses.

Local Palestinian councils renovate and widen internal roads that, due to lack of alternatives, become main roads. In a few places, such as the Hebron and Tulkarem areas, the local councils paved new roads between villages after their access to main roads was cut.[96] Thus, new roads connect Palestinian villages, roads that are not obligated to the Israeli spatial design and thus subvert the attempt to divide the land into cells and to manipulate movement toward the checkpoints.

Sometimes the physical resistance occurs in the most oppressive location, the checkpoint itself. As Rema Hammami describes it:

> Checkpoint workers [porters carrying materials, goods, and even people through the no-driving zone of the checkpoints] constantly subverted physical boundaries: at night they stealthily pushed concrete blocks a few more inches apart to make way for horse carriages, or trampled the edges of newly-made dirt barriers so that porter carts could get to the other side. And through both necessity and ingenuity, they reclaimed the space of the checkpoint from being purely a site of oppression and brutality into the one where livelihood, social life and even sociability could be recovered.[97]

Communication also furthers resistance. Communication networks, informing people about checkpoints and blockages, have developed over the years. Though the Israeli authorities never give notice of movement restrictions, the local radio and television channels do the job. Just as in other places, the daily weather forecast advises people on what to wear, a news segment informs Palestinians about the day's conditions of movement and blockages. Drivers have developed a sign language to inform each other of surprise checkpoints or the presence of military forces on the road. Taxi drivers use their radio networks and mobile phones to warn each other of military forces they have encountered and to channel whoever they can onto alternative routes.

Currently, the lives of Palestinians can be summarized as a double-faced mode of action: steadfastness and smuggling. Steadfastness, *sumud* in Arabic, is an old practice that is the main means of resistance to the occupation, antedating and complementing violent resistance. It has been expressed by building homes in the absence of a permit, knowing full well that they are under constant threat of demolition; by cultivating lands despite the uncertainty and the frequent possibility of confiscation; by reviving the memory of villages destroyed in 1948 and keeping the keys to destroyed houses; but mainly by refusing to emigrate, in spite of the difficulty of living under the occupation. Today, however, *sumud* is expressed mainly by maintaining a routine in spite of the checkpoints.[98]

Concurrently, there are constant attempts to smuggle. In the face of spatial constraints aimed at minimizing movement, Palestinians aim to cross the lines to get to work, to study, to receive medical treatment, to visit relatives, and so on. Palestinians try to smuggle goods, a work force, at times explosives, but always, first and foremost, themselves.

The Palestinian situation is thus integrated into the global rationale of barriers and smuggling. In Israel/Palestine, one group can move freely, while the other is constrained. The walls, like those built these days elsewhere on the periphery of the rich world, are meant to be semipermeable. The wall erected along the U.S.–Mexico border is intended to limit movement only from the south. These walls were designed to stop the smuggling of drugs, goods, and people, and to fix the flow of capital in the desired direction.

The difference lies in the fact that in the OPT, there is also an inner division of the land. This is different from a more or less distinct line separating "here" from "there," with passage allowed in only one direction, as is the situation with regard to the Separation Wall. In the West Bank, there are innumerable boundaries, fluid and changing. Crossing them is prohibited, but they are not defined as "here" and "there," "inside" and "outside." The movement regime in the OPT produces a state of affairs in which nearly every movement involves a transgression, and almost all Palestinians are therefore "traffic violators."

Daily movement, in spite of hardships and the a priori "traffic violations," gives the space new significance and loads it with Palestinian use values. The struggle for space, or rather for its use, is carried out through small daily activities: bypassing checkpoints, risk taking, and generally insisting on using the space. In other words, in the OPT, smuggling *is* steadfastness.

NOTES

1   Torsten Hägerstrand, *Innovation Diffusion as a Spatial Process* (Chicago: University of Chicago Press, 1967).

2   See Kevin Lynch's research on cognitive maps, for example in *The Image of the City* (Cambridge, MA: The MIT Press, 1960).

3   Anthony Giddens, *The Constitution of Society* (Cambridge: Polity Press, 1984).

4   This is the sum of the settlements' municipal area. See the report by B'Tselem, the Israeli Information Center for Human Rights in the Occupied Territories, authored by Yehezkel Lein, "Land Grab: Israel's Settlement Policy in the West Bank," (May 2002), available online http://www.btselem.org/Download/200205_Land_Grab_Eng.pdf (last accessed July 14, 2008).

5   Michel de Certeau, *The Practice of Everyday Life* (Berkeley: University of California Press, 1988), part III.

6   United Nations Office for the Coordination of Humanitarian Affairs, "West Bank Closure Count and Analysis" (January 2006), available on-line at http://www.humanitarianinfo.org/opt/docs/UN/OCHA/OCHAoPt_ClosureAnalysis0106_En.pdf (last accessed July 14, 2008). The maps and the spatial analysis that follow are based on these data. The most updated data at time of publishing are those of September 2008. According to OCHA there were at that date 533 unmanned blocks and 93 manned checkpoints.

7   See Israel Kimchi (ed.), *The Security Fence in Jerusalem: Implications on the City and its Inhabitants* (Jerusalem: Institute for Israel Studies, 2006) (in Hebrew).

8   Meron Rapoport, "Ghost City," *Ha'aretz,* November 18, 2005.

9   See below page 213.

10 See the B'Tselem report by Yehezkel Lein, "Forbidden Roads: The Discriminatory West Bank Road Regime" (August 2004), available on-line at http://www.btselem.org/Download/200408_Forbidden_Roads_Eng.pdf (last accessed July 15, 2008).

11 B'Tselem report by Ron Dudai, "No Way Out: Medical Implications of Israel's Siege Policy" (June 2001), available on-line at http://www.btselem.org/Download/200106_No_Way_Out_Eng.rtf (last accessed July 15, 2008). For a similar analysis, see Neve Gordon and Dani Filc, "The Destruction of Risk Society and the Ascendancy of Hamas," in this volume.

12 A-Tufah checkpoint, which separated Han Yunes from the Al-Mawasi area in the Gaza Strip, was closed at the end of March 2002 for fifty consecutive days. The occupation authorities did not announce anything at any point about the estimated closure period. See the B'Tselem report by Shlomi Swisa, "Al-Mawasi, Gaza Strip: Impossible Life in an Isolated Enclave" (March 2003), available on-line at http://www.btselem.org/Download/200303_Al_Mwassy_Eng.pdf (last accessed July 15, 2008).

13 Hägerstrand, *Innovation Diffusion as a Spatial Process.*

14 *Ibid.*

15 "Place," according to Edward Relph, is a location in space that has something special, that is, it is a location containing human significance exceeding its designated functional role, while a "placeless place" is the cold, alienated, and uniform location. The classic examples of a placeless place are McDonald's branches and shopping malls. Edward Relph, *Place and Placelessness* (London: Pion, 1976).

16 Azmi Bishara, *Yearning in the Land of Checkpoints* (Tel Aviv: Babel, 2006) (in Hebrew), p. 29.

17   Anthony Giddens, *A Contemporary Critique of Historical Materialism, vol. 1: Power, Property and the State* (London: Macmillan, 1981), p. 37.

18   Cited in *Ibid.*, p. 62.

19   See Gary A. Kreps, "Disaster as a Systemic Event and Social Catalyst," in E. L. Quarantelli (ed.), *What is a Disaster?* (London: Routledge, 1998), pp. 31–56.

20   The Separation Wall with its passages, is an aberration of this logic, as will be discussed later.

21   See Adi Ophir and Ariella Azoulay, "The Order of Violence," in this volume.

22   See Neve Gordon, "From Colonization to Separation: Exploring the Structure of Israel's Occupation," in this volume.

23   The army has defined certain areas as "special security zones," which really are death zones. Anyone entering these areas, which are unmarked and whose existence has not been announced in any way, puts his or her life at risk.

24   Reviel Netz, *Barbed Wire: An Ecology of Modernity* (Middletown, CT: Wesleyan University Press, 2004).

25   On the way in which the American use of barbed wire to divide space mortally injured the population of Native Americans, see Olivier Razac, *Barbed Wire: A Political History* (New York: The New Press, 2002). Nevertheless, this injury was a byproduct of limiting agricultural plots, whereas in the Boer War, the primary purpose was to manage and dominate people.

26   In the "Seam Zone" enclaves and in East Jerusalem, inhabitants must produce valid proofs in order to confirm their residency in the restricted area. Failing to do so for any reason (for example, being in the neighboring village at the census time, or the unilateral movement of the "border" by Israeli forces) turns the person into an "illegal resident" in his or her own home. See for example, Akiva Eldar, "Illegal Residents in Their Own Homes," *Ha'aretz,* September 14, 2004; and Meron Rapoport, "There are No People in This Photograph," *Ha'aretz,* January 21, 2005. See also the discussion about the Seam Zone below.

27   Order Regarding the Regulation of Land and Water (Judea and Samaria) (No. 291), 1968.

28   B'Tselem, "Land Grab."

29   *Ibid.*

30   *Ibid.*

31   *Ibid.*

32   Elisha Efrat, *Geography of Occupation: Judea, Samaria and Gaza Region* (Jerusalem: Carmel, 2002) (in Hebrew), p. 76.

33   B'Tselem, "Limitations on Building of Residences on the West Bank" (August 1990), available on-line at http://www.btselem.org/Download/199008_Limitations_on_Building_Eng.doc (last accessed July 16, 2008).

34   B'Tselem, "Land Grab."

35   *Ibid.* The limitations on construction are not a new method, but rather one that was widely used in Arab villages and towns within "Israel proper," that is, west of the Green Line. The municipal boundaries marked by the Ministry of Interior reduced the average municipal area by 64 percent in comparison with the "village lands" area of the British Mandate. Therefore, while the Arab population constitutes about 18 percent of Israel's total population, the municipal areas of their settlements make up only 2.5 percent of Israel's land. Following the fixing of boundaries, the constructed area within Arab villages and towns is sixteen times that of 1948. Planners for Planning Rights (Bimkom), "Widening Municipal Areas

for the Arab sector" (in Hebrew), available on-line at http://www.bimkom.org/pressView. asp?publicationId=20 (last accessed July 16, 2008).

36   Akiva Eldar and Idith Zertal, *Lords of the Land: The Settlers and the State of Israel 1967–2004* (Tel Aviv: Dvir, 2004), (in Hebrew), p. 400.

37   B'Tselem, "Land Grab."

38   Planners for Planning Rights (Bimkom), "Appropriation of Space: Planning and Un-planning at the West Bank as a political tool" (in Hebrew), available on-line at http://www.bimkom. org/publicationView.asp?publicationId=36 (last accessed July 16, 2008).

39   The method started following the High Court of Justice decision in the Elon Moreh case, rejecting the security argument as a basis for the seizure of land to establish the settlement. The petitioners submit affidavits of former senior military officials that question the secu- rity need in building a settlement in the heart of a densely populated area. In addition, the settlers themselves submit an affidavit that avoids the security pretext and claim they have a complete and unconditional right to settle everywhere in the West Bank. Following the court's decision, Israel had to seek for new ways of seizing Palestinian land on which to build settlements.

40   Interview with Talia Sasson, author of the *Opinion Concerning Unauthorized Outposts,* March 17, 2006.

41   Order Regarding Government Property (Judea and Samaria), section 2C, in B'Tselem, "Land Grab."

42   Since 1983, the heads of villages or neighborhoods, the *mukhtars,* have been the only source of information for the populace. Since then, the custodian has stopped attaching to the order a map showing the declared land borders. See Raja Shehade, *Occupier's Law, Israel and the West Bank* (Washington, D.C.: Institute for Palestine Studies, 1988), p. 30.

43   Order Regarding Government Property (Judea and Samaria), section 5.

44   Efrat, *Geography of Occupation,* p. 56.

45   Excluding East Jerusalem, in which about 180,000 settlers lived at that time.

46   Gush Emunim, *Master Plan for Settlement in Judea and Samaria* (1980) (in Hebrew), p. 15.

47   B'Tselem, "Land Grab."

48   Ministry of Agriculture and the Settlement Division of the World Zionist Organization, *Master Plan for Settlement of Samaria and Judea, Development Plan for the Area for 1983– 1986.*

49   One example is the 300-inhabitant settlement Shim'a, on a main road in the south of the West Bank. The built area of the settlement is quite limited, just 66 acres, including the outpost to the south of it, but its municipal boundaries are 2,650 acres—forty times the built area.

50   B'Tselem, "Land Grab."

51   Talia Sasson, *Opinion Concerning Unauthorized Outposts,* p. 84. For the full report in Hebrew, see http://www.pmo.gov.il/NR/rdonlyres/0A0FBE3C-C741-46A6-8CB5-F6CDC042465D/0/ sason2.pdf (last accessed October 2008). For an English summary see Talia Sasson, Summary of the Opinion concerning Unauthorized Outposts (March 2005), available on-line at http:// www.mfa.gov.il/MFA/Government/Law/Legal+Issues+and+Rulings/Summary+of+Opinion +Concerning+Unauthorized+Outposts+-+Talya+Sason+Adv.htm (last accessed July 17, 2008).

52   Efrat, *Geography of Occupation,* p. 149.

53   *Ibid.*

54   Amira Hass, "To Drive and Not to See Arabs," *Ha'aretz,* January 22, 2003.

55 Lein, "Forbidden Roads."

56 Which are about 0.14 percent of West Bank Palestinians. *Ibid.*

57 Quoted in Eldar and Zertal, *The Lords of the Land,* p. 410.

58 Order Regarding Security (Judea and Samaria) (No. 378), 1970, Declaration of the Closure of an Area (Israeli Communities).

59 *The State Comptroller Report no. 56a for the Year 2005* (in Hebrew), pp. 263–66.

60 Eldar and Zertal, *Lords of the Land,* p. 422.

61 Which is not a safe place, either. Many Palestinians have been killed in their homes, schools, yards, and so on. The common excuse cited by the IDF spokesperson is that they were hurt by a "stray bullet" fired in an incident nearby in which shooting was "legitimate."

62 Not necessarily as a result of fear for their lives, but also because of the fear of being caught by a military jeep and having to undergo questioning, humiliation, and even beatings. Therefore, although there is no law that prohibits Palestinians from walking along the roads, most of them avoid it out of fear. Interview with *Ha'aretz* reporter in the OPT Gideon Levy, March 22, 2006.

63 Meron Rapoport, "Evyatar Cohen Will Not Divide Jerusalem," *Ha'aretz,* January 20, 2006.

64 See for example the B'Tselem's report by Antigona Askar, "Means of Expulsion: Violence, Harassment and Lawlessness toward Palestinians in the Southern Hebron Hills" (July 2005), available on-line at http://www.btselem.org/Download/200507_South_Mount_Hebron_Eng.pdf, and "Free Rein: Vigilante Settlers and Israel's Non-Enforcement of the Law" (October 2001), available on-line at http://www.btselem.org/Download/200110_Free_Rein_Eng.pdf (both last accessed July 16, 2008).

65 In some cases, there is extensive fencing along main roads of the West Bank, physically preventing pedestrian and vehicular passage.

66 One should not confuse the 101 "land cells" previously mentioned with the 190 "islands" of Areas A and B within Area C. While the latter are quite stable, being, at least officially, part of reciprocal negotiations, the former are the effects of tentative and changing de facto limits on Palestinian movement as imposed by Israel.

67 Razac, *Barbed Wire,* p. x.

68 The outposts are often seen as a problem to Israel's relations with the United States, since the Israeli government is said to be committed to the evacuation of all the outposts built after March 2001, or as a symbol of the lawlessness on part of the young generation of settlers, the "youth hill." But they are rarely understood as a problem in itself, due to the harsh effects they have on the Palestinian environment and daily life. The same goes for the disengagement plan, which is often presented as "the beginning of the end of the occupation," or for the plans for the separation of movement.

69 Talia Sasson's *Summary of the Opinion Concerning Unauthorized Outposts* distinguishes between two kinds of outposts—those established before and after March 2001, the time when Ariel Sharon became prime minister. The opinion notes that there are 753 families in the first type and 600 individuals in the second.

70 On the case of Modi'in Illit, see also Gadi Algazi, "Matrix in Bil'in," in this volume.

71 It should be noted that the Israeli High Court of Justice ordered the dismantlement of 1.7 kilometers of the separation barrier near Modi'in Illit and the return of more than one thousand dunams to residents of the village of Bil'in. The justices held that the route was not based on security reasons and was planned so as to include future neighborhoods in *Modi'in*

Illit. HCJ 8414/05, *Yassin vs. The State of Israel.* Since January 2005, the villagers of Bil'in, together with Israeli leftist activists, had waged a continuous nonviolent struggle against the separation barrier. On the Court's decision see Orna Ben-Naftali, Aeyal M. Gross, and Keren Michaeli, "The Illegality of the Occupation Regime," in this volume.

72 "The security concept according to which the IDF will provide defense in any place where an Israeli lives has had a particularly sad outcome. Every settler who wishes to build his house in a given place, even without permission, without authority, and against the law, is defended by the army. The result of these acts is that the IDF's deployment in the area is determined at the end of the day not by the military commander, but by the settlers." *Opinion Concerning Unauthorized Outposts,* p. 342.

73 In these outposts, the houses are built consciously at a great distance from each other. "Thus an outpost inhabited by only a few families succeeds in spreading itself over dozens and sometimes hundreds of acres." Nadav Shragai, "'Consciously We Have Already Won,' Say the Inhabitants of Hill 725," *Ha'aretz,* May 31, 2006.

74 A road connecting the easternmost outpost to the Gitit settlement in the Jordan Valley was paved, creating a Jewish-controlled line stretching all the way from Nablus to the Jordan Valley.

75 Order Regarding Defense Regulations (Judea and Samaria) (No. 378), 1970, Declaration Regarding Closure of Area No. s2/03 (Seam Area).

76 See, for example, the B'Tselem report by Yehezkel Lein, "Nu'man, East Jerusalem: Life under the Threat of Expulsion" (September 2003), available on-line at http://www.btselem.org/Download/200309_Numan_East_Jerusalem_Eng.doc (last accessed July 18, 2008).

77 From the beginning of the Israeli withdrawal from the Gaza Strip (mid-August 2005) to the time of writing these lines (January 2008), Karni checkpoint—the only active transit point for goods moving in and out of Gaza—has operated only part of the time and never to its full capacity. Since Hamas won the elections and later took control over Gaza, the checkpoint has been closed most of the time. For 2007 data, see Palestinian Trade Center (Paltrade), Gaza Terminals Movement Monitoring: Monthly Report (January 10, 2008), available on-line at http://www.paltrade.org/cms/images/enpublications/GAZA_TERMINALS_Report_DECEMBER%202007.pdf (last accessed July 18, 2008).

78 See United Nations Relief and Works Agency, UNRWA Emergency Appeal 2006, available on-line at http://www.un.org/unrwa/emergency/appeals/2006-appeal.pdf (last accessed July 18, 2008).

79 Akiva Eldar, "UN Organizations Warn: Gaza Is on the Verge of Humanitarian Catastrophe," *Ha'aretz,* April 4, 2006. On the "catastrophization" of Gaza, see Ariella Azoulay and Adi Ophir, *This Regime Which Is Not One* (Tel Aviv: Resling, 2008) (in Hebrew), part 3, chap. 10, and Adi Ophir, "The Politics of Catastrophization: Emergency and Exception," in Didier Fassin and Mariella Pandolfi (eds.), *Contemporary States of Emergency: The Politics of Military and Humanitarian Interventions* (New York: Zone Books, 2010).

80 *Ha'aretz,* December 18, 2005.

81 See Eyal Weizman, "Tanato-tactics," in this volume.

82 James Ron, *Frontiers and Ghettos: State Violence in Serbia and Israel* (Berkeley: University of California Press, 2003).

83 *Ibid.,* p. xii.

84 Thirty-four Wall passages are planned in addition to seventy to seventy-five agricultural gates, meant to enable villagers to work their lands on the "Israeli" side of the barrier.

85   "Checkpoint," in Hebrew, is *machsom,* which means "barrier."

86   Interview with Baruch Spiegel, February 17, 2006.

87   Nitzan Cohen, "Did Someone Give You Something to Pass?" *Ha'aretz,* June 24, 2005.

88   Interview with Baruch Spiegel, February 17, 2006.

89   Below are the planned passage times for Palestinian pedestrians:
      a. Security check for a pedestrian without luggage—11 to 13 seconds.
      b. Security check for a pedestrian with luggage/special populations—20 to 24 seconds.
      c. Checking of permits for a Palestinian holding a "smart card" and passing through a manned post, including biometric identification—13 to 17 seconds.
      Quoted from the passages contract.

90   So that Israel can avoid accusations of apartheid, Palestinians will be formally permitted to drive on Israeli roads, but their doing so will involve many checkpoints. The security system therefore expects them to prefer the smooth driving available on Palestinian roads. Amira Hass, "IDF Paves Roads for the Palestinians: Will Drive on Different Levels Than the Israelis," *Ha'aretz,* March 23, 2006.

91   Amir Rapaport, "The Bank's Roads Separation Plan," NRG, February 24, 2006 (in Hebrew), available on-line at http://www.nrg.co.il/online/1/ART1/052/490.html (last accessed November 30, 2008).

92   Arnon Regular, "Qalandia: The Passage Will Open as a Border Passage to Israel," *Ha'aretz,* March 20, 2006.

93   Daniela Mansbach, "From Checkpoints to 'Passages': Canceling the 'State of Emergency' for Maintaining 'Bare Life,'" paper presented at a workshop "Bare Life," Van Leer Institute in Jerusalem, September 19, 2006. See also Meron Rapoport, "Checkpoints under Contract," *Ha'aretz,* September 28, 2007.

94   Gilles Deleuze, "Postscript on the Societies of Control," *October* 59 (Winter 1992): pp. 3–7.

95   De Certeau, *The Practice of Everyday Life,* p. 98.

96   Hass, "IDF Paves Roads for the Palestinians."

97   Rema Hammami, "On the Importance of Thugs: The Moral Economy of a Checkpoint," *Middle East Report* 231 (Summer 2004): p. 28

98   *Ibid.,* p. 18.

· **LICENSE GIVEN BY THE CIVIL ADMINISTRATION TO OPERATE A BUS LINE** between the Nablus encirclement and the Jericho encirclement in both directions. The license forbids entry to Area A of the West Bank and states that "the passengers will board/exit only along the route from encirclement checkpoint to encirclement checkpoint."

· **LETTER FROM THE IDF SPOKESPERSON TO B'TSELEM** regarding special security zones.

המנהל האזרחי ליהודה ושומרון
המפקח על התחבורה
רישיון להפעלת קו שרות

בתוקף סמכותי על פי צו בדבר תעבורה (יהודה והשומרון) (מספר 1310) – התשנ"ב –
1992 ותקנות התעבורה (יהודה והשומרון) התשנ"ב – 1992 .
אני נותן בזה רשיון להפעלת קו שרות ציבורי ל :
שם בעל הרשיון : **חברת אוטובוסים אל-תמימי** כתובת : **שכם.**
תוקף רשיון זה מיום : **19.06.2003** עד יום : **18.08.2003.**
מוצא–יעד : **כתר שכם- כתר יריחו וחזרה.**
מסלול הקו : **כתר שכם- חוורה- ציר אלון–ציר 90 –כתר יריחו.**
תחנות : **לאורך הדרך .**
מחיר הנסיעה המאושר : **25 ש"ח .**
זמני הנסיעה : **אוטובוס אחד מכל כיוון.**
כמות האוטובוסים בקו : **10 .**
מספר הרישום של האוטובוס בקו : **34-121-70.**
תנאי הרשיון

1. רשיון זה הינו בר-תוקף כאשר צמוד אליו רשיון רכב ותעודת ביטוח בתוקף.

2. האוטובוס חייב להיות תמיד במצב תקין וראוי לשימוש וממלא אחר הוראאות כל דין .

3. האוטובוס יהיה בבעלותו של הבעל הרשום ברשיון .

4. אין להעביר רשיון זה לאחר ויש להחזירו לרשות עם פקיעת תוקפו .

5. בעל הרשיון, עובדו או הפועל בשמו או הבא מכוחו יפעיל את האוטובוס בהתאם למהלך קו הנסיעה ובהתאם למסלול תנסיעה שנקבע לו ברשיון זה או בהוראאות ר רשות. אין לחזור או לקיים תחנה סופית אחרת לפני שהאוטובוס הגיע לתחנת חיעד הסופי. של חקו .

6. בעל הרשיון חייב להגיש לרשות העתק מאושר מלוח זמני תנסיעות בקו, שיכיל את מספר הנסיעות בכל יום .

7. בעל הרשיון חייב להפעיל את האוטובוס בקו לפי חלוח האמור בתנאי (5) ואין לשנותו ללא היתר מאת הרשות.
הופר תנאי מתנאי רשיון זה או נעברה עבירה על כל דין בקשר עזו חסעת האוטובוס זכאית הרשות להתלות את ההיתר ואו לבטלו .

8. רשיון זה בתוקף רק לאחר שהתקבלו כל האישורים הביטחוניים הדרושים גם לגבי תחנות המוצא והיעד, התחנות והמסלול.

9. היתר זה מותנה ב:

א. האוטובוס ישהה במשך הלילה מחוץ לשטחי הרש"פ (שטח A).

ב. האוטובוס לא יכנס בשום אופן לתחום A במשך שעות הפעילות ואנוסעיים יעלו/ירדו אך ורק לאורך מסלול הנסיעה ממחוץ כתר ממחוסם מתר.

המפקח על התחבורה
יהודה ושומרון

מוגבל

מקום : בית אל
תאריך : 18.06.2003

Civil Administration for Judea and Samaria
Transportation Supervisor
License to Operate Service Line

Pursuant to my authority under the Order Regarding Transportation (Judea and Samaria) (Number 1310), 5752—1992, and the Transportation Regulations (Judea and Samaria), 5752—1992,

I hereby grant a license to operate a public service line to:

Name of license holder: **al-Tamimi Bus Company**   Address: **Nablus**

The license is valid from **19 June 2003** to **18 August 2003**.

Departs—Destination: **Nablus encirclement—Jericho encirclement and back**

Route of the line: **Nablus encirclement—Huwara—Alon Route—Route 90—Jericho encirclement**

Stops: **Along the road**.

Approved price for the trip: **NIS 25**

Number of buses on the line: **10**

License number of the bus on the line: **70-121-34**

[The conditions of the license follow.]

Transportation Supervisor
Judea and Samaria

Place: Beit El
Date: 18 June 2003

1

Futshi — לפור

צבא	התגגה	לישראל
חטיבת	דובר	צה"ל
דסק	ארגונים	בינלאומיים
טל':	03-5694193	03-6080220/358
פקס:		03-6080343
א-ד		2611
א'	בשבט	התשס"ה
11	בינואר	2005

דובר צה"ל
I.D.F Spokesperson

לכבוד
נמרוד אמזלק
בצלם

הנדון: <u>פנייתך לדובר צה"ל</u>
(בהמשך לפנייתך שמספרה: 10722)

פנייתך בנושא שטחים ביטחוניים מיוחדים התקבלה במשרדנו.

להלן התייחסותנו:

לאחר מספר פיגועי חדירה ליישובים ישראליים באזור יהודה ושומרון ובאזור חבל עזה בתקופת אירועי הלחימה הנוכחיים, בהם נרצחו אזרחים רבים, הוחלט על הקפת היישובים הישראליים במעטפת חיצונית של מרכיבי ביטחון, ועוד יצירת מרחב הגנה והתרעה- שטח ביטחוני מיוחד (להלן שב"מ), הנתחם בין שתי גדרות- גדר חיישוב וגדר השב"מ, חמוכרז כשטח צבאי סגור, שהכניסה אליו מתאפשרת בהיתר בלבד.

נכון למועד זה, הוצאו צווים על-ידי מפקד כוחות צה"ל באזור יהודה ושומרון לצורך הקמת שב"מים סביב חמישה יישובים: חרמש, כדים, מבוא דותן, חומש וקריית ארבע. באזור חבל עזה הוקמו שב"מ"ים סביב היישובים נצרים כפר דרום ומורג. אל מול האילוצים והצרכים הביטחוניים, צה"ל יקים שב"מ ביישובים נוספים.

מרחק גדר השב"מ מגדר היישוב אינו אחיד, והוא נקבע באופן פרטני ביחס לכל יישוב ויישוב, ולעתים אף ביחס למקטעים שונים של השב"מ סביב יישוב מסויים, לאור איזון הנערך בין שיקולי זמן ומרחב (הצורך בהתרעה בעת חדירה ליישוב לשם היערכות וכוחות), שיקולים טופוגרפים, מזעור הפגיעה בקניין הפרט ובחופש התנועה, וכיו"ב.

I.D.F. Spokesperson
Israel Defense Forces
IDF Spokesperson Section
International Organizations Desk
Tel: 03-5694193
Fax: 03-6080343
1 Shvat 5765
11 January 2005

Mr. Nimrod Amzalek
B'Tselem

Re: Your inquiry to the IDF Spokesperson
     (in follow up to your inquiry, Ref. 10722)

Your inquiry regarding special security zones was received in our office.

Our reply is as follows:

Following a number of terrorist attacks in which the perpetrators infiltrated Israeli communities in Judea and Samaria and in the Gaza Strip during the current hostilities in which many civilians were murdered, it was decided to surround the Israeli communities with an external envelope of security components while creating a protection and warning space—a special security zone (hereafter SSZ), bordered by two fences—the community's fence and the SSZ fence—which is declared a closed military zone, entry into which requires a permit.

As of the present time, the IDF commander of forces in Judea and Samaria issued orders to build SSZs around five communities: Hermesh, Kadim, Mevo Dotan, Homesh, and Kiryat Arba. In the Gaza Strip, SSZs were built around Netzarim, Kfar Darom, and Morag. Due to constraints and security needs, the IDF will build SSZs in additional communities.

The distance of the SSZ fence from the community's fence is not uniform and is determined individually for each community, sometimes also with respect to certain sections of the SSZ around a specific community, due to a balancing of time and space considerations (the need for warning to deploy troops when there is an infiltration), topological considerations, minimization of the infringement on the right of property of the individual and to freedom of movement, and the like.

בחלק מן המקרים, מצויים מקרקעין פרטיים בתחום השב"מ. יודגש, כי מקרקעין אלו אינם מופקעים או נתפסים, אלא נותרים ברשות בעליהם. חרף העובדה, שהשב"מ מוכרז כשטח צבאי סגור, בעלי הזכויות במקרקעין רשאים להיכנס למקרקעין לצורך עיבודם, בהתאם לנוהל שנקבע לשם כך, שתוכנו יובא לידיעת הנתושבים באמצעות מפקדות התיאום והקישור הגזרתיות.

ביחס לשב"מים שהוקמו, **הוצאו על-ידי מפקד כוחות צה"ל באזור יהודה ושומרון ומפקד צה"ל באזור חבל עזה צווים לתפיסת שטח** - ולא צווי הפקעה. הצווים תחומים בזמן, ומתייחסים לרצועה צרה הכוללת גדר ודרך ביטחון. בעלי הזכויות במקרקעין זכאים לקבל דמי שימוש ופיצויים בגין התפיסה, בכפוף לחוכחת זכויותיהם כנדרש. נשוב ונדגיש, **כי חשטח המצוי בין גדר הישוב לבין גדר חשב"מ לא נתפס ו/או מופקע.**

בהתייחס לחוראות הפתיחה באש הנהוגות בשב"מים צה"ל אינו נוהג לפרט את חוראות הפתיחה באש בחיותם הוראות מבצעיות.

הקמת השב"מים מיושמת כחלק מתפיסת החגנה על חיישובים הישראליים באזור יהודה ושומרון ובאזור חבל עזה. זאת, לאור העובדה שהאוכלוסיה באזור, שהמפקד הצבאי מופקד על שלומה וביטחונה, כוללת אף את אוכלוסיית הישראלים המתגוררים באזור. התפיסה חמשפטית האמורה עוגנה בפסיקות רבות של ביהמ"ש העליון. ניתן לציין, בהקשר זה, את פסק-הדין בפרשת ציר המתפבלים *(בג"ץ 10497/02 עיליית חבריו נ' מפקד כוחות צה"ל).*

יודגש, כי ביהמ"ש העליון אישר לפני כשנה הוצאת צווים לחקמת שב"מ סביב חלק מן היישוב ביתר עילית, וזאת לאחר שהוצגה בפניו התפיסה הביטחונית העומדת ביסוד הפרויקט *(בג"ץ 4462/03 פגון נ' מפקד כוחות צה"ל).* במספר מקרים נוספים נדחו עתירות שהוגשו כנגד הקמת מרכיבי ביטחון ליישובים באזור חבל עזה *(בג"ץ 3441/04 אבן מדין נ' מפקד כוחות צה"ל באזח"ע, בג"ץ 1152/04 עבד אלעז נ' מפקד כוחות צה"ל באזח"ע).*

בברכה,

ב' ליעד גרמוסן, סמל

ירון

פ...

ראש דסק ארמנים בינלאומיים

רב-טוראי בינלאומיים

In some of the cases, private land lies inside the SSZ. It should be noted that this land is not expropriated or seized, but remains the possession of its owner. Notwithstanding the fact that the SSZ is declared a closed military area, the holders of rights in the land may enter the land to work it in accordance with a set procedure whose contents will be announced to the residents through the sectoral Coordination and Liaison Headquarters.

Regarding the SSZs that have been built, **the commander of IDF forces in Judea and Samaria and the commander of IDF forces in the Gaza Strip have issued orders to seize land**, and not expropriation orders. The orders are limited in time and relate to a narrow strip that includes a fence and security road. The holders of rights in the land are entitled to receive usage fees and compensation for the seizure upon proving their rights as required. Again, we note that **the area located between the community's fence and the SSZ fence is not seized and/or expropriated**.

Regarding the regulations for opening fire in SSZs, the IDF does not reveal these regulations, inasmuch as they are operational regulations.

The building of SSZs forms part of a broader vision for the defense of Israeli communities in Judea and Samaria and in the Gaza region, in light of the fact that the population, whose well-being and safety the military commander is responsible for, also includes Israelis living in the area. This legal conception was reaffirmed in many rulings of the Supreme Court. In this context, one may note the Supreme Court's decision in the case of the worshippers' route (**HCJ 10497/02 Hebron Municipality v. IDF Commander**).

It should be stressed that approximately a year ago the Supreme Court approved the orders issued for building a SSZ around part of the Beitar Illit community, after it was presented with the security conception on which the project was based (**HCJ 4462/03 Fanon v. IDF Commander**). In several other cases, the Court rejected petitions against the building of security elements for communities in the Gaza region (**HCJ 3441/04 Abu Madin v. IDF Commander in the Gaza region, HCJ 1152/04 Abed El'az v. IDF Commander in the Gaza region**).

Sincerely,

On behalf of Liad Levi-Mosen, Sergeant
Yaron Pazi, Corporal
Head, International Organizations Desk

Ariella Azoulay

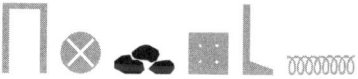

2.1 HEBRON, 2007 The matching stones inlaid in the windows are the visual seal of the confiscation of the house from the Palestinian family who lived in it.

Architectonic schemes by Meira Kowalsky

DAFNA KAPLAN

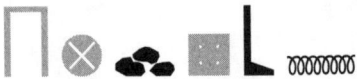

2.2 LUBAN A-SHARQIYAH, NORTH OF RAMALLAH, 2003 Under the trappings of a military outpost—the Israeli flag, barbed-wire fencing and camouflage netting—is a Palestinian home. The army needed to position itself at this site, and the family living there was removed indefinitely.

2.3 HEBRON, 2007 Concrete modules stretch across the street between two houses. Behind them, Jews reside in houses previously inhabited by Palestinians. In front of them dwell Palestinians whose city—over half of it—is blocked to them, and they are prohibited from moving in other parts. In addition to these walls that obstruct movement in the streets, Hebron also contains sixteen manned checkpoints.

2.4 BEIT HANOUN, YEAR UNKNOWN (DURING THE SECOND INTIFADA) A direct hit to the middle of the bridge disabled it. The army, suspecting that launchers of Qassam rockets use this bridge in order to transport rockets, justified blocking any Palestinian movement between Gaza and Beit Hanoun.

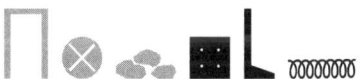

2.5 JAAYOUS, 2002 In places where the Wall has separated Palestinians from their fields, schools, and workplaces, gates have been erected for the local population, open three times a day. Eighty-seven such gates are scattered along the Separation Wall. Every gate is the site of a new waiting line, a tool for stealing time.

2.6 BETWEEN QALQILIYA AND TUL KARM, 2003 At places where the topography has provided a "natural" gap in the Separation Wall, the army makes do with barbed wire.

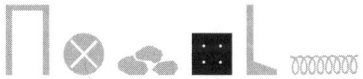

2.7 BEIT UR AL-TAHTA, 2001 Before erecting the Separation Wall, the army delineated separation with concrete blocks such as the one in the photograph. After the
Wall was built, the blocks remained to create "local separations." Hundreds of separation lines now crisscross the West Bank with these concrete blocks. The military
"invention" of providing the Occupied Territories with commodities at back-to-back
installations, where two trucks meet, the one laden with produce, the other empty,
and wares are transferred, has not solved food shortage, so Palestinians improvise
their own "back-to-back" operations over such concrete blocks.

2.8 BEIT UR AL-TAHTA, 2001 Any improvisation is a provocation of the occupier. The abundant rubble from home demolitions had served to cover the concrete blocks and the space in between them that enabled the transfer of goods from one side to the other. The army does not rescind its monopoly, even in the "back-to-back" domain. A while after such an improvised site was installed by Palestinians, the army blocked it.

From Colonization to Separation:
Exploring the Structure of Israel's Occupation

Neve Gordon

Immediately following the 1967 War, the head of Israel's General Security Service, Yosef Harmelin, submitted a proposal to Defense Minister Moshe Dayan elaborating on how he thought the population in the West Bank and Gaza Strip should be governed. Harmelin suggested that the same framework that had been used to manage the Palestinians inside Israel during the period of the internal military government (1948–66) should be adopted in the West Bank and Gaza Strip.[1] Dayan disagreed, maintaining that given the very different social and political situations of the Palestinians inside Israel after 1948 and of the inhabitants of the newly occupied territories, the form of military government established inside Israel should not be emulated.

A relatively small percentage of Palestinians had remained in what became Israel after 1948. The vast majority of leaders and the intelligentsia had fled the urban centers, leaving them practically empty, while the inhabitants who did not leave were mostly unorganized rural dwellers. This, alongside the fact that not long after the war Israel decided to offer these Palestinians citizenship and incorporate them, at least partially, into Israeli society, shaped the forms of control adopted by the internal military government. In the Occupied Territories, by contrast, most of the inhabitants were not displaced during the 1967 War. Both the urban and rural leadership had to a large extent stayed put, and Israel had no intention of integrating these Palestinians into its own citizenry. From Israel's perspective, then, these social and political differences called for a different form of government, and Dayan decided to adopt a more open and less interventionist policy than the one that had been used to manage the Palestinians inside Israel.[2] Israel's intention, according to military reports published after the war, was to implement "a policy of normalization" through the encouragement of self-rule, which would "allow the population of the areas to carry on their life and activities just as they had been used to until the 5th of June 1967."[3] Or as Dayan once put it, the goal was to make the "occupation invisible."[4]

Dayan, it appears, had reached this conclusion even before the war ended. On June 8, just a few hours after the Israeli military captured Jerusalem's Temple Mount, Haram al-Sharif, Dayan visited the site. Noticing that troops had hung an Israeli flag on the top of the al-Aqsa shrine, he asked one of the soldiers to remove it, adding that displaying the Israeli national symbol for all to see was an unnecessarily provocative act.[5] This gesture captures part of Dayan's strategic legacy of trying to normalize the occupation by concealing Israel's presence. It also underscores the profound shift that has taken place in the Occupied Territories, since anyone who visited the West Bank and Gaza Strip in the 1980s and 1990s no doubt noticed Israeli flags fluttering over almost every building that Israel occupied, as well as above every Jewish settlement.

Another significant change that has transpired over the years involves the Israeli government's relationship to trees, the symbol of life. While in 1968 Israel helped Palestinians in the Gaza Strip plant some six hundred and eighteen thousand trees and provided farmers with improved varieties of seeds for vegetables and field crops, during the first three years of the second intifada Israel destroyed more than 10 percent of Gaza's agricultural land and uprooted over two hundred and twenty-six thousand trees.[6] The appearance and proliferation of the flag, on the one hand, and the razing of trees, on the other, signify a fundamental transformation in Israel's attempts to control the inhabitants of the Occupied Palestinian Territories and point to a profound modification in the modes of power employed there. It appears as if Israel decided to alter its methods of upholding the occupation, replacing a politics of life, which aimed to secure the existence and livelihood of the Palestinian inhabitants, with a politics of death.

Military documents, newspaper articles, and a series of reports indeed indicate that the occupation in the late 1960s and 1970s was very different from the occupation in the 1980s and 1990s. The 1980s and 1990s, in turn, witnessed an occupation quite different from the one of the past several years. What spurred Israel to change the way it manages the Palestinian population? How did Israel administer the Palestinian inhabitants during the occupation's first years? And why did it modify the methods it employed to manage the lives of the residents? In this essay, I will begin to address these questions.[7]

REPERTOIRES OF VIOLENCE

While the changes in the Occupied Territories have manifested themselves in all areas of life, they are particularly conspicuous when counting bodies. Between the

	PALESTINIANS KILLED	ANNUAL AVERAGE
June 1967 – December 1987	650	32
December 1987 – September 2000	1,491	106
September 2000 – December 2006	4,046	674
TOTAL	6,187	—

TABLE 1 Number of Palestinians killed by Israel.

six-year period from 2001 to 2007 Israel has, on average, killed more Palestinians per year than it killed during the first twenty years of occupation. Moreover, since the eruption of the second intifada, Israelis have killed almost twice as many Palestinians as they killed in the preceding thirty-four years (see Table 1).[8]

How can one make sense of the increasing violence Israel uses in order to uphold the occupation of the West Bank and Gaza Strip, and why did the Israeli military government radically alter the forms of control it used to manage the occupied Palestinian residents?[9] Those who help manufacture public opinion within Israel claim that the dramatic increase in Palestinian deaths is due to the fact that the Palestinians have changed the methods of violence they employ against Israel and that Israel, in turn, also began using more violent means, which explains the increase in Palestinian deaths. And indeed, the number of Israelis killed has dramatically increased over the years. While during the thirteen-year period between December 1987 and September 2000 422 Israelis were killed by Palestinians, during the six-year period from the eruption of the second intifada until the end of November 2008, 1,062 Israelis were killed.[10] Palestinians, however, might invert this argument, claiming that they have altered their methods of resistance in response to Israel's use of more lethal violence. Even though all such explanations contain a grain of truth, they are symptomatic accounts and do little to reveal the root causes underlying the processes leading to the substantial increase in human deaths. They are therefore not very helpful for those interested in making sense of what has been going on in the West Bank and the Gaza Strip. Although the steady increase in deaths is striking and no doubt an important factor that must be reflected upon, it is merely an effect of other significant changes that have taken place in the Occupied Territories.

It is also worth noting that when comparing the Israeli occupation with other military occupations, the number of Palestinians killed is relatively small. During the U.S. military occupation of Iraq, for example, on average, more civilians have been killed per day than were killed during a whole year in the West Bank and Gaza Strip between the years 1967 and 1987. Moreover, the United Nations reports that during the four-month period from May through August 2006, 12,417 Iraqi civilians were killed, much more than the number of Palestinians killed during four decades of Israeli military rule.[11] The civilian death toll in Chechnya, East Timor, and other areas that have been under military occupation tends to resemble the death toll in Iraq and in certain instances is much higher.[12]

What is common to all these places is that they are part of what Derek Gregory calls "the colonial present," which is characterized, among other things, by two cartographic performances.[13] The first is a performance through which ruptured space is simulated as a coherent state so that in fact sovereignty has to be conjured up to render the categories of political action meaningful. The Occupied Territories after Oslo, as well as Afghanistan and Iraq, are thus described as sovereign states, even though none of these entities is in fact a real state. The second is a performance of territory through which fluid networks such as al-Qaeda are fixed into a bounded space that can then be legitimately bombed and occupied. The artificial ascription of a fixed and well-delineated space to al-Qaeda justifies the bombing and military seizure of this space. Whereas Gregory tries to outline the features common to the colonial present, my objective is to explain the differences between contemporary colonial regimes and the changes they undergo over time. Here, I concentrate on the changes in the Occupied Territories.

One should try and understand why, in comparison with other military occupations, a relatively small number of Palestinians were killed, particularly during the first thirty-four years of occupation, and why, in the last few years, we have witnessed waves of "eruptive violence" in the West Bank and Gaza.[14] The hypothesis I wish to present in the following pages is that certain elements in the structure of the occupation regime, and not political decisions made by any particular politicians or military officer, are responsible for the recent increase in the eruption of violence. I will argue that for many years, the occupation regime's guiding principle was colonization, which involved efforts to exploit the resources in the occupied region (in our case, land, water, and labor) while administering the lives of the colonized population and attempting to normalize the colonial relation. I will show that over time, a series of structural contradictions undermined this principle and gave way in the mid-1990s to another guiding principle—separation. Separation signifies giving up efforts to administer the lives of the colonized population, (except for the people living in the seam zones and in close proximity to the Separation Wall) and insisting on the continued exploitation of nonhuman resources (i.e., land and water). The lack of interest in or indifference to the life of most of the colonized population characteristic of the separation principle helps to explain the recent surge in lethal violence in the Occupied Territories.

However, before describing these two principles further, let me introduce two qualifications to the claim I have just made. First, it is important to note that the diachronic presentation of the two principles is misleading. The two coexisted from the very beginning, contaminating each other, and there is no single historical event that marks the transition from the one to the other. In retrospect, however, it becomes clear that the dominance that the principle of colonization enjoyed during the first three decades of the occupation is now over and that separation has become the guiding principle of the occupation. Second, it is also important to note that despite the seeming dichotomy between exploitation and administration in many colonial contexts, including the Israeli one, the native population was considered at one and the same time as an object of government and administration and as an object of exploitation in the form of slavery or cheap labor.

THE COLONIZATION PRINCIPLE

By "the colonization principle," I mean a form of government whereby the colonizer attempts to manage the lives of the colonized inhabitants while exploiting the captured territory's resources.[15] As Hilla Dayan points out in "Regimes of Separation: Israel/Palestine and the Shadow of Apartheid" in this volume, colonial powers do not conquer for the sake of imposing administrative rule on the indigenous population, but they end up managing the conquered inhabitants in order to facilitate the extraction of resources. When a colonial system acts according to the principle of colonization, it tends to emphasize two forms of power that Michel Foucault described and analyzed in a different context as disciplinary and bio-political and minimizes its recourse to sovereign power.[16]

Disciplinary power strives to normalize power relations through the fragmentation of everyday life, often trying to maximize the economic productivity of the colonized while reducing their political skills. It works on the most detailed and nuanced elements of which everyday interactions consist in order to create and disseminate a whole spectrum of norms and social practices. Disciplinary power works from below, creating uniformity among multiple individuals and introducing enforceable standards on modes of thought and patterns of behavior. Submission is achieved through normalization. At the same time, disciplinary practices also work to differentiate individuals and classes of subjects, ascribing roles and skills to individuals or classes and determining lines of transgression.

Bio-power deals with the population (as opposed to the individual) as a political problem. It does not oppose the deployment of disciplinary power, but includes it and molds it. It is utilized on a different scale and applies a series of unique instruments. Like disciplinary power, it is continuous and dispersed through social space. Bio-power is engaged in a series of processes that have to do with the death rate, life expectancy, the fertility of the population, birth rates, hygiene, vaccinations, common diseases, unemployment rates, and the patterns of employment as varied across age, gender, vocation, per-capita income, and so on. Israel's effort to increase the rate of births that take place in Palestinian hospitals, for example, is an instance of this kind of power. Whereas in the early 1970s only 16 percent of West Bank births took place in hospitals, by 1993, the rate of hospital births had risen to 74.5 percent. This influenced traditional norms and practices and remarkably decreased infant mortality.[17] In order to control the population, bio-power applies statistical and scientific methods, as well as surveillance and supervision that focus on the individual only as part of a multiplicity. This kind of power functions through a series of institutions that coordinate, organize, and regulate medical treatment, economic policy, and the like while at the same time delineating and shaping the political sphere and normalizing fields of knowledge.[18] As I will show in the following pages, in the first years after the 1967 War, bio-power and disciplinary power were both emphasized in order to normalize the occupation by creating prosperity in the West Bank and the Gaza Strip. Likewise, abundant efforts were devoted to erasing all symbols relating to Palestinian nationality.

At the same time, Israel has never avoided using the more traditional kind of power—sovereign power characterized by the sword. When discussing sovereign power, I mean the ability to dictate a certain legal system and to use the military and police in order to enforce or suspend it.[19] This kind of force is operated by the judicial and administrative branches. Often it is controlled from the top down, intermittently. That is, it tends to appear only when the law is violated by certain individuals or when the law is suspended by the sovereign. In our case, the meaning of this kind of power is the application of a legal system that sees every form of Palestinian resistance as terror and the activation of Israeli security forces to repress any kind of terror. At the same time, this legal system has turned into a means of expropriation through which Israel has divested Palestinians of their land and property.

It is important to emphasize that most of the time, the three kinds of power function together as parts of modern forms of administration. Even though these kinds of power coexist, every administration has a different configuration of power, because every administration emphasizes certain kinds of power and restrains others. The particular configuration of power is what determines the guiding principle of an administration and helps us understand why the order of violence changes. This claim coincides, I think, with the differentiation that Foucault poses between sovereign power, which relates to the management and control of territory, and governmentality, which relates to the management of population, inasmuch as that differentiation is not considered to be a binary opposition, but rather a shift in emphasis that stems from a renewed definition of purposes.[20] In other words, in a regime that emphasizes a sovereign form of control, control of the population is important, but the control of territory is the main purpose. Conversely, in a regime operating according to the logic of governmentality, the control of territory remains important, but it is not the only or the main purpose. The difference between the two also leads to a different configuration of power. An administration that operates according to the principle of colonization is closer in the way it operates to the logic that Foucault called "governmentality," because disciplinary power and bio-power are emphasized, whereas sovereign power is restrained. On the other hand, an administration operating according to the principle of separation emphasizes sovereign power and restrains disciplinary power and bio-power. In the first, the control of both population and territory are perceived as purposes, while in the second, the sole purpose becomes the control of territory. A brief historical survey is sufficient to illustrate these differences in emphasis.

After the 1967 War, Israel assumed responsibility for the residents of the Occupied Territories, undertaking the administration of the major civil institutions through which modern societies are managed: education, health care, welfare, and the financial and legal systems. Simultaneously, it began expropriating Palestinian land and water, the most important natural resources in the region. Two weeks after the war, East Jerusalem along with twenty-eight villages were annexed, and about three months later, on September 1967, the first Jewish settlement was built in the West Bank.[21] About 40 percent of the land in the West Bank and Gaza had been appropriated by the time the first intifada erupted in December 1987. Within these first twenty years, Israel had established 125 settlements and transferred about sixty thousand Israeli citizens to the two regions (excluding East Jerusalem).[22]

The colonization principle thus incorporates a certain notion of separation, which one might call the "first separation principle." Levi Eshkol, Israel's prime minister in 1967, clearly articulated this principle during a Labor Party meeting that took place three months after the war in which the consequences of Israel's military victory were discussed. He turned to Golda Meir, who was then the party's general secretary, and said: "I understand…you covet the dowry, but not the bride." The dowry was the land that Israel occupied in June 1967, and the bride was the Palestinian population.[23]

Despite Israel's aversion toward the bride, it considered the Palestinian body to be an extremely important object of management and control, and during the first two decades of occupation, it attempted to rule the population in primarily nonviolent ways. According to a 1970 military report, the "Six-Day War erased the 'Green Line' that used to separate Israel from the areas now administered and it is quite unavoidable and natural that these areas now depend on Israel in all economic matters and services.... The only way to avoid a potential outburst of social forces is to strive continuously for the improvement of the standard of living and the services of this underprivileged society."[24] Therefore, it is not altogether surprising that already in the midst of the war, Israel provided services to Palestinian farmers in order to save crops and to prevent the death of livestock.[25] And when the fighting subsided, Israel established a series of programs to improve economic productivity. Consider, for a moment, a telling passage taken from a 1969 military report.

> In the course of a veterinary action, all cattle herds, about 30,000 heads, were marked, and immunization shots against mouth and hoof disease administered. The cattle are examined for tuberculosis, and sick cows are purchased by the military government for slaughtering without loss to the farmer. The entire poultry stock— about half a million heads—received shots against the New Castle disease. There has been a radical decline in the mortality of poultry as a result of these injections to a very small number this year in comparison with a 60% loss in the past. Thousands of dogs were destroyed to prevent the spread of rabies.[26]

This passage shows that Israel immediately put to use up-to-date forms of surveillance, monitoring the number of cattle and poultry and keeping track of diseases to which the livestock had been subjected and how many had died due to infection. To be sure, it had a vested interest in monitoring and preventing any epidemic from developing, since viruses and diseases do not stop at the Green Line, the pre-1967 border. But it also had an interest in increasing the economic utility of the Palestinian farmers. The introduction of an immunization program had a huge effect on the mortality rate of livestock and substantially raised the productivity of Palestinian farmers. Moreover, Israel's policy of purchasing sick cows from the farmers suggests that it was also genuinely concerned about guaranteeing the livelihood of the local population. The logic was to render the occupied inhabitants docile by raising their standard of living and transforming their lifestyle. Forms of management that promoted a politics of life rapidly became prominent.

The incorporation of Palestinians into the Israeli workforce not only provided cheap labor for the Israeli market, thus satisfying Israel's economic needs, but also had a significant effect on the population's standard of living. According to the Bank of Israel, it was "the chief factor behind the vigorous development [in the Occupied Territories] of the early years."[27] The swiftness of the laborer's incorporation is worth noting. Already in 1968, one year after the war, 6 percent of the

Palestinian labor force found jobs in Israel. By 1974, 69,400 Palestinians worked in Israel and made up 33 percent of the workforce. On the eve of the first intifada (1987), the Palestinian workforce was 277,700, of which 108,900 were employed in Israel (39.2 percent). For so large a percentage of the workforce to work outside the territory in which the laborers reside is a phenomenon unparalleled throughout the rest of the world.[28] These figures are widely regarded as understated, since they take into account only those who found work through formal channels and do not include unregistered workers. The number of unregistered workers fluctuated over the years and has been estimated to be an additional 40 to 70 percent of the total number of workers just cited as entering Israel.[29]

At least during the first years, the Palestinians who worked in Israel earned anywhere from 10 to 100 percent more than they would have if they worked in the territories, depending on their occupation. As a result, the average daily wages of all employees from the West Bank rose by 35 percent in the period from 1970 to 1974 and by 13 percent during the period from 1974 to 1979. In the Gaza Strip, they rose by 50 and 18.4 percent, respectively.[30] Between 1968 and 1972, GNP increased annually by 16 and 20 percent in the West Bank and Gaza Strip, respectively. From 1973 to 1980, the economic growth continued, albeit at a slower but nonetheless very impressive rate, with a 9 and 6 percent annual increase of GNP in West Bank and Gaza, respectively.[31]

One should keep in mind, however, that there is a significant difference between growth and development. Even though the Palestinians experienced a substantial rise in their standard of living, the development of the local economy was obstructed by a series of restrictions and constraints. The Palestinians were not allowed to establish any industry, and Israel's control and continuous expropriation of land and the appropriation of water hindered growth in the agricultural sector. Sara Roy convincingly argues that the Palestinian economy was actually "de-developed," by which she means "the deliberate, systematic destruction of an indigenous economy by a dominant power."[32] Nonetheless, for a few years, Israel's policies managed to produce prosperity in the West Bank and Gaza Strip, which helped mitigate the colonization principle's basic contradiction—the separation of the people and their land—and to undermine widespread political resistance to the occupation.

Indeed, the initial outcome of Israel's policies proved to be beneficial. The dramatic rise in individual prosperity served to conceal the communal stagnation that Israel was creating.[33] Due to the integration of the Palestinian laborers, there was a dramatic decrease in unemployment rates, accompanied by remarkable economic growth, which helped Israel direct the energies of many Palestinians toward increasing their productive capacity. Simultaneously, the military government outlawed all forms of political organizing and forcefully suppressed all resistance, thus ensuring that Palestinian opposition would remain local and sporadic.

In the effort to obfuscate the occupation and incorporate the captured territories into Israel, the government introduced numerous erasure practices, of which the erasure of the international border was crucial. Less than six months after the war, on December 17, the Israeli government began referring to the West Bank as "Judea and Samaria," thus drawing a connection between the state of Israel and the biblical land of Israel.[34] Gradually, the Green Line was erased from all atlases, maps, and textbooks published by the Israeli government, making it nearly impossible for Israeli schoolchildren to learn that Israel's recognized international borders actually pass along the line of the 1949 Armistice Agreements.[35] Not unlike the Palestinian maps that depict all of Mandatory Palestine as "Palestine," Israeli maps depict all of Mandatory Palestine as "Israel," leading many schoolchildren to believe that the recognized borders are south of Rafah and pass through the Jordan Valley.[36]

To reify the erasure of borders, Israel also connected the physical infrastructure between its territory and the regions it had captured. It linked the transport and communication networks of the West Bank and Gaza to Israel proper, making it easy for the increasing number of Jewish settlers and Palestinian laborers to reach Tel Aviv and Jerusalem.[37] Rapidly, almost all of the obstacles characterizing an international border were removed. Any Israeli could drive to the West Bank or Gaza as if he or she was going to visit an adjacent district. Several Israeli "field schools," centers located in hiking areas, operated by the Society for the Protection of Nature in Israel and providing educational facilities, guided tours, and accommodation for hikers were opened in the West Bank, and the Israeli public regularly hiked and picnicked throughout this region. Thousands of shoppers went on weekend excursions to buy cheap produce in the territories. Most of the customs, tariffs, and barriers that typify the exchange of commodities across international borders did not exist. Moreover, at a certain point, the distinction between government expenditures within Israel proper and expenditures in the Occupied Territories was expunged from the annual budget, in effect transforming the entire area from the Jordan Valley to the Mediterranean Sea into one economic unit.

In addition to the spatial changes and the interventions in the economic field, Israel employed disciplinary technologies for managing the population of the Occupied Territories in the legal, education, and medical fields, as well as in numerous other areas, ranging from movement to planning and zoning. In the legal field, for example, it adopted a sui generis interpretation of international law that enabled it to separate the land from its inhabitants. Together with a number of other officials, Meir Shamgar, who in 1967 was the Judge Advocate General and later the president of Israel's Supreme Court, formulated a policy that rejected the applicability to the Occupied Territories of the 1949 Fourth Geneva Convention—the most important humanitarian law pertaining to the occupation of conquered territories and their civilian population.[38] Shamgar's rationale was that the West Bank and Gaza Strip should not be considered occupied territories, because the two regions had been seized by Jordan and Egypt during the 1948 War and thus had never been an integral part of a sovereign state. Consequently, he maintained, the West Bank and Gaza Strip should be considered "disputed," rather than occupied areas.[39] He accordingly advised the government to abide by the Geneva Convention on a de facto rather than de jure basis by respecting its "humanitarian provisions," but he never specified when these provisions should actually be respected.[40] Thus, the land was not subjected to the Geneva Convention, while its Palestinian inhabitants were, but their rights remained ambiguously defined.[41]

Shamgar also insisted that the Eshkol government accept the 1907 Hague Convention, which stipulates that the occupying power should recognize the laws that were in force before the occupation.[42] By June 7, 1967, the military commander had already issued Proclamation No. 2, a declaration dealing with the governance and legal arrangements in the Territories. The laws existing in the territories prior to the occupation were declared valid, provided they did not contradict any legislation issued by the military commander.[43] Accordingly, a complex legal system was put in place composed of laws from the Ottoman Empire, the British Mandate (particularly the emergency regulations of 1945), Jordanian and Egyptian law (depending on the region), and Israeli military orders.

The military orders are decrees issued by the military commander and immediately became law for all Palestinians living in the area.[44] Over the years, the military commanders have used their legislative powers extensively, issuing more than twenty-five hundred orders, which have dealt with a wide range of topics: from military, judicial, and fiscal matters to administrative affairs, including education, welfare, and health and even the status of Jewish settlements.[45] The orders codified Israel's control of the Occupied Territories far beyond the concern for the security of its military forces. Israel's idiosyncratic interpretation of international humanitarian law has had an immense effect on the occupation. Its ingenuity lies, on the one hand, in its effective distinction between the people and the land and, on the other, in the fact that it does not reject the law outright, but rather embraces a selective approach toward the law. Shamgar seems to have recognized that even as Israel suspended significant elements of international law and bestowed on the military commander the authority to cancel and enact domestic laws according to immediate political objectives, it was also crucial to espouse a "rule of law" approach. Adopting laws that had existed before the occupation while making room for the enactment of military orders that could cancel these laws actually enabled Israel to argue that the rule of law reigned in the West Bank and Gaza Strip. In this way, Israel managed to deflect criticism of despotic rule for many years.[46]

Thus, during the period in which the colonial principle reigned, a particular legal system based on multiple legal frameworks was established and used for managing the population. The adoption of several legal frameworks alongside the prerogative powers handed to the military commander enabled Israel to exploit the gaps and contradictions engendered by the different legal frameworks and to use both the laws and the exceptions that the gaps and contradictions made possible in order to control the inhabitants. While the colonial principle is characterized by the deployment of legal procedures and justifications and the exploitation of multiple legal frameworks, as we will see below, the separation principle entails the suspension of the law.

The objective of the legal system and the erasure of the Green Line, as well as of the other disciplinary technologies employed in the Occupied Territories, was different from what it is elsewhere in the world. In most countries, discipline regulates people through processes of incorporation into the state, constituting them as citizens. In the Occupied Territories, by contrast, all forms of social incorporation were partial and always informed by a series of separations. The integration of the Palestinian laborers into the Israeli workforce, for example, was always incomplete. In addition to being paid lower salaries, the Palestinian workers were not permitted to join any of the existing unions within Israel and were not allowed to form their own unions for laborers who worked inside Israel.[47] The truncated economic integration and the consequent perpetual job insecurity reflected the fact that Palestinians were not integrated politically and therefore could not enjoy the rights and status of Israeli workers.[48] As Michael Mann suggests in a different context, their incorporation was "without legitimization."[49]

Because there was never an intention of fully integrating the Palestinian inhabitants and making them part of the Israeli citizenry, the different disciplines and the erasure of the Green Line were never employed to incorporate the Palestinian inhabitants into Israeli society, but rather to constitute them as nonnational subjects. Since the Palestinian national subject was conceived to be a demon of sorts, Israel employed violence to expose and annihilate it. Immediately after the 1967 War, the military imposed curfews, deported leaders, demolished homes, carried out arrests, tortured detainees, and restricted movement. In the West Bank, these kinds of actions were carried out particularly during the first two years, until the occupation was consolidated. In the Gaza Strip, the Palestinians organized armed resistance, but after the opposition was brutally crushed in 1971, Israel changed the repertoires of violence it employed in this region and began implementing measures similar to those utilized in the West Bank, where, during the 1970s, the sword was employed as an ever-lurking threat and only rarely as an actual weapon of annihilation.[50]

The general mood in the Occupied Territories during the first decades was very different than it is today. For several years, the Israeli military government published annual reports entitled *Accountability*, suggesting that Israel felt a need to provide an account of the social and economic developments taking place in the regions that it had captured. In these reports, the civilizing mission of the colonial principle is omnipresent. Israel portrayed itself as bringing progress to the uncivilized Palestinians. The thrust of the claims made in the reports can be summed up in the following way: Due to our interventions, the Palestinian economic, industrial, educational, health-care, and civilian infrastructures have significantly developed.

Many of the military reports also underscore Israel's ongoing efforts to normalize the occupation. The Palestinians had never had a state of their own and had always lived under foreign rule, a fact that made Israel's efforts easier. The ultimate aim of the military government, as pronounced by the first coordinator of government activities in the Occupied Territories, was to create a situation whereby a Palestinian "resident of the area might be born in the hospital, receive his birth certificate, grow up and receive his education, be married and raise his children and grandchildren to a ripe old age—all this without the help of an Israeli government employee or clerk and without even setting eyes on him."[51] If this goal had been reached, the occupation, as Moshe Dayan has put it, would have been invisible indeed.

CONTRADICTIONS

Although Israel succeeded in containing the Palestinian national movement for several years, eventually, its disciplinary technologies of control began producing a series of contradictions that helped empower Palestinian resistance within the Occupied Territories. According to Joel Migdal, for example, the incorporation of Palestinian laborers into the Israeli workforce created two major social cleavages in West Bank villages, cleavages characterized by generational and income gaps.[52] These gaps ultimately weakened the traditional village leadership, since those who worked in Israel became economically independent and were demanding a say in local politics. That is, although the Palestinian laborers then became dependent on Israel for their livelihood, a fact that was used by Israel to expand its control over them, simultaneously, the process of incorporation weakened the control of the traditional elites over these laborers because the economic power which the laborers acquired often put them in a better financial position than the traditional elites. By extension, this process also weakened Israel's control over the laborers, since one of the ways Israel controlled the population was through the elites.[53]

By 1976, when Israel carried out municipal elections in the West Bank, many of the laborers created alliances with the urban Palestinian nationalists, since only through the nationalists could the laborers obtain some form of political power that reflected their economic power. The nationalists ended up winning the elections, dealing a blow to the traditional elites and to the Israeli military government. In other words, Israel's attempt to control the population by providing benefits to the traditional elites failed, not least because the incorporation of young men into the Israeli workforce empowered many workers who were looking for ways of translating their economic achievements into political power. Hence, the integration of workers, which had been used as a technology to manage the population, helped undo another controlling technology—the use of traditional elites to administer the area and repress the national aspirations of the Palestinian subject.

Two other contradictions that undercut Israel's attempts to normalize the occupation were produced as a direct result of the separation between the Palestinians and their land. Simply put, the massive investment in settlement infrastructure and the transfer of thousands of Jewish citizens to the captured territories flew in the face of Israel's insistent claim that the occupation was temporary. One should note that for several years, the "temporariness of the occupation" was deployed as a modality of control. The deliberately temporary nature of arrangements, legal orders, and policies, as well as the temporary or incomplete status of refugees, were all used to thwart resistance and for a while proved to be a very efficient management technique. Along similar lines, the temporary status of the Jewish settlements and bypass roads, which existed for years in an ostensibly suspended state, helped prevent Palestinian opposition. And yet, it did not take a great deal of time before the settlement project exposed, at least to the local inhabitants, the grand lie concerning the temporality of the occupation, rendering this controlling technology less and less efficient.

Simultaneously, the settlement project created a new spatial reality for the dispossessed Palestinians, whose living space was dramatically circumscribed. Because the land was indiscriminately expropriated, the confiscation helped fuse the interests of rivaling *hamulahs* (extended families) as well as the poor and the rich, urban dwellers and rural residents, and Muslims and Christians, thus weakening clan, class, regional, and religious fragmentation. Israel's settlement enterprise consequently helped widen and deepen national awareness among the Palestinian population and ended up reproducing the Palestinian national subject, which Israel incessantly aimed to repress. Moreover, the Palestinians came to realize that the settlements threatened the hope of establishing a Palestinian state in the future. What, in other words, is the point of prosperity if one is dispossessed?

These examples are merely indicative of numerous other contradictions that manifested themselves over the years. They suggest, as Timothy Mitchell has argued in a different context, that disciplines often counteract one another, break down, or overreach. They create spaces for maneuver and resistance and can be turned to counterhegemonic purposes.[54] They accordingly suggest that the colonization principle, and more precisely the contradictions that it created, not only repressed the Palestinian national subject, but also helped construct it, thus empowering the Palestinian resistance movement within the Occupied Territories. All of which helps explain the eruption of the first intifada.

THE SEPARATION PRINCIPLE

At a certain point during the first intifada, Israel realized that the colonization principle could no longer be used as the basic logic informing its control of the West Bank and the Gaza Strip and began looking for a new principle that would allow it to uphold the occupation. The desire to normalize the occupation and successfully annihilate the Palestinian national subject through a series of disciplinary technologies that were supported when need arose by the sword proved to be unrealistic. It took a few years before a clear policy was shaped, but eventually, the separation principle was adopted. As opposed to the colonization principle, which was rarely discussed, the separation principle has been talked about incessantly. The paradigmatic sentence describing this principle is: "We are here, they are there." The "we" refers to Israelis, and the "they" to Palestinians.

While the first principle reflects the logic of the occupation, the second ostensibly offers a solution to the occupation. The key word here is "ostensibly." If truth be told, the second principle does not aim to solve the occupation, but rather to alter its logic. In other words, "We are here, they are there," does not signify a withdrawal of Israeli power from the Occupied Territories (even though that is how it is understood among the Israeli public), but is used to blur the fact that Israel has been reorganizing its power in the territories in order to continue its control over their resources. Thus, the Oslo Accords, which were the direct result of the first intifada as well as of the changing political and economic circumstances in the international realm, signified the *reorganization of power, rather than its withdrawal,* and should be understood as the continuation of the occupation by other means. As one commentator observed early on, Oslo was a form of "occupation by remote control."[55]

If one reads the eight different Oslo agreements that the Israelis and Palestinians signed over the years not as part of a peace process (that is, not in the way they were presented to the public), but rather as texts that depict the modification or replacement of existing controlling technologies in an attempt to outsource responsibility for the population of the Occupied Territories to a Palestinian Authority (PA), then the strategy Israel adopted becomes clear.[56] Instead of reaching a settlement about the withdrawal of Israeli power, the Oslo agreements actually stipulate, in unambiguous language, how Israel's power would be reorganized in three distinct spheres—the civil institutions, the economy, and law enforcement. In exchange for the Palestinian Authority's providing Israel with an array of services, Israel offered the fledgling PA some sort of truncated sovereignty over the people of the Occupied Territories, while it, in turn, continued to control most of the occupied land. The overarching logic informing the different agreements is straightforward: Transfer all responsibilities relating to the management of the population to the Palestinians themselves while preserving control of Palestinian space.

The partition of space and the reorganization of power were intricately tied. Oslo divided the West Bank into Areas A, B, and C, as well as H-1 and H-2 in Hebron and the Yellow and White Areas in Gaza.[57] Areas A, B, and C determined the distribution of powers in the West Bank by creating internal boundaries. These boundaries produced a series of new "insides" and "outsides" within the Occupied Territories, each one with its own specific laws and regulations. While in all three areas the PA assumed full responsibility over the civil institutions, in Area A, which in 1995 amounted to 3 percent of the West Bank's land and 26 percent of its population, the PA was given full responsibility for maintaining law and order. In Area B, which amounted to 24 percent of the land and 70 percent of the population, the PA was handed over responsibility for public order, but Israel maintained overriding responsibility for security. And in Area C, which contained 73 percent of the land and 4 percent of the population, Israel retained full responsibility for security and public order, as well as for civil issues relating to territory (planning and zoning, archeology, etc.). Thus, in 1995, the PA was responsible for managing all of the Palestinian inhabitants, but had full control of only 3 percent of the West Bank's land (the cities Jenin, Nablus, Tulkarem, Qalqilya, Ramallah, Bethlehem, and Jericho). By 2000, following a series of agreements, the relative distribution of the areas had changed, so that Area A contained 17.2 percent, Area B 23.8 percent, and Area C 59.0 percent of the land.[58] Area A was divided into 11 separate clusters, Area B was made up of 120 clusters, while the 64 percent that constituted Area C was contiguous.[59] The areas in which the Palestinians had full control were like an archipelago of sorts, while the areas controlled by Israel were strategic corridors that interrupted the territorial contiguity of the West Bank.

Thus, for all practical purposes, the internal borders dividing areas A, B, and C did not exist with respect to the operation of civil institutions providing health care, education, and welfare: The PA took on full responsibility for the civil institutions serving the Palestinian population as a whole, regardless of where people lived in the Occupied Territories.[60] From 1994 on, the PA relieved Israel of the most difficult aspect of the occupation, while Israel, in turn, kept most of the land under its control. Thus, the division of space within the Occupied Territories not only determined the distribution of certain powers, but also allowed Israel to maintain the distinction between the Palestinian population and their land.

Initially, the reorganization of power and space produced the desired effects. A general quiet replaced the social unrest in the Occupied Territories, permitting a sense of normalcy to take over. The nightly curfews in the Gaza Strip ended, children played in the streets, and schools and universities were opened, as were coffee shops, restaurants, and new hotels. Many of those who had invested much time in the struggle against the Israeli military turned to securing a stable income for their families. For a while, the Occupied Territories experienced a construction boom, particularly in Gaza and Ramallah, and money was invested in infrastructure while numerous cooperation projects between Palestinian and Israeli businesses helped produce an atmosphere of peace. And although three thousand Palestinians remained in jails, the majority of the political prisoners were released by 1996.[61] There was also a sharp decline in the number of Palestinians killed by Israeli security forces. In 1996, for example, 18 Palestinians were killed in the Occupied Territories, in comparison with 155 in 1993. The number of children killed also dropped dramatically. During the three-year period from 1994 to 1996, thirty-five children were killed, while in 1993 alone, forty children were killed, and in 1989, seventy-eight children were killed.[62] The change in the lives of the Palestinians had quite a bit to do with the redeployment of the Israeli military, which, in turn, reduced the price Israel had to pay for the occupation, both politically and economically.

Simultaneously, Oslo managed to undo the first intifada's most important achievements. While the intifada undermined almost all forms of normalization and exposed the occupation for what it was—military rule upheld through violence and violation—Oslo succeeded in normalizing the occupation once again. Moreover, the creation of the PA led to the disappearance of vigorous popular and civil movements that had been the mainstay of the first intifada. As Reema Hamami and Salim Tamari point out, popular committees, neighborhood committees, mass organizations, and most of the political movements that sustained them began to collapse toward the end of the intifada due to Israeli counterinsurgency methods, and their recovery was preempted by the Oslo agreements and the ostensible state-formation process.[63]

Wittingly or unwittingly, the specific organization of space and the transfer of authority over civil institutions to the PA reflects the beginning of a transformation from the principle of colonization to the principle of separation, where the latter does not mean the termination of control, but rather its alteration from a system based on managing the lives of the residents of the Occupied territories to a system that is no longer interested in the lives of the Palestinian residents. Consequently, Israel no longer provides any kind of "account" of the conditions under which the Palestinians are living. One important manifestation of this change is that the Israeli Bureau of Statistics has stopped monitoring any development pertaining to the Palestinian population in the Occupied Territories.

Although the principle informing the occupation changed parallel to the Oslo process, the transformations in the modes of violence were seen only after the eruption of the second intifada. Until then, the Palestinian Authority was responsible for managing the population in the West Bank and Gaza Strip, having taken on this role in 1994. In my book *Israel's Occupation,* I describe the contradictions leading to the outbreak of the intifada, as well as the actions taken to destroy the PA. Here it is sufficient to note that following Israel's assault on the PA, most of the strategies deployed to govern and manage the population were obstructed. Israel did not, however, assume responsibility for the lives of the population, as it had done following the occupation of the territories in 1967, and merely continued to develop forms of population control in the checkpoints and seam zones. Moreover, the outbreak of the second intifada also led Israel to alter its relation to the law. Until September 2000, Israel controlled the inhabitants of the Occupied Territories primarily through the application of multiple legal frameworks—including, to be sure, the enforcement of draconian laws that both legalized the incarceration of thousands of political prisoners and permitted deportations, house demolitions, torture, extended curfews, and other forms of collective punishment. By contrast, one of the most striking characteristics of the second intifada is the extensive suspension of the law under the aegis of the separation principle.

In the first thirty-three years of occupation, any suspension of the law was still considered an exception to the rule, even though the law's actual application did not entail any meaningful administration of justice. In the second intifada, the suspension of the law became the norm. One example of this suspension is Israel's pervasive employment of extrajudicial executions. The fact that not one Israeli soldier has been tried for these killings and that they are part of an overt policy suggests that some of the inhabitants of the Occupied Territories have been reduced to what the Italian political philosopher Giorgio Agamben has called *homo sacer,* people who can be killed without it being considered a crime.[64]

Another example of how the law has been suspended involves the massive destruction of Palestinian homes. During the first four years of the second intifada, the Israeli military demolished over twenty-five hundred Palestinian houses in the Gaza Strip. According to Human Rights Watch, nearly two-thirds of these homes were in Rafah, a densely populated town and refugee camp located on the border with Egypt. As a result, sixteen thousand people—more than 10 percent of Rafah's population—lost their homes, most of them refugees who were dispossessed for a second or third time.[65] To stop these demolitions, a few groups petitioned the Israeli High Court of Justice, which had consistently legitimized demolitions for decades, but which had developed a limited jurisprudence regarding the owner's right to be heard in advance of demolitions.[66] During the second intifada, the High Court of Justice expanded the scope of the military's discretion to dispense with the right to a hearing. The court ruled that the right to due process could be revoked in three instances: if destruction is absolutely necessary for military operations, if providing advance notice would endanger the lives of soldiers, and if providing advance notice would endanger the success of the demolition. Thus, even though before the uprising there were instances in which demolitions could go ahead without a hearing, and although the hearing itself rarely stopped the demolition, according to Human Rights Watch, the cumulative effect of the "three exceptions" rule has been "to give the military discretion to circumvent the already limited role of the Court and to avoid having to justify demolitions in the first place."[67] Both the extrajudicial executions and the house demolitions accordingly indicate that following the implementation of the separation principle, the rule of law in the Occupied Territories has, in many respects, become superfluous.

The crucial point is that with the adoption of the separation principle, Israel has lost interest in the lives of the Palestinians and now focuses almost solely on the Occupied Territories' resources. The checkpoints and seam zones are the exception, since at these locations, Israel continues to monitor the Palestinian subject closely and to disseminate a series of norms through disciplinary practices that aim to teach inhabitants who wish to move the requirements of correct conduct. Israel, in other words, is no longer attempting to normalize the occupation by striving to shape the behavior of the Palestinian population, but rather it aims to shape and administer only the *moving subject*. Following the adoption of the separation principle, only those Palestinians who either want to move within the Occupied Territories or want to exit the region are subjected to Israel's disciplinary practices and must, in order to become moving subjects, adopt a series of normative fiats. Those Palestinians who do not want any contact with Israel must remain within the confines of their refugee camp, village, town, or city. It is therefore not surprising that 85 percent of people in the West Bank did not leave their villages during the second intifada's first three years.[68]

In addition to policing the Palestinian moving subject, Israel has adopted a series of strategies that further contract Palestinian space, primarily through the imposition of internal and external closures, the creation of blockades and check-points, and, more recently, the construction of the separation barrier and the fortification of outposts and settlements. The loss of interest in the lives of the occupied residents and the extensive suspension of the law creates an extremely precarious situation, since it sets the stage for a change in the repertoires of violence and a dramatic increase in the number of Palestinian deaths.

OF GHETTOS AND FRONTIERS

Why, one might ask, has Israel employed more lethal forms of violence after it abandoned the colonization principle and adopted the separation principle? The insights of James Ron, who examined the violence in the Occupied Territories and Lebanon in the beginning of the 1990s, can help us make sense of some of the changes taking place in the West Bank and Gaza Strip.[69] Ron's basic and straight-forward claim is that state violence is shaped by the institutional setting in which it takes place. He employs two spatial metaphors: ghettos and frontiers. Ghettos are areas densely institutionalized by the controlling state, since they are within its legal sphere of influence and serve as repositories for unwanted and marginalized populations. Frontiers, on the other hand, are distinguished from the controlling state by clear boundaries and are only thinly institutionalized arenas. The different institutional settings determine the kind of violence employed. Whereas ghettos are characterized by ethnic policing, mass incarceration, and ongoing harassment, frontiers are more prone to brutal and lawless violence. Ron, who was writing about the 1970s, 1980s, and early 1990s, claims that the Occupied Territories are Israel's ghetto, while Lebanon is its frontier.

The comparison with Lebanon is important. Following the adoption of the separation principle and the dilution of the Israeli bureaucratic and legal institutions in the West Bank and Gaza (a process that began with Oslo), the means of violence that Israel has employed in the Occupied Territories are becoming more and more similar to the ones it uses in Lebanon: F-16 fighter jets, Apache helicopters, and ground-to-ground missiles. Former Shabak head Avi Dichter, who has recently served as a minister in the Israeli government, said as much before Israel's withdrawal from the Gaza Strip. The withdrawal, he asserted, would give Israel more freedom to carry out military operations in the strip.[70] Thus, there seems to be a strong correlation between ghettos and the colonization principle and between frontiers and the separation principle.

Ron provides us with the analytical tools to understand the modifications in the modes of violence and the dramatic changes in the number of Palestinian deaths over the years, yet his metaphors do not exactly correspond to the new reality in the Occupied Territories. While the West Bank and Gaza Strip have been transformed into Israel's frontiers in the sense of the thinning out of institutions aimed at managing the lives of the residents of the Occupied Territories, from a spatial perspective, they have become hermetic ghettos. We are accordingly confronted with a much more complex and dangerous situation than the one that Ron describes.

A few years before the second intifada erupted, Israel began imposing a harsh closure regime on the Occupied Territories, whereby it closed off the Green Line altogether, rendering it illegal for any Palestinian to exit the region regardless of whether he or she held an entry permit.[71] Actually, the closure had begun as a sporadic form of control in 1991 and became more frequent and comprehensive over the years. In 1994, the Occupied Territories were under closure for 43 days; in 1996, the territories were closed off for 104 days; and in 1997 for 87 days.[72] The internal closures had dire results. Nongovernmental organizations estimated that for the duration of each internal closure, about two hundred thousand Palestinians (80 percent of the labor force) were prevented from reaching their workplaces.[73]

Also, in the midst of the Oslo process, Israel built a fence around the Gaza Strip to ensure that all Gazans would be subjected to the closure-and-entry-permit regime. (During those years, many workers succeeded in infiltrating into Israel from the West Bank, despite the closures.) Within a relatively short period, a patrol road and a series of fences fifty-four kilometers long closed off the border between the strip and Israel, leaving only four passageways connecting the two regions (two of which operate in one direction only, from Israel to Gaza) and one more connecting Gaza with Egypt.[74] The Green Line was accordingly converted from a "normally open" border into a "normally closed" one. Only a very small number of Palestinian political leaders and businessmen whom Israel wanted to support and to promote received permits to travel during closures.

Following the outbreak of the second intifada, Israel also imposed an internal closure that restricts movement within the West Bank and Gaza Strip.[75] According to the United Nations Office for the Coordination of Humanitarian Affairs, as of July 2004, over seven hundred physical barriers existed *within* the West Bank — including checkpoints, roadblocks, earth mounds, trenches, and road gates — that divided the region into scores of "clusters," severely curtailing the movement of 2.4 million Palestinians.[76] The Gaza Strip has been periodically cut into three separate regions, with movement from one region to the other denied. After Israel's withdrawal from Gaza in August 2005, it was transformed into a hermetic ghetto, which rendered Israel's violence in the region much more fatal — not only because the Gazans, unlike the Lebanese, have nowhere to flee when Israel bombs them, but because the ghettoization of Palestinian society has been destroying the civilian infrastructure that did exist.

The creation of the hermetic ghetto alongside the economic sanctions that have been imposed on the occupied Palestinians produce unique forms of violence. In addition to the F-16s, Apache helicopters, and missiles, there are walls and fences, roads for Jews only, checkpoints, roadblocks, and panoptic towers that restrict the population's movement while destroying the economy as well as the education, health-care, and welfare systems. The cruel irony is that even though the separation principle presents itself as separating Palestinians and Israelis, the primary contradiction (the attempt to separate the Palestinians from their land) has, with slight alterations, remained intact. Israel has not withdrawn its power from the Occupied Territories, but rather continues to control Palestinian space, both through forms of violence applied by remote control (surveillance aircraft, fighter jets, missiles, etc.) and through the hermetic ghetto, as well as through economic sanctions.

THE NEW VIOLENCE

The separation principle produces a totally different controlling logic from the logic produced by the colonial principle. While during the first decade of the occupation, Israel tried to decrease Palestinian unemployment in order to manage the population, following the advent of the new millennium, Israel intentionally produced unemployment in the Occupied Territories. Whereas in 1992, some 30 percent of the Palestinian workforce was employed in Israel, in 1996, that figure had fallen to 7 percent, and the average rate of unemployment in the territories reached 32.6 percent, rising twelvefold from the 3 percent unemployment in 1992.[77]

Along similar lines, while during the first years of the occupation Israel provided immunization for cattle and poultry, in 2006, it created conditions that prevented people from receiving immunization for themselves. As I show in the contribution to this volume that I wrote with Dani Filc, following the adoption of the separation principle, the health of the Palestinian population deteriorated. The World Bank reports that acute malnutrition affects more than 9 percent of Palestinian children in the territories, and the Food and Agriculture Organization of the United Nations estimated that in 2003, almost 40 percent of the Palestinians in the Occupied Territories suffered from food insecurity.[78] Almost half of the children between six and fifty-nine months old and women of child-bearing age are anemic. It is not only that the Palestinian body is no longer considered to be an important object of management and that Israel has abandoned its objective of constituting the occupied inhabitant as an economically efficient subject, but that it has adopted a series of policies that in effect weaken and destroy the Palestinian body.

Indeed, under the separation principle, the Palestinian body is no longer conceived to be an object that needs to be meddled with and shaped. The military's policy during the second intifada, whereby soldiers shot more than one million bullets within the first month, is poles apart from the policies informing the first years of the occupation and even from Defense Minister Yitzhak Rabin's directive "to break their bones," given to soldiers during the first intifada.[79] The difference between beating and killing reflects the difference between the colonial principle and the separation principle—between shaping the body and crushing it. While during the first twenty years of occupation Israel killed 650 people, in the past six years, it has killed on average more and more Palestinians each year. Israel's use of more lethal violence is, accordingly, not the result of an isolated tactic whose goal is to accomplish certain objectives, such as the repression of the second intifada. Nor can Israel's violence be explained as a response to a more violent resistance. Rather, the different repertoires of violence reflect the transformation from the colonial to the separation principle.

NOTES

A different and much shorter version of this chapter appeared in *Third World Quarterly* 29, no. 1 (2008): pp. 25–44.

1   Ian Black and Benny Morris, *Israel's Secret Wars: The Untold History of Israeli Intelligence* (London: Hamish Hamilton, 1991), p. 239.

2   Shlomo Gazit, lecture, June 10, 2006, Tel Aviv University.

3   State of Israel, Ministry of Defense, Unit for Coordination of Activities in the Territories, *Three Years of Military Government, 1967–1970: Figures on Civilian Activity in Judea, Samaria, the Gaza Strip and Northern Sinai* (Tel Aviv: Ministry of Defense, 1970), p. 4.

4   Cited in Shlomo Gazit, *Trapped Fools: Thirty Years of Israeli Policy in the Territories* (London: Frank Cass, 2003), p. 163.

5   *Ibid.*, p. 162.

6   State of Israel, Ministry of Defense, Unit for Coordination of Activities in the Territories, *Two Years of Military Government, 1967–1969: Figures on Civilian Activity in Judea, Samaria, the Gaza Strip and Northern Sinai* (Tel Aviv: Ministry of Defense, May 1969), p. 39; Amnesty International, *Under the Rubble: House Demolition and Destruction of Land and Property* (London: Amnesty International, May, 18, 2004). In the West Bank, Israel planted one million trees in 1968 (see Jewish National Fund archives file 31235/KKL5, letter dated March 28, 1969), and by 2002, it had uprooted literally hundreds of thousands of trees (see Amnesty International, *Under the Rubble*).

7   For a much longer and more detailed discussion of these questions see Neve Gordon, *Israel's Occupation* (Berkeley: University of California Press, 2008).

8   The numbers in this table are taken from several sources. B'Tselem, The Israeli Information Center for Human Rights in the Occupied Territories, has documented the number of

Palestinians who were killed since the eruption of the first intifada in December 1987. The number of Palestinians killed during the first two decades of the occupation was gathered from several sources. According to the Palestinian Organization of Families of the Deceased, an estimated four hundred Gazans were killed during the first twenty years of occupation. *Ha'aretz,* August 23, 2005. David Ronen claims that 87 Palestinians were killed in the West Bank from the end of the war until December 1967. David Ronen, *The Year of the Shabak: The Deployment in Judea and Samaria, the First Year* (Tel Aviv: Ministry of Defense, 1989) (in Hebrew), p. 57. Meron Benvenisti notes that between 1968 and 1983, 92 Palestinians were killed in the West Bank. Meron Benvenisti, *The West Bank Data Project, 1986 Report: Demographic, Economic, Legal, Social, and Political Developments in the West Bank* (Washington D.C.: The American Enterprise Institute for Public Policy Research, 1986), p. 63. In 1986 and 1987, another 30 were killed. Meron Benvenisti, *The West Bank Data Project, 1987 Report: Demographic, Economic, Legal, Social, and Political Developments in the West Bank* (Washington D.C.: The American Enterprise Institute for Public Policy Research, 1987), p. 42. Al Haq, an affiliate of the Geneva-based International Commission of Jurists, notes that in 1984, 11 Palestinians were killed. *Al Haq's Response to the Chapter on Israel and the Occupied Territories in the U.S.'s State Department, "Country Reports on Human Rights Practices for 1984"* (Ramallah: Al Haq, 1985), p. 5. Thus, the total amount is 620 Palestinians, while there is missing data for 1985 in the West Bank.

9   I refer to the Gaza Strip as part of the Occupied Territories even though Israel dismantled its settlements and withdrew its troops from the region in August 2005. The reason I do so is because Israel is still sovereign both in the traditional sense of being the supreme authority over a given territory and in the sense of exercising a monopoly over the means of movement. See John Torpey, *The Invention of the Passport* (Cambridge: Cambridge University Press, 2000), p. 4.

10   The numbers are taken from B'Tselem's Web site at http://www.btselem.org/English/Statistics/First_Intifada_Tables.asp and http://www.btselem.org/English/Statistics/Casualties.asp (last accessed March 2, 2009).

11   Associated Press, "U.N.: Iraq Civilian Deaths Hit a Record," CBS News, September 21, 2006. In addition to the 6,187 Palestinians who were killed by Israelis (see Table 1), no more than 1,500 Palestinians were killed by Palestinians (see http://www.btselem.org/English/Statistics/Casualties.asp and http://www.btselem.org/English/Publications/Summaries/199401_Collaboration_Suspects.asp, last accessed 12 December 2008). Consult http://www.btselem.org/English/Statistics/Casualties.asp and www.iraqbodycount.org for up-to-date information.

12   In East Timor, for example, an estimated two hundred thousand people were killed out of a population of seven hundred thousand. Mathew Jardine, *East Timor: Genocide in Paradise* (Tucson, AZ: Odonian Press, 1995), p. 7.

13   Derek Gregory, *The Colonial Present: Afghanistan, Palestine, Iraq* (Oxford: Blackwell, 2004), p. 50.

14   See Ariella Azoulay and Adi Ophir, "The Order of Violence," in this volume. My argument differs from Azoulay and Ophir's without contradicting it. What I propose here may instead explain the transformation in "the order of violence" that they describe and the fact that much more eruptive violence has been recently exercised.

15   The colonial enterprise, to be sure, is a multifaceted and complex phenomenon and cannot be defined in one sentence or passage. See, for example, Timothy Mitchell, *Colonising Egypt*

(Cambridge: Cambridge University Press, 1988); Partha Chatterjee, *The Nation and Its Fragments: Colonial and Postcolonial Histories* (Princeton, NJ: Princeton University Press, 1993); David Scott, "Colonial Governmentality," *Social Text* 43 (Autumn 1995): pp. 191–220. Mahmud Mamdani, for example, shows how different native populations (e.g., urban versus rural sectors) were governed entirely differently. Mahmud Mamdani, *Citizen and Subject: Contemporary Africa and the Legacy of Late Colonialism* (Princeton, NJ: Princeton University Press, 1996). For an analysis of the different dimensions and types of the colonial project, see Gershon Shafir, *Land, Labor and the Origins of the Israeli Palestinian Conflict, 1882–1914* (Cambridge: Cambridge University Press, 1989).

16   Michel Foucault, *Discipline and Punish: The Birth of the Prison,* trans. Alan Sheridan (New York: Vintage, 1979); *The History of Sexuality, Vol. 1: An Introduction,* trans. Robert Hurley (New York: Vintage, 1990); *Society Must Be Defended: Lectures at the Collège de France, 1975–76,* ed. Mauro Bertani and Alessandro Fontana, trans. David Macey (London: Penguin Books, 2004); *Security, Territory, Population: Lectures at the Collège de France, 1977–78,* ed. Michel Senellart, trans. Graham Burchell (New York: Palgrave Macmillan, 2007). See also Gordon, *Israel's Occupation.*

17   Cilla Acker, "From Home Delivery to Hospital Delivery: The Transformation of Mother and Child Care in the West Bank," in Tamara Barnea and Rafiq Husseini (eds.), *Cooperate and Separate, Separate and Cooperate: The Disengagement of the Palestinian Health Care System from Israel and its Emergence as an Independent System* (New York: Greenwood Press, 2002).

18   Foucault, *Society Must be Defended.*

19   Michel Foucault, *Power/Knowledge: Selected Interviews and Other Writings, 1972–1977,* ed., Colin Gordon, trans. Colin Gordon, Leo Marshall, John Mepham, and Kate Soper (New York: Pantheon Books, 1980); Carl Schmitt, *Political Theology: Four Chapters on the Concept of Sovereignty* (Chicago, IL: University of Chicago Press, 2006).

20   Foucault, *Security, Territory, Population.*

21   The annexation applied to the territory itself, whereas its inhabitants were given the option to become Israeli citizens, but in order to do so, they had to relinquish their Jordanian citizenship. Only a small number complied. Nonetheless, all of the inhabitants were made permanent Jerusalem residents and could vote for municipal elections. Eitan Felner, *A Policy of Discrimination, Land Expropriation, Planning and Building in East Jerusalem* (Jerusalem: B'Tselem, 1995) available on-line at http://www.btselem.org/Download/199505_Policy_of_Discrimination_Eng.doc (last accessed December 10, 2008); Yael Stein, *The Quiet Deportation: Revocation of Residency of East Jerusalem Palestinians* (Jerusalem: HaMoked and B'Tselem, 1997) available on-line at http://www.btselem.org/Download/199704_Quiet_Deportation_Eng.doc (last accessed December 10, 2008).

22   Meron Benvenisti and Shlomo Khayat, *The West Bank and Gaza Atlas* (Jerusalem: The Jerusalem Post, 1987), pp. 112–13; Sara Roy, *The Gaza Strip: The Political Economy of De-Development* (Washington D.C.: Institute for Palestinian Studies, 1995), pp. 175–81; Yehezkel Lein, "Land Grab: Israel's Settlement Policy in the West Bank" (2002), B'Tselem report available on-line at http://www.btselem.org/Download/200205_Land_Grab_Eng.pdf (last accessed July 14, 2008).

23   The passage is cited in several places, including Shlomo Gazit, *The Carrot and the Stick: Israel's Policy in Judea and Samaria, 1967–1969* (Washington, D.C.: B'nai Brith Books, 1995), p. 135.

24   State of Israel, Ministry of Defense, Unit for Coordination of Activities in the Territories, *Three Years of Military Government, 1967–1970*, p. 4.

25   Shabtai Teveth, *The Cursed Blessing: The Story of Israel's Occupation of the West Bank* (London: Weidenfeld and Nicolson, 1970).

26   State of Israel, Ministry of Defense, Unit for Coordination of Activities in the Territories, *Two Years of Military Government, 1967–1969*, p. 11.

27   Raphael Meron, *Economic Development in Judea-Samaria and the Gaza District: Economic Growth and Structural Change, 1970–1980* (Jerusalem: Bank of Israel Research Department, 1983), p. 6.

28   Central Bureau of Statistics, *National Accountability: Judea, Samaria and the Gaza Strip, 1968–1993*, Central Bureau of Statistics, publication 1012 (Tel Aviv: Central Bureau of Statistics, 1996) (in Hebrew), p. 125.

29   Yehezkel Lein, *Builders of Zion: Human Rights Violations of Palestinians from the Occupied Territories Working in Israel and the Settlements* (Jerusalem: B'Tselem, 1999), p. 8.

30   United Nations, *Report of the Secretary-General, Development and International Economic Co-Operation: Living Conditions of the Palestinian People in the Occupied Arab Territories*, A/35/533, October 17, 1980.

31   Central Bureau of Statistics, *National Accountability*, p. 18.

32   Sara Roy, *The Gaza Strip*, pp. 4, 128.

33   According to the Bank of Israel, average annual GNP growth in the West Bank and Gaza was 14 percent between 1970 and 1975, 7 percent between 1976 and 1980, and 0 percent in 1981 and 1982. Dan Zakai, *Economic Development in Judea-Samaria and the Gaza District, 1981–1982* (Jerusalem: Bank of Israel Research Department, 1985), p. 11.

34   Raja Sheathe and Jonathan Kutras, *The West Bank and the Rule of Law* (Ramallah: The International Commission of Lawyers, 1980), p. 10. According to Shabtai Teveth, the names were altered in March 1968. *The Cursed Blessing*, pp. 258–59.

35   There is one interesting exception. The annual reports published by the Central Bureau of Statistics include a map that demarcates the West Bank and Gaza Strip (all the areas not formally annexed by Israel). See Yinon Cohen, "Sum Thing for Everyone: The Annual Abstract Put Out by the Central Bureau of Statistics Is Much, Much More Than a Dry Collection of Statistics," *Ha'aretz*, November 29, 2002 (in Hebrew).

36   Nathan Brown, "Democracy, History, and the Contest over the Palestinian Curriculum," paper prepared for the Adam Institute, November, 2001, available on-line at http://www.geocities.com/nathanbrown1/Adam_Institute_Palestinian_textbooks.htm (last accessed May 29, 2008).

37   Salim Tamari, "What the Uprising Means," in Zachary Lockman and Joel Beinin (eds.), *Intifada: The Palestinian Uprising against Israeli Occupation* (Boston, MA: South End Press, 1989), p. 128.

38   Lisa Hajjar, *Courting Conflict: The Israeli Military Court System in the West Bank and Gaza* (Berkeley: University of California Press, 2005), p. 56. For a detailed description of the construction of the legal doctrine in the Occupied Territories, as well as Shamgar's role, see chap. 2. Not surprisingly, as chief justice, Shamgar supported Israel's policy of suspending the Geneva Convention on every occasion that rights advocates petitioned for the enforcement of this policy in the High Court of Justice. Thus, one can gain a glimpse of how Israel's judiciary system supported the occupying power on all important matters. See also David

Kretzmer, *The Occupation of Justice: The Supreme Court of Israel and the Occupied Territories* (Albany: State University of New York Press, 2002).

39 Jordan had actually annexed the West Bank, but only England and Pakistan recognized the annexation. Meir Shamgar, "Legal Concepts and Problems of the Israeli Military Government the Initial Stage," in Meir Shamgar (ed.), *Military Government in the Territories Administered by Israel 1967–1980: The Legal Aspects* (Jerusalem: Harry Sacher Institute for Legislative Research and Comparative Law, 1982), pp. 35–36.

40 *Ibid.*, pp. 31–43.

41 Ibrahim Dakkak, "Back to Square One: A Study of the Reemergence of the Palestinian Identity in the West Bank, 1967–1980," in Alexander Scholch (ed.), *Palestinians over the Green Line: Studies on the Relations between Palestinians on Both Sides of the 1949 Armistice Line since 1967* (London: Ithaca Press, 1983), p. 67.

42 The Hague Convention also states that the occupying power must be only the temporary manager and beneficiary of land and other properties in the occupied territories and is not permitted to create permanent "facts on the ground" that will remain in the area after the occupation.

43 In the Gaza Strip, Egyptian law and ordinances continued to be valid, while in the West Bank, Jordanian law and ordinances continued to be valid. Chief Military Command, *Orders and Proclamations, Judea and Samaria, 1968–1972* (Tel Aviv: Israeli Defense Ministry, 1972) (in Hebrew). The Jordanian and Egyptian laws were based on the laws of the British Mandate period. See Sasson Levi, *Local Government in the Administered Territories* (Ramat Gan: Bar-Ilan University, 1977) and Kretzmer, *The Occupation of Justice.*

44 For a discussion of the military orders see Kretzmer, *The Occupation of Justice*, pp. 27–29.

45 Many of these orders undercut international legal provisions that ensured the rights of populations in occupied areas. See Raja Shedadah, *Occupier's Law: Israel and the West Bank* (Washington D.C.: Institute for Palestine Studies, 1985).

46 To support this claim, Israel also set up an elaborate system of military courts, which were manned by military personnel who were responsible for trying those who were suspected of illegal activity. Hajjar, *Courting Conflict.*

47 Lev Grinberg, *The Histadrut above All* (Jerusalem: Nevo, 1993) (in Hebrew).

48 The Palestinian laborers also did not receive the same benefits granted to Israelis, such as bonuses for seniority, and were not incorporated into the Israeli social safety net, which offers Israeli citizens a variety of social security allowances. Emanuel Farjoun, "Palestinian Workers in Israel: A Reserve Army of Labour," in Jon Rothschild (ed.), *Forbidden Agendas: Intolerance and Defiance in the Middle East* (London: Al Saqi, 1984), pp. 111–18.

49 Michael Mann, "The Dark Side of Democracy: The Modern Tradition of Ethnic and Political Cleansing," *New Left Review* 235 (May–June 1999): pp. 18–45.

50 In 1971, General Ariel Sharon, the head of the Southern Command, was asked to suppress Fatah and the Popular Front for the Liberation of Palestine's armed resistance in the Gaza Strip's refugee camps. A fence was erected that surrounded parts of the region as Israeli troops, the Shabak, and Palestinian collaborators combed the area with a list of "wanted" men. The families of these men were also rounded up, and approximately twelve thousand inhabitants were sent to the remote Abu Zneima detention center on the coast of the Sinai Peninsula. An estimated two thousand houses were demolished in refugee camps such as Shati and Jabaliya in order to make it easier for the military to patrol the camps. These

demolitions displaced, again, over fifteen thousand refugees. Simultaneously, curfews were imposed on the camps, adult males were randomly stopped and searched, and several Palestinians were shot and killed for failing "to halt for routine searches." After the armed resistance was crushed, however, Israel emphasized disciplinary forms of control. Aside from the Gaza invasion, coercive methods were only intermittently enforced, and, when they were employed, they were implemented with less intensity.

51 State of Israel, *Three Years of Military Government, 1967–1970*, p. 4.

52 Joel S. Migdal, *Palestinian Society and Politics* (Princeton, NJ: Princeton University Press, 1980), p. 62.

53 On July 19, 1967, Israel organized a conference for the *mukhtars*—the heads of villages or neighborhoods— in Nablus, where they were "warned that they would be punished if foreigners or terrorists would be found in their villages and if they distribute the Communist Party's paper *Al-Itihad.*" Each village *mukhtar* was paid seventy-five Israeli pounds a month, while the second *mukhtar* in the same village was paid fifty. Michael Shashar, *The Seventh-Day War: The Diary of the Military Government in Judea and Samaria* (June–December 1967) (Tel Aviv: Sifriat Poalim, 1997) (in Hebrew), pp. 105 and 161. See also Military Order 176, which authorizes the military commander to dismiss any *mukhtar.*

54 Timothy Mitchell, "The Limits of the State: Beyond Statist Approaches and Their Critics," *The American Political Science Review* 85, no. 1 (1991): pp. 77–96.

55 Meron Benvenisti, *Intimate Enemies: Jews and Arabs in a Shared Land* (Berkeley: University of California Press, 1995). See also in this context Amira Hass, *Drinking the Sea at Gaza: Days and Nights in a Land under Siege* (New York: Metropolitan Books, 1996); Edward Said, *Peace and its Discontents* (New York: Vintage, 1996); Graham Usher, *Dispatches from Palestine: The Rise and Fall of the Oslo Peace Process* (London: Pluto Press, 1999); and Neve Gordon, "Outsourcing Violations: The Israeli Case," *Journal of Human Rights* 1, no. 3 (2002): pp. 321–37.

56 The eight agreements, in chronological order, are the Declaration of Principles on Interim Self-Government Arrangements (September 13, 1993), the Paris Protocol on Economic Relations (April 29, 1994), the Agreement on the Gaza Strip and the Jericho Area (May 4, 1994), the Agreement on Preparatory Transfer of Powers and Responsibilities between Israel and the PLO (August 29, 1994), the Israeli-Palestinian Interim Agreement on the West Bank and the Gaza Strip (also known as Oslo II) (September 28, 1995), the Hebron Protocol (January 17, 1997), the Wye River Memorandum (October 23, 1998), and the Sharm el-Sheikh Memorandum (September 4, 1999).

57 In 1997, Hebron was divided into two parts: H-1 under nominal control of the PA and the smaller H-2 section under the control of the Israeli military. Area H-2 is home to about thirty-five thousand Palestinians and five hundred Israeli settlers. The Old City and the Tomb of the Patriarchs are also located in H-2. The Yellow Areas in the Gaza Strip are more or less equivalent to Area B in the West Bank and amount to 23 percent of the strip, while the White Areas are equivalent to Area A and amount to a little less than 10 percent of the strip.

58 The Agreements were Wye I, II, and III and Sharm I.

59 Yehezkel Lein, "Forbidden Roads: The Discriminatory West Bank Road Regime" (August 2004), B'Tselem report available on-line at http://www.btselem.org/Download/200408_Forbidden_Roads_Eng.pdf (last accessed July 15, 2008).

60 Annex III, Article IV of the Interim Agreement states: "In Area C, in the first phase of redeployment, powers and responsibilities not related to territory, as set out in Appendix 1, will

be transferred to and assumed by the [Palestinian] Council in accordance with the provisions of that Appendix," thus, indicating that even though Israel had full authority over all matters in Area C, the PA took over responsibilities not related to territory.

61 Noga Kadman, "1987–1997: A Decade of Human Rights Violations" (1998), B'Tselem report available on-line at http://www.btselem.org/Download/199801_Decade_of_Violations_Eng.doc.

62 Ibid.

63 Rema Hammami and Salim Tamari, "Anatomy of Another Rebellion," *Middle East Report,* no. 217 (Winter 2000).

64 Giorgio Agamben, *Homo Sacer: Sovereign Power and Bare Life,* trans. Daniel Heller-Roazen (Stanford, CA: Stanford University Press, 1998), pp. 83–85.

65 Fred Abrahams, Marc Garlasco, and Darryl Li, *Razing Rafah: Mass Home Demolitions in the Gaza Strip* (New York: Human Rights Watch), 2004.

66 Kretzmer, *The Occupation of Justice,* 145–64.

67 Abrahams, Garlasco, and Li, *Razing Rafah,* 127–28.

68 Alice Rothchild, "Pitching in for Health on the West Bank," *Boston Globe,* March 6, 2004.

69 James Ron, *Frontiers and Ghettos: State Violence in Serbia and Israel* (Berkeley: University of California Press, 2003).

70 Amos Harel, "Avi Dichter Supports the Disengagement," *Ha'aretz,* June 10, 2005 (in Hebrew).

71 Jewish settlers could continue moving freely across the Green Line, while after Oslo, a very small number of Palestinians received VIP cards and could travel even in times of closure.

72 Lein, "Builders of Zion."

73 Usher, *Dispatches from Palestine,* p. 97.

74 The Palestinians did not oppose the construction of this fence, since it was erected on the Green Line. Yehezkel Lein, "One Big Prison: Freedom of Movement to and from the Gaza Strip on the Eve of the Disengagement Plan" (2005), B'Tselem report available on-line at http://www.btselem.org/Download/200503_Gaza_Prison_English.PDF (last accessed September 19, 2008).

75 See Ariel Handel's "Where, Where to, and When in the Occupied Territories: An Introduction to the Geography of Disaster" and "The Destruction of the Risk Society and the Ascendancy of Hamas," by Dani Filc and me in this volume.

76 See http://www.ochaopt.org/documents/ClosureUpdateOctober2007.pdf (last accessed May 30, 2008).

77 B'Tselem, "The Palestinian Economy during the Period of the Oslo Accords: 1994–2000", available on-line at http://www.btselem.org/english/freedom_of_movement/Economy_1994_2000.asp (last accessed May 30, 2008).

78 Research shows that "malnutrition is a contributing factor in nearly 60 percent of deaths in children for which infectious disease is an underlying cause." Bahn Maharj, Bhandari Nita, and Bahl Rajiv, "Management of the Severely Malnourished Child: Perspective from Developing Countries," *British Medical Journal* 326 (2003): p. 146. Per-capita food consumption declined by a quarter since 1998. Human Development Group, *Supplemental Trust Fund Grant to the Second Emergency Services Support Project, Middle East and North Africa Region* (Washington, D.C.: World Bank, 2002), p. 2.

79 Akiva Eldar, "Popular Misconceptions," *Ha'aretz,* June 11, 2004 (in Hebrew); also Reuven Pedatzur, "More Than a Million Bullets," *Ha'aretz,* June 30, 2004 (in Hebrew).

IMPUNITY: BREAKING THE LAW UNDER THE AEGIS OF THE LAW At the beginning of the second intifada the IDF judge advocate general froze the standing command to open a professional and independent investigation by the Military Police Investigation Unit [MPIU] in every case of injury to civilians who were not taking part in the fighting, and stated that such an investigation would be opened only in special cases at the discretion of the Judge Advocate General's Office. This decision institutionalized the informal policy of lack of law enforcement that guided the military investigation and prosecution apparatus as far back as the first intifada, when IDF investigators and prosecutors intentionally carried out superficial investigations and dragged their feet in collecting evidence and questioning witnesses. According to human rights organizations, since the outbreak of the second intifada, the army opened MPIU investigations in only 5 percent of the cases in which IDF forces killed civilians.

PROCEDURE FOR REPORTING EVENTS RESULTING IN PALESTINIAN CASUALTIES
drafted by the IDF in response to suggestions made by the Association for Civil Rights
in the framework of a petition to the High Court of Justice.

צבא	ההגנה	לישראל
לשכת	ראש המטה	הכללי
טל':		0302-1111
חק	-	563522
י"ח	במרחשוון	התשס"ו
20	בנובמבר	2005

מפצ"ר - לשכת המפקד
דואר נכנס
24.11 2005
מס' סידורי _159946_

לשכת הרמטכ"ל

(לוח תפוצה)

הנדון: נוהל דיווח על אירועים במסגרתם נפגעו אזרחים פלסטינים

1. נוהל זה חל על כל אירוע בו היו מעורבים כוחות צה"ל, במהלכו נהרג או נפצע אדם שלא היה מעורב בלחימה מסכנת חיים. בכל מקרה של ספק בדבר מעורבותו של אדם בלחימה כאמור, יש לפעול לפי האמור בנוהל זה.

2. בכל מקרה בן נהרג או נפצע בלתי מעורב כאמור, ידווח האירוע בנוהל חמ"לים מיידי ללשכת הרמטכ"ל, לאמ"ץ ולפצ"ר. **הדיווח כאמור יועבר לא יאוחר מ- 48 שעות ממועד האירוע.**

3. באחריות המח"יט המרחבי ומי' היחידה של הכוח שביצע הפעולה לוודא צילום ותיעוד זירת האירוע בסמוך להתרחשות האירוע, ככל שאין בכך כדי לסכן הכוחות והדבר מתאפשר בנסיבות העניין.

4. המח"יט המרחבי, מי' חטיבת של הכוח שביצע הפעולה (בדרגת סא"ל לפחות) ומי' המתי"ק חגיזורתי נושאים באחריות להעברת דיווח כאמור בסעיף 1 לעיל, עם חיווודע להם חדבר, מהכוחות הפועלים בשטח או מגורמי הקישור הפלסטינים, בהתאם לפורמט המצורף לנוהל זה. לדיווח יצורפו העתקי יומני המבצעים חנוגעים בדבר, חדווחות היומיים תרלבנטיים וכל חומר רלבנטי אחר. במידה שיוחלט שקיימת מניעה לתיעוד וצילום זירת האירוע, בהתאם לאמור בסעיף 2 לעיל, יפורטו הסיבות לכך בדיווח שיועבר כאמור.

Israel Defense Forces
Office of the Chief of Staff
Tel: 0302-1111   563522
18 Heshvan 5766
20 November 2005

Office of the Chief of Staff

JAG Headquarters—Commander's Office
INCOMING MAIL
24 November 2005
Serial No. 159946

(Distribution List)

Re: **Procedure for Reporting Events Resulting in Palestinian Casualties**

1. This procedure applies to every incident in which IDF forces are involved in which a person not involved in life-threatening combat is killed or injured. In the case of doubt if the person was involved in combat as stated, act according to the provisions of this procedure.

2. In every case in which a noninvolved person as stated is killed or injured, the incident will be reported immediately in war-room procedure to the Chief of Staff's Office, to Operations Branch, and to the Judge Advocate General's Office. **The aforementioned report shall be forwarded no later than 48 hours from the time of the incident.**

3. It is the responsibility of the regional brigade commander and commander of the unit of the force that carried out the action to ensure photographing and documenting the scene of the incident close to the time it occurred, to the extent that doing so does not endanger the forces and is possible under the circumstances.

4. The regional brigade commander, the unit commander of the force that carried out the action (holding the rank of Lt. Col. at least), and the commander of the Coordination and Liaison Office of the sector are responsible for providing the report as stated in Section 1 above, if they are made aware of the incident, by the forces operating in the field or from Palestinian liaison officials, in the format attached to this procedure. Copies of the relevant operations journal, the relevant daily reports, and all other relevant material are to be attached to the report. In the event that it is decided that documenting and photographing the scene of the incident is not possible, in accordance with Section 2 above, the reasons therefore are to be specified in the report that will be provided as stated.

5. בנוסף, בכל אירוע שבו נפגע אדם בלתי מעורב כאמור, יבוצע תחקיר, שיאושר על ידי מפקד הפיקוד/זרוע ויועבר לעיון הרמטכ״ל. באחריות מפקד הפיקוד/זרוע לוודא ביצוע התחקיר, לאשרו ולהעבירו לעיון הרמטכ״ל, תוך 21 יום, לכל היותר. עותק מהתחקיר יועבר לאמ״ץ ולפצ״ר. לתחקיר יצורפו החומרים שנאספו במהלכו, תיעוד האירוע וחומרים נוספים שנאספו (לרבות יומן המבצעים, דוחות יומיים, הקלטות רשת הקשר, תיעוד מכשירי ראיית לילה וכיו״ב).

6. אמ״ץ יבצע מעקב אחר הגעת התחקירים אל מול אירועים, ותעביר דוח תודשי כתוב בדבר סטאטוס ביצוע תחקירים אל מול אירועים. בנוסף, תיעשה ע״י מחלקת-בו״ס ביקורת חצי שנתית, לבדיקת יישום נוהל זה.

7. אחריות אמ״ץ להפיץ נוהל זה באופן מיידי בפקודה מחייבת.

בברכה,

דני חלוץ, רב-אלוף

ראש המטה הכללי

5. In addition, in every incident in which a noninvolved is harmed as stated, a debriefing will be carried out, which shall be approved by the Command/arm and forwarded to the chief of staff. It is the responsibility of the Command/arm to ensure the debriefing is executed and to approve it and forward it to the chief of staff within 21 days, at the most. A copy of the debriefing is to be forwarded to Operations Branch and the Judge Advocate General's Office. The material gathered during the course of the debriefing, documentation of the incident, and other information gathered (including the operations journal, daily reports, radio communications recordings, documentation of night-vision implements, and the like) will be attached to the debriefing.

6. Operations Branch will monitor arrival of the debriefings of incidents and forward a written, monthly report on the status of the execution of the debriefings with respect to incidents. In addition, the Audit and Inspection Department will make a six-month review to check that this procedure has been implemented.

7. Operations Branch is responsible for immediately distributing this procedure in a binding command.

Sincerely,

Dani Halutz, Lieutenant General

Chief of Staff

בלמ"ס

<table>
<tr><td>צבאית</td><td>פרקליטות</td></tr>
<tr><td>דרום/מז"י</td><td>פיקוד</td></tr>
<tr><td>08-8619350</td><td>טל':</td></tr>
<tr><td>08-8619353</td><td>פקס:</td></tr>
<tr><td>20065002382</td><td>חק</td></tr>
<tr><td>תמוז. תשס"ז</td><td>י"ח</td></tr>
<tr><td>2007 יולי,</td><td>4</td></tr>
</table>

לכבוד
מר תום מהגר
רכז תלונות, המוקד להגנת הפרט,
רח' אבו עוביידה 4
ירושלים 97200

באמצעות פקס 02-6276317

א.נ.,

הנדון: **עדכון בחוות דעתנו לתיק מצ"ח אורים מס' 05/99 שעניינו:**
חקירה בנסיבות פציעתו של
_____

1. בבסיס מצ"ח אורים התקבלה הוראת פרקליטות דרום ומז"י, לפתוח בחקירה בדבר
תלונת _____ לפיה בתאריך 27/12/2003 בשעה 11:00 לערך,
בעת שעבד יחד עם חברו באתר בנייה הסמוך לכפר דרום, כוחות צה"ל ששהו במוצב
שעמד בקצה היישוב, פתחו לעברו באש, ללא כל סיבה וכתוצאה מכך נפצע ברגלו.

2. ביום 15.5.07 ניתנה חוות-דעתנו בדבר סגירת תיק החקירה בעניין זה, ללא נקיטת צעדים
משפטיים.

3. מהראיות הקיימות בתיק החקירה עלה, כי בתאריך 27.12.03, בשעת צהריים, זיהו חיילי
צה"ל בעמדה בישוב כפר דרום שני אנשים על גג מבנה הנמצא בהליכי בנייה, כשאחד
מהם עומד והשני יושב ורושם. בשל החשד למעורבותם בפח"ע, בוצע לעברם ירי הרתעתי,
ולאחר שזה לא הועיל – בוצע ירי לכיוון רגליו של אחד מהם.

4. מחומר הראיות לא ניתן לדעת מיהו הכוח הצבאי ששהה במקום, את זהות החייל שביצע
את הירי וזהות הגורם שאישר את ביצוע הירי. מנגד, אף לא קיימים ממצאים
אובייקטיביים (כדוגמת, קליע) היכולים להצביע על קיומו של קשר ראייתי מספק בין
הירי האמור לבין הירי ממנו נפגע המתלונן, ואם אכן הירי האמור הוא זה שגרם לפציעתו.

5. בנסיבות האמורות, בהעדר קישור, מחד, של התלונה לאירוע שדווח בזמן המבצעים ;
ובהעדר ממצאים, מאידך, בדבר זהות הכוח שביצע את הירי הנטען ; וכן נוכח הזמן הרב
שחלף – הוריתי על סגירת התיק בלא נקיטת צעדים משפטיים כנגד מאן דהוא.

בברכה,

רונן שור, רס"ן

סגן פרקליטת פד"ם/מז"י

Judge Advocate General's Office
Southern/Ground Forces Command
Tel: 08-8619350
Fax: 08-86191353
20065002382
18 Tammuz 5767
4 July 2007

Mr. Tom Mehager
Complaints Coordinator, HaMoked: Center for the Defense of the Individual
4 Abu Obeidah Street
Jerusalem 97200   Via Fax 02-6276317

Dear Sir:

Re: **Updating of our opinion in the Urim MPIU File No. 05/99 in the matter of:**
Investigation of the circumstances of injury of _____

1.   At the Urim MPIU base, an order was received from the judge advocate for the Southern Com-
     mand and the Ground Forces Command to open an investigation into the complaint of _____,
     according to which on 27 December 2003, at about 11:00 A.M., while he was working with his
     friend at a building site near Kfar Hadarom, IDF forces at a post at the edge of the community
     opened fire at him for no reason, hitting him in the leg.

2.   On 15 May 2007, we issued our opinion on closing the investigation file in this matter without
     taking any legal measures.

3.   The evidence in the investigation file indicates that on 27 December 2003, at noon, IDF soldiers
     at a position in Kfar Hadarom identified two persons on the roof of a building under construc-
     tion, one of them standing and the other sitting and sketching. Suspecting they were engaged in
     hostile terrorist activity, warning shots were fired at them, and when that did not help—gunfire
     was aimed at the legs of one of them.

4.   The evidential material does not enable identification of the military force that was present at the
     site, the identity of the soldier who fired, or the identity of the person who approved the firing.
     On the other hand, there also are no objective findings (such as a bullet) that might establish a
     sufficient evidential connection between the said firing and the firing from which the complain-
     ant was injured and whether the said firing indeed was that which caused his injury.

5.   Under these circumstances, lacking a connection, on the one hand, of the complaint to an event
     that was reported in the operations journal and the lack of findings, on the other hand, regard-
     ing the identity of the force that carried out the alleged shooting, and also in light of the great
     amount of time that has passed—I ordered that the file be closed without taking legal measures
     against anyone.

                              Sincerely,

                                         Ronen Shur, Major
                                         Deputy Judge Advocate,
                                         Southern Command/
                                         Ground Forces Command

A DECISION NOT TO INVESTIGATE a case of targeted killing.

דואר רשמי
בפקס'
-1-

פרקליטות חיל האוויר
טל: 0398-6468/69/70
פקס: 0398-6316
חק 21 (17) -
י"ט באדר התשס"ו
19 במרץ 2006

לכבוד
מר שלומי סויסה
ארגון "בצלם"

שלום רב,

הנדון: **פנייתך לפרקליט הצבאי הראשי מיום 7.3.06**

1. בפנייתך לפרקליט הצבאי הראשי (הפצ"ר) מיום 7.3.06 התייחסת לפעולת סיכול ממוקד שבוצעה בעזה ביום 6.3.06. אבקש להשיב לפנייה, בשם הפצ"ר.

2. הפעילות שבעניינה פנית נוחקרה ונתעדה על ידי חיל האוויר. אבקש לעדכנך, כי לאחר בחינת החומר הרלוונטי ע"י הפרקליטות הצבאית, הוחלט שאין מקום לפתיחה בחקירת מצ"ח לגביה.

3. החלטה זו נשענת על מספר טעמים, ובהם: הנסיבות הלחימתיות שבהן בוצעה התקיפה; העובדה שהותקפו פעילי טרור, שסיכנו בפעילותם חיי ישראלים; העובדה שנעשה שימוש באמצעי לחימה חוקיים ולגיטימיים; וניתוח צילומי הפעולה, המלמדים כי בזמן אמת, לא יכל מקבלי החהחלטות לצפות את הפגיעה באזרחים, כפי שנגרמה בפועל והתבררה לאחר מעשה.

4. בפנייתך ציינת, כי לפי תוצאות הפעולה, נראה שצה"ל חרג מעקרון הפרופורציונליות. עם כל הכבוד, עמידתה של פעולה במבחן הפרופורציונליות אינה נשקלת רק לפי תוצאות הפעולה, אלא, בראש ובראשונה, לפי המידע והנתונים שהיו בידי מקבלי ההחלטות בעת תכנון הפעולה וביצועה.

5. שמת דגש על כך שהפעולה נעשתה באזור צפוף, תוך סיכון האוכלוסיה האזרחית המתגוררת בו. יש להדגיש, כי צה"ל נוקט אמצעים שונים ע"מ למזער, ככל הניתן, את הסיכון לאוכלוסיה האזרחית בעת ביצוע פעולות סיכול ממוקד. הדבר נלקח בחשבון בעת בחירת אמצעי התקיפה, עיתויה ומיקומה. עם זאת, כאשר פעילי הטרור בוחרים, במתכוון, לבצע את פעילותם הנפשעת מתוך לבה של האוכלוסיה אזרחית, לא ניתן להבטיח, כי אזרחים יהיו בטוחים לחלוטין מפגיעה, כפי שארע, למרבה הצער, במקרה זה. היממנעות מוחלטת מסיכון אזרחים אינה דרישה מציאותית בסוג לחימה הנכפה על צה"ל, ומשמעה מתן חסינות בפועל לפעילי הטרור.

Registered Mail
By Fax

Judge Advocate's Office Air Force
Tel: 0398-6468/69/70
Fax: 0398-6316
21 (17)
19 Adar 5766
19 March 2007

Mr. Shlomi Swissa
B'Tselem

Dear Sir:

Re: **Your inquiry of 7 March 2006 to the judge advocate general**

1. In your letter of 7 March 2006 to the judge advocate general (JAG), you referred to a targeted-killing action that was carried out in Gaza on 6 March 2006. On behalf of the JAG, I would like to reply to your inquiry.

2. The action about which you inquire was investigated and documented by the Air Force. I would like to update you that, after the relevant material was examined by the Judge Advocate General's Office, it was decided there was no cause to open an MPIU investigation.

3. This decision was based on a number of reasons, among them: the combat circumstances in which the attack was carried out; the fact that the attack was directed against terrorist activists, whose activity endangered Israeli lives; the fact that legal and legitimate means of warfare were used; and analysis of filming of the action that indicated that, at the crucial time, the decision makers could not have anticipated harm to civilians, as was caused in fact and was revealed prospectively.

4. In your letter, you stated that, based on the results of the action, it appears that the IDF breached the principle of proportionality. With all due respect, proportionality of an action is not determined solely on the results of the action, but, first and foremost, on the information and data that were in the hands of the decision makers at the time the action was planned and executed.

5. You emphasized that the action was carried out in a crowded area, endangering the civilian population living there. It should be noted that the IDF uses varied means to minimize, as much as possible, the danger to the civilian population in carrying out targeted-killing actions. This is taken into account in selecting the means of attack, its timing, and its location. However, when terrorists choose, intentionally, to carry out their criminal acts from within the heart of the civilian population, it is impossible to guarantee that civilians will be absolutely safe from harm, as occurred, regrettably, in this case. Refraining absolutely from endangering civilians is not a realistic demand in the kind of warfare forced on the IDF and would enable terrorists to act with impunity.

6. מכל מקום, מהחומר הקיים ביחס לפעולה לא עולה חשד לביצועה של עבירה פלילית ע"י גורם צבאי כלשהו.

7. לא נוכל להרחיב מעבר לאמור לעיל או להעביר חומר מפורט נוסף, כיוון שחומר התחקיר חסוי עפ"י חוק.

בברכה,

שרון אפק, סא"ל
פרקליט חיל האוויר

6. In any event, the material regarding the action does not raise a suspicion that any military official committed a criminal offense.

7. We are unable to expand further or to provide additional detailed material, inasmuch as the debriefing material is classified by law.

Sincerely,

Sharon Ofek, Lieutenant Colonel
Judge Advocate Air Force

Regimes of Separation: Israel/Palestine and the Shadow of Apartheid

Hilla Dayan

> If I were to wake up one morning and find myself a Black man, the only major difference would be geographical.
> —John Vorster, prime minister of the Republic of South Africa, 1966–78

Apartheid, one of the infamous regimes of the twentieth century, has been conceived in terms of spatial political separation, or euphemistically as "separate development." Spatial political control promised to keep a citizens' society separate from the disenfranchised masses. Separation meant a coercive reconstitution of noncitizen populations and their living environment. Racist, but not genocidal, apartheid visionaries and practitioners did not seek the systematic annihilation of an out-group population. Rather, the regime and its social base anticipated their own annihilation if they were to let go of command over the movements, places of residence, and labor of that population. Forsaking control spelled disaster. It meant that the state and society, which benefited from an advanced capitalist economy and constituted a polity institutionally fashioned on the traditions of European liberal democracies (particularly those of British colonial forbearers), would be utterly lost. Separation with control, especially from the 1960s on, was thus constantly reconfigured. Experiments with redefining populations and their relation to political space marked a qualitative leap from a classic colonial-era "divide and rule." Despite serious policy-implementation failures, significant tension with capitalist interests, international blows, and pressure mounting from resistance campaigns from within, the Republic of South Africa committed itself to these experiments for decades. And hence, spatial and socioeconomic apartheid survives today long after control and political power have been conceded. The "pathological geography of power," as Ann McClintock aptly describes it, the "only" major difference envisioned by John Vorster, indeed shows no signs of disappearing anytime soon.[1]

In what follows, I argue that a similar long-term commitment to the principles of spatial political control over the mass out-group population began to take a distinct turn in contemporary Israel/Palestine in the aftermath of the first Palestinian uprising in 1987. From the outset, however, it is important to clarify that apartheid in South Africa is neither a precursor to nor repeated in Israel/Palestine, nor is apartheid a conceptual basis for comparing the two countries. The tendency in most comparisons of the state of Israel to the apartheid regime is to take at face value seemingly apparent analogies and to draw straightforward, easy conclusions. The problem with various genres through which comparisons are made is that they attempt to capture complex processes and conditions in occupied Palestine through the lens of extremely narrow and superficial catch phrases about apartheid. Too often, the result yields no more than pedestrian knowledge of both. At the same time, precisely because the historical analogies between Israel and South Africa's settler societies are indeed striking and convincing, countercomparison propagandists attempt to block any informed discussion on the basis of a blank and visceral rejection of the very premise of comparison.[2] South Africa and Israel/Palestine deserve more rigorous analytical consideration than what the popular, academic, and political debate over Israeli apartheid has so far managed to produce. They are paradigmatic cases for anyone interested in the dynamics, systemic features, practices, and trajectories of hegemonic regimes. I proceed by delineating principles identified as sui generis to a political type. Studying the type of regimes I call "regimes of separation" enables an extensive evaluation of their historical singularity. Contributing to existing theories of dictatorship and democracy a new regime type, I hope thus to escape the serious limitations imposed by the comparison discourse.

REGIMES OF SEPARATION: A CONCEPTUAL OUTLINE

Supposedly an anachronistic and exceptional relic of colonialism, one of the fundamentals of the apartheid regime was that it controlled the movements and spatial distribution of disenfranchised populations. Apartheid set a precedent, but not as a system serving capitalist interests, economic exploitation, and racist exclusion, which are the underlining premises of most modern polities. Contrary to conventional wisdom, it was not a deviant regime, but a system of rule that emerged from within the logic of the nation-state form. From the 1960s on, however, the Republic of South Africa sets itself up to implement measures that in unprecedented ways robbed its excluded out groups of the capacity and sources for sustaining an independent existence as collectives and political communities. It did so by force and through a massive border apparatus that allowed it to control the status of populations, their movements, and their means of movement (through identity and travel documents) in a political space in which it functioned as the supreme sovereign.[3]

The ability to delineate finite borders and to control movements across them practically defines all modern polities. However, only rarely is this normal prerogative of states, a monopoly over movement and the means of movement, put to use domestically. A sovereign power that uses this monopoly for the demographic and territorial gerrymandering of a political space containing masses of noncitizens disrupts "the natural order of things for the overwhelming majority of the population," as Ian Lustick puts it.[4] Israel/Palestine is a geopolitical entity where this disruption has taken unique and unprecedented dimensions, especially since the early 1990s. There, a domestic border regime overrides the distinction between domestic and international space. A quintessentially unsettled polity, the state of Israel systematically intervenes in and constructs domestic, semidomestic, and peripheral areas in an attempt to manipulate an entire political space demographically and geographically according to its own design and perceived interests.

Etienne Balibar notes the rise of domestic border grids in his important essay on the transformation of political spaces. While international borders have been the historically overdetermined sites of contestations and exclusions, today, contestations and exclusions are no longer situated "at the border." Borders are not "purely external realities," but are situated everywhere and nowhere. Their multiplicity and ubiquity as a means of demarcating differentiated degrees of citizenship is apparent in virtually all nation-states. Balibar points out the paradox that "the more we reduce border externalities the closer we are to a border operating as a grid…ranging over the new social space, and ceasing simply to border it from the outside." His provocative contention is that such domestic grids now perpetuate a global apartheid in virtually "all societies."[5] Anthony Richmond, analyzing immigration regimes, argues that a new world order defined by restrictions of movement indeed amounts to a global apartheid. Global apartheid in his definition stands for the "forcible isolation of people." It occurs "when separation is imposed by a dominant group upon a less powerful one."[6]

It is highly suggestive to think of apartheid as a grid of differentiation through a border regime and as a regime of forcible isolation of less powerful populations. Balibar's and Richmond's contributions are an invitation to examine seriously how grids of differentiation and isolation work today and how they functioned in the past. We need to know how separation rationalities have been put to work and where they produce acute crises of disenfranchisement and violence today. Considering the commonplace division of political spaces and new developments in the regimentation of borders, it is perhaps risky to single out either South Africa or Israel/Palestine. Yet this is where the longevity and peculiarity of domestic border regimes and of forcible isolation of populations suggests that a certain type (as opposed to a global phenomenon) of a disenfranchising logic is at stake.

Many argue that trends toward globalization of the past two decades brought the once self-evident governmentality of nation-states itself into severe crisis, pointing out that issues of the administration of justice, political claims, economic redistribution, and cultural recognition are no longer confined to domestic spaces. Echoing the notion of global apartheid, they argue that exclusions and disenfranchisment no longer begin or stop at national borders, but are more pervasively global in scope. Nancy Fraser is convinced accordingly that "globalization has put the question of the frame squarely on the political agenda." She critiques theories of globalization for stopping short of addressing the injustices created by the very politics of framing itself. Fraser identifies, for instance, the "Keynesian-Westphalian frame" as a "powerful instrument of injustice." She calls "misframing" a condition in which "the community's boundaries are drawn in such a way as to wrongly exclude some people from the chance to participate *at all* in its authorized contests over justice.... The architecture of the interstate system protects the very partitioning of political space that it institutionalizes, effectively excluding transnational democratic decision-making on issues of justice."[7]

Fraser thus invokes the crisis of the nation-state, whose spatial, political, and social parameters are shaken by globalization, in order to reconsider what she calls the metapolitical dimension: the splitting of political space in a way that unjustly excludes the possibility of developing democratic decision-making membership outside the nation-state. For Fraser, misframing is a broadly defined metainjustice in that it denies participation in frame-making processes by people both domestically and internationally. It skews the political frame.

SKEWED POLITICAL FRAMING

Thinking of the concept of misframing or skewed political framing in the context of global configurations of power indeed suggests new forms of mass disenfranchisements. Yet there is no clear answer as to what actually generates it. Is misframing inherent in the Keynesian-Westphalian frame, in the partitioning of political space to nation-states, an old problem only exacerbated by globalization? Or is it rather the case that the politics of the frame is forced to the fore as a result of the changing nature of the territorial state as an effect of globalization's destabilization of the territorial paradigm of sovereignty?

In either case, Fraser's spatial political metaphor—misframing—captures well the disenfranchising logic of an enforced frame. Let us therefore take this concept momentarily out of the context of current debates over globalization. Misframing may be conceived not as a consequence of globalization or as a byproduct of nation-statism, but as the logic of specific forms of coercive rule. It can describe the skewed correlation between a governmental apparatus and out-group populations that generates intense contestation over the frame. Most nation-states (on their last legs or not) still tend to be stable and uncontested framing entities, largely conforming to a division between domestic and international space. But some hegemonic regimes intentionally override this distinction with their frame-setting agendas and domestic border regimes. Regimes of separation, our cases in point, seek not only to contain, but also to control the distribution of their undesired populations within territories lacking such clear determinacy. Their "solution" to the problem of how to keep a safely separate (and often already ethnically cleansed) polity requires that other peoples be ruled by force. Michael Mann's monumental study *The Dark Side of Democracy* shows that democratic or democratizing nation-states often have sought to oust or expel out groups when domination over a minority population considered problematic is no longer a tolerated option. Regimes of separation, by distinction, develop unprecedented mechanisms of containment, with forcible separation and isolation of masses trapped in their overextended political space.[8]

Semipermanent misframing (and its perverse democratic justification and political authority), together with the ensuing chaos, resistance, and disorder it generates, does not fit comfortably any of our definitions of ethnic or territorial conflict, conventional war, or civil war. The paradigms of imperialism, of old forms of colonialism and of neocolonialism also do not sufficiently explain its sanctioned violence and logic of rule. Colonial powers, after all, did not initially conquer for the sake of imposing a frame of rule on the conquered, but simply ruled in order to extract resources. Conversely, the imposition of coercive rule by regimes of separation is a costly and dangerous enterprise, yet is justified as a necessary evil. Notwithstanding the fact that this imposition serves, in a conventional colonial fashion, the overexploitation of territorial, natural, and labor resources, it also exacts a heavy price from the misframing polity. And yet sustaining the interests of the polity's constituencies, particularly the socioeconomic order from which its elites benefit most, is utterly unimaginable without it. Separation and isolation of out-group populations thus becomes an inescapable reality, a reality manufactured by the political project of separation, rarely challenged from within and pursued at all costs.

MISFRAMING DEMOCRACY AND POLITICAL VIOLENCE

For Fraser, what is at stake, the most pernicious consequence of misframing, is nothing short of a collective "political death."[9] There are concrete political spaces where such an outcome is plausible. These are spaces where hegemonic polities continuously define out groups and their living environment in relation to their own hegemonic order. Misframing must be seen then neither as an incidental nor an abstract form of metainjustice. Hannah Arendt, for instance, argued that exclusion from the realm of the political is chronic, not to say inevitable in a world of nation-states. This was the tragic byproduct of just struggles to obtain and expand citizenship through acts of self-determination. Most acts of self-determination entailed some form of misframing, as the bloody history of ethnic minorities in nation-states clearly demonstrates. But in a regime of separation, the misframing of out groups—not minorities but mass populations—is not a coincidental effect of nation-statism, but its *raison d'état*. The colonial formula is also taken a step further. An insatiable accumulation of territory on which to impose an imperial order by a sovereign endowed with the mission to civilize foreign people in far-away lands is not quite what is ultimately at stake. In regimes of separation, misframing mass populations rather becomes an entrenched, fully internalized and rationalized feature of self-determination. Setting the frame is what the survival of the polity and the nation depends upon.

This misframing is guided by an overarching principle, the principle of fundamental mass disenfranchisement through misframing. This principle emphasizes the dynamic constitution of political space, such that a sovereign power determines the condition of belonging to a political frame—to any or to none—for out groups. This contested constitution takes place on the "metapolitical" level, as Fraser calls it, pointing out the lack of agreement over the political frame. On the metapolitical level, this misframing implies a denial of the right to have rights, as the famous Arendt formulation goes. More crucially even, misframing takes place on the ground, on the level of the phenomena of population. A regime of separation thus proceeds by implementing radical means of manipulating, destroying, and exploiting a physical environment and its populace. It is *fundamental* because it involves the metapolitical dimension. It is a *mass* phenomenon, having an impact on a massive scale, on entire social-political groups and their environment, and finally, it is *disenfranchising* in a series of negations and deprivations.[10]

Separation regimes thus narrowly define the parameters of political existence for specific population groups. Giorgio Agamben's writing on the threshold comes immediately to mind, because this political near death remains close to, yet still at the threshold of actual catastrophic annihilation, mass killing, and genocide.[11] Significantly, in a regime of separation, all attempts at active expulsion or annihilation are subordinated to a higher rationale of containment and control. Out groups are not quite "cleansed" in the territorial sense. That is, they do not disappear from a territory through organized campaigns of killing and expulsion. The most effective efforts at the destruction of their environments, displacement, and political destabilization occur well within the skewed frame. Could chronic violence under such conditions turn into mass killings? One notes, for instance, that the apartheid regime was neither genocidal in intent nor in effect. It did, however, attempt to destroy populations as political communities. In regimes of separation, containment as a strategy for the nonphysical political elimination of out groups is a rather peculiar twist on two fundamental aspects of sovereign power— a monopoly over the means of movement and a monopoly over the distribution of status in the population. Containment is achieved through the imposition of a democratically enabled administrative dictatorship (as I explain in more detail in the next section) and a monopoly over the means of movement through a peculiar border regime. As already noted, monopoly over the means of movement is a normative prerogative of modern sovereignty. When mechanisms of misframing are in place, however, we observe the perversion of this principle. Demarcated outsides are continuously and dynamically distinguished from the democratic core, the inside, while in effect being part of one political space where a sovereign attains full monopoly over the means of domestic and "external" movement. A regime of separation is able thus to construct and maintain artificial, circumscribed environments placed under dictatorial authority. It aims at disrupting the relationship of populations to their geopolitical environment, ensuring their total separation from the misframing polity.

APARTHEID REVISITED

Throughout the decades of apartheid, most South Africans lived under a dictatorship, albeit for the most part not under an official state of emergency. A central organ of the government, a virtual "state within a state," the department that went by different names over the years: the Native Affairs Department, then the Department of Bantu Affairs and Development, and finally, in the euphemistic spirit of reform, the Ministry of Co-ordination and Cooperation orchestrated the coercive administration of populations, generally enjoying the collaboration of the courts, government branches, and the civil service.[12] It single-handedly determined all aspects of life for those it defined as belonging outside the polity, or, in more cynical terms, as "migrants," "aliens," and "surplus populations." This regime included residential and labor placements, draconian restrictions on movement, and forced spatial political affiliation to the Bantustans as remote extensions of its administrative reign of terror. More than the accesses of state violence and military repression, what constituted the gist of apartheid's political authority was the successful normalization and routinization of oppression. When it was gradually conceded that sustaining the matrix of control was unsustainable as a day-to-day practical regime, to a large extent simply because it failed miserably to achieve its own declared goals, apartheid began to unravel. As United Party Member of Parliament Marais Styen put it in 1968, it was a "dinosaur with a massive body and small brain."[13]

The out-group population under apartheid was coerced and conditioned to obey the will (and often whim) of the population-administration authorities, who considered them foreign and whom they considered hostile and foreign. Under the administrative dictatorship of apartheid, encompassing geographically the whole of South Africa (even spilling over to Namibia at some point), the decisions made from the lowest to the highest levels of the bureaucracy were both arbitrary and final, as under an occupation government. The democratic structures of the white polity created a semblance of separate spheres of political authority, but in fact together with the coercive administration constituted a hostile government functioning as a supreme sovereign without consent. As noted above, in the case of apartheid, it was not probable that political violence would or could deteriorate into genocidal catastrophe, harsh as the repression was, because the logic of containment and control charted another course: the implosion of hostile rule and the establishment of a population domain including all within the geographical boundaries of South Africa. What the process of regime collapse did eventually was to bring about on the level of political organization and political authority an end to an "impossible form of government," in Hannah Arendt's terms—the hybrid form combining a liberal democracy at home and rule over "subject races" in the colonies. In South Africa, an impossible government gave way to a possible government, or in other words, to a rehabilitated order of popular sovereignty. It is probably not by chance that the mechanism of coercion most plagued by chaos, inconsistency, and failure—influx control, the attempt to regulate the movement of blacks into urban areas—collapsed first, already in 1985, less than a decade before executive-political apartheid gave way.[14]

Before I examine how influx control, apartheid's domestic control of movement, was actually put to work, it is necessary to stress that although this system dates back to the colonial era, apartheid revolutionized it for its misframing purposes. Countering a tendency toward South African exceptionalism, Mahmood Mamdami maintains that systems controlling labor and the experience of disenfranchised populations in the entire region of sub-Saharan Africa generally were not so markedly different under colonialism and in its aftermath.[15] Indeed, apartheid did not emerge in a historical vacuum, and the experience of colonized populations outside South Africa may not have been less harsh. No doubt apartheid must not be artificially plucked out of the context of the continental experience of colonialism. Still, it cannot be fully appreciated as a political rationale if treated as yet another colonial regime. Apartheid, with obvious continuities with its colonial foundations, was a particular type of regime with a distinct population problem to which it sought to devise unprecedented "solutions." Apartheid was defined more by a series of radical spatial political experiments than by any of its ideological premises and proclamations.

Of the gamut of apartheid's experiments, restrictions designed to curb the flow of populations from the rural to the urban areas dealt the most serious blow to individuals and communities. This flow was viewed as a menace to the integrity of white South Africa. Its management was thus implemented through the systematic supervision of movement, residence, and labor, all with the intention of eventually delegating all "nonwhites" to the rural areas. The microcontrol of movements through pass laws indeed dates back to the slavery era of the eighteenth century. Already in a famous speech in 1942, Jan Smuts compared the likeliness of success of influx control to sweeping back the ocean with a broom. Apartheid in any case would not have existed without such relentless attempts at "sweeping." One must always keep in mind that the impetus of apartheid was not the preservation of a colonial status quo of racial segregation, but the radical reconstitution of populations in their relation to a disenfranchising governmental sovereign. This dynamic constitution, which could not have come about without influx-control mechanisms, entailed varying conditions and degrees of dispossession and destitution.

By the end of the 1950s, the impact of new pass laws and influx-control policies began to be felt as a tidal change. Through pass laws and influx control, movements, residential placements, and labor assignments were controlled in and between prescribed areas. Prescribed areas were any areas declared white, but where a large number of nonwhites lived and worked. The modernization of the pass laws entailed the introduction of a comprehensive scheme that created so-called Group Areas for each of the racially defined groups. Thus there were predominantly "colored," black, or Indian concentrations of populations within townships or populating separate townships altogether. Significantly, while restrictions of movement applied only and categorically to *all* nonwhites, they were internally administered according to bureaucratic categories, and not primarily on a racial or ethnic basis. For instance, members of a black family could have different administrative statuses in a given area—some allowed to "remain" and work, some allowed entry for seventy-two hours only for the purpose of work, and some banned from the area altogether.

Notwithstanding the racist bravado of apartheid demagogues, much depended on the extent to which the ambition to order through separation and isolation of populations could be actually translated into practice. The legal fetish of apartheid has been its most memorable feature, and every intricate minutia of racist legislation was put on record with official diligence. It is nevertheless the principle of despotic administrative rule that gave the regime its institutional force to command daily life.[16] Government departments such as the labor and immigration authorities collaborated with the state within a state. The "bureaucratic behemoth," as Deborah Posel calls the bloated civilian army of 1.2 million, had a very clear goal. The majority of South Africans were to be members of nations other than the South African nation. Under apartheid, most people were to be forced to live in the country of their birth as if on a foreign territory. This de facto and de jure mass denationalization (along with the infamous racial classifications, although those were not novel) was made possible through the creation of a national register, the Population Registration Act, Act No. 30 of 1950. Administrators issued identity cards, which contained information on the racial classification, registered residence, and authorized movements of people, using this quintessential tool of government for the purpose of denationalization. Ironically, by forcing identity cards and travel documents on practically all within its political space, the apartheid regime was compelled to govern the very vast populations it turned into stateless people in their own land. The intention to impose order and sort out populations administratively was quickly overshadowed by more ambitious plans for reordering the political space.

From the 1960s on, a more intense geographic upheaval began, with the administrative reconstitution of colonial-era reserves into Bantustans, beginning with the "independence" of Transkei in 1963. Intensified "disorganization and reorganization of the African population in South Africa" ensued.[17] External border movements remained monopolized by the regime, so even the rulers of the Ciskei and Transkei homelands traveled to advertise their newly "independent" status on South African passports.[18] Internally, waves of relocations and forced removals uprooted millions of "surplus people," mostly from rural lands. This constituted a form of domestic ethnic cleansing — ethnic cleansing without expulsion outside the boundaries of sovereignty. With the bulldozing of entire neighborhoods in urban areas, the population of townships began to swell. New townships and "relocation centers" were erected in haste, lacking even basic amenities. These were the refugee camps of apartheid. The disorganization of political space had only gradually acquired the ultimate rationale of defining all who were nonwhites administratively as *citizens* of homelands, with no recourse to permanent presence (and potential stakes) in the Republic of South Africa. The regime "Plan A" was first to turn populations into refugees by defining them as the official out groups of the South African polity. Only later the *apartheidgedachte* (the idea of apartheid) evolved into manufacturing "for" them a perverse version of self-determination—perverse, since this type of self-determination was not meant to exist outside or independent of the enveloping governmental apparatuses of South Africa.

About eight million people have been officially denationalized by apartheid and about three million forcibly removed. It is difficult to ignore the fact that apartheid was successful in redefining spaces and populations radically and permanently. But despite what may appear to be a staggering success, the situation was never ideal as far as apartheid cabinets and their administrative army were concerned. The more they tightened the controls of movement, the more people found ways to circumvent them. The more the regime depended on the Bantustans as containers, in effect unviable social and economic environments, the more traffic flowed back in desperate search for residence and work in the cities. Gray resistance to pass laws was rampant—the business of buying and selling passes boomed, passes were faked, and many used the simple trick of losing passes and then earning a few months before a new pass book (known as a "reference book") could be issued and then lost again, and so on. The list of "endorsements," papers approved and signed by employers, renters, and township administrative authorities, was so long that there was no practical way to verify all the information. Squatters' camps, "informal settlements," and shantytowns boomed. This is a well-known phenomenon in practically all countries with similarly gigantic economic disparities, yet only from the 1960s on did it become an epidemic in South Africa, making the shantytown population there one of the largest in the world. Needless to say, this was one of the unintended consequences of influx control about which apartheid officials were not very happy. In short, the administration of influx-control and pass laws was a logistical nightmare, closer to a grand failure than to a grand success. One commission after another tried to think of ways to "rationalize" this system.[19]

Absurd as it was, the result of the imposition of an apparatus of control in such a way was nevertheless social and spatial engineering of a breathtaking order of magnitude countrywide. The landscape of white towns, industrial zones with adjacent matchbox townships and squatters' camps, remote settlements, and former relocation zones in rural areas leave one with an eerie impression of uniformity. The impact on individuals and communities differed considerably, though. For instance, not in all cases did people suffer serious degradation in living conditions by being relocated to government-built townships. Still, hardly anyone was left untouched by it. In a recent interview, Deborah Posel pointed out that her classic study of the apartheid state, *The Making of Apartheid,* left unresolved the question of how, despite its own internal contradictions and failures, apartheid actually managed to implement separation. That apartheid was no linear, smooth execution of an ideologically well-conceived plan tells only half of the story. The redefinitions of spaces and populations transformed the physical and social landscape of South Africa well beyond merely heightening earlier segregation tendencies. The dynamics of the sovereign demarcation of outsides and insides was so comprehensive and bewildering in scope that experts believe that at the very least, apartheid's physical legacy is bound to remain a permanent feature of South Africa. According to the leading geographer of apartheid, A. J. Christopher:

> The physical inheritance of the apartheid era will survive for a very long time. Apartheid social engineers were part of a post–World War II global movement of professional planners seeking to construct new and improved living conditions for a "better" society. The physical constructions of the era were substantial and effectively permanent. The fabric of apartheid cities, the homeland settlements patterns and the infrastructure can be adapted but not erased.[20]

Perhaps key to understanding the ultimate success of the spatial and demographic revolution of apartheid, as Ivan Evans has suggested, is the fact that the regime did manage to ensure (by sheer force, but also through more subtle practices) a sufficient degree of submission to and compliance with its spatial-political logic for a very long time.[21] However, success was not solely dependent on administrative despotism, but also on the particular role the administration played within the South African Republic. For the citizen constituency, the state within a state seemed to have managed to address security concerns sufficiently enough without raising too much outrage at misconduct. It kept a semblance of normality and demographic, spatial, and political continuity for the white polity. This helped nourish the illusion that out groups conveniently placed under their thumb occupy a separate planet, an underworld beyond the pale, rather than right next door. A democratic veneer was certainly vital to maintaining this illusion. Depoliticized, bureaucratically spirited debates in the media, in parliament, and following the recommendations of commissions of inquiry focused on how influx-control and pass laws functioned badly or could function better. This maintained a vital horizon of hope that a "cleaner" way of ridding the republic of its problem of population might one day be found.

ISRAEL/PALESTINE: THE SOVEREIGNTY OF "AUSCHWITZ BORDERS"

From the outset, the specter of political incorporation of out-group populations haunted prestate Zionist institutions and, later, successive Israeli governments. The Palestinian catastrophe, al-Nakba, during the short seven months in 1948 in which an estimated seven hundred thousand Palestinians were forced into exile by

Jewish militias following an apparently organized military plan, remained incomplete.[22] Those who remained were placed under a military regime until 1966, and Israel firmly blocked the trickle of returnees during the 1950s. Occasional military raids across the border, including the indiscriminate massacres of villagers, effectively prevented refugee dwellings and shantytowns from forming in the backyards of what became the Jewish-dominated metropolitan area on the coast. The state did establish a complex and highly selective procedure for "family reunification," allowing qualified entry options to some, but kept it under tight control. All the while, a persistent ideological defiance of the armistice lines of 1948 perpetuated an unterritorially bound conception of political space. For Abba Eban, a memorable foreign minister in the 1960s, the 1948 boundaries were reminiscent of the borders of Auschwitz.[23] Curiously, when the "Auschwitz borders" were swiftly overrun in 1967, the encroachment over a mass of undesired population did not immediately present itself as an existential concern. In the first two decades of the occupation, the territories were swiftly, if not officially or legally annexed. The people living there were to be subjects overwhelmed by force, resigned to accept a condition of permanent statelessness alongside and outside Israel proper. Thus, 1967 marked a second wave of mass disenfranchisement through intentional misframing.

This convenient arrangement suffered a devastating blow with the outbreak of the intifada, the first Palestinian uprising, in 1987. It was then that the issue of containing the undesired population arose to unprecedented levels of poignancy. In the 1990s, Israel/Palestine entered into a new configuration of territory and sovereignty. We may identify the years between the first intifada up to the signing of the Oslo agreement as an uncertain transition phase in which there were already early signs of the emergence of a regime of separation. To be sure, the geopolitical rationale of separation with control had been already at work since 1948. The two waves of misframing, in 1948 and in 1967, already had "caged" out-group populations within the exclusive and contentious Israeli polity. But, intervention in the geopolitical environment of the Occupied Palestinian Territories and the regimentation of the everyday life of its population began to change beyond recognition from 1987 to 1993. "Peaceful separation," which took on all sorts of geopolitical shapes and ideological signifiers, was accompanied by new means of control and spatial designs. With the rise of peace on the political horizon, mechanisms of misframing shifted gear, becoming even more pervasive and permanent.[24] Both their scope and their rationale had changed. In the new paradigm, the territories began to be projected as external, while their enemy population became a problem to be dealt with seriously. Since then, and certainly after the second intifada (2000), violent revolts had to be crushed by means so severe in their overall impact that the prominent Israeli sociologist Baruch Kimmerling referred to it as "politicide" — a geopoliticide, one might add.[25] It was "the Auschwitz borders" inverted: an imposition and supervision of borders perceived as the only means for ensuring the survival of the misframing polity.

In what follows, I look closely at the early stages of the 1990s revolution in Israel/Palestine. I discuss three principles already dealt with above in relation to apartheid — despotic administrative rule, domestic borders, and population destabilization through misframing. These are general principles that help explain how the particular disenfranchising, occupying, and territorial sovereign logic in a separation regime is effectively put to work. As early as the transition period of 1987 to 1993, the prerogative of sovereign power in the Occupied Palestinian Territories began increasingly to depend on new practices of administrative rule over populations. The emerging domestic grid of borders and the use of a monopoly over the means of movement began severely to destabilize the population's relation to their environment. The physical aspects of this geopolitical revolution are there for everyone to see: the ever-expanding infrastructure of Jewish settlements, the Separation Wall, the system of bypass roads, and the ubiquity of checkpoints and roadblocks. In addition, there is the less visible operation of an administrative grid whose transformation dates back to the pre-Oslo transition period. Documentation and analysis of the administrative grid is made possible through the depository of a veteran human rights organization, Physicians for Human Rights — Israel. I intermittently interrupt this focus on Israel/Palestine to consider some apartheid mechanisms that help further flesh out principles of separation regimes.

THE PRINCIPLE OF DESPOTIC ADMINISTRATIVE RULE

In 1993, following the Oslo agreement, the West Bank was divided into so-called Areas A, B, and C, and Gaza was partitioned into four areas. In the West Bank, Area A was to become autonomous under the Palestinian Authority, Area B under coordinated Israeli and Palestinian control, and Area C, with the most Jewish settlements, under Israeli control. The interim agreement signed in 1995 established a joint Civil Affairs Coordination and Cooperation Committee, regional committees (for the West Bank and Gaza Strip) and district committees (in the West Bank) whose function would be "coordination and cooperation on civil affairs between the Palestinian Council and Israel."[26] Matters such as passage to and from the West Bank and the Gaza Strip, including crossing points and international crossings, as well as the granting of permits, were to be coordinated along with "other matters of common interest."[27] Each side was to establish and operate District Civil Liaison Offices (DCOs) in major West Bank cities (Jenin, Tulkarem, Qalqilya, Nablus,

Ramallah, Bethlehem, Hebron, and Jericho) and in the Gaza districts. Senior officials were to convene in regular meetings. At the time, the Oslo agreement and its planned interim stages were generally received as a breakthrough formula en route to territorial partition and the establishment of a Palestinian state. The contractual language of Oslo suggests ongoing communication between legal-civilian representatives hammering out mutual interests. The nitty-gritty details, however, often were hashed out solely by and between IDF officers and future Palestinian Authority security officers in meetings that often took place inside Israeli military bases.

Civil affairs in the Occupied Palestinian Territories has been the purview of the military government of the IDF since 1967. The legal bases for the operation of the Israeli administration were the proclamations on law and administration issued soon after the war ended in June 1967, which granted the IDF full appointive and administrative powers of government and legislation. In 1981, under Ariel Sharon as defense minister, a new position was introduced, separate from the IDF military government. It was entitled "Coordinator of Activities in the Territories" (Metaem Ha'Peulot ba'Shtachim), and its job was to "instruct, guide, advise, coordinate, and supervise the activities of all government ministries, the Civil Administration, state institutions, the various public authorities and private bodies in all matters concerning their activities in Judea, Samaria and the Gaza Strip."[28] The coordinator reported to the minister of defense. Civilians employed by the defense ministry and the army unit, known since 1981 as the Civil Administration, reported to the coordinator. The military Civil Administration of the Occupied Palestinian Territories has been entangled in complicated structures over the years. Generally speaking, since 1967, authority over civil affairs in the Occupied Palestinian Territories has been the prerogative of the IDF chief of staff and the defense minister.

The arrangements created by the Oslo agreements did not change this structure of administrative authority in the Occupied Palestinian Territories. Authority remained with the military governor of the territories. According to a former legal advisor of the Israeli Foreign Ministry and one of the architects of the Oslo Agreement, Yoel Zinger.

> The nature of the regime established in the West Bank and the Gaza strip, for the duration of the transitional period, is that of Palestinian autonomy under the supreme authority of the Israeli military government. Israel will continue to be responsible for, among other things, external security as well as the external relations between the West Bank and the Gaza strip.... Unlike the Civil Administration, the military government does not dissolve. Instead, it simply withdraws physically from its former location and continues to exist elsewhere as the source of all authority for the Palestinian Council and the powers and responsibilities exercised in the West Bank and the Gaza strip.[29]

Note that the IDF monopoly over what it already then defined as *external* relations between the West Bank and the Gaza Strip and *external* movement on the boundaries of Areas A, B, and C and via Israel abroad was written into the fine print of various Oslo agreements. The Oslo negotiators cemented the IDF monopoly over all aspects pertaining to passage, permits, and the means of movement in the Occupied Palestinian Territories. The Oslo interim agreements thus retained the supreme authority of the military government in the Occupied Palestinian Territories, with some amendments with regard to the physical location of some IDF bases. Specific areas of civil affairs were delegated to a new body, the Palestinian Authority (PA), operating under the IDF umbrella of overall responsibility for "security."

The old Civil Administration was reborn as District Civil Liaison Offices (DCLs) and District Coordination Offices (DCOs). Shlomo Gazit, a former IDF general and the first military governor of the Occupied Territories, who participated in the Oslo agreement negotiations, explains that while the establishment of the DCOs was supposed to reform a decades-old *structure,* it was never the intention to do away with the *principle* of administrative governance altogether. A crucial component of what was defined as the IDF security responsibility became the monopoly over the means of internal movement. A new system of movement permits and passes was to be created exclusively by means of the DCOs. The DCOs redefined both the means and the rationale of military administration, but the IDF did not make any effort to create even the appearance of a changing of the guard. The same symbol of the old Civil Administration army unit tag remained patched on the uniform of the military governor of the Gaza Strip. He now held the title of "coordinator" in the Gaza DCO, yet his portrait adorned a wall along with the portraits of all former military governors of the strip. This was one link in a long chain of unfortunate mistakes, Gazit laments retrospectively, especially since "to the Palestinians, it seemed to make no difference at all. It was the same mechanism; the same landlord that they hated before."[30]

Let me pause here to consider, in comparison, the administrative machinery of apartheid. Notwithstanding the use of coordination as a euphemism for coercion, absolutely no institutional or historical likeness exists between the South African Ministry of Cooperation and District Coordination Offices in the OPT. The administrative apparatus of apartheid overall involved a huge number of people. It was the occupational vocation for a large segment of the Afrikaner population. This cannot be said about IDF DCOs soldier/administrators, who numbered approximately five thousand and issued 229,150 movement permits in 2003 at the time when restrictions of movement in the OPT peaked and the violent clashes of the second intifada raged.[31] The scale and authority for issuing authorizations of movement under apartheid and in Israel/Palestine are likewise not comparable, not to mention the fact that authorizations of movement have served different functions under the two regimes. The apartheid regime had an economic interest in regulating the flow of laborers in and out of industrial centers and a demographic interest in displacing millions of people out of areas it "reserved" to whites. During the Oslo years, the function of authorizations of movement in the OPT was to control the flow of labor, but by and large also to be able to literally "hermetically close the OPT," as the official language put it. The policy was to restrict to the minimum the number of OPT residents entering Israel proper at Israel's will, with the consequence of eliminating economic ties altogether. Gradually, it became an imperative to be able to bring movement *within* the OPT to a complete halt as well, an imperative that, contrary to IDF propaganda, preceded the suicide campaigns launched by militant Palestinian groups against Israeli civilians.[32] In South Africa, the national security rhetoric often invoked "Communist agitators," which later became simply "terrorists." National security, however, was in fact a relatively weak rationale, if not absent for justifying the influx-control and pass laws.

That said, endowed with the mission and means of imposing despotic administrative rule both the Ministry of Cooperation and Development in South Africa and the District Coordination Offices of the Israeli Defense Force today appear to adhere to a principle that may be summarized as a prerogative administration of movement, an administration directed or set apart for out-group populations. Ultimately, various institutional structures and their peculiar motivations matter less than what the imperatives and assumptions of this operational principle entail. For instance, setting up separate mechanisms for the administration of the movements of out groups entails that movement through political space is not a matter of ordinary individual choice. Movement must be authorized and controlled by the regime. The separate and population-specific administration of movement applies on an individual basis, as well as collectively, targeting all belonging to a population group, albeit in myriad uneven ways.

Apartheid's movement-control formula was the pass book known as *dompas* (stupid passes). The method adopted for the magnanimous task of implementing pass laws and influx-control was paper persecution. Everyone had to obtain papers authorizing daily activities. The pass book functioned not only as an identity card, but also as a labor card, requiring employers to fill in endorsements for their workers. Violators of residential laws, movement restrictions, labor placements, and generally people not carrying a properly kept pass book were prosecuted, penalized, and banished to rural oblivion at an astonishing pace of an average of two hundred and fifty thousand cases a year.[33] At a certain point, employers were also required to report and monitor paper violations. A small pamphlet, *Everybody's*

Guide to the Pass Laws, published by the Black Sash—an organization established in 1955 by white women to assist people in their day-to-day struggles with the apartheid bureaucracy—is a testimony of the obtrusive nature of the paper persecutions. In capital letters, the Black Sash recommends that "every African should keep in his possession all documents he has ever had: such things as birth certificates, baptismal certificates, school certificates, references, housing permits, hospital and clinic cards, prison discharge papers, rent receipts and death and burial certificates."[34] [See excerpt on page 299.] Under a regime of despotic administrative rule, every official paper counts—from the cradle through the prison to the grave.

In the Occupied Palestinian Territories, the IDF Civil Administration monopolized the means of movement through the imposition of identity cards and the issuance of travel documents. Its meddling with civil affairs in the first two decades of the occupation, however, had been a looser, more horizontal and indirect affair. The old Civil Administration relied, for instance, on a minimum of IDF personnel and on tens of thousands of local administrators, as a report from 1979 shows.[35] It was to some degree concerned with maintaining a minimum standard of welfare, and the military government regularly surveyed the Occupied Palestinian Territories to measure indicators of health, education, employment, and industrial production. In another report dating from 1988, for instance, the IDF notes the "remarkable improvement in their [the population's] standard of living," for which it credits itself and even suggests that the improvement "stands as proof of Israel's desire for cooperation and coexistence." The desire to project benevolence is interestingly expressed in this Civil Administration report—at the height of the first intifada. This was notably a time when organized strikes and boycotts against the Israeli administration were in full swing. In the Oslo years, as the institutions of the Civil Administration reappeared in their current DCO form, concern for civil affairs, which later acquired the strange official title of the "fabric of life," narrowed down significantly. Israel sought to relieve itself completely of the responsibility for anything that would have to do with the welfare of the population in the Occupied Palestinian Territories.

And so the control of movement, as well as of the flow of humanitarian aid from donor countries, mainly the European Union, on which the survival of many depends to an appalling degree, became the central target of despotic administrative rule. The DCOs, for instance, issue permits that specify the various "sorts of people" and the permission they have been given to move. For example, "pupils' permits" are issued for twelve-year-olds who are residents of seam zones, usually areas bordering the Separation Wall. Permits to be in a specific area or travel in the Occupied Palestinian Territories include detailed information regarding the destination and purpose of travel. They often specify hours of the day when the permit

EXCERPT FROM *EVERYBODY'S GUIDE TO PASS LAWS,* an undated Black Sash pamphlet (probably from the mid-1960s) that includes notes and tips "to Africans" and "to Employers" on issues such as "How to read a Reference Book," "Making application for a Reference Book," and "How to get permission to enter a prescribed area as a contract worker." [Document source: University of Cape Town Black Sash archive]

Everybody's Guide to the Pass Laws

THIS PAMPHLET has been produced to try to present the laws and regulations which govern the day-to-day life of Africans in the urban areas in a comprehensible form. We hope that it will be of use to both employers and employees and to the thousands of people who have to live their lives by these laws.

It should be noted that this summary has been drawn up in Johannesburg and some of the minor regulations and details may differ in other towns.

We have found that many people are finding themselves in trouble because of regulations they did not comply with in the past.

We wish to stress the following: —

EVERY AFRICAN SHOULD KEEP IN HIS POSSESSION ALL DOCUMENTS HE HAS EVER HAD: SUCH THINGS AS BIRTH CERTIFICATES, BAPTISMAL CERTIFICATES, SCHOOL CERTIFICATES, REFERENCES, HOUSING PERMITS, HOSPITAL AND CLINIC CARDS, PRISON DISCHARGE PAPERS, RENT RECEIPTS AND DEATH AND BURIAL CERTIFICATES.

These papers may well be needed at some time to prove his or her right to be in an area, and some are irreplaceable.

Definitions

A PRESCRIBED AREA is one which has been declared prescribed in the Government Gazette, and in practice means any area which is considered to be a White area, but where a large number of Africans live and work.

SECTION 10 of the Native (Urban Areas) Consolidation Act No. 26/1945 is the most important clause in all legislation affecting Africans. On it depends a person's right to come to, work and remain in a prescribed area.

Notes to Africans

1. You must never write anything in your Reference book or remove anything. You should carry it with you always.

2. You should obtain a visitor's permit if you wish to stay in any area other than the one you are entitled to be in for more than 72 hours.

3. If you should go home on holiday from a prescribed area you should not stay away for more than 264 days. If you do, you may not be allowed to return.

4. If you live in a township with your family you should see that you and your wife, and your children, parents and any relatives in your care are on your housing permit.

5. If you are sending your children out of the area to school you should take them to the superintendent in the area in which you live and explain that they are domiciled with you but are going away to school and will be returning for their holidays and will wish to be registered in your area when they have to take their reference books.

6. If you have rent troubles, arrangements can sometimes be made with township superintendents and welfare officers and employers.

is valid. Most permits are valid only for very brief periods, often just hours, forcing perpetual reapplication. Permits are also issued to "inhibit one's own house" for residents in close proximity to military posts, Jewish settlements, or the Separation Wall. VIPs hold special permits that ease their movement in the Occupied Palestinian Territories. And there are the ubiquitous "humanitarian cases" for which, in addition to regular permits, there are special movement-authorization procedures handled by "humanitarian centers" (a relatively recent development) staffed by DCO soldiers.

During the first intifada, movement through the political space of Israel/ Palestine and between Gaza and the West Bank became simultaneously intolerable and more necessary to monitor. With obvious continuities, there has been a paradigmatic shift. In the first two decades of the occupation, a permit allowing movement worked as a general rule, the exception being when it was retracted to disqualify the individual from entering the Israeli job market. On the external rim, there was a similar general permission to cross over to neighboring countries, known as the Open Bridges policy. During the first intifada, at the same time that the first individual movement authorizations were granted, movement was gradually prohibited until this prohibition now became the general rule.

THE PRINCIPLE OF DOMESTIC BORDERS

The basic ingredients of controlling populations through a draconian monopoly over the means of movement within the Occupied Palestinian Territories—internal curfews, closures, and general authorizations of movement—were at work on a rather small and highly localized scale during the first two decades of the occupation. According to Shlomo Gazit, imposing a curfew used to be a complicated procedure. It passed upward from the lower levels to the highest military levels and passed down again as a command on behalf of the IDF chief of staff. The command would specify the task, the forces designated for its execution, and a clear timeline for a curfew. A curfew recommendation would climb up the bureaucratic ladder on the civilian side, as well, and required the approval of the highest civilian executive, the minister of defense.[36]

In response to the intifada, the Israeli security apparatuses first employed short-term curfews as ways of controlling the uprising, with their outpourings of demonstrating crowds into the streets. In 1991, curfews were frequently used, albeit to a large extent still locally. In the village of Anabta in the Tulkarem region, for instance, between January and March 1991, seventy-four days of curfew were imposed on the population, leaving only seven days without a curfew.[37] In order to enforce its curfews, the military had to dispatch patrols into major cities. Pictures of soldiers storming streets and the alleys of refugee camps, shooting at demonstrators, became iconic media images of the intifada. Gradually, the strategic spatial advantages of closures over curfews became apparent: Closures could be imposed simply by blocking main roads to and from certain areas, significantly reducing the need to risk direct "contact" with the population and the inevitable international embarrassments that accompanied these violent scenes. Although both means, curfews and closures, were used during the first intifada, the frequency and severity of closures increased as rapidly as mass and generally nonviolent resistance declined. In 1991, during the First Gulf War, the concept of a protracted "total closure" pertaining to the entire population of the Occupied Territories was first introduced, and in the following years, total closure was used more frequently and lasted for longer periods of time. Closure began to be applied not only following eruptions of demonstrations or attacks on Israeli citizens (mostly settlers), but habitually around Jewish holidays, periods of heightened tourism in Israel.

In the late 1980s and early 1990s, mass mobilization in the Occupied Territories gave way to occasional "knifing" incidents, random attacks on Israeli-Jewish passersby. In March 1993, a closure was imposed on Gaza after such an incident in Tel Aviv. The closure lasted three days before forty thousand workers from Gaza were allowed to return to work in Israel. General Dani Rothschild, then the coordinator of government operations in the territories, announced with the lifting of this closure that only workers picked up by Israeli employees from the Erez checkpoint were to be allowed in.[38] General Amnon Shahak relayed the IDF version of influx control: "economic pressure pushes 25,000 workers to the checkpoint terminals at Erez each day. They go through physical checkup, sample checkup of vehicles and magnetic card validation."[39] The instability of the flow of Palestinian day laborers became a headache for Israeli employers, who then aggressively lobbied the government to expand the importation of cheaper and "safer" international migrant workers.

The gradual process of disappearing the Palestinian day laborers from the Israeli job market did not, however, put them off the radar. The magnetic cards that Shahak referred to in 1993 had been first introduced in 1986 as digital versions of the old paper entry and work permit. This device contains information identifying a person's security status and other computerized data. Those caught in Israel without valid permits were given a police-issued "prohibition" that appeared on the IDF computer screens. Many others were "prohibited" by the General Security Service for undisclosed reasons. Highly restricted though it was, Palestinian labor in Israel was never completely eradicated or officially banned. In 1999, for example, about one hundred thousand permits to enter Israel were issued to Occupied Palestinian Territories residents, and about thirty thousand workers employed by sixteen thousand Israelis obtained special permits to enter Israel at times of closure "in the framework of a special program of consistent employment [*avoda retzifa*]." That same year, the IDF also approved a "passage quota:" 1000 people from the West Bank and 1000 from Gaza were authorized to move between the strip and the West Bank, in addition to 3,450 employees of the Palestinian Authority.[40] Initially then, general closures turned the West Bank and Gaza Strip into two isolated islands. Soon followed an internal splintering of the Occupied Palestinian Territories by domestic borders in the form of military checkpoints.

In studying how domestic borders worked in South Africa, one encounters the difficult task of following confusingly changing and often overlapping spatial divisions and jurisdictions. The most important local administrative unit of central government in apartheid South Africa was the magisterial district. Magisterial district boundaries typically appeared on cartographic presentations of the state. Municipal boundaries, however, did not appear on the national map series and frequently changed. This is significant, because municipal boundaries were the focal point for the implementation of influx-control and pass laws. The boundaries of the Bantustans, for instance, remained fixed and stable throughout, but were not included in the national map series. Despite periodic proclamations of the Bantustans as "independent" throughout the 1970s, only in a 1985 census did district boundaries actually reflect the Bantustan territories under a complex system of overlapping jurisdictions. This, in turn, substantially modified the entire map of the magisterial districts of South Africa.[41] To make a complicated story short, we need note only that the boundaries of jurisdictions, geographical, and administrative units were subject to very frequent changes under apartheid. Presence inside or outside these flexible territorial units depended less upon the juridical coherence or territorial integrity of areas as such and more on a person's ability to obtain official papers to qualify for being in or entering them.

A particular procedure called "endorsing out" captures the schizophrenic nature of a domestic border regime and sheds light on the principle of domestic borders themselves. The function of a domestic border regime is to determine what individuals belong outside the administrative realm of a common political space. Being "endorsed out" meant that a person no longer "qualified" as the official term put it, for residing in and/or working in a certain area. One could qualify to be in an urban area under "section 10 of the Native (Urban Area) Consolidation Act No. 26" only if able to produce evidence that he or she was born in the urban area or had worked continuously there for ten or fifteen years. The endorsement was forfeited and the person lost his or her credential if, for example, the person left the area for a short period or if a person was sentenced to a fine exceeding 1,000 rand or a term of imprisonment exceeding six months. With the level of random arrests based on violations of pass laws alone averaging two hundred and fifty thousand cases a year, this was a highly precarious credential.

In the Black Sash archive, the bureaucratic haggle over a person's administrative status was recorded in appeals to and responses from the authorities. The Athlone Advice Office of the Black Sash in the Cape Town region, for instance, reported its legal expenses for the year 1969–70 in terms of successes and failures to stave off endorsements out. For example, success was recorded in canceling an endorsement out proving a certain person's registered employment and in diminishing the rate of endorsement out in the area of Stellenbosch through advocacy or legal interventions. Failure, most often due to "broken records," in which case a person "disqualified him/herself," in official language, by not providing proper documentation of consistent whereabouts, laconically appears in this document under the heading "not qualified."[42] In 1973, the Athlone Advice Office also reported the expansion of administrative boundaries and pondered the implication of this with regard to freedom of movement:

> The imaginary line dividing the City Council from the Divisional Council portions of the Cape Peninsula is said to be on the verge of dissolution.... An advantage will be that the Cape Peninsula will form one area, movement within which will be freely allowed; unfortunately, it is to remain separate from the rest of the Western Cape, but that too will become one area. One might reasonably hope that in view of the coming amalgamation, the authorities would exercise their discretionary powers when asked, for instance, to sanction a change of employment between areas within the Peninsula. But no, on the contrary.... Even after April those who have broken their continuous residence in one area by living in another area will not be considered to qualify for permanent residence in either area.[43]

What we learn from this report is that in Cape Town at the time, where even the flat top of Table Mountain has been declared a white area (even though only a white cloth of clouds appeared to occupy it continuously) people could not move freely, even within previously established areas, without risking "breaking records." What mattered most, then, were not the boundaries of the area per se, but the administrative status that people had managed (or failed) to acquire and to retain in relation to it. The implications of endorsement out—not qualifying to be in one area or another—have been of catastrophic proportions to individuals, families, and entire communities.

The operation of this administrative grid functioned as a "soft" or invisible domestic border. In a domestic border regime, boundaries do not distinguish or create *territorial* outsides of political sovereignty. Instead, they set up an internal administration for the purpose of differentiation, separation, and control. It is useful to recall Balibar's point here, that borders exist no longer as purely external realities, but are situated everywhere and nowhere. The principle of domestic borders in separation regimes is a particular manifestation of this situation. Borders cease to operate "externally," distinguishing one sovereign territory from another. Instead, borders function as mechanisms of domestic population differentiation and control.

In the Occupied Palestinian Territories, the administrative status that people have to maintain in relation to the territory is monitored through the use of physical "hard" barriers and in the form of "flying," "spontaneous," and "permanent" military checkpoints. This form of monitoring did not exist in South Africa, where it was difficult to distinguish even the areas of the Bantustans from the rest of the country in the absence of borders or border signs. Over the past few years, Kalandia checkpoint, separating residents of Ramallah from residents of East Jerusalem, evolved rapidly from an improvised military checkpoint into a permanent one. More recently, it began to resemble an international terminal, complete with a parking lot and a visitors' waiting hall. Kalandia is nevertheless an artificial physical and administrative divide, a wedge between Ramallah and East Jerusalem, the largest and most important population centers in the OPT.

The domestic border regime in the OPT thus has both physical manifestations of a static and permanent nature (the Wall, checkpoints turned "international" terminals), and a dynamic grid of administrative differentiation (shifting, arbitrary, and short-term authorizations of movement, categories of authorized residence, and so on, managed ad hoc by checkpoint and DCO influx administrators who are soldiers). In Israel/Palestine, the domestication of borders has had the distinct effect of creating closed-off, prisonlike environments, or in IDF terminology, "land cells," echoing John Vorsters's vision of geographical difference.

THE PRINCIPLE OF POPULATION DESTABILIZATION THROUGH MISFRAMING

In the transition period from 1987 to 1993, when domestic borders just began to appear in their current form, the sovereign monopoly over the "external" boundaries of Israel/Palestine severely destabilized the Palestinian population. Skewed framing was put to work through the use of unprecedented impositions of internal and external exile. Examining a particular mechanism of population destabilization in the transition period sharpens our understanding of the process by which the occupation regime morphed into a regime of separation.

To be sure, policies that force de facto exile on the Palestinian population were in practice long before what is identified here as a transition period to a separation regime. It is common knowledge that arbitrary denials and harassments when crossing the Occupied Palestinian Territories into neighboring countries were practiced before the first intifada. Physicians or patients' appeals to Physicians for Human Rights—Israel between 1988 and 1993 involved requests for assistance in attaining travel permits to leave the Occupied Palestinian Territories and go abroad. The archive of PHR-I contains documents beginning in 1988, the year it was founded in response to the first intifada.[44] The permits that the organization helped people to obtain at the time were issued by the offices of the old Civil Administration, which was responsible for authorizing "external" border movements. Some files contain a description of the medical circumstances of applicants: victims of security-forces shootings, practices of torture, beatings, egregious detention conditions, and medical neglect. In some cases, reentry permits were denied for obscure security reasons. Such was the case of the chief neurologist in the East Jerusalem Al-Mukassad Hospital. In February 1991, Dr. N., a resident of East Jerusalem and a holder of a Belgian passport, was refused entry several times while attempting to return from a visit to Jordan. Only after relentless pressure from Al-Mukassad and PHR-I citing Dr. N.'s vital functions at the hospital was entry granted. Many Palestinians experienced similar difficulties, suggesting that the Open Bridges policy of the first two decades of the occupation did not mean that all traffic was automatically or actually authorized. As a matter of fact, for years, the IDF Civil Administration had an unofficial policy of encouraging emigration from the Occupied Palestinian Territories. The state blacklisted people who at one point became "prohibited" and denied entry or who simply were encouraged to leave and not come back.[45] Some high-profile public deportations took place, usually targeting militant leadership (the most memorable being the 1992 expulsion to South Lebanon of 300 Hamas members by Yitzhak Rabin). While some expulsions were handled in the open, in a much less public fashion, Palestinian administrative detainees, incarcerated without trial for indefinite periods, were forced to negotiate exile periods in return for their release. In one case, according to the veteran human rights advocate Tamar Pelleg Sryck, an administrative detainee was forced not to return for seven years in order to end two years of incarceration without charges or a prospect for a trial.[46] Sordid "deals" such as this were first struck with the General Security Service before being secretly approved by the State Prosecutor's Office.

But a practice I refer to as "forced self-exile" had a particular application in the transition period of the early 1990s. In forced self-exile cases, exit permits from the Occupied Palestinian Territories were to be obtained only provided that a person agreed not to return within the foreseeable future. Although it is difficult to establish a clear statistical picture, it is possible that such random cases found in PHR-I's archive (see below for details) have been merely the tip of the iceberg. In 1990, the organization was not as well known in the Occupied Palestinian Territories as it is today. Moreover, a person's medical condition was perhaps not the only urgent need that could be exploited to extract the improbable promise not to return in exchange for a travel permit. Some traveling abroad to study were also forced to sign a form obliging them not to return. Other human rights organizations may have encountered this practice in other contexts. It is unclear who authored the requirement and what its legal basis is in military or any other law. How it was handled is also unclear. For instance, I know little about whether persons who accepted the imposition in return for an exit permit were in fact allowed to return at the end of their forced self-exile period. Archive findings, nevertheless, conclusively show that it was not an accidental occurrence, but a policy, officially corroborated in IDF responses to inquiries made between 1988 and 1993.

Forced Self-Exile: Sample of Cases Handled by Physicians for Human Rights—Israel

1. A., a resident of Jenin, was shot by IDF soldiers in November 1989. A. was arrested and transferred to an Israeli hospital in Afula. Afula physicians did not remove bullet shrapnel from his chest despite serious pain caused by it, on the premise that this condition did not endanger his life. After A. was released from six months of administrative detention, he applied to the Civil Administration office requesting an exit permit for medical treatment abroad. The Civil Administration made his exit permit conditional on a requirement that he should sign a document that obliged him not to return to the Occupied Territories for a period of three years from the day of his departure. A. refused to sign the document and did not obtain an exit permit.

2. In June 1990, B., a resident of Tul Karem, sustained five shots while an operation of special IDF units took place in proximity to his place of residence. Seriously injured, he was first taken for interrogation and only later transferred to a medical center inside Israel. His spine injury resulted in lower-body paralysis. B. applied to the Civil Administration requesting an exit permit for treatments in Jordan. The Civil Administration made issuing a permit conditional on a requirement that B. would sign a document that obliged him not to return to the West Bank for a period of two years. B. refused to sign the document. He has been prevented from leaving the Occupied Palestinian Territories ever since.

3. PHR-I received a letter from the office of the legal department of the Civil Administration dated September 24, 1990, in response to a request for a permit on behalf of patient C., who sought medical treatment abroad and was refused exit. In the letter, Officer Nava Mantsur stated that "should she submit a request to exit the area for a period of a full consecutive year, and upon providing the appropriate document,

our position in her case will be reconsidered." A similar letter was also received on February 24, 1991, in response to a request for a patient's exit permit, this time stating that the person's exit permit was to be approved, provided that he would spend a period of at least eighteen months abroad from the day of his departure.

4. D., from the area of Bethlehem, had repeatedly requested exit permits since 1988 for medical treatments abroad and was denied. The Civil Administration made his permit conditional on an obligation to not return for a period of five years. The case was brought to PHR-I in March 1990.

5. E., a student from the small village Idna in the West Bank, requested an exit permit for the purpose of attending medical school in Romania. Israeli secret services warned her that she could not obtain an exit permit unless she signed a document obliging her not to return to the West Bank for a period of five years. The case was related as oral testimony to PHR-I in February 1990.

It should be emphasized here that forced self-exile, like the curfew and closure methods used by the IDF from the very beginning of the occupation, was not a new method. It had been nevertheless previously imposed in a quite selective and exclusive manner. The notable innovations in the transition period of the early 1990s were the sophisticated way in which the regime implicated its subjects in their own exile and the widespread and indiscriminate use of the regime's monopoly over the means of movement as a tool for population destabilization. Forced self-exile was nevertheless not a coherent policy. For instance, there are counterintuitive discrepancies in the length of exile. Periods of self-exile range broadly from eighteen months to five years, usually from the day of intended departure. Young men from cities such as Jenin and Tul Karem, where serious clashes with the IDF took place during the first intifada (cases 1 and 2) were required to leave for "only" two to three years, while a period of five years was proposed for a young female student from a small, peaceful village (case 5). The only consistent information in all cases seems to be a document that persons were required to sign. The existence of this paper trail is confirmed in the letters PHR-I received from the legal advisor to the Civil Administration office (September 24, 1990, and February 24, 1991, case 3) and in a more recent sample of a pledge of obligation found in the records of the Association for Civil Rights Israel. [See document on pages 308–309.]

The system of authorizations for internal movement had just taken its first steps while this was happening on the external borders of the Occupied Palestinian Territories. One of the earliest indications I found in the PHR-I archive of authorizations for domestic movement involved special permits issued for all Occupied Palestinian Territories medical staff members. The officer in charge of the health unit at the Civil Administration responded to PHR-I's report on restrictions

AN UNDERTAKING OF A PALESTINIAN STUDENT not to return to the Territories for two years in exchange for being permitted to go abroad to study.

התחייבות

1. אני _____ , ת"ז _____ , מתחייב בזאת לצאת את איזור יהודה
והשומרון (לחלן), "יהאזורים) וכן את שטחי מדינת ישראל ואיזור חבל עזה, לרבות
השטחים שבשליטת הפתפ'חה הפלסטינית, ולא לחזור אליהם עד לסיום לימודיי, ובכל
מקרה לתקופה שלא תפחת משנתיים מיום יציאתי מן האיזור, לפי המאוחר ביניהם.

2. ידוע לי ואני מסכים לכך, כי התחייבותי זו, על פרטיה, מתנאה ותנאי לכך שיותר לי לצאת
מן האיזור, ואלמלא הסכמתי לתנאי זה - לא היה ניתן לי לצאת את האיזור.

3. הנני מתחייב שלא לעסוק בפעילות תבלנית ו/או חבלנית ו/או בעלולה לסכן את בטחון מדינת ישראל
ו/או תושביה וכן את בטחון האיזור ו/או תושביו ו/או בטחון איזור חבל עזה ו/או
תושביו. כמו כן, הנני מתחייב לחימנע מחברות ופעילות בכל ארגון טרור ו/או בכל
ארגון שהוצא מחוץ לחוק באיזור.

4. הנני מבין ומסכים, כי, יציאתי מן האיזור וחזרתי לאיזור לאחר סיום לימודיי יהיו אך
ורק דרך מעבר הגבול גשר אלנבי.

5. ידוע לי, כי אם אפר את חחותחייבותיי המפורטות לעיל, לא תותר יציאתי מן האיזור
בעתיד, ואחיה צפוי לעמשים וקבועים בחוק.

14 - 9 - 2004

_____   _____
החתימה .   התאריך .

c4ε / 9 / 1ε

Undertaking

1. I _____ , I.D. Number. _____ , hereby undertake to leave the area of Judea and Samaria (hereafter: "the area") and the territory of the State of Israel and the Gaza Strip, including the areas under the control of the Palestinian Council, and not to return to them until the end of my studies, and in any event for a period not less than two years from the day I leave the area, whichever is later.

2. I am aware and I agree that this undertaking and the particulars set forth herein constitute a condition for my being permitted to leave the area, and had I not agreed to this condition, I would not be allowed to leave the area.

3. I undertake not to engage in hostile activity that is liable to endanger the security of the State of Israel and/or its residents and the security of the area and/or its residents or the security of the Gaza Strip and/or its residents. Also, I undertake to refrain from being a member and engaging in activity in any terrorist organization and/or any organization that has been banned in the area.

4. I understand and agree that I shall leave the area, and return to the area at the end of my studies, only via the Allenby Bridge border crossing.

5. I am aware that, if I breach my aforesaid undertakings, I shall not be permitted to leave the area in the future, and that I shall be subject to punishment as specified by law.

14 September 2004

_____   _____

Date   Signature on medical staff movements and the lack of access to medical care under curfews on December 4, 1989: "Contrary to PHR's irrelevant and untruthful report…at the beginning of the uprising in Gaza two years ago, special movement in curfew permits have been distributed to all workers of the local health office, numbering 1700, including physicians, nurses and administrative workers."[47] Evidently, because of sustained curfews and closures, the need arose to produce special curfew permits facilitating the movements of this professional sector.

Gradually, blank "humanitarian" movement authorizations were replaced by ad hoc "emergency" permits, yet these exceptions at some point became indistinguishable from other types of permits and frequently did not help those in need of medical assistance. My impression from studying the evolution of the regime of Israeli movement authorizations and restrictions from 1987 to 1993 is that the Civil Administration was scrambling to turn itself into a comprehensive and direct administrative mechanism for the supervision of movement. Significantly, this process of gravitation toward tighter monitoring of everyone's whereabouts had already occurred *before* the Oslo agreement had sealed it with the establishment of the District Coordination Offices. Leaving aside for a moment the institutional dynamic of the Civil Administration, what is curious about the cases of forced self-exile is that they reveal a semirandom deportation method that required no use of explicit violence on the part of the state and that was designed for the population at large. This particular method was only semirandom, since it actually targeted the needy, the sick, and the injured. While previously, political leaders and people suspected of engaging in activities hostile to the state were likely candidates for draconian measures of expulsion, during the transition period from 1987 to 1993, the entire population of the Occupied Territories became equally "suspect."

New methods of deportation, expulsion, and separation or isolation through arbitrary restrictions have developed continuously since then. In May 2006, the Israeli High Court of Justice rejected appeals of a legal ban on family unification in Israel. As a result of an amendment to the Israeli Citizenship Law of 2003, all Occupied Palestinian Territories residents categorically are refused the ability to apply for permits to reside in or obtain civic status in Israel, even when they are married to Israeli citizens. Similar restrictions now also apply to Palestinians carrying foreign passports. Palestinians wishing to enter or exit the Occupied Palestinian Territories who have no passport, or who have a European or American passport, for that matter, can all expect to be banned regardless. Israel in effect imposes a double ban on Palestinian family unification. It does so by controlling Palestinian immigration and residency status on both sides of the Green Line.

Collective and individually tailored bans are staples of regimes of separation. The banning of persons was a daily routine in the restricted universe of apartheid, and here, as well, the banning involved both restrictions on internal movement and external exile. Just as a skewed framing of the parameters of the nation-state severely destabilized the Palestinian population, skewed framing in South Africa enabled the apartheid regime to turn large portions of the population into exiles of one kind or the other.

Based on the Riotous Assemblies Act of 1930, together with the Suppression of Communism Act of 1950, later again renamed the Internal Security Act in 1976, the apartheid regime established its authority to issue "banning orders." Specific movement controls were tailored to specific categories of people. Ban orders were particularly used to curtail activists in the black townships. Measures confined certain people to a particular area, forcing them to report periodically to the police. Another method, house arrest, confined a banned person to a place of residence. Ban orders were valid for a period of five years and could be renewed. The regime crackdown on black leaders most infamously took the form of assassinations, death penalties, cruel practices of torture, confinement, and prolonged imprisonment. Yet for those who escaped actual imprisonment, other restrictions of movement applied. To some, through the Departure from the Union Regulation Act of 1955, the government offered an alternative to imprisonment, which was to leave the country with an "exit permit" once the secretary of the interior has established that they intended to leave the country permanently. In some cases, the state refused to issue passports to agitators such as the famous playwright Athol Fugard. Some were handed instead exit permits. In the usual euphemistic fashion, the exit permit procedure actually was an entry ban.[48] Not granting permission to return, it sent people off into forced exile.

South Africans with exit permits were for the most part the elite few and were fortunate in that they received political asylum outside South Africa. This mechanism was thus a relatively orderly and transparent form of imposing exile. In 1983, Amnesty International reported cases in which people who held pass books and South African birth certificates were held incommunicado for periods of up to twelve months. They were forced to confess that they were aliens, and the regime ordered their deportation to Zimbabwe. From 1983 to 1984, twenty thousand alleged citizens of Mozambique were deported from South Africa this way. According to Amnesty International, a considerable number of them had no country of origin other than South Africa.[49]

The difference between these two methods of deportation is between those who had lost their South African status because of activities perceived as hostile to the regime and those who the regime did not recognize as South Africans in the first place. In the first example, individual passports were denied. In the second, entire groups were summarily ejected. It is worth noting here that the apartheid regime did not see its population problem as a problem confined to the boundaries of South Africa alone. Its impact on the entire sub-Saharan region in terms of the control of population flows as well as in terms of economic, demographic, and territorial gerrymandering time and again transgressed South Africa's colonial boundaries, the prolonged occupation of Namibia being a conspicuous example.

Most South Africans, however, experienced exile and displacement at home. Apartheid did not simply ban people. It ensured that any relation they might have to their environment would be made neither stable nor permanent. No brief account of the phenomenon can do justice to its overwhelming complexity and magnitude.[50] Permits required for residence in townships specified who may or may not visit residents. One also could be endorsed out, crucially, from any peripheral township, not simply from the so-called prescribed (urban) areas. Special powers were given to township administrators to expel from the township the "idle or undesirable," the "redundant," and those "detrimental to the maintenance of peace and order."[51] Adding to a maze of administrative decrees, there were the complications stemming from various statuses of pseudocitizenship and noncitizenship. There were those who remained citizens of South Africa while also obtaining citizenship in the "self-governing" Bantustans, in contrast to those who had been denationalized and who became citizens only of the "independent states." Children born after the date of independence of their respective Bantustans and hence were assimilated to the position of "foreign blacks" sometimes had parents with South African citizenship. Single workers from rural areas who were forced into hostel accommodations in townships acquired the status of "migrants" — alien or foreign workers. In 1984, the South African government allowed 355,560 workers from neighboring countries to enter. They, too, were subject to pass laws and racial and administrative classifications, but nevertheless remained foreign. The categories of alien (noncitizenship status) and migrant worker (labor status) applied to them, as well as to some eight million born South Africans in a clearly intentional conflation.

"Dompas," says Zackie Achmat, a famous anti-apartheid and AIDS activist, "were legal documents which made me a foreigner in my own country."[52] While all individuals had in one way or another to deal with the tyranny of paper persecution on a daily basis, the experience of forced removals, the "exodus," as it was called, of entire communities, differed considerably from one place to the other. Experiments in the actual removal and reconstitution of communities and their environment succeeded to inflict social and economic mayhem in some cases more than in others. Various sorts of methods and degrees of violence, coercion, or persuasion were used to dislocate different groups. Communities mounted varying degrees of resistance, although in many cases, particularly in squatters' camps, people also "moved willingly…because they could have their own homes in the new townships" or simply because they would be deemed qualified by the authorities to live at these new locations

Nevertheless, the dislocation and disorganization of the population of South Africa was broadly envisioned, with the result of displacing millions internally. What made the coinage of "separate development" that sanctioned it, in an attempt to sustain an illusion of the spatial political integrity of a white South Africa, so strong, despite its evident irrationality and unworkability? Not only were the Bantustans widely known by the early 1970s to be unviable political-economic units, but influx-control and pass laws also failed to purge the urban population, at the same time dispossessing rural populations of land. Both "separation" and "development" were bound to fail to produce independent, separate nation-states. But, was this really the intention?

First as the head of the BAD (Bantu Administration Department), apartheid's most infamous executioner, Henrik Verwoerd, already had begun orchestrating mass campaigns of forced removals in the late 1950s. Converting ideological proclamations into practical force, Verwoerd was the quintessential apartheid "bulldozer." He advocated a strong republic that need not worry too much about the economic or political viability of territories or populations. He disregarded, for example, policy recommendations arguing that in order for separate development actually to work, it would be necessary to commit huge resources for the development of the Bantustans. The rhetorical ploys of apartheid indeed called for each citizen to harness a "personal commitment" to "widen your horizons to become nation builders instead of township builders."[53] Yet to put it bluntly, the viability that Verwoerd and apartheid architects worried about was not primarily of any of the "Bantu" nations. Sustaining the Republic of South Africa was the goal, which in the context of South Africa meant a long-term commitment to the political destruction of those nations. It could not have been as hegemonic an idea, surviving as long as it did, if the ruling elite, and Verwoerd most memorably, had failed to convince citizen constituencies that this program, as costly, complicated, and morally abject as it was in the eyes of the rest of the world, was absolutely necessary for the survival of their polity. This nation-building project turned populations in South Africa into stateless people at the mercy of a hostile foreign government.

The principle of population destabilization through misframing or skewed framing in the form of forced (internal and external) exile is the operational side of separation with control. Normally, the expelled are no longer monitored by a regime and are simply taken out of its frame. More frequently, though, in a regime of separation, the function of domestic expulsion, banning, or confinement is to mark people as outside the frame and still to bind them coercively to the misframing sovereign. In multiple ways, both individually and collectively, the undesired population must be reined in by a regime that at the same time attempts to sever any sustained relation it has to its political space. As a consequence, both individuals and communities are under a chronic threat of destabilization through external and internal exile, which more often than not becomes their actual predicament. This feature of a separation regime may or may not have the potential to turn into something else, such as a full-fledged regime of expulsion begetting a more conventional version of ethnic cleansing or even mass (as opposed to chronic) killings and genocide. In light of this principle, we can look back and reflect at forced self-exile in Israel/Palestine during the transition period from 1987 to 1993 as not a particularly coherent, rather low-key, secretive experiment in population destabilization.

It may be, as the South African political analyst Steven Friedman is inclined to believe, that Israel, replicating the high apartheid of the 1960s, had entered its Verwoerdian moment in the twenty-first century, with Ariel Sharon as prime minister and his plans for so-called "unilateral separation."[54] One may be taken by the analogy or reject it outright as an anachronism. Israel's capacity to conceive and to implement programs of population destabilization is, in any case, apparent. A total onslaught on an entire group in an attempt to wipe it out or to oust it from certain territories permanently is carefully avoided. Population problems are taken care of by designing unique, sometimes discrete spatial, administrative, and demographic measures. To accede momentarily to the temptation of the analogy, in contemporary Israel/Palestine, as under apartheid, out groups are offered the choice of actual imprisonment, spatial confinement, self-exile, or internal displacement—all of which point in the direction of creating conditions for a near political death without actually having to kill or expel en masse.

REGIMES OF SEPARATION AS A POLITICAL TYPE

Describing the principles of separation with control by which a regime of separation rules masses of disenfranchised populations obviously invites a more nuanced analysis. Of course, we must then look not only at generic features, but perhaps even more suggestively, at breakdowns, the inevitable systematic failures plaguing this implausible and complex system of domination. The challenge in this regard is to advance a phenomenology and typology of regimes of separation so that the features identified here do not turn into a rigid or arbitrary model bowing to a set of predetermined laws. In addition, one of the difficult questions that this analysis raises is the following: Are there other local, regional, or global instances of regimes of separation, especially recalling Richmond and Balibar and their global or European apartheid thesis? To be sure, this is a highly pertinent question, especially considering the operation of border regimes elsewhere, but one that must be left largely unanswered here.

What I hope to have made sharper by analyzing the regime of separation as a distinct political type is the immediate here and now: the inescapable realities of separation in contemporary Israel/Palestine and the way they have come about. While the geopolitical horizon in Israel/Palestine is uncertain, the already irreversible human and environmental damage of the apparatus of separation with control is not. In the aftermath of the "disengagement" from the Gaza Strip that took place in August 2005, one witnessed the intensification of the use of war apparatuses against civilians, along with a sharp disinvestment of responsibility for the condition created there for a besieged population. Refusing to give up its monopoly over movement, the state of Israel has shown no intention of relinquishing its prerogative as a sovereign over the Gaza Strip. The administrative dictatorship grinds on. The aggressive campaign of the politico-security establishment to continue on the trajectory of separation with control indicates what lies ahead. Pondering whether this strategy is indeed believed to be the most viable for the long haul, I interviewed Reserve General Dani Rothschild, former coordinator of government operations in the territories in his high-tech company office in Kfar Saba, a town to the west of the Separation Wall, which fully encircles the adjacent city of Qalqilya in the Occupied Palestinian Territories with its garish camp towers. He indeed contends:

> Gaza is the model for the future. Why do I need to take care of Qalqilya? We are not inside—we just make sure that [Palestinians] do not enter Israel.... When someone is willing to commit suicide, you cannot deter, you can only block the attempt by halting movement. Freedom of movement is a security issue. After Oslo, we are no longer in control, except for security issues, and movement is one of them. Checkpoints are necessary for security and information, to help us capture suicide bombers. Rabin at the time [of Oslo] did not give up an inch of control over passages and border crossings and rightfully so, otherwise we would have already had al Qaeda in Tel Aviv.[55]

By this logic, in order to defend Israel from al Qaeda, Kfar Saba must continue to strangle the neighboring town of Qalqilya, without taking responsibility for those caged in what once was a thriving commercial center and had now become a ghost town. Rothschild, a labor-oriented ex-general, is genuinely convinced that Israel wants to end the occupation this way. Enforced separation often generates euphoric bravado from the politico-security establishment. High echelons of the IDF consider "what is happening on the ground" as "almost ideal." Thanks to the Separation Wall and the border matrix, for instance, the "quality of intelligence" is better, even more so than in the pre-Oslo days.[56] The reference to the "quality of intelligence" indicates that people confined to "land cells" in the Occupied Palestinian Territories are forced into a sufficient degree of submission and compliance to the apparatuses of surveillance and control. At the same time, a semblance of normality, security, and spatial continuity is artificially, yet effectively manufactured in Israel proper, rarely disturbed by the other inescapable reality — chronic, indiscriminate political violence.

I have not been concerned here with the question of the sameness and apparent identity between the two cases — apartheid in South Africa and separation in Israel/Palestine. This is no mere posture to dissociate myself from the prolific comparative and countercomparative discourse. The aim is rather to make a contribution to the development of a more comprehensive and politically sound appreciation of the revolution of the 1990s in Israel/Palestine, in part by focusing the analytical lens on aspects of apartheid often less known outside South Africa. The philosopher Cornelius Castoriadis makes a convincing argument for taking seriously the fundamental alterity of societies. He calls what institutes society and holds it together the "magma of social imaginary significations." Society is "the work of the instituting imaginary," and it "creates itself as a form (*eidos*) and each time as a singular form," hence: "In its 'materiality,' or 'concreteness,' this or that institution as found in two different societies may appear identical or highly similar; however, this apparent material identity is each time *immersed* in a different magma of different significations, and this suffices to transform such an apparent identity into an actual alterity from the socio-historical point of view."[57]

The flow of the magma of significations is neither predetermined nor replicable. Not to be confused with an enclosed, hermeneutic system of "representations" or "ideas," the magma of significations and effects of which Castoriadis speaks enables us to address a society's "way of living itself and of living the world and life itself."[58] Identifiable organizing and organized forms define every society as it exists and as it is constantly instituted, but these are never permanent or absolute. Society, in Castoriadis's formulation, is under a permanent threat that its "social edifice of significations" will collapse. And thus, "the enemy against which the defenses of society are feeblest is its own instituting imaginary, its own creativity."[59] To put it plainly, the potential for change exists in every society and social order, and change is always a product of the society undergoing it.

These ideas resonate well in the context of Israel/Palestine and apartheid, as the following concluding observations should make clear. What may appear similar in the materiality and concreteness of our cases in point is, from a sociohistorical point of view, not comparable. The reason is that both societies are and have been immersed in entirely different magma of social-imaginary significations at different places and points in time. "Separation," the organizing political trope in Israel/Palestine since the 1990s, is not what "separate development" meant in South Africa in the 1960s or a mere repetition of apartheid. Separation is instead a complex set of hegemonic practices and effects that create quite peculiar inescapable realities that are relevant only in Israel/Palestine. That said, it is not difficult to discern the reasons why the shadow of apartheid looms large over contemporary Israel/Palestine, a fact that does not escape even chauvinist defenders of the Jewish state. Indeed, on a broader social scale, the general outline of the existing order in Israel/Palestine begs for the analogy—separation without sovereignty, the occupation and disenfranchisment of a declared inferior "race," and the forcible separation and isolation of people. While there is no reason to skirt around the shadow, there is some urgency in the need to dispel its mystique.

By introducing the concept of "regimes of separation," I have attempted to show that even though concrete ways of doing things and their material effects are not comparable, it is possible and useful to analyze certain phenomenological aspects as belonging to a distinct political type. By "political type," I mean that certain hegemonic orders share identifiable operational principles and mechanisms for the production of, in our case, deviant political authority. The old apartheid regime in South Africa and the regime in contemporary Israel/Palestine thus belong to a family of democratically enabled dictatorships whose organizing principle is the principle of fundamental mass disenfranchisement through misframing. We are fortunate to be able to say that fundamental mass disenfranchisement through misframing in South Africa is a thing of the past. But, rather than idealizing South Africa's transition to democracy, it is more expedient to study how its socioeconomic-spatial pathology came about. It enables us to think about Israel/Palestine in terms of a grand experiment in the redefinition of political space and in terms of the production of conditions for the near political death of populations.

There is no clear teleological trajectory to the experiments now underway in Israel/Palestine. Apartheid began to unravel from within once the obsession with separation gave way to the acknowledgement of interdependence, once its enormous apparatus of control began to crumble and lose its practical plausibility, and last, but not least, once it became clear that maintaining political power was no longer necessary for keeping much of the socioeconomic order intact. Indeed, despite the swift evaporation of the legal-executive forms of apartheid, the new South Africa, now entering a second postapartheid decade, to a significant degree remains caught in the noose of the old. The ravages of apartheid continue well into this postcolonial, neoliberal epoch. Fundamental mass disenfranchisment is still the lot of millions, mandated not least by the ubiquity of market forces, which some South African revolutionaries turned ruling echelons now valorize. This is partly why it is quite senseless to speak of South Africa as a model for a future "solution" in Israel/Palestine, either in the form of Israelis and Palestinians finding their Mandela or in the form of a one-state solution. Once again, we must keep in mind that a very different magma is seething in the political volcano called Israel/Palestine. If, as Castoriadis says, the enemy of a society is indeed its own instituting imaginary and magma of significations, then society in Israel/Palestine will have to find its own creative ways of collapsing the social edifice of significations on which the current regime of separation depends, reinstituting itself in a new, less objectionable order. The likelihood that this will happen in the foreseeable future is not great. The more implausible the current regime becomes, however, the greater the prospects are that in its already apparent failure, the failure to hegemonize a political community completely, it will eventually be thrown onto the ash heap of history.

NOTES

I wish to extend many thanks to P. W. Zuidhof, Koni Benson, Suren Pillay, Adi Ophir, and Michal Givoni for their invaluable comments. I also thank participants of Van Leer workshops in Jerusalem, Israel, and the history workshop at University of the Western Cape, Cape Town, South Africa where I presented earlier versions of this paper.

1   Anne McClintock, *Imperial Leather: Race, Gender, and Sexuality in the Colonial Conquest* (New York: Routledge, 1995).

2   Even seriously researched, "good" comparisons tend to have a single premise, which is also their necessary conclusion. Usually they negatively argue that Israel is or is becoming an apartheid state and therefore should be censured by the international community. Some comparisons find a positive side to the situation: Israel/Palestine could become a "new" South Africa. Reconciliation is possible if Israelis (!) and Palestinians find their "Mandela" or if a one-state solution course is chosen. See, for example, Heribert Adam and Kogila Moodley, *Seeking Mandela: Peacemaking between Israelis and Palestinians* (Philadelphia: Temple University Press, 2005) and Virginia Tilley, *The One-State Solution: A Breakthrough for Peace in the Israeli-Palestinian Deadlock* (Ann Arbor: University of Michigan Press, 2005). Popular, activist and sociopolitical discourse puts the comparison to use to depict current conditions in occupied Palestine (for example, the "apartheid wall" or "apartheid roads," in virtually all human rights reports published on Palestine), while more resolution-oriented projections tend to come from legal, conflict-resolution, or diplomatic circles concerned with the viability of a two-state solution, for example, Jimmy Carter's *Palestine: Peace, Not Apartheid* (New York: Simon and Schuster, 2006).

3   To the classical formulations of Weber and Marx on the state monopolizing the legitimate

use of force and means of production, John Torpey adds the idea that state formation has necessitated the expropriation of legitimate means of movement. Torpey tracks the development of nineteenth-century European national and international travel documents in John C. Torpey, *The Invention of the Passport: Surveillance, Citizenship, and the State* (Cambridge: Cambridge University Press, 2000).

4   Ian Lustick, *Unsettled States, Disputed Lands: Britain and Ireland, France and Algeria, Israel and the West Bank-Gaza* (Ithaca, NY: Cornell University Press, 1993).

5   Etienne Balibar, "What Is a Border?" in *Politics and the Other Scene,* trans. Christine Jones, James Swenson, and Chris Turner (London: Verso, 2002), p. 84.

6   Richmond offers an empirical sociological analysis of racism and immigration regimes. See Anthony H. Richmond, *Global Apartheid: Refugees, Racism, and the New World Order* (New York: Oxford University Press, 1994), p. 206.

7   Nancy Fraser, *Reframing Justice,* Spinoza Lectures, Department of Philosophy, University of Amsterdam (Assen: Koninklijke Van Gorcum, 2005), pp. 48, 45.

8   Michael Mann, *The Dark Side of Democracy: Explaining Ethnic Cleansing* (Cambridge: Cambridge University Press, 2005).

9   Fraser, *Reframing Justice,* p. 46.

10   Disenfranchisement is used here not in its "weak" sense—that is, when the right to vote is denied. I use it in the "strong" sense to depict a lack of basic conditions for the political, when a meaningful membership in one or any political community is deliberately made impossible. In recent years, residents of the Occupied Palestinian Territories exercised a "right to vote" under conditions imposed by belligerent military occupation. A right to vote under military occupation does not terminate the condition of profound disenfranchisement.

11   Giorgio Agamben, *Homo Sacer: Sovereign Power and Bare Life,* trans. Daniel Heller-Roazen (Stanford, CA: Stanford University Press, 1998); Giorgio Agamben, *Remnants of Auschwitz: The Witness and the Archive,* trans. Daniel Heller-Roazen (New York: Zone Books, 2000).

12   A good reference for the early names for the department is in Ian Evans's list of abbreviations, available on-line at http://www.escholarship.org/editions/view?docId=ft2n39n7f2&chunk.id=d0e94&toc.depth=1&toc.id=&brand=ucpress (last accessed March 3, 2009). All references mentioned on this list are relevant up to the late 1950s. In archive materials from the 1980s, the heading that appears on official letters is of the Ministry of Co-operation and Development.

13   Quoted in Deborah Posel, "Whiteness and Power in the South African Civil Service: Paradoxes of the Apartheid State," *Journal of Southern African Studies* 25, no. 1 (1999), p. 111. This article follows the internal struggle with inefficiency and dysfunction within the "administrative state" as "widening powers and responsibilities were being allocated to an increasingly less qualified or competent civil service" (p. 103).

14   The South African literature on apartheid policies has mostly dealt with the evolution of legislative and policy directives, their impact on labor, and the influence of business interests. See Douglas Hindson, *Pass Controls and the Urban African Proletariat in South Africa* (Johannesburg: Ravan Press, 1987); Deborah Posel, "Influx Control and Urban Labor Markets," in Peter Delius, Philip Bonner, and Deborah Posel (eds.), *Apartheid's Genesis 1935–1962* (Johannesburg: University of Witwatersrand Press, 1993); Elaine Unterhalter, *Forced Removals: The Division, Segregation and Control of the People of South Africa* (London: International Defense and Aid Fund for Southern Africa, 1987); Hermann Buhr Giliomee and Lawrence

Schlemmer, *Up against the Fences: Poverty, Passes, and Privilege in South Africa* (New York: St. Martin's Press, 1985).

15 Mahmood Mamdani, *Citizen and Subject: Contemporary Africa and the Legacy of Late Colonialism* (Princeton, NJ: Princeton University Press, 1996).

16 Ivan Evans, *Bureaucracy and Race: Native Administration in South Africa* (Berkeley: University of California Press, 1997), p. 95. Evans, who studied apartheid administrations and in particular the Department of Native Affairs, is convinced that "the department was more than just central to the apartheid project: the department gave apartheid its particular institutional form" (p. 17).

17 Michael Savage, "Pass Laws and the Disorganization and Reorganization of the African Population in South Africa," paper presented at the Second Carnegie Inquiry into Poverty and Development in Southern Africa, Cape Town, South Africa, April 1984, pp. 38–39.

18 Ran Greenstein, "Citizenship, Land and Political Inclusion: What Can We Learn from the Rise and Demise of Apartheid?" *Law and Government* 10, no. 1 (November 2006): pp. 117–50.

19 On the various strategies of dealing with apartheid's paper persecution, see the South Africa History Project, on-line at http://www.sahistory.org.za, an extremely useful database with chronologies of both grassroots passive and organized resistance (last accessed September 20, 2008). See also Mamphela Ramphele, *A Bed Called Home: Life in the Migrant Labor Hostels of Cape Town* (Cape Town: David Philip Publishers, 1993); Paula Meth, "Rethinking Forced Removals: Diversity and Difference," in Ronnie Donaldson and Lochner Marais (eds.), *Transforming Rural and Urban Spaces in South Africa During the 1990s: Reform, Restitution and Restructuring* (Pretoria: Africa Institute of South Africa, 2002); Koni Benson, "Still Squatting, Still Fighting: A History of African Women Mobilizing Against Forced Removals in Crossroads Cape Town, South Africa, from Apartheid to the Present," Ph.D. thesis, Department of History, University of Minnesota, forthcoming. Annual statistics and detailed information about forced removals and policy recommendations of government commissions of inquiry are available in the South Africa Survey of Race Relations volumes published by the South African Institute of Race Relations.

20 A. J. Christopher, *The Atlas of Changing South Africa,* 2nd ed. (London: Routledge, 2001), p. 238.

21 Evans studies in particular the routinization of oppression through the expansion of administrative law. *Bureaucracy and Race,* p. 18. He argues, moreover, that the imperfections of apartheid's system served its authoritarian logic.

22 Tanya Reinhart, *Israel/Palestine: How to End the War of 1948* (New York: Seven Stories Press, 2002).

23 Eban said this in an interview to the German magazine *Der Spiegel,* November 5, 1969.

24 When "separate development" was conceived in South Africa in the 1960s, it was supposed to inaugurate a new dawn of "racial peace," in the words of Dr. D. F. Malan, the first prime minister of the 1948 apartheid government. Quoted in Richmond, *Global Apartheid,* p. 207.

25 Baruch Kimmerling, *Politicide: Ariel Sharon's War against the Palestinians* (London: Verso, 2006). Kimmerling believed that Sharon's intention in crushing the second intifada was to return Palestinians to a pre-1967 state, that is, to break them as a political community once and for all so that self-determination will be out of the question for the long haul.

26 The Israeli-Palestinian Interim Agreement, September 28, 1995, The Government of Israel and the P.L.O. See Annex I, Article III, item 3. The Oslo documents are published on the Web site

of the Israeli Foreign Ministry, www.mfa.gov.il, under Foreign Relations | Key Agreements (last accessed July 23, 2008).

27   Declaration of Principles on Interim Self-Government Arrangements, September 13, 1993, The Government of Israel and the P.L.O. See Article X, Joint Israeli-Palestinian Liaison Committee.

28   Susan Hattis Rolef, "Military Government," in Susan Hattis Rolef (ed.), *Political Dictionary of the State of Israel* (New York: Macmillan, 1993), p. 221.

29   Amira Hass, *Drinking the Sea at Gaza: Days and Nights in a Land under Siege,* trans. Maxine Nunn (New York: Owl Books, 2000), p. 26.

30   Interview by the author with Shlomo Gazit, October 2004.

31   Figures are available in reports regularly published by the organization MachsomWatch. See http://www.machsomwatch.org/en (last accessed July 23, 2008). Before the outbreak of the second intifada, there were parallel Palestinian DCOs functioning alongside IDF DCOs and under the PA. Since 2000, these have largely ceased to function as a mediating subbureaucracy for the IDF.

32   The first "total closure" was imposed during the First Gulf War in 1991. The first suicide bombing attack on a bus took place in Afula on April 6, 1994. More information is available on the Web site of the Israeli Ministry of Foreign Affairs: www.mfa.gov.il, under Suicide and Other Bombing Attacks in Israel Since the Declaration of Principles (September 1993), found under Terrorism | Terrorism before 2000 (last accessed July 23, 2008).

33   Pass-law persecution practices and imprisonment statistics are described in great detail in Kevin Boyle, *South Africa: Imprisonment under Pass Laws* (New York: Amnesty International, 1986). One particularly egregious practice was to transfer prisoners of pass violations to the custody of white farmers as forced labor to pay back their fines or in exchange for prison terms.

34   Black Sash, *Everybody's Guide to Pass Laws,* approximately dating to the late 1960s or early 1970s.

35   IDF Civil Administration, "Judea and Samaria under Israeli Administration." These reports are to be found in the Civil Administration file at the Moshe Dayan Center for Middle Eastern and African Studies Library, Tel Aviv University.

36   Shlomo Gazit, *Trapped Fools: Thirty Years of Israeli Policy in the Territories* (Or Yehuda: Zmora-Bitan Publishers, 1999) (in Hebrew), p. 49.

37   Physicians for Human Rights, memo on curfew days in Anabta, January–March 1991, available on-line at http://physiciansforhumanrights.org/library/documents/reports/hroh-developments.pdf (last accessed September 20, 2008).

38   *Yediot Achronot,* March 4, 1993 (in Hebrew).

39   *Yediot Achronot,* March 10, 1993 (in Hebrew; my translation).

40   Spokesman Office of the Coordinator of Government Activities in the Territories, February 22, 1999, quoted in B'Tselem, *Human Rights in the Territories Quarterly* 2 (March 1999), p. 7 (in Hebrew).

41   Christopher, *The Atlas of Changing South Africa.*

42   Document on Legal Expense for the year April 1, 1969 to March 31, 1970. Black Sash Athlone Advice Office.

43   Black Sash Athlone Advice Office report, February 1973.

44   PHR-I has more than eleven hundred and fifty members today. The organization runs a mobile clinic in the Occupied Territories in collaboration with the Palestinian Medical Relief

Society and an open clinic in Tel Aviv that provides services for those who have no legal status in Israel and therefore no access to medical treatment. I owe much of the inspiration for this study to my work at PHR-I dealing with the bureaucracy of the occupation in the late 1990s and to Dr. Ruchama Marton, its founder. I thank the PHR-I staff for the generous support during my research at the archive. For more information, see http://www.phr.org.il/phr/.

45 The entry "Military Administration" in *The Political Dictionary of the State of Israel* actually confirms that especially males aged twenty to thirty have been unofficially required not to return for nine months from the time of their exit. Susan Hattis Rolef, "Military Administration," in Rolef (ed.), *Political Dictionary of the State of Israel*, p. 234

46 Pelleg Sryck also knows of a detainee who was forced to sign an agreement that, upon return, he could be again put under administrative detention. Interview by the author with Peleg Sryck, October 11, 2005.

47 Classified letter, dated December 4, 1989, sent by Civil Administration Health Officer David Levanon to the assistant of the Minister of Health, Dror Nagal, in reference to PHR-I's report of October 3, 1989. A copy of this letter was sent to the office of Itzhak Rabin, then minister of defense. (My translation).

48 John Dugard, *Human Rights and the South African Legal Order* (Princeton, NJ: Princeton University Press, 1978).

49 The figures are quoted in Boyle, *South Africa: Imprisonment under Pass Laws*.

50 See also the account in Bernard Magubane, *The Road to Democracy in South Africa, Volume 1: 1960–1970* (Cape Town: Zebra Press, South African Democracy Education Fund, 2004), p. 19.

51 These were legal categories that were specified in pass law stipulations.

52 Achmat has been campaigning for the last decade against the South African government AIDS policies. In Cape Town, January 2006, I watched his film on law under apartheid and in South Africa today, *It's My Life,* with the Transregional Center for Democracy seminar participants. The quote is from this documentary.

53 M. C. Botha, minister of Bantu administration and development in the Verwoerd government in the 1960s. Quoted in Magubane, *The Road to Democracy in South Africa,* p. 40.

54 Interview with Steven Friedman, January 13, 2006. Friedman is an ardent supporter of the Israel-as-apartheid analogy or comparison: "If you want to understand how the [Israeli-Palestinian] conflict is going to unfold, you have to understand the South African case as an analyst. Let's get the red herrings out. If you are looking for a logic and at a trajectory of a society, it is much the same. The analogy enables you to know what to look for."

55 Interview with General (Res.) Dani Rothchild, October 21, 2006.

56 Amos Harel, "What to Do with Positive Statistics" *Ha'aretz,* August 13, 2004 (in Hebrew).

57 Cornelius Castoriadis, *Philosophy, Politics, Autonomy,* trans. David Ames Curtis (New York: Oxford University Press, 1991), p. 147.

58 *Ibid.,* p. 154.

59 *Ibid.,* p. 153.

MOVEMENT PERMITS INSIDE THE WEST BANK In a report published in August 2007, B'Tselem lists nine types of permits for movement inside the West Bank: an encircle-ment-crossing permit, which is given sparingly and enables the holder to leave an area under siege; a humanitarian permit, which allows the holder to leave an area under siege to receive medical treatment; a movement permit for passenger vehicles and another permit for the movement of commercial vehicles, both of which autho-rize movement in certain areas; a movement permit for public-transportation vehicles, needed to operate taxis and buses; a permit given to a permanent resident of the Seam Zone; a day permit to enter the Seam Zone, given selectively to providers of services and to first-degree relatives of residents of the enclaves; a permit to enter the Seam Zone for farming or work purposes; and a permit to enter the Jordan Val-ley, issued to selected persons to provide services and to relatives of residents of the valley. In addition, Palestinians living in the West Bank must obtain a magnetic card if they wish to enter Israel and obtain approval to cross into Gaza. According to figures supplied by the Civil Administration, in 2006, it issued 423,116 permits to leave the West Bank to enter Israel or cross to the Gaza Strip, 40,406 encirclement-crossing permits, and 23,485 Seam Zone movement permits. The criteria for refusing to grant a movement permit and the number of requests that are rejected are generally not made public.

המנהל האזרחי איו״ש
לשכת ראש המנהל
טלפון : 02-9977001/2/3
פקס : 02-9977341
דובר - 1182
כ׳ באלול התשס״ג
17 בספטמבר 2003

המנהל האזרחי איו״ש
לשכת ראש המנהל

לכבוד
יעל שטיין, עו״ד
בצלם

הנדון: **בקשה לפי חוק חופש המידע: היתרי תנועה בתוך שטח הגדה המערבית**

הריני לאשר קבלת מכתבך מתאריך 24 באוגוסט 2003. להלן תשובות
לשאלותייך.

1. המנהל האזרחי החל להנפיק היתרי מעבר בכתר בתאריך 21/1/02. הרעיון
נולד מכורח המציאות הביטחונית המורכבת, המחייבת הטלת כתרים
מתמשכת. בעקבות הקושי שנוצר בתנועות התושבים הפלסטינים, ובייחוד
בתנועות לצרכים הומניטריים, הוחלט להקל על המעבר באמצעות הנפקת
היתרי מעבר בכתר.

2. להלן סוגי ההיתרים בכתר :

א. הומניטרי רפואי
ב. עובדי מנהל אזרחי
ג. אספקת מזון
ד. פינוי אשפה
ה. אחזקת תשתיות
ו. עובד דת
ז. עובד ארגון בינלאומי
ח. מורים
ט. וטרינר
י. גז ודלק
יא. דואר
יב. סוחר
יג. צרכים אישיים
יד. עו״ד
טו. ביקור אסיר
טז. בחינות בגרות
יז. בכיר ברשות הפלסטינית.

Civil Administration Judea and Samaria
Office of the Head of the Administration
Telephone: 02-9977001/2/3
Fax: 02-9977341
Spokesperson—1182
20 Elul 5673
17 September 2003

Civil Administration Judea and Samaria
Office of the Head of the Administration

Ms. Yael Stein, Attorney
B'Tselem

Re: **Request under the Freedom of Information Act: Movement permits inside the West Bank**

I acknowledge receipt of your letter of 24 August 2003. The answers to your questions follow.

1. The Civil Administration began to issue encirclement-crossing permits on 21 January 2002. The idea was necessitated by the complex security situation, which requires imposition of protracted encirclements. As a result of the difficulty that was created with respect to movement of Palestinian residents, especially to meet humanitarian needs, it was decided to ease crossing by granting encirclement-crossing permits.

2. The types of encirclement-crossing permits are as follows:
   A. Medical humanitarian
   B. Civil Administration employees
   C. Food supply
   D. Garbage disposal
   E. Infrastructure maintenance
   F. Religious-affairs employee
   G. International organization employee
   H. Teachers
   I. Veterinarian
   J. Gas and fuel
   K. Mail
   L. Merchant
   M. Personal needs
   N. Attorney
   O. Visiting a prisoner
   P. Matriculation exams
   Q. Senior official of the Palestinian Authority

3. נשיאת היתר תנועה בכתר' אינה נדרשת כל אימת שתושב האזור מבקש לנוע בתחומו, אלא רק בכניסתו ויציאתו מהעיים הנמצאות אותה עת תחת כתר.

4. ככלל, חייתר נדרש מגיל 16 ומעלה, אולם טווחי הגילאים משתנים מעת לעת בהתאם לצרכים הביטחוניים.

5. החיתר ניתן לתקופות שונות, בהתאם לצרכים. התקופות נעות מיום אחד ועד שלושה חודשים.

6. בכל הגזרות קיימת נגישות לחלון קבלת חקהל במפקדות התיאום והקישור. בנוסף, ניתן לפנות למשרדי הקישור הפלסטינים הפועלים מול משרדי התיאום והקישור של המנהל האזרחי, ודרכם לקבל היתרים.

7. כל בקשה להיתר נבחנת לגופה על ידי גורמי מפקדות התיאום והקישור הרלוונטית.

8. כל בקשה להיתר נבחנת לפי מטרת ההיתר המבוקש ובהתאם לשיקולי ביטחון הנובעים מהמציאות הדינמית באזור.

9. היתר בכתר ניתן תוך וזן קצר, מספר דקות עד מספר שעות. במידה ונדרשת בדיקה מעמיקה בעניינו של תושב, ייתכן וההיתר יתקבל לאחר מספר ימים.

10. במידה ובקשת התושב נדחית, נמסר לו כי בקשתו אינה עומדת בקריטריונים. במידה ומדובר בסירוב על רקע ביטחוני או פלילי, נמסר כך לתושב.

11. במקרים המתאימים, ניתן לפנות למשרד היועץ המשפטי לשם בחינה מחדש של הבקשה.

12. להלן נתונים על היתרים שהונפקו ע"פ גזרות ושנים:

סה"כ	יריחו	חברון	בית לחם	רמאללה	שכם	טול כרם	ג'נין	השנה
21545	984	4727	2383	10676	1868	446	461	2002
56751	2067	6213	7850	27538	7351	3359	2377	2003
78301	3051	10940	10233	38214	9219	3805	2838	סה"כ

בברכה,

טליה סומך, סגן
דוברת המנהל האזרחי

3. Holding an encirclement-crossing permit is not needed as long as the resident of the area wants to move about within it, but only upon entry and exit from the towns encircled at the time.

4. As a rule, a permit is needed by persons aged 16 and above, but the age range varies from time to time, depending on security needs.

5. The permit is given for various periods, depending on need. The periods range from one day to three months.

6. In each sector, there is access to a reception window at the Coordination and Liaison Offices. In addition, it is possible to contact the Palestinian liaison offices, which work with the Coordination and Liaison Offices of the Civil Administration and receive permits through them.

7. Every request for a permit is examined on its merits by officials in the relevant Coordination and Liaison Office.

8. Every request for a permit is examined in light of the purpose of the permit requested and according to the security considerations resulting from the dynamic reality in the area.

9. An encirclement permit is given within a short time, several minutes up to several hours. In the event that an in-depth inspection is required in the matter of a resident, the permit might be received after several days.

10. In the event that a resident's request is rejected, he is informed that his request does not meet the criteria. If the rejection is based on a security or criminal background, the resident is so informed.

11. In appropriate cases, it is possible to request the judge advocate's office to reexamine the request.

12. The number of permits granted, by sector and year, are as follows:

Year	Jenin	Tulkarm	Nablus	Ramallah	Bethlehem	Hebron	Jericho	Total
2002	461	446	1868	10676	2383	4727	984	21545
2003	2377	3359	7351	27538	7850	6213	2067	56755
Total	2838	3805	9212	38214	10233	10940	3051	78300

Sincerely,

Talia Somech, Lieutenant
Spokesperson, Civil Administration

REQUEST FORMS for a permit for a permanent resident in the Seam Zone, for an encirclement-crossing permit, for a magnetic card, and for a permit to exit to Israel.

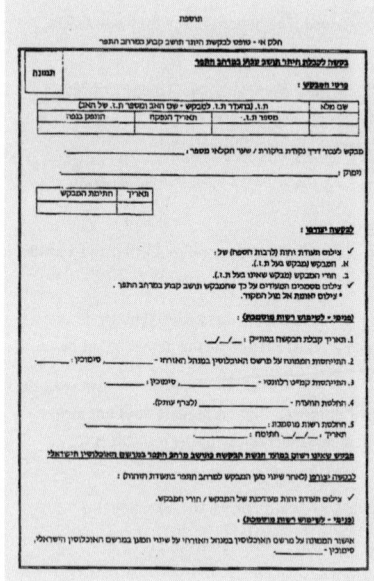

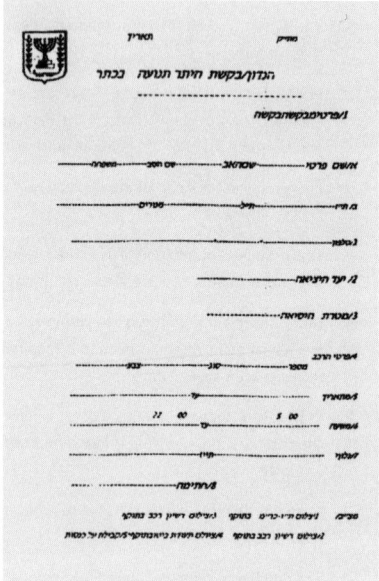

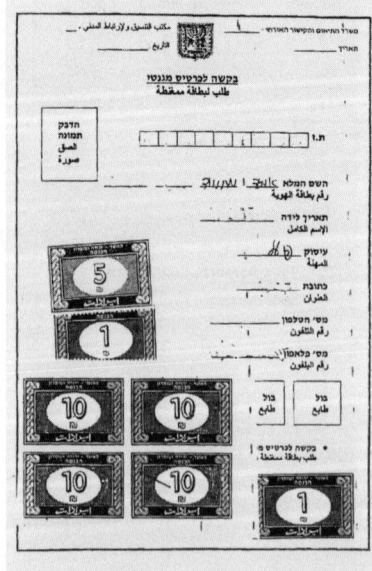

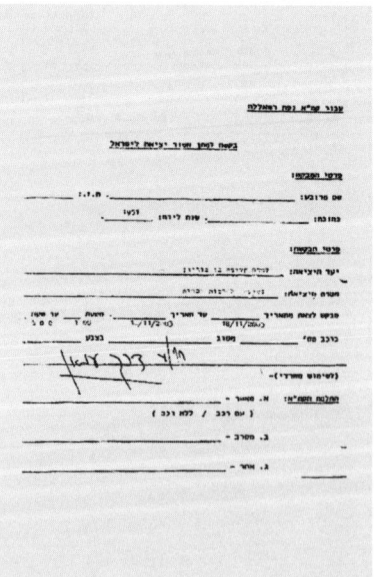

TYPES OF PERSONAL PERMITS TO ENTER THE SEAM ZONE that are issued by the Coordination and Liaison Offices, as specified in the "Regulations Regarding Permits to Enter and Stay in the Seam Zone" of October 2003. The regulations declare the Seam Zone area—the area between the Green Line and the Separation Wall—closed to Palestinians, requiring the residents living in the area and persons visiting there to obtain entry permits.

תוספת

חלק א'

טופס הבקשה	מטרת תכניסה למרחב התפר והשהייה בו
כמפורט בחלק ב' לתוספת	1. בעל עסק במרחב התפר
כמפורט בחלק ג' לתוספת	2. סוחר במרחב התפר
כמפורט בחלק ד' לתוספת	3. מועסק במרחב התפר
כמפורט בחלק ה' לתוספת	4. חקלאי במרחב התפר
כמפורט בחלק ו' לתוספת	5. מורה במרחב התפר
כמפורט בחלק ז' לתוספת	6. תלמיד במרחב התפר
כמפורט בחלק ח' לתוספת	7. עובד הרשות הפלסטינית
כמפורט בחלק ט' לתוספת	8. מבקר במרחב התפר
כמפורט בחלק י' לתוספת	9. עובד ארגון בינלאומי
כמפורט בחלק יא' לתוספת	10. עובד רשות מקומית / חברת תשתית
כמפורט בחלק יב' לתוספת	11. חבר צוות רפואי
כמפורט בחלק יג' לתוספת	12. כל מטרה אחרת

PURPOSE OF ENTRY TO SEAM ZONE AND STAYING IN IT	REQUEST FORM
1. Owner of business in the Seam Zone	As specified in Part 2 of the Schedule
2. Merchant in the Seam Zone	As specified in Part 3 of the Schedule
3. Employee in the Seam Zone	As specified in Part 4 of the Schedule
4. Farmer in the Seam Zone	As specified in Part 5 of the Schedule
5. Teacher in the Seam Zone	As specified in Part 6 of the Schedule
6. Student in the Seam Zone	As specified in Part 7 of the Schedule
7. Employee of the Palestinian Authority	As specified in Part 8 of the Schedule
8. Visitor in the Seam Zone	As specified in Part 9 of the Schedule
9. Employee of international organization	As specified in Part 10 of the Schedule
10. Employer of municipality/infrastructure company	As specified in Part 11 of the Schedule
11. Member of medical staff	As specified in Part 12 of the Schedule
12. Every other purpose	As specified in Part 13 of the Schedule

Ariella Azoulay

ACTIVESTILLS.ORG/ANNE PAQ

3.1 THE SEPARATION WALL IN BETHLEHEM, AROUND RACHEL'S TOMB, 2006 A view from the Ayida refugee camp. The windings of the Wall in Bethlehem. The illegibility of space in this fragment of the Separation Wall delivers its absurdity in a nutshell. The Separation Wall does not delineate a border between two entities that have gone their separate ways, but is a new formation of the occupation's control of the population through separation. The occupier pursues his self-image as separate from those who live in the Occupied Territories, although the means and efforts he invests in maintaining separation impose unceasing friction with them.

3.2 YEAR UNKNOWN (DURING THE SECOND INTIFADA) Heavy boulders block passage on the road leading to Teko'a colony. The separation between Jewish and Palestinian vehicles takes place on roads that lead to this place. Chances that Palestinian traffic will even access this fork are null.

3.3 **KHARBATA, 2005** The high road for Jews, the low road for Arabs.

3.4 NEAR ANATA, EAST JERUSALEM, 2007 Separate roads. Right for Arabs, left for Jews.

IAN STERNTHAL

3.5 GILO, APARTHEID ROAD, 2005

The Colonial Foundations of the State of Exception: Juxtaposing the Israeli Occupation of the Palestinian Territories with Colonial Bureaucratic History

Yehouda Shenhav and Yael Berda

Shortly after the war in 1967 and the occupation of the West Bank and Gaza by the Israeli Army, Israel declared the territories to be a closed military zone.[1] Military rule was established by the military commander of the territories through geographically dispersed military governors known as *moshlim* who ruled distinct areas and who had close contact with the local leadership and a central administrative body that would evolve in 1980 into the Civil Administration of the territories. The Civil Administration had separated the bureaucratic civil administrative apparatus in the territories and the management of the everyday lives of the Palestinians from organized military action, ostensibly creating two bureaucratic spheres of control. As Shlomo Gazit, the first head of the Civil Administration later described it, "We sought to provide law and order to the territories and to differentiate ourselves from the military rule of the Palestinians within the 1967 borders, which we saw as unprofessional."[2] This, however, was not a simple matter, because there was no role model for the Israeli Civil Administration to emulate. In retrospect, Gazit recollected, the colonial model of bureaucracy such as the British employed in India or the French in Algeria never occurred to him as the proper model of control. Rather surprisingly, he evoked the Nazi occupation of Norway as a viable analogous model. The occupation was supposed to run every aspect of human life, from hospitals, municipalities, and schools to the provision of sewage treatment, water, and electricity. The Civil Administration also conducted a population census, which later, in the years following the Oslo accords, would become a powerful tool of population control with the enactment of the permit regime.

During the early years of the occupation (1967–74), the military government's stated guidelines were based on minimum involvement and on maintaining an efficient, fair, and liberal administration.[3] Without claiming sovereignty over the territories and without administrative regulation of their populations, Israel allowed the majority of the Palestinian workforce to enter Israel. In 1970, 5 percent of the Palestinian workforce was employed inside Israel or by Israeli employers. By 1987, over 45 percent of the workforce provided 85 percent of the Palestinian gross domestic product, which gradually created economic dependence among Palestinians on the possibility of entry into Israel, a situation that continued and intensified throughout the "Oslo years."[4] This was due to a relatively free passage of people and goods to and from the Occupied Palestinian Territories (OPT) implemented in 1971 by then defense minister Moshe Dayan as part of the "Open Borders" policy between the OPT and Israel.

The relatively free flow of labor was first obstructed during the uprising known as the first intifada (1987–92). In 1989, the administration first issued requirements for Palestinian workers from Gaza to carry "magnetic cards" as a prerequisite for entry into Israel. The flow of Palestinian labor came to a temporary halt during the 1991 Gulf War, when the Israeli Army introduced intense curfews and local closures in and around towns and villages in the West Bank and Gaza. The general decree allowing the right to free movement between the OPT and Israel was cancelled. It was replaced by a military decree ordering all Palestinians who wished to enter Israel to carry a personal permit.

Then, in 1993, Israel declared the first closure of the borders between the OPT and Israel. It took the form of a state of exception without declaring an end date for the closure. To implement the closure policy, checkpoints were built at various border points.[5] In May 1994, with the signing of the Gaza-Jericho Agreement as part of the Oslo Accords, civil authority and administrative powers in the Gaza Strip were transferred to the Palestinian Authority. The Civil Administration was reduced in size and function, with much of its focus turned from a focus on internal Palestinian civilian life to a focus on Israeli security and monitoring in order to control the movement of Palestinians into Israel for purposes of work, medical care, and religious practice. Annex II of the Oslo Gaza-Jericho Interim Agreement yielded the Joint Civil Affairs Coordination and Cooperation Committee between Israel and the Palestinian Authority (PA) and formed the District Coordination Offices (DCOs) and District Civil Liaison Offices (DCLs) on both the Palestinian and Israeli sides, which were to provide "day-to-day contacts between the two sides as regards matters such as employment permits, hospitalization, transportation licensing, or the transfer of information."[6] The DCOs and DCLs became the double-headed bureaucracy directing the occupation.

The transfer of authority from the Israeli military government and the Civil Administration to the Palestinian Authority shifted the governing paradigm from management of all aspects of Palestinian civil life to control of the Palestinian population seen from the single vantage point of "Israel's security." While relinquishing responsibility for civil affairs, the District Civil Liaison Offices on the Israeli side, together with the downsized Civil Administration, focused on controlling the movement of the Palestinian population. This gave the security apparatuses a key role and conferred on them direct administrative power. Entry into Israel for employment or humanitarian purposes now required a permit. The requests for permits were to be transferred by the Palestinian DCOs to the Israeli military administration using the Israeli registry of the Palestinian population. The double-headed bureaucracy prevented Palestinian individuals from accessing the administrative apparatus, and all requests were passed to the Israeli side through the Palestinian DCOs. This shifted civil responsibility to the Palestinian Authority while retaining Israeli control over security matters, which included denial of entry from the territories into Israel.

Due to the turn of political events and the administrative failure of the Oslo Accords, this double-headed bureaucracy was short-lived. Since the end of the 1990s, the Palestinian DCLs have become mere post offices that deliver requests to the Israeli offices where decisions are made and policies carried out. The joint coordination committees ceased to work effectively in 1996 for political reasons, while increased impediments on the freedom of movement began to take shape in the form of roadblocks, checkpoints, and the omnipresent border police.

The state of exception in the form of military closures took two forms: closures that brought to a halt the entrance of Palestinians to Israel and internal closures that restricted the movement of the Palestinians within the West Bank itself. The closure, a form of control originally enacted for emergency security reasons, was institutionalized as the principal tool of control used by the Israeli Army. These closures had a massive effect on the Palestinian economy, since over 40 percent of Palestinian workers relied on employment within Israel.[7] The DCL's single-headed management remained dysfunctional until October 2000, with the beginning of the second intifada. All connections and liaisons then were halted. Since October 2000, the background to the harsh implementation of the permit regime has been assassinations (euphemized as "extrajudicial killings," or "targeted killings"), massive arrests, night raids on homes and villages, administrative detentions, house demolitions, the takeover of rooms and roofs of Palestinian houses by army units, torture and beatings during interrogations, high fines for traffic violations, and denial of exit into Jordan for security reasons.[8]

This intricate set of laws, decrees, and administrative decisions implemented the impediments to Palestinian freedom of movement to Israel and within the West Bank itself. The permit regime is a bureaucratic apparatus entirely separate from the state bureaucracy within Israel proper. The decrees have been founded on a racial distinction, in that they pertain to Palestinians alone and do not include

Jews, whose settlements in the Occupied Territories have been judged to be illegal under international law. Laws and decrees and their implementation and fundamental civil rights differ greatly between Jews and Arab-Palestinians, even when they commit the same offences in the same territory.[9]

From the end of 2000 on, the bureaucratic labyrinth of the occupation as it operates today began to take its shape. More than two hundred thousand Palestinians were recorded in the DCOs' databases as to be "denied entry for security reasons," meaning they could not obtain magnetic cards, the prerequisite for obtaining permits for entry into Israel and in many cases for traveling in the West Bank between cities and villages.[10] More than sixty-four thousand Palestinians are "denied [entry] for police reasons," which can mean that the person has an unpaid police traffic ticket, or a court case that is in process, or files opened by border police at checkpoints for attempted illegal entry without further legal prosecution. Although denial of entry by the Israeli police is an attenuated classification compared with denial by the General Security Service (GSS), the secret service known as the Shabak, the implications are the same. Both prevent a person from receiving a permit to enter Israel.

Following the renewal of control of the Israeli military bureaucracy over the Palestinian population after October 2000, the GSS morphed from a consultant to the military Civil Administration to an administrative body in itself, holding sole power on classification of Palestinians as security threats. (However, this change has not been officially recorded in published administrative directives, preventing the possibility of legal appeals.)[11] Laws criminalizing the employment of illegal Palestinian workers have set high fines and long prison sentences for Israeli employers who have employed Palestinians for over twenty years. Laws criminalizing drivers caught with Palestinian passengers who lack permits empower border police to impound cars on the spot for thirty days and to press charges against the drivers that result in prison sentences. Palestinians caught in Israel without a permit serve prison sentences of up to two to six months and are usually denied entry for at least two years afterward.

The bureaucracy of the occupation could seem like a dysfunctional mayhem, if some of its recurring exceptions, its efficiency for controlling Palestinian movement, and the racial hierarchy that governs it through separate laws and regulation administered to Palestinians and Jews in the Occupied Territories did not hint at another possibility for the interpretation of its mechanisms and working principles. In this essay, we explore that possibility—the possibility that this seeming patchwork of arbitrary policies is in fact based on a coherent and well-articulated approach to the implementation of a colonial bureaucracy, an approach based on the politics of exception and political theology.

MAX WEBER AND CRITICAL STUDIES OF BUREAUCRACY

How are we to conceptualize and analyze this labyrinth of bureaucratic (dis)order? The traditional model of bureaucracy espoused by liberal political theory and its critique in the tradition of critical theory is inadequate to depict the inner working of the bureaucracy of the occupation. Since Max Weber, and in the wake of his pioneering studies of bureaucracy,[12] the main menace associated with bureaucracy has seemed to lie in its hyperinstrumental rationality. Weber was the first to offer a systematic account of bureaucracy's ideal type—arguing that precision, speed, predictability, coordination, and the reduction of friction raise efficiency to its optimal level and that pure bureaucratic organizations are expected to function according to universal considerations of competency in order to achieve the "very calculability of results."[13] Yet Weber also provided an unambiguous warning about the towering threat posed by bureaucratic domination and its well-organized machinery. Following Weber, Franz Neumann focused more cogently on the disastrous connection between efficient bureaucracy and the loosely integrated apparatuses of the Nazi state terror known as "Behemoth."[14] In the same vein, Max Horkheimer and Theodor W. Adorno underlined the dialectic nature of instrumental rationality, pointing out the displacement of means and goals, as well as the ascent of instrumental reason as a prime ideology,[15] which Zygmunt Bauman later identified as the main impetus behind the "twisted road to Auschwitz."[16] In a different tradition, Hannah Arendt described the bureaucratic mind of Adolph Eichmann, an efficient clerk whose initial organizational task was immigration. She coined the term "the banality of evil" to capture the mechanical, bureaucratic way in which such a mind was involved in the most horrendous atrocities.[17] Arendt, as well as Bauman, have suggested that "moral aloofness" and the "banality of evil" are endemic to the pathologies and abnormal manifestations of a modern rational bureaucracy.[18]

This line of critique, which was developed in the backdrop of horrifying state atrocities during World War II, was indeed eye-opening and instructive. For one thing, it turned the ideal type of bureaucracy on its head. Rather than speed and precision, the critique of bureaucratic reason underscored the ominous nature of the organizational machinery, the detrimental effects of efficiency as an ideology, and the malicious use of its advantages toward particularistic and inhuman ends.

Yet the structure and epistemology of this critique remained anchored in European liberal assumptions about governance and the rule of law as the finest form of modern political rationality. It perceived secular law and secular reason to be the sole arbiters of the modern project of bureaucracy and the topos of its sovereignty at state level.[19] Despite its uncompromising critique, it also accepted the basic European assumptions about the nature of bureaucracy: legal, rather than personal control; rationality, rather than superstition; secularism, rather than theology. At the end of the day, it was believed, the violence and evil produced by modern bureaucracy has resulted from the unexpected consequences of action and the irrational consequences of the rational machinery. However, being European in nature, the critique of bureaucratic reason was particularly oblivious to Western colonialism and imperialism. The liberal features specified above are insufficient in explaining the inner workings of contemporary bureaucratic violence as it emerged in the context of colonial rule and imperial formations of power in general and of contemporary bureaucratic violence as it emerges in the Occupied Palestinian Territories in particular.

It is now a truism that the European powers have used their colonies as laboratories for experimentation with "modern projects." And it was there, in the colonies, that European powers privileged a radically different model of state bureaucracy. In this paper, we invoke an alternative ideal type of bureaucracy that was developed by Lord Cromer during the British rule in Egypt. Cromer's bureaucracy was a sovereign organ for managing the "subject races" in the colonial territories, representing the state's apparatuses and the state's law. This model stood in contradistinction to the liberal model of state bureaucracy developed by Max Weber in Germany.[20] Rather than subscribing to the rule of law, the colonial bureaucracy created and inscribed itself into a political nomos where European liberal law was suspended.[21] This political nomos was founded on a tapestry of European laws and local "traditional laws," as well as abruptly promulgated rules and decrees that allowed for administrative discretion and what Carl Schmitt called constant "decisionism." Thus, colonial state bureaucracy has acted as a fount of sovereignty—as autonomous machinery that has carried the prerogative to decide on the exception to the law and to exercise real and symbolic violence.

Thus, whereas the liberal version of bureaucracy renders the exception undesirable, an indication of malfunctioning, Cromer's colonial bureaucracy is founded on the principle of the exception. We look at colonial sovereignty through the lenses of the exception and explore the concrete practices of rule in which sovereignty as a political category loses its uniform meaning. Furthermore, colonial bureaucracy has employed race as an explicit category for action and differentiation. At times, it also has created and altered racial distinctions to serve its purposes. All in all, it has appeared to the "subject races" as a phantom organ that manufactures miraculous decisions, but that conceals the locus of the decision-making process, the inner working of its machinery, and its criteria for judiciousness.

Our main objective is to describe the morphology of this colonial model of bureaucracy and to suggest that it should serve as the proper framework against which colonial situations should be measured and compared, including the Israeli occupation of the Palestinian Territories. The rest of the essay is structured as follows. First, we discuss the political-theological perspective, which calls attention to the growing phenomenon of rule through the exception, rather than the rule of law, in the postcolonial world, as well as in Western democracies. Second, we present the essentials of Lord Cromer's ideal type of bureaucracy, which challenged liberal universal law and extended racially based political exceptions as the main arbiter of the ruling reality. Thus we offer an alternative ideal type of bureaucracy that introduces racial hierarchies into the administrative structure, rendering Weber's prerequisites for a bureaucracy that operates "without scorn and bias" all but obsolete. Third, we provide several illustrative examples from Egypt, India, and Occupied Palestine to show how the model has been implemented in practice. We end with a theoretical reflection that turns the gaze from the colonies to the metropole. In so doing, we challenge the modernist interpretation of Weber's ideal type and show that the Weberian model itself may be subject to political-theological interpretation, a neglected aspect in the literature on bureaucracy and domination.

POLITICAL THEOLOGY AND THE "STATE OF EXCEPTION"

In his *State of Exception,* Giorgio Agamben examines how the exception has become a permanent working paradigm of Western democracies.[22] For example, in 2001, the United States passed the USA PATRIOT Act,[23] under which it strove to fight terrorism. Under the act, the United States put hundreds of administrative detainees in Guantánamo Bay without trial. Amnesty International reports that these detainees are constantly being tortured: They are nearly drowned in cold water, they receive electrical shocks, and their religious beliefs are ridiculed. The *Washington Post* reported that the United States has incarcerated tens of detainees in secret prisons—known as "black sites" and forming "legal black holes"—which are spread throughout Eastern Europe and around the globe. The lives of these detainees were turned from lives worth living into "bare lives," to use Agamben's terminology. They never stood trial, they do not enjoy basic human rights, and the management of their everyday lives is often outsourced to private contractors. The anomalous nature of this territory and the anomalous status of the law are at stake here. Despite the ruling of the Supreme Court, the American government claims that the Constitution does not apply to the "Guantánamo camp," including Camp X-Ray, and the other "camps" located there. Do sites such as these constitute a territory within the axes of the rule of law, or outside of it? This is the question that Walter Benjamin, Carl Schmitt, and Agamben attempt to address.

In 1921, Benjamin published a rather cryptic article under the title "Critique of Violence" in which he examined the dialectical relationships between violence and the rule of law, between the violence that constitutes the law and the violence that preserves and verifies the rule of law. In contrast to these two sources of violence, the state cannot tolerate "pure violence" (or "revolutionary violence"), which exists outside of the law. Benjamin formulated "pure violence" in religious-theological redemptive language.[24] When Schmitt published his *Political Theology,* he implicitly addressed this theological turn.[25] Schmitt pointed an accusing finger at liberal political theory, which allegedly incapacitated the sovereign by forcing him to rely on and be restricted by the legal rule of law. He criticized liberal law and democratic parliamentary institutions for their lack of "decisionism," that is, for defining sovereignty through the law, rather than through administrative discretion, and for neglect of the exception, that is, how the legal system suspends itself in light of political threats.[26] Instead, he suggested that all significant concepts of modern theory of the state are secularized theological concepts, arguing that the omnipotence of the modern lawgiver is derived from theology. In *Political Theology,* the "Sovereign is he who decides on the exception," suggesting that the exception in jurisprudence is analogous to the miracle in theology.[27] Schmitt did not renounce Benjamin's claim that violence underlies the European democratic parliamentary system itself. He argued that this violence, which liberalism tends to deny, is encapsulated in the figure of the sovereign and is necessary for the survival of the liberal state itself. As we argue below, the violence embedded in the law becomes even more apparent and visible in the colonial system of governance.

Agamben accepts the tenets of political theology and develops the logic of exception, which, he argues, provides a necessary supplement to Michel Foucault's concept of governmentality.[28] In *Homo Sacer,* Agamben invokes a particular model of exception that he draws from the Roman codex, that of the sacred man, who is a person whom people have judged on account of his having committed a crime: *"The sovereign sphere is the sphere in which it is permitted to kill without committing homicide and without celebrating a sacrifice."*[29] Agamben describes how in the so-called "camp" (be it the concentration camp or Guantánamo Bay), life becomes bare, purging the legal persons, the subjectivity, and the biography of its inmates. It is a space in which the rule of law is suspended under the cover of the law. While for Agamben life is the deployment and the manifestation of power, he defines sovereignty as the capacity to manage death and mortality.

Agamben offers a partial genealogy of the state of exception as a paradigm for contemporary democratic governance. He describes its origin in Roman law, in revolutionary and modern France, in the Weimar Republic and the Nazi regime, in Switzerland, Italy, England, and the United States. His frame of reference, however, is Europe, accepting its time and space as given modalities. As Andreas Kalyvas has rightly noted "Unfortunately, *Homo Sacer* returns to a representation of time—the time of sovereignty—as uniform, one-directional, and rectilinear," remaining "within the horizons of the Occidental political tradition, the political destiny of the West."[30]

What is conspicuously absent in this genealogy is the role of the exception in the history of imperialism. This is unfortunate, if only because at the beginning of the twentieth century, Western colonies occupied some 85 percent of the world's territory,[31] and they used alternative models of rule that provide a rich arena in which to study sovereignty. As Nasser Hussain firmly puts it: "Colonialism is the best historical example for any theoretical study of norm and exception, rule of law and emergency." The concept of "emergency" in the colonies was used as an elastic category, stretching over political disturbances such as riots and insurgencies, as well as to allow for colonial capitalism. Because an emergency is a "situation of danger that can never be exhaustively anticipated or codified in advance, and thus the suspension of the law would have to be the result of a conscious decision,"[32] and in colonial bureaucracies, it came to be a decision on which administrators increasingly relied.

Agamben owes some of his insights not only to Schmitt, Benjamin and Foucault, but also to Hannah Arendt.[33] Unfortunately, he fails to take her perspective on imperialism and on "race and bureaucracy" seriously. In *The Origins of Totalitarianism* (1951) Arendt turned her gaze to the increasing gap between the political centers in Europe (the metropole) and the colonies, a gap that she described as the inevitable result of the insatiable appetite of imperialism for new lands. Arendt suggested that when imperial conquerors disengaged from the European state and its democratic laws, they replaced democratic culture with despotism and with coercive rule over the subject races. She pointed to the initial gap between the legal status of citizens in the home country and the subject races in the colonies, which are never full-fledged citizens, as the locus of her political inquiry. When it migrates back home, this gap partially explains the rise of totalitarianism. Arendt's causal reasoning is ambiguous, but there is no doubt that she alludes to political governance that is based on exceptions. For example, she shows how imperial rule rests on abrupt and changing decrees. It is these exceptions that we want to mark out in order to explore the political-theological underpinnings of colonial rule.

We take Arendt's perspective on imperialism seriously and combine it with the Schmittian understanding of the exception. However, instead of treating sovereignty as a formal legal category, we examine it as a sociological praxis full of exceptions, fissures, and fractures. In other words, we suggest studying the concrete practices of rule, practices in which sovereignty as a political category loses its uniform meaning. Indeed, in *Society Must Be Defended*, Foucault suggests decomposing the notion of sovereignty and tracing its ephemeral histories. Adi Ophir delineates this project rather succinctly: "Sovereignty can be described as an Archimedean point that can rescue the political philosophy of the law and the legal philosophy of the political from its vicious circle. Sovereignty at one and the same time is the authority to decide the law in every moment and to dictate the law and the ruling power." Yet Ophir also suggests going one step further and distinguishing between the concept of sovereignty and the "sovereign decision": "We ought to keep a distinction (which Agamben underemphasizes) between sovereignty and the 'sovereign decision' as manifested in concrete governmental reality. We should definitely not transpose the same uniform and unified form of 'sovereignty' to the actual exercise of ruling. In every regime, even in the most atrocious forms of totalitarianism, the sovereign rule negotiates the exception."[34]

This comes close to our definition of sociological praxis. The examination of sovereign practices offers multiple manifestations of sovereignty that cannot be identified with a single privileged point of decision. In the colonial context, this multiplicity takes on an additional meaning. Colonial rule is characterized by a tapestry of multiple partial sovereignties, as well as by a collection of rules and abrupt decrees, both of which challenge the unified concept of sovereignty.

One needs only to consider anticolonial manifestations of resistance in order to realize that legal exceptions, states of emergency, closures, the apprehension of administrative detainees, and assassinations authorized by the state were not issued only in response to the destruction of the Twin Towers in New York in 2001 or to terrorist attacks from Gaza or the West Bank. These also were practices that, from the start, characterized colonial occupations and the racial hierarchy upon which they were founded. The fact that states of emergency overlapped with racialized bureaucracies is well known to the subject races whose life developed into bare existence. Franz Fanon's manifesto *Wretched of the Earth* testifies to the distinction between "legitimate violence" and "illegitimate violence" that characterizes the architecture of the modern European state and shows how the distinction becomes blurred in the colonial context. It also clearly suggests that in the colonial context, the state of emergency has become the rule, rather than the exception. As Benjamin prophetically put it: "The tradition of the oppressed teaches us that the 'state of emergency' in which we live is not the exception but the rule. We must attain to a conception of history that accords with this insight."[35]

The history of imperialism shows that states of exception were ubiquitous and omnipresent in the colonial territories. Colonial governance was entrapped between the desire to export the rule of law to the colonies, on the one hand, and a lack of desire (or ability) to annex those territories or to establish full sovereignty, on the other. Colonial administrators had no imperial handbook about what forms of the law were best to institute in colonial settings. Rather, they treated European legal traditions as a "useful collection from which they might draw selectively in crafting colonial legal systems."[36] The colonizers relied "on the blueprint of metropolitan law for distinguishing among categories of legal actors, and they looked for analogous distinctions in indigenous law," sometimes reinventing what they labeled as indigenous "customary law."[37] Thus, racial distinctions were molded by the sovereign to serve its ruling purposes. On top of that, the church was also a legal authority that profoundly influenced the functioning of colonial law.[38] As a result, the colonies "tend not to be organized under a single, vertically integrated sovereignty sustained by a highly centralized state...rather, they consist in a horizontally woven tapestry of partial sovereignties."[39]

Imperial bureaucrats such as Warren Hastings and Lord Curzon in India, Lord Cromer in Egypt, Lord Charles Somerset at the Cape, Sir Harry Smith in South Africa, Sir George Grey in New Zealand, and Lord Lytton in Afghanistan, among others,[40] created a new political *nomos* that produced anomalous and partial models of sovereignty in which ruling was based on legal patchwork and ad hoc arrangements or exceptions, rather than on the unified liberal rule of law. This resulted in the endless negotiations and disagreements that Ross Johnston called "jurisdictional Imperialism" and that Lauren Benton defined as "jurisdictional politics," "jurisdictional flexibility," and "jurisdictional jockeying."[41] These "anomalous models" have resulted in sites of lawlessness under the auspices of the law: foreign jurisdiction, exterritorial jurisdiction, administrative decrees, partial annexations, combat zones, martial law, and states of emergency.[42] Recently, Ann Stoler has used the concept of "imperial formations," which she defines as "macropolities whose technology of rule thrives on the production of exceptions and their uneven and changing proliferation." We could not describe it better:

> Critical features of imperial formations include harboring and building on territorial ambiguity, redefining legal categories of belonging and quasi-membership, and shifting the geographic and demographic zones of partially suspended rights.... The legal and political fuzziness of dependencies, trusteeships, protectorates, and unincorporated territories were all part of the deep grammar of partially restricted rights in the nineteenth- and twentieth-century imperial world.... Imperial states by definition operate as states of exception that vigilantly produce exceptions to their principles and exceptions to their laws.[43]

It is there, in the colonial territory, that the exception has become a permanent working paradigm of Western democracy. The exception, we should emphasize, is not only the suspension of the law, but also its selective use through a legal and administrative patchwork. The British pictured the colonies as representing "anarchy and confusion, selfishness, cowardice, treachery, unpatriotic betrayals and horrible reigns of terror, the tyranny of the strong."[44] They founded their rule on the concept of divine providence bestowing "law and order" and good governance upon its racialized subjects. British sovereignty—both de facto or de jure—viewed the colony as a feudal state with the queen as the natural sovereign ruling under God.[45] As Bernard S. Cohn firmly put it in the context of India, "The British Monarch rules under God and divine providence. The Viceroy then becomes the physical representative of the divine order and the monarchy."[46]

Not surprisingly, British bureaucracy was anchored in Christian moral code. It allowed for judicial intervention (the analogue of divine miracle) to manufacture uncertainty for its racialized subjects, it was based on personal rule, rather than on formal written documents, and it manufactured capricious administrative decrees, rather than the predictable nature of the rule of law.

The political-theological form of colonial bureaucracy was used to differentiate between different political communities, because it was based on the racial distinction between "Europeans" and "natives," or between "Jews" and "Arabs," in the context of the Palestinian territories.[47] In the economics of the bio-political, racial hierarchies became the definers of life and death, as well as their justification. To be sure, racial hierarchies are sometimes camouflaged and justified by alternative regimes of justifications, be it a national struggle, a security paradigm, a distinction between a friend and a foe, or various other definitions that mask the racial elements. However, as Hussain has suggested, "it is race that undermines the legal identity between metropole and colony."[48] The bureaucracy as a differentiating mechanism between "subjects" who are European citizens and "subject races" who are not is at the core of the foundation of the political order.

PROTOTYPES OF COLONIAL BUREAUCRACY

Quintessential to this system of exceptions was Lord Cromer's model of colonial bureaucracy in Egypt. Cromer provided an alternative ideal type of bureaucracy to Weber's. It was a sovereign organ that was suffused with political-theological and racialized procedures and that manufactured miraclelike decisions. At the same time, it was largely invisible and inaccessible to the subject races.

When Lord Cromer became the British Consul General in Egypt in 1883, the future of colonial rule in Egypt was still uncertain, and at first, he advocated a temporary government and a policy of evacuation of British citizens.[49] As it turned out, Cromer governed Egypt for no less than a quarter of a century, and when he realized that the occupation was enduring, he put forward a set of principles for bureaucratic governance that were later published in his essay "The Government of Subject Races" and in part in *Modern Egypt* (1908).[50] In order to avoid full sovereignty, Cromer and his associates acted according to the Foreign Jurisdiction Act of 1843,[51] which facilitated the use of legal and bureaucratic (along temporal and spatial) exceptions. Cromer explained that the regular rule of law, common in liberal representative democracies, is incompatible with racially inferior groups: "So limited is the stock of political ideas in the world that some modified copy of parliamentary institutions is, without doubt, the only method which has yet been invented for mitigating the evils attendant on the personal system of government. But it is a method that is thoroughly uncongenial to Oriental habits of thoughts."[52]

A similar position and justification was stated by Sir William Jones, a philologist at Oxford, upon the seizure of India. British law could not become the law of India, he proposed, because "a system of liberty, forced upon a people invincibly attached to opposite habits, would in truth be a system of tyranny."[53]

Under the Foreign Jurisdiction Act in Egypt, the colonial bureaucracy would become an effective method of control, which Cromer perceived as an enlightened alternative to the liberal rule of law on the one hand, and the brute use of force, on the other. After all "the sword will assuredly be powerless to defend us for long, and the days of our imperial rule will be numbered," he argued.[54] He assured that no matter what the initial qualities of the bureaucrats are, once entered on the unending process of expansion, they will become "instruments of incomparable value in the execution of a policy of Imperialism."[55] In contradistinction to his role in Europe, the colonial bureaucrat "ceases to be what he was and will start to obey the laws of the process, identify himself with anonymous forces that he is supposed to serve in order to keep the whole process in motion; he will think of himself as mere function…mere instrument."[56] Cromer's vision of imperial bureaucracy did not adhere to stable and predictable laws, employed secretive decision-making processes, and issued capricious bureaucratic decrees. To the subject races, the colonial bureaucracy thus represented an illusive "phantom sovereign" that did not respond lawfully to their appeals and challenges.

Cromer's model of bureaucracy was imbued with strong racial assumptions and procedures, which in turn "necessitated" and legitimized the rule of British imperial bureaucracy over the racialized natives. He was explicit in emphasizing that bureaucratic sovereignty is essential, especially where "the inhabitants of the countries under British rule are not of Anglo-Saxon origin."[57] In his two-volume book *Modern Egypt,* he proposes to accomplish the mission of civilizing the natives—the white man's burden—through a racialized form of bureaucratic apparatus:

> It is for the civilized Englishmen to extend to them the hand of fellowship and encouragement, and to raise them, morally and materially, from the abject state in which he finds them. And the Englishman looks towards the scene of other administrative triumphs of worldwide fame, which his progenitors have accomplished. He looks towards India, and he says to himself with all the confidence of the imperial race—I can perform this task."[58]

The rationale and legitimacy of Cromer's bureaucratic model rests upon what was perceived as the low level of the inferior race: "In fact, the Englishman will soon find that the Egyptian, whom he wishes to mould into something really useful with a view to his becoming eventually autonomous, is merely the rawest of raw material." Furthermore: "Contrast…the European talkative mind, bursting with superfluous energy, active in mind, inquisitive about everything he sees and hears…with the grave and silent Eastern, devoid of energy and initiative, stagnant in mind."[59]

Cromer believed that "so long as British supervision is maintained, the Egyptian will readily copy the practices and procedures of his English teachers," and consequently, the "intellect" of the Oriental worker will "be developed" and "his moral being elevated under British auspices."[60] However, as it was, bureaucratic sovereignty simultaneously manufactured constant decisionism and functioned as a phantom sovereign that concealed its proliferating rules and conduct from the subject races.

Cromer's ideal type of colonial bureaucracy thus exhibited four salient features. First, the bureaucratic sovereign was perceived as an organ that allowed for the suspension of the law and that produced miraclelike interventions. These interventions allowed for a constant state of decisionism. Second, colonial bureaucracy appeared as a phantomlike sovereign. On the one hand, it was omnipresent and ubiquitous, but on the other, it was illusive, and its whereabouts were hard to trace. Third, the bureaucratic sovereign used racial distinctions and procedures to segregate Europeans from local natives. Fourth, colonial rule manufactured endless spatial and temporal exceptions, most of them concerned with freedom of movement. In sum, colonial bureaucracy has functioned as a phantom sovereign and performed miraculous decisions over racialized subjects. We can observe the colonial bureaucracy functioning in this way in three examples from the British Empire—in Egypt, India, and Palestine.[61]

COLONIAL BUREAUCRACY IN EGYPT

The vision of colonial bureaucracy outlined by Cromer was readily materialized in practice. As Timothy Mitchell writes, the British established a system of control in Egypt that, as Cromer admitted, was tantamount to the introduction of legal exceptions.[62] Upon its foundation, the system was based on the so-called "Brigandage Commissions" and was composed of abrupt military raids, secret police, local informants, massive imprisonments, and the systematic use of torture. A decade after they were introduced, these commissions were replaced by a more disciplined and consolidated bureaucratic system. It included selective use of the law, an infinite number of decrees, and an abruptly changing set of rules and regulations about movement in the region. This required competent and knowledgeable professional bureaucrats who were familiar with racial distinctions, as Cromer himself testified: "No man, however experienced and laborious, could properly direct and control the various interests of so vast an Empire, unless he were aided by men with knowledge of different parts of the country, and possessing an intimate acquaintance with the different and complicated subjects involved in the government and welfare of so many incongruous races."[63] The justification for British imperial bureaucracy is particularly blunt (and sanctimonious): "It is important that, in our well-intentioned endeavors to impregnate the Oriental mind with our insular habits of thought, we should proceed with the utmost caution." Further: "Before Orientals can attain anything approaching to the British ideal of self-government they will have to undergo very numerous transmigrations of political thought."[64]

British colonial bureaucrats were perceived as benevolent rulers who provided the foundation for British moral conduct. They possessed the necessary moral virtues to rule the subject races: " He [the bureaucrat] will not be possessed with any secret desire to see the whole of Africa or of Asia painted red on the map."[65] The imperial officials were said to be informed "by the light of western knowledge and experience tempered by local considerations," and they "conscientiously think [what] is best for the subject race."[66] This breed of bureaucrat was placed in every Egyptian village, and a central office was set up to organize the official registration of births. This process required what Lord Cromer called "systematic English inspection" in Egyptian villages. This was applied by force, using police and hired watchmen who "surrounded the village at night; in the morning over 400 were found unregistered, and the Sheick will be tried by court-martial."[67]

Similar methods of supervision and governance were applied to capitalist production in Egypt. This is not surprising, since methods of population control that were initially used for combating insurgencies became institutionalized methods of exercising bio-power through population control in general. Mitchell describes the process in which these methods were used to prevent labor desertion from lands on which colonial crops were grown. In order to coerce villagers to cultivate export crops and deliver them to government warehouses, they used methods such as the regulation of population censuses, taxation penalties, and the usurpation of land. Furthermore, when crop monopolies were met by villager resistance, who deserted their lands which were guarded by the military, and moved to agricultural lands beyond government control, a permit regime was introduced under which permits issued by the military were required for travel outside one's village locality.[68] The land laws and decrees that were issued represented attempts to compel individuals to remain on their lands and to confirm the seizure of lands from those who fled.

Colonial bureaucracy also introduced another land reform, for the Bedouins, a reform directly linked to population control and to infringement on the freedom of movement. Those who had fled and who had lost their lands were offered small plots in exchange for submitting to the authority of the military officer assigned to their locality. As Mitchell describes it:

They were to give the officer a list of the heads of the sections of each tribe, with the number of persons and a description of each individual enumerated "tribe by tribe, section by section, name by name." The officer would then issue a permit with the name, physical description, and tribe of every individual under his authority. A person who wished to move from one tribal section to another, or to another part of the country, required this permit to travel.[69]

This method of control inscribed the exception in space, the reason at this point being economic. As revolts occurred, the reason shifted from the purely economic justification of preventing the desertion of farm laborers to one that prescribed control over those posing a "security threat." Villagers were required to round up "depraved and malicious persons and suspicious characters" in their locality, who were then pressed into labor or sent to the army.[70] If, after the assigned period, the suspicious characters were found to have returned to their district, the head man would be punished. The colonial bureaucracy also placed work gangs under continuous police control, with the police overseeing a system of "tickets" that were handed out to workers in their villages before they traveled to their work sites, "but only to those men whom the local police deemed not to be troublemakers."[71]

Besides the organization of the police force, a system of English inspection was set up within the Ministry of the Interior. "The interior of Egyptian village life was thus to be under continuous supervision."[72] This intervention in capitalist production based on population control and impediments on movement was created under the autonomous political *nomos* of the colonial bureaucracy. In this form, the notion of sovereignty and the notion of governmentality became enmeshed and practically indistinguishable.

Colonial bureaucracy represented the sovereign at every level, from the state to the village. It was based on a repertoire of exceptions that allowed for constant decisionism to manage the racial "other."[73] This form of bureaucracy is characterized by multiple and incoherent sovereign decisions and is therefore polytheistic, rather than monotheistic. This by no means comes close to Weber's ideal type of bureaucracy. It was quintessentially Cromer's.

COLONIAL BUREAUCRACY IN INDIA

This rule by the exception rather than by the rule of law, was not exclusive to Egypt. Cromer himself admitted that the Egyptian case was modeled after the administrative system that had been developed in India and suggested "this portion of the Indian system is deserving of reproduction."[74] The story of British rule of India is one of overcoming the sovereign excess of despotism in favor of a bureaucratic form of government.[75]

The East India Company, which was the first British "sovereign" of India, was gradually transformed from a monopoly trading concern to an administrative structure with an elaborate bureaucracy.[76] The East Indian Company had acquired many of the attributes of a European state. It could wage war, make peace, raise taxes, and administer justice.[77] Until the beginning of the twentieth century, British rule in India was direct, including a huge, multilayered bureaucracy comparable in size to those of the Czarist Russian or Chinese empires.[78] According to Edward Thompson and G. T. Garett's *Rise and Fulfillment of British Rule in India* (1934), colonial bureaucracy was believed to facilitate productive life: the building of irrigation systems and railroads, the conducting of land surveys and censuses, the creation of a police force, all these managed by a trained bureaucracy.[79]

The Charter Act of 1833 offered a systematic codification of Indian criminal and civil law. It was based on a theory of authority that was founded on assumptions about the proper ordering of groups in Indian society and their relationship to the British rulers.[80] Despite relatively coherent proclamations about sovereignty and the rule of law, British rule in India was still based on a patchwork of rules and regulations, elaborated administrative sections, intricate legal divisions, and flexible offices. As one British legal expert has observed, "the administrative frontier [in India] was a moving one,"[81] and the government was styled as imperfect or as half-sovereign.[82] It is evident that the phantom theological sovereign in India manufactured endless exceptions.[83] For example, the British frequently resorted to martial law. Yet British sovereignty did not rest on the authorization of ordinary law, but on the legal maxim *Salus populi suprema est lex* (Safety of the people is the supreme law).[84] Similar to the logic propounded in Egypt, the "necessity" for marshal law was legitimized with racially based justifications about the natives as inferior and as bad subjects of the law. At the very least, it represented a foundational schism in the conceptualization of authority in India between natives and Europeans.[85]

In the mid-nineteenth century, John Stuart Mill clearly formulated a similar position regarding the natives of India: "A rude people...may be unable to practice the forbearances which it [representative government] demands...in such a case, a civilized government, to be really advantageous to them, will require to be in a considerable degree despotic." He further explained that cultural inferiority justifies the suspension of the rule of law: "It is characteristic of born slaves to be incapable of conforming their conduct to a rule or law."[86] What was perceived as racial superiority thus served as rationale for British despotic rule and the suspension of the law. The British in India described the subject races as despotic and autocratic, as lawless and inferior.[87] Lauren Benton shows, for example, that "in nineteenth-century India, whole ethnic communities found themselves defined as being outside the law—as 'criminal tribes'—while in many parts of Africa colonial administrators embraced efforts to shore up, and even re-create in quite distorted forms, 'traditional' law."[88] This is indeed noteworthy, especially since the British at the same time acknowledged the political-theological character of their mandate in India. The first crown charter in India stated, for example, that we are "firmly relying ourselves on the truth of Christianity, and acknowledging with gratitude the solace of religion."[89] Noted above, this meant that since the British monarch ruled under God and divine providence, the viceroy then became the physical representative of the divine order in India.[90] Yet because British assault on Indian society was so fierce culturally and religiously, large segments of the Indian population came to reject it and to promote counterideologies and reactions, the most famous being the Great Mutiny and Civil Rebellion of 1857.[91]

On April 13, 1919, the British authorities in Punjab declared that the residents were forbidden to leave the city or to gather in processions and assemblies. The city was observing the fourth day of a general strike, and there were funerals being held for people shot by the military a few days earlier. On top of that, many people had come to the city to celebrate the Hindu New Year. The local sovereign, General Dyer, had found out that residents were planning a procession in Jallianwala Bagh at 4:30 p.m. and mobilized his troops and armored vehicles. Jallianwala Bagh was an unused area in the shape of an irregular rectangle about two hundred and fifty yards long and two hundred yards wide. General Dyer stationed his troops around the rectangle. Then, without warning, he opened fire, and the firing lasted for ten to fifteen minutes. When it was over, the official estimate was that 379 people were killed, with thousands seriously injured.[92] After this event, the Amritsar Massacre of 1919, public discourse in England focused on the need to adopt emergency measures in advance, based on the Indian subjects' ignorance of the law and the natives' lack of sufficient respect for the legal system.

Furthermore, martial law in India was not just a means for restoring order, but also for reestablishing the general authority of the colonial bureaucracy. A British committee that studied another case in Gujranwala found that colonial bureaucrats had resorted to "fancy punishments" as ways to reinforce the general notion of authority and order. Thus, a local bureaucrat issued the infamous "salaaming [greeting] order," which required Indians to leave their wagons and greet European officers. When pressed by the committee to explain the purpose of such an order, the commander insisted that it was used to reinforce a general sense of respect for the sovereign. As Hussain argues, "it is a purely nonmediate form, purely performative, the purpose of which is the sheer manifestation of power itself. It is a form of violence that Benjamin called 'mythical violence.'"[93]

After 1945, during the period known as "decolonization," the state of emergency became a ubiquitous model for rule in the colonies: Malaya, Rhodesia, Cyprus, Palestine, Nigeria, Uganda, Burma, Morocco, Algeria, and Kenya, among many others.[94] Under the state of emergency, the colonial states fought "hostile elements," and suspects were massively arrested and incarcerated in imperial camps. States of emergency provided the colonial empires with a breathing space to fight insurgencies,[95] and they were institutionalized in European law, as well.[96]

CONCEPTUALIZING COLONIAL BUREAUCRACY IN OCCUPIED PALESTINE

The features of the colonial bureaucracy suggested by Cromer and implemented in India and Egypt are clearly present in the ways that the movement of Palestinians is managed in the Israeli Occupied Territories in the West Bank. Operating in the background of physical, military violence, the bureaucracy of the Israeli occupation takes its form based on racial separation in the law and law's implementation and in the way it organizes time and determines and controls space. The construction of separate roads, the separation of territories—practices formed under the pretext of security needs (which create a hierarchy of space)—were all based on the inhabitants' racial characteristics. The exceptions in law, space, and time provide the organizational universe of the permit regime, the heart of the bureaucracy of the occupation. The permit regime forms a racialized bureaucracy that uses the "security threat" as a basis for the miraculous interventions. The following offers glimpses of the inner workings of these exceptions in space and time, which have become the institutionalized rules of the permit regime.[97]

The management of the permit regime is characterized by colossal inefficiency, unpredictability, unaccountability, conflicting orders, unpublished rules, and what seems to be a chaotic handling of administrative matters. This, however, has produced an incredibly effective machine for achieving its ultimate goals: controlling the Palestinian population, placing impediments on the freedom of movement, atomizing Palestinian society, and creating "procedural bare life."[98]

The definition of what constitutes a "security threat"—and the bureaucratic inner workings that produce it—executed through an intricate set of constantly changing and unpublished security criteria, follows hidden procedures and appears on the scene as an administrative "miracle," to use Schmitt's analogy. This racialized profiling procedure is based on an all-powerful instant *classification as security threat* that overrides other procedures and renders all hitherto administrative procedures obsolete. Its justification relies on the belief that inside every Palestinian—regardless of age, residence, or profession—hides the ghost or demon of a Palestinian terrorist. The official policy of the Ministry of Defense was expressed in a letter from the Office of Coordination of Government Activities in the Occupied Territories to a human rights organization. The letter explicitly refers to the sovereign inability to differentiate between a friend and a foe. The Ministry of

Defense claimed that impeding the freedom of movement is necessary to fight terror and is therefore justified:

> One of the phenomena encountered by the Israel Defense Forces in its fight against Palestinian terrorists is the total and intentional insignificance [i.e., indistinction] created by the terrorists between themselves and the innocent Palestinian population. The Palestinian terrorists operate within the civilian population, dressed in civilian clothes, through assimilation into the population and exploitation of its patronage. Houses, hospitals, ambulances, religious institutions, schools—are all exploited by the terrorists as cover for their activities.[99]

In other words, every Palestinian is a potential terrorist, which provides the justification for a racialized regime, with the declaration of someone as a "security risk" acting as the ubiquitous, omnipotent, miraculous intervention that can be applied abruptly to anyone, immediately implying identification, separation, and exclusion. The status of "denied for security reasons" prevents one from obtaining a magnetic card, but can also mean frequent checks at checkpoints, denial of passage from one area of the West Bank to another, and harassment by border police. And because the criteria for identification, separation, and exclusion as a security threat are never articulated and constantly changing, they never have been part of a rational discourse that can be argued, debated, or questioned. When presented with the demand for published criteria for denial of passage on a security basis, the Department of Population Registry of the military advisor in Judea and Samaria replied that the criteria could not be published for security reasons. This practice collapses the distinction between one's race and one's potential threat to security.

The General Security Service denies entry on the basis of general, changing, and unpublished criteria or on the basis of "specific information." Many cases of this categorization can be linked to the refusal of a Palestinian to collaborate with the GSS in supplying information or to the fact that a member of his or her family is incarcerated in criminal or administrative detention. Denial of entry by the police can occur for many reasons, one of them being that one has not paid a traffic ticket. Tickets can be paid in Israeli post offices that one cannot reach without a permit. Other reasons for this type of denial include the existence of an open police file or court case or because of criteria of the recently formed Denied Entry Department of the police headquarters.[100]

Not surprisingly, in a system administered by phantom decision makers, the Israeli government and the office of the prime minister, officially in charge of the General Security Service, deny the very existence of the procedure of classification of Palestinians as denied for security reasons. In November 2005, in a letter from the media advisor of the prime minister's office to attorney Limor Yehuda from the Association for Civil Rights in Israel (ACRI), the prime minister's office claimed they had no knowledge of such procedures and wrote vaguely that "prevention on the basis of security relates to an action a person wishes to make."

The classification "denied entry for security reasons" provides a powerful tool for the GSS to recruit collaborators and informants, offering them a Faustian deal — lifting the classification of security threat and receiving a permit in exchange for working for and providing information to the GSS. This ongoing practice creates suspicion and atomization within the innermost family and community circles in Palestinian society. As Arendt has phrased it, alluding to government-imposed terror of this sort:

> The effectiveness of terror depends almost entirely on social atomization. Every kind of organized social opposition must disappear before the full force of terror can be let loose. This atomization — an outrageously pale academic word for the horror it implies — is maintained and intensified through the ubiquity of the informer, who can be literally omnipresent because he is no longer merely a professional agent in the pay of the police but potentially every person one comes in contact with.[101]

Since the reasons for a denial are unknown, and since almost any political participation is considered problematic because of the criminalization of membership in organizations, criteria for "correct behavior" remain a hidden matter. Political participation, even on a community level, publishing articles and leaflets, is criminalized. The more one is associated with activity in the public sphere, the less chance one stands of obtaining one's right of passage. Participation in the Palestinian political community of any kind is viewed as a threat to the sovereignty of the security apparatus. The Palestinian whose freedom of movement is impeded by the permit regime remains in a permanent state of waiting, aware of the possibility of restriction of movement on entering Israel, whether in order to travel in the West Bank, to cross the Separation Wall, or to cross the bridge to Jordan.

The "state of waiting" — a source of incredible uncertainty — is yet another powerful force of control, preventing long-term and short-term planning and the management of economic and social structures that require freedom of movement and contact. For a traveling Palestinian, not only the General Security Service, but the individual soldier at the checkpoint *is the law,* exercising sovereign decisions. As one low-ranking officer told an American professor who has supported Palestinian human rights organizations and who was denied entry into the West Bank at the Allenby Bridge: "For you, right now, I am the chief of staff. Maybe even the prime minister."[102] The powerful position of the phantom decision makers of the General Security Service, when it comes to dealings with Palestinians, positions them as half gods, empowered by the force of the total, unappeasable decision based on unknown criteria. The administrative decisions of the security apparatus create a dynamic force that is independent of government decisions and is influenced only by general, vague instructions that can be interpreted and reinterpreted at the site and on the spot.

THE OCCUPATION OF TIME

The exceptions by which the bureaucracy of the occupation rules occur as exceptions in time and exceptions in space.[103] In the District Civil Liaison Offices we have the opportunity to glimpse into the control mechanism of the occupation of time. There are currently nine regional DCLs in each area of the OPT, run by the Israeli Army's Civil Administration. In order to reach a DCL, Palestinians must pass various checkpoints, which function as labyrinths, checkpoint after checkpoint, some permanent and others random (called "flying checkpoints"), most of them operating from 6:00 a.m. to 7:00 p.m. The entrance to the DCL is another checkpoint. The hours when the DCLs are functioning are unknown, even when there is a sign posted with opening times. Sometimes the computer systems are down, other times, the DCL is closed for renovation. Sometimes the long lines of people are told to wait until 1:00 p.m., and other times, they are told to come back tomorrow.

Even during the hours that the DCLs are open, usually only from one to two of four windows are open to receive requests. People invest ample amounts of time in returning again and again to the DCL, because of the dire need for and scarcity of various permits allowing for movement. For instance, the DCL in Hawara, in charge of the area of Nablus, has jurisdiction over 319,453 Palestinians. The head officer of the DCL claims that the DCL services 180,000 people. During 2003, for example, 7351 permits were issued; only 2.3 percent of the population received a permit. Even when most visits to the DCL are futile, people return to this site of the perpetual administrative production of uncertainty. The sense of uncertainty is aggravated when closures take place. When border or internal closures occur, no requests are processed, regardless of their nature, besides medical emergency cases involving life-threatening situations. The dates of closure are unpublished and unknown, except for recurring closures during the Jewish holidays. Therefore, temporal uncertainty is an omnipresent feature of the bureaucracy of the occupation.

CLOSURE: WHEN THE ARMY REPLACES THE MOON

In the racialized theological bureaucracy of the occupation, the apparatus takes charge over the elements of nature, rendering their functions obsolete and replacing them. The sun and the moon determine day and night, the passing of time, as well as the division of the weekday, the time of sleep and waking, work days and holidays. In Palestine, besides the Gregorian calendar introduced at the time of the British Mandate, the Islamic calendar is followed. The Islamic calendar is governed by the moon. However, control over Palestinian freedom of movement by the Israeli Army not only has impeded the ability to move, travel, and satisfy the basic needs of life, but has literally and practically changed the definition of time. The Palestinian calendar is no longer determined by the lunar cycle, but rather by the decisions of military officers and by General Security Service recommendations. The Separation Wall, barbed-wire fences, surveillance cameras, the active presence of the border police, roadblocks, and checkpoints have altered the definition of Palestinian time. The Palestinian kilometer, although it remains the same physical distance as the Israeli kilometer, has become much longer, measuring the time it takes a Palestinian to travel it.[104] One cannot plan a journey, go to work or school, or go shopping without encountering a military obstruction in some form.

Closure brings even this obstructed movement to a halt. Closure means that no Palestinian can enter Israel legally through the permit regime (work permit, residence permits, or humanitarian permits), which is entirely suspended except for extreme humanitarian exceptions decided at the discretion of the military commander. During a closure, the entire bureaucratic apparatus of the occupation ceases to function, and no requests for permits or magnetic cards are processed. For example, during 2002, 240 days of closure were enforced. In 2005, full closure was enacted for 132 days, and in 2006, 127 days of closure were enforced.

Closure is enacted for a variety of reasons. Many of them pertain to the events of the Israeli and Jewish calendars. During religious holidays or Israeli national holidays or during a diplomatic visit of leaders or officials from Europe or the United States, closure is in effect. Closure has also been used as a tool in political negotiations. Due to closure, the Palestinian calendar ceases to be relevant. The times of work and the carrying out of life are determined by the army, not by the moon. Palestinian workers try to coordinate their movements according to the Jewish holidays and plan their time according to the Israeli calendar. However, even when the holiday's date is known, the exact timing of the closure is not known in advance. Moreover, the dates of closure are not directly publicized, and sometimes they are publicized in the Israeli press only. The longest closure in 2006 lasted from Passover through Holocaust Remembrance Day, Memorial Day, and Independence Day, which was a long weekend during the April–May 2006 closure — it lasted for forty-four days.

THE IRRELEVANCE OF THE SUN

During days when entry is permitted, workers rise at 2:00 and 3:00 in the morning to get to work on time, since the waiting time at the checkpoints can easily take over three hours. Sunrise has ceased to govern the time of awakening. At the Erez checkpoint, before the complete restriction on the entry of Gazan workers into Israel, which continues as these lines are written, workers coming from

Gaza would arrive at 1:00 or 2:00 in the morning to take their places in the queue and then sleep on pallets made of cardboard. The time of awaking and sleeping is calculated by the time it takes to ride to and pass through an unknown number of checkpoints, including changing taxis at different roadblocks and checkpoints, since obtaining a permit for a Palestinian car is incredibly difficult. The calculation of time includes security checks, the probable traffic jam at checkpoints, and the consequences of meeting a harassing soldier or border policemen, who hold up Palestinians for various reasons every day. For those without magnetic cards or those classified as "denied entry," the probability of getting stopped rises exponentially, and any calculation of time becomes virtually impossible.

SOVEREIGNTY OVER TIME

In 2003, the Palestinian Authority enacted daylight savings time one week earlier than the Israeli government. This single act of sovereignty over time created chaos at the checkpoints, most of which close at 7:00 in the evening. During this week, people left work at 6:00 p.m. in Palestine and arrived at the checkpoints at what was nearly 8:00 p.m. in Israel, finding themselves trapped. The soldiers at the checkpoints surrounding Nablus said that the checkpoint was closed according to their time, no one was permitted to pass through, and it was not their fault that the Palestinian Authority decided to do "whatever it wanted" and push the clocks back an hour. People simply could not reach their homes. The soldiers told the passengers that it was not their problem that the Palestinians has decided to take the time into their own hands, and for security reasons, the checkpoints closed at 7:00. The week of chaos ended when the Israeli Ministry of the Interior enacted daylight savings time over its territory, restoring the relationship between Palestinian time at the checkpoints and Israeli time. These closure practices, together with the permit regime of movement, have created an occupied time, a colonial time that alters the concept of the collective, family, and personal time of Palestinians at any given moment.

THE PHANTOM SOVEREIGN

Besides the unknown dates and times of waiting for administrative decisions, the most potent, unknown variable in the bureaucracy of the occupation is the identity of the officials who possess administrative discretion in decision making. As we have noted, the sovereign in the Occupied Territories is a phantom sovereign. The military commanders who sign permits are hardly ever remotely connected to a decision to grant a permit. Orders for closed military zones are hardly ever published or presented to Palestinians, and those who issue them remain permanently anonymous. The identity of the General Security Service decision makers is unknown, and they cannot be contacted unless they decide to summon a person who requests a permit for an interview. Usually, soldiers eighteen to twenty years old doing their obligatory military service are the only ones to come in direct contact with such people, but they do not make decisions, except for the decision to allow or to refuse one entry into the DCL in order to make a request, and they rarely have knowledge of the apparatus' policy beyond their specific duties. At any rate, most attempts to trace the origin of power are futile. Conflicting orders issued by the Civil Administration, the local army commanders, the Ministry of Defense, the General Security Service, the police, the border police, the Ministry of Labor, and the Ministry of the Interior may seem to be simply an inefficient mayhem, merely the kind of dysfunction apparent in bureaucracies of various kinds. However, as the residents of the Occupied Territories experience it, without being able to identify any official who is accountable and without knowledge of the structure and process of the decision-making body, its protocols, or its directives, the system of bureaucratic control of movement of the Palestinian population is incredibly powerful and effective. The phantom sovereign is sovereign nonetheless.

TURNING THE GAZE BACK TO THE METROPOLE: REVISITING WEBER'S THEORY OF BUREAUCRACY

The political-theological model of colonial bureaucracy that we have examined here differs markedly from the ideal type developed by Max Weber in *Economy and Society* for liberal civil society in Europe.[105] As we saw, although they are very different from one another, the colonial bureaucracies in Egypt, India, and Palestine have four shared common methods of control.[106] First, a decision on a state of exception analogous to the intervention of a miracle allows for the suspension of the law. In Egypt and India, the occasion for the "miracle" is one of economic need: exploitation of labor and land; in Palestine, it is the existence of a national/ racial conflict and the need to protect Jewish settlers. In all cases, when a measure is introduced for reasons of emergency, it becomes an institutionalized, normalized practice. Even in the cases where the occasion for the original miraclelike intervention is not the infamous "security threat," once there is an outcry or revolt by the subject population, the basis for the reasoning underpinning the intervention shifts to issues of security. Second, in all cases, an intricate bureaucratic system is formed, including many administrative and executive bodies, that functions as a phantom sovereign in the experience of the subject peoples. The presence of authority is ubiquitous, omnipresent, and yet unnamed and not available for any process of appeal. Third, the colonial bureaucracies employ the notion of race to differentiate the metropole from the subject peoples and as a basis for administrative action. And fourth, as methods of control, colonial bureaucracies produce exceptions along spatial and temporal dimensions, principally as ways of regulating freedom of movement.

Weber conceptualized bureaucracies as instruments that secure rationality and predictability: "precision, speed, unambiguity, knowledge of the files, continuity, direction, unity, strict subordination, reduction of friction and of materials and personal costs" raise efficiency to its optimal level. According to this view, the prevalence of uncertainty creates irregularities and complications in planning, standardization, precision, consistency, and the causal linkage between means and ends.[107] Cromer's vision of imperial bureaucracy, on the other hand, provided room for secretive decision-making processes and the issuance of capricious bureaucratic decrees.[108] Cromer believed that colonial rule necessitated flexible structures and needed significant freedom and liberty to issue unpredictable decrees in order to respond to changing conditions and shifting grounds in the colonies.[109] He established the justification for an imperial political-theological bureaucracy based on the inferiority of the "subject races." It possessed mysterious, secretive, unpredictable and arbitrary features. This freedom it achieved by the suspension of the law and the bureaucratic rule by administrative decree.

We have shown that colonial rule was based on fractured sovereignty, selective enforcement of the rule of law, and political-theological bureaucracy resulting in legal and administrative exceptions. We have argued that it is essential to take into account these features in conceptualizing the contemporary violence exerted by those who consider themselves representatives of "Western democracies." We now turn our gaze from the postcolony to the metropole by reexamining Weber's theory of bureaucracy.

Max Weber provided the first systematic formulation of rationality in the social sciences. Integrating social theory with neo-Kantian philosophy and the German institutional school of economics, his work resulted in methodological as well as historical observations about rationality. In his methodological writings, Weber suggested that systems of rationality could be reconstituted as ideal types for the study of social objects. In his historical writings, he examined different aspects of rationality (e.g. action, decision, and systematized worldviews) and applied rationalization—the cultivation of rationality in Western society—to diverse spheres of life, such as religion, law, and economics.

However, Weber's impressive legacy on rationality generated unbridgeable contradictions. Most notable are those between the universality of heuristic devices, on the one hand, and the idiosyncrasy of social processes, on the other; between the intentionality of action and its unintended consequences; and between Kantian-like "objective" ideal types and the subjective meaning of action. Weber's analysis established well-known contradictions between the peculiar historical aspects of charismatic authority and the ahistorical nature of its routinization; between free choice or moral judgment and the constraints imposed by the iron cage of rationality; and between the impersonal nature of instrumental rationality and the highly personal nature of value rationality. Weber believed that only the coexistence of such negating perspectives—historical and ahistorical, subjective and objective, idiographic and nomological, normative and value-neutral—provides the social sciences with tools to analyze the richness of social action in changing historical patterns. Weber understood the impossibility of his position, and he reconciled himself to the limit of social sciences as a peculiar cultural artifact in a given historical moment. Weber did not abandon his incommensurable dualisms. On the contrary, he foresaw that the strength of the social sciences lies in maintaining this ambivalence.

Many intellectuals were intrigued with the nature of Weber's dualistic epistemological framework, but often ignored one dimension of his work or another. For example, American sociologists refused to accept the Janus-faced features of his formulation and relied on the modernist, ahistorical nature of his work on bureaucracy and legitimation.[110] Following Talcott Parsons, they perceived Weber's work as a "generalized theory of authority." They borrowed his thesis on the ascendancy of rationality and left out his critical views about domination. They subscribed to a reified prescription that emphasized the consensual and ahistorical nature of authority and abandoned the historical and phenomenological nature of Weber's rationality. Something of this sort has happened in interpreting the intellectual association between Weber and Schmitt.

The modernist interpretation of Weber's political theory offers three historical, progressive, and consecutive phases of legitimacy: charismatic (personal), traditional, and legal. The postcolonial perspective, on the other hand, offers a hybrid fusion of all three models and allows for their simultaneous appearance: personal influence and sovereign decisionism, together with multiple assisting legalities and bureaucracies.[111] A careful reading of Franz Neumann's *Behemoth* shows that he already had suggested that the bureaucratic model of the Nazi terror state represents a fusion of two kinds of rule: charismatic and bureaucratic.[112] Wolfgang Mommsen has persuasively argued that Weber's threefold model of legitimacy should be reinterpreted in terms of three different, but complementary, issues.

First, his model of legitimacy never suggested that these are three consecutive phases, and in fact, "all forms of domination encountered in empirical reality are mixtures of these three pure types."[113] Weber never ruled out the possibility of charismatic leadership, even in highly bureaucratized societies.

Second, Weber never defined autocratic leadership. His model was based on the basic idea that charisma is the source of all creative leadership. Traditionally, it had been seen as a divine gift by which "God himself had designated certain persons as leaders."[114] Weber substituted for the religious meaning of charisma a phenomenological one, but in fact, his concept was still heavily freighted with political theology. This was best manifested in what he called "plebiscitarian leader-democracy."[115] The British theologian John Milbank has presented ample arguments that attest to the theological roots of Weber's concept of charisma and of charismatic leadership.[116]

Third, Weber's model of legitimacy never included in its scope an epistemological sphere of illegitimacy. As Mommsen again remarks, "the concept of 'illegitimate rule' turns up in Weber's sociology only once and there it refers to the medieval city state." Thus, in Weber's sociological theory of "legitimate rule," "there is no room for illegitimate forms of domination."[117] It does not allow for a distinction between government by consent and tyrannical dictatorship. He seemed to have assumed that every stable political system appears to enjoy the consent of the governed. In a letter to Robert Michels in 1908, he shows intolerance of the theory of the "sovereignty of the people." "The true will of the people ceased to exist for me years ago," he says. Parliamentary democracy was for him "mere ideological trash."[118] Weber believed that the main purpose of politics is to bring strong leaders with genuinely charismatic qualifications into power.

This interpretation of Weber's model of legitimacy comes close to both Schmitt's and Benjamin's notions of political theology. In 1919, a year before his death, Weber had argued that "there is, however, only the choice between leader-democracy with a 'machine' [i.e. a highly bureaucratized party organization that is completely subservient to the political leader] and leaderless democracy, that is to say the rule of professional politicians without a calling, i.e. without the inner charismatic qualities that make a leader."[119] As Mommsen correctly noted, "When he [Weber] argued that it is the charismatic qualification of leaders which matters whereas the democratic institutions are mere functional machinery in their hands, he overstated his own case and came dangerously close to the 'Fuhrerprinzip,' the Fascist leadership principle."[120] According to this interpretation, Weber stood the liberal model of legitimacy on its head and insisted on a scheme in which the creation of the political is designed from top down.[121] Furthermore, Weber expressed clear dissatisfaction with liberal legal formalism, suggesting instead the need for independent political leaders who stand above party machines. He judged the "Caesarist transformation of leadership selection" to be unavoidable, and he viewed the "will of the people" as pure fiction and formal legality as an effort to minimize the rule of man over man.[122] Weber was Schmitt's chief witness for his thesis that "faith in legality of the parliamentary legislative state had to a great extent hardened into mere formalism."[123]

Mommsen argues that Schmitt's infamous thesis about sovereignty "already appears implicitly in Weber's work."[124] Thus, in Weber's work, "the Reich president was essentially conceived as a counterweight to the petty activities of a leaderless parliament and as a valve for the emergence of leadership in a bureaucratic society that tended to leaderlessness."[125] After all, "an increase in the power of the nation state and the selection of leaders who are charismatically gifted within a society hardened into bare legalism."[126] This analysis suggests that Weber perceived bureaucracy as a counterpart to strong personal leadership and opened the space for the antiliberal political decisionism strongly manifested in Carl Schmitt's definition of sovereignty. Raymond Aron has argued that "this re-interpretation of Weberian politics caused an outrage because it robbed the new German democracy of a 'founding father.'"[127]

This observation presents a tough challenge to contemporary Western democracies whose audacious violation of the rule of law calls for a new model of political theory. In particular, they need to ask to what extent they can perceive themselves as secular and liberal in light of their theologically based political foundations—which they tend to deny. This is particularly crucial in light of the gross epistemological asymmetry in the political literature by which the fusion of sovereignty and theology tends to be underplayed in observations about the West and overplayed in observations about the East and the global South.

We believe that the colonial model of bureaucracy as represented by Cromer's ideal type sheds this asymmetry unambiguously. While the colony is a site in which we observe the relationships between bureaucracy, law, and violence most lucidly, it also emphasizes the way that the law—any law including the metropole's law—originates in violence.[128] While martial law was proclaimed most vigorously in the colonies, its sources remained the laws of Europe. Not only that, but the relationship between the colony and the metropole exerts a constant movement between them. As Hussain put it in the context of British rule of India, the exception "could not be exclusively situated in the colonial realm; its ideological consequences would inevitably return to Britain itself."[129] This movement should be carefully traced and followed in a comparative study of metropole-colony relationships.

This conclusion suggests two particular lessons regarding the nature of the Israeli occupation of Palestinian territories and its political framework. First, the notion of legitimacy through charismatic rule is mistaken for legitimacy through exception. The army official and especially the representative of the General Security Service, on site, represent a colonial bureaucracy in which charisma is ushered in by the singular, ultimate power to decide, which in turn raises the status of the security official to that of a half god, able to inflict "procedural violence" at any moment, thus creating unbearable conditions of life. "Security theology," as it collapses the distinction between race and security on the basis of a continually constructed and institutionalized "emergency" situation of "clear and present danger" is thus again mistaken for charismatic leadership.

Second, and more importantly, colonial rule in the territories does not follow the contours of Weber's rational model of bureaucracy. Rather, it is based on a series of exceptions, on racial supremacy, and on particularistic assumptions of governance. The bureaucracy of the occupation retains the administrative memory and paradigms of colonial bureaucrats, whose principles of government are an opposite mirror image of the Weberian model and include unpublished rules, flexibility, total discretion, secrecy, and different rules for different categories of people based on race, with *ira et studio* ("scorn and bias"), rather than without it, as Weber proscribed, perpetuated by an imminent security threat and a constant classification process distinguishing between friend and foe. The bureaucracy of the occupation is an administrative weapon that employs procedural violence as a tool for managing a population engaged in a conflict. And yet, critics and supporters of this mode of administration alike continue to view it as a dysfunctional bureaucracy, rather than as one that follows a model that differs from Weber's classical model bureaucracy. This view, which follows the framework of bureaucracy in liberal democracies, creates an epistemological lacuna. The interpretation we have proposed above views the aggregation of exceptions to the rule as the foundational principle of the bureaucracy itself, rendering it functional and effective for the exacerbation of control and domination over the colonized.

The permit regime, although not unique to the Palestinian case, forms a framework for the control of civilians and does not engage directly in physical violence and death, but rather in the denial of conditions of life and the perpetuation of a social, economic, and political implosion. The bureaucracy of the occupation relies on a complex system of administration that does not begin and end with the military, but permeates the administrative borders of Israel proper. No ocean separates metropole and colony, Israel and the OPT, but the twenty-minute ride between the two, quite exceptionally, leads to a particular administrative planet where colonial bureaucracy produces the possibility of occupying not only space, but time itself.

Yet Israeli bureaucrats, academic researchers, and Palestinian subjects still look for elements representing the rational model. If we may put it this way, Weber's model of bureaucracy serves as an illusionary framework that forges false consciousness for both the Palestinian subjects and the ruling bureaucrats. While numerous observers have attempted to conceptualize the bureaucratic model of rule and to emphasize its dysfunctional forms, at the same time, they have overlooked the inner workings of the colonial form of bureaucracy that is actually in operation in the Occupied Territories.

To be sure, false consciousness does not necessarily conform to the Marxist's interpretation of it. It is a cognitive schema that shapes the consciousness of both the colonizer and the colonized. The application of the rational model as a cognitive schema helps colonial bureaucrats manage their everyday lives and offers a language for rational communication. The disparities between the rational model and the actual colonial model are perceived and interpreted as deviations from the rule, rather than as the rule itself. This "mistaken" diagnosis is therefore functional, rather than dysfunctional, for further domination by the colonizer.

NOTES

We thank Adi Ophir, Michal Givoni, Ronen Shamir, Gideon Kunda, Khaled Fourani, Alexandra Kalev, and Michal Frenkel for excellent comments on earlier drafts.

1   This declaration has some precedents. From 1949 to 1966, the Palestinian citizens of Israel were put under severe military rule. One can easily expect that some practices traveled from this experience into the new regime in the Occupied Territories. This resemblance or continuity, however, has never been studied systematically, but it suggests a link between the 1948 occupation and the 1967 occupation. To be sure, although we speak here about the occupation that took place in 1967 and after, we do not subscribe to the position of the Zionist left in Israel that acknowledges the occupation in 1967, but denies that what happened in 1948 was an occupation, as well.

2   Interview with Shlomo Gazit, the military coordinator of operations in the territories and the first head of the Civil Administration (1968–74), June 9, 2006, Tel Aviv University.

3   *Report on the Occupied Territories, 1967–1974.* Ministry of Defense and the Coordination of Government Activities in the West Bank and Gaza Strip (June 1975) (in Hebrew).

4   Eitan Diamond, "Crossing the Line: Violation of the Rights of Palestinians in Israel without a Permit," B'Tselem report (March 2007), available on-line at http://www.btselem.org/Download/200703_Crossing_the_Line_eng.pdf (last accessed July 25, 2008).

5   In December 2007, B'Tselem reports, the army maintained sixty-six checkpoints in the territory of the West Bank, posing a great impediment to freedom of movement, since every passenger was checked. Thirty-six more checkpoints were on the Green Line border and were manned around the clock. Some were at gates in the Separation Wall, some on the roads. Sixteen more checkpoints were partially manned or had a watchtower. Twelve checkpoints existed within the city of Hebron. In December 2007, there were 459 unmanned blockades by cement blocks, dirt mounds, and areas that had been dug up to prevent passage. There also were forty-one roads, spanning 700 kilometers, that Palestinians were prevented from using and that were restricted to use by Israelis in the West Bank. B'Tselem press release, December 31, 2007, available on-line at http://www.btselem.org/english/press_releases/20071231.asp (last accessed July 25, 2008).

6   Gaza-Jericho Interim Agreement Annex II, Protocol Concerning Civil Affairs, Article 1 (a) (2) (c), available on-line at http://www.mfa.gov.il/MFA/Peace%20Process/Guide%20to%20 the%20Peace%20Process/Gaza-Jericho%20Agreement%20Annex%20II (last accessed July 25, 2008).

7   Yehezkel Lein, "Builders of Zion: Human Rights Violations of Palestinians from the Occupied Territories Working in Israel and the Settlements," a B'Tselem report (August 1999), available

on-line at http://www.btselem.org/Download/199908_Workers_Eng.doc (last accessed July 25, 2008).

8   B'Tselem reports that from October 2000 to December 2007, 4,330 Palestinians were killed by Israeli armed forces, 864 of them under the age of eighteen. Of these, 2,056 were not engaged in combat when killed. In the same period, 1,130 Israelis were killed, 119 under eighteen. See http://www.btselem.org/English/Statistics/Casualties.asp (last accessed March 3, 2009). Until 2005, when the policy was stopped by the Civil Administration, 668 homes were demolished as a form of punishment. See http://www.btselem.org/English/Punitive_Demolitions/Statistics.asp (last accessed March 3, 2009). In 2005, 29 people were killed in "targeted assassinations" and 70 in 2007. During 2007, 840 prisoners were in administrative detention during 2007 without being charged with an offense. See http://www.btselem.org/English/Administrative_Detention/Statistics.asp (last accessed March 3, 2009).

9   On the coexistence of the two legal systems, see Orna Ben-Naftali, Aeyal M. Gross, and Keren Michaeli, "The Illegality of the Occupation Regime: The Fabric of Law in the Occupied Palestinian Territories," in this volume and the sources cited there. Here is one example: If a Palestinian from the OPT and an Israeli citizen or resident are arrested for participation in a demonstration or for entering into a closed military zone at the exact same time and place, the disparity in rights and consequences is great. The Israeli usually will be released by the police after a few hours or brought before a civil court twenty-four hours after his or her arrest, usually to be released on self-bail. The Palestinian can be arrested for four days, then will be brought before a military judge and will face a trial that can result in prison sentences anywhere from a month to three months.

10   Interview with Dov Zdaka, former head of the Civil Administration (1998–2002), December 2006.

11   Interview with Dov Zdaka, 2006.

12   Max Weber, "Characteristics of Bureaucracy," in *From Max Weber: Essays in Sociology,* trans. and ed. H. H. Gerth and C. Wright Mills (Oxford: Oxford University Press, 1946).

13   *Ibid.,* p. 96.

14   Franz Neumann, *Behemoth: The Structure and Practice of National Socialism* (1942; New York: Harper Books, 1963).

15   Max Horkheimer and Theodor W. Adorno, *Dialectic of Enlightenment* (1944; New York: Continuum, 1994).

16   Zygmunt Bauman, *Modernity and the Holocaust* (Ithaca, NY: Cornell University Press, 1989).

17   Hannah Arendt, *Eichmann in Jerusalem: A Report on the Banality of Evil* (New York: Viking Press, 1963), p. 60.

18   There are additional arenas in which this structure of modern bureaucracy is manifested, for example, in the sphere of industry, in formal organizations, and in the processes of institutionalization. See Harry Braverman, *Labor and Monopoly Capital: The Degradation of Work in the Twentieth Century* (New York: Monthly Review Press, 1974); Richard Edwards, *Contested Terrain: The Transformation of the Workplace in the Twentieth Century* (New York: Basic Books, 1979); Michael Burawoy, *Manufacturing Consent: Changes in the Labor Process under Monopoly Capitalism* (Chicago: University of Chicago Press, 1979); W. Richard Scott, *Organizations: Rational, Natural, and Open Systems* (Englewood Cliffs, NJ: Prentice Hall, 2003); and James C. Scott, *Seeing Like a State* (New Haven, CT: Yale University Press, 1998). We excluded these areas from the current discussion, which pertains solely to political theory.

19   Achile Mbembe, "Necropolitics," *Public Culture* 15, no. 1 (2003): pp. 11–40.

20 Pierre Bourdieu provides a historical description of the emergence of the bureaucracy of the European state, focusing on its institutionalization and its putatively natural appearance. He describes the state as a culmination of a process in which different species of capital are consolidated: the capital of physical force or instruments of coercion, economic capital, cultural capital, and symbolic capital. Bourdieu focuses on the conflictive and coercive elements that were used not only externally, but also internally, including seizures, arrests, imprisonments, and a writ of restraint binding on all parties. "Rethinking the State: Genesis and Structure of the Bureaucratic Field," in Pierre Bourdieu, *Practical Reason: On the Theory of Action* (Stanford, CA: Stanford University Press, 1998), pp. 35–74. By focusing on the conflictive history of bureaucracy's emergence, this description resonates well with Michel Foucault's account of sovereignty and Walter Benjamin's account of violence. See Michel Foucault, *Society Must Be Defended: Lectures at the Collège de France, 1975–76,* ed. Mauro Bertani, Alessandro Fontana, and François Ewald, trans. David Macey (New York: Picador 1997); Walter Benjamin, "Critique of Violence," trans. Edmund Jephcott, in *Walter Benjamin, Selected Writings, Volume 1: 1913–1926,* ed. Marcus Bullock and Michael W. Jennings (Cambridge, MA: Harvard University Press, 1996), pp. 237–52.

21 See also Carl Schmitt, *The Nomos of the Earth* (1950; New York: Telos Press, 2003).

22 Giorgio Agamben, *State of Exception,* trans. Kevin Atell (Chicago: University of Chicago Press, 2005).

23 The all-caps name is an acronym for the act's real title, the Uniting and Strengthening America by Providing Appropriate Tools Required to Intercept and Obstruct Terrorism Act of 2001.

24 Benjamin, "Critique of Violence," in *Walter Benjamin Selected Writings, Volume I: 1913–1926,* ed. Howard Eiland and Michael W. Jennings (Cambridge, MA: Harvard University Press, 1958), pp. 247–52.

25 Carl Schmitt, *Political Theology: Four Chapters on the Concept of Sovereignty* (1922; Cambridge, MA: The MIT Press, 1988). On Schmitt's text as a response to Benjamin's "Critique of Violence," see Agamben, *State of Exception,* chap. 4.

26 Schmitt, *Political Theology,* p. 14.

27 *Ibid.,* pp. 5, 36.

28 Michel Foucault, "Governmentality," trans. Rosi Braidotti and rev. Colin Gordon, in Graham Burchell, Colin Gordon, and Peter Miller (eds.), *The Foucault Effect: Studies in Governmentality* (Chicago: University of Chicago Press, 1991), pp. 87–104.

29 Giorgio Agamben, *Homo Sacer: Sovereign Power and Bare Life,* trans. Daniel Heller-Roazen (Stanford, CA: Stanford University Press, 1998), p. 83.

30 Andreas Kalyvas, "The Sovereign Weaver: Beyond the Camp," in Andrew Norris (ed.), *Politics, Metaphysics, and Death: Essays on Giorgio Agamben's "Homo Sacer,"* (Durham, NC: Duke University Press, 2005), pp. 107–34. Ronit Lentin also provides a feminist critique, speaking particularly about what she labels the "femina sacra." See Ronit Lentin, "'Femina Sacra': Gendered Memory and Political Violence," *Women's Studies International Forum* 29 (2005): pp. 463–73.

31 D. K. Fieldhouse, *The Colonial Empires: A Comparative Survey from the Eighteenth Century* (New York: Delacorte Press, 1967).

32 Nasser Hussain, *The Jurisprudence of Emergency: Colonialism and the Rule of Law* (Ann Arbor: The University of Michigan Press, 2003), p. 19.

33 For example, Agamben echoes the distinction that Arendt borrowed from Aristotle between *zōe* and *bios* as two forms of life (Hannah Arendt, *The Human Condition* [Chicago: University

of Chicago Press, 1958]) and her analysis of stateless people (Hannah Arendt, *The Origins of Totalitarianism* [New York: Harcourt, Brace and World, 1951]).

34   Adi Ophir, "Introduction to *Homo Sacer*," in Lavie Shai (ed.), *Technologies of Justice* (Tel Aviv: Ramot) (in Hebrew), pp. 360, 377.

35   Walter Benjamin, "On the Concept of History," trans. Harry Zohn, in *Walter Benjamin, Selected Writings, Volume 4: 1938–1940*, ed. Howard Eiland and Michael W. Jennings (Cambridge, MA: Harvard University Press, 2003), p. 392.

36   Lauren Benton, *Law and Colonial Cultures* (Cambridge: Cambridge University Press, 2002), p. 261.

37   *Ibid.*, p. 18.

38   *Ibid.*, p. 13; Sally Engle Merry, "Law and Colonialism," *Law and Society Review* 25, no. 4 (1991): pp. 889–922; Sally Falk Moore, "Treating Law as Knowledge: Telling Colonial Officers What to Say to Africans about Running 'Their Own' Native Courts," *Law and Society Review* 26, no. 1 (1992): pp. 11–46.

39   Jean Comaroff and John Comaroff (eds.), *Law and Disorder in the Postcolony* (Chicago: University of Chicago Press, 2006).

40   Peter Burroughs, "Imperial Institutions and the Government of Empire," in Andrew Porter (ed.), *The Oxford History of the British Empire: The Nineteenth Century* (Oxford: Oxford University Press, 1999), pp. 170–97.

41   Ross Johnston Ross, *Sovereignty and Protection: A Study of British Jurisdictional Imperialism in Late Nineteen Century* (Durham, NC: Duke University Press, 1973); Benton, *Law and Colonial Cultures,* pp. 20, 104, 172.

42   See, for example, Timothy Mitchell, *Colonising Egypt* (Berkeley: University of California Press, 1988) and Hussain, *The Jurisprudence of Emergency.*

43   Ann Laura Stoler, "On Degrees of Imperial Sovereignties," *Public Culture* 18, no. 1 (Winter 2006): pp. 126, 132, 134.

44   Bernard S. Cohn, "Political Systems in Eighteenth-Century India," in *The Bernard Cohn Omnibus* (New Delhi: Oxford University Press), p. 483.

45   Bernard S. Cohn, "African Models and Indian Histories," in *The Bernard Cohn Omnibus,* p. 216.

46   *Ibid.*, p. 219.

47   See Ronit Lentin (ed.), *Thinking Palestine* (London: Zed Books, 2008) and Theo David Goldberg, "Racial Palestinization," in *ibid.*, pp. 25–45.

48   Hussain, *The Jurisprudence of Emergency,* p. 113.

49   Roger Owen, *Lord Cromer: Victorian Imperialist, Edwardian Proconsul* (Oxford: Oxford University Press, 2004).

50   Evelyn Baring, Earl of Cromer, "The Government of Subject Races," *Edinburgh Review,* January 1908, pp. 1–27; Evelyn Baring, Earl of Cromer, *Modern Egypt,* 2 vols. (New York: Macmillan, 1908).

51   Peter Burroughs, "Imperial Institutions and the Government of Empire," in Andrew Porter (ed.), *The Oxford History of the British Empire: The Nineteenth Century* (Oxford: Oxford University Press, 1999), p. 191.

52   Cromer, "The Government of Subject Races," p. 13.

53   Bernard S. Cohn, "Anthropology and History in the 1980s," in *The Bernard Cohn Omnibus,* p. 68.

54   Cromer, "The Government of Subject Races," p. 6.

55   Evelyn Baring, Earl of Cromer, letter to Lord Salisbury, 1899, quoted in Arendt, *The Origins of Totalitarianism,* p. 95.

56   *Ibid.* In conceptualizing colonial bureaucratic sovereignty, Cromer criticized the "Continental school of bureaucracy," which refers to the French system of direct rule. "Over-centralization is a danger which should be carefully shunned," he suggested. He disparaged the centralized structure and "the tendency of every French central authority…to allow no discretionary power whatever to his subordinate," resulting in a reciprocal tendency of the subordinate "to lean in everything on superior authority." In contrast to the French model, the British model offered a decentralized bureaucracy that "pervades the whole British administrative system, and that has given birth to a class of officials who have both the desire and capacity to govern." Decentralized structure and its irregular form of exceptions should not be regarded as a menace to the empire's rule of law, he argued. After all "the British official…whether in England or abroad, is an Englishman first and an official afterwards. He possesses his full share of national characteristics." Cromer, "The Government of Subject Races," pp. 15–16.

57   Cromer, "The Government of Subject Races," p. 1.

58   Cromer, *Modern Egypt,* p. 2:130.

59   *Ibid.,* 2:131, p. 2:148.

60   *Ibid.,* 2:155, p. 2:143.

61   In accounting for the following examples, please note that they by no means attempt to be exhaustive or representative. They are used as illustrations only, to underscore our arguments.

62   Mitchell, *Colonising Egypt,* p. 97. Martial law was a frequent manifestation of the exception in the colonies. As Hussain persuasively argues in his excellent analysis in *The Jurisprudence of Emergency,* it carried different meanings in Europe and in the colonies. Based on cases from Punjab and St. Thomas, Hussain shows how the use of martial law in the colonies were suffused, both in practice and in theory, with racialized definitions and interpretations.

63   Cromer, "The Government of Subject Races," p. 16.

64   *Ibid.,* p. 14.

65   *Ibid.,* pp. 1–2.

66   *Ibid.,* p. 6.

67   Mitchell, *Colonising Egypt,* pp. 97, 96.

68   Timothy Mitchell, *Rule of Experts: Egypt, Techno-Politics, Modernity* (Berkeley: University of California Press, 2002), pp. 60–61; Mitchell, *Colonising Egypt,* pp. 40–43.

69   Mitchell, *Rule of Experts,* p. 62.

70   Mitchell, *Colonising Egypt,* p. 97.

71   *Ibid.*

72   *Ibid.,* p. 98.

73   Ilana Feldman, in "Government without Expertise?: Competence, Capacity and Civil Service Practice in Gaza, 1917–67," *International Journal of Middle East Studies* 37 (2005) describes the British rule of Gaza and Palestine after 1917. Despite the fact that she adopts a completely secular position, she still argues in favor of what she labels "Palestinian peculiarity" (p. 489).

74   Cromer, "The Government of Subject Races," p. 16.

75   Hussain, *The Jurisprudence of Emergency,* p. 38.

76   Bernard S. Cohn, "The Study of Indian Society and Culture," in *The Bernard Cohn Omnibus,* p. 148.

77   Cohn, "Anthropology and History in the 1980s," p. 58

78   John W. Cell, "Colonial Rule," in Judith M. Brown and William Roger Louis (eds.), *The Oxford History of the British Empire, vol. 4, The Twentieth Century* (Oxford: Oxford University Press, 1999), p. 236.

79 Cited in Hussain, *The Jurisprudence of Emergency,* p. 39.

80 Bernard S. Cohn, "Representing Authority in Victorian India," in *The Bernard Cohn Omnibus,* p. 632.

81 Bernard S. Cohn, "From Indian Status to British Contract," in *The Bernard Cohn Omnibus,* p. 468.

82 Johnston, *Sovereignty and Protection,* p. 217.

83 There is a vast literature that describes the contradictions and cultural clashes between the rulers and the ruled, as well as the cultural transformations and cultural machinations in and around these differences. Ranjit Guha articulated this as a paradox in which the law was intended to serve as the basic defining principle of colonial rule, "indeed as a primary signifier of British dominance in the subcontinent corresponding in function and structure to the hegemonic signifier of Rule of Law in metropolitan Britain." Ranjit Guha, "Introduction," in *The Bernard Cohn Omnibus,* p. xvii. Yet it is exactly the law that became an instrument for producing rifts and cleavages and an arena for struggle over issues such as decisionism versus the lack of decisionism, personal versus contractual relations, and equality versus inequality before the law. Bernard S. Cohn, "Some Notes on Law and Change in North India," in *The Bernard Cohn Omnibus,* pp. 568–71.

84 Hussain, *The Jurisprudence of Emergency,* p. 102. As Hussain argues, "a given act of violence contains no integral difference whether executed by those under legal authority or by those set against it" (*ibid.,* p. 107). It is therefore the case that "the law resorting to violence" produces a need for external signature of legality in order to distinguish between the two. As Benjamin taught us, the law fears "revolutionary violence" more than regular crime, since it threatens not so much to transgress the law, but to set up an alternative logic to it.

85 *Ibid.,* p. 80.

86 Quoted in *ibid.,* pp. 119, 120.

87 Bernard S. Cohn, "African Models and Indian Histories," in *The Bernard Cohn Omnibus,* p. 212.

88 Benton, *Law and Colonial Cultures,* p. 15.

89 Cohn, "African Models and Indian Histories," p. 216.

90 *Ibid.,* p. 219.

91 D. A. Washbrook, "India, 1818–1860: The Two Faces of Colonialism," in Andrew Porter (ed.), *The Oxford History of the British Empire, vol. 3, The Nineteenth Century* (Oxford: Oxford University Press, 1999), pp. 395–421.

92 Hussain, *The Jurisprudence of Emergency,* p. 100.

93 *Ibid.,* p. 124.

94 Robert F. Holland (ed.), *Emergencies and Disorder in the European Empires after 1945* (London: F. Cass, 1994).

95 To be sure, the legal exception and the state of emergency were not originally discovered in the colonies. Already in the early nineteenth century, Benjamin Constant had identified the fact that freedom is threatened by the frequency of emergency rulings by both right-wing and left-wing politicians. Constant issued a stern warning about the institutionalization of emergencies in political practice. See Fontana Biancamaria (ed.), *Constant: Political Writings* (Cambridge: Cambridge University Press), p. 143. Yet it was in the colonies where the state of emergency was practiced time and again and where it was institutionalized through the use of racialized bureaucracies. Arendt has pointed this out, although Agamben does not pick it up. In *Homo Sacer,* Agamben mentions only in passing the colonial Spanish history

in Cuba and that of the English in South Africa as two territories into which the exception was extended.

96 For example, in order to fight the protest of North African immigrants in Paris in September 2005, the state enforced an emergency law that had been legislated in the context of the Algerian War.

97 In this context, we focus mainly on permits requested by Palestinian workers for labor purposes only. However, permits are needed for movement within the West Bank, for humanitarian reasons such as medical treatment and accompaniment of sick persons, and for access to holy sites. Denial for security reasons affects the right to exit to Jordan over the Allenby Bridge.

98 See Hohaida Ghanim, "Biopower and Thanato-politics: The Case of the Colonial Occupation of Palestine," in Ronit (ed.), *Thinking Palestine,* pp. 65–81.

99 Letter of Colonel Daniel Beaudoin, head of the Foreign Relations Branch, Coordination of Government Activities in the Territories, Israel Ministry of Defense, to Physicians for Human Rights, June 4, 2004.

100 The category of "denied entry" issued by the General Security Service includes two hundred thousand Palestinians, while those "denied entry" by the Israeli police numbers sixty-four thousand.

101 Hannah Arendt, *On Violence* (New York: Harcourt, Brace and World, 1970), p. 55.

102 Exchange between Allenby Bridge security guard and M. N., June 2006.

103 Amal Jamal, "On the Voyages of Racialized Time," in Yehouda Shenhav and Yossi Yonah (eds.), *Racism in Israel* (Tel Aviv: Ha'Kibutz Ha'Meuchad and the Van Leer Institute, 2008) (in Hebrew), pp. 348–80.

104 See Ariel Handel's essay, "Where, Where to, and When in the Occupied Territories: An Introduction to Geography of Disaster," in this volume.

105 Max Weber, "Characteristics of Bureaucracy," in *From Max Weber: Essays in Sociology,* trans. and ed. H. H. Gerth and C. Wright Mills (Oxford: Oxford University Press, 1946), p. 463.

106 One major difference in the bureaucracy in Palestine stems from the conflicting claims on land and the need to separate the Palestinian minority in Israel from the Palestinians in the Occupied Territories in order to maintain demographic hegemony, as well as the "security needs" of the Jewish settlers that produce a massive separation based on racial and national identity.

107 Yehouda Shenhav, "Fusing Sociological Theory with Engineering Discourse: The Historical and Epistemological Foundations of Organization Theory," in Knudsen Christian and Haridimos Tsoukas (eds.), *The Oxford Handbook of Organization Theory: Meta-theoretical Perspectives* (Oxford: Oxford University Press, 2003), pp. 183–209; Yehouda Shenhav, *Manufacturing Rationality: The Engineering Foundations of the Managerial Revolution* (Oxford: Oxford University Press, 1999); and Yehouda Shenhav, "Manufacturing Uncertainty and Uncertainty in Manufacturing: Managerial Discourse and the Rhetoric of Organization Theory," *Science in Context* 7 (1994): pp. 275–305.

108 Michal Frenkel and Yehouda Shenhav, "From Binarism Back to Hybridity: A Postcolonial Reading of Management and Organization Studies," *Organization Studies* 27, no. 6 (2006): pp. 855–76.

109 This point was crucial to Arendt's analysis of totalitarianism, because she saw the growing disparity between the political center and its economic goals on the periphery as endemic to the disintegration of European liberal democracy. It was particularly the gap between the bureaucracy as a form of governance for one's own citizens and bureaucracy as a form of

governance for the noncitizen "subject races" that she saw as crucial to understanding the conditions under which atrocities took place. In this vein, Arendt even made a direct comparison between imperial bureaucracy and the bureaucratic machinery of the Third Reich: "everything was always in a state of continuous flux, a steady stream," a description that "sounded plausible to the student of totalitarianism, who knows that the monolithic quality of this form of government is a myth." Arendt, *The Origins of Totalitarianism*, p. 136. For the relationship between colonial/imperial genocides, administrative massacres, and the Nazi genocide, see also A. Dirk Moses, "Conceptual Blockages and Definitional Dilemmas in the 'Racial Century': Genocides of Indigenous Peoples and the Holocaust," *Patterns of Prejudice* 36, no. 4 (2002): pp. 9–36; Benjamin Madley, "From Africa to Auschwitz: How German South West Africa Incubated Ideas and Methods Adopted and Developed by the Nazis in Eastern Europe," *European History Quarterly* 35, no. 3 (2005): pp. 429–64; and Isabel V. Hull, "Military Culture and the Production of 'Final Solutions' in the Colonies: The Example of Wilhelminian Germany," in Robert Gellately and Ben Kiernan (eds.), *The Specter of Genocide* (Cambridge: Cambridge University Press, 2003), pp. 141–62. They trace the colonial origins of "the Final Solution," "Lebensraum," "concentration camps," and "institutionalized forms of racism."

110 See Shenhav, "Fusing Sociological Theory with Engineering Discourse" for an elaborated discussion.

111 See Wolfgang Mommsen, *Max Weber and German Politics, 1890–1920* (1959; Chicago: The University of Chicago Press, 1984), and Wolfgang Mommsen, *The Age of Bureaucracy: Perspectives on the Political Sociology of Max Weber* (New York: Harper & Row, 1974).

112 Neumann, *Behemoth.*

113 Mommsen, *The Age of Bureaucracy,* p. 74.

114 *Ibid.,* p. 78.

115 *Ibid.,* p. 83.

116 John Milbank, *Theology and Social Theory: Beyond Secular Reason* (Oxford: Blackwell, 1990), pp. 84–98.

117 Mommsen, *The Age of Bureaucracy,* p. 83.

118 *Ibid.,* p. 87.

119 *Ibid.,* p. 90.

120 *Ibid.,* p. 93.

121 Mommsen, *Max Weber and German Politics,* p. 183.

122 *Ibid.,* pp. 186, 189.

123 *Ibid.,* p. 405.

124 *Ibid.,* p. 382.

125 *Ibid.,* p. 383.

126 Weber, quoted in *ibid.,* p. 452.

127 Raymond Aron, *Main Currents in Sociological Thought,* 2 vols., trans. Richard Howard and Helen Weaver (New York: Basic Books, 1967), p. 2:248.

128 Benjamin, "Critique of Violence."

129 Hussain, *The Jurisprudence of Emergency,* p. 114.

A LETTER FROM THE JUDGE ADVOCATE'S OFFICE to an Israeli attorney representing a Palestinian applying for a permit. The Israeli defense establishment refuses to publish the criteria on which it grants or refuses to grant permits to enter Israel. To receive an entry permit and movement permits, Palestinians are at times summoned to a meeting with Shabak agents at a Coordination and Liaison Office, where they are required to collaborate in exchange for obtaining the permit.

אזור יהודה ושומרון
לשכת היועץ המשפטי
ת.ד. 5, בית אל 90631
טל: 711/02-9977071
פקס: 02-9977326
221/00 - 614740
ט' בטבת התשס"ו
9 בינואר 2006

לכבוד
יעל ברדה, עו"ד
פקס: 02-6245463

הנדון : ___ ___ ___ ___ ___ ___ : ת.ז. ___

1. במענה לפנייתך בעניין הנדון, הריני להשיבך, כי האזור הינו "שטח סגור", מכח צו בדבר שטחים סגורים (אזור הגדה המערבית) (מס' 34), תשכ"ז – 1967.
עפ"י צו זה, אסורה יציאתם של תושבי האזור לישראל, אלא אם יש בידיהם היתר יציאה פרטני. לפיכך הרי שאין לאיש מתושבי האזור כל זכות שבדין לצאת לישראל.

2. בדיקתנו העלתה כי מרשך אינו עומד באמות המידה הנוכחיות להוצרת כניסה לישראל של תושבי האזור.

3. אמות מידה אלו נקבעות על סמך הערכת סיכון כללית ופרטנית הנערכת על ידי גורמי הביטחון בשים לב לנסיבות ובהסתמך, בין היתר, על גיל, מצב משפחתי, מקום מגורים ופרמטרים אישיים נוספים.

4. לחווי ידוע לך שאמות מידה אלו משתנות מעת לעת בשים לב להערכת הסיכון הביטחוני של גורמי הביטחון, כנובע מהיקף הפיגועים, זהותם של מבצעי הפיגועים וכיו"ב.

5. בברכה,

טל יחיאב, רב"ס
מש"קית משפטים
מדור מרשם אוכלוסין
בשם היועץ המשפטי

Judea and Samaria
Office of the Judge Advocate
P.O.B. 5 Beit El 90631
Tel: 02-997071/711
Fax: 02-9977326
614740—21/00
9 Tevet 5766
20 January 2006

Yael Berda, Attorney
Fax: 02-6245463

Re: _____ **, I.D. No.** _____

1. In response to your letter in the aforementioned matter, the area is a "closed area" pursuant to the Order Regarding Closed Areas (West Bank) (No. 34), 5727—1967.

    This order forbids residents of the area to exit to Israel unless they have an individual exit permit. Therefore, no resident of the area has any right under law to exit to Israel.

2. Our check indicated that your client does not meet the current criteria for residents of the area to enter Israel.

3. These criteria are established on the basis of a general and individual risk assessment made by security officials, taking into account the circumstances and relying, inter alia, on age, family status, place of residence, and other personal parameters.

4. It should be clearly understood that these criteria change from time to time, depending on the security-risk assessment of security officials resulting from the magnitude of terrorist attacks, identity of the perpetrators, and so forth.

5. Sincerely,

    Tal Yehiye, Corporal
    Legal NCO
    Population Registry Section
    On behalf of the Judge Advocate

From Domination to Destruction:
The Palestinian Economy under the Israeli Occupation

Leila Farsakh

The aim of this essay is to analyze the Palestinian economy of the West Bank and the Gaza Strip, which is on the verge of total collapse. By 2007, Palestinian real per-capita income fell by 40 percent compared with its 1999 levels, and poverty rates soared to over 67 percent.[1] The separation of Gaza from the West Bank in June 2007 only aggravated the economic disparity between the two Palestinian regions, but did not alter their economic demise. On the eve of the Israeli assault on Gaza in December 2008, the strip had no economy to speak of: Food supplies to over 56 percent of its population were insecure, its unemployment rate was over 60 percent, and its private and banking sectors were destroyed.[2] According to the World Bank, the Palestinian economy was kept afloat thanks to donors' aid, which amounted to an annual average of $800 million, or $258 per Palestinian person.[3] This situation stands in complete contrast to what many expected of the Oslo peace process, which was supposed to set the stage for Palestinian economic growth. Indeed, between 1996 and 1999, the Palestinian GDP is recorded to have grown at 8 percent per annum, the banking sector in the West Bank and Gaza boomed, and Palestinian unemployment dropped from 23 percent in 1996 to 11 percent in 1999.[4]

This essay explores the underlying structural mechanisms that brought about such an unstable economic situation and that can explain the contradictions between the expectations set out by the Oslo process and the reality on the ground. It is critical of arguments made by some academics and policy makers that maintain that Palestinian economic problems are mainly tied to the ambiguity of the political project set out by the Oslo peace process and the failure so far to establish a viable sovereign Palestinian state. It argues instead that the failure of the Palestinian economy is a result of a sui generis colonial structure of domination that was set up by al-Naksa ("the setback" in Arabic), or Israeli occupation in 1967. This colonial structure was transformed, rather than abolished with the Oslo peace process. The Oslo years also set the stage for separating the Gaza Strip from both Israel and the West Bank while keeping the West Bank integrated within Israel. It led to the demise of any economically and territorially viable Palestinian independence on any piece of the Occupied Palestinian Territories.

The Israeli-Palestinian conflict has been analyzed as a colonial conflict from a sociological and historical viewpoint, but not always from an economic perspective. The work of Israeli post-Zionist sociologists stressed the importance of Zionism's colonial foundation as a way to understand the nature of Israeli society and polity.[5] They showed that the nature of Israeli democracy and its economy are the outcome of a specific form of colonial control over land and labor that sought to create an exclusivist Jewish state. Palestinian academics and international scholars have also relied on the colonial framework of analysis for explaining the extent of Palestinian dispossession and exploitation under Israeli rule.[6] However, they have not always explained the economic implications and depth of this colonial structure. Over the past decade, there has also been an increasing interest in using the apartheid colonial experience of South Africa as a way to analyze the evolution and implications of the Israeli occupation of the West Bank and Gaza.[7] However, most economists and development specialists have been reluctant to describe the political economy of the Israeli occupation as colonial. Part of the reluctance stems from the fear, mainly in the United States, of being accused of anti-Semitism or unscholarly bias. It also stems from the peculiarity of the occupation from a legal and an economic point of view.

However, analyzing the economics of Israeli occupation of the West Bank and Gaza as colonial is both necessary and useful. It allows for the incorporation of the role of power and domination, and here, specifically, Zionism, in explaining the unsustainable structure of the Palestinian economy and its implications for Palestinian self-government. It is also helpful in analyzing the ways this economic structure evolved over the course of the past forty years as a function of Israeli territorial ambitions and the nature of Palestinian resistance to it, rather than of simply unmediated or rational market forces. It allows, in turn, for a critical understanding of the ways in which a Palestinian state has been economically compromised and how its demise affects the prospects of any other solution to the conflict. Last, but not least, situating the economics of the occupation within a colonial framework of analysis allows for a reconsideration of the role of the international community, particularly after Oslo, in indirectly perpetuating a colonial relation that the international legal system does not legitimize.

In what follows I first describe and analyze the political economy of Israeli occupation pre-1993 and then identify the important structural changes brought about by the Oslo peace process.

DEFINING THE ISRAELI OCCUPATION

It is difficult to analyze the economy of the Israeli occupation within a clear theoretical framework. The literature that focuses on Israeli-Palestinian economic relations in the West Bank and the Gaza Strip tends to describe the Palestinian economy as distorted, stalled, skewed, underdeveloped or "de-developed." On the one
hand, one finds a liberal economistic approach that situates the Palestinian economy within a rationalist liberal framework of analysis. The material produced by
various economic institutions and development specialists in this regard considers
the problems of the Palestinian economy to be a result of failure to allow market
forces to play their role or of political intervention preventing efficient rational
optimal choices from producing sustainable economic growth.[8] On the other hand,
some political economists have emphasized the importance of integrating Israel's
Zionist foundation and motivations, particularly land conquest for the sake of
establishing a strong Jewish state, into the analysis of the Palestinian situation.[9]
They argue that economic exploitation and dislocations that Palestinians experienced are not simply a result of market failure, but of Zionist settlement expansion
into Palestinian land. The mainstream literature, though, tends to avoid describing
the Occupied Territories' economy as living under a colonial regime. Part of the
reluctance stems from the peculiarity of Israeli rule in the Occupied Territories, the
ambiguous legal status of the occupation, and the ambiguity of the phenomenon
of colonialism.

According to Jurgen Osterhammel, colonialism is a relation of domination by
which an invading foreign minority rules over an indigenous population, often to
serve the interests of a metropolis.[10] However, he is also quick to add that colonization is also "a phenomenon of colossal vagueness."[11] Part of the vagueness stems
from the difficulty of distinguishing colonialism from colonization, the former
being a system of domination, while the latter is a process of control that evolves
over time as a result of changing material and international conditions.[12] It also
stems from the risk of essentializing colonialism and the need to distinguish the
political rhetoric of exploitation from the historical specificity of a colonial project.
Understanding the Israeli occupation as a colonial process is particularly challenging, because it posits further the difficulty of identifying the processes by which
a specific form of a military conquest occurring in a postcolonial world and regulated, in principle, by international law can become colonial, despite the attempts
by the international legal system after 1945 to end and delegitimize all forms of
foreign domination.

However, as Caroline Elkins and Susan Pederson, among others, have shown,
colonialism has come in various types. Seventeenth-century and eighteenth-

century New World colonies differed from settler colonial projects of the nineteenth and twentieth centuries insofar as they relied on a mercantile capitalist structure and succeeded in eliminating the indigenous population. Settler colonialism meanwhile came in various variants: The experience of colonial Algeria was not analogous to Japan's colonization of Korea, and the South Africa settler colonial project was different from Israel's creation in 1948.[13] What is colonial about all these projects is that they involved a settler community seeking to dominate and in some cases to eliminate the indigenous population in order to create an exclusive polity of settlers. They fundamentally sought to expropriate land already inhabited by others. They differed in the way they dealt with the four elements central to any colonial endeavor: relations with the indigenous population, control over the land, the overall economic structure of domination, and the relation to the metropolis from which the colonial project emanated.

Relation with the indigenous population, including questions of subordination or elimination of the indigenous population, as well as the issue of their legal representation and rights in comparison to the settlers, have been of primary importance. Directly related to control of the indigenous population and imbricated with it is control over the land, as is the overall economic structure of domination, particularly the way the colonial project has dealt with territorial and labor questions. In what ways and to what end the indigenous population is controlled have direct implications for the ways in which their land is expropriated and how it is put to use by the colonizers, whether for purposes of economic exploitation or for other purposes. Colonial projects have typically been conducted in pursuit of economic gains and wealth, seeking to appropriate rich lands as much as to exploit cheap labor. Finally, colonial projects have not been independent of the international political system in which they appear. Their success or failure has always been tied to the nature of their relation to the metropolis, to the extent to which it helped finance the colonial enterprise, and to whether or not the international legal system upheld that enterprise.

It might not be necessarily evident that by using these criteria, the Israeli occupation of the West Bank and the Gaza Strip automatically can be said to be colonial, for two main reasons. The first is the question of Israel's intention and the extent to which it wanted to occupy the West Bank and the Gaza Strip in 1967 and exploit their land and labor. The second is the more important issue of the legal framework governing the occupation.

Where intentions are concerned, the Israeli official discourse has insisted that the 1967 War was a preemptive war that sought to defend Israel's precarious existence and to deter Arab countries from invading it. The Israeli cabinet debated at the conclusion of the war whether or not to annex the Occupied Territories, but decided not to do so in order to protect the Jewish character of the Israeli state.[14] The Israeli military and political establishment regarded the territorial acquisitions of the 1967 War as bargaining chips to be used for diplomatic gains—namely, the Arab countries' recognition of Israel's existence. While this stand has been challenged by a number of scholars, who have argued that Israel had provoked and intended the 1967 War in order to expand its boundaries,[15] there is no official evidence to support the claim that Israel was in search of new markets or planned to exploit the Palestinian population economically.

However, it can be misleading to establish the colonial foundation of the occupation, or any other form of domination, on the basis of intention. Noneconomic intentions do not prevent colonial processes from being unleashed and having economic dimensions, as the experiences of France in Algeria or the Boers in South Africa, among others, reveal. As has been well documented, the Israeli economy benefited from the Palestinian economy, which was, until 1993, its second export-and-import market, after the United States. As will be shown below, the key question is to identify the economic elements in the structure of domination and the extent to which they forced the Palestinians' dependence on Israel.

On the other hand, the international legal framework governing Israel's occupation of the West Bank and the Gaza Strip contributed to the ambiguity of the Israeli occupation as a typical colonial form of domination. The international community was neither compliant with the occupation nor did it legitimize it the way that the League of Nations acted with regard to the European mandate of Middle Eastern states in the 1920s, for example. The superpowers, as well as the United Nations, condemned the 1967 War and reaffirmed the inadmissibility of the acquisition of land by war. UN Security Council Resolution 242 in November 1967 did not bestow any legitimacy on Israel's occupation of the West Bank and the Gaza Strip and called on it to retreat from the Occupied Territories in exchange for peace. Israel did not and could not claim sovereignty over the West Bank and Gaza, and although it annexed East Jerusalem, this annexation was never accepted by the international community. Moreover, the Fourth Geneva Convention applied to the West Bank and Gaza Strip.[16] This meant that Israel was not allowed to change the demographic, political, or economic structure of the land it took under its control. While Israel has accepted the humanitarian provisions of the Fourth Geneva Convention, the international community has refused Israel's interpretations and has contested many of its actions in the Occupied Territories, the latest example being the July 2004 ruling of the International Court of Justice against the construction of the Israeli Separation Wall in the West Bank.

The international legal framework thus sought to prevent the creation of a colonial relation between Israel and the Palestinian Occupied Territories. This being said, it is important to note that the international community did not ensure that Israel will be compliant. UN Security Council Resolution 242, which became the main reference for peace negotiations, does not specifically address the Palestinian right to self-determination or make the usual reference to other UN resolutions on Palestine, including UN General Assembly resolution 181, which calls for the creation of an Arab state in Palestine. It also did not specify the areas of land that Israel occupied, which meant that Israel could have a margin to maneuver in its redefinition of the 1967 boundaries in any peace negotiation. Moreover, Israel was not faced with any threat of action for any violation, since UN Security Council resolution 242 was adopted under Chapter 6, rather than Chapter 7 of the UN Charter. This meant it was without implementation force. The ambiguity of such an important international resolution made it relatively easy for Israel to pursue its territorial ambitions without fearing major political or military repercussions.

In fact, while the international legal framework sought to distance Israeli rule from being seen as a classical colonial endeavor, a reexamination of Israeli policy since 1967 reveals that Israel's occupation has been colonial insofar as it has consisted of a foreign entity dominating a large indigenous majority for the sake of appropriating its land. It is, however, a distinctive colonial project because of the way Israel dealt with the four key elements central to any colonial project—the subjugation of the indigenous population, the issue of land control, the structure of economic domination, in which the question of labor control was central, and the relation of the colony to the metropolis.

SUBJUGATING THE INDIGENOUS POPULATION AND THEIR LAND

The first distinctive element about Israel's colonial structure of domination is the way Israel dealt with the population that came under its control in 1967 and the central role that the Israeli Army came to play in this regard. In the aftermath of the 1967 War, the Israeli military gained control over about one million Palestinians, which formed 30 percent of the total population under Israeli rule at the time, and of which 70,000 were residents of East Jerusalem and the neighboring villages who immediately became "permanent Israeli residents" after Israel annexed the area in which they lived. As I noted, the Israeli government did not intend to incorporate them into Israel for fear of jeopardizing the Jewish character of the state. At the same time, it could not expel them or force them to leave, as many did in 1948.[17] According to the Fourth Geneva Convention, the military was the only entity allowed to rule over the population of the Occupied Territories until their status was determined. The military had the mandate to ensure security, but not to change the demographic and territorial character of the area.

As is well documented by now, the Israeli government opted for a system of rule that allowed for maximum incorporation of the land while maintaining a soci-etal and geographic separation between Israelis and the indigenous Palestinian population. In this regard, the military played a central role, since it became the tool that allowed territorial and demographic changes to take place, and thereby it sowed the seeds of a colonial relation between Israel and the Occupied Territories. The Israeli military produced over 200 military orders between 1967 and 1970 and established the large Civil Administration apparatus in 1981, institutionalizing the structure that separated Israelis from Palestinians while facilitating the expropria-tion of land in the West Bank and the Gaza Strip. While such a large investment of the occupier's resources is not unique to Israel and can be seen in Japan's coloniza-tion of Korea or Taiwan, for example,[18] it is original insofar as it was not conducted for economic purposes, but rather to expand Israel's 1948 borders. The military became the conduit for land appropriation through its organization of the system of land expropriation and settlement construction. During the first decade of the occupation, the military issued a number of decrees for acquiring land, mainly by declaring them state or absentee land (Military Orders No. 58 and No. 59). It also established a high planning committee composed of military officials that took control of land administration and planning in the Occupied Territories (Military Order No. 418) and created a special department for land transactions and the reg-istration of settlements (Military Order No. 569). Moreover, it prevented Palestin-ians from registering their land and from investing in it without obtaining military approval. The military was thus able to take direct control of 35 to 40 percent of land of the West Bank and the Gaza Strip and to supervise the whole settlement movement, with which it remains closely tied.[19]

As in other colonial processes, the Israeli military created settlements as a way to establish a territorial claim over an indigenously populated area. As Moshe Dayan put it in 1971, Israeli settlements in the Occupied Territories are essential "not because they can ensure security better than the army, but because without them…the IDF would be a foreign army ruling a foreign population."[20] Although doings so was illegal under the Fourth Geneva Convention and numerous UN reso-lutions, Israel built over 178 settlements between 1972 and 2003 and allowed the transfer of 400,000 Israeli citizens into the Occupied Territories, half of whom were transferred during the Oslo years.[21] Half of those live in the eleven settlements of East Jerusalem that Israel considers an integral part of its "unified Jerusalem," but that under international law were considered illegal. The peculiarity of Israeli set-tlements as a central element in the Israeli colonization of the West Bank and Gaza Strip stems in part from the fact that settlers did not come or were not brought in to exploit the Palestinians or in search of economic gains. Unlike the settlers in Algeria, the whites in Kenya or Zimbabwe, or the unionists in Northern Ireland,

Israeli settlers did not so much make their living in the Occupied Territories as use it as a subsidized dormitory. Still in 2000, less than 48 percent of the settlers have worked in the settlements in the West Bank and Gaza Strip, with the majority commuting to Tel Aviv or Jerusalem.[22]

Settlers remain a central pillar of the Israeli colonial structure. They have provided a way to create a claim over Palestinian land and have also allowed the institutionalization of a legal system of segregation, which is a common feature of most colonial projects. The Israeli military instituted two different legal systems in the West Bank and Gaza Strip: one for the settlers and the other for the Palestinians. The settlers were governed by Israeli civilian law, while the Palestinians were ruled by military law. The Israeli military ruled the Palestinians through a series of military orders that combined some aspects of international law governing populations in times of war with specific Israeli concerns for the settlements. The Israeli military governor allowed Israeli citizens to live and work in the West Bank after 1967, although the Fourth Geneva Convention forbids it.[23] Israeli settlers were protected by and accountable to Israeli law, while Palestinians were subject to military law. Settlements remained directly dependent on the army until they were declared towns that became administered like any town in Israel, with rights to local planning, levying taxes, and zoning and urban planning, which were all forbidden to Palestinians. In the ways that it controlled the indigenous population of the Occupied Territories and colonized their land, Israel created a de facto institutionalized system of legal segregation between Palestinians and Israelis, albeit an original one. It was original insofar as Israel did not want to include the Palestinians in its polity as citizens or residents,[24] even as second-class citizens, and could not do so from an international legal point of view. At the same time, it kept their legal and political status unresolved, left to the outcome of the Israeli-Palestinian negotiations.

DOMINATION AND THE ECONOMICS OF OCCUPATION

The way Israel dealt with the Palestinian economy, and particularly with Palestinian labor, is also at the heart of the peculiarity of Israeli occupation as a colonial project. As is well documented by now, Israeli economic policy in the area was not based on any grand strategy for economic exploitation or investment. Chief economists consulted by the military at the end of the Six-Day War argued that economic integration based on free movement of capital and labor across the 1967 borders would be most beneficial to both Israelis and Palestinians in the long run. This is because it would have allowed an efficient allocation of resources between two economies with different resource endowments.[25] The national unity government at the time rejected this suggestion for economic and political reasons. Economically, it was feared that integration would harm Israeli workers, cause a capital flight toward cheaper labor and resources in the West Bank and Gaza Strip, and be detrimental to the Jewish-sector domestic development.[26] Politically, it would have threatened the interests of the Jewish trade-union and agricultural lobbies, as well as posing a complicated challenge to the issue of citizenship rights.

Instead, the military decided to incorporate, rather than to separate, the Palestinian economy into Israel in a way that would facilitate maximum territorial incorporation of the land, but without creating Israeli dependence on Palestinian labor. One of the main factors that prevented Israel from undergoing a South African apartheid or a Zimbabwean colonial experience was an economic structure that refused to rely on indigenous labor. Before 1948, less than 30 percent of the Jewish sector relied on Palestinian/Arab labor, and after 1948, Israeli Arabs came to represent from 15 to 20 percent of the Israeli labor force. In the 1980s, Palestinian labor from the West Bank and Gaza Strip formed from 30 to 40 percent of workers employed in the Israeli construction sector, but since 1967, they have not represented more than 7 percent of the total labor force working inside Israel.[27]

Yet the economics of Israeli occupation has been colonial insofar as it was based on a system of economic integration that made the economies of the West Bank and the Gaza Strip dependent on Israeli demand and regulations and unable to respond to local demand or to create the basis of a viable economy and an independent Palestinian state. While the Israeli occupation might not have been conducted for the purpose of economic exploitation, it was structured to ensure Israel's economic and territorial domination. The economics of occupation relied on four main pillars. The first was an economic policy that was guided by a concern to pacify the Palestinian population economically while keeping Israeli control over the land and preventing any competition from Palestinian goods or factors of production. The second was the integration of the Palestinian economy into Israel through the creation of a "one-sided" customs union that allowed Israeli products free access to the Palestinian markets, but restricted the entry of Palestinian goods, particularly agricultural ones, into the Israeli economy. This customs system enabled Israel to collect and appropriate tariff revenues on goods destined to Palestinian areas, which amounted to approximately from 12 to 21 percent of the West Bank and Gaza Strip GNP between 1970 and 1987.[28] The third pillar supporting the economics of occupation was financial and fiscal restriction. Israel restricted investment and capital flows, something that would have logically flown from Israel into the Occupied Territories because of their lower labor costs. The Palestinian population was also taxed heavily, but investment in local infrastructure remained low.[29] The fourth pillar involved promoting the flow of Palestinian labor into Israel while the Israeli army forbade Israeli workers or businessmen from working inside the Palestinian territories.

As is well documented by now, the economic effects of the occupation between 1967 and 1987 have been the "paradoxical" rise in Palestinian per-capita income alongside diminishing productive capabilities.[30] Per-capita income doubled between 1970 and 1987, and GNP grew by an average of 3 percent per annum. The rise in per-capita income has been sustained thanks to the flow of Palestinian workers into the Israeli economy. Palestinian labor migrants became the key structural link ensuring the flow of this economic system of integration. Palestinian workers employed in Israel represented 45 percent of the Gaza labor force in the mid-1980s and 32 percent of West Bank workers. Their income represented 25 percent of Palestinian GNP and financed the trade deficit formed with Israel. Israel remained the market for 70 percent of Palestinian exports and the source of 90 percent of its imports. Palestinian migrant workers in Israel were the main anchor of Palestinian economic growth, a growth that relied principally on access to Israel.[31]

INTERNATIONAL RELATIONS: THE OSLO YEARS

The Economic Protocol of the Oslo Peace Agreements sought to redress some of the inequalities imposed by Israel's economic management of the Occupied Territories. Its preamble clearly expresses the intention to have the Palestinian economy prosper and be guided by Palestinian interests. Yet the Oslo agreements, like UN Security Council Resolution 242, do not specify the right of Palestinians to a state or to economic independence. More importantly perhaps, they do not specify that their aim is to end the occupation. Instead, they promise to establish an interim Palestinian self-governing authority that will work together with Israel on defining a final-status agreement.[32] Built into the accords was an ambiguity that was in part the result of the decision to defer all discussions on sovereignty, land, and borders to the final-status negotiations.

According to Arie Arnon and Jimmy Weinblatt, the Economic Protocol was an incomplete contract insofar as it did not address the power imbalance between Israel and the Palestinians. It kept Israel in control of the borders as well as in control of major economic decisions that would have a significant effect on the Palestinian economy, such as the scope of trade diversification and the size of labor flows to Israel and of the tax revenues that were to be refunded to the Palestinian Authority. The literature on the economics of Oslo has long debated whether the prospects for Palestinian economic success hinged on the implementation of the Economic Protocol or on its structural flaws.[33] Those who favored the latter perspective have tended to argue that Oslo confirmed the geoeconomic system put in place by the post-1967 military administration.[34] Those who defended the former maintained that Oslo intended to end military control.

A closer look at the Oslo agreement reveals that the peace process neither abolished nor confirmed the geoeconomic structure established in 1967. It did not demolish the political economy of occupation, it reshaped it. It created a new colonial structure of domination that was based on three new foundations. These included the institutionalization of Israeli security concerns as a governing principle in all economic activity, the creation of the Palestinian Authority with limited autonomy, and the transfer of economic management of the Occupied Territories from Israel to international institutions, namely, the World Bank and the International Monetary Fund (IMF).

The institutionalization of Israeli security concerns, while present before 1993, is peculiar insofar as it was done with de facto consent of the newly established Palestinian Authority, a consent that could not have been given before its establishment in 1993. It was rationalized in terms of Israel's defense against the rise in suicide bombings and the political opposition to Oslo. Yet while this opposition strengthened the hold of military considerations, security was embedded in the agreements themselves. It was structured in the scope of jurisdiction that the Palestinian Authority was given, in the way the territorial question was handled, and in the pattern of trade and labor relations created. What is colonial about this new structure is its ability to enable Israel to expropriate more Palestinian land and to control Palestinian mobility and economic conditions. What is new about it is its attempts to obtain a de facto international endorsement of the precedence of Israeli military laws and security concerns over international law in the management of the occupation.

INSTITUTIONALIZING ISRAELI MILITARY CONCERNS The military continued to play a central role in the colonizing process of the West Bank and the Gaza Strip after 1993. While the Oslo agreements allowed devolution of Israeli rule to an elected Palestinian Authority, it did not dismantle the Israeli military infrastructure. Unlike other cases where occupation ended, be it in East Timor, Kenya, or Algeria, cases in which the occupiers retreated, taking their troops, administration, and laws with them, in the West Bank and Gaza, the Israeli military did not retreat, but redeployed. Israeli laws were not abrogated, but were combined with limited Palestinian legislation. The Oslo agreements' modus operandi was to create an infrastructure of cooperation between the Palestinian Authority and the Israeli military through the medium of the Joint Israeli-Palestinian Liaison Committees, which became the agencies for the transfer of authority from the Israeli Civil Administration to the Palestinian Authority. Among the first stipulations of the Oslo Accords was the creation of a Palestinian police force, which is to ensure public order and to cooperate closely with the Israeli side on security issues.[35] The implication of this structure was to allow the Israeli military to have a say in every aspect of Palestinian life.

The institutionalization of security concerns is best exemplified in the way the Oslo Accords dealt with legal claims over land, as well as with the issue of closures, checkpoints, and permits, all of which are key to any prospect for economic growth, let alone independence, in the Occupied Territories. The Interim Agreement kept Israel in control of 59 percent of the West Bank land, which came under Area C.[36] It further supplied a legalistic endorsement of Israel's claim over the land, because the Palestinian Authority agreed to respect the legal rights of Israelis in areas under its control, as well as Israel's sole jurisdiction over the settlements.[37] This endorsement, combined with the fact that the settlements were left out of the interim agreement, made it possible for Israel to colonize more Palestinian land. Between 1993 and 2004, Israel expropriated over 120,000 dunams (29,653 acres),[38] build over seventy-two new settlements and outposts, and transferred a total of 209,000 new settlers into the territories.[39] While this expropriation is still illegal according to the Fourth Geneva Convention, nothing in the Oslo Accords provides the Palestinians with the legal or political measures to stop it.

The institutionalization of Israeli security concerns is also seen in the way the Interim Agreement makes closure not a violation, but an accepted prerogative of Israel. Article IX of the Protocol of Redeployment and Security Arrangements (PRS) clearly states that Israel alone has the right to close its crossing points, prohibit or limit the entry of persons into its areas, and determine the mode of entry of people into its areas (including Area C). It affirms Israel's right to intervene in any Palestinian area at any time in case of perceived threats, including intervening in Areas A and B. Between 1994 and 1999, Israel imposed 484 days of closures, the equivalent of three months per year, and installed as many as 230 temporary or "floating" checkpoints that stalled all sustainable economic activity.[40] While it is true that these closures were imposed in anticipation or as a result of a growing number of suicide bombings in Israel by parties opposed to the peace process, the fact remains that the Oslo structure did not make these restrictions illegal or offer a means to deal with their economic damage.

The institutionalization of Israeli security concerns has created a new form of colonial domination not only insofar as it facilitated the appropriation of Palestinian land, but also in the new mechanisms it created for population control. In contrast to the pre-Oslo years, when population movements across the 1967 borderline were still possible, after 1993, population movements became militarily regulated and restricted. The system of restriction that started to be imposed on Palestinians after the first intifada became more elaborate and institutionalized in the Oslo agreements, particularly with the Protocol on Civil Affairs. Any Palestinian seeking to enter Israel for work needed to apply for a permit issued by the Israeli Civil Administration after undergoing a security clearance.[41] The system was further extended in 1996 with every increase in suicide bombings inside Israel, when the Israeli military made all movement contingent on having a permit. This applied to workers as much as to businessmen, and to women as well as to men.

A WEAK PALESTINIAN AUTHORITY The Oslo agreements allowed the creation of an elected Palestinian Authority, but tied its jurisdiction to Israeli considerations. The jurisdiction of the Palestinian Authority did not emanate solely from the Palestinian electorate or from international law, but rather remained tied to the scope of Israeli redeployment. In this regard, the Palestinian Authority was given mainly functional, rather than full territorial jurisdiction. The Palestinian Authority could thereby run the civilian and economic affairs of 93 percent of the Palestinian people, but could not fully control Palestinian land. Nor could it abolish Israeli laws on land over which it had no direct control. Until 2000, the Palestinian Authority had direct control, but no sovereignty, over only 20 percent of the West Bank land and 70 percent of the Gaza Strip (Area A).

Within this framework, the Palestinian Authority was given the responsibility of managing the Palestinian economy. Its ability to fulfill this role was constrained not only by its limited territorial jurisdiction, but also by the nature of the trade relations established with Israel. The economic protocol of the Oslo II agreement did not abolish the de facto customs unions set in place, nor did it establish a free-trade agreement for fear that it might insinuate notions of territorial demarcations that were left to the final-status negotiations.[42] It instead established a new customs union that allowed for the free movement of capital and gave the Palestinians limited leeway in monetary and trade policy. In monetary policy, the Palestinian Authority was not allowed to issue its own currency, but was able to establish a monetary authority that became responsible for the management of banks and control of financial activity in the area. The Palestinian economy was also allowed to trade directly with Arab and foreign countries for a limited list of goods.[43] However, Palestinian trade remained bound by Israel's trade policy, because Israeli tax rates (both direct and indirect) remained the governing guidelines, as were Israeli standards and import regulations. Israel, though, agreed to remit to the Palestinian economy value-added taxes (VATs) and customs taxes collected on goods specifically destined to the West Bank and Gaza Strip, something it never did before 1994.

In other words, Oslo restructured the nature of Palestinian dependence on Israel. Despite the importance to the Palestinian economy of Palestinian labor migration to Israel, the Oslo agreements did not promise to protect it. At the same time, it did not guarantee the smooth movement of foreign and domestic capital that would generate domestic employment. Meanwhile, the Israeli military and its Civil Administration retreated from being the direct manager of the Palestinian economy to being the gatekeeper of Palestinian finances and access to the world. Customs revenues collected by the Israeli Ministry of Finance on goods imported to the Palestinian economy became the most important source of financing for the Palestinian Authority. It represented 60 to 70 percent of the Palestinian Authority's revenues and 20 percent of the Palestinian GNP.[44] The entity responsible for the transfer of funds was no longer the Civil Administration, but a committee composed of representatives of the Israeli Ministry of Finance, the Israeli military, and the prime minister's office. The Israeli National Security Council, not the Ministry of the Economy, was also directly involved in all meetings with the Palestinian Authority over customs revenues. Customs revenues became one of the major leverages that restricted the Palestinian Authority's scope of action, one solely in Israeli hands. This new pattern of economic relation fosters, rather than ends the colonial structure of the economy insofar as it facilitates the appropriation of Palestinian revenues by Israel. It allows the Israeli military, rather than economic mechanisms of supply and demand, to control labor and population movements within Palestinian areas and outside them. It also restrains Palestinian economic autonomy and ties Palestinian growth to Israeli territorial and unilaterally defined security considerations.

INTERNATIONAL AID The third major structural change brought about by the Oslo Accords is the new central role it gave to the international donor community in managing of the Palestinian economy. The World Bank, the IMF, and the Ad Hoc Liaison Committee (AHLC) became the advisors of the Palestinian Authority, helping it to formulate its economic policy as much as to manage it. The IMF has effectively overseen the Palestinian Finance Ministry, helping it to plan the Palestinian taxation system as much as to supervise its internal accounts. It also has become the interlocutor with the Israeli Finance Ministry, ensuring that customs revenues are being transferred to the Palestinian Authority. The World Bank is the manager of the donors' funds, deciding their allocation by sector as well as by ministry. Between 1994 and 2000, the donor community disbursed $3.2 billion, the equivalent of an annual West Bank and Gaza Strip GDP. This money was put to use in generating employment projects as much as in paying the salaries of the Palestinian Authority's employees and sustaining the Palestinian Authority's budget.[45] After 2000, international aid amounted to over $1.2 billion a year.[46]

The international community has advisory power over the Palestinian Authority and thereby over the economic direction that the latter can take. In line with the policies of the so-called "Washington Consensus" of policy reforms for economies in crisis and its underlying neoliberal philosophy, the World Bank and the IMF sought to lay the foundation of a viable Palestinian economy that would be characterized by a vibrant private sector, free markets, and a responsible, small, and fiscally rigorous public sector. However, they soon found themselves in the paradoxical situation of going against their own recommendations and instead financing policies they have long considered inefficient and have been busy dismantling elsewhere. Thus, while the World Bank and the IMF have been concerned with Palestinian Authority overspending, especially with regard to public employment in a mainly security-related and inefficient administration, they could not stop it. They actually financed such employment, which they deemed necessary to prevent a total collapse of Palestinian income in view of Israel's restrictions on Palestinian labor movement inside the Green Line, the imposition of closures by Israel, and a rise in poverty rates in the West Bank and Gaza Strip. Meanwhile, the private sector has seen its growth curtailed, in part with the rise of monopolies since 1994 and with the disintegration of the rule of law, especially after the second intifada. The international donor agencies often found themselves in a central, though contradictory position of bailing out the Palestinian Authority and making it dependent on them while having to intervene with Israel as a central player. They had power over the Palestinian Authority insofar as they could determine the amount and direction of the aid they gave. At the same time, their ability to make the Palestinian Authority economically viable was constrained by Israel's unwillingness to cooperate. The international community meanwhile could neither dismiss nor challenge Israel, whose sovereignty was not called into question.

The paradox or contradictions in the international institutions' interventions highlight the power asymmetries of the Oslo peace process, as well as the way in which the international community has become indirectly implicated in a relation of domination that it was supposed to help dismantle. This strong international financial intervention raises the question of the extent to which the cost of the occupation is being subcontracted to the international community, which has always refused to legitimize it. This can be all the more problematic if the international community leans toward accepting as given, rather than challenging Israel's actions on the ground. The World Bank report on the disengagement from Gaza, *Stagnation or Survival: Israeli Disengagement and Palestinian Economic Recovery* (2005), does not mention the occupation as the source of the demise of the Palestinian economy, but focuses on the issue of closure. It does not call for abolishing the closures, but rather for finding ways to accommodate them. This is a significant development that reflects the international community's willingness to accept, indirectly, at least, a fundamental colonial relation based on land expropriation and an oppressive mechanism of separation and control in the name of security.

THE ECONOMIC CONSEQUENCES OF OSLO The economic implications of this new structural relation were massive. In terms of income, the Palestinian economy and people suffered under Oslo, largely as a result of the closure system and the inability of the Palestinian Authority or the international community to counter its paralyzing effects. Real GDP per capita shrank by 18 percent between 1994 and 1996 and again by 36 percent between 2000 and 2007.[47] Poverty, defined as individual earnings of less than $2:00 per day, reached 23.2 percent of the total Palestinian population in 1998, touching 46 percent of those living in the Gaza Strip, compared with 15.4 percent of the households in the West Bank. It rose to touch over 60 percent of the West Bank and Gaza Strip population between 2001 and 2007.[48] The economy became hostage to the system of closures and checkpoints, growing when they are not in use and suffering when they are. It was prevented from collapsing thanks to donors' aid that amounted to 25 percent of West Bank and Gaza Strip GDP. Donors' aid replaced the role played by remittances from Palestinian employment in Israel in the pre-1993 era. As economic life became conditional on Israeli security considerations, three major trends developed.

First, public employment became important, especially in Gaza, because workers could not access Israel. Public-sector employment absorbed nearly 30 percent of the Gaza labor force, compared with less than 15 percent of the West Bank's between 1996 and 2000.[49] It replaced the role played by the Israeli labor market for Gaza workers, in particular. Public-sector employment was dominated by security forces, which represented between 60,000 and 80,000 employees out of a total of 110,000 to 140,000 public-sector wage earners.[50] Their wage bill represented a significant drain on the Palestinian Authority's finances, one that was often ameliorated by the international organizations, who ironically opposed public employment.

Second, the Oslo economic and security structure facilitated the creation of monopolies, especially because they were more successful than individual companies in claiming and centralizing customs clearance. These monopolies included Palestinian Authority and private-sector actors closely tied with the procurement of security services and other goods and firmly linked with Israeli military companies or parastatal Israeli monopolies such as cement or tobacco. The development of rent-seeking activities of this sort was unavoidable, but highly costly for the private-sector development that the donor community is keen on developing. They indicate a restructuring of economic dependence on Israel, rather than its elimination. Israel has remained the main source of imports and exports, as well as the gateway to the outside world, while contacts between Israeli and Palestinian businessmen have become solely mediated through a few monopolies with close ties to the security establishments. While the World Bank has long criticized these monopolies, it has acknowledged that Oslo facilitated their creation. It also has ended up accepting them, since they are the only means of collecting customs revenues from Israel, given the framework set out by Oslo's economic protocol.[51]

Third, the economies of the West Bank and the Gaza Strip grew further apart and related differently to the Israeli economy. Trade between the West Bank and Gaza fell by 30 percent between 1993 and 1998, while Gaza's trade with Israel shrank by 25 percent.[52] The Gaza Strip was effectively cut off from Israel, while the West Bank continued to be integrated into Israel. This was most evidently seen in the changing patterns in Palestinian labor mobility. Employment in the Israeli economy represented less than 8 percent of Gaza workers in 1999 and less than 2 percent in 2005, compared with 38 percent in 1992. The figures for the West Bank stood at 25 percent and 12 percent in 1992 and 2005, respectively. These different labor-movement dynamics were only partly explained by the effect of closures and restrictions on people's movement. They are also tied to the military's intention to keep hold of the West Bank by building settlements. The settlement-housing sector stagnated in Gaza, but grew in the West Bank by over 6 percent per annum between 1995 and 2002.[53] Still, in 2006, and despite the al-Aqsa intifada, 55,500 Palestinians from the West Bank, or 13 percent of its employed force, worked in the Israeli economy, reflecting continuous integration of the West Bank into Israel.[54]

THE ECONOMICS OF DISENGAGEMENT

The institutionalization of Israeli security concerns that led to further fragmentation of Palestinian land was consolidated by Israel's response to the al-Aqsa intifada. The violence of the Palestinian response to the failure of Oslo and the continuous occupation was met by the Israeli decision to sophisticate their security measures further. These measures were intended to finalize the separation of Palestinians from Israelis while incorporating the largest amount of land into Israel. They are best encapsulated in the construction of the Separation Wall, the consolidation of the checkpoint system, and the disengagement plan from Gaza.

In June 2002, Israel started to build a wall separating Israel from the West Bank, but whose route did not follow the 1949 armistice line. By 2008, 415 kilometers (or 57 percent of the total size) of the Separation Wall had been constructed, mainly in the northern part of the West Bank, including 89 kilometers built around East Jerusalem. Seventy-nine percent of it ran inside the West Bank, rather than along the Green Line.[55] The Israeli military declared all West Bank land between the security wall and Israel a closed military zone and thus prone to further confiscation. So far, 479,881 dunams of land (1,942,010 acres) is trapped west of the Wall and thus is prone to confiscation, and 44, 273 Palestinians have been trapped in 1,149 localities. Upon its completion, the Wall would leave 395,900 Palestinians (including 220,000 living in the suburbs of East Jerusalem) isolated outside the Palestinian enclaves that the Separation Wall will have created. This is equivalent to 10 percent of the Palestinian population. Meanwhile, the Wall would integrate 90 percent of settlers into the confines of Israel. It would establish a border unilaterally defined by Israel that violates the 1967 boundaries and that leaves the Palestinians with control over less than 53 percent of the West Bank.[56] Although the International Court of Justice and the Israeli Supreme Court ruled against the route in certain, relatively short segments of the Wall, its construction has not stopped. It seals a colonial endeavor of land expropriation that has been going on for forty years.

The construction of the Separation Wall in the West Bank was carried out in tandem with Israel's disengagement plan for Gaza, which was implemented in August 2005. This disengagement was the final step in a process of economic separation from Gaza that was consolidated during the Oslo years. It did not entail the end of the occupation, even as Israel retreated physically from the Gaza Strip and removed the 8,500 settlers who were living in it. In fact, Israel remained in control of the borders, airspace, and economic resources. Gazans are still not free to move outside of the strip or to reach the West Bank, let alone the outside world, without a permit from the Israeli security forces. Since the Israeli and international boycott imposed on Gaza after the election of Hamas in January 2006, the economy of Gaza has not been able to feed its population, let alone trade with the West Bank or the outside world. On the eve of Israeli assault on the Gaza Strip in December 2008, 79.4 percent of the population was living below the poverty line and 56 percent did not have secure access to food. According to the most recent World Bank report, the manufacturing sector was 98 percent inactive, banking had shrunk drastically, and the private sector had been destroyed.[57]

The Israeli disengagement from Gaza offers an idea of what might happen to the West Bank. Before he resigned as Israeli prime minister, Ehud Olmert had promised to disengage from the West Bank according to a "convergency" plan that allows for the incorporation of the major settlement blocks within Israel. Such a unilateral realignment of the 1967 borders will take place along the route traced by the Separation Wall. The war on Lebanon in the summer of 2006 put his plan on hold, but the construction of the Separation Wall continued unabated. The Israeli military has already transformed the formerly mobile checkpoints in the West Bank into large, bureaucratized, entrenched entry terminals that can cater to buses as well as cars, people as well as goods, and that people cannot cross without an Israeli-issued permit. These terminals, be it at the edges of Nablus or Ramallah, are now reminiscent of the processing facilities between Israel and the Gaza Strip—the Karni and Erez crossings. They seek to guarantee security by relying on magnetized searches, cameras, and invisible supervision, rather than by direct searches, thereby reducing the contact between Palestinians and Israeli soldiers. Israel cut the West Bank in eight disconnected Bantustans that are unsustainable economically and at the mercy of the Israeli Army.[58]

The economics of the al-Aqsa intifada and the disengagement consolidated the structure imposed by Oslo. It was based on the institutionalization of Israeli security concerns and confirmed the limits of Palestinian autonomy. Consolidated checkpoints in the West Bank and disengagement further curtailed economic activity, because trade and employment were further restricted. Unemployment by the summer of 2008 touched 55 percent of the Gaza workforce and 25 percent of the West Bank's, and economic activity remained focused on petty trade in what came to be known as "checkpoint economy." Real GDP in 2006 fell by 10 percent, compared with 2005, and is already 40 percent lower its level in 1999. The raids on the Palestinian Authority's offices in 2002 and the election of Hamas in 2006 led to a 61 percent fall in the Palestinian Authority's revenues. In March 2006, Israel decided to withhold customs revenues owed to the Palestinian Authority worth $555 million, the equivalent of two-thirds of its total revenues and 10 percent of the West Bank and Gaza Strip's GDP.[59]

Meanwhile, the past eight years saw the enhancement of the role of the international community as a rescuer of first, rather than last resort. It created a precedent little known in the history of colonialism, since rarely has outside international financial aid been given to a colonized population. The international community, as represented by the international institutions such as the World Bank, IMF, and UN as much as by the burgeoning international NGOs such as Oxfam and Save the Children, actually increased their funds to the West Bank and Gaza Strip and channeled it as emergency support. The donations of the so-called "Quartet," the United States, Russia, the European Union, and the United Nations, managed by the World Bank were mainly used to pay to health workers and civil servants, whose number increased to 160,000 employees. Meanwhile, international NGOs are funneling money to support the Palestinian civil society and NGOs in ways that are compromising the latter's independence. Palestinian NGOs are increasingly pressured to adapt their visions and their projects in line with the international donors' priorities, not necessarily in line with the demands of their local constituencies. Their ability to represent their constituents as well as to be active civil participants is being increasingly curtailed.[60] The economic disparity between locally and internationally funded NGOs as well as between the higher and lower echelons of the NGOs' leadership has also increased, causing great inequality, regionally as well as nationally. Ramallah has been typically capable of recovering much more quickly than Hebron or Gaza in any crisis, thanks to the concentration of the donor agencies in it.

Although provided with good intentions, international aid is becoming a tool that further compromises not only the Palestinian economy, but also its democracy and institutions. The fighting between Hamas and Fatah in Gaza that left Gaza in the hands of the former by June 2007 administered the final blow to whatever remained of the Gaza economy and showed how significant international aid and its boycott can be to Palestinian economic and political viability. International aid has become a structural feature of the Palestinian economy, one that redefines its dependence, rather than ends it. So far, it has proven more inclined to abide by Israeli security considerations than to challenge colonial domination effectively. This, in turn, raises important questions with regard to the responsibility of the international community and the ways in which it needs to make Israel accountable if it is to uphold its commitment to Palestinian independence.

CONCLUSION

The legacy of forty years of occupation for the Palestinian economy is complex, but not rewarding. While Palestinians saw their per-capita income grow during the first twenty-five years of the occupation, their control over their resources diminished. Their prosperity remained tied to having access to the Israeli labor market, since domestic investment and trade were curtailed by Israeli restrictions. The Oslo peace process promised prosperity, but it brought about economic restructuring that deepened, rather than reduced Palestinian dependence on Israel. The Palestinian GDP has fallen by 30 percent over the past fifteen years, Palestinian mobility has become restricted, and Palestinian land has been further fragmented. While Oslo brought about two significant changes in the management of the Palestinian economy, the creation of a Palestinian Authority and the involvement of the international donor community, growth fluctuated and became dependent on international aid and "Israeli security." Since the outbreak of the al-Aqsa intifada, the Palestinian economy and its 4.5 million Palestinian consumers have been saved from total collapse by the injection of over $1022 million a year on average by the international donor community, double the yearly average donated before 2000.[61] Private-sector activity, meanwhile, is estimated to have shrunk by 60 percent.[62]

Since 1967, the Palestinian economy has been subjected to a military rule that de facto laid the foundation for a colonial relation of domination, one that was perpetuated during the Oslo process and that was bound to affect the prospects and nature of a viable political solution. It has not always been easy for economists to situate the Israeli occupation of the West Bank and the Gaza Strip within the analytical perspective of colonization because of the peculiarity of the international legal structure governing the occupation. It has also been politically inappropriate, especially in the United States, to describe the Israeli occupation as colonial. However, this "political correctness" risks accommodating, if not legitimizing a reality it should be criticizing. Calling a spade a spade is necessary in any attempt to understand the destruction of the Palestinian economy and to find the means to stop compromising Palestinian rights in the name of Israel's security. A careful consideration of Israeli territorial, legal, and economic policies in the Occupied Territories indicates that the Israeli occupation is colonial insofar as it is based on a structure of domination that has enabled Israel to appropriate Palestinian land, maintain political and economic hegemony over the Palestinian economic life, and prevent the Palestinians from becoming independent of Israel. This colonial structure underwent an important transformation during the Oslo years, but was not brought to an end, even with the Israeli disengagement plan. It hinges today on the way Israeli security considerations have been institutionalized and have come to dominate every aspect of Palestinian life, on the restraints put on the Palestinian authority, and on the subcontracting of Palestinian economic survival to the international donor community. It has led to the atomization of Palestinian land, the destruction of Palestinian economic activity, and the disintegration of the Palestinian polity.

The political implications of these developments are major. The economic separation of Gaza from Israel and the West Bank that was fostered during the Oslo years was politically sealed with the Israeli disengagement in August 2005. Israeli institutionalization of the permit policy and fragmentation of Palestinian land through closures, checkpoints, and the Separation Wall have made any prospects for a viable two-state solution dismal, if possible at all. Despite its commitment to Palestinian state building as declared in the so-called "road map for peace" outlined by the Quartet and the 2007 Annapolis peace conference, the international community has neither stopped the fragmentation of Palestinian land nor is fostering autonomous development in the Occupied Palestinian Territories. It has not upheld international law and continues to adhere to Israeli security priorities to the detriment of its own commitment to democracy and self-determination. The colonization perspective is analytically useful for its ability to explain the causes of the "distortion" in the Palestinian economy and to identify the structural factors that prevent Palestinian independence. Above all, it is particularly insightful in showing how Israelis and Palestinians are embedded in a dynamic relation of domination that continues to evolve and has so far foreclosed any viable two-state solution to the conflict. It opens, in turn, scope for analyzing what new forms of power and resistance may develop and the inevitability of thinking of new alternatives to the ongoing impasse.

NOTES

1   World Bank, *Investing in Palestinian Economic Reform and Development: Report for the Pledging Conference,* Paris, December 17, 2007, available on-line at http://siteresources.worldbank.org/INTWESTBANKGAZA/Resources/294264-1166525851073/ParisconferencepaperDec17.pdf (last accessed August 23, 2008).

2   World Bank, *Palestinian Economic Prospects: Aid, Access and Reform,* Economic Monitoring Report to the Ad Hoc Liaison Committee, September 22, 2008, available on-line at http://siteresources.worldbank.org/INTWESTBANKGAZA/Resources/AHLCReportSept.08final.pdf (last accessed March 4, 2009).

3   World Bank, *Four Years: Intifada, Closures and Palestinian Economic Crisis: An Assessment* (Washington, D.C.: World Bank, November 2004).

4   See International Monetary Fund, *Economic Performance and Reform under Conflict Conditions,* Middle East Department, WBGS office, Washington, D.C.

5   See, among others, Uri Ram, "The Colonisation Perspective in Israeli Sociology," in Ilan Pappe (ed.), *The Israel/Palestine Question* (London: Routledge, 1999); Gershon Shafir, *Land, Labour and the Origins of the Israeli-Palestinian Conflict, 1883–1914* (Cambridge: Cambridge University Press, 1989); Baruch Kimmerling, *Zionism and Territory: The Socio-Territorial Dimensions of Zionist Politics* (Berkeley: Institute of International Studies, 1983); and Baruch Kimmerling, *Zionism and Economy* (Cambridge, MA: Schenkman, 1983).

6   See, for example, Maxime Rodinson, *Israel: A Settler-Colonial State?* (New York: Monrad Press, 1973); Elia Zureik, *Palestinians in Israel: A Study in Internal Colonialism* (London: Routledge, 1979); and Nasseer Aruri, *Occupation: Israel over Palestine* (Belmont, MA: Association of Arab-American University Graduates, 1989).

7   See, among others, Leila Farsakh, "Introduction: Commemorating the Naksa," *MIT-EJMES* 8 (Spring 2008); Virginia Tilley, *The One-State Solution: A Breakthrough for Peace in the Israeli-Palestinian Deadlock* (Ann Arbor: University of Michigan Press, 2005); Jimmy Carter, *Palestine: Peace Not Apartheid* (New York: Simon and Schuster, 2006); and Leila Farsakh, "Independence, Cantons or Bantustans: Whither the Palestinian State?" *Middle East Journal* 59, no. 2 (2005).

8   See, among others, David Cobham and Noman Kanafani, *The Economics of Palestine* (London: Routledge, 2004); World Bank, *Stagnation or Survival?: Israeli Disengagement and Palestinian Economic Recovery* (Washington, D.C.: World Bank, 2005); Fawaz Gharaibeh, *The Economies of the West Bank and the Gaza Strip* (Boulder, CO: Westview Press, 1985); World Bank, *Developing the Occupied Territories: an Investment in Peace,* 6 vols. (Washington, D.C.: World Bank, 1993); and United Nations Conference on Trade and Development, *Prospects for Sustained Development in the Palestinian Economy of the West Bank and Gaza Strip* (Geneva: United Nations, 1993).

9   See, among others, Leila Farsakh, *Palestinian Labour Migration to Israel: Labour, Land and Occupation* (London: Routledge 2005); Sara Roy, *The Gaza Strip: The Political Economy of De-Development,* 2nd ed. (Washington, D.C.: Institute of Palestine Studies, 2001); and Adel Samara, *The Political Economy of the West Bank, 1967–1987* (London: Khamsin, 1988).

10   Jurgen Osterhammel, *Colonialism: A Theoretical Overview,* trans. Shelly Frisch (Princeton, NJ: Markus Wiener, 1997), pp. 16–17.

11   *Ibid.,* p. 4.

12 See also D. K. Fieldhouse, *Colonialism, 1870–1945: An Introduction* (New York: St. Martin's Press, 1981).

13 Caroline Elkins and Susan Pedersen (eds.), *Settler Colonialism in the Twentieth Century: Projects, Practices, Legacies* (London: Routledge, 2005).

14 See, for example, Shlomo Gazit, *The Carrot and the Stick: Israel's Policy in Judea and Samaria: 1967–1968* (Washington, D.C.: B'nai B'rith, 1995); Yigal Allon "Israel: The Case for Defensible Borders," *Foreign Affairs* 55, no. 1 (October 1976): pp. 38–53; 1976, Baruch Kimmerling, *Zionism and Territory* (Berkeley: University of California Press, 1983); Geoffrey Aronson, *Creating Facts: Israel, Palestinians and the West Bank* (Washington, D.C.: Institute of Palestine Studies, 1987).

15 See, for example, Ibrahim Abu-Lughod (ed.), *The Arab-Israeli Confrontation of June 1967: An Arab Perspective* (Evanston, IL: Northwestern University Press, 1970) and Norman Finkelstein, *Image and Reality of the Israel-Palestine Conflict* (London: Verso, 1995).

16 UN Security Council Resolution 237, June 1967. UN Security Council resolutions are available on-line at http://www.un.org/documents/scres.htm (last accessed August 23, 2008).

17 A total of 300,000 were expelled and displaced as a result of the 1967 War. See Nur Masalhah, *A Land without a People: Israel, Transfer and the Palestinians, 1949–1996* (London: Faber and Faber, 1997).

18 See Jun Uchida, "Brokers of Empire: Japanese and Korean Business Elites in Colonial Korea," in Elkins and Pedersen (eds.), *Settler Colonialism*, pp 153–70.

19 See Raja Shehadeh, *Occupier's Law: Israel and the West Bank* (Washington, D.C.: Institute for Palestine Studies, 1988).

20 Quoted in Aronson, *Creating Facts,* p. 4.

21 See Farsakh, *Palestinian Labour Migration to Israel,* pp. 62–63 and Foundation for Middle East Peace, *Report on Israeli Settlements in the Occupied Territories,* available on-line at http://www.fmep.org/settlement_info/statistics.html (last accessed August 23, 2008).

22 Israel Central Bureau of Statistics, *Labour Force Survey, 2000–2001* (Jerusalem: ICBS, 2003).

23 See Shehadeh, *Occupier's Law,* pp. 79–93.

24 With the exception of East Jerusalemites who became residents, an act considered illegal from an international legal point of view. See UN Security Council Resolution 252, May 1968, UN Security Council resolution 295, September 1971, and UN Security Council Resolution 478, August 1980.

25 See for example Arie Arnon, Israel Luski, Avia Spivak, and Jimmy Weinblatt, *The Palestinian Economy: Between Imposed Integration and Voluntary Separation* (Leiden: Brill, 1997), pp. 2–6.

26 *Ibid.*

27 See Farsakh, *Palestinian Labour Migration to Israel,* p. 87.

28 See, among others, Osama A. Hamed and Radwan A. Shaban, "One-Sided Customs and Monetary Union: The Case of the West Bank and Gaza Strip under Israeli Occupation," in Stanley Fischer, Dani Rodrik, and Elias Tuma (eds.), *The Economics of Middle East Peace: Views from the Region* (Cambridge, MA: The MIT Press, 1993), p. 142.

29 See World Bank, *Developing the Occupied Territories: An Investment in Peace. Volume 2, The Economy* (Washington, D.C.: World Bank, 1993), p. 35; and Jimmy Weinblatt and Arie Arnon, "Sovereignty and Economic Development: The Case of Israel and Palestine," *The Economic Journal* 111, no. 472 (2001): pp. 291–308.

30 Roy, *The Gaza Strip,* pp. 4–8.

31 See World Bank, *Developing the Occupied Territories: An Investment in Peace. Volume 1, Overview* (Washington, D.C.: World Bank, 1993), pp. 25–28, and Farsakh, *Palestinian Labour Migration to Israel,* chap. 2, pp. 37–42.

32 See Article 1 of the Declaration of Principle on Interim Self-Government Arrangements (Oslo I), available on-line at http://www.yale.edu/lawweb/avalon/mideast/isrplo.htm, and "Background" in The Interim Agreement between Israel and the PLO (Oslo II), available on-line at http://www.acpr.org.il/resources/oslo2.html (both last accessed August 23, 2008).

33 For those arguing that the Economic Protocol failed because of poor implementation, see E. Kleiman, "The Paris Protocol and the Future of Israeli-Palestinian Relations," in B. Philippe and C. Pissarides (eds.), *Evaluating the Paris Protocol: Economic Relations between Israel and the Palestinian Territories* (Brussels: European Commission, 1999). For those stressing the structural flaws of the Economic Protocol, see, among others, Farsakh, *Palestinian Labour Migration to Israel;* Noman Kanafani, "Trade—A Catalyst for Peace?," *The Economic Journal* 111 (2001): pp. 276–90; Arnon and Weinblatt, "Sovereignty and Economic Development," and Cobham and Kanafani, *The Economics of Palestine.*

34 See, for example, Sharif S. Elmusa and Mahmud El-Jaafari, "Power and Trade: The Israeli-Palestinian Economic Protocol" in *Journal of Palestine Studies* 24, no.2 (1997); Sara Roy, "De-development Revisited: Palestinian Economy and Society Since Oslo," *Journal of Palestine Studies* 28, no. 3 (1999).

35 Declaration of Principle on Interim Self-Government Arrangements, Article VIII, Article X; The Israeli-Palestinian Interim Agreement on the West Bank and the Gaza Strip (Oslo II), Preamble, Article VIII, available on-line at http://www.mfa.gov.il/MFA/Peace+Process/Guide+to+the+Peace+Process/Declaration+of+Principles.htm (last accessed March 4, 2009).

36 Article XI.c of Oslo II.

37 See Articles 12, 16, 22, and 27 from Annex III of Oslo II.

38 The Palestine Economic Research Institute (MAS), *The Economic Monitor, 1994–2000* (Ramallah: Palestine Economic Policy Research Institute, 2001), p. 161.

39 Foundation for Middle East Peace, *Report on Israeli Settlements in the Occupied Territories.*

40 See Stanley Fischer, Alice Alonso-Gamo, and Uli E.Von Allman, "Economic Developments in the West Bank and Gaza Strip since Oslo," *Economic Journal* 111, no. 472 (2001): pp. 254–75.

41 Annex III, Article 11.2, 11.3, and 11.4, Oslo II.

42 See Kanafani, "Trade—A Catalyst for Peace?"

43 These include the lists A1, A2, and B. Quantities to be imported under these lists are to be determined by some agreed-upon estimates of Palestinian market needs. Imports of goods A1 and A2 are not subject to Israeli imports duties, but are regulated by Israeli standards and regulations.

44 World Bank, *Long-Term Policy Options for the Palestinian Economy* (Washington, D.C.: World Bank, 2002).

45 See World Bank, *Four Years,* pp. 12–40.

46 World Bank, *Palestinian Economic Prospects.*

47 *Ibid.;* Ishac Diwan and Radwān ʿAlī Shaʿbān, Development under Adversity: The Palestinian Economy in Transition. (Washington, D.C.: MAS-World Bank Joint Report, 1999), p. 43.

48 World Bank, *Poverty in the West Bank and Gaza Strip* (Washington, D.C.: World Bank, 2002); World Bank, *Palestinian Economic Prospects.*

49   The Palestine Economic Research Institute (MAS), *The Economic Monitor, 1994–2000* (Ramallah: MAS, 2001), pp. xix–xx.

50   Fischer et al., "Economic Developments."

51   World Bank, *West Bank and Gaza Country Economic Memorandum: Growth in West Bank and Gaza. Opportunities and Constraints,* Internal document, WBGS World Bank Office, September 2006.

52   Farsakh, *Palestinian Labour Migration to Israel,* p. 149.

53   *Ibid.,* pp. 133–37.

54   Palestinian Central Bureau of Statistics (PCBS), *Labour Force Quarterly Survey: July–September 2008* (Ramallah: PCBS, 2008), table 1.1.

55   United Nations Office for Coordination of Humanitarian Affairs (OCHA), OCHA Closure Update, April 30–September 11, 2008, available on-line at http://www.ochaopt.org/documents/ocha_opt_closure_update_2008_09_english.pdf (last accessed January 5, 2009).

56   United Nations Office for Coordination of Humanitarian Affairs (OCHA), *The Humanitarian Impact of the West Bank Barrier on Palestinian Communities* (Ramallah: UN, 2007), pp. 5–7.

57   Poverty is defined as a family of six with an income of 2,300 Israeli shekels—less than four dollars a day. The already high rates of what the UN calls "deep poverty" increased as well. The deep poverty line reflects a budget for food, clothing, and housing only. For a family of six, the deep poverty line in 2006 was 1,837 Israeli shekels. See World Bank, *Palestinian Economic Prospect.*

58   For elaboration on the Bantustans comparison, see Leila Farsakh, "Independence, Cantons or Bantustans."

59   World Bank, *West Bank and Gaza Update,* November 2007, pp. 1–10.

60   See, for example, Joel Beinin and Rebecca Stein, *The Struggle for Sovereignty: Palestine and Israel, 1993–2005* (Stanford, CA: Stanford University Press, 2006); Michael Keating, Ann le More and Robert Lowe (eds.), *Aid, Diplomacy, and Facts on the Ground: The Case of Palestine* (London: Chatham House, 2005); and Islah Jad, "The Demobilisation of the Palestinians Women's Movement in Palestine" *MIT-EJMES* 7 (Fall 2007).

61   United Nations Conference on Trade and Development (UNCTAD), *Palestinian War-Torn Economy: Aid, Development and State Formation* (Geneva: UNCTAD, 2006).

62   World Bank, *West Bank and Gaza Update,* March 2007, pp.1–10.

- **MILITARY ORDER SEIZING THIRTY DUNAMS OF LAND** from al-Nuʿaman village for the purpose of building the Mazmuria commercial terminal along the route of the Separation Wall. Until the Israeli High Court decision in the landmark case of the Jewish settlement Elon Moreh, Israel made extensive use of military orders seizing private Palestinian land to build settlements under the pretext that the land was required "for imperative and urgent military needs." Since 1994, Israel has renewed the use of military seizure orders, this time to build roads for settlers.

- **EVICTION NOTICE** issued by the Custodian of Absentee Land and Government Property in the Civil Administration to farmers from the village of al-Jabaʾa, under the pretext that their land is classified as "state land." Since the beginning of the occupation of the West Bank in 1967, Israel has declared 40 percent of the area "state land," relying on provisions of the Ottoman Land Law of 1858 and taking advantage of the fact that, in 1967, only one-third of the land in the West Bank was registered as privately owned land.

[Documents source: *Monitoring Israeli Colonizing Activities in the Palestinian West Bank and Gaza*, a joint project of the Applied Research Institute in Jerusalem and the Land Research Center]

أمر بشأن وضع اليد على اراضي رقم ٠٥/١٥٥/ت

وفقاً لصلاحيتي كقائد قوات الجيش الدفاع الاسرائيلي في منطقه يهودا والسامره ، وبما انني
اعتقد ان الامر ضروري لاغراض عسكريه، وعلى اثر الظروف الامنيه الخاصه السائده في
المنطقه، والحاجه باتخاذ خطوات لمنع عمليات ارهابية، فاني امر بما يلي :

تعاريف	١.	في هذا الامر:

"الخارطـه"ـ خارطـه بمقيـاس رسـم ١٠٠٠٠٠:١، الموقعـه بتـوقيعي
والمرفقه لهذا الامر وتشكل جزء لا يتجزء منه.

"الاراضي"ـ قطاع الارض المعلم بخط بالون الاحمر في الخارطة،
مجمل مساحته ٣٠ دنم ، والموجود في اراضي القرى:

اراضي بيت ساحور (غير طابو):
حوض ١٣ـ موقع : نعمان.

اراضي بيت لحم (غير طابو):
حوض ١٣ـ موقع: عرد القشه

وضع اليد	٢.	اعلن بهذا على وضع اليد على الاراضي لاغراض عسكريه ولاجل اقامة نقطة فحص لنقل البضائع.

الحيازه	٣.	قوات جيش الدفاع الاسرائيلي تضع اليد على الاراضي والحيازه المطلقه بها تعطى لضابط الاراضي في قيادة المنطقة الوسطى بواسطة الضابط لشؤون وزارة الدفاع في الادارة المدنية.

تسليم	٤.	نسخ من هذا الامر والخارطة المرفقه له تسلم، بقدر الامكان، لاصحاب الاراضي او المتصرفين بها من قبل مكتب التنسيق والارتباط بيت لحم.

نشر	٥.	أ. ١) الاعلان عن توقيع هذا الامر يعلم، بقدر الامكان، لاصحاب الاراضي او المتصرفين بها بواسطه نشره في مكتب التنسيق والارتباط بيت لحم في الاراضي، وبكل طريقه اخرى ملائمه.

٢) يعلن في الاعلان عن موعد الجولة التي تنفذ على يد مكتب
التنسيق والارتباط بيت لحم من اجل التعرف على الاراضي.

ISRAEL DEFENSE FORCES

Order Regarding Seizure of Land Number T/155/05

Pursuant to my authority as commander of IDF forces in the Judea and Samaria region, being of the opinion that military necessity so dictates, and in light of the special security situation in the region and the need to take the measures necessary to prevent terrorist attacks, I hereby declare as follows:

Definitions   1.   In this order:

"**the map**"—the map with the scale of 1:10,000, signed by me and attached to this order and constituting an integral part thereof.

"**the land**"—the strip of land in the total area of some thirty dunams marked by a red line on the attached map and located on the land of the villages:

Land of Beit Sahur (not arranged):
Block 13—mawaqa: Nu'aman.
Land in Bethlehem (not arranged):
Block 13—mawaqa: Ard al Fatza.

Seizure of land   2.   I hereby declare that the land is to be seized for military needs, for the purpose of institutionalizing a terminal for the crossing of goods.

Possession   3.   The land shall be seized by IDF forces and sole possession of it handed over to the land officer in Central Command headquarters through the staff officer for Ministry of Defense matters in the Civil Administration.

Delivery   4.   Copies of this order and the attached map of the order will be delivered, to the extent possible, to the owners or possessors of the land by the Bethlehem DCL.

Publication   5.   A.   1)   Notice that I have signed this order will be brought, to the extent
possible, to the attention of the owners or possessors of the land, by publishing it in the Bethlehem DCL, posting it on the land, and in any other way deemed appropriate.
2)   The notice shall state the time of a tour that will be made by the Bethlehem DCL to show the land.

ب. نسخ من هذا الأمر ومن الخارطه المرفقه له توضع لاطلاع المعنيين
في الاماكن التاليه:

١. مكاتب التنسيق والارتباط بيت لحم.
٢. مكاتب المستشار القضائي للمنطقه يهودا والسامره.
٣. مكتب الضابط لشؤون وزارة الدفاع في الاداره المدنيه.
٤. مكتب المسؤول عن الاملاك المتروكه والحكوميه فـي الاداره
المدنيه.
ج. نسخة من الاعلان والخارطه تعلق على لوحة الاعلانات في مكاتب
التنسيق والارتباط في بيت لحم لمدة ١٠ ايام منذ نشر الخبر ،
كالمذكور في البند الصغير (أ).

٦. حق الادعاء   يحق لاصحاب الاراضي أو المتصرفين بها أن يقدموا اعتراضاتهم على
هذا الأمر خلال ٧ ايام من يوم تنفيذ الجوله، كالمذكور في البند(أ)
بواسطة مكتب الارتباط والتنسيق بيت لحم او ديوان المستشار القضائي
للمنطقه.

٧. رسوم استعمال   يحق لاصحاب الاراضي أو المتصرفين بها التوجه لمكتب الارتباط
   والتعويضات   والتنسيق بيت لحم الاستفسار عن حقهم للحصول على
رسوم استعمال وتعويضات جراء وضع اليد.

٨. بدء سريان   يبدأ سريان هذا الأمر من يوم توقيعه حتى يوم ٢٠٠٧/١٢/٣١.

٩. الاسم   يسمى هذا الأمر : "الامر بشأن وضع اليد على اراضي رقم ١٥٥/٠٥ت
(يهودا والسامره) ٢٠٠٥،٥٧٦٠.

٢٠٠٥ _____
٥٧٦٠ _____

يئير نفيه، الوف
قائد قوات جيش الدفاع الاسرائيلي
في منطقه يهودا والسامره

		B. Copies of this order and the map attached hereto shall be deposited for study by interested persons at the following locations:

B. Copies of this order and the map attached hereto shall be deposited for study by interested persons at the following locations:
1) The Bethlehem DCL.
2) The office of the legal advisor for Judea and Samaria.
3) The office of the Ministry of Defense security officer in the Civil Administration.
4) The office of the Custodian of Abandoned and Government Property in the Civil Administration.

C. Copies of the seizure order and map shall be posted on the bulletin board in the Bethlehem DCL offices for a period of 10 days from the day of publication of the notice, as stated in subsection (A).

Right to be heard   **6.**   Owners or possessors of the land will be allowed to submit objections to this order, through the Bethlehem DCL or the office of the judge advocate for the area, within seven days from the day the tour is conducted, as stated in section 5(A) above.

Clarification of entitlement to usage fees and compensation   **7.**   Land owners shall be permitted to seek clarification from the Bethlehem DCL regarding their entitlement to receive usage fees and compensation.

Commencement of validity   **8.**   This order shall remain in force from the day it is signed until 31 December 2007.

Name   **9.**   This order will be called "Order Regarding Seizure of Land No. T/155/05 (Judea and Samaria), 5765—2005.

Date: 23 Av 5765
23 August 2005

Yair Naveh, Major General
Commander of IDF Forces
in Judea and Samaria

צבא הגנה לישראל
جيش الدفاع الإسرائيلي
الممثل المسؤول لمنطقة يهودا والسامرة
الإدارة المدنية لمنطقة يهودا والسامرة
المسؤول عن الأملاك الحكومية
مديرية المركز لرصد ...
وحدة التفتيش المركزية
إخطار بوجوب الإخلاء

لحضرة _____

العنوان رقم الهوية	اسم العائلة	اسم الجد	اسم الأب	الاسم الشخصي

1. ... لعام 1967، ... (رقم 1006) لعام 1982. ...

1. استنادًا إلى الصلاحيات المعطاة إليّ بموجب الأمر بشأن الممتلكات الحكومية (يهودا والسامرة) (رقم ٥٩) لعام ١٩٦٧ وبموجب المادة (٢) من الأمر بشأن التعيينات والصلاحيات حسب قانون المحافظة على أراضي وممتلكات الدولة (يهودا والسامرة) (رقم ١٠٠٦) لعام ١٩٨٢، أقرر بعد ما يوجد بحوزتكم/م الأراضي الموصولة أدناه بشكل غير قانوني

المكان		
... 208BS/620 175		
... 208270/620130 في مساحة منتظم حوض		
208/85/620 115		
208290/620		

وصف الأراضي والتعيين: ...

2. ...

2. يُطلب منكم/م رفع يدكم عن الأراضي وإعادة وضع الأراضي إلى ما كان عليه سابقًا خلال ٤٥ يومًا من يوم تسليم هذا الأمر. في حالة عدم قيامك بذلك سوف تقوم السلطة المختصة بإجراء الإخلاء ويحق لها تحميلك/م تكاليف الإخلاء.

3. ... 45 يوم من يوم تسليم الأمر ...

3. يحق لكم/م تقديم اعتراض على هذا القرار إذا رغبت/م في ذلك للجنة الاعتراضات ... الموجودة في معسكر ... خلال ٤٥ يومًا من يوم تسليم هذا الإخطار.

يحق لكم أيضًا أن تستوضح عن تفاصيل بخصوص هذا الإخطار في مكتب وحدة التفتيش في مكتب التنسيق والارتباط _____ هاتف/فاكس _____

تاريخ	...	رقم الهوية	الاسم الكامل

5. بتاريخ _____ في الساعة، تسلمتُ هذا المستند بـ ٣ نسخ ...

6. ...

6. اسم الهيئة
6.1 اسم المفتش _____

التوقيع	العائلة	التاريخ	المنصب	الاسم

Israel Defense Forces
Civil Administration for Judea and Samaria
The Custodian of Government Property
Central Inspection Unit
Warning on Requirement to Vacate

Renewed Order 427

Squatting B 46/05

Dear   *Possessor of the property*
_____
       First name   Father's name   Grandfather's name   Family name   ID   Address

1. Pursuant to my authority under the Order Regarding Government Property (Judea and Samaria) (No. 59), 5727—1967, and under section 2 of the Order Regarding Appointments and Powers under the Preservation of Lands and State Assets (Judea and Samara) (No. 1006) Law, 5742—1982, I determine that you unlawfully hold the land described as follows:

   Place *Jaba'a*   Datum Point *208135/620145; 208270/620130; 208185/620110*
   (in an arranged area)   Block _____   Lot _____

   Description of the land and the squatting: *terraces of about 400 meters, preparing and plowing land + planting about 120 olive trees, grapevines, and pomegranates*

2. You are hereby required to vacate the land and return the land to its previous condition within 45 days from the day of delivery of this order. If you do not act as aforesaid, the competent authority will carry out the eviction and be permitted to charge you the costs of the eviction.

3. If you wish, your may appeal this decision to the Military Arrangements Committee located at Ofer Camp within 45 days from the day of delivery of this warning.

4. You may seek clarification about this warning at the Inspection Unit at the *Etzion* DCL, telephone/fax *02/9703884*.

   Delivered to *posted on the aforesaid land in three copies and photographed*.

   _____   _____   _____   _____
   FULL NAME   I.D.   THE CONNECTION   SIGNATURE OF RECIPIENT

5. In the absence of the possessor at the site, I hung the warning in *three* copies and photographed the hanging of the warning.

6. Inspector's name

   [illegible]   [illegible]   21 Jan. 2008
   _____   _____   _____   _____   _____
   NAME   POSITION   DATE   HOUR   SIGNATURE

Cultivating Dependence: Palestinian Agriculture under the Israeli Occupation

Caroline Abu-Sada

> Many peasants had to give up working the land for want of the essential force of traction, given that the livestock had been generally decimated during or after the regrouping. But especially because, in addition to the pure and simple prohibition to move about in certain zones, the excessive remoteness of the lands and the limitations applied to displacements, there were the innumerable military annoyances, the controls, the laisser-passer and the obligatory routes and schedules.
> —Pierre Bourdieu and Abdelmalek Sayad, *Le déracinement: La crise de l'agriculture traditionnelle en Algérie*

The above epigraph,[1] which could equally well refer to the situation of Palestinian farmers under Israeli military occupation, comes from a detailed study of how the French colonizer reshaped the agricultural sector to establish and solidify its control over Algeria, and rural Algeria, in particular. The revamping of land registration played a major role in enabling this control. Property laws passed by the French administration put an end to communal property and created individual property. Changes in the land-ownership system affected the tax system and the coherence of the rural areas. It disorganized the "uncontrollable" countryside in the attempt to reinforce French colonial rule. From 1954 to 1957, thousands of farmers were displaced from their villages in the context of the "no-go" zones that the French army established to empty the countryside and avoid influence of the "rebels" on the rural population. Villagers were regrouped in centers next to military posts so the army could control the population more closely and prevent contact between the population and the National Liberation Army. The French Army then applied the *"terre brûlée"* strategy: it burned down the villages, the crops, and the livestock. The French used all available means to force the farmers to abandon their land and property. By 1960, at least three million people—the farmers uprooted by the

French Army and the rural dwellers who made an exodus to the cities—had been internally displaced in Algeria.[2]

A similar process occurred in India, where British rule reshaped Indian agriculture to serve its own commercial and political interests. The British colonizers introduced a new kind of cottonseed, one more suitable for the British cotton-weaving machines, and declared Indian cotton to be far lower in quality. This move made the farmers dependant on agricultural inputs not commonly used in India and on modes of production unsuitable for Indian agriculture. Cotton production in India failed to recover from the crisis brought about by British colonization, and the dramatic drop in revenue caused many farmers to commit suicide:

> Indian cottons were bred to withstand the vagaries of the variable Indian climate and cultivation practices were done to minimize the cotton plants' vulnerability to pests. The traders were oblivious to these niceties; they wanted quantity production conveniently delivered at central points, to be conveyed overseas as efficiently as possible. For this purpose, the Indian varieties and trade practices were unsuited and so were branded "inferior," and a systematic process of change initiated to mold them to the new demands.[3]

The British rulers followed the traders' advice to "improve" the Indian cotton and make it more suitable for export. They did this by various means: introducing exotic, high-yield seeds; establishing government farms to prove the superiority of the exotic seeds and their cultivation practices over the Indians' seeds and practices; dispatching American planters to introduce new techniques of cultivation; introducing machines for cleaning and pressing cotton; and investing in infrastructure for transportation of the cotton to the ports and for irrigation of the crops to increase yields. In addition, the taxation system reduced Indian farmers to dire poverty and subsequently made them dependent on the governmental strategy. Indigenous processing techniques, which were crucial for the maintenance of the quality of the cotton, came under strain and were eventually replaced by the faster machines from the West, which yielded products of questionable quality. As C. Shambu Prasad contends, "This was in keeping with Britain's policy of converting India into a source of raw material and a market for finished products."[4] In brief, the British colonizer used heavy taxation and the promotion of exotic seeds detrimental to local cotton cultivation to restructure the Indian cotton sector totally so as to maintain total control over the farmers and make them dependent upon the British colonizers.

These radical changes in agriculture provide a prism for analyzing colonialist control. The colonizer targets the agricultural sector and transforms it to serve as a captive market for finished goods and as a source of raw materials. Laws and regulations dealing with land and access to water, agricultural inputs such as fertilizers, and markets are used to support the colonizer's own production needs and access to markets. Under colonial rule, agriculture is more vulnerable than other sectors of the economy because it is one of the privileged ways to ensure that the local population's food needs are met. As I will attempt to demonstrate in this essay, part of Israel's policy has been and is to convert Palestine into a captive market for Israeli finished goods. Moreover, Israel's strategy has been and is to exert full control over the Palestinian economy, allowing no access to the outside world that could help the Palestinians reduce their dependence on Israel and giving them no means to develop their own viable economic system. This strategy entails a systematic undermining of the Palestinian agricultural sector, which, following the outbreak of the second intifada, became vital for the Palestinians' basic survival.

The second intifada, which started in September 2000, has severely affected the livelihood of both rural and urban Palestinians. The closure of the Israeli labor market to Palestinian workers halted almost completely the cash flow between the intertwined economies and left many Palestinians without any source of income or any prospect for earning a livelihood. Traditionally an important part of the economy, agriculture came to play an even more important role in the Palestinian economy. The share of the agricultural sector in the Palestinian GDP, which had decreased from 35 percent in 1990 to 7 percent in 2000, rose to 11 percent in 2004 and 12.5 percent in 2005. The percentage of Palestinians employed in agriculture followed the same course. It fell from 26 percent in 1980 to 12.6 percent in 1999 and then increased to 16 percent in 2004 and 14.6 percent in 2005.[5] This latest increase is a direct result of the closure of the Israeli labor market: Palestinian employment in Israel and in the settlements has declined by 67 percent since 2000.[6] The Palestinians have turned to agriculture to cope with the increasing hardship they face in their daily lives and to ensure they have sufficient food for themselves; indeed, they consume most of what they produce. Agriculture functions as a shock absorber whereby many Palestinians who lost their source of income went back to cultivating their lands, primarily to put food on the table. As agriculture became a means of survival for Palestinians, whoever controlled agriculture ultimately controlled the entire Palestinian population. The Israelis understood this fact of life very well.

Long before the second intifada, Palestinians returned to the land as a way to resist the military occupation. At the end of the 1970s and the beginning of the 1980s, passive resistance (*sumud* in Arabic) within the Palestinian territories joined Palestinian political activism organized from outside the territories in opposition to the occupation. Palestinian land became the symbol of Palestinian identity, and Palestinians developed survival strategies focused on the rural economy. They sought self-sustainability and economic disengagement from Israel. To achieve this, they mobilized the poor, mostly from the villages, by means of alternative structures that were decentralized, open, and democratic and by volunteer work, as well. This new mobilization was sustained by a network of national institutions that promoted self-help throughout the Palestinian population while questioning the traditional, elitist, and nationalist ways to achieve development.[7]

The prohibition by Israel of Palestinian political parties brought the national movement to the understanding that without the help of the official structure of mass organizations, political action was limited. Among the leftist parties, the Palestinian Communist Party, the only party whose leaders lived in the territories, took the leadership in carrying out this new strategy and formed the first mass organization, The Union of Palestinian Medical Relief Committees, in 1979. The Palestinian Agricultural Relief Committees (PARC) were created in 1983 by three agronomists who studied in the USSR. The Union of Agricultural Work Committees (UAWC), which was closer to the Popular Front for the Liberation of Palestine, was formed in 1986. Both organizations, which are the largest Palestinian agricultural organizations today, were based on an original model. The idea was to create farmers' and women's committees throughout the West Bank and to help them cultivate the land so as to minimize the chance that the Israeli military authorities would confiscate it. Both organizations also helped farmers adopt modern farming practices to better compete with Israeli agriculture. The popular committees and mass organizations provided the infrastructure of the first intifada, which was an uprising generated from within the Palestinian population.[8] They constituted a new elite, which stood in opposition to an old, traditional urban elite.[9] Yet their activity did not impede the implementation of Israeli policy. Twenty years later, the problems of Palestinian farmers continue to grow.

Today, cultivating land under occupation is a challenge that more and more Palestinian farmers cannot afford. At the same time, Palestinian society is becoming more and more dependent on the occupying neighbor and on humanitarian and international aid for its survival. The Palestinian agricultural sector does not produce enough to meet the people's food needs, and the population relies on food imports. According to the Palestinian Ministry of Economy, prior to 1971, Palestinian agricultural imports and exports were nearly equal, an average of $20 to $30 million a year. Today, imports greatly exceed exports. Strong domestic demand, limited land and water resources, and Israeli control of the borders and of the movement of goods and people have impeded the export market. As a result, agricultural imports have increased from $21 million in 1971 to $109 million in 1984 and $400 million in 1997, with Israel supplying 95 percent of agricultural imports.[10] Impeding access to land, water resources, and markets is an efficient way for Israel to prevent the expansion of a healthy Palestinian agricultural sector that could help Palestinians become self-reliant. Controlling agriculture in Palestine is one of the means Israel uses to control the population and make the Palestinians totally dependent on agricultural imports from Israel and on foreign assistance.

This process corresponds to what Sara Roy has referred to as "de-development" in her important research on the Gaza Strip.[11] According to the de-development thesis, Israeli measures not only affected the development of Palestinian economy and agriculture, they also prevented it from getting back on track in the future. Roy contends that the dedevelopment of the Gaza Strip was carried out by a set of policies: the expropriation and dispossession of lands, water resources, and other natural resources; the integration and externalization of the Gazan economy vis-à-vis the Israeli economy through the Civil Administration; and the deinstitutionalization of existing Palestinian structures. Roy demonstrates Israel's aim to expropriate Arab resources and make them available for Israeli use and points to water, land, settlements, housing, and investment policies as having an overwhelming effect in permanently dispossessing Palestinians of economic resources.

In an article published in 1999, Roy is even more insistent in her analysis of Israeli policies: "In fact, not only has the peace process failed to mitigate—let alone end—de-development, it has accelerated the process by introducing into the Palestinian economy new dynamics that have further attenuated an already diminished socioeconomic base."[12] Increased territorial fragmentation, very little or no access to markets, and intensive closures have deepened the dedevelopment process and further impoverished the Palestinian population. As Roy predicted, in these conditions, economic activity has returned to a more traditional, circumscribed, and autarkic base, further contributing to the de-development process. Agriculture is a good example of the process whereby, rather than moving toward an integrated economy, Palestinians are advancing toward individual production units.[13]

As in other colonial settings, Palestinian agriculture under Israeli rule encapsulates the logic of control that is exercised in other domains of the society and economy. To the extent that it involves access to lands, access to water, and access to markets, agriculture encompasses the main physical, economic, and political aspects of the occupation.[14] Yet the Israeli-Palestinian case differs from other cases of colonial domination for various reasons. Unlike Britain/India or France/Algeria, the two territories are close, and Israeli military rule is easier to implement. The small size of the Palestinian territories makes it easier to divide and control by closures, checkpoints, roadblocks, bypass roads, and the like. Because of the geography and as a result of the policy of economic integration adopted by Israel at the beginning of the occupation and pursued in a different form following the Oslo process, the Israeli and the Palestinian economies are closely linked. Moreover, unlike other examples of colonial transformation of colonized agriculture, the establishment of Israeli control over Palestinian agriculture and its erosion and/or destruction was a silent process during most of the occupation.

Agriculture became an issue only in recent years, when it became a principal source of living, on the one hand, and was systematically targeted by the occupation regime, on the other. Although agriculture plays a prominent role not only in the basic survival of the Palestinian population, but also in its political and cultural identity (the olive tree and *sumud,* the steadfast devotion to the land, are symbols of the Palestinian struggle for independence), the increased Israeli control over Palestinian agriculture has received very little attention from human rights organizations and in the scholarly literature on the Israeli occupation.

THE PARIS PROTOCOL: A DEAD LETTER

Palestinian agriculture is regulated by the Gaza-Jericho Protocol on Economic Relations, known as the Paris Protocol, the economic-relations agreement signed between Israel and the PLO on April 29, 1994, as part of the Oslo agreements. Like other internationally recognized agreements, the provisions of this protocol are only partially implemented by Israel. The severe restrictions on movement, travel, and the transportation of products imposed by Israel in recent years constitute a clear violation of the protocol's provisions and have had a very negative impact on Palestinian agriculture and the economy.[15] Yet even before the outbreak of the second intifada and the turning of the Paris Protocol into a dead letter, the biased design of the agreement already reestablished the occupier/occupied relation that it was intended to overturn.

Article VI of the Declaration of Principles, signed by Israel and the PLO on September 13, 1993, transferred powers and responsibilities to the Palestinians in the areas of education, culture, health, social affairs, taxes, and tourism, and did not include agriculture. The Israeli-Palestinian Interim Agreement on the West Bank and the Gaza Strip, also known as Oslo II, was concluded on September 26, 1995 and signed in Washington two days later. It prepared the second stage of Palestinian autonomy after the transfer of powers by dividing the Palestinian territories into three areas: Area A (which covered 3 percent of the land area), in which the Palestinians were given complete control over civil matters and internal security; Area B (24 percent of the land area), in which the Palestinians were given complete control over only civil matters and the responsibility for internal security was divided between the two sides; and Area C (73 percent of the land area), in which Israel maintained total control over civil and security matters.

On May 28, 1994, the Palestinian Authority assigned its first sixteen ministerial portfolios. The agriculture portfolio was not among them. In 1995, the Ministry of Agriculture became the last ministry to be created. From the beginning, it was highly criticized because many of the staff had worked for Israel's Civil Administration. These appointments raised the tensions that had already existed between the agricultural organizations, which antedated the Palestinian Authority and which were well established and professional, and the new ministry. International donors further destabilized the relations between the agricultural organizations and the ministry, who competed for funding.[16]

By the time of the Camp David summit in July 2000, Israel held total control of 59 percent of the West Bank (Area C), where the bulk of Palestinian farmland was located, and security control over 23.8 percent of the West Bank (Area B), where the Palestinian Authority held civilian control. Thus, Israel held effective control over 82.8 percent of the West Bank, while the Palestinian Authority had complete control over noncontiguous areas (Area A) amounting to 17.2 percent of the land area.[17] Following the Oslo agreements, Israel established a system of checkpoints and a permit regime for movement from the West Bank to Jerusalem and within the West Bank. It built a fence around the Gaza Strip and controlled the movement of Palestinians wanting to go from the Gaza Strip to the West Bank or to enter Israel.

The fragmentation of the West Bank and its separation from the Gaza Strip increased after the outbreak of the second intifada, when Israel divided the Palestinian territories into segments and impeded movement between them. The spatial division, coupled with the system of permits put in place in 1999, greatly affected Palestinian agriculture. Given that most of the farmland in the West Bank was in Area C, under full Israeli control, some farmers had to request permits to gain access to their own land. More complicated problems also occurred. For example, farmers from Zubeidat, in the Jordan Valley, live in Area B, which is under joint Israeli-Palestinian control, and their land is in Area C, which is under complete Israeli control. A roadway built for settlers, Road 90, separates the farmers' land from their homes. If they want to repair or replace the irrigation system in their fields, a task that entails digging under Road 90 and connecting the pipes to the well that is located in Area B, they need to obtain the army's approval. Such approval has never been given. To complicate matters further, the construction of the Separation Wall has de facto annexed approximately one hundred and twenty-five thousand acres of fertile farmland. Farmers who own land on the Israeli side of the wall have to obtain special permits — "green permits" — to reach their land. The permits are hard to obtain, in part because of the difficulty of proving ownership of the land.[18]

The fragmentation of the Palestinian territory also affects the work of the Ministry of Agriculture, whose staff does not have free access to lands and farmers in Area C. If it wants to intervene in Area C, where most of the farmland is located, the ministry must ask the Israeli authorities for permission. The Israelis have sole control over the matter and do not have to justify denying entry. Palestinian agricultural NGOs, through their farmers' committees throughout the West Bank, have easier access. This advantage of the nongovernmental sector undermines the ministry's legitimacy.

The Paris Protocol is Annex IV of the Gaza-Jericho Interim agreement signed earlier that year. It consists of eleven articles that delineate the future economic relations between the two sides during the interim period. According to the Palestinian Ministry of Economy, the Paris Protocol was intended to improve cooperation between Israelis and Palestinians in four ways: by creating a unified tariff and foreign-trade regime, by establishing fiscal and monetary relations (the VAT, customs, banking matters), by improving coordination, and by allowing the free movement of goods, people, and labor.[19] According to the protocol's preamble, it is intended to improve the economic relations between the sides with the hope that economic development would increase the momentum toward peace:

> The two parties view the economic domain as one of the cornerstones in their mutual relations with a view to enhance their interests in the achievement of a just, lasting and comprehensive peace. Both parties shall cooperate in this field in order to establish a sound economic base for these relations, which will be governed in various economic spheres by the principle of mutual respect of each other's economic interests, reciprocity, equity and fairness.[20]

The Paris Protocol established a number of regulations to promote free trade between Israel and the Palestinian territories. Palestinian products were not to be subject to export restrictions; trade to and from the West Bank and the Gaza Strip had full access to Israeli ports; Palestinian imports and exports were granted equal treatment at Israeli ports, except regarding security measures; and bilateral trade agreements between Israel and other parties applied in the West Bank and the Gaza Strip. However, the Paris Protocol was designed for Israel's advantage. Its principal effect was to institutionalize Palestinian dependence on Israel and increase the integration of the Palestinian economy within the Israeli economy. Israel's obstacles to free trade and the free movement of labor during the second intifada reinforced a tendency that was already present during the Oslo years.

According to the Israeli human rights organization B'Tselem, "The model established in the Protocol is known as a 'customs union,' the primary characteristic of which is the absence of economic borders between members of the union. The practical effect of selecting this model was preservation of the economic relations that had existed until then, i.e., a Palestinian economy integrated in and dependent on the Israeli economy."[21] The protocol ignored the unequal status of the two sides: one controlling the borders and the import-export facilities, the other a newly appointed national authority with little experience in economic and trade matters.

The second intifada halted the already harsh implementation of the protocol. Coordination ceased. The Joint Economic Committee, which was charged, pursuant to Article II, with overseeing implementation of the protocol, has not met since 2000. Palestinian customs activity at the borders (Rafah, the Allenby Bridge, Damiah) was stopped in October 2000 and has not recommenced. The Palestinian Authority was never permitted to exercise its entire Article III powers and responsibilities in the sphere of imports and customs policy and procedures and never exercised control on the import-export facilities. At times, Israel used the import taxes and levies that, under the protocol, it collected for the Palestinian Authority as blackmail to achieve its ends. Thus, after the Palestinian elections in 2006, Israel started using the transfer of the tax revenues as a tool to pressure the Hamas-led government.

Israel has applied the Paris Protocol selectively and unfairly since the outbreak of the second intifada. But most importantly, the Israeli system of checkpoints and physical obstacles has violated the protocol's fundamental principle of the free movement of goods, people, and labor. As of January 2006, Israel had placed some five hundred physical obstacles (dirt mounds, concrete blocks, and trenches) throughout the West Bank, which, together with the checkpoints, the Separation Wall, and the extremely poor road network, impede the transportation of goods.[22] The Paris Protocol states in Article VIII that "there will be free movement of agricultural produce, free of customs and import taxes, between the two sides." The reality is different. Palestinian products undergo security checks at multiple checkpoints within the West Bank. At some checkpoints, Israel requires transfer of the goods from one truck to another (the back-to-back method): the goods are unloaded, the army conducts its security check, and the goods are then reloaded onto another truck on the other side of the checkpoint. The back-to-back system severely impairs the quality of the Palestinian goods, a result of overhandling and lying on the ground under the sun waiting to be checked and reloaded. According to the Ministry of Agriculture and farmers, the back-to-back method has increased the cost of transportation within the West Bank by 200 percent.[23] As one supermarket owner in Ramallah said, "It is now far less expensive to bring products from Tel Aviv than from Jenin."[24]

The Paris Protocol seemingly promoted a principle of reciprocity whereby "the agricultural produce of both sides will have free and unrestricted access to each other's markets."[25] However, the restrictions on movement result in increased Palestinian imports from Israel at the expense of Palestinian products and provide Israeli traders with a captive market. Thus, despite the trade agreements concluded between the Palestinian Authority and Egypt, Saudi Arabia, Jordan, the European Union, the United States, and Canada, among others, the Palestinians remain totally dependent on Israel in trade matters. Israel accounts for 70 percent of Palestinian imports and 90 percent of Palestinian exports. The balance-of-trade deficit ranges from 60 to 75 percent, an indication of an economy utterly reliant on imports.[26] While Israeli farmers have free access to the West Bank and Gaza Strip markets, Palestinian agricultural exports to Israel are highly regulated and restricted. As PalTrade, the Palestinian Trade Center, a nonprofit organization, has pointed out: "The movement of agricultural goods between the two sides has been severely restricted when these products are from Palestinian origin, while Israeli products are allowed to flow with great ease and facilitation into the Palestinian Territories."[27] In the shops in Ramallah and Nablus, over 60 percent of the dairy products are Israeli. The Palestinians produce dairy goods, but the restrictions on movement make it very difficult to transport the products from Hebron, the site of the main Palestinian dairy company, to the northern West Bank. With the loss of income and the grave economic conditions, people cannot afford to be patriotic when making their food purchases.

Israel systematically blocks, directly and indirectly, the importation of Palestinian products. For example, the olive-oil sector is the backbone of Palestinian agriculture, yet Israel imports olive oil from other countries. In 2003–4, Israel produced 3,000 tons of olive oil and imported 10,500 tons. In 2004–5, Israel produced 9,000 tons of olive oil and imported 7,500 tons. That same year, 10,000 tons of olive oil was produced in the Palestinian territories.[28] This phenomenon violates Section 12 of Article VIII (Agriculture) of the Paris Protocol, which states that "the two sides will refrain from importing agricultural products from third parties, which may adversely affect the interests of each other's farmers." According to the Israeli Federation of Chambers of Commerce, in 2004, Israel imported olive oil at a value of $6,907,000.[29]

BARRIERS TO TRADE

Israeli administrative, logistical, and security measures have severely impeded Palestinian trade within the Palestinian territories and abroad. The access of Palestinian goods to markets is prevented at three different levels. First, within the West Bank and the Gaza Strip, restrictions on movement confine the delivery of products to markets within the farmers' local areas. As mentioned, the restrictions also drive up transportation and per-unit costs, thus distorting the price. Second, the farmers are denied access to Israeli markets. And third, Israel controls Palestinian access to international markets via its monopoly on exporting and its control of all seaports and airports. In doing so, Israel violates Section 11 of the agricultural provisions of the Paris Protocol, according to which "the Palestinians will have the right to export their agricultural produce to external markets without restrictions, on the basis of certificates of origin issued by the Palestinian Authority."

Moreover, Agrexco, the main Israeli exporter of agricultural products, has a monopoly on the export of agricultural goods from the Gaza Strip. It is therefore virtually impossible for the Gaza growers to build an identity in foreign markets or even to know where their produce is sold. A study that the Mattin Group prepared for the Netherlands Minister of Development Cooperation on the marketing of strawberries from Gaza noted the obstacles posed by the lack of transparency and accountability in the existing marketing arrangements and by Agrexco's effective monopoly position.[30] In the past, Agrexco's unique ability to arrange the secure and expedited shipment of highly perishable strawberries across the Gaza border to European destinations via Ben-Gurion Airport was a key factor in maintaining its monopoly position. The emergence of competing Israeli exporters reduced, but did not eliminate Agrexco's advantage. Dependence on Israeli exporters to arrange for the shipment of Gaza strawberries to European markets continues to harm the sector and critically affects the feasibility of options that do not rely on Israeli marketing firms. The Mattin Group's report pointed out that:

> Even before deducting special cross-border logistics and security inspection costs and cooperative service fees from the prices paid by Agrexco to Gaza farmers for their exportable output, the weekly export prices paid to the Gaza farmers were found to be consistently lower than the prices Agrexco was paying to a small number of Israeli farmers supplying the same European panelist channels during the same week. In the 2001–2002 season, the weekly prices the Israeli farmers received were on average approximately 25 percent higher than those paid to the Gaza cooperatives before the deduction of extra logistics and security inspection costs from the Gaza prices, and about 35 percent higher after that deduction.[31]

The report further states that, owing mainly to restricted access to Israel's markets and low Palestinian internal market prices, the exporting Gaza farmer is typically able to realize less than 60 percent of the revenue realized on nonexported output by the exporting Israeli farmer. This restricted access is the largest single factor penalizing Gaza farm production.[32]

The commercial links between Agrexco and the Palestinian cooperatives were established during the first years of the Civil Administration. The Israeli company oriented the cooperatives' production toward exports because it was more beneficial to the company and was a way to provide goods for the lucrative European market at a time when Israeli production was insufficient to meet the demand there. For this reason, the products primarily available now in the Gaza Strip are strawberries, cherry tomatoes, peppers, and cut flowers, all originally designed for the European market. The problem with these products is that when the crossing point is closed and the goods cannot be exported, they cannot be marketed in the Gaza Strip, where the residents need rice, sugar, and wheat, rather than strawberries and cut flowers. This is especially true after the borders have been closed for a long time.

In a survey conducted by PalTrade, Palestinian businessmen described Israel's management of land, sea, and airports as poor, unpredictable, and expensive. "For exporting and importing products via Ben-Gurion Airport, unlike Israelis, Palestinian businesses can only use cargo planes due to the Israeli regulations against Palestinian exporters using passenger planes. This restriction causes delays and extra costs to the Palestinian trader especially when it comes to the transport of agricultural goods." PalTrade also pointed out that Israeli customs authorities do not accept imports marked as exempted from duty under the European Union–Palestinian Authority agreement of 1997.[33] Palestinian importers face additional requirements for the entry of the goods. The nontariff barriers are gradually weakening Palestinian trade, especially for agricultural products, because of their fragility. As a result, according to the Palestinian Ministry of Economy, Palestinian agricultural suppliers pay transaction costs at least 70 percent higher than Israeli companies for identical exports. One farmer said:

> Before this agreement [the Paris Protocol], we could sell a ton of bananas for 800 Jordanian dinars. Now, we can hardly get 150 dinars for it. An Israeli farmer can sell his bananas at 2 shekels a kilo and they receive a 2.40-shekel subsidy from the government. So they sell a kilo for 4.40 shekels, while we can only sell it for 0.9 shekels. How can we survive? There is no reason to pick the bananas; it isn't worth it.[34]

A close examination of the state of agriculture in the Gaza Strip demonstrates both the hardships of farming under the occupation and the benefits that Israel reaps from Palestinian dependence in this domain. The high population growth in the Gaza Strip reduces the land available for agricultural use. The amount of farmland in the Gaza Strip has dropped from 45,000 acres to between 25,000 and 27,000 acres over the past decade, a decline of 45 percent.[35] According to Union of Agricultural Work Committees, the Israeli Army has destroyed more than 15,000 acres of farmland since September 2000.[36] For example, according to a report by the United Nations Office for the Coordination of Humanitarian Affairs (OCHA), land covered by trees in the area of Beit Hanoun in the northeastern Gaza Strip, where the IDF conducted intensive leveling of orchards under the explanation that they provided cover for militants that were firing rockets into Israel, fell by 62 percent, from 47.5 hectares to 18.2 hectares. Vegetation as a percentage of wooded land dropped from 49.9 percent to 22.4 percent; 47.5 percent of the land in the area was found "bare," compared with 18.7 percent in October 2001, and the extent of uncultivated land has risen from 20.3 hectares to 51.5 hectares.[37] Because of the lack of land, farmers are intercropping—growing several crops on the same plot, for example, growing green beans on top of strawberries.

Israel's disengagement from the Gaza Strip did not improve Gaza's economy and agricultural production, which even deteriorated in its wake. Despite commitments to extend the operating hours and increase activity at the Karni crossing by the government of Israel and the Palestinian Authority under the Agreement on Movement and Access, signed under the auspices of U.S. Secretary of State Condoleezza Rice and the special envoy for Gaza disengagement from "the Quartet" (as the consortium of the United States, Russia, the European Union, and the United Nations is known) and ex-president of the World Bank, James Wolfensohn, in November 2005, there has been little progress in this regard. From January 1, 2006 to March 19, 2006, Karni was closed 60 percent of the time, almost two out of every three days.[38] It should be noted that even when the crossing is closed, goods are sometimes allowed to enter the Gaza Strip to avoid a humanitarian catastrophe. But the crossing is closed for exports from the Gaza Strip, resulting in the loss of profit on tons of agricultural produce, which are destroyed because the Israeli authorities do not open the crossing for exports. From February 22 to March 8, 2006, Palestinian farmers destroyed forty tons of strawberries a day at a loss of $816,960.[39] According to the Interim Association Agreement signed between the PLO and the European Union in 1997, which exempts certain agricultural products from taxation on entry to the European market, Gazan strawberries enter the EU market tax free from November 1 to March 31. Israeli policy at the Karni crossing and the resultant loss suffered by Palestinian farmers makes Israeli produce more competitive in the European market at the expense of Palestinian goods. Indeed, the manner in which Israel operates the Karni crossing proves that the restrictions on movement of Palestinian goods are intended primarily to advance Israeli economic interests and that security considerations are secondary.

Not only has Israeli policy rendered the Paris Protocol meaningless, it has subjected the Palestinian agricultural sector to increasing regulation and control. On August 28, 2005, while the international community was praising the disengagement, the head of Central Command, Major-General Yair Naveh, issued a military order that was intended, according to the IDF, to prevent weapons and other forbidden materials, such as chemical fertilizers used in making bombs, from being smuggled into Israel or the West Bank under the guise of agricultural goods.[40] The order allows officials, in the words of the IDF, to "monitor the standards of agricultural produce and determine that it meets the necessary health and safety requirements." The order requires that fresh agricultural produce destined for Israel or industrial sites in the West Bank be transported by truck using specified crossings. Persons violating these provisions are subject to five-year prison sentences.

This military order is a disaster for the Palestinian agricultural sector, and it further isolates the agricultural communities of the West Bank. Many informal shops were set up along the settlers' roads inside the West Bank, along Palestinian roads, and even in villages on the Israeli side of the Green Line. Many Arab Israelis went to the West Bank to buy vegetables and fruits, in part to maintain ties with Palestinian communities. The new policy will destroy this informal economy and thus harm the Palestinian farmers who set up roadside stands to market their produce and will further separate the Palestinian populations on the two sides of the Green Line. It clearly benefits Israeli companies who buy Palestinian products, who will be able to pay a lower price because of the lack of demand. Because the checks are not systematic, the new policy cannot be considered a health measure and clearly appears to be a means to increase control over the movements of goods.

CONCLUSION

It is important to highlight the more silent processes and mechanisms used by the occupation regime to control the Palestinian territory and population. In the agricultural sector, which receives little media and public attention, Israeli policies consist, in Sara Roy's term, of a steady process of "de-development" that undermines Palestinian agriculture and impedes its revival in the future. Israel does this in multiple ways.

First, it reduces production capacity, denying access to agricultural inputs such as fertilizers and limiting access to land and water resources. Second, the restrictions on movement severely impede trade within the Palestinian territories and the export of produce from the territories to Israel and elsewhere. Third, Israel discriminates against Palestinian products, in addition to taking advantage of the provisions of the Paris Protocol, which favors Israeli interests and whose partial implementation aggravates the already terrible state of Palestinian agriculture. Finally, the structural transformation of the Palestinian agricultural sector is hampered by the Palestinian Ministry of Agriculture's lack of control over the sector and the ministry's continuing struggle to survive due to the financial crisis of the Palestinian Authority, on the one hand and the competition it faces from nongovernmental organizations, on the other. At the same time, Palestinian NGOs, which concentrate on emergency projects such as rehabilitating water sources and reclaiming land to mitigate Israeli military actions, do not have the resources to engage in development projects. Donor states and international organizations, too, are primarily funding emergency projects. Thus, the Palestinian National Agricultural Plan, which was prepared prior to the outbreak of the second intifada, never had a chance to be implemented, and the Palestinian Authority was unable to draft an emergency plan afterward. As a result, the agricultural sector has been deprived of long-term planning and meaningful reform. Israel's colonial policy is definitely to control Palestinian agriculture as much as possible by means of control over water, land, markets, and the movement of goods and persons while turning the Palestinian territories into a captive market for Israeli products. Palestinian agriculture, not to speak of the whole economy, has been damaged to such a point that it will take a long time before it can get back on track.

Agriculture, which the Palestinian Agriculture Relief Committees still refer to as the backbone of Palestinian society, has become necessary for survival in Palestine. To meet the needs of the present state of emergency and to enable future economic development, it is necessary to give greater attention to agriculture and to protect it to the greatest extent possible.

A SIGN NEXT TO A GATE IN THE SEPARATION WALL According to a survey conducted by OCHA and UNRWA in 2006, only twenty-six gates in the Wall were open to Palestinians on a regular basis, typically for short periods in the early morning, noon, and late afternoon. Many gates are "seasonal" and open only for a limited period during the olive harvest. [Source: UN Office for the Coordination of Humanitarian Affairs, Occupied Palestinian Territory]

APPENDIX 1: THE CONSTRUCTION OF THE SEPARATION WALL AND THE CREATION OF THE SEAM ZONE

Only 20 percent of the route of the Separation Wall runs along the Green Line. According to the United Nations Office for the Coordination of Humanitarian Affairs (OCHA), the Wall, together with the Seam Zone, that is, the area that constitutes the buffer zone between the Green Line and the Wall, covers around 15,000 acres of West Bank land and encloses approximately 10 percent of the territory of the West Bank and East Jerusalem.[41] To build the Wall, the Israeli military has confiscated large areas of fertile land.

Since the Israeli Army declared the buffer zone a "closed military area," farmers who have land on the Israeli side of the Wall must apply for permits issued by the Israeli authorities in order to gain access to their land, which they reach by passing through agricultural gates in the Wall. [See photo on page 428.] Israel has no plan to annex the buffer zone and makes no claim over the land. Even so, the authorities require the farmers to prove ownership of the land before allowing them to enter, fully aware that the land-registration process started under Ottoman rule was never completed and that it is extremely difficult to prove ownership in many cases. Laborers and tenants are especially liable to be refused access to their lands. In addition, misspellings or any inconsistency between the name as it appears on the person's identity card and the land-registration record are grounds for denial of a permit. A report by OCHA and UNRWA (the United Nations Relief and Works Agency for Palestinian Refugees) published in July 2007 found that only 40 percent of farming families had been issued permits.[42]

Security reasons are the grounds for 5 percent of permit-application rejections; the remaining 95 percent of the rejections are for failure to provide sufficient proof of ownership.[43] In 2005, the Israeli authorities placed another restriction on access to land: A grandson is not entitled to a permit if he did not take the relevant administrative steps before his grandparents died. The result has been a reduction in the number of permits issued. Also, since 2005, the permits state the specific gate the residents must use to cross into the buffer zone and get to their land. The Wall's crossing gates are supposed to open at set times during the day, but, in practice, farmers are dependent on the goodwill of the soldiers on duty.

The lack of free access and the permit regime make it impossible for the farmers to tend to their fields and orchards properly. As a result, they fear that their land is going to be annexed by Israel: According to the Absentee Property Law, land that has not been cultivated for three years can be declared state land.

APPENDIX 2: THE JORDAN VALLEY

The vital importance of the Jordan Valley in Israeli colonization strategy already was manifest in the Alon Plan of 1967, the first colonization plan for the West Bank. The Alon Plan called for the annexation of one-third of the West Bank, the establishment of around thirty settlements in the area, and the creation of a security zone in the Jordan Valley. Accordingly, the Jordan Valley was the site of the first Israeli settlements in the newly occupied territories.

The total area of the Jordan Valley is 175,000 acres. It contains 100,000 acres of potential farmland, only 50,000 of which is under cultivation. The remaining area has been seized for the settlements (10,000 acres), or has been declared a closed military zone. The gradual expansion of settlements in the area has been accomplished on potential farmland. Access to land close to the settlements is forbidden, even for grazing livestock.

The hotter climate of the Jordan Valley, which lies below sea level, gives it a comparative agricultural advantage. It is a natural greenhouse in the winter, enabling the earlier production of most agricultural products. Its climate is also ideal for certain agricultural products such as dates and bananas that require hot temperatures. Because they have been permitted to draw water only from the shallow aquifer for decades, Palestinian farmers have been irrigating their fields with poor-quality, saline water. The anarchic use of fertilizers has damaged the soil. Under these circumstances, the farmers need to concentrate on growing dates and other crops that can withstand salty soil.

Because of its importance as a border area and the site of settlements, Israel has isolated the Jordan Valley from other Palestinian areas since the start of the second intifada. The Tayaseer checkpoint isolates the Tubas District from the northern Jordan Valley, the Al-Hamra checkpoint isolates Nablus and the northern districts from the middle Jordan Valley, Jericho is besieged by two checkpoints, isolating it from the rest of the Jordan Valley, and other checkpoints isolate the southern part of the Jordan Valley. This isolation has affected the size of cultivated plots, the movement of farmers, the flow of inputs and outputs—principally fertilizers and agricultural products—and marketing the crops. The journalist Amira Hass writes:

> Restrictions on the movement of Palestinians in the Jordan Valley were imposed at the start of the Intifada and were gradually expanded. But the sweeping prohibition regarding entry into the area by Palestinians was imposed, in fact, after security responsibility in Jericho was given back to the Palestinians on March 16, 2005.... In addition to affecting others, the prohibition also applies to thousands of residents of towns and villages in the northern West Bank such as Tubas and Tamun, most of whose lands are in the Jordan Valley and some of whose residents have been living there for many years.[44]

People who for years have earned a living by seasonal agricultural work for Palestinians in the Jordan Valley and an unknown number (apparently several thousand) of Bedouins and sheep-herders are also greatly affected by the restrictions, which have caused significant losses to the industry and forced many farmers to abandon their land and farming.

The Palestinian NGOs Network announced on February 23, 2006:

> As a consequence of the permit and closure policy, agricultural produce from the Jordan Valley cannot be properly marketed. The transportation of produce through the various checkpoints is often hampered and, as a consequence, has been left to rot on the ground or used to feed sheep and goats. Recently, the Israeli government also closed the terminal for agricultural products in Bardala so that farmers were and are not allowed to take their products to Palestinian markets in Nablus and Jenin or to other areas of the West Bank. The only exit remains the Beit She'an terminal, which they are not permitted to use.[45]

NOTES

This article was written in 2006, and most of the data upon which it is based dates from that period. Some was Web-based and is no longer available on-line.

1 The source is Pierre Bourdieu and Abdelmalek Sayad, *Le déracinement: La crise de l'agriculture traditionnelle en Algérie* (Paris: Éditions de Minuit, 1964), p. 47.

2 *Ibid.,* p. 13.

3 C. Shambu Prasad, "Suicide Deaths and the Quality of Indian Cotton: Perspectives from the History of Technology and the Khadi Movement," *Economic and Political Weekly,* no. 5 (January 1999), available on-line at http://www.epw.org.in/epw/user/viewAbstract.jsp (subscription required).

4 *Ibid.*

5 Nitham Ataya, "Agriculture is a Key Pillar in the Palestinian Economy," Palestinian Agricultural Relief Committee (2005); Palestinian Central Bureau of Statistics (PCBS), under "Agricultural Statistics, Various Data," available on-line at http://www.pcbs.gov.ps/DesktopDefault. aspx?tabID=4022&lang=en (last accessed September 24, 2008); Caroline Abu-Sada, "ONG et construction étatique: L'expérience de PARC dans les Territoires Palestiniens (1983–2005), Institut d'Études Politiques de Paris, Ph.D. thesis, 2005; Caroline Abu-Sada "Farmers Under Occupation: Palestinian Agriculture at the Crossroads," unpublished research paper, Oxfam, Great Britain, 2006. The slight decrease from 2004 to 2005 can be explained by two reasons: first the seasonal pattern of olive production (the main Palestinian agricultural production), with one good year followed by a bad one, and second, by the fact that work in agriculture is mainly informal and family based and as such may not be properly reported.

6 Abu-Sada, "ONG et construction étatique."

7 Dina Craissati, "Social Movements and Democracy in Palestine: Politicization of Society or Civilization of Politics?" in *Orient,* no. 37 (1996). See also Rema Hammami, "NGOs: The Professionalisation of Politics," *Race and Class* 37, no. 2 (October–December 1995): pp. 51–63.

8 On this original model, see Joost R. Hiltermann, *Behind the Intifada: Labor and Women's Movements in the Occupied Territories* (Princeton, NJ: Princeton University Press, 1991).

9 For the earlier period of this phenomenon, see Hammami, "NGOs." On the recent trends, see Sari Hanafi and Tabar Linda, *The Emergence of Palestinian Globalized Elite: Donors, International and Local NGOs* (Ramallah: Institute of Jerusalem Studies and Muwatin, 2005), and Abu-Sada, "ONG et construction étatique."

10 Interview with officials of the Ministry of Economy, Ramallah, November 18, 2005, and PCBS, "Agricultural Statistics," data on imports and exports, pp. 96–97 (no longer available on-line; last accessed 2006).

11 Sara Roy, *The Gaza Strip: The Political Economy of De-Development* (Washington, D.C.: Institute for Palestine Studies, 1995).

12 Sara Roy, "De-Development Revisited: Palestinian Economy and Society since Oslo," *Journal of Palestine Studies* 28, no. 3 (1999): pp. 64–82.

13 On this matter, see United Nations Special Coordinator for the Middle East Peace Process (UNSCO), "The Economic Fragmentation of the West Bank (2005), available on-line at http://www.unsco.org/Documents/Special/FINAL%20FE%20text%20for%20printing.pdf (last accessed August 25, 2008) and UN Food and Agriculture Organization (FAO), "Strengthening Resilience: Food Insecurity and Local Responses to the Fragmentation of the West Bank," available on-line at http://www.chs.ubc.ca/archives/?q=node/779 (last accessed March 5, 2009). The cutting of international aid following the election of the Hamas-dominated

parliament and the nomination of a new government further harmed the Palestinian economy. The reduction in aid has created structural weaknesses that will be hard for the Palestinians to overcome. Many Palestinians have already sold their assets, have cut back on food intake, leading to an increase in malnutrition, have removed their children from schools, and the like.

14   I will not specifically deal with the water problem and the land issue in this essay, though both are crucial to an understanding of agriculture under the occupation. For an overview of the Israeli confiscation of Palestinian lands by declaring them state land, see Ariel Handel, "Where, Where to, and When in the Occupied Territories: An Introduction to Geography of Disaster," in this volume. Regarding the water problem, a few figures will give an idea of its magnitude. Although the World Health Organization (WHO) sets minimal water consumption at 100 liters per capita per day (l/c/d), Palestinian consumption is 50 to 70 l/c/d. By comparison, Israeli consumption is 400 l/c/d, with Israeli settlers in the Palestinian territories consuming 800 l/c/d. Sonia Nettnin, "Why a Water Crisis Still Exists in Gaza," June 10, 2005, available on-line at http://usa.mediamonitors.net/Headlines/Why-a-Water-Crisis-Exists-in-Gaza (last accessed March 5, 2009). The water resources in the Palestinian territories are scarce and are inequitably distributed between the two populations. In the Gaza Strip, overpumping of the aquifer has made the water salty and unsuitable for human consumption most of the time. Seventy percent of the Palestinian water sources are used for agriculture purposes.

15   The Palestinian Trade Center (PalTrade), *Trade Impediments* 1, no. 5 (2005): p. 2, available on-line at http://www.paltrade.org/cms/images/enpublications/Trade_Impediments_-_Issue_5.pdf (last accessed August 25, 2008).

16   See Abu-Sada, "ONG et construction étatique."

17   Sara Roy, "Ending the Palestinian Economy," *Middle East Policy* 9, no. 4 (December 2002): p. 126.

18   For more information on the permit system and the consequences of the Wall, see United Nations Office for the Coordination of Humanitarian Affairs (OCHA), "Humanitarian Impact of the West Bank Barrier, Special Focus, Crossing the Barrier: Palestinian Access to Agricultural Lands" (January 2006), Update no. 6, (November 2006), available on-line at http://www.un.org/unrwa/access/OCHABarRprt_Updt6_En.pdf (last accessed March 5, 2009).

19   Interview with officials of the Palestinian Ministry of Economy, June 15, 2005.

20   Paris Protocol, Preamble, April 29, 1994, Annex IV of the Gaza-Jericho Interim Agreement, available on-line at http://www.palestinecenter.org/cpap/documents/economic.html (last accessed August 25, 2008).

21   B'Tselem, "The Paris Protocol," available on-line at http://www.btselem.org/English/Freedom_of_Movement/Paris_Protocol.asp (last accessed August 25, 2008).

22   United Nations Office for the Coordination of Humanitarian Affairs (OCHA), January 2006, available online at www.ochaopt.org under "Closure Maps."

23   Interviews with residents of Jenin, Tulkarem, Tubas, and Ramallah, May–September 2005.

24   From an interview conducted on July 16, 2005.

25   Paris Protocol, Article VIII, section 10.

26   Palestinian Central Bureau of Statistics (PCBS), under "Agricultural Statistics." See also United Nations Food and Agriculture Organization and World Food Programme, *Comprehensive Food Security and Vulnerability Analysis* (2007), "Executive Summary" available on-line at http://www.ochaopt.org/documents/CFSVA_Executive_Summary.pdf (last accessed April 15, 2009).

27   The Palestinian Trade Center (PalTrade), *Trade Impediments* 1, no. 5 (2005): p. 2.

28   The figures are taken from the International Olive Oil Council, www.internationaloliveoil.org (last accessed on June 2, 2006 and no longer available on-line).

29 The breakdown by countries was Spain (50 percent), Jordan (36), Italy (5), Turkey (5), Portugal (3.3), the United States (0.4), Germany (0.3), Egypt (0.26), and Greece (0.02). (Percentages exceed 100 percent because of rounding.)

30 The Mattin Group, *What Way Forward for the Gaza Strawberry Sector*, prepared for the Netherlands Minister of Development Cooperation, unpublished report, March 2003. The Mattin Group is a research group based in Ramallah that specializes in trade and international human rights law issues.

31 *Ibid.*, p. 16.

32 Prior to the 2001–2 season, Agrexco exported Gaza Palestinian strawberries under Israeli certificates of origin and labeled them "Product of Israel" in contravention of the European Community's and the European Free Trade Association's trade agreements with Israel. In November 2001, Agrexco corrected these improper practices and modified the labeling, certificate of origin, and phytosanitary procedures substantially in accord with the European Community–PLO Interim Association Agreement. It introduced a new proprietary brand, "Coral," and began marketing Gaza strawberries as "Palestinian products" through the same distribution channels.

33 The Palestinian Trade Center (PalTrade), *Trade Impediments* 1, no. 5, p. 3.

34 Interview with the author, Jordan Valley, February 13, 2006.

35 United Nations Office for the Coordination of Humanitarian Affairs (OCHA), "Beit Hanoun Satellite Image Analysis of Vegetation Loss 2001–2004," available on-line at http://domino.un.org/UNISPAL.NSF/3822b5e39951876a85256b6e0058a478/0a118693de831bd5852570670051409e!OpenDocument (last accessed September 2, 2008).

36 Union of Agricultural Work Committees, interview with the head of the Gaza Strip Office, October 18, 2005.

37 OCHA, "Beit Hanoun Satellite Image Analysis of Vegetation Loss 2001–2004."

38 United Nations Office for the Coordination of Humanitarian Affairs (OCHA), "Gaza Strip Situation Report: The Humanitarian Impact of the Karni Crossing Closure: Bread Running Out in Gaza," March 19, 2006, available on-line at http://www.humanitarianinfo.org/opt/docs/UN/OCHA/ochaSR_Gaza190306.pdf (last accessed September 2, 2008).

39 United Nations Food and Agriculture Organization and World Food Programme (WFP), "Market Report no. 3," 2005.

40 "IDF to Allow Produce Transfer from West Bank," *Jerusalem Post*, August 30, 2005, p. 2.

41 United Nations Office for the Coordination of Humanitarian Affairs (OCHA), "The Humanitarian Impact of the West Bank Barrier on Palestinian Communities, March 2005" (no longer available on-line; last accessed 2006).

42 United Nations Office for the Coordination of Humanitarian Affairs (OCHA), "Three Years Later: The Humanitarian Impact of the Barrier Since the International Court of Justice Opinion," OCHA Special Focus, July 9, 2007, available on-line at http://www.ochaopt.org/documents/ICJ4_Special_Focus_July2007.pdf (last accessed September 2, 2008).

43 United Nations Office for the Coordination of Humanitarian Affairs (OCHA), "Barrier Stops Palestinians Accessing Land" (November 2006), available on-line at http://www.ochaopt.org/documents/OCHA_Special_focus_8_Nov_2006_Eng.pdf (last accessed March 5, 2009).

44 Amira Hass, "Israel Cuts Jordan Rift from West Bank," *Ha'aretz*, February 13, 2006.

45 "The Jordan Valley Annexation." Call for action and international solidarity with the Palestinian people in the Jordan Valley, by the Palestinian Non-Governmental Organizations' Network (PNGO), February 23, 2006 (no longer available on-line; last accessed 2006).

Ariella Azoulay

4.1 ROAD 443, 2006 The arrangement in a straight line—like objects in a showcase—of the various items seen in the photograph differentiates them from the scrap thrown at random into the plot directly behind them. Beyond this formal difference—random piling versus orderly arrangement—their presence at the roadside might seem odd to strangers from countries where civil space has not been corrupted by occupation or apartheid. In this local space, however, such signs—a watchtower, camouflage netting, a field latrine, concrete segments "sewn" to each other to form a wall, chicken-wire

Architectonic schemes by Meira Kowalsky

435

fencing—and their unexplained combination are a familiar sight to both Israelis and Palestinians. Even when each of these items separately does not "iterate" its "intrinsic" meaning, and even when the logic of their syntax is hardly decipherable, they produce general "sayings" such as "the army is here" or "there are Palestinians nearby." The relative intelligibility of these phrases for passersby is due to the fact that such sayings are present in many different places and are perceived as an obvious part of the landscape. Their familiarity enables them to appear later in different contexts without standing out as odd or being taken for what they are in fact—tools of harassment.

Beyond the general meaning of such phrases, whose fleeting and repeated familiarity suffices to naturalize them, for the people who experience them closely on an everyday basis, they contain concrete and immediate meanings that shape people's movement in space. Israelis—especially soldiers and colonists—see them as means of protection from Palestinians, and they soon learn to operate them and to expand their uses. They perceive Palestinians as the human raw material to be directly processed with these tools. The Palestinians, especially those who have not given up their basic right to move in space and are forced to be subjected to the use of these tools, recognize each of these components and know how to decipher the nuances of their syntax. Most of them develop such interpretation skills in order to lighten—even if slightly—the burden that such components place in their path. Some of them do this in order to resist—violently or nonviolently—the blunt way in which such tools deny them freedom of movement in public space.

The bluntness of such tools is part and parcel of a comprehensive logic of the occupation regime, meant, at any given moment, to reiterate to the Palestinians their subjugation through instruction, deed, and sign. This bluntness aims to spread into various dimensions of existence, including the interpretative plane—the ways in which Palestinians will decipher the various signs. Thus, for example, the army persists in showing Palestinians watchtowers such as the one in the photograph as supervisory elements in space, even though the second intifada yielded a crop of hundreds of reinforced pillbox posts, making the watchtowers less and less necessary. Most of the older watchtowers have been covered with camouflage netting and a decoy guard dummy of the type used for target practice placed inside. Several times a day, soldiers climb up the post with provisions so that it will not occur to the Palestinians that the tower is empty and that for a given amount of time they have been left unsupervised.

In the picture, a segment is seen of an entire compound surrounding a blocking post. If the frame were wider, one would see a checkpoint, located a bit farther on the right. The purpose of the checkpoint—filtering and even totally denying entry to Palestinians who might come from villages such as Kharbata or Beit Likia to Jerusalem—is achieved more effectively when the road leading to it is already lined with policing signs that make the rules and their authorized makers clear to Palestinians.

MIKI KRATSMAN

4.2 AZOUN ATME, 2006 Blockage points are usually a part of an entire compound, some of it visible, the rest invisible, some of it permanent, other parts temporary, sprawling around the blockage point. Photographs documenting checkpoints and barriers usually present only a segment of the entire spatial compound, which consists of the total spatial distribution of a military force and which changes according to specific geographic-topographical conditions and updated intelligence on the movement of Palestinians in the area. Normally, however, every such segment embodies the principle of the whole: organizing space in a way that ensures Israeli control and sovereignty and Palestinian subjugation and obedience. The fear that such power relations will be disrupted and that the Palestinians might move out of their assigned places accounts for the expanding architecture of fear that creates compounds of spatial control.

A small, but typical section of this architecture is seen in the photograph. A violent uprising of Palestinians—present and past, individual and collective—against the rules of the game imposed upon them is usually translated into an upgrading of the protection level of the security forces and the proliferation of components that aim to subjugate the Palestinians to the rules of the game and restrict their movement ever more tightly.

The concern for the soldiers' safety—metonymically perceived as the concern for the Jewish citizens of the state—has been constructed for years as an objective above and beyond any discussion or debate, and any deployment on the ground is considered and measured mainly with this concern in mind. The stalled lives of hundreds of thousands of Palestinians are taken into consideration only within a secondary discourse that deals with reducing the negative effects of the concern for the soldiers' security. Thus, after the army callously spreads its forces inside the civil life space of the Palestinians, it initiates various "humanitarian" actions in order to minimize to a certain extent the damages it inflicts upon them and to show some consideration for their lives. But humanitarian concern is shown within the invariable assumption that when Jewish lives are to be protected, the lives of Palestinians are dispensable.

The Palestinian uprising against this assumption is perceived as a direct threat to the soldiers. The soldiers, sensing the threat to their lives from the moment they step inside the Occupied Territories, wish to protect themselves and remove this threat. In order to protect the soldiers and give them a sense of security, the army constantly improves the inner syntax of the blockage compounds: Instead of exposed watchtowers, it installs reinforced concrete spires with narrow observation slits at the top, enabling monitoring through remote control. Instead of bare ground on the way to the checkpoint, the army spreads barbed-wire spirals. Instead of dirt or paving, the army lines the road or path with tin sheets that produce noise when anything or anyone moves on them. Instead of raising fences that are man sized, fences two and three stories high are erected when necessary. Instead of wire fences, the army places modular concrete walls. Instead of permitting an uncontrolled stream of people to flow, the army slows down movement by narrowing passages.

MIKI KRATSMAN

4.3 AZOUN ATME, 2006 For Israelis, such tools as shown in the photographs embody the "no choice" assumption. Not only is the landscape in these pictures familiar, it even gives most Israelis a sense of security: shreds of camouflage netting, various metals, shades of khaki, shooting slits, field glasses. These tools aim to quench the visceral fear that afflicts Israelis when they drive on these roads paved on Palestinian soil, roads that whisper to them that around the next curve, someone is lying in wait, ready to pounce. Someone is probably sitting in that army trailer, watching over the road, someone leaning out the top of the tower with his gun drawn, ready to snipe at anyone who would wish them harm. Sometimes they even suffer from these tools themselves, when they happen to get stuck in a line of waiting cars, for example, stalled as a result of a flying checkpoint that the army is "forced" to place on a road that Palestinians were not even supposed to use, but they realize there is "no choice." They understand that the Wall and the pillbox posts are now the landscape with which they must live, day in, day out. This plight seems minimal to them, compared with the benefit attributed to these tools, and in any case, their suffering as a result is immeasurably less than the Palestinians'.

4.4 MAKKABIM CHECKPOINT, 2001 Most of the time, Israelis who—daily—cross checkpoints of the type placed along apartheid Road 443 speed on without stopping. The concrete cubes placed in three half lines across the road require them to slow down and slalom in between them for a very short distance, after which they acceler- ate back to their normal driving speed. Palestinians are not supposed to drive here— although their banning is not anchored in any writ of law—and from the dominant Israeli point of view, those living in the villages should find themselves some source of livelihood that does not necessitate travel by car. The fact that before the road was widened (on lands confiscated from Palestinians) and traffic on it restricted to Jews alone, it was a central artery used by Palestinians to move between the south- ern Ramallah region and villages lying to its southwest—this fact is meaningless. An unstressed routine seems pervasive at this checkpoint and others like it, thanks to the hundreds of checkpoints and barriers throughout the West Bank. The minimal block- age tools throughout this checkpoint prove the effectiveness of the other blockage points, with which it creates a single continuity.

This minimalism indicates that this tool is actually meant only to confirm that other tools, at different points in space, have already done the job and distanced the Palestinians from here. Police presence at such checkpoints, too, is meant as a final backup to prevent entry of Palestinians who have dared and managed to make their way to the road in spite of the costly means placed as obstacles.

There are sufficient clauses in the current traffic laws that they can be found to have violated to prevent their entry. The Israeli flag stuck on top of the guard shack embodies perhaps more than anything else the place where the Israeli sovereign now prefers to show his clout.

4.5 WEST BANK, 2004 Digging a ditch across a road that only Palestinians are allowed to use is a way to ensure that Palestinians will not be able to reach the roads serving Jews on a daily basis, as in the Makkabim or Atarot areas. A wide and relatively deep ditch is opened in the middle of the road, assuring not only that Palestinians will not reach the mixed roads, but also that their lives will proceed very slowly, with many disruptions, and that not much time will be left for other matters beyond the basic concerns of livelihood and daily survival. The army does not make do just with digging a ditch, however. Like a gardener regularly and devotedly visiting and tending his plants, the soldiers devotedly frequent these barriers to make sure that Palestinians have not sabotaged them. The development of tools to ensure that Jewish traffic along the roads and at other checkpoints will not be disrupted is the outcome of the occupier's dual effort: on the one hand, to separate Jews from Palestinians, and on the other to be "there," occupying the place of separation in order to preserve partition and ensure its existence. These blocked roads are not included in the 734 kilometers of apartheid roads that the Palestinians are not permitted to travel at all.

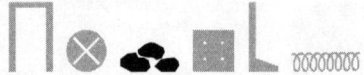

4.6 BEIT LIKIYA, 2001 Some of these barriers are produced with an ecological rationale. The army recycles for other uses the debris that it produces when it demolishes houses. This pile is one of 208 heaps of rubble placed at the entrance to villages or as barriers on roads and one of 486 blockage points of various types scattered at different points in the West Bank in addition to the 100 permanent checkpoints and numerous "flying" checkpoints on which there are no precise data. The explicit purpose of such blockages is the prevention of vehicular traffic. But when debris is scattered from one side of the road to the other, pedestrian movement is blocked, as well. Only people young enough to climb these artificial hills can cross. Behind one another, in single file, they create a virtual path of sorts to the left of the barrier, each in turn deepening the footsteps of his predecessors. They know that the gap and discrepancy between their fate and the free movement enjoyed by those traveling the road to their right will assure that the occupation regime to which they are subjugated will not reign forever.

MIKI KRATSMAN

Π⊗⊹▪L ⦚⦚⦚⦚⦚⦚

4.7 FLYING CHECKPOINT, TRANS-SAMARIA ROAD, 2001 The Trans-Samaria Road (Road 5) stretches from northern Tel Aviv in the west to the Ariel colony and Samaria (the northern West Bank) in the east. The eastern part of this road was paved in the 1990s on Palestinian lands, mostly for the use of Jews. The fantasy was of total control in a sterile zone, but the presence of Palestinians necessitates the disruption of the relative calm in which the Jewish population rides these roads as their very own and requires the erection of "flying checkpoints." A platoon commander who served for two years at the checkpoints says: "You get out there and identify areas where Palestinians travel the roads, and you put up a flying checkpoint." The flying checkpoint has evolved and become a mobile unit ready for use at any moment—two iron rods with a red-and-white stripe in the middle, two spikes on a rope, spike strips on the asphalt, a Stop sign and a Slow sign. The soldiers serving in the Occupied Territories must maintain such a kit in their vehicles when they go out on patrol. Its availability enables the soldiers immediately to carry out the "full blockage" or "partial blockage" of Palestinians' lives.

The commander:

A flying checkpoint is an assignment, by all means.... It could be the result of an intelligence alert, or because we haven't been there for quite a while and need to be seen
everywhere. And then we say "Let's put up a checkpoint between this village and that
hamlet." It usually happens at unexpected times....

A checkpoint has to be a surprise.... The bad guys need to know we're always
around. We expect the [Palestinians] to go from there to the village and tell others
"The army is everywhere."

The army has to seem present everywhere in order to keep the Palestinians from
rebelling, but also because of the invincible fear that some of them might indeed
rebel. The Palestinians have managed to etch into the soldiers' minds the fact that
they can always surprise them, appear, and resist. Before it is a violent power, such
resistance is first and foremost a political power, the power of people to act freely
as they combine their actions with those of others. They cannot be deprived of this
power except by exterminating them as human beings. But Israel exterminates only
individuals in its targeted killings. Whoever has not been targeted and killed might
produce violence, and therefore Israel cannot be free of the fear that all those who
have not been targeted and killed might produce violence. The soldiers in the photograph, protected with their bulletproof vests, armored vehicle, helmets, and goggles,
try to preserve the surprise element on their side and the side of their mates who are
just now putting up a flying checkpoint on the road. Since the rules of the game here
are not agreed upon by the two sides, the battle of this flying checkpoint, too, will be
decided only sporadically, through either obedience or violence.

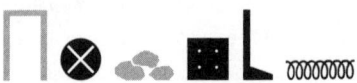

4.8 AL-TUFAH CHECKPOINT, 2003 The components of this checkpoint—concrete cubes, sandbags, plastic barriers, tin sheets, and barbed-wire spirals—are no different from those used at other checkpoints. But its syntax, looking like a random collection of patches that have sprawled with time, is gradually disappearing. It is being replaced by a lean, tight, sterile syntax of modern installations that are supposed to provide a constructed answer to problems that here were given local, improvised solutions. The new installations remove some of the visual "disturbances" in sight: The Palestinians are required to walk amid potholes, and the path indicated by sharp rock shards is a dangerous tripping ground. The route is not clearly marked or bounded by fences that would protect the soldiers against some Palestinian outburst, and the relations between the heart of the checkpoint and its periphery are no longer differentiated. In spite of its disorder and the improvisation that is evident in every connection made between its components, one of the army's guiding principles in administering the movement of Palestinians is present here: narrowing movement into a single file of individuals kept as distant from one another as possible. In current military lingo, this is called "laning." It not only assures control over the actions of those waiting in line, but also prevents the checkpoint area from becoming an agora, a public space where the many assemble and become a power that—together—determines the conditions of its own existence.

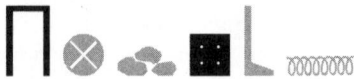

4.9 HUWWARA CHECKPOINT, 2003 The longer the checking of individuals at the head of the waiting line takes, the longer the line stretching far beyond the end of the shed that the army provides grows. But as the line at this checkpoint grows longer and the dangers it entails increase, the army diffuses pressure to other places and produces a general slowing down of the system. Thus, too, the soldiers are sometimes required to throw a concussion grenade to straighten up the line. Most of the time, when the width and length of the line is under control, one soldier suffices to get back in line any person who dares step out of it.

ACTIVESTILLS.ORG/YOTAM RONEN

4.10 QALANDIYA CHECKPOINT, 2007 No doubt these installations are more photo-genic—the waiting hall is spacious, the ceiling high, the shed has ample room for everyone, the ground is paved, the colors are not depressing, there are taps for the thirsty and an ashtray for the smokers. Everything indicates that the quality of life of those having to pass the checkpoints has been taken into consideration.

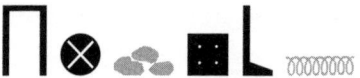

4.11 BEIT FURIQ CHECKPOINT, 2004 Alongside the new and relatively spacious installations, which only a very small percentage of the Palestinian population can enjoy, another species of new installation has been developed, containing nearly everything necessary, but without wasting a single centimeter of air or ground space. The width of the turnstile bars has been reduced from 80 to 60 centimeters, and the ceiling has been planned to be precisely high enough so that no one will be injured by it, but also so that no one might feel that the sky is the limit. Even slits for daylight have been preplanned so that crowding will not become unbearable.

DORIT HERSHKOWITZ

4.12 HUWWARA CHECKPOINT, 2006 The necessary minimum does not omit gender considerations: A narrow cubicle is ready and waiting for the invasive body search of women, requiring privacy.

4.13 HUWWARA CHECKPOINT, 2007 The ongoing enforcement of the policy of slowing down traffic in the Occupied Territories is supposed to reduce pressure at the checkpoints. Different tools "lane" the Palestinians into long waiting lines in order for them to reach the new metal detectors in an orderly, restrained manner. Sometimes it works, as on the day this photograph was taken.

4.14 WATCHTOWER AT THE ENTRANCE TO HEBRON, JANUARY 2006 In order for this sophisticated pillbox post to be effective and enable remote control, numerous ground troops are needed to go on doing the "dirty work." The only way to make this work cleaner is to slow down the Palestinians altogether and make them stay away from public space. The army can also provide food directly to their homes in order to ensure calm and reassure the soldiers who, fearful, hide behind protected shooting slits.

4.15 THE EREZ CROSSING INTO ISRAEL, 2007 The door opens, and a lone Palestinian enters the cell. Another door closes behind him. He receives a laconic instruction to raise his hands, the check is carried out, the front door opens, and the Palestinian can now leave this place to his successor. The checking itself is not time consuming, but the way there might consume about half a workday. Should one file a complaint for lost working hours? Invasion of privacy? Discrimination? Complain to whom?

The Destruction of Risk Society
and the Ascendancy of Hamas

Neve Gordon and Dani Filc

When faith is lost, there is no security.
—Muhammad Iqbal, cited in the Hamas Charter

The increasing popular support for Hamas in Palestinian society, culminating in the organization's landslide victory in the democratic elections of January 25, 2006, is intricately tied to and informed by the mechanisms of control that Israel has employed in the Occupied Territories over the past few years and, more specifically, is related to the profound effect these mechanisms have had on Palestinian society. Founded in Gaza at the beginning of the first intifada (December 1987) by Sheikh Ahmad Yassin, Hamas experienced ups and downs for many years.[1] However, with the eruption of the second intifada in September 2000, its fortunes began changing, and since then, it appears as if there is little one can do to stop the organization's upward surge. Considering that Hamas's ultimate objective is the establishment of an Islamic state in Mandatory Palestine and reforming society there in the spirit of "true" Islam, the movement's increasing popularity threatens the forces sympathetic to the secular democratic state, as well as the two-state solution. What, one might ask, enabled Hamas to garner so much support?

Khaled Hroub suggests that the organization's popularity stems from its being seen as the voice of Palestinian dignity and the symbol of the defense of Palestinian rights at a time of unprecedented hardship, humiliation, and despair, which have followed the historic concessions made by the Palestinian Authority (PA) in the framework of the Oslo process.[2] Surely, the relative success of Izzeddin al-Qassam, Hamas's military wing, in attacking Israeli targets has also increased the organization's popularity, as has Hamas's reputation for clean conduct, modesty, and honesty, which have been pointedly contrasted with the conduct and corruption of many PA officials.

Shaul Mishal and Avraham Sela add that Hamas's success in winning over the masses has to do with its increasingly pragmatic approach, one characterized by support for the short-term objective of a Palestinian state in the West Bank and Gaza Strip while still maintaining the long-term goal of establishing an Islamic state that would replace Israel. They propose that "Hamas's decision-making processes have been markedly balanced, combining realistic considerations with traditional beliefs and arguments, emphasizing visionary goals but also immediate needs."[3] Most commentators agree that Hamas has also benefited from the extensive welfare services that it offers to all Palestinians regardless of their religious belief or political affiliation.[4]

While these insights undoubtedly help explain why Hamas has gained massive popular support, they do not address a key social process that has been taking place in the West Bank and Gaza Strip since the outbreak of the second intifada. Employing insights from risk theory,[5] in this essay, we argue that Hamas's ascendancy is also informed by the collapse of the system of securities in the Occupied Territories. Using the health-care system as a case study, we show that endemic uncertainty has taken over Palestinian society. This uncertainty has, in turn, helped undermine the rationality of risk society—the possibility of calculating risks in order to arm oneself against future ill fortune—thus facilitating the emergence of a different rationality more susceptible to the appeals of Hamas. In other words, we contend that the destruction of the mechanisms that offer security and in this way ensure social stability makes room for a postmodern fundamentalist rationality.

RISK SOCIETY: THEORETICAL BACKGROUND

The calculation of risk in many ways characterizes modernity. By risk society, we mean a society that develops a system of strategies and technologies to secure and manage the lives of its members by anticipating hazards, in this way striving to domesticate the future. Regardless of whether risks are real or constructed, they are rendered calculable and governable, and the calculability of risks has become an important element of the rationality through which society and its institutions are organized, monitored, and regulated.[6] Although risk theory has been discussed at length since the early 1980s,[7] much of the current literature suggests that, at least on one level, we are moving "beyond" risk society, in the sense that many of the risks confronting global society can no longer be calculated or controlled.[8] The very idea of controllability, certainty, or security, which is so fundamental to the original concept of risk society, collapses in light of global ecological, genetic, and nuclear risks.

Taking into account some of the ideas integral to this literature, we return here to the insights of one particular understanding of risk, the one associated with Michel Foucault's notion of governmentality.[9] We use the term "risk society" in order to denote a certain kind of rationality that had been developed in order to manage and regulate the population and thus to guarantee the stability of a specific hegemonic order. Accordingly, the calculability of risks is not only used to control society in a restrictive way, but often improves people's life conditions and may also help engender a certain kind of solidarity.

François Ewald points out that one of the prominent characteristics of risk society is the development of insurance, whose major objective is to calculate ostensibly unpredictable consequences and to provide a safety net for the members of society against an array of "accidents," ranging from car-related and work-related accidents through sickness, infirmity, and old age, all the way to natural disasters such as floods and fires. Considered as separate events, accidents seem random, but when put in the context of a population, they can be treated as predictable and calculable. One can predict, for example, that next year within a given society, a certain number of people will be diagnosed with cancer; the only unknown variable is who will be diagnosed with the disease. All members of society are at risk, and while the level of probability alternates—some have a higher risk (e.g., smokers) and others a lower risk (e.g., athletes)—most people would prefer to have insurance so that if diagnosed with cancer, they can receive medical treatment.

The historical development of this idea was lucidly formulated in the late nineteenth century by the French legal scholar Albert Chaufton:

> Man first thought of insuring his shipping against the risks of navigation. Then he insured his houses, his harvests, and his goods of all kinds against risk of fire. Then, as the idea of capital, and consequently also that of insurable interest, gradually emerged in a clear form out of the confused notions that previously obscured them, man understood the he himself was a capital which death could prematurely destroy, that in himself he embodied an insurable interest. He then devised life insurance, insurance that is to say against the premature destruction of human capital. Next he realized that if human capital can be destroyed, it can also be condemned to disuse through illness, infirmity and old age, and so he devised accident, sickness and pension insurance. Insurance against unemployment or premature destruction of human capital is the true popular form of insurance.[10]

Insurance is accordingly a contractual agreement. Each member contributes to a common fund and expects to receive support if he or she is subjected to misfortune. This is extremely important because it shows that insurance collectivizes risk and in this way creates a grouping of human interests, constituting a mode of association among the different members of society. When insurance is planned and applied by public, nonprofit institutions such as social security, it can represent a form of interage, interclass, intergender and interethnic solidarity. But it is nonetheless a contractual solidarity based on narrow interests. The goal of insurance, Ewald claims, is to discipline the future by providing for it in advance through a series of calculations that arm oneself against ill fortune. Insurance thus replaces the uncertainty characterizing the so-called "natural" or "divine" order and introduces some form of stability in its stead.

The ability of modern society to respond to the arbitrariness of fate by making the incalculable calculable helps explain certain technologies by which society is managed and stabilized. Think what would have happened if the U.S. government had not bailed out the insurance companies after 9/11. The outrage of the people who lost loved ones and livelihoods could have threatened the Bush administration. Thus, the government assures the permanence of insurance institutions, and by guaranteeing their security, the government also guarantees its own existence. By disciplining the future, one disciplines the present.

Whether insurance is provided as a commodity (by private enterprises) or as a right (by the state) makes a significant difference concerning not only ideas about equity and justice, but also the possibility of democratic control. Several scholars make this distinction, describing a process whereby, as a result of the privatization of the welfare state, insurance is outsourced to nonstate institutions while social agents are encouraged to manage themselves. This is called the "new prudentialism." Under the "new prudentialism" the individual is constituted as a free agent, so that "responsibilities for risk minimization become a feature of choices that are made by individuals, households and communities, as consumers, clients and users of services."[11] The state abdicates its responsibility for risk management, and this responsibility is assumed by multiple and often competing actors that offer an array of services—for example, private health insurance, schools, community policing—to citizens qua consumers and clients. On a deeper level, individuals and communities assume the role of managing their own lives, while the state takes on "less a directive and distributive role, and more a coordinative, arbitratory and preventive one."[12]

In the following pages, we show that the processes taking place in the Occupied Palestinian Territories problematize the logic described in the literature on risk. At this stage, we will only say that the possibility of calculating risks—which informs the rationality of risk society—has in many respects been undermined. In the Occupied Territories, the rationality of risk that offered security and in this way guaranteed political, social, and economic stability is in retreat, and in its place a postmodern Islamic fundamentalist rationality is emerging that is shaped both by its opposition to modernity and colonialism and by its incorporation of certain elements integral to modernity. It is precisely the destruction of risk society and the emergence of a postmodern religiosity that has benefited Hamas.

With the collapse of risk society, one is thrown to the mercy of fate, charity, and faith, because many of the instruments and mechanisms used to control the different situations in which risk becomes concrete are no longer available. This is especially true concerning health and health care. The collapse of risk society undermines practices that can prevent, postpone, or enable people to avoid or to cope with illness and disease. Within this context, the very conception of the individual as a free agent who can both choose among different providers of risk-management services while at the same time managing himself or herself becomes meaningless. The accentuation of faith becomes commonsensical, and a fundamentalist worldview based on the adoption of a logic that both highlights divine ordinance and embraces a critique of colonialism and modernity while appropriating certain modern practices gains credence.

THE PALESTINIAN HEALTH SYSTEM PRIOR TO THE SECOND INTIFADA

We chose to focus on the health-care system not only because it is one of the institutions that employs the rationality of risk in a pronounced way,[13] but also because medicine plays a central role in modern governmentality and deals both with the management of populations and the discipline of the body.[14] Moreover, as Bryan Turner points out, in contemporary Western societies, medicine and public health have in many respects replaced religion as central institutions governing the conduct of human bodies, thus suggesting that their collapse makes room for the resurgence of a religious worldview.[15] Before examining the state of the Palestinian health-care system following the outbreak of the second intifada, we provide a thumbnail sketch of the period during which Israel had full control over the Palestinian health-care system (1967–94) and the phase following its transfer to the Palestinian Authority in the framework of the Oslo process (1994–2000). Our objective in these sections is to show how the organization of the health-care system was informed by the logic of risk.[16]

THE HEALTH-CARE SYSTEM IN THE OCCUPIED TERRITORIES, 1967–94

Immediately following the 1967 War, Israel took over the administration of all Palestinian civil institutions, including the health-care system. The residents of the newly occupied West Bank and Gaza Strip were initially regarded as people living under *temporary* Israeli control (unlike the residents of East Jerusalem, whose partial integration into Israeli society was seen as the "price" Israel had to pay for annexing the city on June 27, 1967), and their affairs were managed by the military government.[17] In 1981, the Israeli Ministry of Defense created the Civil Administration and transferred authority over all civil institutions, including the health-care system, to the latter, a move that can be understood as an attempt to "normalize" and hence perpetuate the occupation. The Palestinian health-care system was run by two Israeli medical officers, one in the West Bank and the other in the Gaza Strip. The Israeli Ministry of Health supervised only epidemiological developments liable to present danger to public health within Israel proper, but had little if any authority in the Occupied Territories.

From the outset, the Israeli military government emphasized public health, while development of a robust Palestinian health-care system that could provide services similar to the ones in Israel was never part of its objectives. This policy reflected the entire Israeli colonial project in the Occupied Territories, where investment in infrastructure was, on the whole, for the benefit of Jewish settlers and where there was no real intention of providing the "natives" with the infrastructural support that would make them independent.[18] Indeed, Israel's ongoing policy was to foster Palestinian dependence, which was used as a mechanism to manage and control the population of the Occupied Territories.

With respect to public health, among Israel's first priorities were the control of vaccine-preventable diseases, the implementation of a broad immunization program, and the creation of mechanisms of epidemiological surveillance.[19] The centrality of a public-health approach within the occupied health-care system was inspired by a number of fears. From the occupier's standpoint, the outbreak of disease in the West Bank and Gaza Strip could potentially put the Israeli population at risk; it could lead to social upheaval within the territories; and it would definitely increase the cost of the occupation.[20]

The Palestinian population in the territories was accordingly considered by the occupying power as a "population at risk" (paradoxically, the Israeli population, as a result of the occupation, is also considered at risk), and those in charge of health in the Israeli Ministry of Health produced a great amount of data about it, beginning with a population survey held immediately after the 1967 War and followed by seemingly endless surveys of personal hygiene, sanitary conditions, and diseases. Reports published by the Israeli Ministry of Health in 1994 contain tables and graphs starting from 1970, three years after the occupation began, which describe the success of "Vaccination of Preventable Diseases in the West Bank and Gaza," the "Introduction of New Vaccines to Routine Immunization Schedules," the "Immunization Program for Infants and Schoolchildren," an "Analysis of Tetanus Cases (adult and neonatal)," as well as analyses of diphtheria, poliomyelitis, measles, hepatitis, pulmonary tuberculosis, and so on. In addition, Palestinian medical institutions were instructed to submit monthly reports to the military government (until 1981) and to the Civil Administration (until 1994) on medical, fiscal, and administrative activities.[21]

The administration of health care in the Occupied Territories did not respond only to "pure" medical needs, but was also part of a strategy of surveillance and of managing the population. Consider the changes in child-delivery practices. While during the early 1970s only 16 percent of deliveries in the West Bank took place at hospitals, by 1993, this figure had risen to 74.5 percent. Hospital delivery changed traditional norms and practices, submitting the individual to the requirements of risk management. Simultaneously, hospital delivery diminished the number of perinatal mortalities, making delivery a more foreseeable event, thus disciplining both the individual and the future.[22] For the most part, however, the Israeli authorities prioritized the management of risk at the level of the population and did not allocate many resources to individual risk management, which is much more expensive.[23]

Monetary considerations also impeded the promotion of secondary and tertiary services, which include specialist care provided in ambulatory form at outpatient clinics and more intensive, usually high-tech care and treatment provided for hospitalized patients. Both secondary and tertiary services require high capital investments and operating costs, complex biomedical technology, firm regulatory standards, and highly trained personnel, while primary care consists of much cheaper ambulatory, low-tech care provided by nurses, family physicians, general practitioners, or pediatricians. Throughout the first twenty-seven years of occupation, the development of secondary and tertiary services was extremely slow and consistently lagged far behind those offered within Israel. The Palestinians hospitals' maintained only a basic level of care and were characterized by a high degree of inefficiency and ineffectiveness. Between 1967 and 1984, for example, the number of hospital beds in the Occupied Territories actually decreased while the population doubled.[24] Many areas of medical expertise were never established in the territories, while other basic medical fields were only semifunctional.[25]

The fact that the secondary and tertiary health-care systems in the Occupied Territories remained dependent on Israel and never became self-sufficient was used to manage the population and keep it under surveillance. For instance, cancer patients who needed to undergo radiation treatment had to be referred to Israeli medical institutions. The Civil Administration often covered the referral costs to Israel for members of its insurance program, which was introduced in 1974 by the military government.[26] Yet those patients who required treatment outside the territories also needed the security approval of the Israeli General Security Service in order to receive a permit to enter Israel. Thus, becoming a member of the insurance program did not ensure that one would be transferred to an Israeli hospital; one at times had to promise to collaborate with Israel. Doctor Ephraim Sneh, who headed the Civil Administration between 1985 and 1987, states that upon taking office, he found an Israeli policy intended to pressure Palestinians into collaborating on various levels: "The motto was 'If you behave, you will receive; if not, you won't.'" "The policy," he continues, "wasn't explicit, but it was known to all the involved parties, and mentioned in internal discussions."[27]

An article written by Doctors Yitzhak Sever and Yitzhak Peterburg, who served as chief medical officers for the Civil Administration in the West Bank and Gaza Strip, respectively, affirms that the health-care system's three major objectives were to provide basic health services at a low price, to help the occupying forces manage the Palestinian population, and to contain epidemics so that they would not pass the Green Line and threaten Israeli citizens. "It was clear," the two doctors write about the health-care system they directed, "that Israel had to care for the local populations in the territories and ensure high standards of public health and reasonable medical care.... The overall goal was to keep the population satisfied and quiet, and to provide a stable, calm, and reasonable background for future negotiations that would lead to a political solution."[28] Sever and Peterburg demonstrate that the health-care system was used as a central instrument of governmentality in the Occupied Territories, as it is in all risk societies.

Even though the occupying power kept the level of the health-care services in the West Bank and Gaza Strip far below those offered in Israel and hindered the development of a health-care system independent of the occupying machine, the health status of the Palestinians was enhanced during the first twenty-five years of the occupation. Basic health indicators improved dramatically during the first two decades of occupation, with the infant mortality rate falling from about 60 per 1000 in 1970 to 27.2 per 1000 in 1993 and life expectancy rising from 48 to 69.2 years between 1970 and 1993. There are several reasons for this improvement, ranging from the provision of universal primary health care, including immunization and vaccination; to the systemization of hospital deliveries; to substantial economic growth, which also entailed an upgrading of the food basket and its nutritional value. The basic health indicators show that Palestinians were also better off than the inhabitants in neighboring countries, where in 1993, infant mortality and life expectancy were, respectively, 55 per 1000 and 62 years in Egypt, 36 per 1000 and 68 years in Jordan, and 40 per 1000 and 67 years in Syria. Nonetheless, the same indicators remained much lower than in Israel, where infant mortality and life expectancy in 1993 were 9 per 1000 and 77 years, respectively.[29] Thus, the administration of the health-care system exercised a weak pastoral power that improved the condition of the population in several respects, combined with disciplinary techniques that allowed for its surveillance and control.[30]

The health-care system in the Occupied Territories, however, also was characterized by fragmentation. In addition to the governmental health-care system that was run by Israel, there were four additional operators of health services in the West Bank and Gaza Strip: the United Nations Relief and Works Agency (UNRWA), nongovernmental organizations (NGOs), charitable organizations, and private providers. UNRWA has been responsible for providing health-care services for Palestinian refugees since the early 1950s. It offers hardly any secondary and tertiary care—it operates only one small hospital in Qalqyilia—and has always emphasized integrated primary health-care services. Over the years, it has implemented effective preventive primary health care: maternal and child health and family-planning services, as well as control of communicable and noncommunicable diseases.[31] Thus, through its public-health programs, UNRWA played a central role in helping the occupying power manage the Palestinian population.

The nongovernmental sector emerged in the 1970s, slowly creating an important network for health-care delivery in the West Bank, Gaza, and East Jerusalem. At the outset, this sector provided secondary and tertiary care and by 1992 was responsible for over 40 percent of Palestinian hospital beds. About half of the hospital beds were located in East Jerusalem, which housed the largest and most specialized secondary and tertiary care services available to Palestinians. Yet not unlike the governmental hospitals, the nongovernmental facilities provided mostly basic services that remained far behind the services offered by Israeli hospitals.[32] Following the eruption of the second intifada and the erection of the Wall in East Jerusalem, West Bank and Gaza Strip residents could not reach the hospitals and clinics in East Jerusalem, and their occupancy rate rapidly dwindled. These hospitals can no longer be considered part of the Palestinian health-care system simply because they are inaccessible to the population of the Occupied Territories. Therefore, they are no longer part of the mechanisms that help control risks. We return to this point later.

While many of the health-related NGOs initially offered secondary and tertiary care, following the outbreak of the first intifada in December 1987, the provision of primary services was compromised, and a plethora of popular health organizations emerged, focusing mostly, but not exclusively, on primary and preventative health care. A 1992 survey of the West Bank identified seventy-five clinics operated by charitable societies, located in seventy communities, thus servicing 30 percent of the rural population.[33] Already then, clinics administered by the Zakat Committees, which are directly associated with the Hamas, constituted the largest proportion of charitable clinics in the West Bank (26 percent), which was not considered a Hamas stronghold. Yet the charitable sector "possessed some resemblance to the private sector in terms of the absence of consistent guidelines and standards governing the delivery of both curative and preventative services."[34] This contrasts with the planning and calculability upon which risk society is built. Finally, the 1992 West Bank survey identified 150 private clinics in eighty rural communities.

Over the years, the Palestinian health-care system was maintained at a level that satisfied the goals set by the occupying power. Relatively good primary services were offered, ensuring that communicable and noncommunicable diseases were contained, yet the secondary and tertiary systems remained underdeveloped. This fulfilled at least four objectives. First, it kept down the cost of running the occupied health-care system, if only because primary health services are much less expensive than secondary and tertiary care. Second, the establishment of universal primary services helped ensure that there would not be an outbreak of disease that could, in turn, lead to high financial expenditures and to social upheaval. In other words, the primary services helped discipline the future, as much as possible, in order to keep the population quiet and manageable and expenses affordable. Third, the primary services also ensured that no diseases would spill over into Israel, suggesting that the services offered in the territories were also important for managing the population inside Israel proper. It is no coincidence that the health protocols of the Oslo agreements stated that the PA will continue to implement the immunization and vaccination programs that Israel developed in the territories.[35] Finally, Israel maintained the secondary and tertiary services in the Occupied Territories at such a level so as to ensure that the Palestinians would continue to be dependent on the services offered in Israel proper and used them as a means of exercising disciplinary control over the occupied population.

THE PALESTINIAN HEALTH SYSTEM, 1994–2000

Even though Israel retained extensive economic and military control in the West Bank and Gaza Strip after the transfer of authority to the PA, the latter took upon itself full responsibility for the health of the Palestinian population. According to the 2000 annual report of the Palestinian Ministry of Health (PMH), the routine immunization program had been maintained, while the health-insurance scheme was dramatically expanded, covering around 53 percent of the population.[36] However, the quality of secondary and particularly tertiary services remained low, and investment in their development actually decreased. The per-capita governmental expenditure on health care for 2000 was $30.40, much lower than the expenditure in 1996 of $42.70 and even lower than the Civil Administration per-capita expenditure in 1993 of $33.80.[37] According to the Palestinian Central Bureau of Statistics, the total per-capita health expenditure (governmental and nongovernmental) in 2000 was $121.60, indicating that governmental expenditure constituted less than

30 percent of the total expenditure on health care. By comparison, in Israel, per-capita expenditure on health care in 2000 was $1,609, of which 70 percent was government funded.

The discrepancy between these figures is revealing for a number of reasons. First, one notices that after a short-term increase in government spending on health care following the transfer of authority to the PA, health expenditures dropped dramatically. Second, the relatively low level of governmental expenditure reveals that the Palestinian health-care system was totally dependent on the nongovernmental sector.[38] This was surely part of the inheritance of the first twenty-seven years of occupation, since during that period, the nongovernmental sector was developed by Palestinians in order to fill acute needs that were not satisfied by the Civil Administration while simultaneously serving as a form of resistance to the occupation. Moreover, under the auspices of the World Bank, the Palestinian Authority initiated an aggressive policy of rapid privatization, transforming the West Bank and Gaza into one of the most privatized political entities in the world.[39] The fact that the PA did not increase the government's role in supplying health-care services had even more serious ramifications once the second intifada erupted, since it became relatively easy for competing forces to take over because the government services were relatively weak.

Finally, the level of expenditure on health care suggests that while the PA managed to maintain an adequate primary health-care system, the Palestinians continued to be dependant on external health-care systems for advanced services — that is, on Israel, Egypt, and Jordan. Initially, the PA signed a contract with Israeli hospitals about patient referrals, and for a couple of years patients who could not be treated in the Occupied Territories were transferred to Israeli hospitals. When expenses grew and money dwindled, the PA stopped referring patients to Israel and established contractual relations with hospitals in Jordan and Egypt, where hospitalization costs were much lower. Referrals to these hospitals lasted until the eruption of the second intifada.

In sum, primary health-care services were maintained between 1994 and 2000, and insurance coverage expanded. In real terms, health-care expenditures actually decreased, and consequently, there was no substantial advance with respect to the development of secondary and tertiary services. Due to budgetary constraints, the referral system continued to be minimal, dramatically shrinking over time.[40] Overall, however, a level of consistency regarding health-care services was sustained, even though the quality of services was low in comparison with what prevailed in Israel. The Palestinian residents knew more or less which services were available and where and when they could receive them, so that in fact, the logic of risk society was upheld.

Perhaps the most devastating consequence of the second intifada is that it has destroyed vital social securities and has engendered endemic uncertainty in the West Bank and Gaza Strip. Within a very short period, Israel imposed harsh restrictions on movement, destroyed the Palestinian infrastructure supporting bare life, and triggered an economic disaster in the territories. All three processes occurred in tandem, and their combined effect in many respects undermined the very possibility of planning for the future.[41] Conditions became particularly critical after the Israeli military offensive dubbed Defensive Shield (April 2002), in which the West Bank was reoccupied. The fledgling Palestinian entity lost even the limited sovereignty it had gained, and Israel, for all practical purposes, became sovereign. At this stage, the Palestinian health-care system was seriously compromised, and efforts to control the Palestinian population by managing their lives through the strategies employed in a risk society were overshadowed by military interventions and economic strangulation.

In the following pages, we identify three major processes that led to the health-care system's breakdown during the second intifada: the severe deterioration in financial circumstances and its effect both on the population and on health-care services, the growth in the needs of the population due to the economic crisis and the Israeli siege, and the harsh restrictions on freedom of movement.

ECONOMIC CRISIS

According to the World Bank, following the outbreak of the intifada, an economic crisis erupted in the West Bank and Gaza Strip that "seriously compromised household welfare."[42] Real GDP per capita in 2005 was about 31 percent lower than it was in 1999.[43] Moreover, in 1999, financial aid per capita amounted to $181.60, while in 2002, it was $500.30, almost half of the per-capita gross national income for that year. Thus, within less than three years, the Palestinian territories had been transformed from a semi-self-sufficient financial entity into a charity-dependant entity. Yet even the impressive amount of financial aid offered to the Palestinians by the international community has not been enough to sustain the population. Due to the various restrictions placed on the movement of people, labor, and goods and on the transfer of revenues collected by the Israeli government on the PA's behalf, the Palestinians have experienced a contraction in real personal incomes of almost 40 percent between the third quarter of 2000 and the third quarter of 2002—despite the more than doubling of annual donor disbursements in the same period.[44] Using a $2.10-per-day poverty line, an estimated 60 percent of the population was poor by December 2002, three times the amount documented on the eve of the intifada. Accordingly, the number of poor tripled, from 650,000 to 1.9 million. It is worth noting that in the Gaza Strip, the situation is worse than in the West Bank, with a poverty rate of 75 percent. Furthermore, the poor have gotten even poorer. In 1998, the average daily consumption of a poor person was equivalent to $1.47 per day; by 2003 it slipped to $1.32.[45]

The 2003 annual Palestinian government budget on health-care was $98.4 million, or $26.30 per capita. Taking into account inflation, this amounted to about half the 1996 per-capita government health-care expenditure of $42.70.[46] On the one hand, the population had very little buying power with which to purchase services, while on the other, the per-capita governmental budget had shrunk by half. As the health-care services deteriorated due to budgetary constraints, there was also a rapid decline in the number of people covered by the governmental health-insurance program. While in 1999, over 53 percent of the population was covered, by 2003, the number fell to 38 percent. Due to the economic crisis, the Palestinian Ministry of Health has begun publishing regular requests for donations of essential drugs, because it does not have the capital to purchase the drugs it needs for day-to-day operations. The Health Ministry claims that shortages of drugs have actually caused significant reductions in the provision of services. Thus, the already impoverished health-care system sustained a major financial blow, and the amount and level of services provided deteriorated even further. Simultaneously, Palestinians found it more difficult to purchase services due to monetary constraints.

GROWING NEEDS AND REDUCED SERVICES

During the second intifada, the Palestinian population experienced an exponential growth in health-care needs. The health status of the population deteriorated as a result of both direct violence and the general relapse in living conditions. The exponential growth in unemployment and poverty, the widespread and rampant destruction of infrastructure, as well as severe problems in water supply and sanitation had a significant and detrimental effect on the health-care needs of Palestinians in the Occupied Territories.[47] The World Bank reports that acute malnutrition affected more than 9 percent of Palestinian children in the territories, and the Food and Agriculture Organization of the United Nations estimated that almost 40 percent of the Palestinians in the Occupied Territories suffer from food insecurity.[48] Almost half of the children between six and fifty-nine months old and women of child-bearing age are anemic. Child mortality increased substantially in 2002 and there has been a 58 percent increase in the number of stillbirths due to poor prenatal care, to become the second leading cause of death overall.[49] The number of children suffering from acute infectious diarrhea as a consequence of the worsening quality of drinking water and sanitation greatly increased. The measured contamination rate was 59 percent, up from a baseline of 20 percent, indicating that the quality of piped water supplied to the inhabitants is nearly as bad as tanker water.[50]

The conflict itself has also had a devastating impact on the provision of health-care services. According to the Palestinian Red Crescent Society, four years of intifada have left over thirty thousand Palestinians injured, suggesting that about 1 out of every 100 Palestinians was wounded.[51] Whereas some of the Palestinians probably suffered from minor injuries that necessitated little medical attention, thousands required substantial and prolonged medical treatment. The demand for blood-transfusion services increased by 178 percent between 2000 and 2003; in 2003, hospital emergency wards treated 749,318 injuries, an increase of 52.6 percent over the year 2000.[52] Thus, the already dilapidated Palestinian health-care services had to cope with a massive influx of additional patients whose medical needs resulted directly from the conflict. In addition, the World Health Organization reports that primary-care clinics have experienced a dramatic overload in their work, not least due to obstacles in accessing hospitals.[53]

In spite of the tremendous growth in needs, the provision of health-care services has decreased since the outbreak of the second intifada. The ongoing curtailment of movement alongside direct destruction has hindered access to health-care services and reduced the number of services supplied. Collected data reveals that 28.6 percent of families who needed curative services did not obtain medical care because medication was not available, 32.9 percent said they had no money, 26.6 percent could not reach a health-care center, and 16.8 percent reported that the doctor could not reach the health-care center.[54] Moreover, a decrease in the immunization rate has been reported, especially in remote areas, and preventive services such as Hepatitis B vaccination and screening for phenylketonuria were severely diminished as a consequence of the decrease in hospital births.

FREEDOM OF MOVEMENT

Notwithstanding the importance of the economic crisis and the impact of the armed conflict, one cannot understand the situation in the Palestinian territories without taking into account the harsh restrictions on movement.[55] Following the outbreak of the second intifada, Israel implemented a total closure on the West Bank and Gaza Strip, denying Palestinians residing in these regions the right to enter occupied East Jerusalem, where the major Palestinian secondary and tertiary medical centers are located, and Israel proper. Simultaneously, Israel also imposed an internal closure that restricts movement within the West Bank and Gaza Strip. According to the United Nations Office for the Coordination of Humanitarian Affairs, as of July 2004, over 700 physical barriers existed *within* the West Bank—including checkpoints, roadblocks, earth mounds, trenches, and road gates—that divide the region into scores of "clusters," severely curtailing the movement of 2.4 million Palestinians.[56] The Gaza Strip has been periodically cut into three separate regions, with movement from one region to the other denied. The effect of these restrictions on movement on the provision of regular health-care services and emergency medical aid, as well as on access to work and school, has been devastating. Moreover, the already deteriorating situation has been constantly aggravated as construction of the Separation Wall deep inside Palestinian territory continues.

The restriction of movement effectively cuts the majority of the population off from secondary and tertiary health-care facilities. A number of incidents of new-borns who died because Palestinian women in labor were delayed at checkpoints or prevented from reaching medical facilities have been well documented and publicized, but they represent only a fraction of cases whereby restrictions on access to medical care have led to injury or death.[57] Not surprisingly, hospital facilities are operating at an extremely low capacity. St Luke's hospital in Nablus reports a 49 percent decline in general practitioner patients, a 73 percent decline in specialty services, and a 53 percent decline in surgery—at a time when needs have actually grown and there is an insufficient number of hospital beds.[58]

The seemingly endless number of physical barriers has not only violated the rights of Palestinians by impeding their access to medical facilities, but, on a deeper level, these barriers have distorted basic conceptions of time and space.[59] In the Occupied Territories there is no longer any way to calculate the relation between the two, a fact that helps produce widespread uncertainty.

This graph exemplifies how the relationship between time and space has been ruptured. The distance between a patient's house and the hospital is 20 kilometers. The dotted line on the bottom of the graph represents how much time it would take to reach the hospital under normal circumstances. The hyphenated line above it takes into account the time it would take to reach the hospital if a physical barrier blocked the way and one would have to find an alternative route. The hyphenated line on the far left represents the movement during a curfew, when one is basically confined to the home. The most important line in the context of our discussion is the heavy black line that represents an encounter with a manned military checkpoint, since the checkpoint, more than anything else, shatters the relation between time and space. Even during curfews, when people are confined to their homes, uncertainty is not as potent as it is at the checkpoint.

The black circle represents the manned checkpoint and the black lines connected to it exemplify some of the possible scenarios that could follow once Palestinians reach the checkpoint. The soldiers might allow the Palestinians to pass and

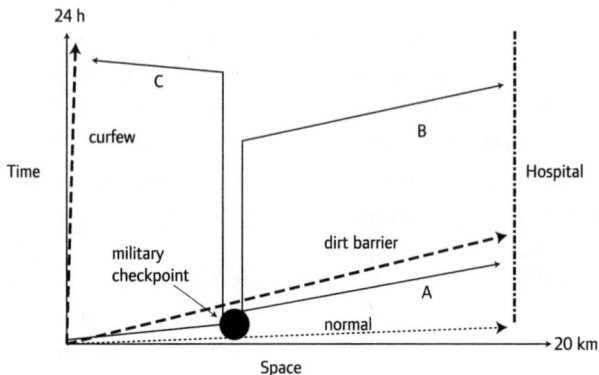

they would then reach the hospital faster than if they came across an unmanned physical barrier (Line A). It could be that they have to wait a few hours and are then permitted to pass (Line B). It could also be that they are made to wait many hours before they are instructed to return home (Line C). The crux of the matter is that the whole process is often determined according to the whim of the soldier at the checkpoint and therefore is totally arbitrary. Moreover, the actual journey to a hospital is frequently more uncertain than this graph indicates, since there are often a number of military checkpoints and dirt barriers between a patient's house and the hospital. And while a patient might pass a few barriers and checkpoints, he or she could be instructed to return home at the next checkpoint.

The curfews, checkpoints, and barriers affect everyone, not only the sick and health-care professionals. They rupture the relationship between time and space that most people living in Western countries take for granted. Thus, the restrictions on movement as well as the destruction of the infrastructure supporting bare life create a profound sense of disorientation. The possibility of calculating the future is accordingly undermined, and one tends to lose one's sense of control. It is as if one is left at the mercy of fate, charity, and faith.

THE BREAKDOWN OF SECURITY AND THE RISE OF HAMAS

As a result of the situation just described, four major processes have been unfolding in the Occupied Territories. First, the conditions that enable the management of risk (some form of predictability) have disappeared. This is extremely important for understanding Hamas's ascendancy, since the ills that befall us lose much of their providential meaning if there is a possibility of calculating the future and if society can become the general arbiter answerable for the causes of our destiny. In risk society, dialysis patients or pregnant women know that they can reach a hospital and receive treatment within a certain period of time, while healthy people know they will receive medical treatment if diagnosed with cancer. Conversely, when existence becomes totally insecure and uncertain, one often witnesses the delaicization of the world, a situation in which God becomes the ultimate—and sole—guarantee of justice and well-being. Moreover, the conception of the individual as a free agent who can make plans for the future that informs the rationality of risk society becomes meaningless when endemic uncertainty reigns, as does the notion of choosing among security providers that characterizes the "new prudentialism." Faith can consequently become the source of hope and guarantee, particularly when the proponents of this faith supplement their appeal with a scathing critique of the repressive political and economic structures and offer social services that mitigate the suffering.

Second, social calamity produces new populations that need assistance just in order to survive. As one member of an Islamic charity stated, "The novelty of this uprising is that it has engendered new types of need, which has increased the number of eligible beneficiaries and diversified the social groups requiring such assistance."[60] These new groups currently include landowners, shopkeepers, and those whose homes have been demolished by Israeli bulldozers—in other words, these new groups are not just the poor. Third, an institutional vacuum is created, making room for institutions that have characteristics that antedate the development of risk society. Following the eruption of the second intifada, NGOs and charitable organizations rapidly became the major welfare service providers in the territories, reaching about 60 percent of the total number of beneficiaries, followed by the United Nations Relief and Work Agency (UNRWA) (more than 34 percent) and the Palestinian Authority (only 6 percent).[61] Finally, the destruction of risk rationality ruptures social cohesion, because the general political regulations and institutions that lead to the deindividualization of society through the grouping of human interests (e.g., social security) have disappeared. In other words, solidarity—in its contractual as opposed to ethnocultural or religious sense—is undermined, making room for other forms of solidarity.

The significant point is that these dire developments can also be conceived as an opportunity, and Hamas knew how to benefit from them. The organization continued its policy of providing assistance on the basis of socioeconomic need, rather than religious or political criteria, so that families in economic distress did not need to be Hamas members or even practicing Muslims in order to qualify for aid. As the chairman of an Islamic charity noted, "The increase in poverty has vastly increased the pressure upon our organization, because we are receiving many more applications than before."[62]

The charitable organizations associated with Hamas quickly became very prominent in the Occupied Territories. A report on Islamic social-welfare activism suggests that by 2001, Islamic organizations were collectively the largest food donor in the occupied Palestinian territories after the United Nations Relief and Work Agency. Rema Hammami, a sociologist from Birzeit University, reports that according to surveys undertaken to assess emergency and relief provisions during the intifada, between 10 and 18 percent (depending on the period) cited Zakat, Islamic Charity, as the organization that had provided support. The charities associated with Hamas were again second only to UNWRA and offered more emergency services and financial relief than the Palestinian Authority. The role of secular NGOs was so minimal that they were presented in the survey under the category of "other."[63] This point is crucial, since it indicates that Hamas's charitable and health-care institutions, which are characterized by the absence of consistent guidelines and standards governing the delivery of services, have grown dramatically while the secular NGOs, which were developed according to broad nationwide plans and some form of calculability—the characteristics of risk society— have failed to benefit from the situation.

On the one hand, Hamas's network of social welfare and health-care facilities resembles the kind of charity networks that antedated risk society. There is no overall program or plan that links the different health providers so as to create an efficient and effective national health-care system. The haphazard and makeshift way the network of charity organizations operates contrasts with the planning and calculability upon which a risk society is built. On the other hand, Hamas does not conform to the characteristics of prerisk-society institutions. It has not abandoned the notion of modern solidarity that uses collective action, planning, prevention, and insurance to cope with natural disasters, disease, and other ill fortunes. For example, Hamas's network of health-care facilities adopts certain practices and insights that belong to risk society, such as preventative medicine and medical screenings. Thus, the destruction of the Palestinian risk society has not entailed a return to the past, but on the contrary, it has made room for the appearance of a postrisk social movement.

Even though Hamas has adopted certain premodern characteristics, like most other contemporary Islamist movements, it is a postmodern phenomenon.[64] Although Hamas espouses a "grand narrative" and, in this sense, rejects a key postmodern edict, the organization is very critical of the Enlightenment project, "the assumption of universal progress based on reason," and the modern Promethean myth of humanity's mastery of its destiny and its capacity to resolve all of its problems.[65] Moreover, Hamas does not advocate a straightforward return to the literal understanding of the holy texts, since the movement combines its appeals with an unwavering attempt to intervene in the political system, mobilize the Palestinian inhabitants, and create a vibrant organization for assuming and retaining political power.[66] In other words, Hamas has managed to gain the support of the masses because it has in many ways adopted a postrisk rather than a prerisk rationality.

The movement's ascendancy, as we have tried to show, is not only due to its reaction to Israel's colonial project, but is also an effect of this project. Paradoxically, the critique of postcolonial Western domination and cultural imperialism is also tied to different modern phenomena, such as the expansion of higher education, urbanization, and the emergence of vast markets for inexpensive Islamic books and newspapers and the proliferation of religious radio and television programs.[67] Along similar lines, Hamas, like other Islamist movements, has been shaped through its interaction with globalization.[68] The deconstruction of the universal pretensions of European civilization, Haldun Gülalp convincingly claims in a slightly different context, has led to a growing recognition that the West, too, is a provincial culture with its own hegemonic project. This recognition has allowed alternative visions of civilization to gain currency. Thus, it is no surprise that anti-Western Islamist themes that champion the periphery against the center found enthusiastic audiences among a new generation of students and other intellectuals who conceive religious culture not as a return to the past, but as a site of social innovation.[69] Many of Hamas's leaders fit this description to a tee, because they are doctors, engineers, lawyers, and other professionals whose religious sense of justice is, in several respects, postnationalist and postsocialist and represents an answer to modernity's unaccomplished promises.[70] So while Hamas supporters contest the absolute certainties and unfulfilled promises propagated by the West, they adopt many aspects of modernity.[71] Hamas, accordingly, is no different from other Islamist movements that constantly utilize modern technologies, relying heavily on state-of-the-art machinery and gear to achieve their objectives, and this is especially so concerning health-care services.[72]

In prerisk societies, as Ewald claims, humans were "juxtaposed alongside one another in society," while in risk societies, insurance has substantially contributed to building solidarity, since "reciprocal penetration of souls and interests establishes a close solidarity among [human beings]."[73] Not unlike what prevails in risk society, solidarity is a central component of Hamas's social-welfare network, so central that it is mentioned several times in the organization's charter.[74] Article 20 claims that the "Muslim society is a society of solidarity (altakaful alajtimai)," and Article 21 states: "Social solidarity means giving aid to the needy, both material and moral, or helping take certain actions. It is incumbent upon the members of the Islamic Resistance Movement to look after the needs of the people in the [same] way they look after their own interests sparing no effort in realizing and maintaining them."[75] Hamas's conception of solidarity, however, is different from the one that develops in risk society, because its production does not rely solely on common institutional interests, but is also formed through faith and fraternity.

The writers of the previously mentioned report on Islamic social-welfare activism conclude that while it is impossible to measure the effect of Hamas's charitable work on its popularity, the organization's positive image is significantly related to the efficiency of its social services, particularly when compared with the Palestinian Authority's weaknesses.[76] Taking into account both the scope of the services that Hamas offers and the sense of solidarity that it provides, this conclusion is surely accurate, yet it substitutes the symptoms for the causes. The question is not whether Hamas's social-welfare organizations have helped it garner popular support, but rather why Hamas's charity network has been so successful. The answer to this question becomes apparent once one takes into account the destruction of Palestinian state institutions alongside the collapse of all sources of social security and the creation of endemic uncertainty. Within this context, the rationality of risk that informs modern society is suppressed, and for many people, a postmodern form of religion that combines faith with a harsh critique of Israel's colonial project becomes the only door of hope.

Hence, the claim that Hamas's popularity results from its charity and healthcare network conceals two key issues. First, it elides the fact that Israel has produced a situation where there is desperate need for charity institutions. On a deeper level, though, it obscures how a complete sense of uncertainty influences the ways in which people think and act. Many secular organizations offer social-welfare services—the Union of Palestinian Medical Relief Committees, for example— yet unlike Hamas, they have not been empowered by the situation. The reason is that the rationality that informs their activities is a modern one, based on the calculation of risk. Alongside the critique of Israel's policies and the provision of social services, Hamas accentuates the importance of faith, fate, and divine ordinance, a worldview that rings true within a context of widespread destruction and absolute uncertainty. Indeed, Hamas's notion that "when faith is lost, there is no security" (the Hamas Charter) postulates an insecure and uncertain world where God is the ultimate—and sole—guarantee of justice and security. But simultaneously, it also embraces many of the features developed during modernity, ranging from modern technologies to cutting-edge forms of political action.

Consider a June 2003 interview, in which Hamas leader Abdul al-Aziz Rantisi was asked whether his training as a physician did not contradict his hawkish position in Hamas (the interview took place about a year before he was assassinated). Rantisi replied:

In 1985, soldiers besieged my clinic in Khan Yunis for 45 days and prevented my little patients from getting to me. That decision was made in order to prevent Dr. Mahmud al-Zahar [another Hamas leader] and me from establishing a nursing college. At the same time, an Israeli girl, whose father was a police officer in Khan Yunis, fell ill. The treatment in Tel Aviv was unsuccessful. They told him that only Rantisi knows how to treat her. So he came to me. Really. I don't remember what she had. At first I hesitated. I thought about all the Palestinian children who did not receive treatment. But in the end I agreed. Allah [wanted her to get well] and within 24 hours she was well.[77]

While Rantisi's reply has many dimensions, what interests us here is the way in which he invokes Allah. He is asked about the significance of his training as a physician, the influence of science and the scientific method on his political thought, and in response, he portrays the medical field as if it is ultimately determined by God, rather than by scientific knowledge and expertise. Rantisi knows that the technological capabilities and medical expertise in Gaza are inferior when compared with the services offered in Israel and that, therefore, from a medical perspective, a patient can receive much better treatment in Israel. In the interview, he intimates that he has an advantage over his Israeli counterparts because God is on his side, indicating that according to his worldview, medicine is subsumed under divine ordinance and faith. At the same time, though, he does not abandon or forsake medicine, but keeps on practicing it.

RISK THEORY REVISITED

Our interrogation of the Palestinian health-care system suggests that the logic informing Israel's military occupation has changed over the years.[78] While during the first two decades of the occupation Israel attempted to manage the Palestinian inhabitants by providing them with some form of security against future ill fortunes, since the eruption of the second intifada, Israel has striven to control the Palestinians by producing insecurities and endemic uncertainty. Israel's violent destruction of the Palestinian infrastructure of existence and societal securities has empowered Hamas—one of Israel's worst enemies. This corroborates Susan Buck-Morss's theoretical claim concerning the "dialectic of power," the notion that power produces its own vulnerability.[79]

Our findings also lend themselves to a number of theoretical inferences about risk theory. First, the destruction of the Palestinian risk society actually exposes a social process that has been neglected in the literature on risk. While risk scholars emphasize the impossibility of calculating certain risks due to global processes such as ecological destruction and the threat of nuclear attacks by state and nonstate actors, our case study suggests that an increasing number of local processes are also making it impossible to calculate risks. Focusing on Israel's occupation, we have underscored how practices employed to manage and control the Palestinian inhabitants have engendered a sense of arbitrariness and thus have rendered it virtually impossible to calculate the future. Even though Palestinians in the Occupied Territories have become accustomed, particularly in the past six years, to the wanton destruction of buildings and infrastructure, extrajudicial executions, acute poverty, random checkpoints, and the draconian permit regime, their intimate familiarity with this reality does not yet entail that they can carry out the kind of planning that diminishes and distributes risks.

Second, there seem to be numerous differences in the way global and local processes operate. Global processes are more or less indiscriminate regarding the populations they affect, although their effect is often mediated by an array of social factors. Ecological disasters, for example, tend to affect the population in developed countries less severely than they do in underdeveloped ones, the rich less than the poor. By contrast, local processes that produce endemic uncertainty often target particular populations located on the lower end of the social ladder: the poor, women and certain ethnic, religious, or national groups. While we have not conducted in-depth research in other geographical areas or on other sectors of society, parallel processes can, it seems, be identified in Darfur, Iraq, Chechnya, Afghanistan, and other conflict-ridden zones where the local population or sectors within it are subjected to endemic uncertainty. This uncertainty, we maintain, is often intentionally created and used as a weapon in order to advance political objectives. But conflict zones are not the only regions where local processes render it impossible to calculate risks. Similar developments are also beginning to unfold—although with less intensity—in several liberal democracies. We are referring specifically to processes relating to the dismantlement of the welfare state, which is leaving more and more people without homes, basic health care, and even food, not to mention pensions and other forms of security.

Third, these local processes are undermining the very rationality upon which risk society is based. While historically there has been an intentional attempt to make risk calculable in order to advance specific social, economic, and political objectives, our case study suggests that currently, risks are intentionally being rendered incalculable in order to advance new objectives, not the least of which are the restriction of political action and the dramatic curtailment of the public domain. Finally, the destruction of the rationality of risk that offers security and in this way ensures social stability makes room for a postmodern fundamentalist rationality.

The local processes that we have described raise several disturbing questions, two of which we would like to briefly discuss here. First, how do these local processes affect the individual members of society? Second, what are the political ramifications of such processes? While each of these issues deserves to be dealt with at length, here we can only provide some tentative and cursory answers.

Invoking the insights of Hannah Arendt as a supplement to risk theory, we think, can be beneficial. Arendt would have probably claimed that insofar as people cannot plan ahead, they are transformed into *animal laborans,* humans whose activities focus on the biological processes that sustain life. Our findings indeed suggest that most Palestinians are currently driven by the imperative of securing life's necessities—defense, food, shelter, and reproduction—a task that is accomplished on a day-to-day basis by the family, which is frequently aided by charity organizations. The two other forms of human activity identified by Arendt, work and action, are, in turn, undermined. According to an Arendtian analysis, the reduction of human activity to *animal laborans* has far-reaching implications for the political realm, since it leaves little if any room for political action, the activity in which humans can begin something new through deeds and speech. Arendt states that when humans are transformed to *animal laborans,*

> what [is] left [is] a "natural force," the force of the life process itself, to which all men and all human activities [are] equally submitted...and whose only aim, if it [has] an aim at all, [is] survival of the animal species man. None of the higher capacities of man [is] any longer necessary to connect individual life with the life of the species; individual life [becomes] part of the life process, and to labor, to assure the continuity of one's own life and the life of his family, [is] all that [is] needed.[80]

Indeed, in *The Human Condition,* Arendt decries the ascent of *labor,* since its domination binds humans to necessity and leads them to lose all sense of what constitutes true freedom and collective public life. One does not need to adopt Arendt's strict dichotomy between the private and public or between the political and economic realms to appreciate that when the members of society are reduced to *animal laborans,* the public domain dramatically shrinks, and political action—in the Arendtian sense—is undermined. On the one hand, with the amplification of labor, individuals are isolated, because they concentrate on securing life's necessities; therefore their propensity to act politically is greatly reduced. On the other hand, they lose their singularity and become mere particles in a mass. "What makes mass society so difficult to bear," Arendt claims, "is not the number of people involved, or at least not primarily, but the fact that the world between them has lost its power to gather them together, to relate and to separate them."[81] Arendt accordingly claimed that the preoccupation, engrossment, and fixation with the life process leads to depoliticization, to the turning away from the affairs of the world. She may have added that in the Occupied Territories, the political also has been destroyed, because politics tends to be obliterated where violence reigns. Such a claim is informed by the Aristotelian assertion that speech is a necessary condition of politics, along with Arendt's insight that violence is incapable of speech, and "speech is helpless when confronted with violence."[82]

However, we disagree with Arendt's assessment that such processes destroy the political or political activity per se, particularly because we consider both violence and fixation on the life process as concrete manifestations of a certain kind of politics. In this sense, we are more in tune with the insight made by Walter Benjamin in his "Critique of Violence," where he underscores that violence is integral to politics, in both the enforcement of law and the resistance to it.[83] Accordingly, the second intifada and Israel's reaction to it are political, despite the violent character of these events. We do think, though, that the processes we have described point to the dramatic diminishment of the public domain in the Occupied Territories, and thus Arendt's insights become useful for understanding how the individual and the political are affected. The existence of the public domain is the condition of possibility for a *political activity of a certain kind,* one that is informed by open debate and the ability to bring about social change through discussion and persuasion.

So if until now we have argued that the destruction of the rationality of risk facilitates the rise of Hamas, since it makes room for a postmodern religious rationality that both emphasizes faith and divine ordinance and critiques the colonial and imperialist projects of the West, here we would like to add that both the individual concentration on securing day-to-day necessities and the consequent shrinking of the public domain that are the effects of the impossibility of calculating risks have also contributed to Hamas's ascendancy. Moreover, it appears that while the curtailment of the public domain and the decline of political action are direct consequences of endemic uncertainty, the rise of fundamentalism is actually coincidental to them. Accordingly, we do not propose that the destruction of the rationality of risk necessarily leads to the rise of postmodern fundamentalism. Rather, we merely claim that the diminishment of the public domain makes the adoption of a fundamentalist position that espouses both a single truth and the view that certain people have access to that truth and can direct all others toward it much more compelling. This is only one of many possibilities, and the reason it occurred in the West Bank and Gaza Strip is due, at least in great part, to the fact that an already vibrant postmodern religious movement existed there and was able to take advantage of the situation.

Recent developments in Lebanon seem to suggest that we could be witnessing a pattern, both in terms of Israel's military logic and in terms of the effects of its military actions on risk society, the public domain, and the ascendancy of postmodern religious fundamentalism. In its attacks against Lebanon during the summer of 2006, Israel targeted the country's civilian infrastructure, destroying many of the mechanisms through which risk is managed. Even though the attacks targeting the civilian infrastructure received wide international attention, they constituted merely an intensification of an Israeli strategy that had been in place for about three decades. This strategy, we contend, has helped strengthen Hezbollah. Interestingly, before the 2006 War, Hezbollah was beginning to lose ground in Lebanon precisely because there was a dramatic drop in Israeli interventions, particularly those targeting the civilian infrastructure. Israel's decision to renew its strategy of bombing civilian sites ended up empowering the organization, so that today, there is a greater possibility that Hezbollah will be able to take control of the political institutions in Lebanon, just as Hamas did in the Occupied Territories.

A cursory examination suggests that in other areas of the world, the reduction of the individual to an *animal laborans* and the shrinking of the public domain are becoming manifest due to specific local processes that undermine the possibility of calculating risk. It appears that for large segments of the affected populations, the rationality of risk—even in its reduced and individualized form of the "new prudentialism"—does not exist. Their conduct is not governed by the technologies of modern governmentality or by neoliberal technologies of "enterprising" the self, but by oppression, exclusion, and sheer force, accompanied by the suspension of the law.[84] Such a situation, as we have tried to show, does not leave much room for the modern republican model of political life.

NOTES

A much shorter and less developed version of this chapter originally appeared in the journal *Constellations*. We would like to thank Michel Feher, Michal Givoni, Adi Ophir, and Catherine Rottenberg for their comments on earlier drafts.

1   Hamas is a direct extension of the Muslim Brotherhood. The term "Hamas" is an abbreviation of Harakat al-Muqawama al-Islamiyya, the Islamic Resistance Movement.

2   Khaled Hroub, *Hamas: Political Thought and Practice* (Washington, D.C.: Institute for Palestine Studies, 2000).

3   Shaul Mishal and Avraham Sela, *The Palestinian Hamas: Vision, Violence, and Coexistence* (New York: Columbia University Press, 2000), p. 3.

4   Khaled Hroub, "Hamas After Shaykh Yasin and Rantisi," *Journal of Palestine Studies* 33, no. 4 (Summer 2004): pp. 21–38 and Hamas; International Crisis Group, "Islamic Social Welfare Activism in the Occupied Palestinian Territories: A Legitimate Target?" *Middle East Report* no. 13, April 2, 2003, available on-line at http://www.crisisweb.org/home/index.cfm?id=1662&l=1International Crisis Group 2003 (last accessed April 7, 2008); Mishal and Sela,

The Palestinian Hamas; Sara Roy, "Hamas and the Transformation(s) of Political Islam in Palestine," *Current History* 102 (2003): pp. 13–20. According to the International Crisis Group,
Hamas devotes between 85 and 95 percent of its estimated U.S. $70 million annual budget
to an extensive social-services network. "Islamic Social Welfare Activism in the Occupied
Palestinian Territories," p. 13.

5   Ulrich Beck, *Risk Society: Towards a New Modernity* (London: Sage 1992) and *World Risk Soci-
     ety* (Oxford: Polity Press 1999); Mitchell Dean, "Sociology after Society," in David Owen (ed.),
     Sociology after Postmodernism (London: Sage, 1997) and "Risk, Calculable and Incalculable,"
     in Deborah Lupton (ed.), *Risk and Sociocultural Theory: New Directions and Perspectives,*
     (Cambridge: Cambridge University Press, 1999); Mary Douglas and Adam Wildavsky, *Risk
     and Culture: An Essay on the Selection of Technological and Environmental Dangers* (Berke-
     ley: University of California Press, 1982); François Ewald, "Insurance and Risk," in Graham
     Burchell, Colin Gordon, and Peter Miller (eds.), *The Foucault Effect: Studies in Governmen-
     tality* (London: Harvester Wheatsheaf, 1991) and "Two Infinities of Risk," in Brian Massumi
     (ed.), *The Politics of Everyday Fear* (Minneapolis: University of Minnesota Press, 1993);
     Paul Higgs, "Risk, Governmentality, and the Reconceptualization of Citizenship," in Graham
     Scambler and Paul Higgs (eds.), *Modernity, Medicine and Health* (London: Routledge, 1998);
     Deborah Lupton, *The Imperative of Health: Public Health and the Regulated Body* (London:
     Sage, 1995) and *Risk* (London: Routledge, 1999).

6   Lupton, *Risk*, pp. 7–36.

7   See Douglas and Wildavsky, *Risk and Culture.*

8   Barbara Adam, Ulrich Beck, and Joost Van Loon (eds.), *The Risk Society and Beyond* (Lon-
     don: Sage, 2000); Beck, *Risk Society* and *World Risk Society*; Ewald, "Two Infinities of Risk."

9   Burchell, Gordon, and Miller (eds.), *The Foucault Effect*; Dean, "Sociology After Society" and
     "Risk, Calculable and Incalculable"; Higgs, "Risk, Governmentality, and the Reconceptualiza-
     tion of Citizenship"; Lupton, *The Imperative of Health*; and Pat O'Malley, "Risk, Power and
     Crime Prevention," *Economy and Society* 21, no. 3 (1992): pp. 252–75. While much of the risk
     literature that focuses on governmentality discusses the ways the individual is led to man-
     age himself or herself—e.g., Dean, "Sociology after Society,"; Higgs, "Risk, Governmentality,
     and the Reconceptualization of Citizenship"; and Lupton, *The Imperative of Health*—in this
     essay, we do not deal with this issue.

10   Cited in Ewald, "Insurance and Risk," pp. 204–5.

11   Dean, "Sociology after Society," p. 218.

12   *Ibid.*, p. 223.

13   Scambler and Higgs (eds.), *Modernity, Medicine and Health*; Lupton, *The Imperative of
     Health*; Alan Petersen "Risk, Governance and the New Public Health," in Alan Peterson and
     Robin Bunton (eds.), *Foucault: Health and Medicine* (London: Routledge, 1998).

14   Petersen and Bunton, *Foucault: Health and Medicine.*

15   Bryan Turner, "Theoretical Developments in the Sociology of the Body," *Australian Cultural
     History* 13 (1994): p. 27.

16   Surely the logic of risk antedates Israel's occupation of the West Bank, Gaza Strip, and East
     Jerusalem. For a discussion of the historical development of the health-care system in Pal-
     estine during the Ottoman era and the British Mandate, consult His Majesty's Government,
     *A Survey of Palestine: Prepared in December 1945 and January 1946 for the Information of
     the Anglo-American Committee of Inquiry,* vols. 1 and 2 (Washington D.C.: Reprinted by the
     Institute of Palestine Studies, 1991); Nira Reiss, *Health Care of the Arabs in Israel* (Boulder,

CO: Westview Press, 1991); Sandy Sufian, "Arab Health Care during the British Mandate, 1920–1947," in Tamara Barnea and Rafiq Husseini (eds.), *Cooperate and Separate, Separate and Cooperate: The Disengagement of the Palestinian Health Care System from Israel and its Emergence as an Independent System* (New York: Greenwood Press, 2002), pp. 9–30. For a description of the years East Jerusalem, the West Bank and Gaza Strip were occupied by Jordan and Egypt consult Amin Khatib, "Eyewitness Account: Origins of the Palestinian Health System in the West Bank under Jordanian Rule and the Rise of Non-Governmental Organizations," in Barnea and Husseini (eds.), *Cooperate and Separate, Separate and Cooperate,* pp. 31–40, and Riad Zanoun, "The Long Road to Independence in Health: A Personal Account," in Barnea and Husseini (eds.), *Cooperate and Separate, Separate and Cooperate,* pp. 135–48.

17   Hadas Ziv, *A Legacy of Injustice: A Critique of Israeli Approaches to the Right to Health of Palestinians in the Occupied Territories* (Tel Aviv: Physicians for Human Rights, 2002).

18   See Neve Gordon, "From Colonization to Separation: Exploring the Structure of Israel's Occupation," in this volume.

19   Yitzhak Sever and Yitzhak Peterburg, "Israel's Development and Provision of Health Services to the Palestinians in the West Bank and Gaza, 1967–1994," in Barnea and Husseini (eds.), *Cooperate and Separate, Separate and Cooperate,* p. 46.

20   Neve Gordon, *Israel's Occupation* (Berkeley: University of California Press, 2008).

21   Tamara Barnea and Irah Kaneman, "Data for Policy and Data Policy: Information Gathering for Management, Monitoring, Planning and Reporting," in Barnea and Husseini (eds.), *Cooperate and Separate, Separate and Cooperate,* pp. 57–66.

22   Cilla Acker, "From Home Delivery to Hospital Delivery: The Transformation of Mother and Child Care in the West Bank," in Barnea and Husseini (eds.), *Cooperate and Separate, Separate and Cooperate,* pp. 87–98.

23   Whereas within the paradigm of public health the population is at risk, within the paradigm of therapeutic medicine, the individual is the one at risk. When a population's and an individual's health are constantly at risk, surveillance is essential in order to manage and diminish the risk. The risk of the individual is managed through technologies of control administered by health professionals and through technologies of the self administered by the individual himself or herself. Alan Petersen, "Risk, Governance and the New Public Health," in Petersen and Bunton (eds.), *Foucault: Health and Medicine.*

24   Union of Palestinian Medical Relief Committees, *Into the Third Decade, Building a Palestinian Health Movement* (Ramallah: UPMRC, 2002).

25   Neve Gordon, Rela Mazali, and Nogah Ofer, *The Occupied Health Care System* (Tel Aviv: Physicians for Human Rights, 1993).

26   The estimated percentage of families covered by the health-insurance scheme has varied enormously, yet it appears that it ultimately reached a level of about 30 percent. Jon Pedersen and Rick Hooper (eds.), *Developing Palestinian Society: Socio-Economic Trends and Their Implications for Development Strategies* (Oslo: Fafo Institute for Applied Social Science, 1998). All the Palestinians who worked for the Civil Administration, whether in education, health, or any other civil institution, had their insurance fees deducted automatically from their salaries.

27   Ephraim Sneh, "There Is Another Way: An Attempt to Switch from Occupation to Governance," in Barnea and Husseini (eds.), *Cooperate and Separate, Separate and Cooperate,* p. 125.

28   Sever and Peterburg, "Israel's Development and Provision of Health Services to the Palestinians in the West Bank and Gaza," pp. 44–46.

29   Gordon, Mazali, and Ofer, *The Occupied Health Care System,* pp. 5–14.

30   Michel Foucault, "Afterword: The Subject and Power," in Hubert L. Dreyfus and Paul Rabinow (eds.), *Michel Foucault: Beyond Structuralism and Hermeneutics* (Chicago: University of Chicago Press, 1982), pp. 208–26.

31   United Nations Relief and Work Agency (UNRWA), *Annual Report of the Department of Health, 2003,* available on-line at http://www.un.org/unrwa/publications/pdf/ar_health2003.pdf (last accessed September 3, 2008).

32   Tawfiq Nasser and Mordechai Shani, "The Development of Palestinian Hospital Services," in Barnea and Husseini (eds.), *Cooperate and Separate, Separate and Cooperate,* pp. 203–16.

33   Mustafa Barghouthi and Ibrahim Diabes, *Infrastructure and Health Services in the West Bank: Guidelines for Health Care Planning* (Ramallah: HDIP, 1993), pp. 80–83.

34   *Ibid.*, p. 83.

35   Interim Agreement, September 1995, Article XVII.2, available on-line at http://www.acpr.org.il/resources/oslo2.html (last accessed September 3, 2008).

36   Palestinian Ministry of Health, *Annual Report* (Ramallah: PMH, 2000), p. 58. The total number of primary health-care centers in the West Bank and Gaza Strip increased during the Oslo years by about 150 (25 percent), while the number of hospital beds increased by 100 percent. Nonetheless, the number of hospital beds per capita (1 to 744) continued to be lower than the per capita number of beds (1 to 600) recommended by the World Health Organization (WHO).

37   Michaela Pfeiffer, *Vulnerability and the International Health Response in the West Bank and Gaza Strip: An Analysis of Health and the Health Sector* (Jerusalem: WHO, 2001), p. 16; Sever and Peterburg, "Israel's Development and Provision of Health Services to the Palestinians in the West Bank and Gaza," p. 45. Per-capita government expenditure was much lower than in Egypt ($48), Syria ($90) and Jordan ($123). Pfeiffer, *Vulnerability and the International Health Response in the West Bank and Gaza Strip,* p. 16.

38   Mustafa Barghouthi and Ibrahim Diabes, *Infrastructure and Health Services in the West Bank.*

39   Efraim Davidi, "Globalization and Economy in the Middle East," *Palestine-Israel Journal* 7 (2000): pp. 33–38.

40   While in 1995 the PA spent over $14 million on referrals abroad, by 2000, it spent just over $6 million. Palestinian Ministry of Health, *Annual Report* (2000).

41   See also Ariel Handel, "Where, Where to, and When in the Occupied Territories: An Introduction to the Geography of Disaster," in this volume.

42   World Bank, "Supplemental Trust Fund Grant to the Second Emergency Services Support Project," Human Development Group, Middle East and North Africa Region (November 6, 2003), p. 2, available on-line at http://www-wds.worldbank.org/external/default/WDSContentServer/WDSP/IB/2003/11/12/000012009_20031112102457/Rendered/PDF/27199.pdf (last accessed September 4, 2008).

43   World Bank, "West Bank and Gaza Update" (April 2006), p. 3, available on-line at http://siteresources.worldbank.org/INTWESTBANKGAZA/Resources/WBGUpdateEng.pdf (last accessed September 4, 2008).

44   *Ibid.*, p. 4.

45   World Bank, "Supplemental Trust Fund Grant to the Second Emergency Services Support Project," p. 2.

46   Palestinian Ministry of Health, *Annual Report* (Ramallah: PMH, 2003).

47   World Bank, "Supplemental Trust Fund Grant to the Second Emergency Services Support Project," p. 1.

48   Research shows that "malnutrition is a contributing factor in nearly 60 percent of deaths in

children for which infectious disease is an underlying cause." Maharj Bahl, Nita Bhandari, and Rajiv Bahl Rajiv, "Management of the Severely Malnourished Child: Perspective from Developing Countries," *British Medical Journal* 326 (2003): pp. 146–51. Per-capita food consumption declined by one-quarter since 1998. World Bank, "Supplemental Trust Fund Grant to the Second Emergency Services Support Project," p. 2.

49 World Bank, "Supplemental Trust Fund Grant to the Second Emergency Services Support Project," p. 2.

50 World Bank, *Four Years—Intifada, Closures and Palestinian Economic Crisis: An Assessment* (October 2004), available on-line at http://www-wds.worldbank.org/external/default/WDSContentServer/WDSP/IB/2005/07/25/000090341_20050725095832/Rendered/INDEX/329950wbgaza14yrassessment.txt (last accessed December 12, 2008).

51 See http://www.palestinercs.org/Statistics_Arch.aspx (last accessed March 6, 2009).

52 World Bank, *Four Years—Intifada, Closures and Palestinian Economic Crisis.*

53 World Bank, "Supplemental Trust Fund Grant to the Second Emergency Services Support Project," pp. 2–3.

54 Samia Halileh, "The Effects of Israel's Operation Defensive Shield on Palestinian Children Living in the West Bank" (Ramallah: Institute of Community and Public Health Birzeit University, June 29, 2002), available on-line at http://icph.birzeit.edu/Emergencey%20Publications/Child%20Report%20final%202002.doc (last accessed March 6, 2009).

55 See Ariel Handel, "Where, Where to, and When in the Occupied Territories: An Introduction to the Geography of Disaster," in this volume.

56 See http://www.ochaopt.org/documents/ClosureUpdateOctober2007.pdf (last accessed May 30, 2008).

57 Health, Development, and Policy Institute (HDIP), "The Israeli Imposed Closure: The Effect of Closure on Health Care in the West Bank and Gaza Strip" (2003), available on-line at http://www.hdip.org/fact%20sheets/factsheet_health.htm (last accessed September 4, 2008). Since the beginning of the intifada there has been a 29 percent increase in home deliveries within the West Bank. *Ibid.*

58 World Health Organization, "Health Situation of Palestinian People Living in the Occupied Palestinian Territory" (2002), available on-line at http://www.who.int/mediacentre/news/statements/statement04/en (last accessed September 4, 2008).

59 Ariel Handel, "What Is Left of the Palestinian Territories?: A Spatial Look," paper presented at the Politics of Humanitarianism in the Occupied Territories Conference, the Van Leer Jerusalem Institute, April 20–21, 2004.

60 International Crisis Group, "Islamic Social Welfare Activism in the Occupied Palestinian Territories," p. 15.

61 United Nations Office of the Special Coordinator for the Middle East Peace Process and United Nations Office for the Coordination of Humanitarian Affairs, "Food and Cash Assistance Programmes, October 2000–August 2001: A Brief Overview" (Jerusalem: OCHA, 2001), p. 18.

62 International Crisis Group, "Islamic Social Welfare Activism in the Occupied Palestinian Territories," p. 15.

63 Rema Hammami, "Palestinian NGOs, the Oslo Transition and the Space of Development," conference paper, Birzeit University, February 2002, p. 23.

64 Faribah Adelkah, "Transformations of Mass Religious Culture in the Islamic Republic of Iran," in Jeff Haynes (ed.), *Religion, Globalization and Political Culture in the Third World*

(Hampshire, UK: Macmillan Press, 1999); Anouar Majid, "Can the Postcolonial Critic Speak?: Orientalism and the Rushdie Affair," *Cultural Critique* (Winter 1995–96): pp. 5–42; C. A. O. van Nieuwenhuijze, "Islamism: A Defiant Utopianism," *Die Welt des Islams* 35, no. 1 (1995): pp. 1–36.

65   Jeff Haynes, "Religion, Securalization and Politics: A Postmodern Conspectus," *Third World Quarterly* 18, no. 4 (1997): p. 751.

66   Fred Halliday, "The Politics of Islam, A Second Look," *British Journal of Political Science* 25, no. 3 (1995): p. 400.

67   R. Hefner, "Multiple Modernities: Christianity, Islam and Hinduism in a Globalizing Age," *Annual Review of Anthropology* 27 (1998): pp. 83–104.

68   Haldun Gülalp, "Globalization and Political Islam: The Social Bases of Turkey's Welfare Party," *International Journal of Middle East Studies* 33, no. 3 (2001): pp. 433–48.

69   *Ibid.*, p. 443; Adelkah, "Transformations of Mass Religious Culture in the Islamic Republic of Iran."

70   Gülalp, "Globalization and Political Islam," p. 443.

71   Majid, "Can the Postcolonial Critic Speak?" pp. 7–8. Nazir Ayubi claims that it would be a mistake to argue that the form of "Islamic government" found in Iran today, which is greatly influenced by Khomeini's ideas, is in any major sense traditional or conventional. Khomeini did not simply retrieve an old belief system, but rather brought about a reinterpreted and ideologized conception of the old system and saw in the particular combination of modern and traditional one of the reasons for the revolution's initial success. Nazih Ayubi, "The Politics of Islam in the Middle East with Special Reference to Egypt, Iran and Saudi Arabia," in Haynes (ed.), *Religion, Globalization and Political Culture in the Third World,* pp. 86–87.

72   Van Nieuwenhuijze, "Islamism: A Defiant Utopianism," p. 16.

73   Ewald, "Insurance and Risk," p. 207.

74   There are several translations of the Hamas Charter. In this essay we use the one that appears in Mishal and Sela, *The Palestinian Hamas,* pp. 175–99.

75   *Ibid.*, pp. 188–89. The phrase *altakaful alajtimai* means literately "taking on responsibility for each other," or mutual responsibility.

76   International Crisis Group, "Islamic Social Welfare Activism in the Occupied Palestinian Territories," p. 25.

77   Amira Hass, "What the Doctor Orders," *Ha'aretz,* June 22, 2003.

78   See also Neve Gordon, "From Colonization to Separation: Exploring the Structure of Israel's Occupation," in this volume.

79   Susan Buck-Morss, *Thinking Past Terror* (New York: Verso, 2003), p. 23.

80   Hannah Arendt, *The Human Condition* (Chicago: University of Chicago Press, 1958), p. 321.

81   *Ibid.*, p. 52.

82   Hannah Arendt, *On Revolution* (London: Penguin Books, 1963), p. 19.

83   Walter Benjamin, "Critique of Violence," trans. Edmund Jephcott, in *Walter Benjamin, Selected Writings, Volume 1: 1913–1926,* ed. Marcus Bullock and Michael W. Jennings (Cambridge, MA: Harvard University Press, 1996).

84   Giorgio Agamben, *Homo Sacer: Sovereign Power and Bare Life,* trans. Daniel Heller-Roazen (Stanford, CA: Stanford University Press, 1998).

MILITARY PROCEDURES REGULATING THE MOVEMENT OF SICK PERSONS FROM THE FIRST AND SECOND INTIFADA (EXCERPTS) The first procedure that dates from the first intifada reflects the frequent use of curfews and incorporates a clear-cut, binary disntinction between prohibited movement and permitted movement during curfew. The second procedure that was drafted eight years later, when internal closure became general policy, indicates a more flexible and fluid logic of regulation, establishing grades of authorized and unauthorized movement fluctuating in time and place. The IDF was forced to prepare and issue both procedures following petitions to the High Court of Justice filed by Physicians for Human Rights—Israel. The organization contended that the recent procedure has been systematically breached.

<u>נוהל תנועות רופאים וחולים בזמן עוצר</u>

<u>כללי</u>

1. תושבי איו"ש נקלעים לעיתים למצב בו מוטל עוצר על סביבת מגוריהם.

2. במצב עוצר ישנם מקרים בהם נזקק תושב לטיפול רפואי כחד, ומאידך אינו מורשה לצאת מביתו.

3. <u>המטרה</u>

מטרת נוהל זה לקבוע הסדרים לתנועת רופאים, אמבולנסים וחולים בתקופת עוצר במרחבי איו"ש, ובכלל זה מעבר מיהודה לשומרון וההיפך וכן מעבר לירושלים ומירושלים לאזור כל זאת ע"מ לאפשר הספקת שרותים רפואיים באופן תקין וסדיר לתושבי איו"ש.

4. <u>השיטה</u>

א. <u>רופאים, אחיות, צוותי פינוי רפואי:</u>

1) עובדי בתי חולים יורשו להגיע לעבודתם בכית החולים <u>גם</u> במשמרות.

2) עובדי הכריאות החיוניים יצויידרו באישור מיוחד אשר יקנה להם_ןהיתר תנועה בעוצר (מצ"ב דוגמה).

3) הנ"ל יורשו לנוע עם רכב (אמבולנס או רכב ביה"ח או רכב פרטי – הכל לפי העניין וכפי שמצויין באישור). לכל רכב מורשה תנועקף תרית חלון מיוחדת אשר תאפשר לחיילי המחסום זיהוי מהיר של הרכב המורשה.

4) כאשר עובד בריאות חיוני ימצא לנכון לפנות את החולה לבית חולים, הוא יהיה רשאי לעשות זאת ברכב איתו הגיע לבית החולה (אמבולס או רכב אחר המצוייד באישור שניתן לו). ברכב המפנה, אפשר שתהיה <u>בת</u> משפחתו של החולה לצורך לווי_ן + או סיעודו במהלך הפ_ונוי.

5) האישורים יאפשרו גם מעבר מנפה לנפה כולל במצבים בהם קיים_ן סגר בין הנפות.

6) פינוי לישראל (לרבות ירושלים) או מעבר מיהודה לשומרון וההיפך יבוצע <u>אך ורק</u> באמצעות אמבולנס.

7) האמבולנס יצוייד בהיתר יציאה לישראל (כרטיס לבן), בנוסף לאישור הנ"ל (זאת כל עוד מותלה היתר היציאה הכללי מהאזור).

Procedure for Movement of Physicians and Sick Persons during Curfew

General

1. Residents of Judea and Samaria are sometimes caught in a situation in which a curfew is imposed on the area in which whey live.

2. During curfew, there are cases in which a resident needs rapid medical treatment, but is not permitted to leave his house.

3. The objective

   The objective of this procedure is to regulate movement of physicians, ambulances, and sick persons at times of curfew in Judea and Samaria, including movement from Judea to Samaria and vice versa and movement to Jerusalem and from Jerusalem to the region, all for the purpose of enabling proper and regular provision of medical services to residents of Judea and Samaria.

4. The method

   A. Physicians, nurses, medical evacuation teams

      1) Hospital employees will be permitted to get to work in the hospital, also during shifts.

      2) Vital health workers will carry with them a special authorization that permits them to move about in a curfew (a sample is attached).

      3) The aforesaid persons will be permitted to move about with a vehicle (ambulance or hospital vehicle or private vehicle, as the case may be, and as shall be specified in the authorization). A special windshield sticker, which will enable soldiers at the checkpoint to rapidly identify authorized vehicles, will be issued for every authorized vehicle.

      4) When a vital health worker deems it proper to evacuate a sick person to hospital, he will be allowed to do so in a vehicle in which he arrived at the home of the sick person (ambulance or other authorized vehicle). A female member of the family of the sick person is allowed to ride in the evacuating vehicle to accompany the sick person or aid the patient during the evacuation.

      5) The authorizations will also enable movement from sector to sector, including in situations in which a closure exists between the sectors.

      6) Evacuation to Israel (including Jerusalem) or movement from Judea to Samaria and vice versa shall be done only by ambulance.

      7) The ambulance shall have a permit to exit to Israel (white card), in addition to the aforesaid authorization (this as long as the general exit permit from the area is suspended).

ב. <u>תנועת חולים בתקופת עוצר:</u>

1) נפות המנהא"ו יפרסמו ע"ג לוחות המודעות טלפונים של
   בתי"ח, מרפאות, ועובדי בריאות חיוניים (טל' בבית).

2) ככלל, חולה הזקוק לטיפול רפואי דחוף יוכל לפנות למי
   מהטלפונים הנ"ל, ולהזמין ביקור בית של־עובד בריאות
   חיוני.

3) באם <u>אין</u> ברשות התושב טלפון:

   א. !בת משפחתו של התושב תגיע למוכתאר הקרוב למקום
      מגוריו,
      או לטלפון סמוך, או לבי"ח/מרפאה סמוכה (מותר
      תנועה של נשים <u>בלבד</u>).

   ב. המוכתאר יגיע מצוייד באישור זהה לאישור של עובד
      בריאות חיוני ויהיה רשאי להסיע החולה
      לבי"ח/מרפאה הקרוב ביותר (בנוסף לאישור תנופק לו
      תוית חלון לרכב־כנ"ל).

ג. <u>שרותים רפואיים חיוניים</u>

1) בתי החולים (ממשלתי/פרטי/אונר"א) ימשיכו לפעול <u>גם</u> בזמן
   עוצר.

2) מרפאות (ממשלתי/פרטי/אונר"א) ימשיכו לפעול <u>גם</u> בזמן
   עוצר.

3) בתי מרקחת ימשיכו לפעול גם בזמן עוצר. במקומות שניתן,
   יופעלו בתי מרקחת ניידים (כפי שבוצע במהלך מלחמת
   המפרץ), אשר יצויידו באישורים לנוע ולחלק תרגפות מבית
   לבית.

B. Movement of sick persons during curfew

1. The Civil Administration sectors will post on the bulletin boards the telephone numbers of hospitals, clinics, and vital health workers (home telephone numbers).

2. As a rule, a sick person needing urgent medical treatment can call one of the aforesaid telephone numbers and request a house visit of a vital health worker.

3. If the resident does not have a telephone:

A. A member of the family of the resident will go to the *mukhtar* [traditional leader of a village or clan] close to his place of residence, or to a nearby telephone, or to a hospital/clinic nearby (movement is permitted for women only).

B. The *mukhtar* will arrive, with an authorization identical to the authorization of a vital health worker, and be allowed to drive the sick person to the closest hospital/clinic (in addition to the authorization, he will be given a vehicle windshield sticker as mentioned above).

[...]

אוגדת איו"ש 877
א ג " ס
מב - 1197
21 בדצמבר 1999

סכסכסכסכסכסכסכ

מאת: אוגדת איו"ש – ק.אג"ם
אל: חט"מירים – מח"טים, סמח"טים, ק.אג"ם
מחט"ב מג"יב – ק.אג"ם
דע: אוגדת איו"ש – לשכה
אוגדת איו"ש' – מטה

הנדון: <u>נוהל טיפול בתושב ב איו"ש הגניע למחסום במצב חרום רפואי דחוף</u>

א. <u>כללי/חנוהל:</u>

1. נוהל זה מסדיר מקרים בחם מגיע למחסום צח"ילי באיו"ש אדם המצוי במצב חירום דחוף ומבקש לעוברו לצורך הגעח למוסד רפואי בו יינתן לו טיפול רפואי בישראל או באזור בזמן שגרה, סגר או כתר פנימי.

2. ככלל, מפקד' מחסום יאמשר מעברו של אדם במחסום (לרבות כניסתו לישראל) לצורך קבלת טיפול רפואי, אף אם אין בידו היתר כנדרש, אם המדובר במצב חירום רפואי דחוף. כמקרה חירום רפואי דחוף ייחשבו לדוגמא, מצב בו מניעח למחסום יולדת, מצב בו מגיע למחסום מקרה דימום קשה, מצב בו מגיע למחסום מקרה כוויה קשה וכד'.

3. שיקול הדעת| באשר לשאלה אם המדובר במקרה חירום רפואי דחוף, נתון למפקד המחסום. מפקד המחסום יוועץ ככל הניתן במגבלות הזמן, בגורם רפואי.

4. במקרה של ספק בשאלה, אם המדובר במצב חירום רפואי דחוף, יפעל ספקן זה לטובת התושב.

5. חייל מחסום, אשר מובא בפניו מקרה חירום רפואי דחוף, יעביר מיידית את הטיפול במקרה למפקד המחסום.

6. מפקד המחסום ישקול אפשרות ליווי של תושב, המצוי במצב חירום רפואי דחוף, ע"י רכב של כוחותינו וכן אפשרות העברתו של התושב לרכב או לאמבולנס של כוחותינו שיוביל אותו ליעדו.

7. נוהל זה ישוען לכל חיילי צח"ל ומ"צב במחסומים.

Judea and Samaria
Division 877
Operations Branch
Oper. 1997
21 December 1999

From: Judea and Samaria Division—Operations Branch officer

To: Regional Brigades—Brigade commanders, deputy brigade commanders, Operations Branch officers
Border Police Brigade Headquarters—Operations Branch Officer

cc: Judea and Samaria Division—Office
Judea and Samaria Division—Headquarters

Re: Procedure for handling a resident of Judea and Samaria who arrives at a checkpoint in an urgent medical condition

1. This procedure regulates cases in which a person in an urgent medical condition arrives at an IDF checkpoint in Judea and Samaria and wishes to cross so he can reach a medical institution where he will be given medical treatment in Israel or in the region, in normal times, closure, or internal encirclement.

2. As a rule, the checkpoint commander will enable passage of a person at the checkpoint (including entry to Israel) to receive medical treatment, even if he does not have the requisite permit, if an urgent medical condition is involved. It is deemed an urgent medical condition, for example, when a woman about to give birth or a person who is bleeding heavily or suffering from severe burns arrives at the checkpoint.

3. The discretion to determine if the case involves an urgent medical condition lies with the checkpoint's commander. The checkpoint commander will consult, to the extent possible under the time constraints, with a medical official.

4. In the event of doubt if the case involves an urgent medical condition, the doubt will be resolved in the resident's favor.

5. A soldier at a checkpoint who is presented with a case of an urgent medical condition will immediately turn the handling of the matter over to the checkpoint commander.

6. The checkpoint commander will consider the possibility of escorting a resident who is in an urgent medical condition with a vehicle of our forces, and also the possibility of transferring the resident to a vehicle or ambulance of our forces, which will take the person to his destination.

7. This procedure will be drilled into all IDF soldiers and Border Police officers at checkpoints.

Palestinian Refugee Camps in the Palestinian Territory: Territory of Exception and Locus of Resistance

Sari Hanafi

> The camps are both the emblem of the social condition created by the coupling of war with humanitarian action, the site where it is constructed in the most elaborate manner, as a life kept at a distance from the ordinary social and political world, and the experimentation of the large-scale segregations that are being established on a planetary scale.
> —M. Agier, "Between War and City: Towards an Urban Anthropology of Refugee Camps"

Palestinian nationalist discourse used to rely on two main pillars: al-Nakba and the right of return of refugees.[1] To maintain the strength of this discourse, Palestinian nationalists took the camp as the primary unit used to maintain Palestinian identity in Arab host countries. However, using the camp setting to reinforce nationalism is not unique to the Palestinian case. Burundian refugees in camps in Tanzania cultivated their Hutu nationalism, while those who dwell in the towns identified themselves as "out of the group."[2]

For humanitarian organizations, the camp remains the most suitable spatial configuration for the control and surveillance of refugees. It is, in fact, an imposed form, because refugees themselves generally resist their confinement to such a space. According to statistics from the UN High Commissioner for Refugees, in 2002 only 38 percent of the world's refugees were camp dwellers, while 20 percent were urban-zone dwellers. When it comes to the Palestinian case, the average rate of refugees inside camps is fairly significant at 29 percent, but in Gaza and in Lebanon, these rates hold great significance, because the percentage registered with the United Nations Relief and Works Agency for Palestine Refugees in the Near East (UNRWA) rise to around 50 percent (See Table 1). Palestinian refugees (about 5.3 million worldwide) constitute approximately 17 percent of the total number of refugees in the world.

REGION OR COUNTRY	NUMBER OF CAMPS	REFUGEES INSIDE THE CAMPS	REFUGEES OUTSIDE THE CAMPS	TOTAL NUMBER OF REFUGEES	PERCENT INSIDE THE CAMPS	PERCENT COMPARED WITH LOCAL POPULATION
Jordan	10	283,183	1,497,518	1,780,701	15.9%	32.8%*
West Bank	19	181,241	506,301	687,542	26.4%	31.4%**
Gaza Strip	8	471,555	490,090	961,645	49%	78.4%**
Lebanon	12	210,952	189,630	400,582***	52.7%	10.7%*
Syria	10	112,882****	311,768	424,650	26.6%	2.4%*
TOTAL	59	1,259,813	2,995,307	4,255,120	29.6%	—

   * Statistics dating from 2006

   ** Extrapolation based on the 1997 Census by the Palestinian Central Bureau of Statistics (PCBS)

   *** Although there are 400,000 Palestinian refugees registered with UNRWA, it has become increasingly common to suppose that only half that many, perhaps up to 250,000 refugees, are actually residing in Lebanon. Jon Pedersen, "Population Forecast of Palestinian Refugees 2000–2020," in Laurie Blome Jacobsen (ed.), *Finding Means, UNRWA's Financial Crisis and Refugee Living Conditions: Socio-economic Situation of Palestinian Refugees in Jordan, Lebanon, Syria, and the West Bank and Gaza Strip*, Fafo Report 427, volume 1 (Oslo: Fafo, 2003).

   **** This figure does not include the dwellers of Yarmouk camp, which is the biggest Palestinian camp in the world, because it is not an official camp for UNRWA.

TABLE 1 Palestinian refugees registered at UNRWA (2006).

For sixty years, the space of the refugee camps in the Palestinian Territory was treated as a space of exception and an experimental laboratory for control and surveillance. This state of exception was not promulgated by any one sovereign. Many actors involved in the different modes of governance have been contributing to the suspension of law in this space under the cover of laws and regulations themselves. These actors involved in the politics of space are mainly the Israeli authorities, the Palestinian National Authority (PNA) and, to a lesser degree, the United Nations Relief and Works Agency for Palestine Refugees in the Near East (UNRWA), in addition to different local political commissars.

What is the effect on the socioeconomic situation of the inhabitants as well as on the political and national identities of dwelling in such camps? Many studies that I have conducted in the past concerning the Palestinian diaspora demonstrate a substantial difference in terms of socioeconomic status, living conditions, and identity formation between those who are camp dwellers and those who are urban city dwellers.[3] This essay develops this notion further. I begin by presenting a comparative overview of the living conditions of Palestinian camp dwellers. I then argue that there are major differences between closed and open refugee camps and that the camp setting as a closed space is not a "natural" setting, but rather has its raison d'être in disciplinary power, control, and surveillance and in deploying the state of exception. Contrary to those who consider the absence of refugee camps as a determining factor in diluting the refugees' national identity with that of the host country, I argue that the relationship between national identity and residential setting is very weak. The camps create a new, much more urban identity, rather than a national one.

While UN Security Council resolutions, human rights law, and international law, including the United Nations Convention Relating to the Status of Refugees, have acknowledged or provided a legitimacy for the refugees' claims and rights of return or integration,[4] Israel and the host countries have not respected these rights. In addition to that, the demographic expansion and structural changes that have taken place in the camps since their establishment have brought them ever closer to being slum areas and underdeveloped urban sprawls.

This study is based on several years of fieldwork, including interviews with the populations of the Palestinian refugee camps and those who govern the camps, not only in the Occupied Palestinian Territories but also in Lebanon, Syria, and Jordan. Modes of governance were one of the foci for the interviews.

PALESTINIANS IN CAMPS: CLOSED VERSUS OPEN SPACE

Can space be a major factor in shaping the living conditions of a population? I will argue that, with regard to the creation of endemic poverty in some Palestinian refugee communities, two chief factors contribute to this condition: being confined in slums in urban areas, and, consequently, being discriminated against in the labor market.

Although Palestinian refugee camp dwellers by and large enjoy adequate health and education services thanks to UNRWA, they are disfavored and overlooked in the socioeconomic plans of the host countries. While differences between camp dwellers and refugee urban dwellers (off-camp dwellers) in Syria and to a lesser extent in Jordan are minimal,[5] the gap between camp and off-camp dwellers in Lebanon and in the Occupied Territories is enormous. This can be explained by the fact that the camps in Jordan and Syria constitute, by and large, open spaces regulated by the host state, while in the Palestinian territories and Lebanon, they are set in closed spaces.

I define "open space" as both urban and societal. Open urban space is regulated by the host country to look like any residential low-income neighborhood, allowing it to be connected to the surrounding cities and villages. From the societal

COUNTRY/REGION	DISCRIMINATION IN THE LABOR MARKET	TYPE OF CAMP	RATE OF POVERTY COMPARED WITH THE LOCAL RATE
Egypt	Yes	No camps	Similar
Syria	No	Open space	Similar
Jordan	No	Open space	Similar
Gaza Strip	No	Semiclosed space	Slightly higher
West Bank	No	Closed space	Higher
Lebanon	Yes	Closed space	Higher

TABLE 2 Relations between poverty rate, type of camp, and discrimination in the labor market.

point of view, camp dwellers are relatively integrated socially and economically into the surrounding neighborhood and labor market. A "closed space" does not meet at least one of these conditions. Camps organized as closed spaces constitute either urban enclaves or satellites located at the urban periphery, all lacking in green spaces, with poor access to surrounding neighborhoods and to the labor market and with poor housing.

Previous studies of refugee camps have shown correlations between the relative poverty rates of Palestinian refugees and the poverty rates among the respective local populations in different localities.[6] Two related factors are worth noting in this context: discrimination against Palestinian refugees in the labor market and the type of residential area where they live. As one can clearly see from Table 2, it is only in both Lebanon and the Occupied Palestinian Territories (mainly the West Bank) that the poverty rate is higher compared with the local population, despite the fact that in the Occupied Palestinian Territories there is no institutional discrimination in the labor market.[7] This discrimination certainly plays a partial role in the poverty rate noticed in Lebanon. Therefore, the factor contributing to the production of a high poverty rate shared by refugees in Lebanon and the Occupied Palestinian Territories is the feature of closed space. This demonstrates how salient such a space is, in regard to not only refugees' living conditions, but also to their urban identity and their relationship to Palestinian nationalism, as we will see later. It should be mentioned, though, that this analysis by country does not in any manner suggest homogeneity inside each respective country, mostly because of the location of the camps. Some camps are located in an urban context, while other camps are situated at the urban periphery, and a number of them are isolated camps in a rural setting. The differences between these camps are sometimes huge.

According to various surveys in Jordan and Syria by the Norwegian Institute for Applied Social Science (Fafo), the living conditions of Palestinian refugees outside the camps is not much different from that of the general population in the host country.[8] The situation of refugees living in camps, however, is worse than that of those living off camp, and this is true in every host country. But even so, the camp populations do not all face the same rate of poverty and deteriorating living conditions, nor do they constitute the main poverty problem of the host countries. Only in Lebanon do all indicators surveyed by Fafo show that living conditions in the camps are worse than in any off-camp area.[9]

In 1982, in the Palestinian territories, UNRWA ceased distribution of food rations to all registered refugees and began to focus instead on those refugees most in need, the special hardship cases (SHCs).[10] These cases represented about 6 percent of the total registered Palestinian refugees in 2000. Proportionately, Lebanon has the highest percentage of SHCs (about 11 percent of the Palestine refugees in Lebanon benefit from the SHC program), while Jordan has the lowest percentage (about 3 percent). The rate of SHCs in the West Bank is 7.8 percent. This difference is explained by the fact that the level of socioeconomic integration of refugees in Jordan is highest, while in Lebanon it is the lowest of UNRWA's areas of operation.

Even though education levels are generally good, thanks to UNRWA, in Lebanon, 60 percent of Palestinian youth aged eighteen to twenty-nine do not finish their basic education. In the Occupied Palestinian Territories, girls tend to drop out of high school before graduation due to early marriages and, as a consequence, illiteracy rates for females are higher than the rates for males. The incompatibility between the relatively high level of education and the low socioeconomic status of camp dwellers arises from the fact that people whose economic status has improved usually leave the camps for the cities, where work is more readily available.

Over 54 percent of homes in refugee camps in the Occupied Palestinian Territories lack proper sanitary installations for drinking water. Yet the most serious sanitary problem concerns the density of population inside the camp: 30 to 40 percent of the homes have a density of three to eleven people or more, causing huge environmental problems. The buildings are often heaped in narrow alleys with no natural light, exposed to hazardous building materials, inadequate temperature control, and poor ventilation.

The situation of the refugee camps and the poverty rate in both Lebanon and the Occupied Palestinian Territories thus is very distinct from the situation in other camps. At least in Lebanon, the difference is attributed not only to the spatial marginalization of the camps, but also to institutional discrimination in the labor market. In addition, there are other factors that play a less significant role in this distinctive poverty rate, such as class-selective migration patterns.[11] As already mentioned, in the Occupied Palestinian Territories, people often leave the camp once their financial situation permits them to do so. This does not hinder some people from choosing to stay in the camp, because it is the place where they weave their social networks, but when the crowdedness takes its toll, people tend to leave. According to a Shaml survey (see below), two-thirds of the camp dwellers would be willing to move out of the camp if their financial situation improved.

CAMPS IN THE OCCUPIED PALESTINIAN TERRITORIES

Contrary to the ideologically driven claims of two Israeli anthropologists, Emanuel Marx and Yoram Ben-Porath, who perceived the Palestinian refugee camps as a normal urban space undergoing a process of assimilation into the syntax of the city,[12] the camp is an entity that carries with it the weight of the history of the Palestinian exodus and resistance, and it is very difficult to pretend that it is just another normal space. Let us scrutinize the urban situation of camps in the Occupied Palestinian Territories.

According to UNRWA, in 2006, 664,104 of the 1,587,920 Palestinian refugees in the Occupied Palestinian Territories lived in camps: 26.4 percent of the refugees in the West Bank and 49 percent of the refugees in Gaza (see Table 1). Camps have better health and educational services, but higher unemployment than urban and rural areas (21.5 percent in camps, compared with 17.2 percent and 16 percent respectively in urban and rural areas).[13] Many shelters in the camps are unhealthy and unsafe. Poor construction of the barracks means scorching temperatures during the summer and freezing conditions during the winter. Water seeps through leaks and holes in the roofs, and the shelters become infested with rodents and insects.

This situation was confirmed by the survey conducted by the Palestinian Diaspora and Refugee Center, Shaml, among Palestinian refugees.[14] This survey illustrates how the camp dwellers feel about the urban problems in their life. According to this survey, two-thirds of camp dwellers felt that their home was too small for their families, half felt that the camps do not meet their basic needs, and 57 percent stated that the camps lacked proper health conditions. Moreover, poverty in the camps is more structural, because camp dwellers lack even that small piece of land that allows other Palestinian families to grow vegetables for private consumption. The Palestinian Central Bureau of Statistics also provided valuable data regarding this issue. Relatively more camp dwellers work for the Palestinian National Authority where the salary is very modest, and fewer work for international organizations other than UNRWA.[15] Approximately a third of camp dwellers and villagers work in the private sector, as opposed to 46.6 percent among city dwellers.[16]

Society in the Occupied Palestinian Territories is highly fragmented. Its fragmentation reflects its naturally fragmented geography, the traditional division between villages and city dwellers, the dissection of Palestine into the West Bank and Gaza as a result of the 1948 War, and further forced fragmentations introduced by the occupation regime. But it is also a result of the reproduction of differences between refugees and local residents and between those who returned to the territories after the Oslo Accords and all the rest. Culturally and socially, refugees in the territories are relatively well integrated into society when they live off camp, but much less so when they live inside the camps. When one looks at lifestyles and class membership, the evidence is clear. For instance, 40 percent of the refugees living off-camp have at least one family member married to a nonrefugee, as opposed to 20 percent of camp dwellers.[17]

In the Occupied Palestinian Territories, the camps have become a symbol of territorial illegitimacy due to two processes, one imposed from above and one that has developed from below. Imposed from above, the general fragmentation of Palestinian space that the Israeli military has forcefully created and that the regime of movement control has imposed have made living conditions in the camps even harsher.[18] Today, to be able to live safely in a West Bank camp, you must recognize the camp borders and armored vehicles, and you must learn to live with barbed wire, gates blocking the roads, and infinite waiting periods at checkpoints. Since the construction of the Separation Wall, the case of the Shufat camp in Jerusalem has constituted a very flagrant example. While the camp dwellers have Jerusalem IDs, they are separated from the vital spaces of job markets, services, and socialization inside Jerusalem. The fragmentation of space, the regime of movement control, and the Separation Wall intensify the domino effect caused by long-standing processes of bio-politics, colonization, and ethnic cleansing that the colonized Palestinian people have resisted. However, the refugee camps are not the only camps in the Occupied Territories nowadays. The closure of the Gaza Strip, the construction of more and less temporary barriers, and the drawing of borders throughout the West Bank create other camps of all sorts, closing off Palestinian villages and cities and "protected" enclaves for settlers.[19] Barbed wire and surveillance form a unique colonial device of the spatial application of ruling power. The refugee camps have now become symbols of territorial illegitimacy, a fact arising from the sovereign proclamation of a state of exception.

The Palestinian National Authority's position toward this issue is very complex. While the PNA has developed some projects for the camps, the camps are still conceived as enclaves under the responsibility of the international community and in particular the United Nations Relief and Works Agency. In fact, the PNA reinforced the division of space into refugee and nonrefugee areas by excluding the camps from urban or infrastructural projects. For instance, the recent committee that supervises the work on the master plan for three municipalities, Bireh, Ramallah, and Bitonia, ended up without any representative of the three refugee camps located in the area. Thus, the question is not how many projects the PNA has executed in these camps, but the fact that these camps are considered even by the PNA as spaces of exception without agency. The representatives on such committees are elected by the residents who live in the area for which the master plan is designed, and hence this particular plan will reflect the power relations between the three towns without giving a voice to the refugees. This lack of representation is consistent with the fact that in general, camp dwellers in the West Bank do not vote and are not represented in the Palestinian political bodies.

In processes that have operated from below, the refugee camp has emerged as a heterotopic place in the Foucauldian sense of this term,[20] an area disconnected from the social and urban tissues in the neighboring areas. But this heterotopic place is not characterized merely by its isolation from its surroundings, but rather by different spatial urban rules projected into the same spatial unit, for instance, being excepted from regulation by the urban municipality, but regulated by informal negotiations between neighbors. These different formations coexist without either of them being derived from or reduced to the other. They constitute a space of tension revolving around deviation, marginality, and contradiction: a space of total control in which acts of resistance and transgression nevertheless take place. The disconnection of the refugee camps from their environment has happened gradually and was accelerated by local elections from which the refugee camps' dwellers have been excluded. Having the significance of a gray zone of ambivalence, neither completely internal nor entirely external to the society at large (or both internal and external at the same time), these closed spaces are extraterritorial, not truly belonging to the place, subsisting "in," but not being part "of" the space that they physically occupy.

This ambivalence and delegitimization has an effect on the social identity and self-identification of the refugee-camp dwellers. Local camp identity becomes a decisive factor in producing both local and national identity. Thus, although the Shaml survey found that a vast majority of camp dwellers were proud of their camp identity, some, notably those in the Shufat camp, hid from their colleagues the fact that they lived in the camp. Any minor social dispute between city people and camp dwellers quickly escalates, as in the clashes between people in Kalandia camp and Ramallah during 2001 and 2002.[21] Many years of double marginalization from the Israeli military authorities, on the one hand, and from the PNA and local Palestinian authorities, on the other, has made these areas resemble many slums that sprawl around the world—the suburbs of Paris, for instance. Thus, one cannot understand the problems of refugee camps unless one studies them as urban sites.

Finally, the camp dwellers deeply sense their marginality and wish to transform their camps into something better. According to the 2003 survey by the Palestinian Center for Policy and Survey Research (PSR), half of the refugees surveyed would not mind being settled outside their camps and would accept radical improvement of their camp. In particular, 87 percent wanted to vote in municipal elections (when the camp is inside the city—and three-quarters wanted to do so when it was outside), and about half favored enlarging the camp inside the city limits.

CAMPS AS BIO-POLITICAL SPACE

The bio-power exercised by humanitarian organizations has created categories for those in need with the effect of depoliticizing them.[22] Refugees are transformed into bodies to be fed and sheltered while being deprived of their political existence. Humanitarian law used to refer to "protected people,"[23] but current humanitarian practices focus mainly on "victims" or, at times, "survivors" in order to sound more positive. By classifying people as victims, the basis of humanitarian action is shifted from rights to welfare. In disaster areas—the space of exception— values of generosity and pragmatism obscure any references to the rights and responsibilities of the people concerned (refugees, humanitarian organizations, international community, etc.) that would endow them with their own agency.

However, throughout the years, the activities of refugee organizations (the list is long: the Nansen Bureau for Russian and Armenian Refugees in 1921; the High Commission for Refugees from Germany in 1936; the Intergovernmental Committee for Refugees in 1938; the International Refugee Organization of the United Nations in 1946; UNRWA in 1950; and up to the present, the UN High Commission for Refugees since 1951) have been limited according to their statutes to "humanitarian and social" issues while excluding political issues.[24] With refugees often stripped of their political existence and identities and reduced to their status as individuals in need of shelter and food, as bare life, the entire refugee question has been transferred to the hands of the police and military forces, on the one hand, and to apolitical service organizations such UNRWA, on the other.[25]

When reconsidering the emergence of the urban identity of the camp, it becomes clear that the identity and political status of camp dwellers are related to the very nature of the camp and to its segregation and isolation as a distinct and enclosed spatial unit. Refugees who are not camp dwellers tend quickly to establish good relationships with their host society and to escape the status of "victims." As a closed space, the camp forms the conditions that facilitate the use of bio-politics by the host countries and by UNRWA, because refugees are gathered in a centralized and controlled place where they can be under constant surveillance. This "care, cure, and control" system has transformed refugee camps into disciplinary spaces.[26] In the pretext of facilitating the provision of services, the camp is conceived as the only workable possible form of space, as if outside the camps, the distribution of food and other services to the refugees would have become almost impossible. In the Palestinian context, however, the problem does not lie only with the spatial nature of the camp, but also with the mandate of UNRWA, the main provider of services in the camp.

UNRWA, which was created in 1950 as a refugee organization specifically dedicated to the Palestinian refugees was established as a service provider. Its UN mandate included neither de jure protection of refugees nor their return to their homes. Despite its very strict mandate, in the past fifteen years, there have been cases in which the organization acted beyond the letter of the mandate, for example, when it provided "passive protection" for Palestinian refugees during the first intifada. Since a donors' meeting in Geneva in 2004, the organization has started linking service provision to advocacy, and recently, a rights-based approach to its humanitarian mandate has been emerging. One can notice relatively strong language used in UNRWA publications to attract the attention of the international community to the continuous plight of Palestinian refugees.[27] However, taking into account housing, children's and women's rights, and other rights does not mean that the right of return has become part of UNRWA's advocacy strategy. In spite of the importance of UNRWA publications for mobilizing the international community, the very concept of refugees as an artifact of victimization discourse obstructs the possibility of resistance that seeks to advance their return and statehood. The United States and some of UNRWA's European donors consider that if UNRWA goes in the direction of looking for a durable solution such as settlement and return, it will undergo a dangerous politicization, although UNHCR's case has shown that being involved in the search for durable solutions does not conflict with an essentially humanitarian mandate.[28] As the new UNRWA discourse appeared, Karen Koning AbuZayd, commissioner-general, subtly revealed the tension between what is political and what is humanitarian in her statement at the Host and Donors Meeting held in Amman on December 11, 2006:

> I refer to the issues surrounding the tension that frequently appears between the preoccupations of States on the one hand, and humanitarian questions on the other. This tension is manifested in a variety of ways. One of its most striking manifestations is the contrast between the readiness of states to fund emergency responses, compared to their failure to address the questions of international law and politics that cause these emergencies. That tension is clear in the way in which the urgency

to resolve underlying questions of justice and peace for Palestinians is somehow divorced from the challenge of providing for their human needs.

We believe that these tensions and contradictions can — and should — be avoided, particularly in the Palestinian arena where political, security, humanitarian, development and refugee issues are often virtually indistinguishable. The issues are too tightly interwoven to allow the luxury of a fragmented approach. An approach in which security and political questions are deemed to supersede or override humanitarian and protection issues is unrealistic and simply not sustainable....

These questions recall an important aspect of UNRWA's evolving role. I am referring to our role as a global advocate for the care and protection of Palestine refugees. This role is implicit in our mandate and in our identity as an Agency that ultimately derives its authority from the General Assembly and the Charter of the United Nations....

We do not assume this role lightly. We are fully aware that the legitimacy of our advocacy role rests on remaining within the boundaries of our humanitarian mandate. We are cognizant of the fact that the boundaries that separate the humanitarian from the political are indistinct at best, but nevertheless real. We have no illusions about how high the costs would be if we were to stray too far, and we have no desire whatsoever to jeopardize the international credibility we have worked so hard to create and maintain. That would be a price we are not prepared to pay.[29]

While UNRWA has played a very important role in empowering Palestinian refugees by providing education, health services, and sometimes employment, this has not been sufficient to get the Palestinians beyond the threshold of poverty and isolation and to allow their integration into the host society. Due to its mandate, UNRWA has been unable to seize the opportunity and promote some changes in the situation of the Palestinian refugees. The recent involvement of UNRWA in the reconstruction of the Jenin refugee camp after its partial destruction by the Israeli occupation army in 2001 is revealing in this sense. Instead of alleviating the crowdedness of the camps by returning some refugees to their place of origin (a third of the Jenin's refugees come from the village of Zaraan, located some 17 kilometers west of the city), UNRWA pursued only two options: rebuilding the camp while respecting its boundaries or asking the Jenin municipality to allocate a piece of land to allow its expansion.

Maintaining the camps as temporary space has as one major consequence: the further marginalization of the refugee population. Furthermore, since the 1950s, one of its indirect consequences has been emigration, not only to the Gulf area, but also to North America.[30] The result of maintaining refugees in camps so as to keep them operational in the political struggle and ready for the refugees' return was relocating the refugees farther from their place of origin and keeping them in a state of double alienation: both from their place of origin and from the urban and social domains in the host country's society.

This double alienation is related not only to spatial suspension, but also to temporal suspension. These refugee camps, characterized by what the French anthropologist Michel Agier calls "frozen transience," are an ongoing, lasting state of temporariness. As in the prisons and "hyperghettos" scrutinized by Loïc Wacquant, camp dwellers "learn to live, or rather survive, in the here-and-now, bathed in the concentrate of violence and hopelessness brewing within its walls."[31]

CLOSED CAMPS AS A SPACE OF EXCEPTION

Unlike the camps in Syria and Jordan, which function as open spaces, the closed camps in the West Bank are spaces of exception. They are subjected to bio-power and the use of the state of exception put into play by different actors, including the Israeli ruling apparatuses, the PLO, and UNRWA, among other emerging actors, who act as different sovereigns over the camp. Some surveys and many studies have been undertaken by Israel to provide demographic information on the camp dwellers for the purposes of surveillance and disciplinary power. This is a peculiar kind of bio-politics, not one that is concerned to maximize the health and wealth of the population, but quite the opposite, to establish a delicate balance in which both the well-being of the population and especially the extent of the physical terrain on which it exists are minimized without being eliminated altogether. The sovereign, according to the German philosopher Carl Schmitt, is the one who proclaims the state of exception. He is not characterized by the order that he institutes through the constitution, but by the suspension of that order.[32] The politics of exception has been bluntly or subtly exercised against these urban places since the establishment of these camps. But how exactly has this occurred?

A politics of exception has been exercised against these urban places on two levels: by instituting exceptions to the law and by abandoning any effort at urban planning. While the PNA and the Israeli authorities generally have exercised their presence in the Occupied Palestinian Territories by the rule of law, they have abandoned the camps and allowed them to become spaces devoid of laws and regulations. The urbanization process then takes on a wild nature stemming from the absence of planning policies and, in particular, the nonenforcement of construction laws. Everyone builds as he or she sees fit, and the result is hundreds of illegal buildings spreading in all directions. This process of urbanization in the unregulated camps has resulted in a large amount of the population suffering from poverty in the slum areas surrounding the cities.

In this situation, nothing is legally defined. Everything is suspended, but upheld without written documents concerning this suspension. Most of the camps in the Occupied Territories have been under the jurisdiction of the PNA since the Oslo Accords. This authority created a local committee in each camp. However, the camps are actually governed by a web of complex power structures composed of the local committee, notables,[33] family linkages, political factions, imams, PLO popular organizations (workers, women, engineers, etc.), different NGOs,[34] women's program centers (WPCs),[35] community rehabilitation centers (CRCs),[36] youth activities centers (YACs),[37] and UNRWA directors. These camp leaders have imposed measures that are changing as the balance of power between these different groups changes. Nowadays, the leading actor is the local committee. At times, family linkages are very important, as is the case of Dir Ammar, where committee membership is always determined by the number of families. Each extended family has to be represented on the committee. However, whether family-based or factionally based, the committee is often considered illegitimate, not only because it is nominated by the PNA or by the political factions, but also because there are rivalries and conflicts between groups or subdivisions belonging to the same political parties.[38]

The interviews we conducted in different camps showed how camp populations have lived with the disarray caused by this state of exception. According to an old woman refugee expressing her anger: "Who can I complain to when my neighbor builds a second and third floor without leaving any proper space for my apartment?" Many interviewees used the word "chaos" to describe the situation in the camps.

What seems to be chaos is regulated by an internal mode of governance[39] which is not based on the absence of law, but on the exclusion by the sovereign(s) of the population from the space where the law is supposed to operate: "Camps are under the UNRWA," declared one camp dweller in the Al-Amari camp in the vicinity of Ramallah, while for others, it is the PNA that exercises governance. Few consider the local committee as the sovereign in camp. The camp dwellers are excluded from the sphere of the city while at the same time included in it with respect to security arrangements and taxation. This flexible use of law and its suspension justifies the use of the space of exception as a way to understand the relationship between the space of the camps and the space of the cities. At times, however, the situation comes closer to a state of a void, filled in a very ad hoc way as the result of the architecture of the power structure. The presumed sovereign suspends the laws in the camp area to make it a quasi-lawless area and to bring it to the point that it becomes hardly controllable, while local actors will compete as putative sovereigns in order to rule the camp. In many cases, as my fieldwork suggests, they create a state of void due to the unresolved conflicts between the competing factions and the destructive nature of their competition.

The state of exception, according to Giorgio Agamben, is the suspension of law by one sovereign. However, in the case of the Palestinian refugee camps, we have a tapestry of multiple partial sovereignties: a quasi-real sovereign such as the PNA, but also phantom sovereigns such as UNRWA, in addition to a web of actors who contribute to the state of exception and the suspension of laws.

And UNRWA is indeed a phantom sovereign.[40] What is important, Michel Foucault reminds us, is not the power that stems from the exercise of sovereignty, but rather the effects of power that a governmental technology generates. While UNRWA was not intended to govern the camps, nor does it pretend to do so, many camp dwellers nevertheless ascribed to it the status of a sovereign. Many among the camp dwellers we interviewed consider UNRWA responsible for the disorder in the camps. UNRWA calls its representatives in the camps "camp directors," a title definitely carrying symbolic violence—the violence of occupying a ruling position without acting accordingly. This confusion is not due to any cognitive disorder on the part of the refugees, but rather stems from the historical role played by UNRWA directors in not merely providing services, but also in administering and coordinating many aspects of the refugees' lives. By substituting for an absent sovereign and by exercising governmental functions designed for and addressed to camps dwellers only, UNRWA too actually constitutes the camp as a zone of exception and reproduces the territorial illegitimacy that characterizes the camps.

However, this state of exception is exercised not only by the sovereign, but also by the actors themselves. Agamben fails to account for the agency of the actors resisting the "total institution" of the camp. He conceives the camp as a paradigmatic place of modernity and modern politics, using concentration camps such as the Nazi camps as an emblematic example.[41] Agamben conceives the camp as a zone of indistinction between the public and the private, fact and norm, law and life, where inmates are nothing but submissive subjects who follow myriad orders and regulations into which the sovereign decision on the exception is disseminated. However, the Palestinian refugee camps are places of resistance and transgression, where agency does not express itself only in the actions of resistance, but also in the use of the same mode of power: the state of exception.

Discursively, many actors, often the political commissars of these camps and what I call the "local sovereigns," insist on the exceptional status of the camps while refusing to submit them not only to the Israeli power, but also to the local Palestinian municipality and the urban sphere of Palestinian society,[42] if only by evading tax collection or by failing to pay water and electricity fees. The same power strategy is used by these political commissars to keep their authoritative power without any sort of election. This refusal comes from the need to maintain a status quo in which the majority of the camps' popular committees are nominated by the various Palestinian factions. The creation and maintenance of this status quo is a political process in which the camp population is not represented and many are alienated by it. Many interviews that we conducted in refugee camps in the West Bank and Lebanon show the growth of a pervasive, often angry disillusionment with any kind of politics, either secular or mainstream religious, especially with the onset of factional strife in Gaza and the destruction of Nahr al-Bared in northern Lebanon.

Ever since the arrival of the PNA, the police have not been able to penetrate the camps without negotiating with the powerful actors who decide whether to cooperate or not, case by case. The camp population resorts to imams and local notables, as well as to local security leaders, in any quarrels or problems before going to the police. While such conflict-resolution methods have been rather successful throughout the Israeli occupation, refugee camps no longer enjoy harmonious communitarian structures headed by local notables (mukhtars). Since the end of the 1970s, we have witnessed the emergence of a new elite whose legitimacy is based on the Palestinian national struggle. This situation was changed after the launching of the Oslo process, because participation in this struggle alone is no longer sufficient for someone to become a power broker.

Many stories that we have collected show the problem of this multiplicity of actors governing the camp. In Amari, a camp in the vicinity of Ramallah, for example, when an internal conflict over sexual harassment ended in violence, at first, an imam intervened, and then the matter was taken up by the local committee.[43] Sandi Hilal, in her work on the Dehisha camp, has demonstrated the complexity involved in resolving problems of land ownership between this camp's two neighboring villages, Doha and Artas. Five people have already been killed in fighting associated with this conflict.[44]

CONCLUSION

The space of the camps has five principal functions: as a place of habitat, as an economic space, as a space of memory and identity affirmation, as a space for exercising power,[45] and as a place of military resistance. These functions render the camp a laboratory of Palestinian society and of a Palestinian state in the making, but also an experimental laboratory for control and surveillance and a technical model of repression developed by its sovereigns' know-how, a technology implemented and deployed in other parts of the world that do not "behave" properly. We live in a world where enclaving undesirable, risky groups and confining them to spaces of exception is seen as the very condition for the "free" circulation of "civilized" people in the global archipelago.[46] In addition to that, in case this enclave becomes dangerous, it can be destroyed. The destruction of the Jenin camp by Israeli forces in 2001 projects the image of Agamben's concept of *homo sacer.* Camps, such as the Jenin camp, have become "sacred" spaces in that they are spaces where the inhabitants can be "eliminated" by anyone without being punished through internal or external mechanisms and without even proper attention from the Palestinian public sphere. However, the refugee camps have also become a laboratory for resisting both the Israeli occupation and the unpopular power of the Palestinian National Authority. Actually, the camps, which, compared with the cities, benefited little from "the peace process," were invested politically by Hamas and the Islamic Jihad organizations.

The most extreme situation can be found in Lebanon, where the refugee camps are also closed. According to the French anthropologist Bernard Rougier, Lebanese refugee camps have emerged as a sort of laboratory or microcosm for the vast range of thought relating to politicized Islamism.[47] However, the question with regard to the refugee camps in general is not the emergence of a new Islamist ideology such as al-Qaida's, but the advent of a new mode of action. My interviews with the Syrian Palestinian refugee camp dwellers who have gone to fight with al-Qaida in Iraq show clearly that they are fighting against the American project in the region, and not against Western values. In the Palestinian territories, the ideology developed is a nationalistic Islamist one in the form of Hamas and the Islamic Jihad organization.

The portrait I have drawn here, though seemingly dark and threatening, does not concern all the refugee camps in Lebanon and the Occupied Territories to the same degree. The different functions that the camps serve have created a Palestinian sociospatial dynamics based on three aspects: territorial permanence (a place of stability and continuity), communitarian space (a place of ongoing social interactions), and a space of contact and conflict with the surrounding communities. However, few camps are economically integrated with their surrounding areas, and they are largely disconnected from the urban fabric. Contrary to many researchers who conflate economic integration of the camps with urban and social integration, the difference is huge. The camps are not different in this respect from ghettos and other enclaves that have been traditionally integrated with their cities economically, but not socially.

While looking at the refugee camps as extreme cases located on the legal edge, as existing in some times and places in a state of exception and in others as a state of void, I have applied a distinction between open and closed camps. The closed camps are zones of exception, albeit under different modalities ordered by various types of phantom like sovereignties—national, international, and local. Where Palestinian refugees are constituted as bare life and subjected to extreme legal conditions, by revolting and resisting these conditions, they express their agency and transgress the role assigned to them by their oppressors and the many sovereigns that oppression has made possible.

The dominant Palestinian and humanitarian organizations' imaginary discourses have narrated the conflict in terms of human suffering and victimhood. Portraying closed camps as museums of suffering has enabled such narratives. Moreover, these spaces are considered the primary units for constructing and reproducing the refugees' identity as Palestinians. As a result, the camp as a quasi-political entity has been investigated by social scientists, journalists, and experts and has been shown to reproduce the structure of pre-1948 Palestinian society, including the reproduction of the place of origin inside the camps, as if Lobieh, Safad, and so on could be reproduced in the Jalazon or Nahr al-Bared camps. This ethnicization of the refugees' history overlooks the importance of the economic, social, and cultural relationships with the host countries, relationships to which very few ethnographic studies paid adequate attention.[48]

The image of the refugee in the Arab region is confined to those who dwell in miserable camps, and not necessarily extended to those who have been uprooted and dwell outside their country and region. The assumption in popular thought and within the scholarly community has been that the more miserable the camp, the less likely it is that people would want to settle in the host countries and would ultimately insist on returning to their homes in Palestine. The discourse of misery revolves around stagnation, control, and the silencing of camp dwellers. Yet, the relationship between Palestinian national identity and belonging and the type of residential area is very loose. There is no relationship between place of residence and taking a clear political position in favor of insisting on the right of return.

The right-of-return movement has emerged in Europe and North America, rather than in the Arab world. One needs not be a member of a closed refugee camp to advocate the right of return and the maintenance of a Palestinian identity. Contrary to the popular belief that the camp nurtures the Palestinian national identity, however, the camps, where radical national movements mingle with religious conservatism, have produced a new rebellious urban identity, rather than a national one.

Many scholars, in the name of supporting the Palestinian national movement, are unaware of the form of totalitarian nationalism being cultivated in the camps. To echo Philipp Misselwitz, the lyric image of the camp as an iconic symbol of struggle should not hide the fact that this same weapon has been used for internal fighting and to challenge the authority of the PNA and its conception of the project of national liberation.[49]

New, emerging discourses, such as those of Khaled Hroub and Oraib Rantawi, argue that the "right of return," as a key political demand, should not contradict the "right to survive."[50] They allude to a form of camp nationalism based on an abstract discourse of the right of return that is threatening the survival of the Palestinian national movement and even the Palestinians as a nation.

We must rethink the refugee camp as a space of radicalism. There is a real need to empower camp dwellers by giving them the right to access and use their neighboring cities and by radically improving the urban conditions of their space. This will not be possible without connecting the camps to the urban tissue of the neighboring cities and creating a transparent mode of governance based on local elections.

I am not advocating a tabula rasa approach, but rather the rehabilitation of the refugee camps and their design as an urban space. This rehabilitation should be carried out not only with reference to the camps' political and social status, but also with regard to their becoming part of the city, and not an oppositional element in relation to it, as in the Yarmok refugee camp in Damascus or the Al-Wihdat camp in Amman.[51] An urban master plan based on rehabilitation should take into account the physical, socioeconomic, and cultural fabric of the concerned spaces. A bottom-up participatory approach should be used to outline the differentiated needs of the Palestinian refugee population: women, men, children, the working class, the middle class, and so on.[52] A solution grounded in the right of choice (between return and settling in the host country, in the Occupied Palestinian Territories, or in other countries), and close cooperation (not competition) between the PNA, UNRWA, and the local committees would take the first steps toward alleviating the problems of the refugees. Alleviation would form the basis for empowering the refugees as transnational subjects.

Some efforts to bring this about and to include the camps in the state's urban infrastructure are being made in Jordan and to a lesser extent in Syria, but nothing has yet been initiated by the Lebanese government and the PNA. These authorities should recognize the transnational and flexible nature of the identity and citizenship of the refugee community.[53] There is no opposition between rehabilitation of a place where refugees live and the ardent desire of some of them to return to their land or to the homes of their parents. A refugee is able to place himself or herself in a succession or a superposition of many temporalities or spaces of reference. This is why improving the refugee camps cannot be interpreted as an attempt made by UNRWA to undermine the right of return, even though some political commissars (like some leaders of popular committees) oppose by populist agitation the camp-improvement initiatives.

Throughout the debate of whether or not to maintain the status quo in the refugee camps, the individual Palestinian is invisible. The political insistence of the status quo is in fact a mirror image of the humanitarian organizations' deployment of bio-political practices that depoliticize Palestinian lives. On both ends of the spectrum of refugee discourse, the Palestinians are mere figures: demographic artifacts and a transient political mass waiting for return. Between the humanitarian discourse in the zones of emergency, on the one hand, and the status-quo discourse on the other, the rights-based approach for the Palestinians as individuals and collectives, as refugees, as citizen-refugees with civil and economic rights, as well as bearers of what Henri Lefebvre called "the right to the city,"[54] is lost.

NOTES

I would like to thank readers of earlier versions of this paper, especially Adi Ophir, Michal Givoni, Yael Berda, Ray Jureidini, Marwan Khawaja, Aage Tiltnes, Manal Kortam, and Rima Rassi.

1   Al-Nakba is the Palestinian catastrophe of 1948.

2   According to Liisa Malkki: "In contrast [to the nationalists in the camps], the town refugees had not constructed such a categorically distinct, collective identity. Rather than defining themselves collectively as 'the Hutu refugees,' they tended to seek ways of assimilating and of manipulating multiple identities—identities derived or 'borrowed' from the social context of the township. The town refugees were not essentially 'Hutu' or 'refugees' or 'Tanzanians' or 'Burundians' but rather just 'broad persons.'... They were creolized, rhizomatic identities— changing and situational rather than essential and moral.... In the process of managing these 'rootless' identities in township life, they were creating not a heroized national identity but a lively cosmopolitanism." Liisa Malkki, "Speechless Emissaries: Refugees, Humanitarianism, and Dehistoricization," in Karen Fog Olwig and Kirsten Hastrup (eds.), *Sitting Culture: The Shifting Anthropological Object* (London: Routledge, 1997), pp. 67–68.

3   Sari Hanafi, *Entre deux mondes: Les hommes d'affaires palestiniens de la diaspora et la construction de l'entité palestinienne* (Le Caire: CEDEJ, 1997).

4   Sari Hanafi, "Opening the Debate on the Right of Return," *Middle East Report,* no. 222 (Spring 2002).

5   In Syria and Jordan, refugees enjoyed access to free education, relatively egalitarian job opportunities, and easily crossed national borders for work abroad.

6   Sari Hanafi, "Vivre dans le camp, vivre ailleurs: Les palestiniens réfugiés en Egypte et dans les Territoires Palestiniens," *Bulletin de l'Association des Géographes Français* 83 (2006): pp. 76–92.

7   Of course, what I am describing here is true on one level, but not on another. It holds when comparing the camp populations in Jordan and Palestinian territory with the country average. However, in both places, there are large population groups with even much poorer living

conditions. See Marwan Khawaja, "Migration and the Reproduction of Poverty: The Refugee Camps in Jordan," *International Migration* 41, no. 2 (2003).

8 M. Arneberg, *Conditions among Palestinian Refugees and Displaced in Jordan,* Fafo Report 237 (Oslo: Fafo, 1997). Actually, the difference in living conditions of the Palestinian refugees between those who are camp dwellers and those who live off camp is more important than what is mentioned in the Fafo surveys. I am basing my estimation here on my anthropological observations, as well as on statistics from the Syrian and Palestinian Central Bureaus of Statistics. Fafo usually conducted its surveys in the refugee camps or at Palestinian gathering sites. However, Palestinian refugees also live in cities, where they integrate with the local population. Thus, it is usually very hard to identify them.

9 J. Hanssen-Bauer and L. B. Jacobsen, "Living in Provisional Normality—The Living Conditions of Palestinian Refugees in the Host Countries of the Middle East," paper presented at the Stocking II Conference on Palestinian Refugee Research, International Development Research Centre, Ottawa, June 2003.

10 Those who benefit from the SHCs are the "most disadvantaged and vulnerable refugees, such as women whose husbands have died or whose husbands have divorced or abandoned them, the elderly, the chronically ill, refugees with disabilities, or the very young." UNRWA provides these groups with direct material and financial assistance. See http://www.un.org/unrwa/programmes/rss/specialhardship.html (last accessed September 5, 2008).

11 William J. Wilson is one of the architects of this thesis, arguing that the movement of middle-class blacks from inner-city neighborhoods resulted in the concentration of a much poorer segment of the black population in these communities. William J. Wilson, *The Truly Disadvantaged: The Inner City, The Underclass, and Public Policy* (Chicago: University of Chicago Press, 1987) cited by Khawaja, "Migration and the Reproduction of Poverty," p. 29.

12 Emanuel Marx, "The Social World of Refugees: A Conceptual Framework," *Journal of Refugee Studies* 3, no. 3 (1971): pp. 189–203; Emanuel Marx and Yoram Ben-Porath, *Some Sociological and Economic Aspects of Refugee Camps on the West Bank* (Santa Monica, CA: RAND, 1971).

13 All the following statistics are drawn from the 1997 census, unless mentioned otherwise. Hussein al-Rimmawi and Hana Bukhari, *Population Characteristics of the Population Refugee Camps,* Analytical Report Series no. 3 (Ramallah: Palestinian Central Bureau of Statistics 2002) (in Arabic). No reliable survey has been conducted since.

14 As a team leader, I conducted this survey between January and October 2003. Five-hundred and sixty open questionnaires were completed by refugees and nonrefugees living in the camps and outside them.

15 Camp-dwelling Palestinian National Authority workers amounted to 27.4 percent of those employed, compared with 9.5 percent and 12.8 percent in urban and rural areas, respectively.

16 Al-Rimmawi and Bukhari, *Population Characteristics of the Population Refugee Camps,* pp. 23–24.

17 These figures are according to a survey by the Palestinian Center for Policy and Survey Research (PSR). The survey was conducted between January 16 and February 5, 2003, targeting 1,498 Palestinian refugee households distributed among 150 localities in the West Bank and Gaza Strip.

18 See Ariel Handel, "Where, Where to, and When in the Occupied Territories: An Introduction to the Geography of Disaster," and Hilla Dayan, "Regimes of Separation: Israel/Palestine and the Shadow of Apartheid," in this volume.

19 Ariella Azoulay and Adi Ophir, "The Ruling Apparatus of Control in the Occupied Territories," a paper presented at the Politics of Humanitarianism Conference, the Van Leer Institute, April 20–21, 2004.

20 Michel, Foucault, "Of Other Spaces," *Diacritics* 16, no. 1 (Spring 1986): pp. 22–27.

21 Events that the author witnessed at the time. See also Peter Lagerquist, "Ramallah Day," *New Left Review* 14 (March–April 2002), available on-line at http://www.newleftreview. org/?view=2378 (last accessed September 5, 2008).

22 On Foucault's concept of bio-power, see Michel Foucault, *The History of Sexuality, Vol. 1: An Introduction* (New York: Vintage Books, 1990).

23 See, for instance, Erika Feller, Volker Türk, and Frances Nicholson (eds.), *Refugee Protection in International Law: UNHCR's Global Consultations on International Protection* (Cambridge: Cambridge University Press and UNHCR, 2003).

24 Giorgio Agamben, "We Refugees" (1997), trans. Michael Rocke, available on-line at http:// www.egs.edu/faculty/agamben/agamben-we-refugees.html (last accessed September 5, 2008).

25 It is interesting to note that as an academic discipline, "refugee studies" is mainly conceived as a study of the humanitarian condition of refugees that usually ignores their political condition. As Mallki has noted, "refugee studies" has uncritically imported its main theoretical ideas, often on an ad hoc basis, from other scholarly domains, especially development studies. Malkki, "Speechless Emissaries," p. 599. The discipline has often been functionalist, and the questions it studies are shaped by the international organizations that fund it, while issues such as protection are still very loosely articulated with respect to refugees' political rights. A similar critique has been expressed by scholars such as Guglielmo Verdirame and Barbara Harrell-Bond, Michel Agier, and Fabienne Le Houérou, among others, writing about the practices of the UNHCR concerning their management of the refugee flow. See Guglielmo Verdirame and Barbara Harrell-Bond, *Rights In Exile: Janus-Faced Humanitarianism,* Studies in Forced Migration, vol. 17 (New York: Berghahn Books, 2005); Agier, "Between War and City"; and Fabienne Le Houérou, *Migrants forcés éthiopiens et érythréens en Égypte et au Soudan: Passagers d'un monde à l'autre* (Paris, l'Harmattan, 2004).

26 Elia Zureik, "Theoretical and Methodological Considerations for the Study of Palestinian Society," *Comparative Studies of South Asia, Africa and the Middle East* 23, nos. 1–2 (2003): p. 156; Julie Peteet, *Landscape of Hope and Despair: Place and Identity in Palestinian Refugee Camps* (Philadelphia: University of Pennsylvania Press, 2005), p. 45.

27 As a sign of this positive change in the discourse of the UNRWA, see, for example, the presentations of Lex Takkenberg and Anders Fange at the International Conference organized by Al-Quds University in Jerusalem, The Palestinian Refugees: Conditions and Recent Developments, on November 25 and 26, 2006. For UNRWA's mission statement, see www. unrwa.org.

28 Lex Takkenberg, "The Search for Durable Solutions for Palestinian Refugees: A Role for UNRWA?" in Eyal Benvenisti, Chaim Gans and Sari Hanafi (eds.), *Israel and the Palestinian Refugees* (Berlin: Springer, 2007).

29 See http://www.un.org/unrwa/news/statements/2006/hdm_Dec06.html (last accessed September 5, 2008).

30 Sari Hanafi, *Entre deux mondes: Les hommes d'affaires palestiniens de la diaspora et la construction de l'entité palestinienne* (Le Caire: CEDEJ, 1997).

31 Agier, "Between War and City," p. 318.

32 Giorgio Agamben, *Homo Sacer: Sovereign Power and Bare Life,* trans. Daniel Heller-Roazen (Stanford, CA: Stanford University Press, 1998).

33 The social structures of the camps are very diverse. In the Jalazon camp near Ramallah, for example, there is a tribal structure, because the camp is divided into quarters, each inhabited by refugees from a specific village, while in the Balata camp in Nablus, the old notables are not important, and a new elite has emerged from the strong presence of Palestinian political factions.

34 In many camps, the social role of NGOs is much more important than that of the political factions. However, some of these NGOs are connected to different political factions. Interviewees reported a climate of mistrust against the NGOs. Sari Hanafi and Linda Tabar, *The Emergence of a Palestinian Globalized Elite: Donors, International Organizations and Local NGOs* (Ramallah: Muwatin and Institute of Jerusalem Studies, 2005).

35 Beginning in the early 1950s and until 1987, UNRWA set up women's training centers that provided courses in sewing, health education, and nutrition or home economics. Since 1987, the women's program centers have included legal literacy programs and legal advice bureaus, which provide awareness training and advice on a wide variety of legal and civic matters. In 2005, the program was able to respond to the needs of 18,000 women of different ages.

36 There are over 6,700 people who are being assisted through the CRCs. The activities at the CRCs include programs devised to respond to the needs of the visually impaired, classes for children with cerebral palsy, classes for the mentally disabled, and the provision of occupational therapy, medical diagnosis and evaluation, and speech therapy.

37 Youth activities centers have offered sport and recreational facilities, adult education, leadership training, civic awareness, and community action programs to thousands of participants since 1959. In 2006, The YACs offered services to more than 12,000 youth. All CRCs and YACs are financially self-supporting; eight of the seventy-one WPCs are financially self-supporting; fifty-four have reached partial financial sustainability, and only nine centers are still totally dependent on UNRWA's support.

38 Yousef Hoshieh, discussion in the Community Involvement and Spatial Representation Workshop, UNRWA, Ramallah, October 5, 2006, unpublished document.

39 Rima Hammami, discussion in the Community Involvement and Spatial Representation workshop, UNRWA, Ramallah, October 5, 2006, unpublished document.

40 On this point, see Yehouda Shenhav and Yael Berda, "The Colonial Foundations of the State of Exception: Juxtaposing the Israeli Occupation of Palestinian Territories with Colonial Bureaucratic History," in this volume.

41 Agamben, *Homo Sacer,* pp. 168–69, 174–75.

42 I am referring here to the discussion in the workshop organized by the Department of Palestinian Refugee Affaires (one of the departments of the PLO) in Ramallah in which many members of local committees opposed the idea that municipal urban regulations should be applied to the camp space.

43 Information based on fieldwork conducted in the late 1990s.

44 Interview with Sandi Hilal, January 2006.

45 Mohamed Kamel Doraï, *Les réfugiés palestiniens au Liban: Une géographie de l'exil* (Paris: CNRS Éditions, 2006).

46 Alessandro Petti, *Arcipelaghi e enclave: Architettura dell'ordinamento spaziale contemporaneo* (Rome: Bruno Mandadori, 2007).

47 Bernard Rougier, *Everyday Jihad: The Rise of Militant Islam among Palestinians in Lebanon* (Cambridge, MA: Harvard University Press, 2007).

48 Zuriek, "Theoretical and Methodological Considerations for the Study of Palestinian Society," p. 159.

49 Interview with Philip Misselwitz, June 2007.

50 Khaled Hroub, "Between the Right of Return and the 'Right to Survive!,'" *Al-Ayyām,* June 8, 2007. See also the interview with Oraib Rantawi, "Palestinian Refugees in Jordan Fear for Their Rights," available on-line at http://www.voanews.com/english/archive/2005-02/2005-02-04-voa28.cfm (last accessed March 7, 2009).

51 Concerning the rehabilitation of the refugee camp in Syria, the example of the Neirab camp is very compelling. I am referring to UNRWA Neirab Rehabilitation Project: Project Briefing, March 2003 (unpublished document).

52 One should salute the impetus that UNRWA currently has to improve the camp situation in all their areas of intervention. *Housing & Camp Improvement Unit Concept Paper—Executive Summary* (unpublished document from UNRWA). The UNRWA project led by the German architect Philipp Misselwitz regarding the rehabilitation of the refugee camps also deserves praise.

53 Sari Hanafi, "Finding a Just Solution for the Palestinian Refugee Problem: Toward an Extraterritorial Nation-State," in Mahdi Abdul Hadi (ed.), *Palestinian-Israel Impasse: Exploring Alternative Solutions to the Palestine-Israel Conflict* (Jerusalem: PASSIA, 2005), pp. 187–204.

54 Henri Lefebvre, *Le droit à la ville* (Paris: Anthropos, 1968).

Matrix in Bil'in: Colonial Capitalism
in the Occupied Territories

Gadi Algazi

The occupation of the Palestinian territories is basically a colonial process carried out under the protective shield of Israel's military control. This has often been overlooked: Daily oppression and blatant infringements of human rights have consistently deflected attention from the structural processes transforming the social and economic landscape of the Occupied Territories. Prevalent perceptions of the Israeli-Palestinian conflict in general and the occupation in particular, seen through the prism of international relations and interstate conflict, often have not only obscured the enormous disparity of power between Israel and the Palestinians by suggesting a false symmetry, they also have focused attention time and again on official declarations and political symbols and away from the humble facts of land and water, the distribution of resources, and emerging regimes of movement. But the reality of the conflict is colonial—one that is determined, first and foremost, by facts on the ground, by bulldozers and fences, colonies and water wells. Settler colonialism does not exhaust itself in diplomatic maneuvers or spectacular acts of violence. It is first and foremost a social and economic process that changes nature itself and the fabric of social life, reallocates resources, and leaves people dispossessed. Its results are hence always, in a sense, irreversible: Social reality cannot be simply restored to its pristine state. This does not entail accepting its outcomes as given or giving up prematurely the struggle to end it. One can—and should— confront its evils and seek to bring about a measure of justice, but this entails a long and painful struggle against a new social and economic reality.

Israel's colonial project in the Occupied Territories has three main pillars: a web of settlements, a network of roads, and a system of roadblocks, checkpoints, and barriers. The settlements control essential resources, cut up the occupied area, and create a colonial frontier that is constantly on the move, pushing the dispossession process further.[1] The roads separate colonial masters from their subjects. They enable the army and the settlers to control space and serve as a network of additional barriers separating Palestinian villages and towns. The system of roadblocks and barriers, travel permits and terminals, concrete walls and fenced enclaves keep the indigenous population locked up under constant supervision, free only to manage its own hardship.

The greatest failure of the Israeli left and of all the opponents of the occupation is in confronting the settlement project. Significant political protest accompanied only the very early stages of the settlement process, mainly at the end of the 1970s, and a few conspicuous settlement projects such as Hebron and Abu Ghneim/"Har Homa," south of Jerusalem. To an extent, this is typical of situations in which colonial policies of establishing facts on the ground bring about a radical transformation in the fabric of social life: Political discussion tends to lag behind the rapid changes, exposing the limitations of traditional forms of political protest. Yet there was more to it: When Ariel Sharon promised in 1983 one hundred thousand settlers in the Occupied Territories, he was derided. The establishment of a regime of checkpoints and roadblocks during the 1990s failed to attract proper attention. Amira Hass's articles depicting the reality taking shape in the Occupied Territories during the years of the "Peace process" were perceived as dealing with the minutiae of human rights and everyday life under the occupation, rather than as a timely warning against a comprehensive political strategy.[2] The roads built throughout the territories during those years were considered bitter pills that must be swallowed for the sake of "the process." The examples can be multiplied: Conceiving the occupation as a merely "political" issue, a matter of borders and diplomatic arrangements, and ignoring the depth of the social and economic transformations lying at the heart of every colonial process prevented the opponents of the occupation from facing them. The Israeli left failed to notice how economic deprivation and social misery within Israeli society were used to advance the colonial process and hence has not sought ways to undermine the social alliances upon which it rests.

The social and economic transformations of Israeli society in the 1980s and 1990s also radically reshaped the realities of the Occupied Territories. With waves of accelerated privatization after 1985, social polarization within Israel intensified to an unprecedented extent. The modest achievements of the early 1970s in key areas such as education, housing, labor, and health were undermined rapidly by successive governments. Accelerated privatization went hand in hand with a colonial project heavily subsidized by the same state that shrank from public investment in social services within its pre-1967 borders. Israeli colonialism changed its face at the same time. The hard-core settlers of the ultranationalist right were gradually joined by a host of new social groups—from upper-middle-class settlers looking for an improved quality of life, through new immigrants channeled to the Occupied Territories by state authorities and Zionist institutions, to poor Israeli citizens seeking to better their lives and in search of public housing and state subsidies.

The establishment of an almost permanent closure of the West Bank and Gaza after 1993, preventing hundreds of thousands of Palestinians from entering Israel, should equally be seen not only in the context of Israeli-Palestinian political conflict, but also in the context of the evolution of Israel's political economy. Israeli capitalism made Palestinian workers superfluous, sentencing them to horrific poverty and hardship while seeking to modernize itself rapidly and to renegotiate its place in global markets. On the one hand, the closure became a permanent fact, and the Occupied Territories were henceforth subjected to a regime of checkpoints and roadblocks anticipating their total fragmentation after October 2000. On the other hand, the influx of cheap foreign labor force—more than a million Jewish immigrants and several hundred thousands migrant workers, as a rule employed as contract labor—granted Israeli capitalism a new momentum.

This is not to deny the role of politics and the state in renewing the Israeli occupation. In fact, Ariel Sharon, the true architect of Israel's post-1967 colonial project, played a key role not only in shaping the master plan for the settlements in 1977–78, but also in broadening the social base of Israeli colonialism, catering not only to the ultranationalist Zionist vanguard, but also to the upper middle class and—eventually—to the poor and underprivileged. At one end of the rapid process of social polarization in Israel, the 1980s and the 1990s gave shape to a new upper middle class thirsty for a better quality of life and for social distinction. Quality-of-life settlements became a respectable option, which ultimately brought the settlement project closer to hearts of the middle class: gated communities planted in the colonial landscape, just beyond the Green Line, conveniently connected to the center, free of Arabs and poor people.[3]

At the other end of the social structure, poor families and young couples of modest means, especially large ultraorthodox families with few alternatives, began to populate urban settlements in the West Bank. We are often reminded that in the 1990s, during the years of the Oslo "peace process," the number of Jewish settlers in the Occupied Territories doubled. One often forgets, however, that a large majority among them consisted precisely of such settlers, not the intransigent nationalist zealots who so easily capture the public imagination. Coming to terms with the challenge they pose is an urgent task. To illustrate the entanglements and contradictions involved in this phenomenon, I would like to focus in the following on one such settlement, Modi'in Illit.

MODI'IN ILLIT AND BIL'IN

Modi'in Illit is one of the largest Israeli settlements in the West Bank. It was founded in 1996, three miles east of the Green Line, Israel's pre-1967 border, under the shadow of the Oslo "peace process" by a group of private entrepreneurs. It is situated some twenty miles east of Tel Aviv and eight miles west of Ramallah on what once were the orchards, fields, and pastures of five Palestinian villages: Nil'in, Kharbata, Saffa, Bil'in, and Dir Qadis.[4] Although a latecomer among Israeli settlements, it soon became one of the fastest-growing colonies in the West Bank, with a population of over 35,000 in 2007; the Housing Ministry projects 150,000 residents by 2020. Along with the huge ring of Israeli-only housing around Greater Jerusalem, the eastward sprawling conurbation of Ma'ale Adumim and other rapidly expanding settler towns such as Ariel, Karnei Shomron, Betar Illit, and others in the cluster of settlements at Gush Etzion, it is part of a rash of new building that has transformed the West Bank landscape.

Modi'in Illit is not the work of messianic settler-zealots, but of a heterogeneous sociopolitical alliance that links real-estate developers, capitalists seeking the opportunity to profit from land confiscation and government subsidies, politicians driving forward the colonization project—and captive labor. Its development is part of a larger project, begun in the 1980s, that aimed both to establish enclaves in the Occupied Territories for wealthy, more "mainstream" settlers and to dissolve the Green Line by creating "facts on the ground"—linking the new settlements to communities inside the Green Line while expanding the latter in the direction of the Occupied Territories. Its very name, "Upper Modi'in," misleadingly suggests that it is part of the town of Modi'in, situated some miles away on the Israeli side of the pre-1967 border.

With the post-Oslo expansion of West Bank settlements in the mid-1990s, thousands of housing units were built in Modi'in Illit in violation of the law— and with the ex post facto approval of the local council. In one area, the council whitewashed the illegal construction by making retroactive adjustments to the zoning plan. According to a 1998 investigation, the entire Brachfeld Estate—built on the lands of Bil'in and comprising several thousand housing units—was thrown up without construction permits, though naturally, not one of these houses was demolished when this fact was revealed. The close cooperation between the Modi'in Illit Council and powerful private entrepreneurs, who were granted special benefits and no-bid contracts, is well documented in the state comptroller's report.[5] Again and again the council sought to justify its cozy relationship with the investors, arguing that the private contractor "has already built housing units and other projects in the area" and that there is "an urgent need to complete the

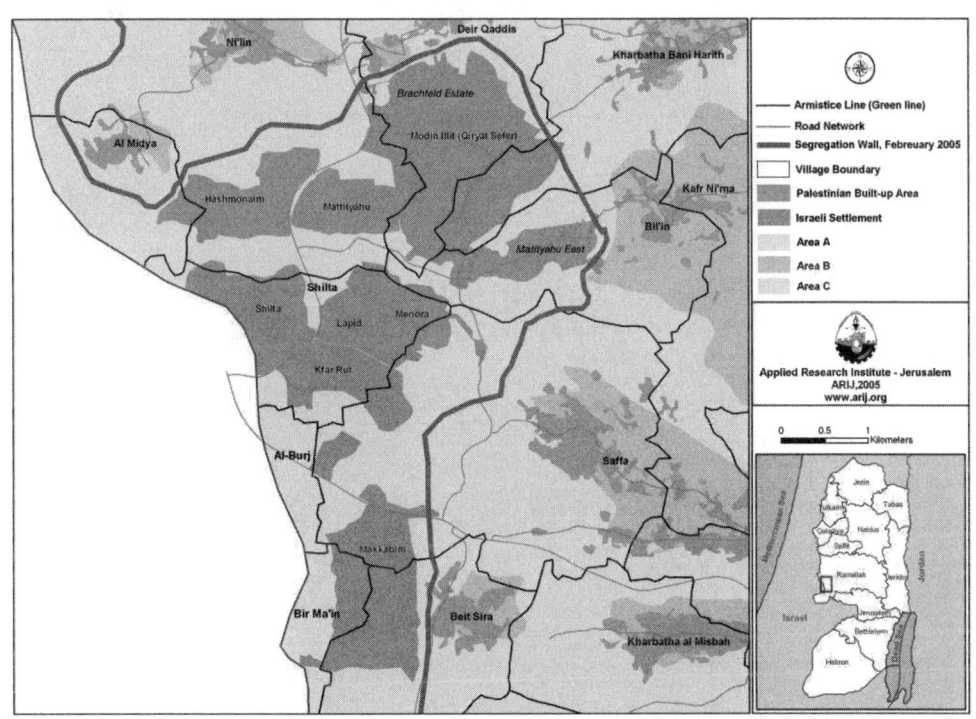

Modi'in Illit and the surrounding Palestinian communities. [Source: Applied Research Institute, Jerusalem, 2005 (map slightly modified)]

project." The state comptroller also determined that the Modi'in Illit Council collected only 10 percent of the taxes that the developers owed on the lands and that the council "offset the debts it was owed" from the two main developers of the settlement "by means of shady bookkeeping involving future building projects, even before receiving the required permits for their construction."

All this is not a matter of mere corruption or mismanagement, but a structural feature of the colonial frontier: Unregulated settlement activity creates possibilities for vast profits at the expense of the human and natural environments. In Israel's Wild East, the need to establish "facts on the ground" gives developers a free hand. The political urgency of the colonization process works in tandem with investors' attempts to secure quick profits.

The second Palestinian uprising (October 2000) impeded the expansion of most Israeli settlements. Yet its defeat, and especially the construction of the Separation Wall and the political shelter provided by Sharon's "disengagement plan," gave the expansion of Modi'in Illit and similar settlements a further boost. With the de facto annexation of the West Bank lands lying between the Wall and the pre-1967 border, real-estate developers could now promise the luxury and security of gated communities to wealthy Israelis, while the local Palestinian inhabitants were barricaded out of sight.

At the same time, generous government subsidies offered jobs, housing, and social services unobtainable in Israel proper, a powerful magnet for those struggling to subsist. Precisely because they are not based solely on the messianic fervor of hard-line settlers, but also offer answers to real social needs, these settlements are able to broaden the power base of the colonization movement, forging a powerful alliance of state, political, and capitalist interests, well-off home buyers and those suffering real hardship, such as large families looking for cheap housing or new immigrants dependent on government subsidies and seeking social acceptance. It is they who pay the price for the hostility that the Wall generates among those whose land it robs.

The construction of the Wall around Modi'in Illit is swallowing up another 445 acres (about 2,000 dunams) of Bil'in farmers' lands, in addition to what had already been stolen. In this part of Palestine, as throughout much of the Mediterranean basin, farmers have traditionally lived in small villages, rather than on isolated farmsteads, and go out each day to cultivate their family holdings in the surrounding area. To wall off the village is thus a brutally simple way of robbing these families of their ancestral lands. The inhabitants of Bil'in have fought the construction of the wall that separates them from their lands both by legal means and through popular, nonviolent struggle. They have filed a petition to the High Court of Justice and, since February 2005, they have demonstrated every Friday, hand in hand with Israeli peace activists and international volunteers, in front of the developers' bulldozers and the IDF troops accompanying them. They have joined a series of Palestinian villages—Jayyous, Biddu, Deir Ballut, Budrus, and others—leading campaigns of nonviolent resistance against the Wall. Often coordinated by the local Popular Committees against the Fence—though often with little support from the official Palestinian leadership—these campaigns have achieved some modest successes, impeding or slowing down the advance of the separation barrier or deflecting its course so as to regain some of their lost vineyards and fields.

More than two hundred people have been injured in the violent dispersal of the joint Israeli-Palestinian demonstrations in Bil'in, and many have been arrested under various pretexts. Forces of the Israeli Army, the Border Guard, Israeli police, and private security firms have been used against the protesters. Clubs, tear gas, rubber bullets, and live fire have taken a heavy toll. With late-night sweeps and arrests, Israeli forces have tried to deter the members of the Popular Committee of Bil'in who, even in these times of hatred and fear, steadfastly adhere to the principles of nonviolent resistance and open cooperation with Israeli opponents of the occupation. The prison service even sent in its special Masada unit, police provocateurs disguised as Palestinians, who tried to whip up the crowd and incite demonstrators to use force against the soldiers.[6] Only the determination of the members of the Popular Committee of Bil'in prevented these provocations from causing an uncontrolled escalation that could have ended with the loss of life.

Meanwhile, construction had already started on some of the newly expropriated land, even before the Bil'in villagers' case had been heard. It was, indeed, the real-estate investors and developers who insisted on this particular route for the Wall, to encircle land they had already earmarked for future settler housing. The main entrepreneurs involved in the expansion of Modi'in Illit are Lev Leviev, one of Israel's most powerful businessmen and an owner of Africa Israel Investments; Leviev's business partner Shaya Boymelgreen, an American real-estate investor; Mordechai Yona, former head of the Contractors Association who founded Heftsiba, the company building the neighborhood Matityahu East; and Pinchas Salzman, an orthodox businessman. Green Park, one of the developments being built on the land robbed from the Bil'in peasants, is already under construction by Leviev and Boymelgreen's Danya Cebus company, a subsidiary of Africa Israel—a massive $230 million project, with 3,000 apartments planned.[7]

Serious financial interests are thus involved in the struggle over Bil'in's farming land. They have received substantial assistance from two bodies with claims to legal ownership of much of it: the Custodian of Absentee Property and the Land Redemption Fund (LRF). The Custodian of Absentee Property is a governmental agency officially entrusted with the management of "absentee land." It has played a key role in taking possession of Palestinian land, initially that belonging to refugees within Israel and, more recently, in the Occupied Territories, as well. When Bil'in residents appealed to Israel's High Court of Justice to change the route of the Separation Wall, it was revealed that the state custodian had served as a cover for the settlers. In a special report, two Israeli human rights organizations uncovered these "revolving transactions": The settlers "transfer the land they purchased to the Custodian, who declares it state land. This enables the planning process to start. The Custodian allocates the land to the purchaser in the framework of the planning-authorization agreement, and then for development, for no consideration."[8] The Land Redemption Fund was established some twenty years ago by hard-line settlers (former Gush Emunim leader Zvi Slonim, Sharon aide Avraham Mintz, and Brooklyn-born terrorist Era Rapaport)[9] with the goal of coordinating the takeover of Palestinian land in areas targeted for settlement expansion. Arab straw men act as mediators in the land deals, posing as buyers, while the actual purchasers are Israeli investors.[10] These methods were also used to take possession of Bil'in's lands.[11]

The project is thus inextricably political and economic: Colonization and annexation yield enormous profits. Among the LRF's donors can be found the same capitalists who appear elsewhere as settlement builders and real-estate investors. They donate considerable sums to the radical settlers' fund, and not out of political conviction alone, for there is a profit to be made. The same alliance can be encountered elsewhere in the West Bank. The LRF is also the investor behind the expansion of the Tzufin settlement on lands robbed from Jayyous—another Palestinian village set to lose most of its resources with the construction of the Separation Wall. Here, an elevenfold expansion of the settlement is under way, and the developer is once again a real-estate company controlled by Leviev.[12]

The people of Bil'in have indeed scored some significant achievements. In September 2007, Israel's High Court of Justice ruled against the current route of the barrier and ordered the state to prepare within a reasonable time a proposal for an alternative route that would allow the inhabitants of Bil'in to access their lands.[13] More than a year after the court's decision, the fence still had not been moved (December 2008). In a separate ruling, the Israeli court recognized that the whole neighborhood Matityahu East in Modi'in Illit had been built illegally, as the residents of Bil'in claimed, but failed to order its demolition.[14] Meanwhile the construction company building Matityahu East went insolvent, and its CEO, Boaz Yona, fled the country. The company's financial difficulties were owed not least to Bil'in's persistent struggle, which prevented the investor from completing the building project. Beyond causing some serious damage to the developers making profits from the settlement's expansion, slowing down the advancing fence, and perhaps changing its route, the people of Bil'in and their allies provided a model of stubborn popular resistance against the Separation Wall and the occupation.

GLOBAL, DIGITAL, AND COLONIAL

In Modi'in Illit, the old economy of contractors and developers meets the new economy of high-tech development. Faced with competition from low-paid computer programmers in India and elsewhere, several software companies have opted for what they term "offshoring at home" — that is, in Israel's colonial backyard. In Modi'in Illit, such companies as Imagestore, Citybook, and, most prominently, Matrix, one of Israel's largest Internet technology (IT) companies, have opened development centers, using low-paid ultraorthodox women workers in the state-subsidized settlement. Matrix's development center has been named Talpiot — after the IDF's elite unit. Its Web site promises "the quality, performance and professionalism of a modern, Western country, at third world prices!"[15] As Matrix CEO Mordechai Gutman explains, outsourcing to East Asia is not all perfect:

> Long distances, cultural and language differences, different time zones, as well as rising wages and high turnaround rates, all combine to reduce the attractiveness of development in these countries. To tackle the problem, Matrix has set up a development center in Israel, employing a highly qualified workforce at competitive rates.... [At Talpiot], religious women gain employment in development centers close to their home, in a homogeneous environment that provides for their specific needs.... Because the religious population competing for the jobs faces relatively low living costs, Matrix is able to provide its local offshore outsourcing services to customers at prices similar to those in Far East countries, but with the advantages of...geographic and cultural proximity.[16]

Glossed over in this "proximity" is the fact that Matrix's "offshore outsourcing" operation in Modi'in Illit takes place in the Occupied Territories and that the "low cost of living" is due to the substantial subsidies advanced by the state for the expansion of the settlements.

As its Web site explains, Matrix, through its wholly owned subsidiary Sibam, is one of the largest IT suppliers to the IDF and the Israeli security forces, as well as to government ministries, energy and transport sectors, and the Knesset. It also leads the market in banking-information systems, "providing consulting services for most of Israel's commercial banks, mortgage banks, credit card companies and insurance companies."[17] At a June 2004 meeting of IT firms with the Knesset's Science and Technology Committee attended by Finance Minister Benjamin Netanyahu, a request by Matrix CEO Mordechai Gutman for state assistance to enable them to compete with cheap programmers in India was warmly received. As both Netanyahu and the committee's chairman agreed, "the range of interests you represent here, around the table, is also the interest of the state."[18]

DOCILE LABOR

The state indeed sustains Matrix's venture in Modi'in Illit. Not only are the workers' wages subsidized by the government for at least five years, but the colonial project continues to put at the disposal of the developers, contractors, and high-tech firms the cheap, stolen land of the local farmers, as well as the public resources, policemen, and soldiers necessary to secure it—and a captive and disciplined workforce. The company's use of ultraorthodox women's labor is a much-publicized feature of Matrix's "offshoring at home" operation in Modi'in Illit. At the beginning of 2008, around 400 women were employed.[19] At the Talpiot software development center, the Jewish dietary rules of *kashruth* are observed, and there are separate kitchens for women and men. There is also a "pumping room" for women to nurse their babies. "Although many are mothers of six, they miss fewer days of work than a mother of two in Tel Aviv," an Imagestore project director in Modi'in Illit told a journalist. "These women have no issues. They just work. No smoking or coffee breaks, chatting on the phone, or looking for vacation deals in Turkey. Breaks are only for eating, or pumping breast milk in a special room. Some women can pop home, breast-feed and come back."[20]

The Matrix development center is strictly kosher, with two local rabbis to supervise the site. "We painstakingly uphold every kosher rule," say the company's directors, "so as not to lose rabbinical approval." In exchange for the rabbinical seal, the investors get obedient kosher girls. The rabbis play a crucial role in instilling capitalist work discipline. The ominous word *gezel*—a loaded moral term in the Jewish religious tradition, meaning taking by force and robbery—is applied, not to the lands of Bil'in, but to "stealing" the employer's time through idle talk. Visiting journalists are struck by the silence at the workplace:

> Personal conversations in the work room of Matrix's development centre are forbidden, not only between men and women, but among the women. "They pay you for eight hours of work," says Esti [one of the workers], "so they expect you to work. If someone is talking too much…someone else will tell her "Hey, that's *gezel*," as though we are taking from the company. Once we asked if we could take a break of five minutes for prayer, but the rabbi said that the ancient Sages didn't take a break but would call out the Shma while working, and thus we can put off the prayer until after the working day."[21]

The "girls" are described as diligent, efficient, and exceptionally productive workers—every human-resource manager's dream. The punctilious adherence to the rules is maintained even when the bosses are not present. Esti's group supervisor is usually in the city of Petach Tikva. But even so, with the ecology of mutual pressure among the women, the rules are upheld. "We are accustomed to rigor and obedience," she says with half a smile. "We have gotten used to not doing forbidden things even when no one is looking, because there is someone watching from above."[22] The Matrix recipe is a new combination of reciprocal social control among workers, of surveillance and discipline with rabbinical authority.[23]

How much are they paid? During the first six months, which includes a comprehensive government-sponsored computer-programming course in Java and the Microsoft .NET Framework, the women earn $435 per month, or 2,000 shekels. After that, they receive the minimum wage, which stood at $725 per month at the end of 2005. From their second year, they get $1,045 per month—compared with perhaps $3,500 or $4,000 per month for an experienced programmer in Israel and over $5,500 per month in the United States. In addition, the state subsidizes Matrix's Talpiot center by $215 per month for every worker. There are no bonuses, and the women are tied to the company for at least two years. They have to pay a fine equivalent to two months' salary if they want to quit.[24] The company's PR department is careful to explain that the wage rates in Modi'in Illit have nothing to do with the exploitation of cheap labor. They do not reflect the relative productivity of the "girls" or the price of their services in the international market, but rather "their low cost of living." As one of their religious leaders explained to another Israeli reporter: "The ultraorthodox community is used to living on nothing, so making a little is a lot for them."[25]

CANNON FODDER?

Israeli press reports of the workers at the Talpiot center give the impression of an encounter with a remote and exotic tribe whose women are given to strange rituals and high birth rates. Despite their strange ways, the writers emphasize, these women can be trained for productive labor. They are content with very little and are disciplined and obedient, thanks to the priests of the tribe, who add their authority to the employers' commands. Great is the fortune of Israeli capitalists! Faced with the challenges of globalization, they have no need to search for cheap, docile labor in faraway countries. They have found it in their own colonial backyard. But if these descriptions are reminiscent of Max Weber's invocation of pious female workers and the Protestant ethic, such idealized representations should not be taken for everyday reality. The ultraorthodox women working for Matrix surely find their own ways to circumvent rabbinical injunctions and shop-floor control.

In addition, there are pressing material reasons for obedience to the prevailing labor discipline. Where else can these women work? They are often the sole wage earners in large families in which husbands are expected to devote themselves exclusively to learning. One of the female managers of the project openly states: "There is no work in Modi'in Illit, and women do not have cars to travel anywhere else. Most of them have no driver's license, making it crucial that there is a place of employment close to home."[26] The rate of car ownership in Modi'in Illit is among the lowest in the country—sixty vehicles per thousand of population—and there are no industrial areas. Modi'in Illit and Betar Illit, the two large ultraorthodox urban settlements in the West Bank, account for more than a quarter of all Jewish settlers in the West Bank. According to the most recent survey, they are also the two poorest Jewish communities in Israel and the Occupied Territories.[27] This is the law of the stick and the carrot—and the stick is the same stick, unemployment and poverty, that also drives Palestinian workers in Israel and the Occupied Territories to participate as day laborers in building the settlements and the Separation Wall. They are victims of colonial capitalism, like many others who are being incorporated into the settlement process through the exploitation of their social distress. But what future awaits them and their children, as long as their existence is based on theft of land and serving as a human wall, a target for the hatred of the dispossessed Palestinians?

Two years ago, speaking to a reporter from *Ha'aretz,* some of the residents of Modi'in Illit emphasized that they did not think of themselves as settlers. It is the housing shortage that pushes large untraorthodox families into the settlements, where they find public housing and government assistance that do not exist within Israel. In the settlement of Betar Illit and in Modi'in Illit, a two-bedroom apartment costs less than $100,000. The mechanisms that incorporate people into the colonial process, making them settlers despite themselves, occasionally emerge into the open. In 2003, the mayor of Betar Illit, Yitzhak Pindrus, went so far as to tell the reporter that the ultraorthodox were sent to the Occupied Territories against their will "to serve as cannon fodder." "But even if they didn't come here for ideological reasons," responded the spokesman for the Settlers' Council with confidence, "they won't give up their homes so easily."[28]

The colonization process is built not just on capitalist expansion, but on social misery and poor people's pressing needs, just as the Separation Wall is built on fears, real and imagined, amplified by daily propaganda. It draws in young couples from the slums of Jerusalem and enrolls new immigrants from the Russian Federation who may find themselves sent to settle Ariel, for example, in the heart of the West Bank. Large ultraorthodox families, too, gain access to subsidized housing only by joining the settlement project. All these can find themselves defending the occupation in order to defend the fragile social existence they have built for themselves under the guidance of government authorities, the settler movement, and private capital.

Matrix employs around 2,300 persons. Its profits rose by 48 percent in 2005 and by a further 78 percent in 2006. Its valuation on the Tel Aviv Stock Exchange stands at around half a billion shekels (around $100 million). Matrix is controlled by Formula Systems, of the Formula Group, with worldwide sales of $500 million.[29] It is also quite vulnerable to public criticism and boycott. Matrix, for instance, is the primary distributor of one of the most popular commercial versions of the Linux operating system—Red Hat. What would happen if Linux users were to announce a boycott of Matrix until it withdraws its investments from the Occupied Territories, or if they were to put pressure on the public institutions that are among its clients? Among others, the Hebrew University, the Weizmann Institute of Science, Ben Gurion University, and my own Tel Aviv University have all purchased Red Hat licenses from Matrix. What if users were to threaten to boycott the companies—such as Oracle—who use the services of the Talpiot development center in the settlement of Modi'in Illit? This does not apply to Israel alone: Matrix represents some of the most important international companies. All are vulnerable to public pressure from opponents of the settlements.[30] And what of Formula Systems, which owns Matrix? Formula Systems is very sensitive to its public image. It takes pains to present itself as a socially responsible company. Its customers, too, can demand that Formula stop supporting the building and expansion of settlements in the occupied West Bank.

It has sometimes been suggested that the dynamic of capitalist modernization would compel Israel to abandon its attachment to old-style colonialism. The case of Matrix in Bil'in demonstrates that Israeli capitalism can be both colonial and digital, occupying both global markets and frontier settlements, campaigning both for unbridled privatization and for heavy government subsidies. Left to itself, it will neither extricate itself from colonial expansionism nor exert pressure on the state to do so—that is, unless Israeli colonialism becomes an overwhelming liability and resistance by the colonized and their allies forces a change of course.

NOTES

Previous versions of this essay have been published in Hebrew on *Haokets* Web site (www.haokets.org) and later in *Theory and Critique* 29 (2006): pp. 173–92. A modified English version was published in *New Left Review* 40 (July–August 2006): pp. 27–37. This is a revised and expanded version.

1   See Idit Zertal and Akiva Eldar, *Lords of the Land: The War for Israel's Settlements in the Occupied Territories, 1967–2007* (New York: Nation Books, 2007).

2   See Amira Hass, *Reporting from Ramallah: An Israeli Journalist in an Occupied Land* (Los Angeles: Semiotext(e), 2003), and *Drinking the Sea at Gaza: Days and Nights in a Land Under Siege* (New York: Metropolitan Books, 1999).

3   Gadi Algazi, "The Upper-Class Fence," *The Occupation Magazine*, June 21, 2005, available online at http://www.kibush.co.il/show_file.asp?num=5086 (last accessed on May 7, 2008).

4   Nir Shalev, "The Wall in Bil'in and the Eastward Expansion of Modi'in Illit," *Indymedia/ HaGada HaSmalit*, September 11, 2005, available on-line at http://www.kibush.co.il/show_file.asp?num=8767 (in Hebrew) (last accessed May 7, 2008).

5   *Israel's State Comptroller's Report*, no. 51a (2000), pp. 201–18 (in Hebrew).

6   Meron Rapaport, "Bil'in Residents: Undercover Troops Provoked Stone-Throwing," *Ha'aretz*, October 14, 2005.

7   Sharon Kedmi, "Dania Cebus Is to Build in Modi'in Illit," *Globes*, August 15, 2004 (in Hebrew). On their Web sites, Africa Israel Investments and Danya Cebus do not mention their construction projects in the Occupied Territories and speak only of building "throughout the State of Israel."

8   See Yehezkel Lein and Alon Cohen-Lifshitz, "Under the Guise of Security: Routing the Separation Barrier to Enable the Expansion of Israeli Settlements in the West Bank," a Bimkom/ B'Tselem report, December 2005, available on-line at http://www.btselem.org/Download/200512_Under_the_Guise_of_Security_Eng.pdf (last accessed September 6, 2008).

9   Shalom Yerushalmi, "Every Prime Minister Who Gave Away Eretz Yisrael Was Hurt (an Interview with Era Rapaport)," *Ma'ariv*, April 5, 2002 (in Hebrew).

10   Shosh Mula and Ofer Petersburg, "The Settler National Fund," *Yedi'ot Aharonot*, January 28, 2005 (in Hebrew).

11   Akiva Eldar, "Documents Reveal West Bank Settlement Modi'in Illit Built Illegally," *Ha'aretz*, January 3, 2006; "State Mulls Criminal Probe into Illegal Settlement Construction," *Ha'aretz*, January 8, 2006.

12   Ada Ushpiz, "Fenced Out," *Ha'aretz*, September 16, 2005.

13   HCJ 8414/05 (September 4, 2007).

14   HCJ 143/06, 1526/07 (September 5, 2007).

15   The Talpiot web site is http://www.talpiot-it.com (last accessed November 22, 2008).

16   Mordechai Gutman, "Offshore in Israel—The New Direction in Developing Software for Organizations at High Quality and Low Cost," available on-line at http://www.matrix.co.il/Matrix/he-IL/Contents/Headlines/Off%20Shore.htm (in Hebrew) (last accessed September 6, 2008).

17   See the Matrix company profile at http://www.matrix.co.il (in Hebrew) (last accessed September 6, 2008).

18 *Protocols of the Knesset's Commission on Science and Technology,* June 29, 2004 (in Hebrew).

19 Ido Solomon, "An Experienced Male Programmer Is Worth 2 Ultraorthodox Women," *Ha'aretz* —*The Marker,* December 11, 2007 (in Hebrew).

20 Ruth Sinai, "Modi'in Illit: The Zionist Response to Offshoring," *Ha'aretz,* September 19, 2005.

21 Yoni Shadmi, "Globalization Killed the High-Tech Star," *Ma'ariv,* November 11, 2005 (in Hebrew).

22 *Ibid.*

23 An uncritical report evokes a similar image of labor discipline and social control in Citybook, another firm based in Modi'in Illit: Tulli Pikarsh, "Women Are Tabu," *Hatzofeh,* December 9, 2007 (in Hebrew).

24 Shadmi, "Globalization." The numbers are based on the exchange rate of the new Israeli shekel (NIS) at the end of 2005; recent reports confirm the emerging picture, with allowance made for the low exchange rate of the U.S. dollar against the shekel.

25 Galit Yemini, "Indian Labour? Matrix is Hiring Orthodox Women," *Ha'aretz,* January 17, 2005.

26 Eli Shimoni, "Who Can Find an Orthodox Java Wife?" YNet, September 23, 2005 (in Hebrew).

27 The Israel Central Bureau of Statistics, "Characterization and Classification of Local Authorities by the Socio-Economic Level of the Population 2001," February 2004 (in Hebrew).

28 Tamar Rotem, "The Price is Right," *Ha'aretz,* 23 September 2003.

29 See http://www.formulasystems.com (last accessed September 6, 2008).

30 A partial list of clients on Matrix's Web site includes PeopleSoft, bmc Software, Red Hat, Compuware, Business Objects, Verity, Vignette, iona, WebMethods, and BindView, among others.

Ariella Azoulay

5.1 AL-FURADDIS VILLAGE, HEBRON REGION, 2008 The heavier rubble has been removed. The site where the house once stood is covered with masonry shards, like an expensive vase that has been smashed to smithereens.

5.2 HEBRON, 2003 As in some delicate filigree, building blocks have been removed from the metal rods, and the house now resembles a transparent hothouse. Here and there, concrete beads hang from the ceiling, as if someone had tried to regulate the entry of light.

5.3 ANATA, EAST JERUSALEM, 2006 Clothes torn out of the closet add some color to the stone mosaic. Does the child, whose gaze lingers from the neighboring hill on the geometry flowing out of what once was a house, identify familiar shapes?

5.4 JENIN REFUGEE CAMP, 2002, AFTER OPERATION DEFENSIVE SHIELD The massive destruction of about five hundred houses, most of them in the Hawashin neighborhood, created vast "plazas" inside the camp's dense fabric. The rubble layer covering them created a potholed texture that hampered movement in the camp and created local gatherings. New hills, too, consisting of the remains of pulverized houses, contributed to the camp's altered topography.

5.5 WALAJA VILLAGE, 2007 The houses of the Gilo colony seen in the background have been sanctioned by the law. The Palestinian house in Walaja was defined by the same law as illegally built and was demolished.

ACTIVESTILLS.ORG/YOTAM RONEN

5.6 **RUINS OF A HOUSE ON THE ROAD FROM A-RAM TO RAMALLAH** At times, the stones are elegantly compressed and create a pile bearing no traces of the house from which it was generated. The clean ground around it reinforces the illusion that these are, perhaps, stones meant for masonry and building.

5.7 ISSAWIYA, EAST JERUSALEM Several days later, as the site of a demolished house loses its aura, passersby throw empty bottles or refuse bags into the empty space, where they blend in with the rubble.

Thanato-tactics

Eyal Weizman

Throughout the years of the second intifada, a major Israeli effort was directed at the development of airborne assassinations and the specific technology related to it. From what was often described as a "rare and exceptional emergency method," it has become the Israeli Air Force's main form of attack in the Gaza Strip. According to Ephraim Segoli, a helicopter pilot and former commander of the air force base in Palmahim, located halfway between Tel Aviv and Gaza, from which most assassination raids have been launched and where now the largest fleets of remotely controlled killer drones are located, airborne "liquidations are the central component of IDF operations and the very essence of the 'war' it is waging." Segoli, speaking in May 2006, claimed, furthermore, that "the intention to 'perfect' these operations meant that Israel's security industries have...started concentrating [much of their efforts] on the development of systems that primarily serve this operational logic."[1]

According to data collected by the human rights organization B'Tselem, from the beginning of the intifada to February 2008, 376 Palestinians were killed in targeted assassinations. Only 227 of those were the intended targets for assassination. The rest were Palestinians who happened to be in the wrong place at the wrong time. About fifty of those were children.[2] The assassinated included many of the political and military leadership of Hamas, as well.

What follows deals with the methods—technological, operational, legal, and other—that form the basis of these operations and asks how they interact. How do these tactics of assassination intersect with political considerations and calculations? How does the Israeli government and military seek to justify these assassinations, legally, morally, and politically?

Beyond thinking of targeted assassination as a direct, preemptive response to terror, the aim here, an update and revision on my previous research on the subject,[3] is to show how Israeli security organizations conceived assassination as a central component in a political "project" and as an attempt to generate a degree of control over Palestinian politics and the population at large. It asks, following Achille Mbembe's essay "Necropolitics," "What is the relationship between politics and death" that these efforts form?[4] How, after the evacuation of the ground surface of Gaza, did bodies, rather than territories, or death, rather than space, turn into the raw material of Israeli sovereignty?

TARGETING

Segoli explained that targeted assassinations are "a success story based upon a high degree of cooperation between the General Security Service (GSS) and the air force."[5] Above all, airborne targeted assassinations were fed by the information and organizational powers that the GSS developed under Avi Dichter, director of the GSS from 2000 to 2005, who gained considerable popularity with the public and with the prime minister, Ariel Sharon, as a result of their "success." The efficiency of the operations has relied on the close networking between the intelligence provided by the GSS, fast-tracked political decisions, and the strike capacity of the air force. The GSS drafts the death lists and recommends the time of the operation (once included, rarely has a name been removed from them alive); it provides the files on each person to be liquidated (including details of their involvement in the resistance and their prospective danger to Israel); a special ministerial committee gives its approval (the typical length of deliberation is fifteen minutes, and there are generally no objections); and the air force does the killing.[6]

Each targeted assassination is a large-scale operation that integrates hundreds of specialists from different military branches and security apparatuses. Beyond its reliance on background intelligence (much of it gathered in mass arrests and from Palestinians stopped at checkpoints), targeted assassination depends on sharing real-time information between various agents, commanders, operators, and different military planes and on their ability to act upon it. After a Palestinian is put on the death list, he is followed, sometimes for days, by a "swarm" of different kinds of unmanned aerial vehicles. Often, different swarms follow different people simultaneously in different areas of the Gaza Strip. In this way, the security services establish the targeted person's daily routines and habits and maintain continuous visual contact with him until his killing.[7] As well as being cheaper to operate, unmanned drones have the advantage over manned planes or helicopters because they can remain in the air around the clock, some for as long as thirty hours, and because their formations circulate in relatively small areas while providing a multiplicity of angles of vision. Moreover, drones are quiet and barely visible to the human eye. This is the reason that beginning in 2004, the air force started to shoot its missiles from drones, rather than from its more visible battle helicopters. A swarm of various types of drones, each circulating at a different altitude, up to a height of 30,000 feet, is navigated by a GPS system and woven by radio communication into a single synergetic reconnaissance and killing instrument that conducts the entire assassination operation. Some drones are designed to view the terrain vertically in order to establish the digital coordinates of a targeted person, while others look diagonally, in order to distinguish facial features or identify a vehicle's license plates. Some drones are designed to intercept radio signals and mobile-phone transmissions, while others can carry and shoot missiles. With the development and proliferation of drone technology, "very few Israeli soldiers [are] in the airspace over Gaza," and "the air is mainly filled with Golems." It is "an army without soldiers."[8]

Airborne assassinations depend as well on other mechanisms within Israel's system of domination. While targeted assassinations are explained as the alternative to collective punishment, to hardships imposed on the "uninvolved population," and to mass incarcerations, they are dependent on intelligence obtained in those mass incarcerations and interrogations. They rely, primarily in the West Bank, upon seducing Palestinians into collaboration in exchange for travel and work permits. The checkpoints themselves are part of Israel's "surveillance assemblages." In them, it is easy for the General Security Service to make contact with its informers without raising suspicions.

The clandestine Unit 504, jointly operated by military intelligence and the GSS, is responsible for the forced recruitment of Palestinians into collaboration. From one of its bases south of Haifa, where it also maintains Facility 1391, a Guantánamo Bay–style secret prison for "administrative detainees," Unit 504 trains groups of Palestinians to mark targets, plant and detonate bombs, or "shake the tree for the air force."[9] In previous years, members of this Palestinian military unit of the IDF would splash ultraviolet paint on the roof of a car to identify the target for a pilot to destroy.[10]

The missiles aim most often at a vehicle, but increasingly, and since Palestinians now often take the precaution to walk, also at pedestrians. Each assassination thus juxtaposes different spaces and domains: a control room in central Tel Aviv in which young soldiers navigate remotely piloted drones and missiles, as in a live computer game, into the narrow, dusty alleys of Gaza's refugee camps, where young Palestinians end their lives.

The IDF employs the sanitizing term "focused obstruction" or "focused preemption" (*sikul memukad*) to describe these assassinations. Such rhetoric is repeated by most of the popular Israeli media, which conceals as far as possible the real impact of the killings, mostly avoiding mentioning the names of Palestinian civilians killed in Israeli attacks and the display of the corpses, blood, and body parts—the very images on which it lingers when covering the aftermath of a Palestinian terror attack. Indeed, the Israeli media's use of selective imagery allows it to project assassination not only as necessary, but also as ethical, rhetorically legalizing it by what Neve Gordon has called "the discursive production of a pseudo-judicial process."[11]

One of many counterpoints to these digitized visions of "precision" killing was provided by Aref Daraghmeh, a witness to an August 2002 targeted assassination in the village of Tubas in the West Bank, who has provided the following testimony for B'Tselem:

> The helicopter...fired a third missile towards a silver Mitsubishi, which had four people in it. The missile hit the trunk and the car spun around its axis. I saw a man stepping out of the car and running away. He ran about 25 meters and then fell on the ground and died. The three other passengers remained inside. I saw an arm and an upper part of a skull flying out of the car. The car went up in flames and I could see three bodies burning inside it. Three minutes later, after the Israeli helicopters left, I went out to the street and began to shout. I saw people lying on the ground. Among them was six-year-old Bahira.... She was dead.... I also saw Bahira's cousin, Osama.... I saw Osama's mother running towards Bahira, picking her up and heading towards the a-Shifa clinic, which is about 500 meters away. I went to the clinic and saw her screaming after seeing the body of her son, Osama.[12]

OPERATIONAL PLANNING

The operational aspect of airborne targeted assassinations relies on military developments that originated in Israel's war in Lebanon during the 1980s and 1990s. In February 1992, Hezbollah Secretary General Sheikh Abbas Mussawi was the first to be killed in an airborne assassination when a group of Israeli helicopters flying inland from the Mediterranean Sea attacked his convoy, killing him and his family. The first airborne targeted assassination in Palestinian areas took place on November 9, 2000, when an Israeli Apache helicopter pilot launched a U.S.-made Hellfire antitank missile at the car of a member of Tanzim al-Fatah organization, Hussein Muhammad Abayit, in Beit-Sahur, near Bethlehem, killing him and two women, Rahmeh Shahin and Aziza Muhammed Danun, who happened to be walking by the car when it exploded in the middle of their street. The IDF's spokesperson announced that the killing was part of "a new state policy."[13] Since 2002, however, it has been Gaza that has become the world's largest laboratory for airborne assassinations.[14] The U.S. administration feebly protested Israeli assassinations, demanding through diplomatic channels that Israel merely "considers the results of its actions." Meanwhile, different branches of the U.S. security forces, themselves engaged in unacknowledged assassinations using unmanned drones began to "examine Israeli Air Force's performances and results in order to draw lessons for its own wars."[15]

The planning and execution of these operations follows the principles of air force operational planning. The unit of "operational analysis" is part of the Israeli Air Force's "operational group" and is responsible, together with various intelligence agencies, for planning and optimizing bombing missions. There are three levels according to which bombing is planned: mechanical, systemic and political.

At the mechanical level, planning is concerned with the matching of munitions with targets—calculating what size and what type of bomb is needed to destroy a particular target; what amount of explosives is needed to destroy a car, a building of a particular size, a tunnel, or a bunker. The mechanical level involves calculations by civil engineers and blast experts assessing the structure of the target and the quality of its construction. Military engineers then use a computer program to determine the munitions, attack angle, and time of day that will ensure the destruction of the target with the minimum use of munitions, destruction, and death to bystanders.

In the context of targeted assassinations, the mechanical level is concerned with the development of the warhead, the explosives used within it, and the accuracy of its delivery. Like the knife of the guillotine, the warhead and other innovations in the technologies of bombing aimed at making killing more efficient and "civilized" in fact enable its routine and frequent application. I will return to this point at a later part of the essay. In this role—as the designer and employer of the knife of the guillotine—the unit of operational analysis has been criticized at least twice, once for the use of excessive force and the other for excessive caution. The first case involved the decision, on July 23, 2002, to use a one-ton bomb to destroy a residential building in Gaza where the leader of Hamas's military wing, Salah Shehadeh, was spending the night, causing several buildings to collapse, killing Shehadeh and additional fourteen Palestinian civilians, more than half of them children. In the second case, two years later, the operational analysis unit was criticized for allocating a quarter-ton bomb for the attack on a meeting of Hamas's leadership. The bomb failed to cause the collapse of the building, allowing the leaders to escape unharmed from the ground floor.

The second level of planning is the systemic. The function of the unit of operational analysis extends beyond the planning of physical destruction. It attempts to predict and map out the effect that the destruction of a particular target might have on the enemy's overall system of operation. Following the principles of "system analysis,"[16] the enemy is understood as an operational network of interacting elements. In air force targeting theories, cities, societies, and political regimes are vulnerable because of their reliance on networked infrastructures that sustain life. When translated to its war with the Palestinians, the killing of members of Palestinian organizations is similarly thought of in relation to a systemic logic. Unlike state militaries, much of whose power is grounded in physical infrastructure and equipment, in the case of the Palestinian resistance, the infrastructure of resistance is the people themselves.[17] The effectiveness of the Palestinian resistance is grounded in its people and in the efficiency of the relations between them: political and spiritual leaders, spokespersons, financiers, commanders, experienced fighters, bomb makers, and recruiters. The killing of a key individual is conceived in terms similar to the destruction of a command-and-control center or a strategic bridge. Both are intended to trigger a sequence of systemic "failures" that will disrupt the enemy's system, making it more vulnerable to further military action.[18] "Operational shock" is best achieved, according to the military and the GSS, when the rhythms of these operations is rapid and the enemy system is not given time to recover between attacks.[19]

The third level of planning is political. Aerial bombing has had a political dimension from the inception of air forces between the First and Second World Wars. In his 1921 *The Command of the Air,* the Italian Giulio Douhet recognized the effects of bombing on civilian and military morale. Air power could break a people's will by destroying a country's "vital centers," he argued. Douhet identified the six basic target types as industry, transport, infrastructure, communications, government, and "the will of the people." The first four are types of targets related to targeting's military-systemic logic, while the last two could be attributed to political/psychological objectives. The political objective of targeting is to compel the enemy leadership to negotiate a surrender on the attacker's terms. Douhet was explicit about the fact that air war calls for the manipulation of civilian fear and suffering in order to achieve its political aims and that according to these terms, an air war could be considered a terror war.[20] When considering the political rationality of targeting, the killing of the uninvolved civilians that the military calls "collateral damage" could no longer be simply considered as the byproduct of the intention to hit military targets, but rather as the very aim of the bombing.

Often, the political logic of targeting is hidden behind military rhetoric that argues for the logic of bombing according to the first two levels of planning, the mechanical and systemic, which are considered legal according to international law. For example, in Israeli military announcements during the 2006 War between Israel and Hezbollah, Israeli targeting was explained according to a military logic: the destruction of airports, bridges, Hezbollah offices, launching sites, supply lines, infrastructure, and so on. It presented civilian casualties as the regrettable side effects of its attempts to hit military or dual-use targets. However, the destruction of homes and the killing and displacement of civilians was the main leverage of political pressure. This set of calculated acts has precedents in the logic of Israel's military interventions in Lebanon, which often aimed to manipulate differences and existing hostilities within Lebanon's complex social-political-ethnic fabric. The bombing in the 2006 War, according to Israeli speakers, aimed to turn the Lebanese populace against Hezbollah—a stratagem that was based on the assumption that a cold political calculus can triumph over vengeful rage in time of war. The creation of civilian casualties and their justification as "collateral damage" was part of an attempt to create a human catastrophe that could not be tolerated internationally and that would thus precipitate international intervention on Israel's terms. The bombing of Shiite towns and villages in the south was meant to force hundreds of thousands of civilians to flee northward toward Beirut. There, Israel hoped, their presence would put pressure on the government, who would in turn put pressure on the Hezbollah leadership to stop its military activities and disarm. Needless to say, these tactics led to crushing strategic failures. The refugees had neither the inclination nor the power to pressure the government in Lebanon or Hezbollah, and the bombings created nothing but public outrage and further support for Hezbollah.[21]

"TECHNOLOGY INSTEAD OF OCCUPATION"

Perennial overoptimism regarding air power has led successive generations of airmen to believe that unprecedented technological developments would allow wars to be won from the air, with bombing to intimidate politicians into submission and native populations to be managed by air power. The role of this new technology was to reduce uncertainty and increase control. The fantasy of a cheap aerial occupation, or "aerially enforced colonization," is as old as air forces themselves. In the 1920s, Winston Churchill, as minister of war and air, was fascinated with what he perceived to be the economically efficient, quick, clean, mechanical, and impersonal alternatives that air power could provide to the otherwise onerous and expensive tasks of colonial control. Emboldened by a murderous aerial attack on a tribal leader in Somaliland in 1920 that put down a rebellion, he suggested that aircraft be further adapted to the tasks of policing the empire. In 1922, Churchill persuaded the British government to invest in the air force and offered the Royal Air Force 6 million pounds to take over control of the Mesopotamia (Iraq) operation from the army, which had cost 18 million thus far.[22] The policy, called "control without occupation," saw the RAF successfully replacing large and expensive army contingents. Sir Percy Cox, the high commissioner in Baghdad, reported that by the end of 1922, "on [at least] three occasions demonstrations by aircraft [have been sufficient to bring] tribal feuds to an end. On another occasion planes…dropped bombs on a sheik and his followers who refused to pay taxes, held up travelers and attacked a police station."[23] Arthur "Bomber" Harris (so called after his infamous bombing campaigns on German working-class districts when commander of the RAF's bomber wing during World War II) reported after a mission in Iraq in 1924: "The Arab and Kurd now know what real bombing means, in casualties and damage. They know that within 45 minutes a full-sized village can be practically wiped out and a third of its inhabitants killed or injured."[24] The methods pioneered in Somaliland were also applied by the RAF against revolutionaries in Egypt, Darfur, India, Palestine (mainly during the 1936–39 Arab revolt),[25] and in Afghanistan's Jalalabad and Kabul. Anticipating the logic of targeted assassinations, Harris later boasted that the Afghan war was won by a single strike on the king's palace.[26]

Similar belief in "aerially enforced occupation" allowed the Israeli Air Force to attempt to replace the network of lookout outposts woven through the topography of the terrain by translating categories of "depth," "stronghold," "high point," "closure," and "panorama" into "air-defense in depth," "clear skies," "aerial reconnaissance," "aerially enforced closure," and "panoramic radar." With a "vacuum cleaner" approach to intelligence gathering, sensors aboard unmanned drones, aerial reconnaissance jets, attack helicopters, unmanned balloons, early warning Hawkeye planes, and military satellites capture most signals out of Palestinian airspace. Since the beginning of the second intifada, the air force has put in hundreds of thousands of flight hours, harvesting a stream of information through its network of airborne reconnaissance platforms, information that was later put at the disposal of different intelligence agencies and command-and-control rooms.

Distinctions must be maintained, however, between the kind of operation that the IDF conducts in Gaza (ever more so after the "evacuation") and those in the West Bank. The degrees of violence that Israel employs in Gaza greatly exceed the levels of violence employed in the West Bank. These differences in military approach are shaped by differences in degrees of control over the territory and the population. In the West Bank, Israel has a massive civilian presence of about half a million settlers and an extensive ground military presence, whereas even before the evacuation, Gaza was always considered a territory that it is hard for ground troops to enter. Whereas Israeli soldiers have broken into all Palestinian cities, villages, and refugee camps in the West Bank again and again, they have done so much less often in the larger and more impoverished refugee camps of Gaza. The evacuation of Gaza sharpened this tendency, and the strip was thereafter controlled primarily from the air, but also from the territorial waters off its coast-line and through border terminals along its fences.

In the West Bank, as its former chief commander, Yair Golan, mentioned in 2007, the military seeks to maintain a constant degree of "effective friction" for both operational and intelligence purposes, bringing the Palestinian civilian population into constant contact with Israeli soldiers and other security personnel.[27] The tactics of constant friction are maintained by the presence of settlements, roadblocks, checkpoints, and military offices for civilian administration. They control the population by constant harassment, as well as by modulating flows of various kinds: people, goods, and services. Aerial assassinations in the West Bank have indeed ceased after Operation Defensive Shield on April 2002, when the IDF destroyed organized Palestinian police and military forces, as well as many government offices, and reinstated complete ground control over Palestinian population centers. Since the end of 2002, assassinations in the West Bank have been undertaken from the ground, many of them under the pretext of arrest operations. According to figures released by B'Tselem, between 2004 and May 2006, Israeli security forces killed 157 persons during operations referred to as "arrest operations."[28] The most common justification for IDF killings conducted during ground raids in the West Bank is that the victim "violently attempted to resist arrest," but ground forces do not always allow militants to surrender and often try to steer them away from it.

The legal framework for targeted assassinations has developed in response to the pace of events. Immediately after the start of the second intifada, the head of the IDF's International Law Department, Colonel Daniel Reisner, stated that due to the heightened level and frequency of Palestinian violence, Israel could start defining its military operations in the Occupied Territories as an "armed conflict short of war," which placed the intifada in the context of international law, rather than criminal law.[29] Such a definition implied that, for the purpose of their killing (but not their internment), members of militant Palestinian organizations could be seen as combatants and thus attacked at will, not only when in the process of a hostile action or while resisting arrest.[30] Given that in international law, distinctions between "inside" and "outside" regulate the logic of security operations ("internal" operations are perceived as policing or security work; "external" ones as military) and that the definition of "inside" depends upon whether a state has "effective control" over the territory in question,[31] the evacuation of the Gaza Strip strengthened Israel's conviction that targeted assassinations are legal and has made their use more frequent. Politically, Israel expected that once it had evacuated the settlements and had retreated to the international border around Gaza, the international community would be more tolerant of these forms of military action.[32] This implies that the tactics of airborne assassinations have developed in response to the Israeli military ceding territorial control, or otherwise, that the evacuation could be thought of as a means to facilitate the continuation of assassinations.

Indeed, the tactical precondition for Israel's policy of territorial withdrawal was that its security services be able to maintain domination of the evacuated areas by means other than territorial control. The members of an IDF think tank called the Alternative Team involved in rethinking Israeli security after the evacuation of Gaza admitted: "Whether or not we are physically present in the territories, we should still be able to demonstrate our ability to control and affect them."[33] The occupation that they conceived to follow the supposed end of the occupation—that is, the domination of Palestinians after the evacuation of the ground space of the Gaza Strip and parts of the West Bank is completed—was alternately referred to by these and other military planners as the "invisible occupation," the "airborne occupation," or "occupation in disappearance."[34]

The ability of the Israeli Air Force to maintain a constant "surveillance and strike" capability over Palestinian areas was one of the main reasons for the Sharon government's confidence in and popular support for unilateral ground withdrawals and for accordingly transforming the logic of occupation. Sharon's sacking of Chief of Staff Moshe Ya'alon and his replacement with the pilot and former air force commander Dan Halutz several months before the ground evacuation of Gaza testified to the perceived offset of military emphasis from the ground to the air and to the Israeli government's acceptance of Halutz's mantra "technology instead of occupation."[35] Halutz, as head of the air force, supervised almost one hundred operations of targeted assassinations. Until the result of the 2006 War in Lebanon made him realize otherwise, he was known as the strongest proponent of the claim that airpower can gradually replace many of the traditional functions of ground forces. In a lecture he delivered at the military's National Security College in 2001, he explained that "the capability of the air force today renders some traditional assumptions— that victory equals territory—anachronistic,"[36] and he even suggested any subsequent war in Lebanon could be won from the air. "Why do you need to endanger infantry soldiers?" he asked. "I can resolve the entire Lebanon [situation] from the air in 3 to 5 days—a week, maximum."[37] The approach that Halutz promoted was drafted in a military publication that was handed out to members of the senior staff in April 2006, two months before the second Lebanon war, explaining that in future conflicts, new military technology would allow for the transformation of warfare from conflicts based on maneuvers to conflicts based on "standoff capacity, precise fire and the deadly effects of invisible forces, without the need to resort to occupation and with minimum friction with the enemy and the civilian population." The publication further emphasizes the importance of generating an "effect" on the enemy's leadership, either by searing their consciousness or by their "decapitation."[38]

While previously the IDF would cordon off an area with fences and earth dikes and place checkpoints on the approach roads, the airborne occupation of Gaza enforces its closures by leafleting villages and refugee camps around the area to be shut off, declaring it off-limits and then targeting whoever tries to enter. In this manner, the evacuated settlements of the northern part of Gaza have remained under closure ever since the 2005 evacuation. Following the evacuation, a procedure, code named A Knock on the Door, replaced military bulldozers with bomber jets for the purpose of demolishing houses. This new method involves an air force operator telephoning the house to be demolished, as happened on August 2006 at the a-Rahman family home in Jabalia refugee camp. On Thursday, August 24, 2006, at 11:30 in the evening, someone called the telephone at the house of Abed a-Rahman in Jebalia, claiming to be from the IDF.

> The phone had been disconnected because the bill had not been paid to the Palestinian phone company, but was activated for the sake of this conversation. The wife of Abed a-Rahman, Um-Salem, answered the phone.... [On the other side of the line, a voice] said "evacuate the house immediately and notify the neighbors." She asked "who is talking?" and was answered: the IDF. She asked again, but her interlocutor had hung up. Um-Salem tried to use the phone, but it was disconnected again.... The entire family left the house without having the possibility to take anything with them. At 24:00, the house was bombed by military helicopters and was completely destroyed.[39]

This shows that the "evacuation" thus could not be thought of as an act of decolonization, but rather as the reorganization of state power and control and the enactment of a technocolonial rule.

THE POLITICS OF KILLING

For targeted assassinations to assume the preeminence that they have among all other Israeli techniques of domination, they have had to rely upon not only the maturing of operational and technological developments, but also on legal and popular support. When all these components were put in place, less than a year after the beginning of the intifada, and with successful assassinations carried out routinely since then, the appetite for assassinations has grown. A central factor helping maintain a high level of popular support for targeted assassinations was the daily terror alerts that the GSS under Avi Dichter routinely released. Their average during the height of the intifada, from 2001 to 2003, was between forty and fifty a day, and Israeli popular public support for targeted assassination, which seemed not only a response, but a suitable revenge, as well, stood at about 80 percent.[40] In government meetings called to authorize the attacks, Sharon's enthusiasm for successful attacks encouraged the GSS and the military to pursue such operations with greater vigor. Given the high level of Israeli public support for targeted assassinations, no government minister could afford to let slip his or her opposition to the policy or to the timing of a particular assassination as recommended by the GSS, lest it be leaked to the media.

The partial relinquishment of control and the selective absence of government from these decisions brought about the growing autonomy of the security services, which started leading the pace of events. With targeted assassination, security operatives thus filled the political vacuum of the intifada years, dictating developments on the ground. From their own perspective, the GSS and the military believed that targeted assassinations provided the government with "military solutions to situations that were thought of as militarily unsolvable." As the intifada wore on, an obsession with assassination gripped the entire Israeli security system, so much so that in a 2002 meeting called to discuss the assassination of several Palestinian leaders, a military officer suggested conducting one killing every day as a matter of policy. The minister of defense thought it was "indeed an idea," and Sharon seemed excited, but the GSS recommended that the idea be dropped, because it was supposed to be for the GSS, not the military, to decide where and when Palestinians should be killed. (At that point, in any case, killings were already being carried out at an average rate of one every five days.)[41] The military and the GSS, confident of their ability to hit anybody anywhere, at any time, started publishing in advance the names of those to be killed.[42] According to a June 2003 statement by then Chief of Staff Ya'alon, targeted assassinations became the continuation of politics by other means. "Liquidations," he claimed, "gave the political levels a tool to create a change of direction."[43]

The effects of targeted assassination on political developments were varied. One of its effects was assuring that no diplomatic process "forced" on Israel could occur. Whenever a political initiative, local or international, seemed to be emerging, threatening to return the parties to the negotiating table, an assassination followed and derailed it. Until the opening of government and GSS archive, it would be hard to establish this intention beyond a doubt, but the following examples demonstrate a clear pattern of action whose intention is the radicalization of conflict when its level could be subdued. On July 31, 2001, the Israeli Air Force bombed an apartment building in Nablus in which a Hamas officer was located, killing two Hamas leaders, Jamal Mansour and Jamal Salim, and two boys, bringing the end of a nearly two-month-long Hamas cease-fire. The January 2002 killing of Ra'ad Karmi, a leader in Fatah's own militant group, al-Tanzim, in the preparation of which the GSS has already invested millions of shekels, was not prevented, although the killing was certain to bring about the collapse of a cease-fire that started in December 2001 and to bury an American diplomatic initiative. The assassination led to the spate of Palestinian suicide attacks of February and March 2002. On July 23, 2002, a day before al-Tanzim was to announce a unilateral cease-fire, Salah Shehadeh was assassinated, foreclosing this development. A year later, at the beginning of the summer of 2003, another type of cease-fire, a hudna, or tactical truce, was declared, and another American diplomatic initiative was launched. As it was being formulated, on June 10 2003, the military attempted to assassinate Abdul al-Aziz Rantisi, a political leader from the Hamas. A few weeks later, Israeli security forces targeted al-Tanzim militant Mahmoud Shawer in Qalqiliyah, derailing the initiative completely. On December 1, 2003, the same day that the Geneva Initiative was launched, the IDF conducted a massive operation attempting to kill Sheikh Ibrahim Hamed, head of Hamas in Ramallah. In June 2006, just as Mahmoud Abbas was about to declare a referendum vote on a progressive political initiative of the "prisoners' document,"[44] Israel targeted Jamal Abu Samhadana, the commander of the Popular Resistance Committees in Gaza, and the idea for the referendum was cancelled.

From the very start of the intifada, Palestinian political leaders were targets of assassinations. At the end of August 2003, government authorization was given to kill the entire political leadership of Hamas in Gaza without further notice. A place on the assassination list was assured, according to Israeli speakers, to anyone who had crossed the threshold of being involved in planning terror attacks, but in fact, the entire political wing of Hamas was placed on it, regardless of whether or not the target was directly involved in operational planning. The method was referred to as opening the "hunting season"—the first leader to reveal himself would be the first to be killed. The stated intention was to weaken Hamas, which led the armed resistance against Israeli settlers, civilians, and the military and to reinforce Fatah's position in the Gaza Strip. The first one to be killed under these instructions was Ismail Abu Shanab, a relatively moderate political leader of Hamas who was targeted on August 21, 2003. On March 22, 2004, Israel assassinated the spiritual leader of Hamas, Sheikh Ahmed Yassin. A month later, on April 17, 2004, Yassin's successor, Abdul al-Aziz Rantisi was killed. Dichter explained that the reason for these assassinations was to strengthen the position of Abbas and the moderates in the "Palestinian street." At the beginning of 2006, when the "moderates" were ousted by the newly elected Hamas government, Defense Minister Shaul Mofaz repeated the warning, promising that "no one will be immune," including the Palestinian prime minister, Ismail Haniyeh.[45] The logic behind these "decapitations" assumed that new leaders would not be as experienced as those killed and that the relative power of their organizations within the field of Palestinian politics would thus decline. "Killing," according to Shimon Naveh, "injects energy into the enemy system, disrupting its institutional hierarchies," although, as Naveh has said, "there can be no precise prediction of the outcome of these killings," the effect, according to the IDF, is a degree of institutional and political chaos that allows Israeli security forces to sit back and see "how the cards fall."

Not only assassination, but also its suspension, is being used as a weapon. Suspended credible threats of killing generate political effects regardless of the actual assassination taking place. The practical confirmation of this principle was paradoxically pronounced with its cancellation. In July 2007, as part of a package of gestures that the Israeli government "granted" to the Palestinian government of Mahmoud Abbas, Israel announced not only the release of Fatah prisoners (so that they fight Hamas in the West Bank), but also pardons for other activists who were on its target list. The IDF and the GSS offered, under certain conditions that included travel restrictions, to remove from these lists a number of Fatah activists and announced that they will not further pursue attempts for their arrest or assassination. The enthusiastic acceptance by these wanted Palestinians of the conditions imposed by the Israeli security forces demonstrated the pressure that Palestinian militants felt being on Israel's death lists. At several other points during the intifada, Israel's suspension of targeted assassinations was itself used as an incentive to reach a cease-fire on Israel's term.

"Radical" Palestinian leaders could be assassinated to open the way for a more "pragmatic" politics. "Pragmatic" leaders could be assassinated in order to open the way for direct confrontation or to stave off a diplomatic initiative. Other assassinations could have been undertaken in order to "restore order," others still to "create chaos"; some assassinations would be undertaken simply because they could be undertaken and because no one happened to intervene to stop the assassination machine. Theorizing about the political effects of targeted assassinations has thus become almost an industry unto itself, heavily populated with intelligence analysts, game theorists, and other statistically oriented behavioral scientists— many of whom seem addicted to a jargon that is aimed at making unthinkable state behavior appear intelligent, responsible, rational, and inevitable.

A considerable part of Israel's security logic of assassination is grounded in the bias of Israel's intelligence agencies toward personality analysis. The Israeli sociologist Gil Eyal demonstrated that, following a long Orientalist tradition, the Israeli intelligence services have tended to seek motives for political developments, as well as for terror attacks, not in responses to a history of repression or in pursuit of rational political goals, but in the personal irrationalities, idiosyncrasies, and inconsistencies of Arab leaders.[46] When undertaken, political and economic analysis generally has provided no more than a context for the work of psychological profiling.[47] The natural consequence of this logic has been the belief that in killing, Israel's security services remove not only a leader, but also the cause of a political or security problem. Understanding of the resistance to the occupation, in turn, has similarly been bound up with a focus on certain key figures, while the causes behind it have been ignored.

Although so much effort has been put into modeling enemy behavior, and the security services remain confident in their methods, years of targeted assassinations have not managed to limit violence, nor have they reduced Palestinian motivations for resistance, or strengthened President Mahmoud Abbas, or reinforced "the moderates in the Palestinian street." On the contrary, assassinations have fed the conflict by seeding terror, uncertainty, and rage and by promoting social chaos, creating further motivations for violent retaliations and dramatically increasing Palestinian popular support for acts of terror.

Assassinations thus have contributed to the actual emergence of the threat they were purportedly there to preempt. In this respect, Israel's security organizations have not "restored order," but have been acting instead as the agents of chaos. Israeli order is preserved by the systematic destruction of Palestinian order.

The power of targeted assassinations to affect politics has been most strongly felt within the Israeli political system itself. In the half year from the beginning of 2004, when the political debates regarding the evacuation of Gaza settlements began, to June 6, 2004, when the "disengagement plan" came to a vote and was authorized by the Israeli government, targeted assassinations were accelerated, leading to the death of thirty-three Palestinians. In anticipation of the evacuation operation itself, scheduled for August 2005, the level of assassinations increased again, with July 2005 being the bloodiest of that year. This bloodshed helped Sharon present himself as "tough on terror" while pursuing a policy that was understood in Israel as left leaning. In this manner, targeted assassinations and the supposed ability of the Israeli Air Force to maintain a constant "surveillance and strike" capability over Palestinian areas paradoxically increased the support for "territorial compromise" embodied in the ground evacuation of Gaza.

THE "HUMANITARIAN" WAR

The policy of targeted assassination continuously interacted with domestic and international criticism of it to the effect of generating technological and procedural innovations that purportedly aimed at its self-moderation and at reducing the death of bystanders. The transformation in the procedures and technology of airborne assassinations accelerated after the protests that followed the death and destruction caused by the 2002 attack on Salah Shehadeh and increased significantly following the announced refusal of several Israeli Air Force Reserve pilots to take part in such missions if called to do so.[48] On the one hand, the security forces sought to improve legal arguments and moral justifications for the assassinations, and on the other, they sought to improve the precision of intelligence and attacks so that fewer bystanders would get hurt. The first approach was exemplified by an IDF invitation to Asa Kasher, a distinguished professor of philosophy at Tel Aviv University, to provide an ordered ethical defense for targeted assassinations. The resulting "principles of military ethics in fighting terror," developed with a team of officers of the IDF's National Defense College, exemplified the intersection of military efficiency with ethical considerations. It emphasized the standard of self-defense and outlined the military's obligation to reduce the level of civilian casualties. Assassinations were argued for not as retribution for acts of terror already committed, but as responses to the potential of future threats. Unlike acts deemed illegal under criminal law, airborne executions should be considered legal (and moral) if responding not to what a person has done, but to what he may do. The document has been approved by the chief of staff and accepted as IDF standard ethical reference for these attacks.[49] Around the same time the air force began to employ operatives whose task was to minimize "collateral deaths." Using cameras on auxiliary drones, they observed the surrounding context of an impending attack in order to judge the "safest" moment to launch missiles. These specialists have effectively become the "trigger" of the operation, deciding to what level of danger Palestinian bystanders can be acceptably subjected. As one of these operators explained to me, they see their work not as facilitating assassinations, but as saving lives, minimizing the slaughter that would undoubtedly have occurred were they not there to maintain vigilance.[50] I will later return to this line of justification.

Three years later, responding to the widespread condemnation of a March 2006 attack that killed a man and two children, the chief of the air force, Eliezer Shakedy, called a press conference at which he claimed that the air force makes "superhuman efforts in order to reduce the number of innocent civilian casualties in aerial strikes."[51] To prove his claims, he projected charts that numerically "demonstrated" how the air force had reduced the ratio between the victims of aerial raids that it defined as "combatants" and those victims it was willing to concede were "noncombatants" or "uninvolved civilians"—from the death of one "uninvolved person" for every target of assassination in 2002 to one civilian death for every twenty-five targets killed in 2005, he claimed.[52] Data collected by the Israeli human rights organization B'Tselem show that the military figures were skewed—

largely because the military included within the definition of "combatants" any adult man who happened to be in the vicinity of the assassination,[53] but even according to their own and to Palestinian studies, the number of "noncombatant" victims has radically decreased.

The change was due both to technological innovations in the warhead and the missile system and to a change in the command and regulation of these attacks. Most technological developments were related to the mechanical level of the attacks— the design of the warhead. As part of its attempt to reduce unintended casualties, Israel's Armament Development Authority, Rafael, developed the Spike missile to replace the U.S.-made Hellfire—a laser-guided antitank missile—for the purpose of targeted assassinations. The Spike is itself a small, joystick-navigated "kamikaze" drone with an "optical head."[54] Rafael also developed the Firefly, a missile with an even smaller warhead.[55] Clips from the "kamikaze" cameras on "smart missiles" and from other airborne sensors were routinely broadcast in the popular media to support IDF refutations of Palestinian accusations of indiscriminate killing and to focus political and public resolve for the further application of this tactic. The images and videos from these munitions are thus as much a media product as they are "operation footage."[56]

In the summer of 2006, a new type of explosive started to be used in missiles shot in targeted assassinations. That new munitions were used became apparent when doctors in Gaza hospitals started receiving Palestinian victims with horrifying burn wounds, amputations, and internal burns never seen before. A former Israeli Air Force officer and head of the IDF's weapons-development program, Yitzhak Ben-Israel, explained that these new munitions—referred to as "focused lethality munitions" or "munitions of low collateral damage"—were designed to produce a blast more lethal, but also of smaller radius than traditional explosives. "This technology allows [the military] to strike very small targets...without causing damage to bystanders or other persons." Medical and forensic research led an independent Italian investigative team to believe that these munitions were dense inert metal explosives, or DIMEs.[57]

At the end of November 2006, again in response to local and international protests regarding the killing of civilians, the Israeli government wanted to demonstrate that it was acting to regulate targeted assassinations further. It established a "legal committee" to rule on the assassination of individuals, with the assassination of senior political leaders subjected to the opinion of the attorney general. A few weeks later, on December 14, 2006, in response to petitions by the Public Committee Against Torture in Israel and the Palestinian Society for the Protection of Human Rights and the Environment (known by its Arabic acronym, LAW), the Israeli High Court of Justice issued a ruling in which other regulatory directives were outlined: Assassinations could take place only when there is "well-founded, strong and persuasive information as to the identity [of the person assassinated] and his activity"; if they could help curtail terror attacks; if other, more moderate uses of force, such as arrest, cannot take place without gravely endangering the lives of soldiers; and if the assassination does not lead to "disproportionate collateral harm to innocent civilians."[58]

Whether or not these measures have reduced and will reduce the deaths of bystanders in targeted assassinations, a critical perspective cannot allow this possible outcome to exonerate the act. Instead, it must contend with the nature of the claims that these and other military developments in the technology, techniques, and proficiency of targeted assassination will eventually bring about fewer unintended deaths. Otherwise, one would have to accept the Israeli terms of a necro-economy in which a "lesser evil" or "lesser evils," represented by a lower body count, should be measured against an imaginary or real, present or future "greater evil" in the form of more suffering and death on both sides.[59]

The problem of the "lesser evil" presents itself as the necessity for a choice of action in situations where the available options seem to be limited. The condition by which choice presents itself affirms an economic model embedded at the heart of ethics according to which various forms of suffering can be calculated (as if they were algorithms in mathematical minimum problems), evaluated, and acted upon. The articulation of the dilemma of the "lesser evil" has its origin in the classical philosophy of ethics and in theology and has been invoked in a staggeringly diverse set of contexts—from individual situational ethics through political choices to international relations. Significantly, it has recently been prominently invoked in the context of attempts to govern the economics of violence in the context of the "war on terror" and to moderate the power of brutal regimes, but also in maneuvering through the paradoxes and complicities of human rights and humanitarian aid.

In relation to the "global war on terror," the terms of this argument were recently articulated by the human rights scholar and now deputy leader of the Liberal Party of Canada, Michael Ignatieff. Ignatieff claims that in the "war on terror," democratic societies may need to establish state mechanisms that would regulate the breach of some rights and allow their security services to engage in other covert and unsavory state actions—in his eyes, a "lesser evil"—in order to fend off or to minimize potential "greater evils" such as terror attacks.[60] Ignatieff is even willing to consider Israeli targeted assassinations under conditions similar to those articulated by the Israeli High Court of Justice as "qualifying within the effective moral-political framework of the lesser evil."[61] For Alan Dershowitz, one of the most vocal apologists for Israel in the United States, "targeted assassination

[is] the polar opposite of collective punishment" and is therefore not only legal, but, under the conditions stated above, ethical.[62]

In the terms of this necroeconomy, targeted assassinations are to be understood as the "lesser evil" alternative to possible greater evils that could occur to Israelis, but that could occur as well to the Palestinians themselves. Israel, which undertakes these operations, would like Palestinians to understand that, beyond protecting its own population, the use of targeted assassinations helps it restrain more brutal measures that would affect the entire Palestinian population, with targeted assassinations killing only—or mostly—those "guilty." According to former Chief of Staff Ya'alon, "focused obstructions are important because they [communicate to the Palestinians that we] make a distinction between the general public and the instigator of terror."[63] As I mentioned above, however, the intelligence necessary for targeted assassinations relies on "collective measures" such as mass arrests and the checkpoint/terminal system.

However, as Adi Ophir has suggested, this conception of the "lesser evil" is problematic even according to the terms of its own proposed economy. The economy of violence assumes the possibility of a lesser means and the risk of more violence, but questions of violence are forever unpredictable. The supposed "lesser evil" may always be more violent than the violence it opposes, and there can be no end to the challenges that stem from the impossibility of calculation. A less brutal measure is also a measure that may easily be naturalized, accepted, and tolerated.[64] When exceptional means are normalized, they can be more frequently applied. Elevating targeted assassinations into a legally and morally acceptable practice makes them part of the state's legal options, part of a list of counterterrorism techniques, with all sense of horror lost. Because they help normalize low-intensity conflict, the overall duration of this conflict can be extended, and finally, more "lesser evils" can be committed, with the result that the greater evil is reached cumulatively. "Lesser evils" can thus bring about greater evils, even according to the very economy they invoke.

However, because "lesser-evil" arguments measure and compromise only Palestinian life and rights for the sake of Israeli security, which stands as a nonnegotiable or unmeasured absolute value, they cannot be understood as properly moral arguments and should simply be understood according to the Israeli utilitarian logic of warfare, its efficiency, and the way it is mediated locally and internationally. Cases of colonial powers seeking to justify themselves with the rhetoric of improvement, civility, and reform are almost the constant of colonial history.

An analogous phenomenon that can help clarify the paradox of the "lesser evil" can be observed in the IDF's use of rubber-coated steel munitions. Soldiers believe that "rubber bullets" are nonlethal munitions and that their use demonstrates restraint in situations that are not life threatening. But this perception leads to their more frequent and indiscriminate use, causing death and permanent injury to many Palestinian demonstrators, mainly children.[65] Similarly, the purported military ability to perform "controlled," "elegant," "pinhead accurate," and "discriminate" killing can bring about more destruction and death than "traditional" strategies do, because these methods, combined with the manipulative and euphoric rhetoric used to promulgate them, induce decision makers to authorize their frequent and extended use. The illusion of precision, here part of a rhetoric of restraint, gives the military-political apparatus the necessary justification to use explosives in civilian environments where they could not be used without injuring or killing civilians. The lower the threshold of violence that a certain means is believed to possess, the more frequent its application tends to become.

The "lesser evil" approach that has sought to moderate Israel's war on the Palestinians and to normalize Israeli control led the IDF to inaugurate, in the middle of 2003, the program Another Life, whose aim was to "minimize the damage to the Palestinian life fabric in order to avoid the humanitarian crisis that will necessitate the IDF to completely take over the provision of food and services to the Palestinian population."[66] This program has turned "humanitarianism" into a strategic category in Israeli military operations and has influenced the design of its various instruments of control. Indeed, "humanitarian" has become the most common buzzword in various matters of occupation design, with the designation of "humanitarian gates," "humanitarian terminals," "humanitarian technology," and "humanitarian awareness," as well as—according to a procedure already put in effect since the beginning of the intifada—a "humanitarian officer" (usually a middle-aged reserve soldier) employed in checkpoints to smooth the process of passage and to mediate between the needs of Palestinians and the orders of soldiers.

The paradox of the lesser evil further affects most practitioners who operate the various systems in the ecology of the occupation: the army commander who, according to international law, is responsible for the territories under his domination and who attempts to administer Palestinian life (and death) in an enlightened manner; the security agents who introduce new spatiotechnological means of domination (arguing for them as more humane) and who generate new types of powers; human rights organizations and lawyers who lodge petitions challenging the legality of those means and powers and thus affirm the logic of the system as a whole; the humanitarian agent providing life-sustaining substances and medical help and who thus sustains the occupation; the politicians, the intellectuals, the Palestinian administrator, and not least the Palestinian civilian who is the subject of this regime.

In regard to the humanitarian agents, Israel's system of domination has learned to use the work of Palestinian, international, and Israeli organizations to fill the void left by a dysfunctional Palestinian Authority and to manage life in the Occupied Palestinian Territories. In spite of the fundamental moral differences between these groups, the logic of the lesser evil allows for moments of cooperation between organizations whose stated aims are widely different. Indeed, the urgent and important criticism that peace organizations often level at the IDF to the effect that it is dehumanizing its enemies masks another, more dangerous process by which the military incorporates into its operations the logic of, and even seeks to cooperate directly with, the very humanitarian and human rights organizations that oppose it. Israeli theorist Ariella Azoulay has claimed that although it has brought the Occupied Territories to the verge of hunger, the Israeli government tries to control the flow of traffic, money, and aid in such a way as to prevent the situation reaching a point of total collapse because of the international intervention, possibly under a UN mandate, that might follow.[67]

It is in this "pragmatic" approach that the principle of the "lesser evil" justifies and naturalizes crimes and other forms of injustice and masks political responsibilities. By accepting the necessity to choose the "lesser evil," oppositional and advocacy groups accept the validity of the systems that have imposed these choices, blocking possible ways to struggle against and refute the logic and validity of the governmental rationality that grounds them. Writing about the collaboration and cooperation of ordinary Germans with the Nazi regime, mainly by those employed in the Civil Service (but also by the Jewish councils set up by the Nazis), Hannah Arendt explained that the argument for the "lesser evil" had become one of the most important "mechanisms built into the machinery of terror and crimes." She explained that "acceptance of lesser evils [has been] consciously used in conditioning the government officials as well as the population at large to the acceptance of evil as such," to the degree that "those who choose the lesser evil forget very quickly that they chose evil." She further claimed that even for the practical consequences, it is always better if enough people refuse to participate in criminal state behavior, rather than engage in moderating it.[68]

Against all those who stayed in Germany to make things better from within, against all acts of collaboration, especially those undertaken for the sake of the moderation of harm, against the argument that the "lesser evil" of collaboration with brutal regimes is acceptable if it might prevent or divert greater evils, she called for individual disobedience and collective disorder. Participation, she insisted, communicates consent. Moreover, it hands support to the oppressor. When nothing else is possible, to do nothing is the last effective form of resistance, and the practical consequences of refusal are nearly always better if enough people refuse. In her essay "The Eggs Speak Up," a sarcastic reference to Stalin's dictum that "you can't make an omelet without breaking a few eggs," Arendt pleaded for "a radical negation of the whole concept of lesser evil in politics."[69]

The moral principle of the "lesser evil" could be discerned in the legal category of "proportionality" employed by the High Court of Justice when it was called to rule on matters relating to "security" and "human rights" considerations in the context of the occupation. According to the principle of "proportionality," the state must weigh its alternative security measures in a way that balances security needs against the livelihood of the Palestinian inhabitants. Because of the constant international criticism of the occupation, it is always in the interest of the state to moderate its violence and take into account the "humanitarian issues" arising from the occupation, thereby deflecting attention from the fundamental illegitimacy of the entire project. Although it often has seemed as if the Israeli High Court of Justice has adopted a profoundly adversarial position toward the government, by moderating the attitudes of the military and "balancing" rights against security, the court has effectively taken part in the very logic by which the occupation works.[70]

Furthermore, when, in the aftermath of the court's rulings, the military itself began using the vocabulary of international law, principles such as "proportionality" started to become compatible with military goals such as "efficiency," helping make military action more economical. In this sense, the "lesser evil" argument relates to the discursive nature of warfare and especially to the discursive nature of low-intensity war.

Military threats can function only if gaps are maintained between the *possible* destruction that an army can inflict in the application of its full destructive capacity and the *actual* destruction that it does inflict. Restraint is what allows for the possibility of further escalation.[71] A degree of restraint is thus part of the logic of almost every conventional military operation: However bad military attacks may appear to be, they could always get worse. At the moment when this gap between the possible and the actual application of force closes, war is no longer a language, and violence is stripped of semiotics and simply aims to make the enemy disappear as a subject.[72]

The promoters of the instruments, techniques, and rhetoric supporting such "lesser evils" believe that by developing and perfecting them, they actually exercise a restraining effect on the government and on the rest of the security forces, which would otherwise succeed in pushing for the further radicalization of violence, and that targeted assassinations are the more moderate alternative to the devastating capacity for destruction that the military actually possesses and would unleash in the form of a full-scale invasion or the renewal of territorial occupation, should the enemy exceed an "acceptable" level of violence or breach some unspoken agreement in the violent discourse of attacks and retaliations. Confirming this logic, only a few weeks before the June 2006 invasion of Gaza, air force chief Shakedy, arguing for targeted assassinations, explained that "the only alternative to aerial attacks is a ground operation and the reoccupation of Gaza" and that targeted assassination "is the most precise tool we have."[73]

The reoccupation of Gaza starting in June 2006 and the Lebanon war of July–August 2006 demonstrated that more destructive alternatives are always possible, especially when the "unwritten rules" of low-intensity conflict are perceived to have been broken. From the June 28 kidnapping of an Israeli soldier in Gaza and until December 2006, over 500 Palestinians were killed, including 88 minors, and more than 2,700 injured.[74] Forty-six million dollars worth of infrastructure, including a power plant, and 270 private houses and residences, was destroyed. This should be understood as an eruption of violence meant to sustain the threat of greater measures. In terms of their justification, targeted assassinations thus exist at the middle of the spectrum between war and peace.

Naturally, I am not suggesting that "greater evils" should be preferred to lesser ones or that wars should be more brutal. Rather, I am suggesting that we question the very terms of the economy of evils, the system that has presented to us its choice as inevitable. The dilemma, if we are still to think in its terms, should thus not be only about which of the bad options to choose, but whether to choose at all and thus to accept the very terms of the question. When asked to choose between the two horns of an angry bull, Robert Pirsig suggested alternatives: One can "refuse to enter the arena," "throw sand in the bull's eyes," or even "sing the bull to sleep."[75]

The positioning of the lesser-evil dilemma is integral to political militarism—a culture that sees violence as a permanent rule of history and thus military contingencies as the principal alternative available to politicians. Israeli militarism accordingly always has sought military solutions to political problems.[76] Locked within the limits defined by the degrees of violence, Israel continually forecloses the exploration of other avenues for negotiations and participation in a genuine political process. At the beginning of 2006, Chief of Staff Dan Halutz expressed this view when he stated that the intifada is part of an unresolvable permanent conflict between Jews and Palestinians that started in 1929. The military, according to Halutz, must therefore gear itself to operate within an environment saturated with conflict and in a future of permanent violence. With this, he echoed an often-recurring claim within Israeli security discourse, as when in June 1977, Foreign Minister Moshe Dayan explained the presumption that Israel's conflict with the Palestinians could be "solved" was fundamentally flawed. "The question was not, 'What is the solution?' but 'How do we live without a solution?'"[77] The "lesser evil" approach thus relates to Israeli unilateralism, to the perception that there is no partner, and to the idea of infinite conflict. Territorial, ground occupation is thus projected as a "necessary evil" in the West Bank and assassinations as a "necessary evil" in Gaza. In the absence of both options—a political solution, on the one hand, or the possibility of a decisive military outcome, on the other— the Israeli military thus merely "manages the conflict." The ideology of the lesser evil, the lesser-evil occupation, has thus replaced the political horizon and a quest for justice. At the beginning of 2006, Halutz still thought that the precision methods of the Israeli Air Force would help keep the conflict "on a flame low enough for Israeli society to be able to live and to prosper within it."[78] This projection of endless war in all likelihood will fulfill itself.

NOTES

1   Interview with Ephraim Segoli, Tel Aviv, May 22, 2006.

2   B'Tselem, "Statistics: Fatalities," available on-line at http://www.btselem.org/English/Statistics/Casualties.asp (last accessed May 10, 2008).

3   See chap. 9 in Eyal Weizman, *Hollow Land: Israel's Architecture of Occupation* (London: Verso, 2007).

4   In "Necropolitics," Achille Mbembe follows Michel Foucault to argue that sovereignty is located not only within the institutions of the geographically defined nation-state or, as postmodern thinkers suggest, within the operational networks of supranational institutions, but in the capacity of power to make decisions regarding life and death. According to Foucault, the other side of the politics that engages with the management of life (bio-politics) is the administration of death (thanato-politics). See Michel Foucault, *Society Must Be Defended: Lectures at the Collège de France, 1975–1976,* ed. Mauro Bertani, Alessandro Fontana, and François Ewald, trans. David Macey (New York: Picador, 2003), p. 25, and Achille Mbembe, "Necropolitics," *Public Culture* 15, no. 1 (Winter 2003): pp. 11–40.

5   Interview with Ephraim Segoli, Tel Aviv, May 22, 2006.

6   See Raviv Druker and Ofer Shelah, *Boomerang* (Jerusalem: Keter Press, 2005) (in Hebrew), pp. 161–216.

7   Aharon Yoffe, "Focus Preemption, Chances and Dangers," *Nativ* 109, no. 2 (March 2006) (in Hebrew). See also Yedidia Ya'ari and Haim Assa, *Diffused Warfare: War in the 21st Century* (Tel Aviv: Miskal—Yediot Aharonot Books and Chemed Books, 2005) (in Hebrew), p. 37. The book is the summary of positions developed within the so-called "Alternative Team" and under the influence of the Operational Theory Research Institute (OTRI). Yedidya Ya'ari, the former commander of the Israeli Navy, and Haim Assa, a former member of a comparable Israeli Air Force think tank, directed the team. Affiliated with it were air force pilot Dror Ben David, Brigadier General Gadi Eisenkott, and Brigadier General Aviv Kochavi. General Benni Gantz was assigned to implement this study within the Israeli Defense Forces. The Alternative

Team was operating in cooperation with the U.S. Transformation Group under the U.S. secretary of defense, Donald Rumsfeld. In 2006, the Israeli chief of staff, Dan Halutz, dismantled the Alternative Team. There were a large number of parallel and smaller teams with similar aims, as well, such as the Military Research Centre for the Study of the Tactical Environment, directed by Gabrial Siboni. On the latter, see Gabrial Siboni, "The Importance of Activity," *Bamahane* (In the Camp), the IDF's official journal, December 31, 2004, (in Hebrew), pp. 14–18.

8   Interview with Brigadier General (ret.) Shimon Naveh, former director of the OTRI in the IDF. All the following quotes from Naveh are based on interviews conducted on September 15, 2005 (by telephone), March 7, 2006 (by telephone), and April 11, 2006 and May 22–23, 2006 (at an Israeli Army Intelligence military base in Glilot, near Tel Aviv). All transcripts and translations to English of the interviews were sent to Naveh for confirmation of their content. All future references to the interview refer to those above unless mentioned otherwise.

9   Interview with former member of Unit 504, May 2006, who preferred to remain anonymous.

10   Robert Fisk, "Death by Remote Control as Hit Squads Return," *The Independent,* May 13, 2001.

11   Neve Gordon, "Rationalizing Extra-Judicial Executions: The Israeli Press and the Legitimization of Abuse," *International Journal of Human Rights* 8, no. 3 (Autumn 2004): p. 305. In 2005 *Ha'aretz,* Israel's liberal daily, started to publish, as a matter of policy, the names of Palestinians killed by Israel in all its military operations.

12   B'Tselem, "IDF Helicopter Missile-Fire Kills Four Palestinian Civilians and Wounds Dozens," August 2002, available on-line at http://www.btselem.org/English/Testimonies/20020831_ Tubas_Killing_Witness_Aref_Daraghmeh.asp (last accessed September 6, 2008).

13   Orna Ben-Naftali and Keren Michaeli, "'We Must Not Make a Scarecrow of the Law': A Legal Analysis of the Israeli Policy of Targeted Killings," *Cornell International Law Journal* 36, no. 2 (Spring 2004): p. 234 n. 22.

14   See Naomi Klein, "Laboratory for a Fortressed World," *The Nation,* July 2, 2007: "Another star of the Paris Air Show will be Israeli defense giant Elbit, which plans to showcase its Hermes 450 and 900 unmanned air vehicles. As recently as May, according to press reports, Israel used the drones on bombing missions in Gaza. Once tested in the territories, they are exported abroad: The Hermes has already been used at the Arizona-Mexico border."

15   In November 2002, a car travelling in a remote part of Yemen was destroyed by a missile fired from an unmanned Predator drone, killing six suspected members of al-Qaeda. While the U.S. administration did not publicly acknowledge responsibility for the attack, officials let it be known that the CIA had carried it out. The June 2006 killing of Abu Musab al-Zarqawi and the January 2006 attempt to kill Ayman al-Zawahiri were undertaken from the air. Previous strikes killed Mohammed Atef, al-Qaeda's military chief, and Hamza Rabia, a senior operative in Pakistan. Currently, the U.S. military plans to double the number of Predator and Global Hawk drones used for surveillance and targeting. See Anthony Dworkin, "The Yemen Strike: The War on Terrorism Goes Global," Crimes of War Project, November 14, 2002, available on-line at http://www.crimesofwar.org/onnews/news-yemen.html (last accessed September 6, 2008); Chris Downes, "'Targeted Killing' in an Age of Terror: The Legality of the Yemen Strike," *Journal of Conflict and Security Law* 9, no. 2 (2004): pp. 277–79.

16   Ludwig von Bertalanffy defines a system as a complex of interacting elements. Thus, a system's problems, according to Bertalanffy, are problems of the interrelations of a great number of variables that occur in the field of politics, economics, industry, commerce, and

military conduct. See Ludwig von Bertalanffy, *General System Theory: Foundations, Development, Applications* (New York: George Braziller, 1976). In military discourse, systems analysis originated after the end of World War II and was instrumental in the conception in 1982 of the U.S. military doctrine of "Airland Battle," which emphasized targeting an enemy at its systematic bottlenecks—bridges, headquarters, and supply lines—in the attempt to throw an enemy's system of operation off balance. It was conceived to check Soviet invasion in Central Europe and was first applied in the Gulf War of 1991. The advance of this line of thinking led to the development of the Network-centric Warfare Doctrine in the context of the Revolution in Military Affairs (RMA) after the end of the Cold War. (In fact, what the military refers to as "networks"—implying the nonhierarchical cooperation of dispersed parts—should technically be referred to as "systems," which are distributed structures with a centralized command.) In the context of the IDF, systems analysis is used in both the air and ground forces. One of the main promoters of systems theory and analysis is Shimon Naveh. (See note 8.)

17 The idea of people as infrastructure was developed in another context—that of African cities. See AbdouMaliq Simone, "People as Infrastructure: Intersecting Fragments in Johannesburg," *Public Culture,* no. 3 (Fall 2004): pp. 407–29.

18 This logic was reflected in a March 2006 presentation to U.S. security personnel at the Washington, D.C. Brookings Institution by Avi Dichter, the former chief of Israel's General Security Service. Dichter, the driving force behind the tactical success and frequent application of targeted assassinations, observed that "by eliminating…generators of terror through arrests (the preferred method) or by targeted killings (if absolutely necessary), a state can greatly disrupt the operations of terrorist organizations." See: Avi Dichter and Daniel Byman, "Israel's Lessons for Fighting Terrorists and Their Implications for The United States," Analysis Paper Number 8, March 2006, the Saban Centre for Middle East Policy at the Brookings Institute, Washington, D.C.

19 Interview with Brigadier General (ret.) Shimon Naveh.

20 Giulio Douhet, *Command of the Air* (1921; London: Ayer Publishing, 1942). The full text is available on-line at http://www.airforcehistory.hq.af.mil/Publications/fulltext/command_of_the_air.pdf (last accessed September 6, 2008).

21 However, an important distinction must still be maintained. The military approaches that the IDF employs in Lebanon are strategically distinct from those employed in the Occupied Palestinian Territories. According to the political scientist James Ron, in Lebanon, Israel employed degrees of violence that greatly exceed those employed in the Occupied Territories, and consequently, casualty figures in Lebanon were much higher than those in the West Bank and Gaza. Ron explains that these differences in military approach are shaped by differences in degrees of control over territory and population. In the Occupied Territories, enclosed within Israeli-controlled territory, Israel still bears some responsibility for the welfare of the populations, whereas in Lebanon—which is completely beyond the state's frontier—the civilian population could be attacked with ferocity without economic and other repercussions to Israel. James Ron, *Frontiers and Ghettos: State Violence in Serbia and Israel* (Berkeley: University of California Press, 2003).

22 Sven Linqvist, *A History of Bombing,* trans. Linda Haverty Rugg (New York: New Press, 2000), entry 101.

23 Philip Anthony Towle, *Pilots and Rebels: The Use of Aircraft in Unconventional Warfare, 1918–*

1988 (London: Brassey's Defence Publishers, 1989), p. 17; David Willard Parsons, "British Air Control: A Model for the Application of Air Power in Low-Intensity Conflict?" *Airpower Journal* (Summer 1994), available on-line at http://www.airpower.maxwell.af.mil/airchronicles/apj/apj94/parsons.html (last accessed September 7, 2008).

24 Quoted in Lt. Colonel David J. Dean, USAF, "Air Power in Small Wars: The British Air Control Experience," *Air University Review* 34, no. 5 (July–August 1985).

25 Dean, "Air Power in Small Wars." David Omissi, *Air Power and Colonial Control: The Royal Air Force 1919–1939* (Manchester: Manchester University Press, 1990). David MacIsaac, "Voices from the Central Blue: The Air Power Theorists," in Peter Paret, *Makers of Modern Strategy, From Machiavelli to the Nuclear Age* (Oxford: Oxford University Press, 1986), pp. 624–47, especially p. 633.

26 Linqvist, *A History of Bombing,* entry 102.

27 Brigadier General Yair Golan, in a discussion with the research group for the study of the catastrophization in the Occupied Territories at the Van Leer Jerusalem Institute, April 20, 2007.

28 Ronen Shnayderman, "Take No Prisoners: The Fatal Shooting of Palestinians by Israeli Security Forces during 'Arrest Operations,'" B'Tselem, May 2005, available on-line at http://www.btselem.org/Download/200505_Take_No_Prisoners_Eng.pdf (last accessed September 7, 2008). See also Al-Haq, "Indiscriminate and Excessive Use of Force: Four Palestinians Killed During Arrest Raid, May 24, 2006," available on-line at http://www.alhaq.org/etemplate.php?id=8 (last accessed March 7, 2009).

29 David Kretzmer, "Targeted Killing of Suspected Terrorists: Extra-Judicial Executions or Legitimate Means of Defense?" *The European Journal of International Law* 16, no. 2 (2005): pp. 196, 207.

30 Press briefing by Colonel Daniel Reisner, director of the International Law Department of the IDF Legal Division, Israeli Ministry of Foreign Affairs, November 15, 2000, available on-line at http://www.mfa.gov.il/MFA/MFAArchive/2000_2009/2000/11/Press%20Briefing%20by%20Colonel%20Daniel%20Reisner-%20Head%20of (last accessed September 7, 2008).

31 The Israeli legal scholar Eyal Benvenisti claimed that the proper measure to judge whether Israel continues to be bound by the obligations of an occupying power is the facts on the ground: "If there were areas under Palestinian control, they were not subject to Israeli occupation." See Eyal Benvenisti, "Israel and the Palestinians: What Laws Were Broken," Crimes of War Project, available on-line at http://www.crimesofwar.org/expert/me-intro.html (last accessed September 7, 2008). Charles Shamas, a Ramallah-based legal expert, joined others in claiming that since Israel still exercises effective control over movement between localities, over the supply of goods, and over access to natural resources, it has in effect authority over the enactment of Palestinian legislation and therefore continues to be bound by the duties of an occupying power. Compare, as well, Baruch Kimmerling's notion of "system of control" in "Boundaries and Frontiers of the Israeli Control System," in Baruch Kimmerling (ed.), *The Israeli State and Society: Boundaries and Frontiers* (Albany: State University of New York Press, 1989), pp. 265–84.

32 Indeed, since the evacuation of Gaza, the IDF became even more willing to employ violence against the Palestinians. In 2006 alone, Israeli forces killed 405 Palestinians in Gaza, half of them civilians, including 88 minors. During the same year, Israel killed 22 Palestinians in targeted assassinations. Following a certain decline in 2007 (293 Palestinians killed in Gaza,

approximately one-third of them civilians) the level of violence peaked again in the beginning of 2008: According to B'Tselem, in only one week, from February 27 to the afternoon of March 3, 106 Palestinians were killed in the Gaza Strip, at least 54 of whom were civilians. In June 2006, Israel bombed the electric grid in Gaza, cutting off 700,000 people from electricity, and has repeatedly restricted electricity and fuel supplies to Gaza ever since. For data on causalities see, respectively: B'Tselem: "683 people Killed in the Conflict in 2006," available on-line at http://www.btselem.org/english/press_releases/20061228.asp; B'Tselem, "Human Rights in the Occupied Territories, 2007 Annual Report," at http://www.btselem.org/Download/200712_Annual_Report_eng.pdf; and B'Tselem, "Contrary to Israel's Chief of Staff, at least Half of Those Killed in Gaza Did Not Take Part in the Fighting," press release, March 3, 2008, at http://www.btselem.org/english/Press_Releases/20080303.asp (all last accessed September 7, 2008).

33 Ya'ari and Assa, *Diffused Warfare Century,* pp. 9–13 (all translations from Hebrew are mine).

34 The last of the terms was coined in a joint program between the former commander of a fighter squadron, Dror Ben David, and researchers at the Operational Theory Research Institute.

35 Halutz constantly defended the technology behind his airborne assassinations, even when it regularly has taken the lives of many bystanders. When asked for his reaction to the death of many civilians in an operation of targeted assassination, he famously retorted, "If you want to know what I feel when I release a bomb, I will tell you: I feel a light bump to the plane as a result of the bomb's release. A second later, it's gone, and that's all. That is what I feel." See Vered Levy-Barzilai, "Halutz: The High and the Mighty," *Ha'aretz Magazine,* August 21, 2002.

36 Israel Harel, "The IDF Protects Itself," *Ha'aretz,* August 29, 2006.

37 Amir Rapaport, "Dan Halutz is a Bluff, Interview with Shimon Naveh," *Ma'ariv,* Yom Kippur Supplement, October 1, 2006. (in Hebrew)

38 Ofer Shelah and Yoav Limor, *Captives of Lebanon* (Tel Aviv: Miskal—Yedioth Aharonoth Books and Chemed Books, 2007) (in Hebrew), p. 199.

39 Darryl Li, "Gaza Consultancy—Research Findings, 20 to 27 August 2006," draft submitted to B'Tselem, September 10, 2006. Testimony number 3287. Unpublished.

40 A *Ma'ariv* Gallup Poll of August 10, 2001 revealed that 76 percent of the public polled supported assassinations. In later years, and in particular as a result of the killing of many bystanders, public support dropped considerably. In June 2003, at the start of the campaign to assassinate the leadership of Hamas, an opinion poll by the daily newspaper *Yedioth Ahronoth* found that 58 percent of Israelis polled said the military should at least temporarily discontinue targeted killings. After the "disengagement" from Gaza and a quite persistent rocket shelling on neighboring Israeli towns and villages, support for assassination grew again. On January 6, 2003, *Ha'aretz* estimated this support to be more than 80 percent. See Druker and Shelah, *Boomerang,* p. 216.

41 *Ibid.,* p. 161.

42 "The IDF Published a List of Seven 'Assassination Candidates,'" *Ha'aretz,* July 6, 2001.

43 Ya'ari and Assa, *Diffused Warfare,* p. 147. Druker and Shelah, *Boomerang,* p. 162 and n. 96.

44 Officially called the National Conciliation Document of the Palestinian Prisoners, "the prisoners' document" was written by Palestinian prisoners in Israeli jails. In it, representatives of Fatah, Hamas, Islamic Jihad, the Popular Front for the Liberation of Palestine (PFLP), and the Democratic Front for the Liberation of Palestine (DFLP) tried to articulate policy posi-

tions that would reconcile the various factions.

45 Quoted in Amos Harel and Arnon Regular, "IAF probe: Civilians Spotted Too Late to Divert Missiles in Gaza Strike," *Ha'aretz,* March 7, 2006. See also Soha Abdelaty, "Intifada Timeline, September 30–October 6, 2004," *Al-Ahram Weekly Online,* at http://weekly.ahram.org. eg/2004/710/fo5.htm (last accessed September 7, 2008); and Vincent Cannistraro, "Assassination Is Wrong—and Dumb," *Washington Post,* August 30, 2001.

46 For many years, Yassir Arafat remained at the top of Israel's Most Wanted list. The *dibbuk* haunting Israeli security services, Arafat's "irrational character" was blamed for almost every political stalemate or outbreak of violence. Chief of Military Intelligence Amos Gilad, who developed a personal obsession with him, described Arafat thus: "Mentally, Arafat feels at his best when he is surrounded by a reality of flames, fire, suffering and blood." Only an explicit promise extracted from Sharon by George W. Bush prevented the IDF from doing what it really wanted to do and assassinate Arafat himself. Gil Eyal, *The Disenchantment of the Orient: Expertise in Arab Affairs and the Israeli State* (Palo Alto, CA: Stanford University Press, 2006), p. 290 n. 93, 189.

47 Eyal, *The Disenchantment of the Orient,* p. 183.

48 Chris McGreal, "We're Air Force Pilots, Not Mafia. We Don't Take Revenge," *The Guardian,* December 3, 2003.

49 The principles of the military ethics of fighting terror were developed by a team of the IDF's National Defense College, headed by Major General Amos Yadlin, then commander of the college. The team included other officers with experience in such military activities, as well as experts in international law and ethics. The final document, produced by Yadlin and Asa Kasher, was presented to the IDF chief of staff and to generals involved in fighting terror. The document was approved, and besides being used in different stages of the education of officers, is currently being used for the preparation of proposed explanatory guidelines for a variety of specific situations and operations. Asa Kasher and Amos Yadlin, "The Military Ethics of Fighting Terror: An Israeli Perspective," *Journal of Military Ethics* 4 (2005). See also Asa Kasher and Amos Yadlin, "Assassination and Preventive Killing," *SAIS Review* 25, no. 1 (2005): pp. 41–57.

50 Interview with an Israeli Air Force operator of unmanned drones, April 2005. The operator's name cannot be revealed.

51 Harel and Regular, "IAF Probe."

52 Further data published in *Ha'aretz* states that between 2002 and 2003, 50 percent of people killed were uninvolved civilians, that in 2005, the number dropped to 3.5 percent, that in 2006, when attacks accelerated after the abduction of an Israeli soldier, it was 10 percent, and that in 2007, it dropped again to its lowest level, between 2 and 3 percent. Amos Harel, "Precise Military," *Ha'aretz,* December 30, 2008.

53 Amos Harel, "Nothing 'Surgical' about Air Force Attacks in Urban Areas," *Ha'aretz,* June 22, 2006. The B'Tselem figures are available on-line at http://www.btselem.org/English/ Statistics/Casualties.asp (last accessed September 7, 2008).

54 David A. Fulghum and Robert Wall, "Israel Starts Reexamining Military Missions and Technology," *Aviation Week,* August 20, 2006.

55 Laura Blumenfeld, "In Israel, a Divisive Struggle over Targeted Killing," *Washington Post,* August 27, 2006.

56 Indeed, during the 1991 Gulf War, the public was fed images of "kamikaze bombs"—smart

bombs or laser-guided munitions—as proof of the technological superiority and surgical skills of the U.S. military. Harun Farocki, "War From a Distance," lecture delivered at the Academy of Fine Arts, Vienna, January 13, 2005.

57 Quoted in Meron Rapoport, "Italian TV: Israel Used New Weapon Prototype in Gaza Strip," *Ha'aretz,* October 12, 2006. These weapons are made of a carbon-fiber casing filled with tungsten powder—a metal capable of conducting very high temperatures. Upon detonation, the tungsten particles are propelled outward in a relatively small (about four meters), but very deadly cloud, causing severe burns, amputated limbs, and internal burns.

58 HCJ 769/02, *The Public Committee against Torture in Israel v. The Government of Israel.* Previous petitions to the High Court of Justice against targeted assassinations (for example HCJ 5872/2002, M. K. Muhammed Barake vs. Prime Minister and Minister of Defense) were dismissed.

59 "Evil" in this context is best understood, following Adi Ophir, as a category displaced from the realm of the divine or diabolical and relocated in a social order in which suffering and pain could have been, but were not prevented. See Adi Ophir, *The Order of Evils: Toward an Ontology of Morals,* trans. Rela Mazali and Havi Carel (New York: Zone Books, 2005). "Evils can only be justified by appealing to more grave hypothetical evils that could have been caused if the prevention or disengagement actions would have taken place" (section 7.100, p. 339). "The justification displaces the discussion from one order of exchange, in which the one harmed tries to create a link between damage or suffering and compensation, to another order of exchange, in which the defendant tries to create a link between evils that occurred to possible evils that might have occurred" (section 3.432, p. 152).

60 Michael Ignatieff, *The Lesser Evil: Political Ethics in an Age of Terror* (Princeton, NJ: Princeton University Press, 2004).

61 According to Ignatieff, assassinations should be "applied to the smallest number of people, used as a last resort, and kept under the adversarial scrutiny of an open democratic system." Furthermore, "assassination can be justified only if…less violent alternatives, like arrest and capture, endanger…personnel or civilians…[and] where all reasonable precautions are taken to minimize collateral damage and civilian harm." *Ibid.,* pp. 8, 129–33.

62 Alan M. Dershowitz, *The Case for Israel* (Hoboken, NJ: John Wiley & Sons, 2003), p. 173.

63 Quoted in Amos Harel and Avi Isacharoff, *The Seventh War* (Tel Aviv: Miskal—Yedioth Aharonoth Books and Chemed Books, 2004) (in Hebrew), p. 343.

64 Ophir, *The Order of Evils,* section 7.100, p. 339; sections 7.2 and 7.3, pp. 327–29. See, also, for example, section 7.335, p. 375.

65 Iris Giller, "A Death Foretold: Firing of 'Rubber' Bullets to Disperse Demonstrations in the Occupied Territories," B'Tselem, November 1998, available on-line at http://www.btselem.org/Download/199812_Death_Foretold_Eng.rtf (last accessed September 7, 2008).

66 Harel and Isacharoff, *The Seventh War,* p. 343.

67 Ariella Azoulay, "Hunger in Palestine: The Event That Never Was," in Anselm Franke, Rafi Segal, and Eyal Weizman (eds.), *Territories, Islands, Camps and Other States of Utopia* (Cologne: Walter Koening, 2003), pp. 154–57. According to the chief of military intelligence, Amos Gilad, "hunger is when people walk around with a swollen belly, collapse and die. There is no hunger in the Palestinian territories." Druker and Shelah, *Boomerang,* p. 329. Since Hamas was elected to power in January 2006, Israel has used the weapon of economic strangulation as a means of political pressure, withholding all Palestinian tax monies—about

$60 million a month—that it is legally obligated to transfer to the Palestinian Authority. Israel has also mobilized the international community to suspend aid until Hamas recognizes "Israel's right to exist" and enters into a political process. However, the international boycott of Gaza residents to pressure the Hamas government has been counterproductive, with both Israel and donor countries desperately seeking a way out.

68   Hannah Arendt, *Responsibility and Judgment* (New York: Schocken Books, 2005), p. 36.

69   Hannah Arendt, "The Eggs Speak Up" (1950), in *Essays in Understanding, 1930–1954: Formation, Exile, and Totalitarianism,* ed. Jerome Kohn (New York: Schocken, 2005), pp. 270–84; see especially p. 271. Arendt claims that Stalin's "only original contribution" to socialism was to transform the breaking of eggs from a tragic necessity into a revolutionary virtue.

70   David Kennedy, *The Dark Side of Virtue: Reassessing International Humanitarianism* (Princeton, NJ: Princeton University Press, 2004). See, in particular, the chapter "Humanitarianism and Force," especially p. 295. See also discussion of this issue and of Kennedy's ideas in an article by his former student, Aeyal M. Gross, "The Construction of a Wall between The Hague and Jerusalem: The Enforcement and Limits of Humanitarian Law and the Structure of Occupation," *Leiden Journal of International Law* 19 (2006): pp. 393–400, and "Human Proportions: Are Human Rights the Emperor's New Clothes of the International Law of Occupation?" *The European Journal of International Law* 18, no. 1 (2007): pp. 1–35.

71   See Ariella Azoulay and Adi Ophir, "The Order of Violence," in this volume.

72   Beyond their meaning in the total mobilization of society, "total wars"—marking the other limit of the conceptual spectrum—are wars that no longer allow any communication to take place. Colonial wars have often been total wars, because the "natives" were not perceived to share the same "humanity" as the colonizers and thus could not be considered a party capable of rational behavior and discourse. Terror is "total," as well, because, most often, it places no legal or moral limits on violence and makes no distinction between innocence and guilt. Moreover, it acts to attack the very possibility of discourse. Degrees and distinctions are precisely what make war less than total.

73   Quoted in Harel, "Nothing 'Surgical.'"

74   B'Tselem, "683 People Killed in the Conflict in 2006."

75   Robert Pirsig, *Zen and the Art of Motorcycle Maintenance* (New York: Bantam, 1974), pp. 229–30.

76   On Israeli militarism, see Uri Ben-Eliezer, "Post-Modern Armies and the Question of Peace and War: The Israeli Defense Forces in the 'New Times,'" *International Journal of Middle East Studies* 36 (2004): p. 50. See also Uri Ben-Eliezer, *The Making of Israeli Militarism* (Bloomington: Indiana University Press, 1998), pp. 1–18; Baruch Kimmerling, *The Invention and Decline of Israeliness: Society, Culture, and the Military* (Berkeley: University of California Press, 2001), p. 209; and Michael Mann, "The Roots and Contradictions of Modern Militarism," *New Left Review* 162 (March–April 1987).

77   Dayan's quote is from Foundation for Middle East Peace, "Sharon's Enduring Agenda: Consolidate Territorial Control, Manage the Conflict," *Report on Israeli Settlement in the Occupied Territories* 14, no. 1 (January–February 2004), available on-line at http://www.fmep.org/reports/archive/vol.-14/no.-1/PDF.

78   Amir Oren, "The Tenth Round," *Ha'aretz* weekend supplement, January 14, 2006.

STRATEGIC HUMANITARIANISM In recent years, the occupation regime has made broad use of the humanitarian ethics of "the lesser evil" in an attempt to moderate the harsh consequences of the exacerbated oppression of the Palestinians and to stabilize Israeli control in the territories. The inflation of the humanitarian discourse has reached its peak in the attempts to regulate and rationalize the operation of the checkpoints.

מתי"ק   חברון   חטמ"ר   יהודה

הנחיות מעבר במחסומי תשגב

1. הסגר נועד למנוע יציאה וכניסה של בני אדם ורכב מתחום העיר חברון ואליה.

2. על אף זאת וכדי לאפשר קיום חיים סבירים יורשו לעבור במחסומים כל אלה שיפורטו מטה.

   א. תומני רפואי

   אמבולנסים, רכב צוותי רפואה, משאיות תרופות, כל אדם המבקש לעבור כדי לקבל טיפול רפואי וחכל ע"פ שיקול דעת מפקד המחסום שיחוייב לנהוג לקולא במקרה של ספק.

   ב. מזון ומים

   משאיות מזון כולל חלב, ירקות ותערובת לבהמות וכמובן כל מיכליות חמים.

   ג. דלק וגז

   לכל סוגיו

   ד. רכבי עירונית חברון

   רכבי חתברואה, מים, חשמל, מכבי אש וכדו'.

   ה. בעלי התרים לישראל

   כל אדם הנושא היתר כניסה לישראל יוכל לעבור במחסומים עם רכבו.

   ו. היתרים של המת"ק

   כל אישור בכתב של המתי"ק יכובד הן לרכב וחן לבני אדם.

   ז. תמשורת ורכבים דיפולמטים - תנועה חופשית.

3. הנחיות אלה מתעדכנות מדי יום ולכן יכול שיחולו שינויים.

ברוך נג, אלי"מ   --יואל-שהון, אלי"מ
רמתי"ק חברון   מתי"ט חטמי"ר יהודה

מנגבל

Hebron DCL   Judea Regional Brigade

Directives on Crossing at Closure Checkpoints

1. The closure is intended to prevent the exit and entry of persons and vehicles to and from the city of Hebron.

2. Notwithstanding this, and to enable a reasonable life, all of the following will be allowed to cross the checkpoints.

   A. Humane medical
      Ambulances, medical-team vehicles, trucks carrying medicines, every person wanting to cross to receive medical treatment, all at the discretion of the checkpoint commander, who will be lenient in case of doubt.

   B. Food and water
      Trucks carrying food, including milk, vegetables and grain for livestock, and of course every water tanker.

   C. Fuel and gas
      Of all kinds.

   D. Hebron municipality vehicles
      Sanitation, water, electricity, fire department vehicles, and the like.

   E. Persons holding permits to enter Israel
      Every person holding a permit to enter Israel may cross the checkpoints with his vehicle.

   F. DCL permits
      Every written permit issued by the DCL will be honored, both with respect to vehicles and persons.

   G. Media and diplomatic vehicles—free movement.

3. These directives are updated daily, so changes might occur.

Baruch Nager, Colonel   Yigal Sharon, Colonel
Head, Hebron DCL   Commander Judea Regional Brigade

ETHICAL TRAINING Simulation of a case drawn from *Values in Combat—Checkpoints*, an IDF pocket booklet on "Ethical analysis of incidents in the checkpoints mission" (front cover, above). The booklet, used for training soldiers, is accompanied by a video produced by the IDF's Education Corps as a basis for discussions that commanders are supposed to conduct with their soldiers about dilemmas arising at checkpoints. The purpose of the discussions, as stated in the booklet, is "to strengthen the soldier's ability to analyze incidents in checkpoint missions on rational and not emotional grounds, exercising value-based discretion, with the objective of improving the soldier's' functioning in carrying out the checkpoint mission." The document is undated, but apparently was issued in 2004–2005.

אירוע א'

"קצין, מותר או אסור לעבור?"

אזרח ישראלי ערבי תושב ירושלים מגיע למחסום בדרכו חזרה עם משאית עמוסה סחורה. החייל לא מאפשר לו לעבור, למרות שלפני שעה קלה אמר שיוכל לעבור. מצב זה נוצר כיוון שהפקודות השתנו בשעה האחרונה. נתקיים ויכוח קולני בין נהג המשאית לחייל. לאחר שיחה קצרה של הנהג עם הקצין מהמחסום, הקצין משתכנע ומאפשר לו לעבור למרות הכל ואאת ללא בדיקה ביטחונית כנדרש.

נקודות מרכזיות העולות מהאירוע:

- הפקודות לא תמיד ברורות לחייל בשטח
- הפקודות וההנחיות מתחלפות לעיתים בתדירות גבוהה וגורמות לא אחת לבלבול בשטח
- לחייל בשטח לא ברור מדוע שונתה מדיניות המעבר במחסום
- החייל חושש מטעות בהפעל"ת שיקול דעת מול פקודות ("בסה"כ אני חייל במחסום ולא פותר בעיות")
- הפער בין סמכויות החייל לבין סמכויות הקצין

Incident 1

"Officer, is it permitted or forbidden to cross?"

An Arab Israeli citizen, resident of Jerusalem, arrives at a checkpoint on his way home with a truck full of goods. The soldier does not let him cross, even though a short time earlier he said he could cross. This situation arose because the commands changed in the last hour. The truck driver and the soldier get into a loud argument. After a brief conversation between the driver and the checkpoint officer, the officer is convinced and allows him to cross, despite everything, without conducting a security check as required.

Main points arising from the incident:

- The commands are not always clear to the soldier in the field.

- The commands and directives change very frequently and often lead to confusion in the field.

- It is not clear to the soldier in the field why the checkpoint-crossing policy was changed.

- The soldier fears making a mistake in exercising his discretion in the face of commands. ("Basically, I am a soldier at a checkpoint and do not solve problems.")

- The gap between the soldier's powers and the officer's powers.

10

פרק א' - שאלות מנחות:

מטרת פרק זה לעורר מודעות למקרה שהוקרן ולפתוח את הדיון שבפרק הבא (ב').

מפקד - ערוך שיחה פתוחה ללא ביקורת בה כל חייל יתייחס בחופשיות לשאלות המנחות.

תגובות אופייניות	שאלה מנחה
החייל שקרן, הצבא מבולבל, החייל לא בר סמכא ממלא פקודות, עצבני, מאבד עשתונות, כועס, מתוסכל, משימת החיילים שוחקת	מה מרגיש נהג המשאית? מה מרגיש החי"ל?
◾ **בעד תגובת החייל:** כי ביצע את הפקודות, כי הפקודות לא נחרות לו, כי המשימה שלו שוחקת, כי זה היה שיקול דעתו ולא הוא שינה את הפקודה, כי נהג המשאית צעק, כי אם יפעל בניגוד לפקודה החדשה הוא עלול להיעשש, כי "במלחמה כמו במלחמה" לפעמים הפקודות מתחלפות, כי "צריך ללמד אותם מי הקובע פה"	העלה טיעונים בעד ונגד פעולת החייל
◾ **נגד תגובת החייל:** כי איבד את העשתונות, כי הנסיח דבר שלא בשליטתו, כי לא העלה את הבעיה לקצין בעצמו, כי יצא מופסד וחתוש, כי יצא "האיש הרע" כי נפי שהוודה למצלמה, המציאות דינמית ועל כן החייל לא אמור להבטיח הבטחות, הוא אמור להתייחס למצב כיים ולא למצב עתידי	
◾ **בעד תגובת נהג המשאית:** כי החייל הנסיח לו, כי מניע לו לחזור לביתו, כי אי אפשר להיות באי ודאות כזו שמתחליפים פקודות בכל רגע, כי בולט שהחייל מניב אמוציונאלית, כי הוא אזרח ישראלי	מה תחושותיך לגבי המצב כו נתזן נהג המשאית?

תגובות אופייניות	שאלה מנחה
◾ **נגד תגובת נהג המשאית:** כי אין מטמשעות להבטחות בעל פה, כי זו לא זכותו לדבר עם הקצין כפי שהוא סען	
◾ **בעד תגובת הקצין:** כי הבין שהחייל טעה, כי הפעיל את שיקול דעתו וסמכות, כי מנע פגיעה מיותרת באזרח ישראלי	העלה טיעונים בעד ונגד פעולת הקצין
◾ **נגד תגובת הקצין:** כי שבר סמכות של החייל (היה צריך להעביר הנגה"ה דרום), כי אם מותר לעבור - עליו ליידע את החייל בכן מראש, כי לא ביצע פקודה	

פרק ב' - דיון

מטרת פרק זה לקיים דיון ולהציע דרכי פעולה.
יש לעודד את החייל להעלות מקרים דומים שנתקל בהם או מקרים שלדעתו הוא עלול להתקל בהם.

עורר דיון בשאלה:

באיזה אופן מצפה המערכת שהחייל יפעל במקרה זה?

שאלות מנחות תוך כדי דיון:

◾ במה צדק החייל ובמה טעה בתהליך וביחס לנהג המשאית? האם החייל הגיב אמוציונאלית בלבד (כאשר לא בדק את המשאית בפועל)?

◾ כיצד היה על החייל לפעול מרגע שהגיע הנהג חזרה למחסום? (לפנות לקצין? לקבל החלטה בעצמו? לבדוק מול המכ"ל? וכו')

◾ מה גרם לכן שהחייל יצא בתחושה קשה מהמקרה?

◾ מה יכול החייל לעשות כדי להימנע מסיטואציה לא נעימה זו? (ליזום בעצמו פניה לקצין? להבין שהוא מבצע פקודות ולעיתים יש בהן שינוי? וכו').

Commander—hold an open discussion, without criticism, in which each soldier relates freely to the following questions:

Guiding question	Typical responses
What does the truck driver feel?	The soldier is a liar, the army is confused, the soldier is not the one possessing authority.
What does the soldier feel?	He is carrying out orders, nervous, loses his head, angry, frustrated, his mission wears him out.
Raise arguments for and against the soldier's action.	**In favor of the soldier's response:** He carried out the command; the commands were not clear to him; he is worn out by his mission; he used his discretion and he wasn't the one who changed the command; the truck driver shouted; if he violated the new command, he might be punished; "in war as in war"; sometimes commands are changed; "they have to be taught who makes the decisions here."
	Against the soldier's response: He lost his head; promised something he had no control over; he did not raise the problem to the officer by himself; he ended up defeated and weak; he came out "the bad guy," as he admitted to the camera; the situation is dynamic, so the soldier is not supposed to make promises; he is supposed to relate to the existing condition and not a future one.
What do you feel regarding the situation in which the truck driver found himself?	**In favor of the truck driver's response:** The soldier promised him; he prevented him from getting home; it is impossible to live in uncertainty like that when commands are changed from one moment to the next; the soldier clearly responded emotionally; he is an Israeli citizen.
	Against the truck driver's response: Verbal promises are meaningless; it was not his right to speak with the officer as he contended.
Raise arguments for and against the officer's action.	**In favor of the officer's response:** He understood the soldier erred; he exercised his discretion and authority; he prevented unnecessary harm to an Israeli citizen.
	Against the officer's response: He damaged the soldier's authority (he should have transmitted the directive through him); if it is permitted to cross, he should inform the soldier in advance; he did not carry out a command.

FROM FRICTION POINTS TO INSPECTION POINTS Conclusions of the committee headed by Brigadier General (ret.) Baruch Spiegel, appointed by the Ministry of Defense to examine the functioning of the checkpoints. The committee's full report was never made public, but excerpts were published in the media in the summer of 2004. [Document source: NRG Web site]

---

1. **GENERAL**

A. **Background**

1. In Judea and Samaria, inspection points (closure checkpoints, encirclement checkpoints, flying checkpoints) and gates along the Seam Zone fence are in operation.
2. The purpose of the inspection points (checkpoints): thwart hostile terrorist activity, prevent the crossing of persons not permitted to cross, and grant crossing to the population permitted to cross.
3. The activity at the checkpoints is a major part of the operational experience and of the "fabric of life" in general with which the IDF and the other security forces engage.
4. The nature of the activity at the checkpoints and gates is unique. On the one hand, it encompasses threats to the lives of the soldiers, and on the other hand, the contact with the population creates incidents of harm to dignity, inappropriate conduct, and becoming significantly worn out.
5. To this was added activity along the separation fence and its gates. The activity in the Seam Zone has become a permanent, ongoing mission that requires a combined and proper operational-civilian response.
6. The building of the fence with its gates and inspection points requires optimal deployment while maintaining the balance between the security need and providing a response for the "fabric of life" of the population.

B. **Basic Assumptions**

1. The checkpoint /inspection points and the gates at the present time and in the future appear to be major meeting and friction points between the IDF and the Palestinian population.
2. The population must be separated from terrorists and terrorist entities. Alongside the war on terrorism, a dignified and human "fabric of life" should be maintained to the extent possible.
3. It is necessary to continue to maintain a balanced and combined security-civilian policy that provides a necessary security response alongside proper conduct of life of the population in the area.

C. **Purpose of the examination**

Formulate recommendations relating to management of the (examined) checkpoints/gates at the weak points, "the bottlenecks," and other flaws with the objective of improving and rendering more efficient the treatment of the needy population.

2. **PRINCIPAL PROBLEMS**

A. Continued assimilation of "iron rules," principles for a "common language," and systemic and uniform commands and procedures regarding the operation/functioning of the checkpoints.

B. Lack of clarity, interpretation, and uniformity in movement and crossing procedures.

C. Behavior, disciplinary, ethical, and moral problems. Lack of response to learning lessons, rapid debriefings, timely enforcement and punishment.

D. Lack of an institutional response in preparation, training, training in advance of combat, on-site training, and criticism.

E. Worn-out soldiers and commanders.

F. Lack of necessary personnel to provide a proper professional response (primarily at busy times).

G. Lack of sufficient physical, organizational, and technological infrastructure, which impairs efficiency and regular functioning for the crossing of the population and vehicles.

H. Lack of inspection, identification, and discovery means.

I. Absence of uniformity, continuity of action, defined times, and orderly procedures at gates in the fence.

J. Erosion of the IDF's credibility and image by the international community and foreign entities operating in the area.

SCHEMATIC DRAWING OF AN INSPECTION POINT Along with the attempt to rationalize the operation of the checkpoints deep inside the West Bank, Israel has built new
checkpoints in the Seam Zone that are based on a different planning and operational
scheme. These checkpoints, which are intended to be operated by private companies,
are designed as modern terminals and are equipped with devices intended to enable
more efficient and rapid crossing while reducing contact between the inspectors and the
inspected. The following drawing, entitled "Crossing of Pedestrians from Israel to Judea
and Samara/from Judea and Samaria to Israel," was included in a tender for bids to
operate the checkpoints in the Seam Zone published by the Israeli Ministry of Defense.

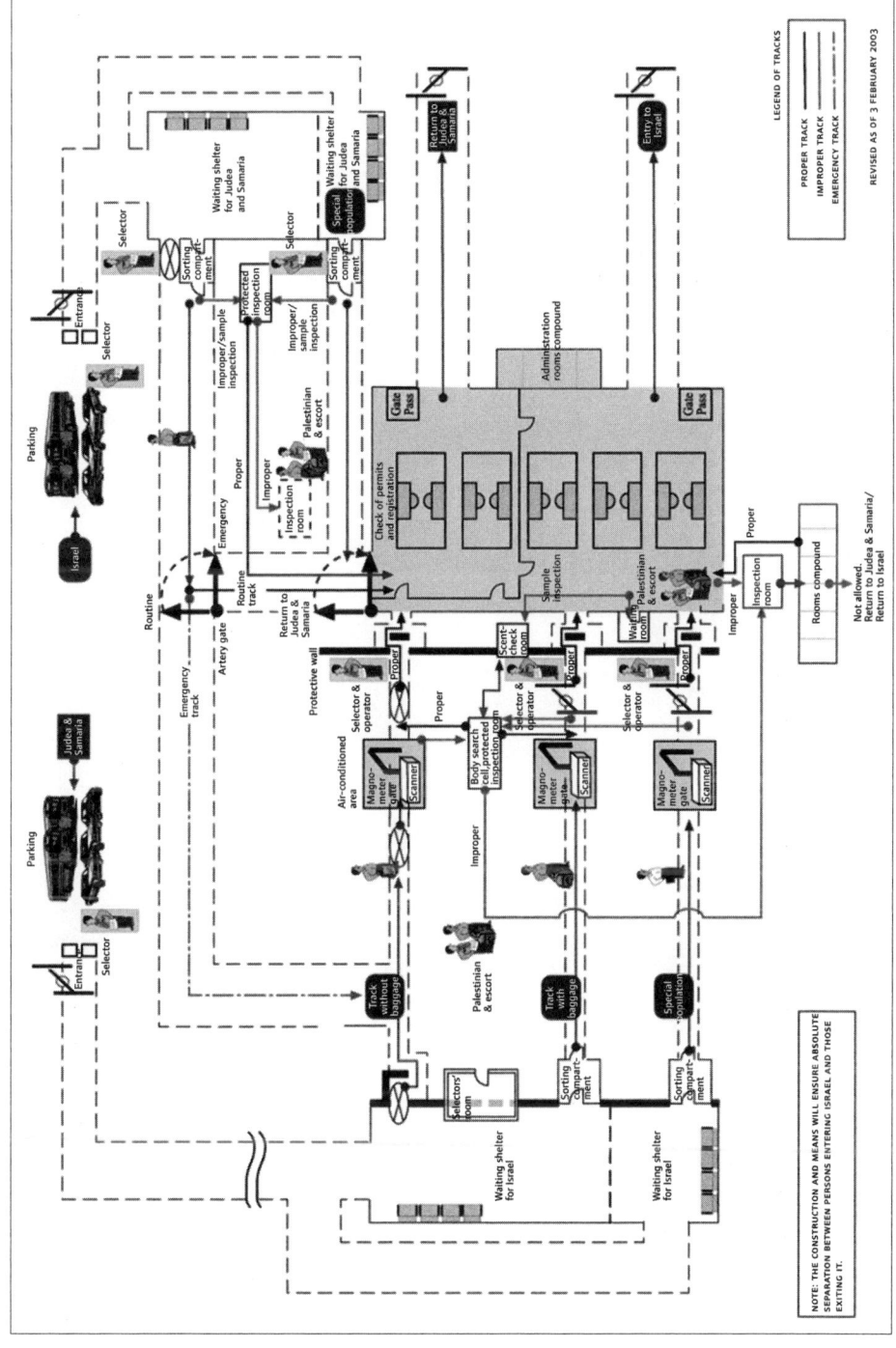

LEGEND OF TRACKS

PROPER TRACK
IMPROPER TRACK
EMERGENCY TRACK

REVISED AS OF 3 FEBRUARY 2003

NOTE: THE CONSTRUCTION AND MEANS WILL ENSURE ABSOLUTE SEPARATION BETWEEN PERSONS ENTERING ISRAEL AND THOSE EXITING IT.

Occupation as Disorientation:
The Impossibility of Borders

Ronen Shamir

> The first man who, having enclosed a piece of ground, bethought himself of saying "This is mine," and found people simple enough to believe him, was the real founder of civil society. From how many crimes, wars, and murders, from how many horrors and misfortunes might not any one have saved mankind, by pulling up the stakes, or filling up the ditch, and crying to his fellows: "beware of listening to this imposter; you are undone if you once forget that the fruits of the earth belong to us all, and the earth itself to nobody."
>
> —Jean-Jacques Rousseau, *Discourse on the Origin and Basis of Inequality among Men*

Gideon Levy, a veteran observer of the Israeli-Palestinian conflict, ventures into nostalgia when he writes:

> Last Saturday I was reminded of the old yellow signs that read STOP! BORDER AHEAD. They marked the end of the world. We expanded since then. And so we took a ride and found ourselves in the middle of a Palestinian village, at the heart of Intifada Land. Scared, I was reminded of the traveling instructions that Jewish settlers follow: Always carry a gun, and an escape hammer, and have a fire extinguisher within reach. Always turn down the volume of the radio so you can hear noises outside, always assign your passengers to look in different directions. We did not have all this. We could only turn the radio down. So we sped away, back to the Promised Land on the other side of the Green Line. And I wished we could go back to the good old habit of marking the border.[1]

Since the "expansion," it has become commonplace to speak of "The Occupation" as a temporal and spatial configuration relating to the 1967 military takeover of the West Bank and Gaza Strip. Somewhat more expansively, "The Occupation" also relates to the Golan Heights and to the periodic incursions of the Israeli Army into southern Lebanon. Used in that way, the idea of the "The Occupation" in fact conceals more than it reveals. It seems to speak of a delimited space, a temporal and spatial exception, something "out there," whereas the occupation is in fact an all-encompassing sociopolitical configuration: a deliberate dissection of space along multilayered lines of partition and a normative reality of strategically shifting borderlands. From an analytical point of view, the occupation (rather than "The Occupation") is the overriding governmentality of Israel, a rationality of government held, applied, sustained, and perfected by state institutions and ordinary citizens since 1948.[2] Delimiting "The Occupation" as an exceptional reality therefore unintentionally conceals the all-pervasive presence of the occupation.

I grew up in an upscale neighborhood in northern Tel Aviv. It was called Tzameret (Top). Next to Tzameret, with no physical barriers to set it apart, in fact in perfect topographical harmony with it, were the remains of the formerly Palestinian township of Jamusin. Its inhabitants had been deported, and most of their houses had been destroyed, providing space for new middle-class and upper-middle-class Jewish neighborhoods. But some houses remained and clung to Tzameret in an intimate physical proximity. In the mid-1960s, when I grew up, it was officially called Giv'at Amal (Labor Hill) and was inhabited by blue-collar Jews from Arab countries. Nobody called it "Giv'at Amal"—we didn't, the white boys in Tzameret, nor did they, the black boys in Giv'at Amal. "Jamusin" it was, and "Jamusin" it remained. Black it was and black it remained. I now live in suburbia, in a kind of an upscale semigated community, called Tzamarot (Tops). I drive to my office at Tel Aviv University almost daily. The campus stands on what once had been the Palestinian village of Sheikh Muneis. For all practical purposes, the Palestinians who once resided in Jamusin and Sheikh Muneis had been rendered invisible, whether through displacement, exile, or death. Some places have lost their names. Some places have acquired names precisely to commemorate their disappearance. The Har-Gilo (Hebrew for Mount Gilo) area, site of Jewish settlements around Jerusalem, had once been called Ras Beit Jala (Arabic for Mount Beit Jallah). Palestinians now refer to it as Jabal-Ma-Rakh (Mountain that Went Away), and there are other places that they now refer to in terms of Ma-Rakh (Gone).[3]

The project of decoupling population and territory is an ongoing one, ceaselessly operating at both the collective and individual levels, targeting people and places. Military, economic, and psychological pressures create incentives for immigration. To travel away from home, to move across the lines, to forget about time, are occasions for losing one's ability to claim a coupling. Miriam Halil Salam Abu El Tin was born in 1952 in the town of Beit Jala, near Jerusalem, which came under Israeli control in 1967. A year later, at the age of sixteen, she moved to Amman,

Jordan, where she married. She then moved with her husband to Kuwait, a place where she became a mother. Four years later, at the age of twenty, Miriam was granted permission to visit her parents and siblings in Beit Jallah. Miriam then decided to apply for the status of permanent resident. She was refused and petitioned Israel's High Court of Justice. The court established that sixteen years of growing up in Beit Jallah were not equivalent to four fertile years in Kuwait. Two of the justices explained that Miriam had left her home of her own free will and that she had established a new home and "even gave birth to children" in Kuwait. They therefore concluded that Miriam had "deserted her parents' home" and that her "ties to the territories" had been permanently severed. A third justice explained that the court followed the Geneva Convention, which stipulates that individuals under occupation who wish to leave the occupied area should be allowed to do so. Yet, the justice reasoned, the Geneva Convention does not stipulate that those who were allowed to leave retain the right to return. As a Palestinian, you can check out anytime you like, but can return, conditionally, only on humanitarian grounds. Miriam had to leave.

Still, projects for rendering suspect populations invisible are hardly ever fully realized. Cracks remain. "While dispossession is complete, displacement is not."[4] A town whose inhabitants stay, refugees who try to return, deportees who challenge administrative orders, and persons who engage in a protracted civic and armed struggle are disturbing, undermining and frustrating the project of rendering the population invisibile. Complementary devices must also be invoked, this time relying on technologies of hypervisibility. Spying, targeted killings, surveillance, detection and inspection, distribution of magnetic cards, and minute record keeping target each individual. The suspect population in general has to be watched. Nothing is too small to count, and no object is too minor to register.[5] Those Palestinians who had not been rendered invisible en masse during the War of 1948 and remained on the Israeli side of the Green Line were subjected to an administrative regime dispensing permits to live, work, and move on the basis of individual scrutiny. One of the primary functions of this regime had been to divide the territory so as to establish distinct coordinates for Israeli-Arab movement within the space shared with Jews:

> Whenever they wanted to venture away from their places of residence they had to report to the military governor and to obtain a personal permit which determined not only the destination and the date but also the time of departure and return. A permit was required for all purposes, for traveling to work or for business, medical treatment or visits to relatives—a wedding, a funeral, a medical operation or going out to watch a movie—everything required permission."[6]

Internal boundaries were created, a grid of physical and administrative barriers that fashioned a two-layered space, subjecting Israeli Jews and Israeli Arabs each to a different matrix of mobility. What had been originally invented within the Israel of the 1947 armistice lines had later been applied, more brutally, to the Occupied Territories.[7] One observer thus talks about the "politics of verticality": a territorial ecosystem of externally alienated, internally homogenized ethnic enclaves located next to, within, above, or below each other, spaces where intricate frontiers are invented, temporary borders are drawn up, partitions are imagined, new devices are conceived, all obeying an overriding logic of retaining control over the airspace above and the terrain beneath.[8]

In the case of *Ayoub v. Minister of Defense*, the Israeli High Court of Justice justified the legitimacy of Jewish settlements in the West Bank in panoptic terms:

> There is no doubt that the presence of [Jewish] settlements in an administered territory significantly contributes to the security situation in that area and makes the work of the army easier. One does not have to be an expert on security to understand that subversive elements operate more easily in a space inhabited only by sympathetic or indifferent residents than in a space where there are also people who keep an eye on them and are willing to report suspicious movements.[9]

Jewish settlements thus serve as watchtowers and Jewish settlers as megaprison guards whose role is to spy, inquire, follow, and report on a terrain where subversive elements and suspicious movements are forever present.

Where mine fields, barbed wire, STOP! BORDER AHEAD signs, political armistice lines, military security zones, diplomatic Green and Purple Lines, and a security fence work in the service of invisibility, roadblocks, checkpoints, observation towers, and administrative and judicial permit regimes work in the service of hypervisibility. The space in between technologies rendering a population invisible and technologies rendering it hypervisible is marred by virtual and actual lines of separation that are drawn everywhere, inscribed in a topography of gated communities, fortresslike settlements, prisons and detention camps, bypass highways, and segregated towns. All in all, the governmental logic of occupation is an "antiborder" logic. Borders presuppose some recognition of the other, even a certain respect for the other. The governmental logic of the occupation does not presuppose an equal other, but a dangerous other, calling for either elimination or segregation. Or both. Borders, no matter how arbitrarily drawn, are testimonies of sovereignty. The governmental logic of the occupation substitutes the violent appropriation of territory for legitimate sovereignty. In the absence of permanent, mutually recognized borders, the physical space under effective control becomes a chaotic ensemble of micropartitions, experienced and acted upon tentatively, negligently, and arbitrarily.

Barta'a had been a single village before 1949. The armistice line agreed upon between Jordan and Israel, however, split the village into two, one part in Israel, the other in Jordan. It seems that the surveyors who drew a green line on their maps considered the valley that cuts across the village to be a natural border, rendering half of the village invisible and the other half subject to hypervisibility. "Maybe," writes David Grossman, "they didn't know what they were doing."[10] In the absence of borders, the Simmelian dimensions of distance and proximity lose their analytical validity and are replaced by an everyday-life phenomenology of cultural and political disorientation. Dissociation through exclusion and partitioning, to paraphrase Georg Simmel, becomes an elemental form of socialization.[11]

"What are the limits of Palestine? Where does it end and where does Israel begin, and are those limits spatial or temporal or both?" asks one Palestinian scholar.[12] Foucauldian-style spatial imageries are undermined. Michel Foucault invokes a powerful opposition—historically crystallized between the seventeenth and nineteenth centuries—between the treatment of the leper and the treatment of the plague. The leper "gave rise to rituals of exclusion." The leper was governed through a system of binary divisions between one set of people and another. The leper was transferred, deported, locked away, left to his doom in a mass among which it was useless to differentiate, rendered invisible through "exile enclosure." The plague triggered new forms of response, based on multiple separations and individualizing distributions. Against the leper and his separation came the plague and its segmentations. The leper had been marked and distanced. The plague invited finely tuned selections and distinctions, the careful partitioning of space, with each street placed under surveillance, each resident required to report in the window to the count call of sentinels. Once again, closure reigned, but now it was space as a whole that was ordered, divided, managed: not by exclusion, but by division. The plague gave rise to a new modality of power: spatial partitioning. Inspection becomes a prime concern, the gaze becomes alert everywhere, and all is recorded, measured, assessed, registered. The plague was met by a strict spatial and temporal order, ushering in the political dream of the penetration of regulation into the smallest details of everyday life, a utopia of a perfectly governed space and the population within it, deploying technologies of surveillance, registration, and minute instructions for governing the self. A principle of rendering one invisible governs the government of the leper. A principle of hypervisibility governs the government of the plague.[13] Foucault offers us a historical account of the substitution of one modality of power for another. Yet the occupation is a regime that simultaneously relies on both modalities of power, driven by the utopia of invisibility and compelled to address its never fully realizable dream by subjecting its fugitives and survivors to a hypervisible matrix.

Foucault offers us a distinction between the singled-out leper, distinguished by his separation from the rest, and the population as a whole, where everyone may become contagious, where everyone is a potential suspect. The occupation is a regime that seeks both exclusion and partitioning. The occupation is a cartographic effort to create both horizontal maps, separating territories and populations from each other, and vertical maps, dividing space as a whole so as to impose different coordinates of mobility on rulers and ruled. The principles of invisibility and hypervisibility mutually support each other, complement each other, interchangeably deployed, treating the suspect population as both objects of power (punished through exclusion) and subjects in power (disciplined through spatial policing.) Yet both projects are forever incomplete. They are marred with transgressions and evasions. In fact, they not only presuppose such transgressions and evasions but invite them; they breed both the impossibility of borders and the reality of infiltration.

I became scared of the black kids of Jamusin only when they came to us. I never thought twice before walking to the grocery of Ezra, in the middle of Jamusin, to buy candies and ices. I liked going to Ezra. I would walk along the little streets of Tzameret, basking in green, and smoothly cross into Jamusin. It was amazingly trivial. The street kept its width and pace—it just became unpaved. And the green was gone. It was dusty, instead. I crossed into Jamusin as a wandering child, as a consumer of candies. Technically, the black kids of Jamusin could also easily cross into Tzameret. They sometimes did, but we made sure that their crossing would be felt—both by us and by them—as odd, awkward, suspicious. The crossing of the black kids into our neighborhood bore the marks of subversive infiltration.

Infiltration across the Green Line had been a permanent feature of the Israeli experience before 1967 and, later, ever since the first intifada (1987). At times a thief, at times a refugee seeking a way back home, at times a suicide bomber, at times a desperate laborer, at times a guerilla fighter, the Palestinian "infiltrator" has represented a bodily reality of unchecked suspect movement in space. A whole range of state practices and policies were shaped in the shadow of "infiltration," periodically culminating in counterinfiltration activities, further compromising the integrity of sovereignty, further subverting the possibility of borders. Whereas infiltrators are labeled as subversives, counterinfiltrators are admired as heroes. As a child, I devoured the stories about Commando Unit No. 101. Active in the 1950s, the unit specialized in infiltrating the 1949 armistice lines, carrying out what were officially considered to be "retaliation attacks" against Arab infiltration. Uri Milstein, a military historian, also wrote for children, vividly narrating the actions of Unit 101 as heroic adventure stories. Meir Har-Zion (Mount of Zion) was the most famous fighter of the unit. "They were brave; they penetrated, and they navigated. They ventured out again. Light weapons, rubber shoes and sour candies. 'When I walk the hills for hours,' Har-Zion confesses, 'I suck on sour candies instead of cigarettes and gum.'"[14]

Urban street skateboarders come to mind. Viewed as delinquents by some and as creative adventurers by others, skaters write and rewrite, inscribe and reinscribe the physical boundaries of urban space, exposing ledges, sidewalks, steps, and rails as invisible borders, simultaneously subverting them and mocking their arbitrariness.[15] Likewise with infiltration and counterinfiltration, the notion of borders becomes vague, tentative, disorienting.

Fahed Quasme and two other Palestinian leaders had been deported by helicopter to Lebanon in May 1980. In absentia, they petitioned Israel's High Court of Justice, arguing that they were deprived of their legal right to appeal to an administrative committee with authority to review the legality of the deportation as stipulated by law. The court concurred, and the deportees were allowed to return so they could exhaust the legal remedies available to them by appealing to the committee. Fourteen years later, Israel deported 400 Hamas leaders. Loaded on buses, the deportees were transferred to Lebanon. Their petition to the High Court of Justice raised the very same procedural argument invoked in *Quasme*. The court concurred this time around, as well. The justices ruled that the 400 deportees had a right to appeal to the administrative committee. Yet rather than ordering their return, the court ruled that "the committee would be able to hold its meetings at any place where the Israeli Army is able to secure the committee's adequate functioning."[16]

Physical control of land thus becomes paramount, sovereignty only secondary. The cultural language that seeks to establish a border as a marker of national distinction is constantly undermined by the logic of occupation, surrendering to another cultural language that sustains, if not celebrates, the open frontier,[17] a space that simultaneously licenses incursions and infiltrations and renders invisible—and thereby vulnerable to excessive violence—the suspect population "behind" it. But this is never one-sided. Palestinian workers find their way across the roadblocks. Palestinian terrorists find their way across the checkpoints. The lines are constantly breached, newly imagined, redrawn. Partition is acted upon, performed.

A Palestinian farmer gives his account:

> Here's my story of the border. In 1948, an engineer of the Jordanian Army arrived with guards and staff. He took out the map and ordered them to paint border markers with whitewash right outside our house. The house was here, and our land farther away. He placed the border right outside our house. I said, "That's no good. Either you put the house and the land in Jordan, or the house and the land in Israel."

But our house was in Israel and our land in Jordan. [He said:] "The map is like that and I can't change it." The moment his back was turned, I pulled up the markers and moved the border to include our land. I even whitewashed them again to look as good as new. That's how the state grew by 2000 hectares."[18]

The very same transience also serves the unbearable lightness of colonization: Kuneitra is a Syrian town ruined in the War of 1973. Keshet was an embryonic Jewish settlement established on the outskirts of Kuneitra. The 1973 armistice line left Keshet on the Syrian side. Nothing but a scattered line of barrels tentatively marked the cease-fire line to be. At night, the settlers repositioned the barrels so as to include Keshet on the Israeli side.[19]

Occupation as a rationality of government is hegemonic, incorporating even its defiance. Gvul, in Hebrew, stands for both a limit and a border. The occupation is about setting limits and boundaries, and yet has little to rely on by way of drawing borders. The occupation is about divisions, and yet each division further undermines the very notion of bounded sovereignty. Yesh Gvul (There Is a Limit/Border) is a political movement supporting soldiers who refuse to serve in the Occupied Territories. It draws a line: Yes to military service within the Green Line, no to military service across it. But the Green Line is just that, an arbitrary and tentative and forever challenged twilight zone. Thus, even the limited political ambition to end "The Occupation" has nothing more to rely on than the 1949 armistice line, turned into the 1967 armistice line, drawn on maps with a green pencil during the UN-brokered talks between Israel, on the one hand, and Egypt, Jordan, Syria, and Lebanon on the other.

In the absence of borders, and yet with a utopia of invisibility as an underlying logic, all kinds of new partition lines are imagined, constructed, dreamt of. New walls are being built, new security zones created. New citizenship laws are conceived. In desperation, unilateral "disengagement" plans become political tropes, "naturally" following the logic of the occupation. Social scientists try to catch up, searching for a language and a conceptual toolbox that may make sense of the chaotic, multilayered space. James Ron's approach is particularly appealing. Ron employs an opposition between two spatial metaphors: frontiers and ghettos. Ghettos are configured to maximize visibility, characterized by spatial policing, mass incarceration, and the strict surveillance of movement. Still, the minute detection of life in the ghetto underwrites techniques that are essentially about the managing of life. Frontiers, on the other hand, are the unbounded zones beyond which lie the invisible population or what had been so rendered. Frontiers mark the end of responsibility, thereby substituting the more brutal techniques of taking life for those techniques designed to manage it. In these terms, experimentation with unilateral "disengagement" plans, almost counterintuitively, does not mark the ghettoization of Palestinian territories, but rather the opposite, their transformation into uninhabited frontiers.

Yet as with lepers and plagues, the logic of occupation does not easily succumb to the analytic neatness of opposing spatial forms. Frontiers and ghettos are inscribed into and on top of each other, interchangeable, capricious, substituting hypervisibility for invisibility, back and forth as political circumstances allow, as notions of responsibility shift, as bureaucratic imperatives permit. The logic of the occupation really knows only one rule: Both frontiers and ghettos rely on spatial demarcations that are hostile to borders. The result is that the logic of the occupation sustains the impossibility of establishing borders, frustrating any coherent paradigm of peaceful neighboring. It speaks of lepers in the plague.

NOTES

1   Gideon Levy, *The Twilight Zone: Life and Death under the Israeli Occupation, 1988–2003* (Tel Aviv: Babel, 2004) (in Hebrew; my translation), p. 33.

2   The occupation has its roots in Zionist techniques of redeeming the land.

3   David Grossman, *Yellow Wind* (Tel Aviv: Ha-Kibbutz HaMeuchad, 1987) (in Hebrew) p. 29. Available in English as *The Yellow Wind*, trans. Haim Watzman (New York: Farrar, Straus and Giroux, 1998).

4   Nicholas Blomley, *Unsettling the City: Urban Land and the Politics of Property* (New York: Routledge, 2004), p. 106.

5   James Ron, *Frontiers and Ghettos: State Violence in Serbia and Israel* (Berkeley: University of California Press, 2003).

6   Tom Segev, *Israel in 1967* (Jerusalem: Keter, 2005) (in Hebrew; my translation), p. 82.

7   Ariel Handel, "Technologies of Spatial Uncertainty in the Occupied Territories: An Introduction to a Geography of Disaster," *Theory and Criticism* 20 (2008) (in Hebrew).

8   Eyal Weizman, *Hollow Land: Israel's Architecture of Occupation* (London: Verso, 2007).

9   *Ayoub v. Minister of Defense*, HCJ 610/78 33 (2) 113, 119.

10 Grossman, *Yellow Wind*, p. 93.

11 Kurt Wolff, (ed.). *The Sociology of Georg Simmel* (New York: The Free Press, 1950), p. 416.

12 Rashid Khalidi, "Contrasting Narratives of Palestinian Identity," in Patricia Yaeger (ed.), *The Geography of Identity* (Ann Arbor: University of Michigan Press, 1996), p. 187.

13 Michel Foucault, *Discipline and Punish: The Birth of the Prison* (New York: Vintage Books, 1995), p. 198.

14 Uri Milstein, *Secret Commando Unit 101* (Tel Aviv: Ramdor, 1968) (in Hebrew), p. 177.

15 Taro Nettleton, "Streetstyle: Skateboarding, Spatial Appropriation, and Dissent," *Post Road Magazine*, issue 8 (2005), available on-line at www.postroadmag.com/8/criticism/Streetstyle.phtml (last accessed September 8, 2008).

16 HCJ 5973/92, *ACRI v. Minister of Defense*, 47 (1) 267.

17 Adriana Kemp, "Talking Boundaries: The Making of Political Territory in Israel 1949–1957," Ph.D. thesis, Tel Aviv University, 1997 (in Hebrew).

18 *Route 181: Fragments of a Journey in Palestine Israel,* a film by Michel Khleifi and Eyal Sivan, Montreal Sourat Films, Sindibad, WDR, 2004 (in Hebrew; my translation).

19 Danny Rubinstein, *On the Lord's Side: Gush Emunim* (Tel Aviv: Hakibbutz Hameuchad, 1982) (in Hebrew), p. 56.

- **INVESTIGATION SHEET OF PERSON SUSPECTED OF STAYING ILLEGALLY IN ISRAEL** In recent years, Israel has significantly reduced the number of Palestinians permitted to enter its territory, closely monitored entry, and mounted police hunts to capture those who sneak in. This policy is carried out under the protection of the Separation Wall and its supervised crossing gates and is aided by a "demographic" rhetoric that views Palestinians as threats. Large numbers of Palestinians who fail to receive permits to enter Israel sneak into the country to work and earn a living. In the security jargon, they are referred to as "persons staying illegally" (PSIs). Most Palestinians caught by the police inside Israel—thousands every week—are returned to the east of the Green Line without interrogation and without any legal proceedings being initiated against them. Many suffer police abuse when caught.

- **NOTICE FROM THE POPULATION ADMINISTRATION** refusing to make an appointment to submit a request for family reunification. The notice is addressed to a Palestinian woman who is an Israeli citizen and who wants to arrange residency status for her husband, a resident of the Occupied Territories. The temporary amendment to the Nationality and Entry into Israel Law, which was first enacted in 2003 and which has been extended a few times since then, greatly limits the granting of status in Israel to Palestinian residents of the Occupied Territories who are married to Palestinian citizens of Israel. The temporary provision, which was approved by the High Court of Justice, applies only to requests for family unification with Palestinians and citizens of enemy (that is, Arab) countries.

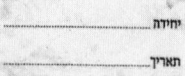

משטרת ישראל
شرطة إسرائيل

יחידה ....

תאריך ....

الوحدة ....

التاريخ ....

גיליון חקירת חשוד בעבירת שב"ח

מס' זהות ותח רقم الهوية	שם משפחה اسم العائلة	שם פרטי الاسم الشخصي	שם האב الأب	שם הסב الجد	שם האם الأم

כתובת العنوان		טל' בית هاتف	ניד الجوال

מקום לידה مكان الولادة	תאריך לידה تاريخ الولادة	מצב משפחתי الحالة الاجتماعية	דת الدين	אזרחות الجنسية
		☐ רווק أعزب ☐ נשוי متزوج ☐ גרוש مطلق ☐ אלמן أرمل		☐ ישראלית ☐ פלסטינית

בתאריך بتاريخ	בשעה الساعة	במקום المكان	ראיתי את הנ"ל בפני ואמרתי לו: אני איש משטרה رأيت المذكور أعلاه وقلت له أني رجل شرطه

עומד לגבות הודעתך כחשוד בשהייה בלתי חוקית בישראל,
سلطتك أفيدك كمشتبه بإقامته غير شرعيه

מס' אישי الاسم والعائلة	דרגה الرتبة	שם פרטי ושם משפחה הרقم الشخصي ....

בכך שהיום בתאריך .... בשעה .... במקום .... נתפסת ע"י צוות מג"ב בשטח מדינת ישראל
في يوم بتاريخ بالساعة بالمكان قبض عليك فريق حرس الحدود بمنطقة إسرائيلية دخول

כאשר אין ברשותך אישור כניסה לישראל, בניגוד לסעיף 12 לחוק הכניסה לישראל 1952. אין אתה חייב לומר דבר, כל שתאמר עשוי לשמש כראיה נגדך.
إلى إسرائيل، مخالف لبند 12 من قانون الدخول إلى إسرائيل 1952. انك لست ملزم بان تقول أي كلمه، كل ما ستقوله سنسجله وسيكون عرضه لاستعماله كدليل

חימנועותך מלהשיב לשאלות עשרות לחזק את הראיות נגדך.
امتناعك عن الأجوبه يمكن أن يعزز الأدله ضدك.

לאחר שקראתי את הרשום לעיל הנ"ל אישר שהבין את החשד נגדו ואת תוכן האזהרה ואישר זאת בחתימתו.
بعد أن قرأت المكتوب المذكور أعلاه صادق بإمضائه انه فهم الشبهة ومضمون التحذير.

....

חתימת החשוד إمضاء المشبوه ....

תוכן האזהרה והעדות תורגם מעברית לערבית ולהפך ע"י .... חתימה ....

1. האם יש לך אישור כניסה / עבודה לישראל؟ هل لديك تصريح إقامه / عمل في إسرائيل؟   ☐ כן نعم ☐ לא لا
2. האם היה לך בעבר אישור כניסה / עבודה לישראל؟ هل كان لديك تصريح إقامه / عمل في إسرائيل في الماضي؟   ☐ כן نعم ☐ לא لا
3. האם אתה יודע שצריך אישור כזה؟ هل تعرف انك بحاجة إلى تصريح؟   ☐ כן نعم ☐ לא لا
4. לצורך מה הגעת לישראל؟ لماذا دخلت إلى إسرائيل؟ ....
5. מהיכן נכנסת לישראל؟ من أي مكان دخلت إلى إسرائيل؟ ....
6. כמה פעמים נכנסת לישראל؟ كم مره دخلت إلى إسرائيل؟ ....
7. איך הגעת למקום בו נתפסת ע"י צוות מג"ב؟ كيف وصلت إلى المكان الذي قبض عليك فيها بيد حرس الحدود؟ ....
8. מי הסיע אותך ומה היה מסלול הנסיעה؟ مع من سافرت، وما هو مسلك السفر؟ ....
9. באיזה רכב הגעת לישראל؟ بأي مركبه دخلت إلى إسرائيل؟ ....
10. במה עבדת בישראל וחיכך؟ ماذا اشتغلت واين في إسرائيل؟ ....
11. מי העסיק אותך בישראל؟ من شغلك في إسرائيل؟ ....
12. כמה שילמו לך עבור העבודה בישראל؟ كم دفعوا لك مقابل العمل في إسرائيل؟ ....
13. עם מי הגעת לישראל؟ مع من دخلت إلى إسرائيل؟ ....
14. האם יש לך מה להוסיף؟ أليك أقوال أخرى؟ ....

זו הודעתי שהוקראה בפני ואושרה ככונה בחתימת ידי.
هذه أقوالي التي قرأت أمامي وصادقت عليها بإمضائي.

חתימת החשוד إمضاء المشبوه	שם המתורגמן .... חתימה	שם גובה העדות .... חתימה ....

ט/3106

(4.06) 600×50

Israel Police Force

Unit...........

Date..........

Investigation Sheet of Person Suspected of Staying Illegally

ID NUMBER	FAMILY NAME	FIRST NAME	FATHER'S NAME	GRANDFATHER'S NAME	MOTHER'S NAME
ADDRESS			HOME TELEPHONE		MOBILE PHONE
PLACE OF BIRTH	DATE OF BIRTH	FAMILY STATUS ☐ SINGLE ☐ MARRIED ☐ DIVORCED ☐ WIDOW		RELIGION	NATIONALITY ☐ PALESTINIAN ☐ JORDANIAN

On .... at .... o'clock at .... I saw the aforesaid in front of me and told him:

I, a police officer (personal no.) .... (rank) .... (first and last name) ....

am about to take your statement as a person suspected of staying illegally in Israel, in that on

.... at .... o'clock at .... you were caught by a Border Police team in the

territory of the State of Israel without a permit to enter Israel, in violation of sec. 12 of the Entry

into Israel Law, 1952. You may remain silent, anything you say may be used as evidence against you.

Your refusal to respond may strengthen the case against you. After I read the above, the aforesaid

person confirmed that he understands the suspicion against him and the content of the warning, and

confirmed this with his signature.

....

Signature of the suspect

The content of the warning and the testimony was translated from Arabic to Hebrew and vice-versa

by .... Signature ....

1. Do you have a permit to enter/work in Israel? ☐ yes ☐ no
2. Did you ever have a permit to enter/work in Israel? ☐ yes ☐ no
3. Do you know that you need a permit of this kind? ☐ yes ☐ no
4. For what purpose did you come to Israel? ....
5. Where did you enter Israel?..
6. How many times have you entered Israel? ....
7. How did you get to the place where you were caught by the Border Police? ....
8. Who transported you and what was the route? ....
9. In which vehicle did you arrive in Israel? ....
10. What work did you do in Israel and where? ....
11. Who employed you in Israel? ....
12. How much did they pay you for the work in Israel? ....
13. Who was with you when you arrived in Israel? ....
14. Do you have anything to add? ....

This is my statement, which was read before me and is confirmed as correct by my signature.

....

NAME OF SUSPECT   NAME OF TRANSLATOR   SIGNATURE   NAME OF PERSON TAKING THE TESTIMONY   SIGNATURE

מדינת ישראל
משרד הפנים
לשכת מנהל האוכלוסין תל - אביב

לכבוד حצ' :

التاريخ:
ת"ז رقم الهوية:
תיק رقم الملف:

הנדון: בקשה לקבלת מעמד לבן/ת זוג חזר
الموضوع: طلب الحصول على وضع لزوج/ة أجنبي/ة

1. הריני להודיעך כי בהמשך לבקשתך לקביעת תור לשם הגשת בקשה לקבלת מעמד לבן/ת זוג זר/ה, בשלב זה לא יקבע תור לאור העובדה שאינכם עומדים בגדרי התיקון לחוק האזרחות והכניסה לישראל (הוראת שעה) תיקון תשס"ה - 2005 מיום 1.8.05.

أعلمك بأن طلبك لتحديد موعد لتقديم طلب لحصول على وضع للزوج/ة الأجنبي/ة في هذه الأثناء لم يوافق عليه وذلك بسبب عدم توفر الشروط والتعليمات التي تم تحديدها من قبل قانون المواطنة والدخول إلى إسرائيل (تعليمات الساعة) تصحيح 2005 من يوم 1.8.05.

☒ בן זוגך תושב האזור מתחת לגיל 35 זוגך מן منطقة السلطة الفلسطينية عمره أقل من 35 عامًا.

☐ בת זוגתך תושבת האזור מתחת לגיל 25 زوجتك من منطقة السلطة الفلسطينية عمرها أقل من 25 عامًا.

2. אם בכל זאת ברצונך לקבוע תור לשם הגשת בקשה תוך תשלום אגרה, אנא הודיענו במכתב חזר.

إذا أردت بالرغم هذا تحديد موعد لتقديم الطلب ودفع الرسوم الرجاء إبلاغنا بواسطة مكتوب آخر.

3. במידה ובן/ת הזוג חזר/ה נמצא/ת בישראל, הרי שעליה/ה לעזוב את הארץ **לאלתר**.

في حالة وجود الزوج/ة في إسرائيل أعلمك بأنه يتوجب مغادرته/ها البلاد فورا.

4. היה ובן/ת הזוג לא י/תצא את הארץ כאמור, יוצא כנגדו/ה צו הרחקה על פי חוק הכניסה לישראל, התשי"ב, על כל המשתמע מכך.

في حالة عدم مغادرة الزوج/ة البلاد وحسب قانون الدخول لإسرائيل سيصدر قرار إبعاد ضده/ها مع التنوية بهذا.

5. בכבוד רב,
مع فائق الاحترام.

(סרוב לקביעת תור)

בברכה מع فائق الاحتراد
מנהל הלשכה مدير الدائر

רחוב דרך מנחם בגין 125 מיקוד 67012 טלפון:03-7632534 פקס:03-7632533
כתובתנו באנטרנט :WWW.PNIM.GOV.IL
מרכז מידע ארצי: 3450*

משרד הפנים עם הפנים קדימה, בשבילך ולמענך!

STATE OF ISRAEL
MINISTRY OF THE INTERIOR
Population Administration Office Tel-Aviv

Tel-Aviv
4 February 2007
Itzik Hobness
Senior Coordinator

Re: Request to receive status for foreign spouse

1. Please be informed that in handling your request for scheduling submission of a request for a status for a foreign spouse, at this stage, submission will not be scheduled because you do not meet the provisions of the amendment to the Citizenship and Entry into Israel Law (Temporary Provision), 5765—2005, of 1 August 2005.

   ☒ Your husband is a resident of the area and under age 35
   ☐ Your wife is a resident of the area and under age 25

2. If you would like, in any case, to schedule submission of a request, which entails payment of a fee, please inform us in writing.

3. In the event that your foreign spouse remains in Israel, he/she must leave Israel immediately.

4. If your spouse does not leave Israel as stated, an order to remove him under the Entry into Israel Law, 5712—1952, will be issued, with all that entails.

5. Sincerely,

Greetings,
Office Director

Tel-Aviv
4 February 2007
Itzik Hobness
Senior Coordinator

125 Menachem Begin Blvd 67012 Tel: 03-7632534 Fax: 03-7632533
Our Website: www.pnim.gov.il
National Information Center: *3450
Ministry of the Interior Moving Forward, for You and For Your Sake!

Chronology of the Occupation Regime, 1967–2007

Ariel Handel

1967

JUNE 5 — War breaks out between Israel, Egypt, Syria, and Jordan. When it ends, Israel controls the West Bank, the Gaza Strip, the Golan Heights, and the Sinai Peninsula.

JUNE 7 — Proclamation No. 1 is posted on Palestinian houses as the Israeli military forces advance. It states: "The Israel Defense Forces have today entered the area and taken control and responsibility for maintenance of public order and safety." This proclamation and other orders that would be issued subsequently had already been drafted by the Judge Advocate General's Office in the early 1960s as part of a legal framework for a future military government in occupied territory. Also on June 7, Proclamation No. 2 is issued, which grants the military commander sole executive and legislative power in the territory occupied, with the power to repeal or suspend every local law, cancel every decision made under law, ignore the provisions of international law, dismiss every official, elected or appointed, and make and repeal regulations. Over the years, Israel will issue more than twenty-five hundred orders arranging all areas of life in the Occupied Territories.

JUNE 7 — The Israel Defense Forces (IDF) destroy three villages ('Imwas, Yalu, and Beit Nuba) in the Latrun enclave, near the main Jerusalem–Tel Aviv Road, and their eight thousand inhabitants are forced to go by foot

eastward, to the Ramallah area. Three days later, most of the Maghariba neighborhood, near the Wailing Wall, is demolished to build an open area for Jewish worshippers. In general, however, unlike the situation following the 1948 War, most of the Palestinian towns and villages are left standing. Exceptions are the villages in the Latrun enclave and the refugee camps in the Jordan Valley, which are demolished soon after the war and their fifty thousand residents evacuated. Extensive use of house demolition begins immediately after the war. A report published by the Israeli League for Human and Civil Rights states that, by April 1968, 5,367 houses had been demolished, 1,830 of them in the three villages that had been totally destroyed.

JUNE 13 — The military government announces that every citizen in the West Bank will be allowed to move to the Kingdom of Jordan and organizes special transportation service for Palestinians wanting to move. During and after the war, between two hundred thousand and two hundred and fifty thousand Palestinians fled or were expelled to Jordan.

JUNE 15 — A Directors-General Committee is established to solve civil and economic problems arising in the Occupied Territories. The committee is composed of the directors-general of several ministries and is chaired by the director-general of the Ministry of Finance. A Coordination

Committee is also established to coordinate the handling of political and security matters and is headed by an army officer. The Ministerial Committee for the Administered Territories that established the Directors-General Committee states: "The inclination is to cover the costs to meet civilian needs from the resources of the Territories.... Government ministries will not allocate funds from their budgets to fund the civil tasks related to the Territories."

JUNE 18 — Order No. 25 is issued. It prevents property and land transactions without the authorities' approval.

JUNE 19 — The government makes its first decision relating to the fate of the territories occupied in the war, stating that they are to be held in trust until a peace agreement is signed. The decision states that the Gaza Strip would remain under Israeli control in any event and that no decision on the West Bank would be made at the present time.

JUNE 20 — The Palestinian Liberation Organization (PLO) announces that its main headquarters will be moved to the Occupied Territories.

JUNE 27 — Israel annexes East Jerusalem, along with twenty-eight other villages, a total area of seventy square kilometers (Jordanian East Jerusalem comprised only six square kilometers), the borders of the annexed area being based on the principle of "maximum land area, minimum number of Arabs." In a census taken shortly after annexation, sixty-six thousand Palestinians are found to be living in the city. They are offered an Israeli identity card in exchange for relinquishing their Jordanian citizenship. Almost no Palestinian takes the offer. The Palestinians in the city are then given Israeli resident cards, which grant them only some civil and political rights.

JULY — Order No. 58 and Order No. 59 are issued. They state, respectively, that absentee property and enemy civilian property will be handed over to the state. Under Order No. 58,

in the coming five years, Israel will transfer to its ownership some 7.5 percent of West Bank lands. By 1979, Israel will take ownership, under Order No. 59, of about 13 percent of the West Bank.

JULY — Israel allows West Bank Palestinians who fled to Jordan during the war to return to their homes, provided that they do so within thirty days. The deadline is extended a few times. In a period of two and a half months, some fourteen thousand refugees of the one hundred and twenty thousand who submitted requests return. Over the next five years, Israel allows some forty-five thousand refugees to return to the West Bank. Males aged sixteen to sixty are not allowed to return.

JULY 2 — The Knesset decides to adopt a dual judicial system whereby offenses committed by Israelis in the Occupied Territories will be heard by courts in Israel.

JULY 13 — The "Alon Plan" (its official name is "The Future of the Territories and the Handling of Refugees") is presented for the first time. It will be the basic plan for Israeli settlement in the territories during the first decade of occupation, although it is never formally approved. The principal elements of the plan: the Jordan River is Israel's eastern border; the Jordan Valley, the southern Hebron Hills, East Jerusalem, and Gaza will be annexed and undergo large-scale settlement; no settlements will be established in crowded Palestinian areas, which will be given autonomy; a number of refugees from the Gaza Strip will be resettled in the West Bank.

JULY 16 — Buses are allowed to travel between Gaza and the West Bank.

AUGUST — The Directors-General Committee and the Coordination Committee that were appointed two months before to handle, respectively, the civil and security affairs of the government in the Occupied Territories are unified. A coordinator of government operations in the territories is appointed as head of the unified committee. Subordinate to both the defense minister and the IDF General Staff, the coordinator carries out civil and military functions.

AUGUST 22 — Order No. 92 is issued. The order expropriates all the water resources in the West Bank.

AUGUST 31 — Jerusalem's Old City is declared a site of antiquity, and no building is permitted until an archaeological survey is conducted.

SEPTEMBER — The first census is taken in the Occupied Territories: The West Bank (including East Jerusalem) has 667,200 residents, and the Gaza Strip has 389,700.

SEPTEMBER 1 — The Pan-Arab summit in Khartoum decides on "the three noes": no to recognition of Israel, no to negotiations with Israel, and no to signing an agreement with it.

SEPTEMBER 4 — A general strike in schools in the West Bank in protest against annexation of East Jerusalem and the prohibition on using dozens of textbooks lasts for some two months.

SEPTEMBER 10 — Israel expropriates one hundred thousand dunams of land (approximately twenty-four thousand acres) to build five army bases in the West Bank.

SEPTEMBER 21 — The first deportation: The chief *qadi* (Moslem religious judge) of the West Bank, Abed al-Hamid a-Ziyah, is accused of incitement and is deported to Jordan.

SEPTEMBER 27 — The first settlement, Kfar Etzion, is established on the ruins of a Jewish settlement that was destroyed in the 1948 War.

NOVEMBER 6 — Israelis are allowed open entry into the Occupied Territories.

NOVEMBER 9 — Prime Minister Levi Eshkol makes a request to the head of the World Zionist Organization for assistance from the WZO's Settlement Division in establishing new settlements in the Occupied Territories.

NOVEMBER 15 — The cabinet approves Defense Minister Moshe Dayan's plan for an "invisible

administration" in the territories. The principal elements of the plan are inconspicuousness, lack of interference, "open bridges" between the West Bank and Jordan, and free movement between the West Bank and the Gaza Strip and between the territories and Israel.

NOVEMBER 22 — The UN Security Council adopts Resolution 242. The main sections call for the "withdrawal of Israeli armed forces from territories occupied in the recent conflict," for a "just settlement of the refugee problem," and "for guaranteeing the territorial inviolability and political independence of every State in the area." Almost immediately, Egypt and Jordan accept the resolution. Israel accepts it the following month. For years, the Palestinians have reservations about the resolution because it minimizes the Palestinian issue to the refugee problem, ignoring the Palestinians' demand for self-determination.

— The judge advocate general, Meir Shamgar, allows Palestinians to petition the Israeli High Court of Justice. The High Court of Justice (which is also the Supreme instance in the Israeli court system) exercises judicial review over the other branches of government. In the absence of objections by the Judge Advocate General's Office, the Supreme Court recognizes the standing of Palestinian residents of the Occupied Territories. Over the years, the High Court of Justice will deny the vast majority of the petitions filed by Palestinians.

1968

FEBRUARY 1 — Customs duties between the Occupied Territories and Israel are abolished.

MARCH — In response to the increase in the military and ideological power of Palestinian organizations, the PLO, in particular, in the Occupied Territories and Jordan, Israel attacks PLO bases in Kafr Karameh, a village in Jordan. The operation ends with heavy losses on both sides. The Palestinians claim victory.

MARCH 1 — The status of the territories is officially changed from "enemy territories" to "administered territories."

MARCH 18 — Order No. 234 states that every male Palestinian over sixteen years old must have an identity card and carry it with him at all times.

APRIL 12 — A group of Jews led by Rabbi Moshe Levinger goes to the Park Hotel in Hebron to celebrate the Passover Seder and then refuses to vacate the premises. In May, the settlers move into the military government's building in the city, and in September, they begin to build their houses nearby.

JULY 7 — The Ministerial Committee for Economic Matters allows the employment of Palestinian workers in Israel, stating that "they will receive wages equal to that of an Israeli worker…and all the [tax and social] deductions will be made that are deducted from Israeli workers." Before the year is out, 6 percent of the Palestinian workforce is working in Israel. Tax money is the main source for the military government's budget. As for Social Security, although Palestinians pay it, they do not benefit from it.

JULY 19 — The general curfew that has been in force in the West Bank since the 1967 War is lifted.

AUGUST 1 — The first attack is perpetrated against Israeli civilians inside the Green Line, the armistice line established between Israel and its neighbors, Egypt, Jordan, Lebanon, and Syria, after the 1948 War. An explosive device is hurled at the Orient Café in Jerusalem.

SEPTEMBER 4 — Defense Minister Moshe Dayan proposes a plan for the establishment of four Jewish cities in the West Bank near major Palestinian cities. In the first phase, each city is to house a few thousand families. Dayan's plan is seen as a response to the "Alon Plan" and as an attempt to jeopardize it.

NOVEMBER — The Employment Service of Israel's Ministry of Labor sets up the first local office in the Occupied Territories. By 1976, there will be thirty-four such offices. However, most of the Palestinian workers in Israel will be employed not through the offices, but through direct contact with employers and through "workers' markets" on the outskirts of the cities.

— In the course of 1968, three settlements are established as NAHAL (Fighting Pioneer Youth) outposts, all in the Jordan Valley. NAHAL units receive military combat training and function as founding groups for new settlements.

1969

JANUARY 1 — Order No. 291 freezes a Jordanian law arranging for the registration of West Bank residents' rights to their land. For historical reasons, more than 70 percent of the land in the West Bank had not been registered in the Tabu (Land Registry) prior to the freeze. The freeze would facilitate the later declaration of Palestinian lands as "state lands" and their expropriation for the establishment of the settlements.

JUNE — A general strike is held to mark the two years since the 1967 War. In response, Israel deports nine strike leaders to Jordan.

DECEMBER — Order No. 363 forbids construction, use, and grazing on nature reserves. Some 5 percent of the West Bank will ultimately be declared nature reserves.

1970

MAY 1 — Order Concerning Security Provisions (No. 378) is issued. It includes ninety-seven main sections that grant the IDF numerous powers, for example, in carrying out arrests and administrative detention, conducting searches, confiscating property, closing institutions or certain areas, and restricting the freedom of movement.

SEPTEMBER — "Black September." Following an alleged attempt to assassinate Jordan's King Hussein and the hijacking of three planes by Palestinian terrorists, a hijacking that ended on Jordanian land, where the hijackers blew up the empty planes in front of TV cameras, the tension between the Hashemite Kingdom of Jordan and Palestinian resistance organizations increases and turns into open hostilities. The Jordanian Army attacks the Palestinian organizations, and after ten months of fighting on and off, the organizations are expelled from Jordan and reorganize in Lebanon.

OCTOBER 5 — The report of the UN Special Committee to Investigate Israeli Practices Affecting the Human Rights of the Population of the Occupied Territories states that Israel uses torture when interrogating Palestinians.

NOVEMBER 30 — The first NAHAL outpost in the Gaza Strip, Kfar Darom, is established.

DECEMBER — The army begins an operation, headed by OC Southern Command Ariel Sharon, to eliminate Palestinian resistance, mainly in refugee camps in the Gaza Strip. The operation follows a wave of armed resistance in the strip that began at the end of 1968. At first, Palestinian violence was primarily directed at alleged Palestinian collaborators and subsequently included attacks on security forces and Israeli civilians. During the operation, Israel builds a fence around the refugee camps in the strip, imposes curfew on them, and Israeli troops, together with the Shabak (the General Security Service) and Palestinian collaborators, make incursions into the camps to locate wanted persons. Some twelve thousand men are detained and taken to the Abu-Zneimah Detention Center in the Sinai Peninsula. About two thousand houses, in which some fifteen thousand people lived, are destroyed during the operation.

— The Gaza Strip is connected to the Israeli electricity grid.

— An army report summarizing three years of Israeli control of the Occupied Territories states: "The Six-Day War obliterated the 'Green Line' that separated Israel from the Territories," and "the only way to prevent potential insurrection is to constantly seek to improve the standard of living and services."

— In 1970, 1,261 Palestinians are administratively detained and held without trial. The number drops the following year, to 445. Between 1973 and 1977, about forty Palestinians a year, on average, are held in administrative detention.

1971

APRIL 1 — Order No. 418 enables Israel to alter the planning system in the West Bank that had existed under Jordanian rule, reducing the involvement of Palestinians in planning processes. A High Planning Council composed of military and civilian Israelis is given the exclusive power to grant construction permits and to "amend, cancel, or suspend for a specified period the validity of any plan or permit."

AUGUST 1 — In a military operation in Gaza, thousands of Palestinians are removed from the Jabalya refugee camp and taken to other camps in the strip. The action is taken so the army can demolish buildings and establish wide "security roads" in areas that were used to conceal cells of Fatah and the Popular Front for the Liberation of Palestine. The attempt to move tens of thousands of Palestinians from Gaza to the West Bank will stop, following the growing resistance of the residents, at the end of the month.

— Attorney General Meir Shamgar states that the Fourth Geneva Convention does not apply in the Occupied Territories, but despite this, Israel will act in accordance with the humanitarian provisions of the convention and of the Hague Convention.

1972

MARCH 9 — The IDF spokesperson announces the fencing of land in the Rafah Salient "for security reasons." The action dispossesses and expels some fifteen hundred Bedouin families living in the area, which will later become the town of Yamit.

MARCH 28 — The first municipal elections are held in the West Bank. Both Jordan and the PLO call upon the Palestinians to ban the elections. Under Jordanian municipal law, only about 5 percent of the West Bank population is eligible to vote (for instance, refugee camp dwellers are excluded). Traditional forces affiliated with Jordan win.

JULY — Israel eliminates the military resistance in the Gaza Strip. Aggressive incursions by the IDF, under Ariel Sharon's command, and strenuous efforts by the Shabak force the Palestinian combatants into the refugee camps. In the camps, the IDF begins to pave roads "the width of a tank," causing massive destruction of houses and infrastructure, to enable army access and make it impossible for Palestinian combatants to hide there. The demolition is presented as part of a plan to relocate refugees in new neighborhoods in the strip in a way that would contribute to the "solution of the refugees problem." Eventually, some twelve thousand refugees would move out of the camps to newly constructed neighborhoods in the Gaza Strip.

JULY 2 — A general exit permit is issued whereby residents of the Occupied Territories are allowed to enter Israel without an individual permit. The general permit is not in force from 1:00 a.m. to 5:00 a.m., yet many Palestinian workers remain in Israel through the night.

— The military government approves the expansion of Birzeit College and its reestablishment as Birzeit University. Over the years, the university will have to face extended periods of closure, the expulsion of teachers and administrators, the banning of books and journals from entering the university, and the nonissuance of permits for non-Palestinian teachers.

— Over 5,000 Palestinians of the Gaza refugee camps are transferred to the town of Al-Arish in the Sinai Peninsula as part of a plan to resettle Palestinian refugees. The plan will fail and most of the refugees return to Gaza.

1973

JULY — The so-called Forced Operation begins, in which police and officials from the Labor Ministry enter *moshavim* (agricultural communities) looking for Palestinian workers who stayed overnight in Israel in violation of the general exit permit. The workers are sent back to the Occupied Territories, and the employers are fined. The operation stops with the outbreak of war in October.

OCTOBER 6 — The Yom Kippur/October War breaks out between Israel and Syria and Egypt. During the war and for a short time afterward, Palestinian resistance grows. In response, Israel carries out large-scale arrests, blows up dozens of houses, and sets up dozens of checkpoints throughout the West Bank. During the war, Palestinians are not allowed to enter Israel.

— The Palestinian National Front (PNF) is founded as an arm of the PLO in the Occupied Territories, its purpose being to organize mass resistance to the occupation. Its activities include the encouragement of strikes and demonstrations by labor unions, student councils, and women's organizations.

— In 1973, Israel imposes more stringent criteria for approval of requests for family unification between Palestinians in the diaspora and Palestinians living in the Occupied Territories, but the criteria are not made public. As a result, the number of approvals falls sharply. According to one estimate, between 1973 and 1983, only one thousand or so requests were approved each year, on average. In comparison, between 1967 and 1973, the Israeli authorities granted an average of seventy-five hundred approvals. In 1979, one hundred and fifty thousand requests for family unification remained pending.

1974

FEBRUARY 4 — Gush Emunim, the flagship movement of religious-ideological settlement in the Occupied Territories, convenes for the first time.

JUNE 7 — The Elon Moreh seed group goes onto the land for the first time at the old train station in Sebastia. It is the first attempt to establish a settlement in a crowded Palestinian area in the heart of the West Bank and is contrary to the Alon Plan's guidelines for settlement in the territories.

NOVEMBER 22 — The UN General Assembly recognizes the right of the Palestinians to self-determination and grants the PLO permanent observer status in all UN institutions. Strikes and demonstrations break out throughout the Occupied Territories. Israel sets up checkpoints and sends in large numbers of troops to prevent Palestinians from assembling.

— Thirty-two percent of Palestinian labor force is employed in Israel.

1975

APRIL 20 — The settlement of Ofra is founded under the guise of a work camp for the fencing work being done at a nearby army base.

AUGUST 15 — Under pressure from settlers in Hebron, the worshiping arrangements are changed at the Cave of the Patriarchs/Ibrahimi Mosque. Palestinians in the West Bank demonstrate in response.

SEPTEMBER 21 — The settlement of Ma'ale Adumim is founded. It will later be declared the first city in the Occupied Territories and will remain the largest settlement in the West Bank until 2004.

NOVEMBER 10 — The UN General Assembly adopts a resolution classifying Zionism as a form of racism.

DECEMBER 1 — After a number of failed attempts, Gush Emunim settlers from the Elon Moreh seed group obtain government approval to remain in the West Bank. Following

a compromise, they move to the Qedum army base and two years later establish the settlement Qedumim.

1976

JANUARY 18 — Netzer Hazani becomes the first NAHAL outpost turned over to civilian hands in the Gaza Strip.

MARCH — Widespread demonstrations break out in the territories, held this time with PLO participation. Israel makes an effort to downplay their significance.

APRIL 12 — The young, nationalistic generation wins the municipal elections in the territories, held this time with PLO approval. The PLO gains strength.

MAY 12 — The United States expresses its opposition to Israeli settlement anywhere in the Occupied Territories.

AUGUST — A wave of commercial strikes breaks out in the West Bank, especially in Nablus, as a protest against the payment of exorbitant taxes. Israel imposes collective punishment on the city.

— The Israeli Council for Israeli-Palestinian Peace (ICIPP) is founded. Its members include Uri Avneri, Reserve Major-General Matti Peled, and the former secretary-general of the Labor Party, Lova Eliav. The group openly meets with a senior member of the PLO, Issam Sartawi. Following the meeting, they transmit messages from Sartawi to Prime Minister Yitzhak Rabin, offering Palestinian recognition of the state of Israel and the establishment of a Palestinian state in the Occupied Territories, both contrary to the official PLO stance at the time. Contacts with Rabin yield no result.

1977

MAY 17 — Dramatic political change in Israel: Menachem Begin and the Likud Party gain control of the government and promise to promote substantial growth in settlements. The government abandons the Alon Plan, removes the limitations on settlement, and encourages settlement in Samaria (the northern West Bank) and in densely populated Palestinian areas. During the period of right-wing governments that follows (1977–84), some seventy new settlements are established, and the number of settlers rises dramatically, reaching thirty-five thousand. The massive settlement growth begins in 1982, following completion of the peace agreement with Egypt and the evacuation of the Israeli settlements in the Sinai. Many of the settlements take the community-town form: spacious homes with yards and the residents working outside the settlement mainly west of the Green Line. This model opens the way for building settlements in places where the land is not contiguous or convenient for development and thus facilitates maximum use of state lands in the Occupied Territories.

JUNE 19 — The *Sunday Times* INSIGHT team reports that "Israel tortures Arab prisoners" and cites the following practices: suspension of the detainee by the hands and the simultaneous traction of his other members for hours at a time until he loses consciousness, burns with cigarette stubs, blows by rods on the genitals, tying up and blindfolding for days (in one case, for seven days), bites by dogs, and electric shocks at the temples, mouth, chest, and testicles.

— A-Najah National University in Nablus is founded.

1978

APRIL 1 — The Israeli peace movement Peace Now holds its first demonstration in Tel Aviv, calling for Israeli concessions in negotiations with Egypt. The movement, established by a group of reserve-duty officers and soldiers, quickly becomes the principal extraparliamentary force in Israel calling for withdrawal from the Occupied Territories and evacuation of the settlements.

JULY 27 — Israel begins to build the Trans-Samaria Highway, which connects Ariel and settlements in Samaria to the center of the country. The highway plays a major role in expanding the settlement enterprise deep into the West Bank.

SEPTEMBER 17 — The Camp David Accords are signed. They comprise two framework agreements, one for peace between Israel and Egypt and the other an overall peace agreement for the Middle East. Israel relinquishes the Sinai Peninsula, and the Palestinians in the West Bank and in the Gaza Strip are granted autonomy.

NOVEMBER 14 — According to press reports, the military government severely controls political gatherings in the Occupied Territories, doing so by enforcing a Jordanian law whereby the organizers of gatherings must provide in advance a list of the speakers and their speeches to the military government.

— In response to the Camp David Accords, which provide the Palestinians with autonomy, but not with an independent state, Palestinians found the National Guidance Committee. Its purpose is to create united and effective resistance to the occupation. This body, which would become the leading supporter of the PLO in the Occupied Territories following the banning of the Popular Front, will itself be banned at the end of 1982.

— Order No. 752 is issued. The order arranges the establishment of "Village Associations," which are designed to operate as a counterweight to the national movements active in Palestinian cities. The associations are intended to serve as an alternative leadership supporting Israel and are funded, and subsequently also armed, by Israel. In 1984, Israel gives up hope that the Village Associations will have a significant political effect in the territories and withdraws its support.

— Matityahu Drobless, head of the Settlement Division of the World Zionist Organization, presents a plan to establish sixty town and village settlements in the West Bank. Five years later, he will submit a revised plan calling for the settlement of an additional one hundred thousand settlers.

— The Islamic University in Gaza is founded.

1979

MARCH 15 — The High Court of Justice gives its decision regarding the Beit El settlement. The Palestinian owners of the seized land contend that the establishment of a civilian community does not meet the security needs for which the land was taken. The High Court rules in favor of the state, holding that the settlements fulfill a security need.

OCTOBER — The Palestinian National Front, which classifies itself as the arm of the PLO in the Occupied Territories, is banned.

OCTOBER 22 — The High Court decides the Elon Moreh case, rejecting the security argument as a basis for the seizure of land to establish the settlement. Unlike the Beit El case, this time, the petitioners submit affidavits of former senior military officials that question the security need in building a settlement in the heart of a densely populated Palestinian area. In addition, the settlers themselves submit an affidavit that avoids the security pretext and claim they have a complete and unconditional right to settle everywhere in the West Bank. Following the court's decision, new ways are found to seize Palestinian land on which to build settlements. At the instruction of Pli'a Albeck, senior assistant to the state attorney, Israel takes advantage of provisions of an Ottoman law that applies in the Occupied Territories, which states that unregistered lands (accounting for two-thirds of the West Bank) that are not cultivated for a certain period of time can be declared "state lands." Over the years, Israel will declare close to 30 percent of the West Bank "state lands."

— Order No. 783, relating to the administration of regional councils, grants the Jewish councils powers over a substantial portion of the West Bank while denying the same powers to the Palestinian councils. Order No. 892, which will be issued in 1981, grants similar powers to Jewish local councils. These orders expand the application of Israeli law in the Occupied Territories, not only personally with respect to the settlers, but also to the extensive lands of the regional and local councils and pave the way for control of large sections of land. Within a few years, settlements will control about 42 percent of the land in the West Bank.

— The Union of Palestinian Medical Relief Committees (UPMRC) is founded by a group of Palestinian doctors and health professionals affiliated with the Palestinian Communist Party. The UPMRC focuses on bringing primary health care and health education to rural areas in an attempt to diminish Israel's control and dominance of Palestinian health care.

1980

JANUARY 29 — Following the High Court's decision, the Elon Moreh settlement is moved to Mount Kabir, several kilometers north of its original site.

JANUARY 30 — The first killing of a settler occurs when Yehoshua Saloma is shot to death in the open-air market in Hebron. Settlers in the city riot. The day after the killing, a group of settlers from Kiryat Arba squat in abandoned buildings in the heart of Hebron.

APRIL 15 — Israel cancels the municipal elections scheduled for later in the month out of concern that the nationalist-oriented Palestinian organizations will increase their power.

MAY 2 — Six settlers are killed in Hebron, after which Israel deports the mayors of Hebron and Halhul and the *qadi* of Hebron.

JUNE 2 — The Jewish underground carries out its first terrorist act, aimed at the mayors of Nablus and Ramallah, who are severely injured.

JULY 30 — The Basic Law: Jerusalem is enacted by the Knesset. The law declares the "unified" city to be the eternal capital of the Jewish people. The law is declarative, having no practical significance.

1981

JANUARY 26 — The military government issues orders prohibiting building in the Bethlehem and Jenin areas near roads that surround army bases and settlements.

APRIL 29 — Following criticism by the High Court of Justice regarding enforcement of the law on settlers in the Occupied Territories, the Justice Ministry establishes a committee headed by Deputy Attorney General Yehudit Karp. Its purpose is "to guarantee, to the extent possible, that suspected cases of offenses committed by Israelis in Judea and Samaria against Arab residents of the area are investigated swiftly, substantively, and efficiently." The committee's conclusions, which will be published only in 1984, are unequivocal: The police are not fulfilling their commitment to the High Court to prevent, to the extent possible, illegal acts by settlers. The committee states that the number of files closed on grounds of "offender unknown" is greater than is customary, that police officers are lenient toward settlers who do not cooperate when being investigated, and that in some files, it appears that no action was taken to locate the offenders.

NOVEMBER — The Civil Administration is established. Its official purpose is to implement the "autonomy for residents" plan that Israel committed to in the framework of the peace agreement with Egypt. The coordinator of government activities in the Occupied Territories is from now on subordinate to the IDF chief of staff, rather than to the defense minister, and the involvement of army commanders in the daily decisions relating to the lives of the local population increases.

NOVEMBER — A two-week strike occurs by professionals in Gaza against new taxes imposed by the military government. In response, Israel imposes fines, arrests professionals, and closes shops and pharmacies.

NOVEMBER — The Birzeit Solidarity Committee is founded in Tel Aviv. It provides one of the first frameworks for cooperation between Israelis and Palestinians other than by anti-Zionist groups.

1982

SPRING — A wave of uprisings against Israel breaks out in the Occupied Territories. Thirty-one Palestinians are killed and 365 are injured.

MARCH 12 — Israel dismisses ten mayors in the West Bank and Gaza and appoints Israeli army officers in their stead. With the dismissals, Israel's relative tolerance toward individuals and institutions propounding a Palestinian nationalist stance ends. Later, travel restrictions are placed on workers' leaders, heads of charitable societies, newspaper editors, and others. Israel also imposes regional travel restrictions, detains individuals, increases the pace of house demolitions, and closes schools.

APRIL — The Ministerial Committee for Settlement allows the establishment of settlements under private initiatives, thus approving the purchase of land in the territories by private persons while ending the Jewish National Fund's monopoly on land acquisition.

JUNE 6 — Israel invades Lebanon in what it calls Operation Peace for the Galilee. The attack is aimed at the PLO bases and institutions in Lebanon and seeks to establish a "new order" north of Israel. Despite statements that the operation is limited in scope and duration, the IDF reaches the outskirts of Beirut in a few days. Palestinian neighborhoods and refugee camps in Tzor, Tzidon, and other areas south of Beirut and in the capital itself are attacked. The war continues for months and years.

AUGUST 21 — Following two months of siege on Beirut and thousands of civilian casualties, an agreement mediated by the United States allows

PLO forces to leave the city without surrendering to the Israeli Army. The Palestinian forces disperse to a few Arab countries. PLO headquarters moves to Tunis.

SEPTEMBER 18 — Militiamen from the Christian Phalangists, Israel's allies in Lebanon, massacre some eight hundred and fifty people in the Sabra and Shatila Palestinian refugee camps. IDF troops who are spread out around the camps and who had some intelligence on the forthcoming assault and on the massacre as it is taking place do nothing to prevent the massacre. A week later, hundreds of thousands of Israelis demonstrate in Tel Aviv and demand appointment of a commission of inquiry. The commission will be established a few weeks later. Its report will be published in February 1983 and will eventually lead to the removal of Ariel Sharon from the Defense Ministry.

DECEMBER — The government presents a master plan for the development of Judea and Samaria. The plan foresees the settlement of some seventy-five thousand settlers in thirty-five new settlements.

— In 1982, the trend in the farming sector in the Occupied Territories turns sharply down, recording a decline in farming income for the first time. This decline, a permanent trend in the coming years, further encourages employment in Israel and abandonment of the land and indirectly enables Israel to expand the declaration of uncultivated land as "state lands."

— Responsibility for the water economy in the Occupied Territories is transferred from the IDF to Mekorot, the Israeli water company. In the mid-1990s, 83 percent of the water drawn from the Occupied Territories goes to Israel, where per-capita water consumption is almost four times higher than in the Occupied Territories.

— Yesh Gvul, a peace movement supporting Israeli soldiers who refuse to serve in Lebanon and in the Occupied Territories, is founded. Over the years, more than three thousand soldiers will refuse to take part in IDF actions in the Occupied Territories, with some three hundred and fifty of them being sentenced to military prison for their refusal.

1983

JANUARY — PLO leader Yasser Arafat and its senior member Issam Sartawi publicly meet with Uri Avneri, Matti Peled, and Ya'akov Arnon of the Israeli Council for Israeli-Palestinian Peace. Several weeks later, Arafat and Sartawi are severely criticized during the Palestinian National Council meeting for having met with Israelis. In the following April, Sartawi is shot dead because of his many meetings with Israelis by an assassin from the Abu Nidal organization, which rejects any contact with Israel.

JANUARY 20 — Israel deports thirty-four lecturers from West Bank universities who refuse to sign a statement declaring that they do not support the PLO.

JULY 26 — Members of the Jewish underground attack the Islamic College in Hebron, killing three persons and injuring dozens.

— Israel adopts more stringent criteria for family unification. Requests by residents of the Occupied Territories married to a person from abroad are now examined on the basis of two considerations: governmental considerations, which generally means giving a benefit to families of collaborators and, from time to time, to wealthy Palestinians who promise to invest in the territories, and exceptional humanitarian cases. As a result of the more stringent criteria, the number of approvals for family unification drops by one-third.

— The Palestinian Agricultural Relief Committees (PARC) is founded by a group of Palestinian agronomists and engineers affiliated with the Palestinian Communist Party. PARC strives to reduce agricultural dependence on Israel and to prevent the expropriation of land by helping Palestinian farmers to adopt modern cultivation practices. Its main strategy is to promote the formation and consolidation of local farmers' committees. PARC and other organizations of its kind will constitute the social infrastructure of the first intifada.

1984

APRIL 12 — Israel again suspends municipal elections in the Occupied Territories. Six months later, the High Court of Justice approves the decision.

APRIL 12 — Four Palestinians from the Gaza Strip take control of an Egged bus on the No. 300 line, on its way from Tel Aviv to Ashkelon, and hold the passengers hostage, intending to bring about the release of Palestinians imprisoned in Israel. The hostages are freed by military action, one woman passenger and two of the four abductors being killed during the action. The other two Palestinians are captured, shackled, and taken by soldiers to a nearby field, where, under the orders of the head of the Shabak, Avraham Shalom, they are killed by blows to the head with a rock. The public is told that all the abductors had been killed in the military action. A few days later, the newspaper *Hadashot*, unhindered by censorship order, publishes a picture showing one of the abductors alive after the action and accuses the Shabak of whitewashing the killing of the abductor. Following the affair, Shalom resigns, along with other Shabak heads. All the Shabak members involved in the incident are ultimately pardoned by Israel's president, Chaim Herzog.

MAY 24 — An indictment is filed against twenty-seven members of the Jewish underground. They are accused of murder, attempted murder, and membership in a terrorist organization. Thirteen of them will be convicted on the latter charge—two sentenced to life imprisonment, one to nine years' imprisonment, and the others to sentences of three to four years' imprisonment. Within a few years, most of the members of the underground are freed. Those sentenced to life imprisonment are released after serving less than seven years in jail.

SEPTEMBER 13 — National unity government is inaugurated in Israel. Shimon Peres is the first to serve as Prime Minister.

— The Knesset adopts a law amending and extending the Defense (Emergency) Regulations, opening the way for applying Israeli statutory law to residents of the settlements without the need for a separate amendment of each particular statute. Prior to this, certain laws were extended to cover Israeli "residents of the region."

1985

JANUARY 14 — The government decides to withdraw the IDF from Lebanon in stages while maintaining a security zone north of the international border. The IDF does not leave Lebanon completely until July 2000, following fierce resistance by Hezbollah forces, which include suicide attacks.

FEBRUARY 3 — Operation Obstructions is carried out by more than one thousand settlers, who block twenty-eight traffic arteries in the Occupied Territories and search Palestinian vehicles. The action comes on the backdrop of stone throwing at settlers, with the settlers wanting the army to take more aggressive action against Palestinians.

MAY — The Jibril deal is completed, in which 1,150 Palestinian prisoners are released in exchange for the return of three Israeli soldiers who were being held captive in Lebanon. Settlers raid a few of the released prisoners' houses in the West Bank, beat Palestinians, destroy property, and make threats.

JULY 9 — An order directs all newspapers published in the Occupied Territories to print, for free, notices of the military government. The editors object.

JULY 21 — The Council of Kiryat Arba decides to forbid Arabs to enter the settlement and work there.

SEPTEMBER 7 — Thousands of soldiers are dispatched to the Occupied Territories in response to growing Palestinian resistance. In the previous six weeks, there were twenty-six attacks on Israelis in the Occupied Territories and in Israel, and six Israelis were killed. Israel declares extensive areas in the West Bank a "closed military area."

SEPTEMBER 22 — Settlers join an arrest-and-search operation that the IDF carries out in al-Amari refugee camp following attacks on Israeli vehicles.

— As a condition for handling family-unification requests, the Civil Administration demands that the person for whom the request is made does not remain in the Occupied Territories from the moment that the request is submitted to the time a decision is reached. Following the new requirement, the Civil Administration stops handling the cases of persons (primarily women) who are staying at the time in the territories. As a result, many of the persons waiting for approval of the requests stay in the region illegally.

— The trade deficit between the Occupied Territories and Israel rises by 49 percent in 1985, reaching $219 million. Palestinians have become a captive market of Israel.

1986

APRIL 10 — At a gathering of the Labor Party, Prime Minister Shimon Peres declares that Israel recognizes the Palestinians as a people. His statement provokes harsh criticism.

MAY 6 — Minister of Industry and Trade Ariel Sharon directs that every Palestinian product from the Occupied Territories be clearly marked as such. His reason is that "they threaten Israeli products by means of unfair competition."

AUGUST — The Ministry of Industry and Trade budgets millions of dollars to establish four new industrial areas in the Occupied Territories and to expand ten others.

AUGUST 6 — In response to a series of meetings between Israeli leftist activists and representatives of the PLO, the Knesset enacts a law that prohibits Israelis from meeting with PLO members. Offenders face three years' imprisonment.

DECEMBER 19 — The Ansar II Detention Camp, in Gaza, is closed, following many complaints of abuse and poor conditions. Most of the prisoners are released. Only three months later, the camp reopens.

1987

FEBRUARY 20 — Ehud Barak, head of the Central Command, declares that the character of the Palestinian enemy has changed. According to him, the IDF is no longer pitted in battle in the territories against terrorists, but mainly against indigenous ideologies and ideas that flourish when countered with force."

MARCH 26 — About one thousand Palestinian prisoners jailed in the Kfar Yona, Nablus, and Hebron prisons go on a hunger strike to protest their detention conditions. Within a week, the number of prisoners on strike will rise to four thousand.

APRIL 11 — Israeli Foreign Affairs Minister Shimon Peres and King Hussein of Jordan sign the London Agreement. The agreement outlines a framework for an international conference under UN supervision whose purpose is a solution of the "Palestinian problem." The agreement further stipulates that the Palestinians would be represented in the conference by the Jordanian delegation and that the PLO was not to attend. The agreement is seen as a last-chance attempt to promote the "Jordanian option," the resolution of the Palestinian issue through a form of "power sharing" between Israel and Jordan over the West Bank population. In May, Prime Minister Shamir will veto the agreement in the Israeli Cabinet.

MAY — The Defense Ministry bows to settlers' pressure and executes a list of reprisal measures handed to it by a body called "Citizens of *Yesha*" (an acronym for Judea, Samaria, and the Gaza Strip) following attacks on settlers. The list includes the mass arrest of prominent Palestinian leaders, closure of universities, and curfews.

MAY 14 — Head of the Central Command Barak reveals that the IDF had recently developed improved, nonlethal riot-control techniques for use against Arab demonstrators.

JUNE 7 — It is revealed before the Knesset Financial Committee that the Civil Administration collected $235 million in direct and indirect taxes from the Occupied Territories, a sum exceeding its annual allocated budget.

JUNE 8 — Israeli military authorities ban fishing in the Gaza Strip by Palestinian residents for an indefinite period of time. Between fifteen hundred and two thousand families in the region, mainly in the Shati refugee camp, depend on fishing for their livelihood.

AUGUST — A computerized database on the Palestinian population is set up by the Civil Administration. It will serve as a basis for issuing movement and exit permits in the future.

OCTOBER — The Landau Commission, which was appointed to examine the interrogation methods used by the Shabak, permits the use of "nonviolent psychological pressure of a vigorous and protracted interrogation" and "moderate physical pressure." The commission states that the interrogators act within the provisions of the "necessity defense," which, if proven, relieves them of any criminal responsibility.

NOVEMBER — The Israeli movement The Twenty-First Year: Against the Occupation is founded. It supports acts of practical opposition to the occupation, such as refusal to serve in the Occupied Territories, a boycott of products made in the settlements, and a cessation of trips and excursions in the Occupied Territories.

DECEMBER 6 — Israel detaches the Jewish neighborhoods in East Jerusalem from the Arab electricity grid and connects them to the Israeli electricity grid, thus further blurring the Green Line. A short time later, the franchise license of the East Jerusalem electric company expires, and for the first time, the Israeli electric company supplies electricity to the entire Occupied Territories.

DECEMBER 9 — The first intifada erupts. Following a traffic accident in which an Israeli truck driver kills four residents of the Jabalya refugee camp in the Gaza Strip, and the rumor spreads that he did so in a deliberate act of revenge, widespread demonstrations break out. These are accompanied by harsh clashes with the army in the Gaza Strip and later in the West Bank and East Jerusalem. It takes Israel a few weeks before it realizes that a new phase in Palestinian resistance has begun.

— The National Insurance Institute, Israel's social security administration, starts to implement a decision designed to encourage Palestinian residents of East Jerusalem to move to the West Bank. Some thirty thousand Palestinians, who are holders of Jerusalem identity cards, but who no longer live in the city, start receiving old-age pensions, maternity grants, and other allowances that are not normally granted to Palestinian residents of the territories.

— In order to garner support in the West Bank, Jordan creates a propaganda machine, including radio and television programs and a newspaper, that stress Jordanian-Palestinian "unity of fate." Jordanian measures are complemented by Israeli censorship of attacks on King Hussein in the Palestinian press.

1988

JANUARY 3 — Following the outbreak of the intifada, deportation orders are issued for Palestinian leaders and activists.

JANUARY 21 — The media reports that soldiers were instructed to "break the arms and legs" of Palestinians as a means of punishment.

FEBRUARY — All universities and colleges in the Occupied Territories are closed by military order for two years.

MARCH 14 — Following distribution of a pamphlet by the Unified National Leadership demanding that all Palestinians working for the Israeli Civil Administration resign and the pressure and threats that come in its wake, more than four hundred Palestinian police officers resign.

MAY — A permanent night curfew is imposed on the Gaza Strip. The curfew remains in force for six years.

JULY — A new procedure in the Occupied Territories: The Civil Administration uses different markings on the identity cards of Palestinians and adds restrictions to the cards that state "The holder of this card is not allowed to exit for Israel." A few months later, the Civil Administration will issue green identity cards (most residents of the Occupied Territories carry orange or red cards) to persons who are not permitted to exit the territories.

JULY 31 — King Hussein announces his decision "severing the administrative and judicial connection" between the Kingdom of Jordan and the West Bank.

AUGUST — The IDF begins to use rubber-coated metal bullets to disperse demonstrations. A sharp increase in the number of Palestinian casualties follows.

AUGUST — Israel bans the Palestinian popular committees.

OCTOBER 25 — Reuters exposes the existence of the undercover IDF units Shimshon and Duvdevan and that they carry out extrajudicial executions.

NOVEMBER 15 — The Palestine National Council decides to accept UN Resolution 242, which recognizes Israel. Yasser Arafat declares the establishment of a Palestinian state in exile. Electricity in the Occupied Territories is cut off to prevent Palestinians from watching the TV broadcast. Twenty-two countries immediately recognize the Palestinian state. From now on, this day will be commemorated as Palestinian Independence Day.

DECEMBER 17 — Order No. 1262 is issued. The order conditions the issuance of almost every kind of license and permit—including permits to leave the territories, work permits, drivers' licenses, car registrations, building permits, permits to set up a business, and the like—on the payment of taxes. The taxes that the residents of the Occupied Territories have to pay are 35 percent higher, in real terms, than those paid by Israeli citizens.

— Three Israeli human rights organizations are founded: B'Tselem, Physicians for Human Rights, and Rabbis for Human Rights. These organizations will document violations of human rights in the Occupied Territories, file petitions in the High Court of Justice, offer medical and practical assistance to Palestinians, and engage in public advocacy.

1989

APRIL — At the recommendation of the High Court of Justice, a military appeals court is founded and sits in Ramallah. Prior to establishment of the court, appeals of the decisions of military courts were referred to the military commander and almost always denied.

JUNE — Palestinians from the Gaza Strip who work in Israel are required to have a magnetic card that contains updated information on their "security history" and on the payment of taxes and water and electricity bills. The holder must renew the magnetic card yearly. The card will be used not only to regulate and monitor entry into Israel, but also as a means to pressure workers to collaborate with the Shabak. This is the first restriction placed on the general exit permit that was declared in 1972. The directive is later applied also in the West Bank and is made a condition for obtaining a work permit.

SEPTEMBER 14 — The army changes its open-fire regulations. Soldiers are allowed to fire at masked, unarmed persons.

SEPTEMBER 28 — Israel declares Hamas to be a terrorist organization and makes membership in it a crime. Previously, Israel was said to nurture the Islamic organizations, or at least to turn a blind eye to their growth, so as to provide a counterweight to the nationalist movements.

1990

OCTOBER — Preparations for a war in the Gulf. Fearing attacks by Iraqi missiles carrying chemical warheads, the Israeli government decides to distribute gas masks to all citizens and residents. Following an intervention by the High Court of Justice, the distribution will include Palestinian residents of the Occupied Territories.

— Israel sets up checkpoints and builds dirt mounds to re-mark the borders of greater Jerusalem in an attempt to separate East Jerusalem from the rest of the West Bank. Israeli authorities start to monitor where East Jerusalem Palestinians live and to deny them residency if they transfer their "center of life" outside the city. This policy will be more actively enforced beginning in 1995.

1991

JANUARY — As part of the "security measures" undertaken by Israel in the eve of the Gulf War, the general exit permit that was issued in 1972 is cancelled. Every resident of the Occupied Territories wanting to enter Israel must have an individual permit. In addition, Israel declares a full closure of the Occupied Territories, which will last for forty-one days. This policy is enforced only partially and will be enforced to a significantly greater extent beginning in March 1993.

JANUARY 15 — America-led coalition forces attack the Iraqi Army in Iraq and Kuwait. Within days, Israeli cities would be attacked by Iraqi

(conventional-warhead) missiles. Under American pressure, Israel abstains from retaliation.

MARCH — A report by B'Tselem describes the Shabak's interrogation and torture techniques, which include food and sleep deprivation, imprisonment in isolation, covering the detainee's head with a dirty sack, beatings, and use of the "banana" technique, in which the detainee's legs and hands are tied in a way that causes his body to arch backward.

MARCH 31 — Palestinians are prohibited from entering Israel in private vehicles.

SEPTEMBER 12 — President George H. W. Bush conditions the granting of loan guarantees to Israel on a freeze in settlement activity.

SEPTEMBER 18 — Abie Nathan, peace activist and director of The Voice of Peace radio station, is sentenced to fifteen months in prison for having violated the law prohibiting meeting with PLO members.

OCTOBER 30 — The Madrid Conference begins. Following the Iraqi surrender and the end of the Gulf War, the international conference is called by the foreign ministers of the United States and Russia in an attempt to achieve peace in the Middle East. The conference is attended by Israel and by almost all the Arab countries. The Palestinians are represented by a joint Jordanian-Palestinian delegation; the Palestinian members of the delegation are approved by the PLO, but are not its officials. The conference leads to direct talks between Israel and the delegations from Syria, Lebanon, and Jordan-Palestine.

DECEMBER 15 — Palestinians are forbidden to approach within 150 meters of intercity roads in the Occupied Territories.

1992

FEBRUARY 19 — Ma'ale Adumim is declared the first Israeli city in the territories.

NOVEMBER 22 — The newly elected government headed by Yitzhak Rabin decides to freeze settlement activity in the territories, except within the borders of the existing communities and based on approved outline plans. Order No. 1385, issued a few months later, freezes all planning processes for building in the territories. The government's decision is considered to have spurred the establishment of illegal outposts by Israeli settlers that starts in the mid-1990s and that increases in number during the beginning of the next decade. From 1992 to 1996, the years of Labor Party rule, no new settlements are built. However, the number of settlers grows by 40 percent, reaching one hundred and forty thousand, not including the Jerusalem area.

DECEMBER — Following the kidnapping and killing of a border policeman by Palestinians, Israel deports 415 Hamas members to Lebanon. One group of deportees returns in October 1993 and the others two months later.

1993

MARCH — Israel begins to enforce the prohibition on entry of Palestinians into Israel, including East Jerusalem. Only Palestinians carrying individual permits are allowed to exit the Occupied Territories. Israelis (including Palestinian citizens of Israel) are forbidden to enter the Gaza Strip without a permit, which is given for one day only.

APRIL 16 — The first Palestinian suicide attack. A booby-trapped car explodes at a rest stop in the Jordan Valley, killing a Palestinian employee and injuring seven soldiers.

JULY — Following an increase in the building, development, and rapid occupancy of Jewish neighborhoods in East Jerusalem, Jews for the first time become a majority there (one hundred and sixty thousand Jews, compared with one hundred and fifty-five thousand Palestinians).

AUGUST — Israel sets a quota on family unification for the first time—no more than 2,000 requests will be approved annually. The quota

does not meet the population's needs, and families have to separate during the long wait for their request to be approved.

SEPTEMBER 13 — The Declaration of Principles (the Oslo I agreement) is signed in Washington. The agreement includes reciprocal Israel-PLO recognition and deals with interim arrangements ahead of the establishment of Palestinian self-government in the Gaza Strip and Jericho area and the holding of free elections to a legislative council. The parties agree to postpone the discussions on the final-status arrangements on issues such as Jerusalem, refugees, settlements, and security arrangements. The signing follows secret negotiations over two years, most of which were held in Norway.

— The building of bypass roads in the West Bank reaches its peak following the Oslo Accords and in the framework of the IDF's plans for redeployment. This year, Israel begins the building of more than one hundred kilometers of new roads in the West Bank, which amount to more than 20 percent of all road-construction started by Israel in 1993.

1994

FEBRUARY 25 — Baruch Goldstein, a settler from Kiryat Arba, murders 29 Palestinian worshipers and wounds 125 others in the Cave of the Patriarchs/Ibrahimi Mosque in Hebron. In demonstrations following the incident, nine Palestinians are killed by Israeli security forces. Among the measures Israel takes to "restore public order" is closure of a-Shuhada Street, the main street in the Old City of Hebron, to Palestinian vehicles. A state commission of inquiry, headed by Justice Meir Shamgar, which is appointed following the incident, criticizes the police for not being sufficiently active with respect to the settlers. The commission recommends a number of reforms regarding enforcement of the law on settlers in the West Bank, the major reform being concentration of investigative powers in the hands of the police.

APRIL 29 — The Paris Protocol, which regulates economic relations between Israel and the Palestinian Authority (PA), is signed. Among its provisions, the protocol establishes a customs union between Israel and the PA. Israel undertakes to allow free access of Palestinian workers into Israel and of Palestinian goods to the Israeli market, as well as to transfer to the PA the customs, VAT, and employment taxes that it collects for it. Ever since, Israel has been using transfer of these monies as a means of pressuring the Palestinian Authority.

MAY 16 — The IDF withdraws its forces from the Gaza Strip, except for the settlements and the roads leading to them. For the first time in seven years, the night curfew on the Gaza Strip is removed.

JUNE — Following the recommendation of the Shamgar Commission, which investigated the massacre in Hebron, the SHAI (Samaria and Judea) District of the Israel Police is formed for the purpose of improving law enforcement on the settlers. However, the district will be understaffed and will not be accorded sufficient technical facilities.

JULY 1 — Following the signing of the Declaration of Principles, Yasser Arafat and the top PLO leadership arrive in Gaza from Tunis. Four days later, Arafat is declared president of the Palestinian Authority. The PA begins to assume authority for civil matters (education, health, welfare, and so forth) in the self-government areas—the Gaza Strip and the Jericho area.

SEPTEMBER — Following a number of suicide attacks carried out by the Hamas in response to the massacre in Hebron, the Ministerial Committee for General Security Service Matters expands the permission for using torture that was given by the Landau Commission and allows the Shabak to use "increased physical pressure" in its interrogations.

DECEMBER 10 — The Nobel Peace Prize is awarded to Yasser Arafat, Yitzhak Rabin, and Shimon Peres.

1995

JANUARY — Following terrorist attacks in Israel, the Israeli government establishes two committees to formulate a "separation plan" that will detach Israel from the territories, one headed by the minister of internal security, Moshe Shahal, which is directed to examine the security aspects of the separation, and one headed by the former director-general of the Finance Ministry, David Brodet, to examine the economic aspects. The Shahal Committee recommends establishment of a "Seam Zone" containing physical obstructions that extend for 320 kilometers, only 29 kilometers of it being a fence. It also recommends a permit regime for Palestinian entry into Israel, establishing organized crossing points, reducing the entry of vehicles from the West Bank, and employing a method of controlled transfer of goods into Israel.

MARCH — The Brodet Committee, appointed to examine the economic aspects of separation between Israel and the territories, issues the following recommendations: conditioning Palestinians entry into Israel upon security checks, increased law enforcement on Palestinians who enter Israel without a permit and on their employers, establishing an international Israeli-Palestinian institution to protect investment in the territories from political risks, and establishing a commercial zone alongside Israel's border to reduce the entry of vehicles carrying goods from the territories to Israel.

JUNE — Having already issued magnetic cards to Palestinian workers from the Gaza Strip, Israel also issues magnetic cards to Palestinian workers from the West Bank. The workers must carry the cards along with their permits to enter Israel.

SEPTEMBER 28 — Israel and the PLO sign Oslo II. This agreement divides the West Bank into Area A (an area that will eventually encompass 18 percent of the West Bank and that includes the main Palestinian cities except for Hebron, in which the Palestinian Authority has responsibility for all matters), Area B (which will eventually encompass 22 percent of the West Bank, in which the Palestinians control civil matters and Israel controls security), and Area C (which will eventually encompass 60 percent of the West Bank, in which Israel has complete control). In the framework of the agreement, the IDF redeploys and withdraws from Area A. In Area B, Israeli and Palestinian security forces conduct joint patrols, and District Civil Liaison Offices (DCLs) and District Coordination Offices (DCOs) are established to promote coordination and cooperation between the Israeli authorities and the Palestinian Authority. With the beginning of the second intifada, the DCOs' activity focuses on issuing movement permits and permits to enter Israel.

NOVEMBER 4 — Prime Minister Yitzhak Rabin is assassinated at the end of a peace rally in Tel Aviv by Yigal Amir, a twenty-seven-year-old law student.

— The Gaza perimeter fence is built. Over the years, various areas near the fence will be classified a "special security zone" into which soldiers are permitted to fire without warning.

— The Ministry of the Interior starts to implement a policy of "quiet deportation" in East Jerusalem. Relying on statutes, regulations, and administrative stratagems, the ministry revokes the residency status of Palestinian residents of East Jerusalem who have moved outside Jerusalem's municipal borders, including temporary stays abroad.

1996

JANUARY 5 — Israel eliminates Yehiye Ayash, a senior Hamas explosives expert. Hamas promises revenge.

JANUARY 19 — The Palestinian Authority holds its first elections. Yasser Arafat is elected president; Hamas and other opposition groups ban the elections.

FEBRUARY–MARCH — A wave of suicide attacks in Israel: fifty-eight persons are killed and more

than two hundred injured in four suicide attacks within a space of nine days.

MARCH — Israel issues an order directing that all Gazan students studying in the West Bank return to Gaza. Since then, Israel has refused to issue permits for Gazan students to live and study in the West Bank.

MARCH 3 — The government decides to separate the population in Israel from the Palestinian population of the Occupied Territories. To achieve this objective, Israel will set up crossings in the Seam Zone and block other paths by which Palestinians enter Israel.

MARCH 5 — Following a wave of terrorist attacks, Israel imposes a comprehensive closure on the Occupied Territories. Simultaneously, Areas A and B are separated from each other, and an internal closure is imposed on 465 towns and villages. A protracted curfew is imposed on a few villages from which, Israel contends, the attackers came. In addition, the entire jurisdictional area of the settlements, 42 percent of the West Bank, is declared a "closed military area" into which Palestinians are forbidden entry.

AUGUST 2 — The new right-wing government headed by Benjamin Netanyahu removes the restrictions on development of the settlements and ends the partial freeze agreed to in the Oslo agreements. However, from 1996 on only three new settlements will be built, among them Modi'in Illit, a city populated by ultra-religious Jews that will become the most heavily populated settlement. Most of the new construction of houses takes place in new neighborhoods adjacent to established settlements.

SEPTEMBER 23 — Prime Minister Netanyahu orders the opening of the portal of the Western Wall Tunnel to the Muslim Quarter of the Old City in Jerusalem. Bloody rioting and protest actions follow in the Occupied Territories, in which sixty-nine Palestinians and eleven IDF soldiers are killed.

OCTOBER 3 — Israel cuts off internet lines in the Occupied Territories to block the flow of information.

1997

JANUARY 15 — Israel and the Palestinian Authority sign the Hebron Agreement. Under the agreement, Hebron is divided into an area under complete Palestinian control (H-1) and an area in which Israel is responsible for security and the PA is responsible for civil matters (H-2). H-1 encompasses 18 square kilometers, in which one hundred and fifteen thousand Palestinians live; H-2 encompasses 4.3 square kilometers, in which thirty-five thousand Palestinians and five hundred Israeli Jews live.

— Israel significantly expands the outline plans and jurisdictional area of the settlements with the objective of controlling as much land as possible prior to the continuing division of the West Bank into Areas A, B, and C.

1998

AUGUST 31 — Israel installs thirteen electric gates in the Old City in Hebron to control Palestinian movement in the area.

OCTOBER 2 — The IDF blocks the main route connecting the two parts of the city of Hebron (zones H-1 and H-2). The route had replaced a-Shuhada Street as the main road in the city after the latter was blocked following the massacre in Hebron.

OCTOBER 8 — The settlement of Ariel is declared a city, despite the fact that the number of residents in Ariel is only fifteen thousand and does not reach the minimum of twenty thousand residents required to declare a city in Israel west of the Green Line.

OCTOBER 23 — The Wye River peace talks end with the signing of an agreement that calls for Israel's further withdrawal in the West Bank. Under the agreement, Israel will hand over an additional 13 percent of the West Bank to Palestinian Authority control and, in consideration, the PA will take action to stop terrorist acts arising from its territory, collect illegal weapons, act to put an end to incitement, and delete the section in the Palestinian National Covenant that calls for the destruction of Israel.

NOVEMBER 8 — The PLO executive committee ratifies Arafat's letter to the U.S. president, Bill Clinton, nullifying and amending provisions in the Palestinian National Covenant that deny Israel's right to exist.

NOVEMBER 16 — Foreign Affairs Minister Ariel Sharon encourages settlers to "hurry up and seize hills" in order to establish outposts, provoking severe criticism in the IDF.

NOVEMBER 18 — The Civil Administration starts paving five new bypass roads in the West Bank, preparing for the implementation of the second withdrawal according to the Wye agreement.

NOVEMBER 18 — Peace Now reports that Palestinians are allowed to build in only 7.3 percent of the area of East Jerusalem.

NOVEMBER 24 — The Palestinian International Airport opens in Dahania (Gaza Strip). It is operated by the Palestinian Authority, and a limited number of flights to Arab countries take off from there weekly. Israel will bomb the airport in the beginning of the second intifada.

NOVEMBER 26 — The IDF declares that it will not require settlements to raise security fences, due to settlers' concern that marking settlements' borders may limit future expansion.

1999

MAY 4 — Peace Now reveals that even though there are 3,714 vacant apartments in the settlements, 6,608 new apartments are being built.

MAY 11 — Following a decision by Prime Minister Benjamin Netanyahu, a closure order is issued to the Orient House in East Jerusalem, where the PLO headquarters in the city are located. The

High Court of Justice delays the order until after the elections.

JUNE 20 — The Palestinian cabinet calls upon Palestinian workers to stop working in the settlements.

JUNE 21 — The World Bank reports that Palestinians consume the least amount of water in the Middle East. Consumption reaches less than half of the UN standard.

AUGUST 4 — IDF officials tell settlers that most of the thirty-one outposts established illegally after the Wye agreement will not be evacuated.

AUGUST 15 — The IDF decides to change its policy and try stone throwers starting from the age of twelve.

AUGUST 30 — The IDF declares that it will confiscate cars from Palestinians who do not pay traffic tickets.

SEPTEMBER 5 — The Sharm el-Sheikh Memorandum is signed. It states that the withdrawal agreed upon in the Wye agreement will be implemented in three phases until January 2000, that accelerated negotiations will be held on the final arrangement, that Israel will release 350 Palestinian prisoners, and that the construction of a seaport in Gaza will begin.

SEPTEMBER 6 — The High Court of Justice rules that torture is not to be used as a means of interrogation. The justices disallow the use of interrogation methods such as "shaking" of the interrogatee, holding him in painful positions for a prolonged period of time, sleep deprivation, placing an opaque sack on the interrogatee's head, and playing loud music for many hours. In practice, the Shabak will continue to use some forms of torture, especially following the outbreak of the second intifada.

OCTOBER — After a few years' delay, the "safe passage" route—running between the West Bank and the Gaza Strip—is opened for the first time in the southerly direction. Israel had promised to open the route in the framework of the Oslo Accords. Residents of the Occupied Territories have to obtain a permit from Israel to use the passageway and have to undergo stringent security check before starting their journeys. Many Palestinians are allowed to use the roadway only on special buses escorted by the army. Thousands of other Palestinians are absolutely forbidden to use the passageway, even on army-escorted buses. The safe passage remains open for less than one year and is closed by Israel upon the outbreak of the second intifada in September 2000.

OCTOBER 31 — A-Shuhada Street in Hebron is opened to Palestinian movement for the first time since the massacre in the Cave of the Patriarchs / Ibrahimi Mosque (February 1994). The street will be closed again when the second intifada erupts.

— The settlement of Negohot is founded. It is the last settlement whose establishment is officially approved by the Israeli government. During the Oslo years, until the outbreak of the second intifada, the number of settlers living in the Occupied Territories almost doubles, from one hundred and ten thousand, nine hundred in 1993 to one hundred and ninety-one thousand, six hundred in 2000.

2000

APRIL — The IDF conducts a massive exercise dubbed First Gear in preparation for violent clashes that the army thinks might occur if Palestinians lose hope in the peace process. During the exercise, reserve soldiers simulate the reoccupation of Qalqiliya. The exercise results from a thought process carried out by the IDF's Operational Theory Research Institute, which develops combat techniques for low-intensity conflict based in part on postmodern theory.

MAY 22–24 — Unilaterally and hastily, the IDF withdraws from southern Lebanon.

JULY 27 — The Camp David summit ends in failure. Although both sides agree to significant concessions with respect to their previous positions, they do not reach agreement on Jerusalem, the right of return, and security arrangements. Both sides prepare for an escalation of the military conflict while negotiations are still underway. In advance of the summit, the Judge Advocate General's Office prepared new open-fire regulations, allowing soldiers to shoot to kill armed Palestinians in case fighting breaks out in the territories.

SEPTEMBER 28 — The head of the opposition in Israel, Ariel Sharon, makes a provocative and controversial visit to the Temple Mount, despite intelligence warnings that a "bloodbath" might result from the visit. Immediately after the visit, Palestinian demonstrators assault police forces, who respond with rubber-coated metal bullets and tear gas, killing four Palestinians and injuring more than two hundred. B'Tselem contends that the police reacted with excessive force.

SEPTEMBER 29 — The second intifada (the al-Aqsa intifada) breaks out. The army overreacts, firing 1.3 million live bullets in the first month of the intifada.

OCTOBER 1–8 — Twelve Palestinian citizens of Israel and another Palestinian from the Gaza Strip are shot to death by Israeli police forces during protests and demonstrations held in Palestinian towns in the north of Israel in solidarity with the Palestinians in the Occupied Territories.

OCTOBER 5 — The OC Central Command issues an order prohibiting Israelis from entering Area A. The order also applies to residents of East Jerusalem having blue (Israeli) identity cards.

OCTOBER 8 — Israel places an absolute prohibition on Palestinians from entering Israel and closes the "safe passage" between the West Bank and Gaza, the Rafah crossing, and the international airport in Gaza.

NOVEMBER 9 — The first "targeted killing" in the second intifada: Hussein Abiyat, a member of Tanzim, a military faction of the Fatah who was responsible for protracted gunfire at Jerusalem's Gilo neighborhood, is killed in Beit Sahur

by a helicopter missile. In the same attack, two women are killed and three other persons are injured. For the first time, Israel officially admits it carries out targeted killings. Killings of this kind will result, as of December 2007, in the death of 225 Palestinian activists and 147 civilians.

DECEMBER 13 — Settlers declare a "roadblock operation" under the slogan "Get the Murderers Off the Roads" in protest against the failure to enforce the General Staff's directive to prohibit the movement of Palestinian vehicles that are carrying only males, a directive that caused much criticism within the army.

— Israel defines the events in the territories as an armed conflict short of war, which brings with it an easing of the open-fire regulations. The judge advocate general decides to freeze the permanent command to open a Military Police Investigation Unit investigation in every case involving civilian casualties and instead to open MPIU investigations only in special cases.

— The organization Ta'ayush (living together) is founded. The field organization, composed of Arabs and Jews, focuses on solidarity actions in the Occupied Territories.

— Following the outbreak of the second intifada and the significant deterioration of living conditions in the Occupied Territories, the UN Office for the Coordination of Humanitarian Affairs (OCHA) opens an office in the Occupied Territories. Its objective is to enhance coordination between aid agencies operating in the Occupied Territories and to distribute information and analyses on humanitarian matters. OCHA will serve as the main source of information on the closure regime in the Occupied Territories, document the layout of the checkpoints and roadblocks, and periodically prepare and publish maps reflecting the current situation.

2001

JANUARY 8 — Ha'aretz reports that "the IDF allows firing without warning in part of the Occupied Territories."

JANUARY 21 — Israeli and Palestinian leaders meet in Taba in a last attempt to reach an accord ahead of a permanent agreement between Israel and the Palestinians during the premiership of Ehud Barak. The parties discuss all the final-status issues. The talks end because of the parties' feeling that under existing political circumstances, several days before Israeli elections, it is impossible to complete a framework agreement.

FEBRUARY 1 — Israel prevents Palestinians traveling in private vehicles from entering the Gush Etzion area. Israel will later restrict the travel of Palestinians on many other roads without prior notice or existence of any military order. According to a 2004 B'Tselem report, Israel at that time restricted Palestinian travel on 630 kilometers of roadway in the Occupied Territories.

FEBRUARY 4 — The IDF announces an "encirclement" of all Palestinian cities, preventing private vehicles from entering or leaving the cities. It would not be until early 2002 that Israel would begin issuing permits for movement within the West Bank.

FEBRUARY 6 — Special elections for the office of prime minister in Israel: Ariel Sharon wins.

MARCH 2 — Israel cuts a deep trench around Jericho and turns the city into an isolated enclave.

MARCH 21 — Following a petition to the High Court of Justice by Physicians for Human Rights, the army promises that every so-called "land cell" blocked by physical obstructions will have at least one access road that has a staffed checkpoint.

APRIL 16 — Palestinians fire mortars at Sderot. For the first time, the IDF conducts a major operation in Area A in the Gaza Strip. Israel divides the Gaza Strip into three parts.

MAY — "Protective barricades" that prevent the crossing of vehicles begin to be set up at various places along the Green Line.

MAY 6 — The IDF enters Area A in the West Bank for the first time and exits a few hours later.

MAY 18 — The Israeli Air Force mounts its first attack in the West Bank, on the prison in Nablus.

AUGUST — The International Solidarity Movement (ISM) carries out its first campaign, in which fifty foreigners, mostly from the UK and the United States, come to the Occupied Territories to witness the events and protect Palestinian residents from Israeli security forces. By August 2007, more than two thousand foreigners associated with the ISM would come to the Occupied Territories.

OCTOBER 17 — A Popular Front team assassinates minister Rehavam Ze'evi, a leading supporter of the ideology of transfer.

DECEMBER — A permanent checkpoint is set up at Qalandiya. This checkpoint becomes the principal checkpoint between Jerusalem and Ramallah and the rest of the West Bank. It is located inside the Occupied Territories—not along the Green Line—and inside Jerusalem's municipal boundaries, thus separating Palestinian residents of Jerusalem from each other.

DECEMBER 3 — The OC Central Command signs the "encirclement order," declaring all of Area A in the West Bank to be a closed military area requiring a special permit for anybody wanting to move about from place to place in noncontiguous Area A.

— During the course of 2001, Israel builds fences along fifty kilometers of agricultural areas along the Green Line. The construction is called the "agriculture security fence."

2002

JANUARY — Israel begins to issue internal-movement permits in the West Bank. According to the Civil Administration spokesperson, "The idea grew out of the need resulting from the complex security reality, which calls for the imposition of protracted encirclements. Following the ensuing difficulty in the movement of the Palestinian residents…it was decided to ease passage by means of issuing permits to cross an encirclement."

JANUARY 10 — The IDF demolishes sixty houses in the Rafah refugee camp, claiming that the houses are used to conceal tunnels through which weapons are smuggled from Egypt to the Gaza Strip. Two days later, the army demolishes forty more houses. These and other demolitions result in the creation of a 300-meter buffer zone between Rafah and IDF positions near the Egyptian border.

JANUARY 14 — Israel eliminates Ra'ad Karmi, a Fatah activist from Tulkarm, who was allegedly responsible for shooting attacks on both sides of the Green Line. The killing effectively ends a few weeks of relative calm.

JANUARY 20 — The IDF takes control, for the first time since its forces withdrew from the Palestinian cities in 1995, of a Palestinian city, Tulkarm, for a day.

FEBRUARY — Following suicide attacks, Jerusalem's mayor, Ehud Olmert, decides not to wait for implementation of the government's separation plans and immediately begins to build a fence around Jerusalem at the municipality's expense. Within three months, eight kilometers of relatively simple fences and obstructions are put up around the city.

FEBRUARY — Reserve-duty officers volunteer to serve at checkpoints to handle civil matters. The Seam Zone Volunteer Unit, established at the initiative of the kibbutz movement tasks department, will later be integrated into the IDF, and some four thousand volunteers will serve in the unit in the coming years.

MARCH 27 — Terrorist attack at the Park Hotel, in Netanya, during the Passover Seder. Thirty Israelis are killed.

MARCH 28 — Israel declares the Palestinian Authority an enemy and begins its invasion of the West Bank cities, labeled Operation Defensive Shield. The IDF places Arafat's offices and official residency in the Muqata'a, the PA headquarters in Ramallah, under siege. Arafat will remain in the building for thirty-four days.

The Israeli forces target, among other things, PA governmental offices, causing great damage to administrative facilities and destroying computers and databases. Thousands of Palestinians are detained in extremely crowded and poor conditions in the Ofer Detention Camp near Ramallah and in the reopened Ketzi'ot Detention Camp (Ansar III) in the Negev. The operations result in the killing of 261 Palestinians.

APRIL 2–13 — Fierce battles in the Jenin refugee camp as part of Operation Defensive Shield. Fifty-six Palestinians and twenty-three IDF soldiers are killed. The IDF employs armored bulldozers to widen camp alleys and to demolish houses where Palestinian fighters hide, burying beneath them those who refuse to surrender. The center of the camp is completely destroyed and leveled by the bulldozers. Palestinians claim that the IDF carried out a massacre in the camp.

APRIL 14 — The Israeli cabinet decides to build a permanent barrier in the West Bank. A substantial part of the barrier will not run along the Green Line, but will protrude into the West Bank at distances varying from a few hundred meters to a few kilometers. Later, the barrier's planned route in certain areas will be changed to run closer to the Green Line following decisions of the High Court of Justice that disallow a few sections of the barrier on the grounds that the injury to Palestinian civilians is disproportionate to the security benefit gained from construction of the barrier in those sections. For this reason, the planning and building of the "eastern fence"—which was to run west of the Jordan Valley, along the bottom parts of the mountain range running the entire length of the area— is halted.

JUNE — The number of administrative detainees, which was 80 at the start of Operation Defensive Shield, climbs to 929.

JUNE — The IDF carries out Operation Determined Path, in which more than a million Palestinians are placed under an almost continuous curfew for more than two months.

JULY 22 — Salah Shehadeh, head of the military wing of Hamas in the Gaza Strip, is eliminated by a one-ton bomb dropped by an F-16 aircraft. Also killed in the attack are his wife, his daughter, an assistant, and eleven other civilians, including seven more children. The Israeli Air Force commander and later IDF chief of staff, Dan Halutz, in an interview with *Ha'aretz*, says that the only thing a pilot feels in a case like this is "a slight kick in the wing of the airplane."

JULY 22 — The Knesset enacts Amendment No. 4 to the Civil Wrongs Ordinance, also known as the "first intifada law," which seeks to reduce the state's obligation to compensate Palestinians who are injured by security forces. The definition given to the term "combat action" grants the state broader exemption from liability, and significant procedural limitations are instituted regarding the filing of claims for damages caused in the Occupied Territories from IDF actions that are not combat actions. Among the procedural changes: The period of limitation of action in which the claim must be brought is reduced, and the provisions of the Civil Wrongs Ordinance that switch the burden of proof from the plaintiff to the defendant do not apply in cases that come within the amendment.

AUGUST 12 — Operation Hunt changes the targeted killing policy; whenever the opportunity arises, the IDF is now permitted to target any activist appearing on a list of persons to be eliminated. The elimination is no longer connected to the status of the activist in his organization. Also, there is no longer need for concrete information that the activist is on his way to carry out an attack, thus constituting a "ticking bomb."

— The Shabak Law is passed. For the first time, the powers of the General Security Service, which had operated until then as a legal specter, are prescribed by statute.

— According to the World Bank, between September 2000 and late 2002, the Palestinian economy experienced one of the deepest recessions in modern history. The decline in real per-capita GDP reached almost 40 percent, exceeding the scale of economic losses suffered by the United States in the Great Depression. Unemployment increased from 10 percent of the workforce to an average of 41 percent, and the number of poor persons rose from 20 percent to over 50 percent of the population.

2003

JANUARY — The OC Central Command declares that the "security envelope" surrounding the built-up area of every settlement borders the houses on the edge of the neighboring Arab villages.

MARCH 18 — Mahmoud Abbas is appointed as the first Palestinian prime minister by President Yasser Arafat.

APRIL — The group Anarchists against the Wall is founded. The group undertakes direct action in the struggle against construction of the Separation Wall, organizing joint nonviolent demonstrations of Israelis, Palestinians, and international activists.

APRIL 14 — An advisor to Prime Minister Sharon, Dov Weisglass, delivers to Secretary of State Condoleezza Rice an official letter in which Israel promises, among other things, to establish an Israeli-American team that will establish the "building lines" (the boundaries of the built-up area) for settlements in the West Bank and to hand over within thirty days a list of unauthorized outposts that are to be evacuated, along with the date the evacuation is to take place. None of these promises are kept.

APRIL 30 — President George W. Bush announces the formal release of the "road map" to Israeli-Palestinian peace. The plan aims to lead toward a two-state solution through clearly defined reciprocal steps carried out by Israel and the Palestinian Authority. It includes, in part, the obligation of Israel to evacuate all the outposts established after March 2001 and an obligation on the part of the Palestinians to cease all violence.

JUNE — The United States makes $9 billion in loan guarantees available to Israel without setting any conditions relating to progress in Israeli-Palestinian relations, a freeze on settlements, or the easing of restrictions on the Palestinians. In 1991, granting of the guarantees was conditioned on a freeze on settlements.

JUNE 29 — Palestinian resistance organizations declare a *hudna* (cease-fire) for the first time. The Palestinian Authority accepts security responsibility for the Gaza Strip and Bethlehem. The cease-fire collapses in August, following the renewal of Israel's targeted killing policy and the bombing of a bus on the Number 2 line in Jerusalem.

OCTOBER — Within the framework of building the Separation Wall, the military commander declares the Seam Zone, the enclosed area between the Separation Wall and the Green Line, a "closed area." The order states: "Nobody shall enter or remain in the Seam Zone," and "a person located in the Seam Zone must leave it immediately." This restriction applies only to Palestinians. It does not apply to Israelis, Jews who come within the Law of Return, and foreigners. The order requires Palestinians in the Seam Zone to have permits to enter and remain in their own homes.

DECEMBER 1 — The Geneva Accord is signed. This document, an unofficial outline of a permanent arrangement between Israel and the Palestinians, is the result of discussions held in 2002–3 between teams headed by Yossi Beilin and Yasser Abed Rabbo. Among the main elements of the accord are reciprocal recognition, the cessation of violence, division of Jerusalem, a partial resolution of the refugee problem, a viable border based on the Green Line, and the exchange of territory on a one-for-one basis in a few locations in order to keep some of the more populated settlements within the Israeli border.

DECEMBER 8 — The UN General Assembly requests the International Court of Justice in the Hague to render an advisory opinion on the legality of the construction of the Separation Wall. In the hearings, the Palestinians will claim that the route of the Wall violates international treaties. Israel will not take part in the hearings, but will submit a written statement to the court in which it will challenge the court's jurisdiction and stress Israel's right of self-defense. Both Israel and the Palestinians will conduct a public-relations campaign during the hearings, sending, respectively, grieving parents and farmers cut off from their lands to demonstrations in Hague.

2004

JANUARY 13 — The defense minister, Shaul Mofaz, meets with representatives of donor countries and international humanitarian organizations and requests that they act to prevent the total collapse of the Palestinian Authority.

FEBRUARY — Following a decision to move its route westward, Israel dismantles a section of the Separation Wall east of Baqa a-Sharqiya and runs the section more or less along the Green Line.

FEBRUARY — Work begins on the sunken road between Qalqiliya and Habla, a harbinger of the Everything Flows plan to build a system of separate roads, one set for Israelis and another for Palestinians, that the press will expose in February 2006.

FEBRUARY 2 — Prime Minister Sharon announces the disengagement plan. At the heart of the plan is the withdrawal of army forces from the Gaza Strip and the evacuation of all the settlements there, as well as the evacuation of four settlements (Ganim, Kadim, Homesh, and Sa-Nur) and a few military posts in the northern West Bank. In light of Israel's determination that "there is no Palestinian partner with whom it would be possible to carry out the peace process bilaterally," the government decides to implement the disengagement unilaterally. Under the plan, Israel continues to control the air and sea space of the Gaza Strip and essentially maintains power over the Gaza Strip by "remote control."

Despite this, the government of Israel's decision states that "completion of the plan will negate the force of arguments against Israel as to its responsibility for the Palestinians in the Gaza Strip" and emphasizes that, as a result of implementation of the plan, "there will be no basis for the claim that the Gaza Strip is occupied territory."

MARCH — A committee headed by Reserve Brigadier General Baruch Spiegel, which was appointed to examine the operation of the checkpoints, submits its report to the defense minister. The committee identifies many problems and recommends a reform that will include the establishment of clear procedures for the handling of the Palestinian population, stringent attention to the rules of ethical conduct at checkpoints, a prohibition on beatings, punishment, and humiliation, and reduction of the sweeping movement restrictions in both time and space. Only some of the recommendations are implemented.

MARCH 22 — Israel eliminates the Hamas leader, Sheikh Ahmad Yassin. Yassin was a spiritual and political leader, an old, handicapped man in a wheelchair. The assassination marks Israel's decision to ignore the difference between armed and unarmed members of the Palestinian organizations.

MAY — Israel places a new condition on issuing permits for Palestinian Israelis to stay in the Gaza Strip as part of the "divided families' procedure": Israelis entering the Gaza Strip must remain there at least three months.

MAY — IDF bulldozers destroy 298 houses in the Rafah refugee camp. Some thirty-eight hundred Palestinians lose their homes. In October, Human Rights Watch contends that sixteen thousand persons, almost 10 percent of Rafah's population, lost their homes during the second intifada.

JUNE 23 — A World Bank report states that donors have more than doubled their disbursement levels prior to the intifada, providing an average of $950 million per annum in 2001–3.

Of the estimated $713 million spent in 2002–3 on welfare instruments (food, cash support, job creation), some 97 percent was donor financed.

JUNE 30 — The High Court of Justice gives its decision in Beit Sourik, in which it nullifies for the first time a section of the Separation Wall on the grounds that the route chosen fails to meet the principle of proportionality, whereby there must be a balance between the security gain and the injury to Palestinians. The court orders the state to propose an alternate route.

JULY — Israel seeks to apply the Absentee Property Law in East Jerusalem, under which the property of Palestinian refugees is transferred to the state's custodian of absentee property. The law, whose application had in the past been frozen in East Jerusalem, opens the way to a vast expropriation of property. Following criticism from jurists, the plan is scrapped.

JULY 9 — The International Court of Justice in The Hague gives its decision on the Separation Wall, holding that it is illegal and must be dismantled.

OCTOBER 6 — Dov Weisglass, Prime Minister Sharon's chief advisor, admits in an interview that Israel initiated the disengagement to freeze the peace process.

NOVEMBER 11 — Yasser Arafat dies in a hospital in Paris at age seventy-five. In the preceding weeks, there were conflicting reports about his medical condition and persisting rumors that claimed that he was poisoned.

— The IDF sets up the "crossings apparatus" as part of the Military Police. Checkpoints along the line of the Seam Zone and in the Nablus area are now operated by specialist military units that receive training in carrying out security checks and in human rights.

2005

FEBRUARY 8 — The president of the Palestinian Authority, Mahmoud Abbas, and the Israeli prime minister, Ariel Sharon, hold a summit meeting in Sharm el-Sheikh. At the end of the meeting, the two leaders declare a cease-fire.

FEBRUARY 17 — A committee appointed by the chief of staff, headed by Major General Udi Shani, determines that demolition of the houses of terrorists causes more harm than good and should be stopped. The committee finds that the deterrence gained by demolition of the houses, which is limited in any event, is less significant than the hatred and enmity resulting from the demolitions. The army adopts the recommendations and ceases, as a rule, the use of the demolition of houses as punishment. The demolition of houses on a "security" pretext in Rafah and in other places, and the demolition of houses built without a permit in East Jerusalem and in Area C, continues. The Israeli Committee against House Demolitions estimates that since the beginning of the occupation, Israeli authorities demolished about eighteen thousand houses in the Occupied Territories.

MARCH 8 — Attorney Talia Sasson submits her report, made at the request of Prime Minister Sharon, on the unauthorized settler outposts. Sasson notes the deep involvement of government ministries and the Civil Administration in establishing, budgeting, maintaining, and protecting the outposts, classifying these actions an "institutional breach of the law." The report states that at least half of the 105 unauthorized outposts were built on private Palestinian land, meaning that their establishment cannot be approved retroactively.

MARCH 16 — Palestinians coming from Jordan via the Allenby Bridge (the only entry to the West Bank from abroad) are forbidden to enter via the Jordan Valley, even if they are headed to areas in the northern West Bank. Residents of Jericho wanting to travel north are also forbidden to cross through the Jordan Valley. Later, all Palestinians from the West Bank, except for Palestinians whose registered address is in the Jordan Valley, will be forbidden to enter the area. The prohibition prevents two million Palestinians from entering the valley, and thousands of farmers are unable to get to their farmland. Like most restrictions on movement, this restriction is not incorporated in any military order or regulation.

JUNE — The United States donates $50 million for the establishment of new crossings in the Separation Wall. The money is provided through the humanitarian assistance agency of the U.S. Agency for International Development.

JULY 27 — The Knesset enacts Amendment No. 7 to the Civil Wrongs Law, which exempts the state from responsibility for damages that it causes in "confrontation areas," thereby expanding the exemption provided in Amendment No. 4, of 2002. The amendment, which further diminishes the obligation of Israel to compensate Palestinians injured by its actions, is applied retroactively from the day of the outbreak of the second intifada and also applies to losses resulting from plunder, abuse, needless injury, and so forth. In December 2006, the High Court of Justice nullifies the provision of the amendment that institutes a sweeping prevention on Palestinians from suing Israel for compensation. In response to the High Court's judgment, a bill is submitted to the Knesset (Amendment No. 8) that would institute a similar arrangement using different legal wording.

AUGUST 1 — The Knesset enacts a temporary statutory provision that severely limits family unification between Israelis and Palestinians and prevents spouses from living together in Israel or East Jerusalem. Only Palestinian women aged twenty-five and above and Palestinian men thirty-five and above are allowed a permit to stay in Israel after marrying. The permit does not grant the holder any legal status or social rights. The High Court of Justice, sitting in an expanded panel of eleven justices, sustains the statute by a one-vote majority in May 2006, and the temporary statutory provision is enacted into law soon after.

AUGUST 15 – SEPTEMBER 12 — As part of the framework of the disengagement plan, the IDF evacuates all the settlements in the Gaza Strip and three settlements in northern Samaria and withdraws its forces from the Gaza Strip. All the settlements are completely destroyed, except for the synagogues. Israel continues to control the crossing points between Israel and the strip, the airspace and sea, and the population registry. Israeli citizens are no longer allowed into the Gaza Strip and journalists are required to retain a special permit.

SEPTEMBER 15 — The High Court of Justice gives its decision in Mara'abe, nullifying a section of the Separation Wall that imprisons five Palestinian villages in an enclave between the Wall and the Green Line to enable the Alfe Menashe settlement to remain west of the Wall. In making this decision, the court states that Israel has the right to build the Wall on the eastern side of the Green Line to protect the settlements, and thus rejects the decision of the International Court of Justice.

OCTOBER 28 — The IDF severs the northern West Bank from the rest of the West Bank. Eight hundred thousand Palestinians are not permitted to travel south of Nablus.

NOVEMBER 15 — The Crossings Agreement (officially, the Agreement on Movement and Access), intended to arrange movement to and from the Gaza Strip after Israel's withdrawal as part of the disengagement, is signed. Responsibility over the Rafah crossing is handed over to Egypt and the Palestinian Authority under the supervision of a force from the European Union. Also, Israel undertakes to allow the movement of goods and persons between Gaza and the West Bank and the construction of a commercial seaport and airport in Gaza. Very little of the agreement is carried out. The Rafah crossing is declared an international border, but it is closed for extended periods of time following disputes over the quality of supervision. No crossing is operated between the Gaza Strip and the West Bank.

DECEMBER — The United Nations Relief and Works Agency (UNRWA) finds that 48 percent of the population of the West Bank and 65 percent of the population of the Gaza Strip live under the poverty line, which is set at an income of $2.10 a day.

DECEMBER 29 — Following the firing of Qassam rockets on Sderot and nearby communities, the IDF declares a "buffer zone" in the northern Gaza Strip, into which it shoots to kill by means of artillery fire and munitions delivered from the air.

2006

JANUARY 22 — The Erez checkpoint, at the crossing between the Gaza Strip and Israel, is the first crossing whose operation is handed over to private hands in the framework of a comprehensive program to upgrade the crossings between Israel and the Occupied Territories and turn them into modern terminals. The declared purpose of the plan is to make the crossings more efficient and to improve the service provided to Palestinians. All the crossings, except for one, lie in Palestinian territory, and not along the Green Line.

JANUARY 25 — Hamas wins the elections in the Palestinian Authority. In the months following the elections, Israel and the so-called "Quartet" (the European Union, the United States, the United Nations, and Russia) impose economic sanctions on the PA.

FEBRUARY 17 — An order prohibits Palestinians from entering Israel on roads designated for entry by Israelis. Palestinians are allowed to cross only at eleven crossings, which are intended solely for them.

FEBRUARY 24 — Israel's plan for separate travel on West Bank roads, Everything Flows, is made public. The plan calls for building separate roads for Israelis and for Palestinians covering a distance of about one hundred and forty kilometers. Where the roads intersect, they will be built on different levels. The plan is intended to counter the criticism of Israel for the restrictions it places on Palestinian movement in privately owned passenger cars and to enable steady travel on roads earmarked for Palestinians. Most of the roads intended for Palestinians will be old, narrow roads, and at those sections where the roads are on different levels, an iron gate will be built that will enable Israel to stop the traffic at any time.

APRIL — The army reduces the "safety zone" of artillery fire in the Gaza Strip from 300 meters to 100 meters from built-up areas; 100 meters is the range of possible deviation of the shells fired by the Israeli artillery.

APRIL 14 — For the first time since the disengagement plan was implemented, the IDF enters the Gaza Strip in an attempt to stop the Qassam rocket fire at Sderot and the Gaza envelope communities.

JUNE 25 — Palestinian guerilla forces attack an army post on the Gaza Strip border. Two soldiers are killed, and one, Corporal Gilad Schalit, is injured and abducted. His release is conditioned upon a massive release of Palestinian prisoners. Following the attack, Israel begins Operation Summer Rains, in which air and land attacks on the Gaza Strip increase.

JUNE 27 — Israel bombs Gaza's power station. As a result, seven hundred thousand Palestinians experience severe disruptions of the electricity supply for months. The construction of the power station, as well as its reconstruction after the attack, are paid for by donors' money.

JUNE 28 — The IDF arrests dozens of Hamas leaders in the West Bank, including twenty members of the Palestinian Legislative Council and eight Palestinian Authority government ministers. The action was planned a few weeks earlier and carried out in coordination with the Shabak and the State Attorney's Office. Hamas contends that Israel made the arrests to hold the detainees as bargaining chips for the release of Gilad Schalit.

JULY 12 — Two IDF soldiers, Ehud Goldwasser and Eldad Regev, are abducted to Lebanon by Hezbollah. In response, Israel mounts a major attack on Hezbollah targets throughout Lebanon, including the Shiite quarter of Beirut. According to IDF reports, the Israeli Air Force carries out more than seven thousand bombing sorties in Lebanon. According to figures of the Lebanon government, these forced approximately one million residents of southern Lebanon to evacuate their homes and move to the north and killed twelve hundred people. A large number of land forces are dispatched to Lebanon in a later stage of what has become the Second Lebanon War. The fighting lasts thirty-four days, during which Hezbollah fires thousands of Katyusha rockets at Israel's northern regions, killing fifty-six civilians and soldiers and injuring thousands. With the world's eyes on the north, Israel increases its attacks in the Gaza Strip: 136 Palestinians are killed by security forces while the fighting is going on in Lebanon.

NOVEMBER — Israeli journalists are no longer permitted to enter the Gaza Strip. Israeli authorities cite the possibility of further kidnappings as the main reason for this prohibition.

NOVEMBER 19 — The OC Central Command, Major General Yair Naveh, signs an order prohibiting Palestinians from traveling in a vehicle with Israeli license plates. Following harsh criticism, the order is cancelled.

DECEMBER — Fighting between Fatah and Hamas takes place in the Gaza Strip, with both sides attacking security forces and civilians, resulting in deaths and extensive property damage.

— Following what it classifies as a "refreshing of procedures," Israel prohibits Palestinian residents of the Occupied Territories who hold foreign nationalities from entering the Occupied Territories. Those prohibited include persons who have lived in the Occupied Territories for many years.

2007

MARCH — The United Nations World Food Programme states that, because of the restrictions on movement, the Palestinian economy has become an "island economy" of small areas in which the people run a barter economy, with no trade between cities or between Gaza and the West Bank.

MARCH 17 — Following the Mecca Agreement, signed in February by representatives of Hamas and Fatah, a unity Palestinian government is sworn in. It is headed by Ismail Haniyeh of Hamas, and it contains twenty-five ministers (twelve from Hamas, six from Fatah, and the others independents or from leftist party factions). The objective of the unity government is to stop the internal conflict in the Occupied Territories and to remove the international boycott of the Palestinian Authority following Hamas's victory in the elections.

JUNE 8 — The High Court of Justice sustains the state's position that residents of the Gaza Strip are not allowed to study in Israel. In August, the court rules that residents of Gaza also are not allowed to study in the West Bank. The limited venues of higher education in the Gaza Strip have been further hurt by the prolonged closure of the region.

JUNE 16 — After a week-long battle, Hamas takes control of government institutions in the Gaza Strip and dismisses most of the Fatah-related officials.

JULY 6 — A report by Peace Now reveals that the jurisdictional area of settlements in the West Bank is ten times greater than the settlements' built-up area. Despite the potential for expansion, 90 percent of the settlements seize additional land, mostly private Palestinian lands.

JULY 25 — Relations are renewed between the Israeli and Palestinian District Coordination Offices for the first time since Hamas rule began.

SEPTEMBER 4 — The High Court of Justice orders dismantlement of 1.7 kilometers of the Separation Wall near Modi'in Illit and orders that the state return more than one thousand dunams (247 acres) to residents of the village

of Bil'in. The justices hold that the route was not based on security considerations and was planned to include future neighborhoods in Modi'in Illit. Since January 2005, the residents of Bil'in, together with Israeli leftist activists, had waged a continuous nonviolent struggle against the Separation Wall.

SEPTEMBER 5 — The day after the court's decision in Bil'in, the High Court rules, with respect to another petition, that the houses built illegally on land belonging to Bil'in as part of the Matityahu East neighborhood in the Modi'in Illit settlement do not have to be torn down.

SEPTEMBER 20 — In response to the firing of missiles from the Gaza Strip to the city of Sderot and other neighboring townships, Israel declares the Gaza Strip "enemy territory" and threatens to reduce the supply of electricity and fuel to its residents.

OCTOBER 9 — The IDF issues an order expropriating 1,129 dunams (279 acres) east of Jerusalem. The land is to be seized in order to build a "life fabric road" that will enable "transportation continuity" for Palestinians and to prepare for the building of three Jewish neighborhoods with thirty-five hundred apartments in zone E-1, between Jerusalem and Ma'ale Adumim.

OCTOBER 11 — The High Court of Justice rules that Israeli labor law applies to Palestinians working for Israelis in the Occupied Territories.

OCTOBER 26 — The defense minister, Ehud Barak, approves the disruption of the electricity and gas supply to the Gaza Strip. The supply of diesel fuel, which is used in hospitals and public transportation, will not be interrupted. In a later stage, the supply of diesel fuel will be also decreased substantially, causing severe damage to electricity and water supplies in the Gaza strip.

OCTOBER 29 — Israel allows trucks loaded with shekels to enter the Gaza Strip. The money is intended for paying the wages of Palestinian Authority employees identified with Fatah.

NOVEMBER — The first criminal indictment is submitted under the charges of illegal construction works in the outposts, accusing a settler of concealing an underground electrical cable connecting the settlement Ma'ale Shomron to the nearby outpost El Matan and passing through private land belonging to a Palestinian from the village Thulth.

NOVEMBER 15 — The Knesset confirms an amendment to the Basic Law: Jerusalem. A majority of eighty Knesset members will be required for any concessions in territory or authority in the city.

NOVEMBER 27 — The Annapolis conference convenes. The parties participating are representatives of Israel, the Palestinian Authority, the Quartet, and most of the Arab League nations, including states that do not have diplomatic relations with Israel. The purpose of the conference is to reactivate the peace talks and to set in motion intensive negotiations on a final Israeli-Palestinian peace agreement. It is the first meaningful summit meeting of Israeli and Palestinian leaders since the 2000 Camp David summit and the outbreak of the al-Aqsa intifada.

NOVEMBER 30 — Attorney Talia Sasson, author of the report on unauthorized outposts, warns that the Justice Ministry is preparing the ground for extensive building in the settlements. A ministry proposal presents conduits to legitimize outposts that have been established on private Palestinian lands and to channel governmental funding for illegal outposts. The proposal also acknowledges outposts located several kilometers away from the settlements as "new neighborhoods."

DECEMBER 18 — The IDF reveals that from the beginning of the second intifada, 1,091 criminal investigations were initiated following injury or damage to Palestinian civilians. Indictments were submitted in only 118 cases. Two hundred and thirty-nine shooting incidents were investigated, and in only 30 of them were indictments submitted, resulting in the conviction of sixteen Israeli soldiers. According to B'Tselem reports, 4,330 Palestinians had been killed since the beginning of the second intifada, at least 2,056 of whom did not take part in hostilities.

DECEMBER 21 — Brigadier General Zvi Fogel, who served as OC Southern Command in the beginning of the second intifada, reveals that the IDF had declared "death zones" in Gaza and had bombed populated areas with Flechette shells containing thousands of steel arrows.

Translated by Harold Jacobson. Thanks to Neve Gordon and Shir Hever for helpful comments.

Contributors

CAROLINE ABU-SADA completed her PH.D. at the Institut d'Études Politiques in Paris. Her research dealt with Palestinian nongovernmental organizations and their role in Palestinian state building and focused on the Palestinian Agricultural Relief Committees. She worked as researcher and as food-security analyst for several international organizations in the Occupied Palestinian Territories, including Oxfam Great Britain and the Food and Agriculture Organization. Her publications include *ONG palestiniennes et construction étatique: L'expérience de Palestinian Agricultural relief Committees (PARC) dans les territoires occupés palestiniens, 1983–2005* (Institut Français du Proche-Orient, CNRS, 2007) and "Urgence et développement: L'action des ONG pendant la seconde intifâda," *Études rurales* (2004).

GADI ALGAZI is associate professor at the Department of History at Tel Aviv University and senior editor of the journal *History & Memory*. His research interests include late medieval and early modern social and cultural history, historical anthropology, and the history and theory of the social sciences. His current research project focuses on the shaping of the scholar's way of life and habitus between 1400 and 1600. Among his recent publications: "Scholars in Households: Refiguring the Learned Habitus, 1480–1550," *Science in Context* 16, nos. 1–2 (2003); "Feigned Reciprocities: Lords, Peasants, and the Afterlife of Medieval Social Strategies," in Gadi Algazi, Valentin Groebner, and Bernhard Jussen (eds.), *Negotiating the Gift: Pre-Modern Figurations of Exchange* (Göttingen: Vandenhoeck & Ruprecht, 2003); and "Norbert Elias's Motion Pictures: History, Cinema and Gestures in the Process of Civilization," *Studies in History and Philosophy of Science* 39 (2008). Algazi is a political activist, one of the founders of the Arab-Jewish movement Ta'ayush, and since 2006 has been active in Tarabut–Hit'chabrut.

ARIELLA AZOULAY teaches visual culture and contemporary philosophy in the Program for Culture and Hermeneutics, Bar-Ilan University. She is the author of several books, including *The Civil Contract of Photography* (New York: Zone Books, 2008), *Atto di stato palestina-israele, 1967–2007: Storia fotografica dell'occupazione* (Milan: Bruno Mondadori, 2008), *Once upon a Time: Photography following Walter Benjamin* (Ramat Gan: Bar-Ilan University Press, 2006) (in Hebrew), *Death's Showcase* (Cambridge, MA: The MIT Press, 2001) and (with Adi Ophir) *This Regime Which is Not One: Occupation and Democracy between the Sea and the River* (Tel Aviv: Resling, 2008) (in Hebrew). Azoulay is also a curator and her recent exhibitions include *Constituent Violence: 1947–1950* (Zochrot Gallery, 2009) and *Act of State,* a photographic documentation of forty years of Israeli occupation (Minshar Gallery, 2007).

ORNA BEN-NAFTALI, a graduate of the Tel Aviv University Law Faculty, Harvard University, and the Fletcher School of Law and Diplomacy, is a professor of international law and dean of the Law School, the College of Management Academic Studies, Israel. She served as deputy director-general for academic affairs at the college before proceeding to work for the United Nations Department of Peacekeeping Operations. She is a member of the editorial board of the *European Journal of International Law* and of the executive board of B'Tselem, The Israeli Information Center for Human Rights in the Occupied Territories. Her research focuses on humanitarian law, international criminal law, and law and culture.

YAEL BERDA is a PH.D. candidate in the Department of Sociology at Princeton University. She graduated from the Hebrew University in law and studied toward an M.A. in sociology and anthropology at Tel Aviv University. She has practiced as a human rights lawyer, focusing on cases of violations of the freedom of movement and the freedom of association in the Israeli Supreme Court and in military criminal courts.

HILLA DAYAN studied at the University of Chicago and at the New School for Social Research, New York, where she earned her PH.D. Her fields of expertise are the theory of military occupations, democracy and dictatorship, and the sociology of citizenship, immigration, and border regimes. As a staff member of the Israeli organizations Physicians for Human Rights—Israel and The Association for Civil Rights, she dealt with the bureaucracy of the occupation, torture, and violations of prisoners' rights. Currently, she is a policy advisor for United Civilians for Peace, a coalition initiative of major nongovernmental organizations in the Netherlands.

LEILA FARSAKH is an assistant professor of political science at the University of Massachusetts, Boston, specializing in Middle East politics, comparative politics, and the politics of the Arab-Israeli conflict. She is the author of *Palestinian Labour Migration to Israel: Labor, Land and Occupation* (London: Routledge, 2005) and editor of "Commemorating the Naksa, Evoking the Nakba," special edition of *The Electronic Journal of Middle Eastern Studies* (Spring 2008). She also coedited (with David O'Connor) *Development Strategy, Employment and International Migration: Country Experiences* (Paris: Organisation for Economic Co-operation and Development, 1996). Farsakh has written extensively on issues related to the Palestinian economy and the Oslo peace process, international migration, and regional integration.

DANI FILC, M.D., PH.D., is a senior lecturer in the Department of Politics and Government at Ben Gurion University and chairperson of Physicians for Human Rights—Israel. Among his publications are: *The Power of Property: Israel in the Globalization Age* (edited with Uri Ram) (Jerusalem: The Van Leer Jerusalem Institute, 2004) (in Hebrew); *Hegemony and Populism in Israel* (Tel Aviv: Resling, 2006) (in Hebrew); "The Check-Post, Sovereignty and the Body," *Hagar* 6, no. 3 (2006); and "Neo-liberalism and the Health Business: The Case of Israel," *Critical Social Policy* 25, no. 2 (2005).

MICHAL GIVONI completed her PH.D. studies at the Cohn Institute for the History and Philosophy of Science and Ideas at Tel Aviv University. Her work deals with transnational humanitarianism, contemporary practices of witnessing and testimony, and governmentality in emergencies. She is a postdoctorol fellow at the Department of Sociology and Anthropology at Tel Aviv University and teaches political theory at Ben-Gurion University.

NEVE GORDON teaches in the Department of Politics and Government at Ben-Gurion University. During the first intifada, he was the director of Physicians for Human Rights—Israel. He is the coeditor with Ruchama Marton of *Torture: Human Rights, Medical Ethics and the Case of Israel* (Atlantic Highlands, NJ: Zed Books, 1995), the editor of *From the Margins of Globalization: Critical Perspectives on Human Rights* (Lanham, MD: Lexington Books, 2004), and the author of *Israel's Occupation* (Berkeley: University of California Press, 2008).

AEYAL M. GROSS teaches in the Tel Aviv University Faculty of Law. He received his LL.B. from Tel Aviv University and his S.J.D. from Harvard Law School. He was awarded a diploma in human rights by the European University Institute. He served on the board of the Association for Civil Rights in Israel. In 2007–9, he is a visiting fellow at the Institute of Advanced Legal Studies at the University of London, and is teaching as a visitor at the School of Oriental and African Studies, also at the University of London. His research interests include: international, constitutional, human rights, and humanitarian law, the law of occupation, health rights, sexuality and the law and queer theory, and critical theories of law. He has published and lectured in Israel, Europe, North America, and South Africa. He is the coeditor of *Exploring Social Rights: Between Theory and Practice* (Oxford: Hart, 2007).

SARI HANAFI is an associate professor of sociology at the American University of Beirut and editor of *Idafat: The Arab Journal of Sociology.* Hanafi is a former director of the Palestinian Refugee and Diaspora Center (Shaml). He is the author of numerous journal articles and book chapters on Palestinian refugees, economic sociology, and the sociology of migration. Among his recent books, he has edited a number of volumes: *Crossing Borders, Shifting Boundaries: Palestinian Dilemmas* (Cairo: American University in Cairo, 2008; Arabic version published by the Center of Arab Unity Studies, Beirut); with Eyal Benvenisti and Chaim Gans, *Israel and the Palestinian Refugees* (Berlin: Springer, 2007);and with Sarah Ben Néfissa, Nabil Abdel Fattah, and Carlos Milani, *NGOs and Governance in the Arab World: Issues, Problems and Case Studies* (Cairo: American University in Cairo Press, 2004). He has coauthored with Linda Taber *The Emergence of a Palestinian Globalized Elite: Donors, International Organizations and Local NGOs* (Jerusalem: Muwatin and IPS, 2005) (in English and Arabic).

ARIEL HANDEL wrote a PH.D. dissertation on the regime of movement in the Occupied Territories at the Cohn Institute for the History and Philosophy of Sciences and Ideas at Tel Aviv University. He is the author of several essays on geopolitics in the Occupied Territories.

KEREN MICHAELI is a D.PHIL. candidate at St. Antony's College, the University of Oxford. She is a graduate of Georgetown University (LL.M.) and the Law School of the College of Management Academic Studies, Israel (LL.B.). She is currently a tutor in public international law, international human rights law, and the law of war at the University of Oxford. Her recent publications (coauthored with Orna Ben-Naftali) include: "Justice-Ability: A Critique of the Alleged Non-Justiciability of Israel's Policy of Targeted Killings," *Journal of International Criminal Justice* (2003); "'We must not make a scarecrow of the law': A Legal Analysis of the Israeli Policy of Targeted Killings," *Cornell Journal of International Law* 36, no. 2 (2004); and "The Public Committee against Torture in Israel v. The Government of Israel— A Case Note," *American Journal of International Law* (2007). She is also the author of "The Torture Case + Targeted Killings Case," in *The Oxford Compendium of International Criminal Justice* (forthcoming).

ADI OPHIR teaches philosophy and political theory at the Cohn Institute for the History and Philosophy of Science and Ideas, Tel Aviv University. He is a fellow of the Hartman Institute for Advanced Jewish Studies. His recent books include (with Ariella Azoulay) *This Regime Which Is Not One: Occupation and Democracy between the Sea and the River* (Tel Aviv: Resling, 2008) (in Hebrew), *The Order of Evils: Toward an Ontology of Morals* (New York: Zone Books, 2005), and *Divine Violence: Two Essays on God and Disaster* (Jerusalem: The Van Leer Jerusalem Institute, forthcoming). Ophir was the founding editor of *Theory & Criticism* (in Hebrew), an Israeli journal for critical thought.

RONEN SHAMIR teaches in the Department of Sociology and Anthropology and the School of Law at Tel Aviv University. Using the combined tools of political sociology and the sociology of law, he was among the first in Israel to study the legal architecture of the occupation. Shamir is the author of *The Colonies of Law: Colonialism, Zionism and Law in Early Mandate Palestine* (Cambridge: Cambridge University Press, 2000) and *Managing Legal Uncertainty: Elite Lawyers in the New Deal* (Durham, NC: Duke University Press, 1996).

YEHOUDA SHENHAV (PH.D., Stanford University, 1985) is a professor of sociology at Tel Aviv University and head of advanced studies at the Van Leer Jerusalem Institute. He is also the editor of *Theory & Criticism* (in Hebrew) and senior editor of *Organization Studies*. Among his recent books are *The Arab Jews: A Postcolonial Reading of Nationalism, Religion, and Ethnicity* (Stanford, CA: Stanford University Press, 2006) and *Manufacturing Rationality* (Oxford: Oxford University Press, 2002).

EYAL WEIZMAN is an architect based in London. He studied architecture at the Architectural Association in London and completed his PH.D. at the London Consortium, Birkbeck College. He is the director of the Centre for Research Architecture at Goldsmiths College, University of London. Weizman works with a variety of nongovernmental organizations and human rights groups in Israel/Palestine. He cocurated the exhibition *A Civilian Occupation: The Politics of Israeli Architecture* and coedited the publication of the same title. These projects were based on his human rights research and were banned by the Israeli Association of Architects. They were later shown in the exhibition *Territories* in New York, Berlin, Rotterdam, San Francisco, Malmoe, Tel Aviv, and Ramallah. His books include *Hollow Land* (London: Verso, 2007), *A Civilian Occupation* (London: Verso, 2003), the series *Territories* 1, 2, and 3, *Yellow Rhythms: A Roundabout for London* (Rotterdam: 010 Publishers, 2000), and many articles in journals, magazines, and edited books.

Design and typesetting by Julie Fry
Printed and bound by Maple-Vail